STUDY GUIDE
for use with
McConnell, Brue, and Flynn
MICROECONOMICS

Nineteenth Edition

WILLIAM B. WALSTAD
PROFESSOR OF ECONOMICS
UNIVERSITY OF NEBRASKA–LINCOLN

McGraw-Hill
Irwin

Study Guide for
Microeconomics, Nineteenth Edition
Campbell R. McConnell, Stanley L. Brue, Sean M. Flynn, and William B. Walstad

Published by McGraw-Hill/Irwin, a business unit of The McGraw-Hill Companies, Inc., 1221 Avenue of the Americas, New York, NY 10020. Copyright © 2012 by The McGraw-Hill Companies, Inc. All rights reserved.

1 2 3 4 5 6 7 8 9 0 QDB/QDB 1 0 9 8 7 6 5 4 3 2 1

ISBN 978-0-07-733800-8
MHID 0-07-733800-6

www.mhhe.com

About the Author

William B. Walstad is a professor of economics at the University of Nebraska-Lincoln, where he has been honored with a Distinguished Faculty Award from the College of Business Administration. Professor Walstad also has been recognized with the Henry H. Villard Research Award for his published research in economic education by the National Association of Economic Educators and the Council for Economic Education. He is the editor of the *Journal of Economic Education* and was a former chair of the Committee on Economic Education of the American Economic Association. He is a co-editor and contributor to *Teaching Innovations in Economics: Strategies and Applications for Interactive Instruction*. Professor Walstad received his Ph.D. degree from the University of Minnesota.

To
Tammie, Laura, Kristin, Eileen, Clara, and Martha

Contents

How to Use the Study Guide to Learn Economics

This *Study Guide* should help you read and understand the McConnell, Brue, and Flynn textbook, *Microeconomics*, 19th edition. If used properly, a study guide can be a great aid to you for what is probably your first course in economics.

No one pretends that the study of economics is easy, but it can be made easier with this *Study Guide*. Of course, it will not do your work for you, and its use is no substitute for reading the text. You must first be willing to read the text and work at learning if you wish to understand economics.

Many students, however, do read their text and work hard on their economics course and still fail to learn the subject. This problem occurs because economics is a new subject for these students. They want to learn economics, but do not know how to do it because they have no previous experience with the subject. Here is where the *Study Guide* can help students. Let's first see what the *Study Guide* contains and then how to use it.

■ WHAT THE *STUDY GUIDE* IS

This *Study Guide* contains 24 chapters to support your learning of each of the 24 textbook chapters in *Microeconomics*. There is also one more Study Guide chapter that fully supports the **Web Chapter** for *Microeconomics*. In addition, the *Study Guide* has a **glossary**. This *Study Guide* should give you a complete set of resources to advance your learning of principles of economics.

Each *Study Guide* chapter has 11 sections to give you complete coverage of the textbook material in each chapter. The first five sections help you to **understand** the economics content in each chapter.

1. An **introduction** explains what is in the chapter of the text and how it is related to material in earlier and later chapters. It points out topics to which you should give special attention and reemphasizes difficult or important principles and facts.

2. A **checklist** tells you the things you should be able to do when you have finished the chapter.

3. A **chapter outline** shows how the chapter is organized and summarizes briefly the essential points made in the chapter, including the Last Word.

4. Selected **hints and tips** for each chapter help you identify key points and make connections with any previous discussion of a topic.

5. A list of the **important terms** points out what you must be able to define to understand the material in the chapter. Each term is defined in the glossary at the end of the *Study Guide*.

The next six sections of the *Study Guide* allow you to **self-test** your understanding of the chapter material.

6. **Fill-in questions** (short-answer and list questions) help you learn and remember the important generalizations and facts in the chapter.

7. **True-false questions** test your understanding of the material in the chapter.

8. **Multiple-choice questions** also give you a chance to check your knowledge of the chapter content and prepare for this type of course examination.

9. **Problems** help you learn and understand economic concepts by requiring different skills—drawing a graph, completing a table, or finding relationships—to solve the problems.

10. **Short answer** and **essay questions** can be used as a self-test, to identify important questions in the chapter and to prepare for examinations.

11. **Answers** to fill-in questions, true-false questions, multiple-choice questions, and problems are found at the end of each chapter. References to the specific pages in the textbook for each true-false, multiple-choice, and short answer or essay questions are also provided.

■ HOW TO STUDY AND LEARN WITH THE HELP OF THE *STUDY GUIDE*

1. *Read and outline.* For best results, quickly read the introduction, outline, list of terms, and checklist in the *Study Guide* before you read the chapter in *Microeconomics*. Then read the chapter in the text slowly, keeping one eye on the *Study Guide* outline and the list of terms. Highlight the chapter as you read it by identifying the *major and minor* points and by placing *Study Guide* outline numbers or letters (such as I or A or 1 or a) in the margins. When you have completed the chapter, you will have the chapter highlighted, and the *Study Guide* outline will serve as a handy set of notes on the chapter.

2. *Review and reread.* After you have read the chapter in the text once, return to the introduction, outline, and list of terms in the *Study Guide*. Reread the introduction and outline. Does everything there make sense? If not, go back to the text and reread the topics that you do not remember well or that still confuse you. Look at the outline. Try to recall each of the minor topics that were contained in the text under each of the major points in the outline. When you come to the list of terms, go over them one by one. *Define or explain each to yourself and then look for the definition of the term either in the text chapter or in the glossary*. Compare your own definition or explanation with that in the *text or glossary*. The quick way to find the definition of a term in the text is to look in the text index for the page(s) in which that term or concept is mentioned. Make any necessary correction or change in your own definition or explanation.

3. *Test and check answers.* When you have done the above reading and review, you will have a good idea of what is in the text chapter. Now complete the self-test sections of the *Study Guide* to check your understanding.

In doing the self-test, start with the *fill-in, true-false, multiple-choice,* and *problems* sections. Tackle each of these four sections one at a time, using the following procedures: (1) answer as many self-test items as you can without looking in the text or in the answer section of the *Study Guide*; (2) check the text for whatever help you need in answering the items; and (3) consult the answer section of the *Study Guide* for the correct answers and reread any section of the text for which you missed items.

The self-test items in these four sections are not equally difficult. Some will be easy to answer and others will be harder. Do not expect to get them all correct the first time. Some are designed to pinpoint material of importance that you will probably miss the first time you read the text and answering them will get you to read the text again with more insight and understanding.

The *short answer and essay questions* cover the major points in the chapter. For some of the easier questions, all you may do is mentally outline your answer. For the more difficult questions, you may want to write out a brief outline of the answer or a full answer. Do not avoid the difficult questions just because they are more work. Answering these questions is often the most valuable work you can do toward acquiring an understanding of economic relationships and principles.

Although no answers are given in the *Study Guide* to the short answer and essay questions, the answer section does list text page references for each question. You are *strongly* encouraged to read those text pages for an explanation of the question or for better insight into the question content.

4. *Double check.* Before you turn to the next chapter in the text and *Study Guide*, return to the checklist. If you cannot honestly check off each item in the list, you have not learned what the authors of the text and of this Study Guide hoped you would learn.

■ **WEB CHAPTER FOR *MICROECONOMICS***

The *Study Guide* fully supports the Web-based chapter in *Microeconomics:* Technology, R&D, and Efficiency (Chapter 11W). This chapter is located at *www.mcconnell19e. com*. The *Study Guide* includes full content and self-test materials for this chapter.

■ **GLOSSARY**

All of the important terms and concepts in *Microeconomics* are defined and described in the glossary. It is included in the *Study Guide* for easy reference when you see a term or concept you do not know. It will also aid your work on self-test items in the *Study Guide*.

■ **SOME FINAL WORDS**

Perhaps the method of using the *Study Guide* outlined above seems like a lot of work. It is! Study and learning requires work on your part. This fact is one you must accept if you are to learn economics.

After you have used the *Study Guide* to study one or two chapters, you will find that some sections are more valuable to you than others. Let your own experience determine how you will use it. But do not discontinue use of the *Study Guide* after one or two chapters merely because you are not sure whether it is helping you. ***Stick with it.***

■ **ACKNOWLEDGMENTS**

Special thanks are due to Sharon Nemeth for her hard work in preparing the electronic versions of this *Study Guide*. I am also indebted to Stan Brue, Campbell McConnell, and Sean Flynn for their on-going support during the development of this *Study Guide*. While I am most grateful for all these contributions, I alone am responsible for an errors or omissions. You are welcome to send me comments or suggestions.

William B. Walstad

Limits, Alternatives, and Choices

Chapter 1 introduces you to economics—the social science that studies how individuals, institutions, and society make the optimal best choices under conditions of scarcity. The first section of the chapter describes the three key features of the **economic perspective.** This perspective first recognizes that all choices involve costs and that these costs must be involved in an economic decision. The economic perspective also incorporates the view that to achieve a goal, people make decisions that reflect their purposeful self-interest. The third feature considers that people compare marginal benefits against marginal costs when making decisions and will choose the situation where the marginal benefit is greater than the marginal cost. You will develop a better understanding of these features as you read about the economic issues in this book.

Economics relies heavily on the **scientific method** to develop theories and principles to explain the likely effects from human events and behavior. It involves gathering data, testing hypotheses, and developing theories and principles. In essence, economic theories and principles (and related terms such as laws and models) are generalizations about how the economic world works.

Economists develop economic theories and principles at two levels. **Microeconomics** targets specific units in the economy. Studies at this level research such questions as how prices and output are determined for particular products and how consumers will react to price changes. **Macroeconomics** focuses on the whole economy, or large segments of it. Studies at this level investigate such issues as how to increase economic growth, control inflation, or maintain full employment. Studies at either level have elements of **positive economics,** which investigates facts or cause-and-effect relationships, or **normative economics,** which incorporates subjective views of what ought to be or what policies should be used to address an economic issue.

Several sections of the text are devoted to a discussion of the **economizing problem** from individual or society perspectives. This problem arises from a fundamental conflict between economic wants and economic resources: (1) individuals and society have *unlimited* economic wants; (2) the economic means or resources to satisfy those wants are *limited.* This economic problem forces individuals and societies to make a choice. And anytime a choice is made there is an opportunity cost—the next best alternative that was not chosen.

The economizing problem for individuals is illustrated with a microeconomic model that uses a **budget line.** It shows graphically the meaning of many concepts defined in the chapter: scarcity, choice, trade-offs, opportunity cost, and optimal allocation. The economizing problem for society is illustrated with a macroeconomic model that uses a **production possibilities curve.** It also shows graphically the economic concepts just listed, and in addition it can be used to describe macroeconomic conditions related to unemployment, economic growth, and trade. The production possibilities model can also be applied to many real economic situations, such as the economics of war, as you will learn from the text.

■ **CHECKLIST**

When you have studied this chapter you should be able to

☐ Write a formal definition of economics.
☐ Describe the three key features of the economic perspective.
☐ Give applications of the economic perspective.
☐ Identify the elements of the scientific method.
☐ Define hypothesis, theory, principle, law, and model as they relate to economics.
☐ State how economic principles are generalizations and abstractions.
☐ Explain the "other-things-equal" assumption (*ceteris paribus*) and its use in economics.
☐ Distinguish between microeconomics and macroeconomics.
☐ Give examples of positive and normative economics.
☐ Explain the economizing problem for an individual (from a microeconomic perspective).
☐ Describe the concept of a budget line for the individual.
☐ Explain how to measure the slope of a budget line and determine the location of the budget line.
☐ Use the budget line to illustrate trade-offs and opportunity costs.
☐ Describe the economizing problem for society.
☐ Define the four types of economic resources for society.
☐ State the four assumptions made when a production possibilities table or curve is constructed.
☐ Construct a production possibilities curve when given the data.
☐ Define opportunity cost and utilize a production possibilities curve to explain the concept.
☐ Show how the law of increasing opportunity costs is reflected in the shape of the production possibilities curve.
☐ Explain the economic rationale for the law of increasing opportunity costs.

☐ Use marginal analysis to define optimal allocation.

☐ Explain how optimal allocation determines the optimal point on a production possibilities curve.

☐ Use a production possibilities curve to illustrate unemployment.

☐ Use the production possibilities curve to illustrate economic growth.

☐ Explain how international trade affects a nation's production possibilities curve.

☐ Give other applications of the production possibilities model.

☐ Identify the five pitfalls to sound economic reasoning (*Last Word*).

■ CHAPTER OUTLINE

1. *Economics* studies how individuals, institutions, and society make the optimal or best choices under conditions of *scarcity,* for which economic wants are *unlimited* and the means or resources to satisfy those wants are *limited.*

2. The *economic perspective* has three interrelated features.

a. It recognizes that scarcity requires choice and that making a choice has an *opportunity cost*—giving up the next best alternative to the choice that was made.

b. It views people as purposeful decision makers who make choices based on their self-interests. People seek to increase their satisfaction, or *utility,* from consuming a good or service. They are purposeful because they weigh the costs and benefits in deciding how best to increase that utility.

c. It uses *marginal analysis* to assess how the marginal costs of a decision compare with the marginal benefits.

3. Economics relies on the *scientific method* for analysis.

a. Several terms are used in economic analysis that are related to this method.

(1) A *hypothesis* is a proposition that is tested and used to develop an economic *theory.*

(2) A highly tested and reliable economic theory is called an *economic principle* or *law.* Theories, principles, and laws are meaningful statements about economic behavior or the economy that can be used to predict the likely outcome of an action or event.

(3) An economic *model* is created when several economic laws or principles are used to explain or describe reality.

b. There are several other aspects of economic principles.

(4) Each principle or theory is a generalization that shows a tendency or average effect.

(5) The *other-things-equal assumption* (*ceteris paribus*) is used to limit the influence of other factors when making a generalization.

(6) Many economic models can be illustrated graphically and are simplified representations of economic reality.

4. Economic analysis is conducted at two levels, and for each level there can be elements of positive or normative economics.

a. *Microeconomics* studies the economic behavior of individuals, particular markets, firms, or industries.

b. *Macroeconomics* looks at the entire economy or its major *aggregates* or sectors, such as households, businesses, or government.

c. *Positive economics* focuses on facts and is concerned with what is, or the scientific analysis of economic behavior.

d. *Normative economics* suggests what ought to be and answers policy questions based on value judgments. Most disagreements among economists involve normative economics.

5. Individuals face an *economizing problem* because economic wants are greater than the economic means to satisfy those wants. The problem can be illustrated with a microeconomic model with several features.

a. Individuals have limited income to spend.

b. Individuals have virtually unlimited wants for more goods and services, and higher-quality goods and services.

c. The economizing problem for the individual can be illustrated with a budget line and two products (for instance, DVDs and books). The *budget line* shows graphically the combinations of the two products a consumer can purchase with his or her money income.

(1) All combinations of the two products on or inside the budget line are *attainable* by the consumer; all combinations beyond the budget line are *unattainable.*

(2) To obtain more DVDs the consumer has to give up some books, so there is a *trade-off;* if to get a second DVD the consumer must give up two books, then the *opportunity* cost of the additional DVD is two books.

(3) Limited income forces individuals to evaluate the marginal cost and marginal benefit of a choice to maximize their satisfaction.

(4) Changes in money income shift the budget line: an increase in income shifts the line to the right; a decrease in income shifts the line to the left.

6. Society also faces an economizing problem due to scarcity.

a. *Economic resources* are scarce natural, human, or manufactured inputs used to produce goods and services.

b. Economic resources are sometimes called *factors of production* and are classified into four categories:

(1) *land,* or natural resources.

(2) *labor,* or the contributed time and abilities of people who are producing goods and services.

(3) *capital* (or capital goods), or the machines, tools, and equipment used to make other goods and services; economists refer to the purchase of such capital goods as *investment.*

(4) *entrepreneurial ability,* or the special human talents of individuals who combine the other factors of production.

7. A macroeconomic model of production possibilities illustrates the economizing problem for society. The four assumptions usually made when such a production possibilities model is used are: (1) there is full employment of available resources; (2) the quantity and quality of resources are fixed; (3) the state of technology does not change; and (4) there are two types of goods being produced (**consumer goods** and **capital goods**).

a. The **production possibilities table** indicates the alternative combinations of goods an economy is capable of producing when it has achieved full employment and optimal allocation. The table illustrates the fundamental choice every economy must make: what quantity of each product it must sacrifice to obtain more of another.

b. The data in the production possibilities table can be plotted on a graph to obtain a **production possibilities curve.** Each point on the curve shows some maximum output of the two goods.

c. The opportunity cost of producing an additional unit of one good is the amount of the other good that is sacrificed. The **law of increasing opportunity costs** states that the opportunity cost of producing one more unit of a good (the marginal opportunity cost) increases as more of the good is produced.

(1) The production possibilities curve is bowed out from the origin because of the law of increasing opportunity costs.

(2) The reason the opportunity cost of producing an additional unit of a good increases as more of it is produced is because resources are not completely adaptable to alternative uses.

d. Optimal allocation means that resources are devoted to the best mix of goods to maximize satisfaction in society. This optimal mix is determined by assessing marginal costs and benefits.

(1) The marginal-cost curve for a good increases because of the law of increasing opportunity costs; the marginal-benefit curve decreases because the consumption of a good yields less and less satisfaction.

(2) When the marginal benefit is greater than the marginal cost, there is an incentive to produce more of the good, but when the marginal cost is greater than the marginal benefit, there is an incentive to produce less of the good.

(3) Optimal or efficient allocation is achieved when the marginal cost of a product equals the marginal benefit of a product.

8. Different outcomes will occur when assumptions underlying the production possibilities model are relaxed.

a. Unemployment. When the economy is operating at a point inside the production possibilities curve it means that resources are not fully employed.

b. **Economic growth.** The production possibilities curve shifts outward from economic growth because resources are no longer fixed and technology improves.

(1) Expansion in the quantity and quality of resources contributes to economic growth and shifts the production possibilities curve outward.

(2) Advancement in technology contributes to economic growth and also shifts the production possibilities curve outward.

(3) The combination of capital goods and consumer goods an economy chooses to produce in the present can determine the position of the production possibilities curve in the future. Greater production of capital goods relative to consumer goods in the present shifts the production possibilities curve farther outward in the future because that economy is devoting more of its resources to investment than consumption.

c. Trade. When there is international specialization and trade, a nation can obtain more goods and services than is indicated by the production possibilities curve for a domestic economy. The effect on production possibilities is similar to an increase in economic growth.

9. (*Last Word*). Sound reasoning about economic issues requires the avoidance of five pitfalls.

a. *Bias* is a preconceived belief or opinion that is not warranted by the facts.

b. *Loaded terminology* is the use of terms in a way that appeals to emotion and leads to a nonobjective analysis of the issues.

c. The *fallacy of composition* is the assumption that what is true of the part is necessarily true of the whole.

d. The *post hoc fallacy* ("after this, therefore because of this") is the mistaken belief that when one event precedes another, the first event is the cause of the second.

e. *Confusing correlation with causation* means that two factors may be related, but that does not mean that one factor caused the other.

■ **HINTS AND TIPS**

1. The **economic perspective** presented in the first section of the chapter has three features related to decision making: scarcity and the necessity of choice, purposeful self-interest in decision making, and marginal analysis of the costs and benefits of decisions. Although these features may seem strange to you at first, they are central to the economic thinking used to examine decisions and problems throughout the book.

2. The chapter introduces two pairs of terms: **microeconomics** and **macroeconomics;** and **positive economics** and **normative economics.** Make sure you understand what each pair means and how they are related to each other.

3. The **budget line** shows the consumer what it is possible to purchase in the two-good world, given an income. Make sure that you understand what a budget line is. To test your understanding, practice with different income levels and prices. For example, assume you had an income of $100 to spend for two goods (A and B). Good A costs $10 and Good B costs $5. Draw a budget line to show the possible combinations of A and B that you could purchase.

4. The **production possibilities curve** is a simple and useful economic model for an economy. Practice your understanding of it by using it to explain the following economic concepts: scarcity, choice, opportunity cost, the law of increasing opportunity costs, full employment, optimal allocation, unemployment, and economic growth.

5. **Opportunity cost** is always measured in terms of a forgone alternative. From a production possibilities table, you can easily calculate how many units of one product you forgo when you get another unit of a product.

■ IMPORTANT TERMS

Note: See the Glossary in the back of the book for definitions of terms.

economics	budget line
economic perspective	economic resources
opportunity cost	land
utility	factors of production
marginal analysis	labor
scientific method	capital
economic principle	investment
other-things-equal assumption (*ceteris paribus*)	entrepreneurial ability
	consumer goods
microeconomics	capital goods
macroeconomics	production possibilities
aggregate	curve
positive economics	law of increasing opportunity costs
normative economics	
economizing problem	economic growth

SELF-TEST

■ FILL-IN QUESTIONS

1. The economic perspective recognizes that (resources, scarcity) _____ require(s) choice and that choice has an opportunity (benefit, cost) _____. There is no such thing as a "free lunch" in economics because scarce resources have (unlimited, alternative) _____ uses.

2. The economic perspective also assumes that people make choices based on their self-interest and that they are (random, purposeful) _____. It also is based on comparisons of the (extreme, marginal) _____ costs and benefits of an economic decision.

3. Economics relies on the (model, scientific) _____ method. Statements about economic behavior that enable the prediction of the likely effects of certain actions are economic (facts, theories) _____. The most well-tested of these that have strong predictive accuracy are called economic (hypotheses, principles) _____, or sometimes they are called (laws, actions) _____. Simplified representations of economic behavior or how an economy works are called (policies, models) _____.

4. Economic principles are often expressed as tendencies, or what is typical, and are (fallacies, generalizations) _____ about people's economic behavior. When studying a relationship between two economic variables, economists assume that other variables or factors (do, do not) _____ change, or in other words they

are using the (utility, other-things-equal) _____ assumption.

5. The study of output in a particular industry or of a particular product is the subject of (microeconomics, macroeconomics) _____, and the study of the total output of the economy or the general level of prices is the subject of _____.

6. The collection of specific units that are being added and treated as if they were one unit is an (assumption, aggregate) _____.

7. Two different types of statements can be made about economic topics. A (positive, normative) _____ statement explains what is by offering a scientific proposition about economic behavior that is based on economic theory and facts, but a _____ statement includes a value judgment about an economic policy or the economy that suggests what ought to be. Many of the reported disagreements among economists usually involve (positive, normative) _____ statements.

8. The economizing problem arises because individuals' and society's economic wants for more goods and services or higher-quality goods and services are (limited, unlimited) _____ and the economic means or resources to satisfy those wants are _____.

9. A schedule or curve that shows the various combinations of two products a consumer can (buy, sell) _____ with a money income is called a (budget, marginal cost) _____ line.

10. All combinations of goods inside a budget line are (attainable, unattainable) _____, and all combinations of goods outside the budget line are _____.

11. When a consumer's income increases, the budget line shifts to the (left, right) _____, while a decrease in income shifts the budget line to the _____.

12. The four types of economic resources are

   a. _____

   b. _____

   c. _____

   d. _____

13. When a production possibilities table or curve is constructed, four assumptions are made:

   a. _____

   b. _____

   c. _____

   d. _____

14. Goods that satisfy economic wants directly are (consumer, capital goods) _____, and goods that do so indirectly by helping produce other goods are _____ goods. Assume an economy can produce two basic types of goods, consumer and capital goods. If the economy wants to produce more consumer goods, then the capital goods the economy must give up are the opportunity (benefit, cost) _____ of producing those additional consumer goods.

15. The law of increasing opportunity costs explains why the production possibilities curve is (convex, concave) _____ from the origin. The economic rationale for the law is that economic resources (are, are not) _____ completely adaptable to alternative uses.

16. Optimal allocation of resources to production occurs when the marginal costs of the productive output are (greater than, less than, equal to) _____ the marginal benefits.

17. Following is a production possibilities curve for capital goods and consumer goods.

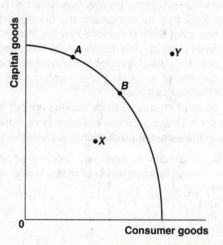

a. If the economy moves from point **A** to point **B**, it will produce (more, fewer) _____ capital goods and (more, fewer) _____ consumer goods.

b. If the economy is producing at point **X**, some resources in the economy are either (not available, unemployed) _____ or (underemployed, overemployed) _____.

c. If the economy moves from point **X** to point **B** (more, fewer) _____ capital goods and (more, fewer) _____ consumer goods will be produced.

d. If the economy is to produce at point **Y**, there must be (unemployment, economic growth) _____.

18. Economic growth will shift a nation's production possibilities curve (inward, outward) _____, and it occurs because of a resource supply (decrease, increase) _____ or because of a technological (decline, advance) _____.

19. An economy can produce goods for the present such as (consumer, capital) _____ goods and goods for the future such as _____ goods. If an economy produces more goods for the future, then this is likely to lead to a (greater, smaller) _____ shift outward in the production possibilities curve over time compared to the case where the economy produces more goods for the present.

20. International specialization and trade enable a nation to obtain (more, less) _____ of output than is possible with the output limits imposed by domestic production possibilities. The gains in output for an economy from greater international specialization and trade are similar to those that occur because of resource (increases, decreases) _____ or a technological (decline, advance) _____.

■ **TRUE–FALSE QUESTIONS**

Circle T if the statement is true, F if it is false.

1. Economics is the social science that studies how individuals, institutions, and society make choices under conditions of scarcity. **T F**

2. From the economic perspective, "there is no such thing as a free lunch." **T F**

3. The economic perspective views individuals or institutions as making purposeful choices based on the marginal analysis of the costs and benefits of decisions. **T F**

4. The scientific method involves the observation of real world data, the formulation of hypotheses based on the data, and the testing of those hypotheses to develop theories. **T F**

5. A well-tested or widely accepted economic theory is often called an economic principle or law. **T F**

6. The other-things-equal assumption (*ceteris paribus*) is made to simplify the economic analysis. **T F**

7. Microeconomic analysis is concerned with the performance of the economy as a whole or its major aggregates. **T F**

8. Macroeconomic analysis is concerned with the economic activity of specific firms or industries. **T F**

9. The statement that "the legal minimum wage should be raised to give working people a decent income" is an example of a normative statement. **T F**

10. A person is using positive economics when the person makes value judgments about how the economy should work. **T F**

11. The conflict between the unlimited economic wants of individuals or societies and limited economic means and resources of individuals or societies gives rise to the economizing problem. **T F**

12. The budget line shows all combinations of two products that the consumer can purchase, given money income and the prices of the products. **T F**

13. A consumer is unable to purchase any of the combinations of two products which lie below (or to the left) of the consumer's budget line. **T F**

14. An increase in the money income of a consumer shifts the budget line to the right. **T F**

15. The factors of production are land, labor, capital, and entrepreneurial ability. **T F**

16. From the economist's perspective, investment refers to money income. **T F**

17. Given full employment and optimal allocation, it is not possible for an economy capable of producing just two goods to increase its production of both at any one point in time. **T F**

18. The opportunity cost of producing more consumer goods is the other goods and services the economy is unable to produce because it has decided to produce these additional consumer goods. **T F**

19. The opportunity cost of producing a good tends to increase as more of it is produced because resources less suitable to its production must be employed. **T F**

20. Drawing a production possibilities curve bowed out from the origin is a graphical way of showing the law of increasing opportunity costs. **T F**

21. The economic rationale for the law of increasing opportunity costs is that economic resources are fully adaptable to alternative uses. **T F**

22. Optimal allocation is determined by assessing the marginal costs and benefits of the output from the allocation of resources to production. **T F**

23. Economic growth means an increase in the production of goods and services and is shown by a movement of the production possibilities curve outward and to the right. **T F**

24. The more capital goods an economy produces today, the greater will be the total output of all goods it can produce in the future, other things being equal. **T F**

25. International specialization and trade permit an economy to overcome the limits imposed by domestic production possibilities and have the same effect on the economy as having more and better resources. **T F**

■ MULTIPLE-CHOICE QUESTIONS

Circle the letter that corresponds to the best answer.

1. What statement would best complete a short definition of economics? Economics studies
(a) how businesses produce goods and services
(b) the equitable distribution of society's income and wealth
(c) the printing and circulation of money throughout the economy
(d) how individuals, institutions, and society make optimal choices under conditions of scarcity

2. The idea in economics that "there is no such thing as a free lunch" means that
(a) the marginal benefit of such a lunch is greater than its marginal cost
(b) businesses cannot increase their market share by offering free lunches
(c) scarce resources have alternative uses or opportunity costs
(d) consumers are irrational when they ask for a free lunch

3. The opportunity cost of a new public stadium is the
(a) money cost of hiring guards and staff for the new stadium
(b) cost of constructing the new stadium in a future year
(c) change in the real estate tax rate to pay off the new stadium
(d) other goods and services that must be sacrificed to construct the new stadium

4. From the economic perspective, when a business decides to employ more workers, the business decision maker has most likely concluded that the marginal
(a) costs of employing more workers have decreased
(b) benefits of employing more workers have increased
(c) benefits of employing more workers are greater than the marginal costs
(d) costs of employing more workers are not opportunity costs for the business because more workers are needed to increase production

5. The combination of economic theories or principles into a simplified representation of reality is referred to as an economic
(a) fact
(b) model
(c) assumption
(d) hypothesis

6. Which would be studied in microeconomics?
(a) the output of the entire U.S. economy
(b) the general level of prices in the U.S. economy
(c) the output and price of wheat in the United States
(d) the total number of workers employed in the United States

7. When we look at the whole economy or its major aggregates, our analysis would be at the level of
(a) microeconomics
(b) macroeconomics
(c) positive economics
(d) normative economics

8. Which is a normative economic statement?
(a) The consumer price index rose 1.2 percent last month.
(b) The unemployment rate of 6.8 percent is too high.
(c) The average rate of interest on loans is 4.6 percent.
(d) The economy grew at an annual rate of 3.6 percent.

9. Sandra states that "there is a high correlation between consumption and income." Arthur replies that the correlation occurs because "people consume too much of their income and don't save enough."
(a) Both Sandra's and Arthur's statements are positive.
(b) Both Sandra's and Arthur's statements are normative.
(c) Sandra's statement is positive and Arthur's statement is normative.
(d) Sandra's statement is normative and Arthur's statement is positive.

10. Assume that a consumer can buy only two goods, **A** and **B**, and has an income of $100. The price of **A** is $10 and the price of **B** is $20. The maximum amount of **A** the consumer is able to purchase is
(a) 5
(b) 10
(c) 20
(d) 30

11. Assume that a consumer can buy only two goods, **A** and **B**, and has an income of $100. The price of **A** is $10 and the price of B is $20. What is the slope of the budget line if **A** is measured horizontally and **B** is measured vertically?
(a) −0.5
(b) −1.0
(c) −2.0
(d) −4.0

12. Tools, machinery, or equipment used to produce other goods would be examples of
(a) public goods
(b) capital goods
(c) social goods
(d) consumer goods

13. An entrepreneur innovates by
(a) making basic policy decisions in a business firm
(b) following government regulations to make a product
(c) coming up with a business idea or a concept
(d) commercializing a new product for a market

14. When a production possibilities schedule is written (or a production possibilities curve is drawn) in this chapter, four assumptions are made. Which is one of those assumptions?
(a) The state of technology changes.
(b) More than two products are produced.
(c) The economy has full employment of available resources.
(d) The quantities of all resources available to the economy are variable, not fixed.

Answer Questions 15, 16, and 17 on the basis of the data given in the following production possibilities table.

	Production possibilities (alternatives)					
	A	**B**	**C**	**D**	**E**	**F**
Capital goods	100	95	85	70	50	0
Consumer goods	0	100	180	240	280	300

15. If the economy is producing at production alternative **D**, the opportunity cost of 40 more units of consumer goods is
(a) 5 units of capital goods
(b) 10 units of capital goods

(c) 15 units of capital goods
(d) 20 units of capital goods

16. In the table above, the law of increasing opportunity costs is suggested by the fact that
(a) capital goods are relatively more scarce than consumer goods
(b) greater and greater quantities of consumer goods must be given up to get more capital goods
(c) smaller and smaller quantities of consumer goods must be given up to get more capital goods
(d) the production possibilities curve will eventually shift outward as the economy expands

17. The present choice of alternative **B** compared with alternative **D** would tend to promote
(a) increased consumption in the present
(b) decreased consumption in the future
(c) a greater increase in economic growth in the future
(d) a smaller increase in economic growth in the future

18. What is the economic rationale for the law of increasing opportunity costs?
(a) Optimal allocation and full employment of resources have not been achieved.
(b) Economic resources are not completely adaptable to alternative uses.
(c) Economic growth is being limited by the pace of technological advancement.
(d) An economy's present choice of output is determined by fixed technology and fixed resources.

19. The underallocation of resources by society to the production of a product means that the
(a) marginal benefit is greater than the marginal cost
(b) marginal benefit is less than the marginal cost
(c) opportunity cost of production is rising
(d) consumption of the product is falling

Answer Questions 20, 21, and 22 based on the following graph for an economy.

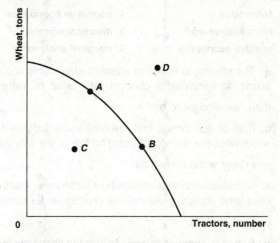

20. Unemployment and productive inefficiency would best be represented in the graph by point
(a) **A**
(b) **B**
(c) **C**
(d) **D**

21. The choice of point **B** over point **A** as the optimal product mix for society would be based on
- **(a)** the state of technology
- **(b)** full employment of resources
- **(c)** the law of increasing opportunity costs
- **(d)** a comparison of marginal costs and benefits

22. Economic growth could be represented by
- **(a)** a movement from point **A** to point **B**
- **(b)** a movement from point **B** to point **A**
- **(c)** a shift in the production possibilities curve out to point **C**
- **(d)** a shift in the production possibilities curve out to point **D**

23. If there is an increase in the resources available within the economy,
- **(a)** the economy will be capable of producing fewer goods
- **(b)** the economy will be capable of producing more goods
- **(c)** the standard of living in the economy will decline
- **(d)** the state of technology will deteriorate

24. Which situation would most likely shift the production possibilities curve for a nation in an outward direction?
- **(a)** deterioration in product quality
- **(b)** reductions in the supply of resources
- **(c)** increases in technological advance
- **(d)** rising levels of unemployment

25. You observe that more education is associated with more income and conclude that more income leads to more education. This would be an example of
- **(a)** the post hoc fallacy
- **(b)** the fallacy of composition
- **(c)** confusing correlation and causation
- **(d)** using the other-things-equal assumption

■ PROBLEMS

1. Use the appropriate number to match the terms with the phrases below.

1. economics	4. normative economics
2. microeconomics	5. macroeconomics
3. positive economics	6. marginal analysis

a. The attempt to establish scientific statements about economic behavior; a concern with "what is" rather than "what ought to be." _____

b. Part of economics that involves value judgments about what the economy should be like or the way the economic world should be. _____

c. Social science that studies how individuals, institutions, and society make optimal choices under conditions of scarcity. _____

d. Part of economics concerned with the economic behavior of individual units such as households, firms, and industries (particular markets). _____

e. The comparison of additional benefits and additional costs. _____

f. Part of economics concerned with the whole economy or its major sectors. _____

2. News report: "The worldwide demand for wheat from the United States increased and caused the price of wheat in the United States to rise." This is a *specific* instance of a more *general* economic principle. Of which economic *generalization* is this a particular example?

_____

_____

3. Following is a list of economic statements. Indicate in the space to the right of each statement whether it is positive (**P**) or normative (**N**). Then, in the last four lines below, write two of your own examples of positive economic statements and two examples of normative economic statements.

a. New York City should control the rental price of apartments. _____

b. Consumer prices rose at an annual rate of 4% last year. _____

c. Most people who are unemployed are just too lazy to work. _____

d. Generally, if you lower the price of a product, people will buy more of that product. _____

e. The profits of oil companies are too large and ought to be used to conduct research on alternative energy sources. _____

f. Government should do more to help the poor.

_____

g. _____ P

h. _____ P

i. _____ N

j. _____ N

4. Following is a list of resources. Indicate in the space to the right of each whether the resource is land (**LD**), labor (**LR**), capital (**C**), entrepreneurial ability (**EA**), or some combinations of these resources.

a. Fishing grounds in the North Atlantic _____

b. A computer in a retail store _____

c. Oil shale deposits in Canada _____

d. An irrigation ditch in Nebraska _____

e. Bill Gates in his work in starting Microsoft _____

f. The oxygen breathed by human beings _____

g. A McDonald's restaurant in Rochester, Minnesota

_____

h. The shelves of a grocery store _____

i. A machine in an auto plant

j. A person who creates a new Web site and uses it to start a successful business _____

k. A carpenter working for a construction company that is building a house _____

5. Following is a production possibilities table for two products, corn and cars. The table is constructed using the usual assumptions. Corn is measured in units of 100,000 bushels and cars in units of 100,000.

Combination	Corn	Cars
A	0	7
B	7	6
C	13	5
D	18	4
E	22	3
F	25	2
G	27	1
H	28	0

a. Follow the general rules for making graphs (see the appendix to Chapter 1); plot the data from the table on the graph below to obtain a production possibilities curve. Place corn on the vertical axis and cars on the horizontal axis.

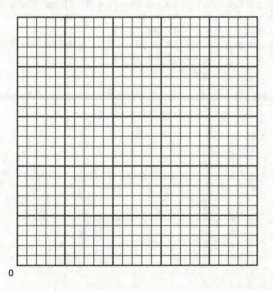

0

b. Fill in the following table showing the opportunity cost per unit of producing the 1st through the 7th car unit in terms of corn units.

Cars	Cost of production
1st	_____
2nd	_____
3rd	_____
4th	_____
5th	_____
6th	_____
7th	_____

c. What is the *marginal* opportunity cost of the 3rd car unit in terms of units of corn? _____

d. What is the *total* opportunity cost of producing 6 car units in terms of units of corn? _____

■ **SHORT ANSWER AND ESSAY QUESTIONS**

1. What are the three interrelated features of the economic perspective?

2. What is the economic meaning of the statement "there is no such thing as a free lunch"?

3. What are the differences and similarities among the terms *hypothesis, theory, principle, law,* and *model*?

4. Why do economists use the "other things equal" assumption?

5. Why are economic principles necessarily generalized and abstract?

6. Explain the difference between microeconomics and macroeconomics.

7. What are some current examples of positive economic statements and normative economic statements?

8. Explain what the term "economizing problem" means for an individual and for society.

9. What is a budget line for an individual? How can it be used to illustrate trade-offs and opportunity costs?

10. What are the four economic resources? How is each resource defined?

11. What four assumptions are made in drawing a production possibilities curve or schedule?

12. What is the law of increasing opportunity costs? Why do opportunity costs increase?

13. What determines the optimal product mix for society's production possibilities?

14. How can unemployment be illustrated with the production possibilities curve?

15. What will be the effect of increasing resource supplies on production possibilities?

16. Describe how technological advances will affect the production possibilities curve.

17. Explain the trade-off between goods for the present and goods for the future and the effect of this trade-off on economic growth.

18. What qualification do international specialization and trade make for the interpretation of production possibilities?

19. Use the production possibilities curve to explain the economics of war.

20. Explain each of the five pitfalls to sound economic reasoning.

ANSWERS

Chapter 1 Limits, Alternatives, and Choices

FILL-IN QUESTIONS

1. scarcity, cost, alternative
2. purposeful, marginal
3. scientific, theories, principles, laws, models
4. generalizations, do not, other-things-equal (or *ceteris paribus*)
5. microeconomics, macroeconomics
6. aggregate
7. positive, normative, normative
8. unlimited, limited
9. buy, budget
10. attainable, unattainable
11. right, left
12. *a.* land or natural resources; *b.* labor; *c.* capital; *d.* entrepreneurial ability
13. *a.* there is full employment and optimal allocation; *b.* the available supplies of the factors of production are fixed; *c.* technology does not change during the course of the analysis; *d.* the economy produces only two products (any order for *a–d*)
14. consumer, capital, cost
15. concave, are not
16. equal to
17. *a.* fewer, more; *b.* unemployed, underemployed; *c.* more, more; *d.* economic growth
18. outward, increase, advance
19. consumer, capital, greater
20. more, increases, advance

TRUE–FALSE QUESTIONS

1. T, p. 4
2. T, p. 4
3. T, pp. 4–5
4. T, pp. 5–6
5. T, p. 6
6. T, p. 6
7. F, p. 6
8. F, pp. 6–7
9. T, p. 7
10. F, p. 7
11. T, pp. 7, 10
12. T, pp. 8–9
13. F, p. 9
14. T, p. 10
15. T, pp. 10–11
16. F, p. 10
17. T, pp. 11–13
18. T, pp. 12–13
19. T, p. 13
20. T, pp. 12–13
21. F, p. 13
22. T, p. 13
23. T, p. 15
24. T, pp. 17–18
25. T, p. 18

MULTIPLE-CHOICE QUESTIONS

1. d, p. 4
2. c, p. 4
3. d, p. 4
4. c, p. 5
5. b, pp. 5–6
6. c, p. 6
7. b, pp. 6–7
8. b, p. 7
9. c, p. 7
10. b, p. 8
11. a, pp. 8–9
12. b, p. 10
13. d, pp. 10–11
14. c, p. 11
15. d, p. 11
16. b, pp. 11–12
17. c, p. 15
18. b, p. 13
19. a, pp. 13–14
20. c, pp. 14–15
21. d, pp. 13–14
22. d, pp. 15–16
23. b, p. 15
24. c, pp. 15–16
25. c, pp. 16–17

PROBLEMS

1. *a.* 3; *b.* 4; *c.* 1; *d.* 2; *e.* 6; *f.* 5
2. An increase in the demand for an economic good will cause the price of that good to rise.
3. *a.* N; *b.* P; *c.* N; *d.* P; *e.* N; *f.* N
4. *a.* LD; *b.* C; *c.* LD; *d.* C; *e.* EA; *f.* LD; *g.* C; *h.* C; *i.* C; *j.* EA; *k.* LR
5. *b.* 1, 2, 3, 4, 5, 6, 7 units of corn; *c.* 3; *d.* 21

SHORT ANSWER AND ESSAY QUESTIONS

1. pp. 4–5
2. p. 4
3. pp. 5–6
4. p. 6
5. p. 6
6. pp. 6–7
7. p. 7
8. pp. 7, 10
9. pp. 8–10
10. pp. 10–11
11. p. 11
12. pp. 12–13
13. p. 13
14. pp. 14–15
15. pp. 15–16
16. p. 16
17. pp. 17–18
18. p. 18
19. p. 14
20. pp. 16–17

APPENDIX TO CHAPTER 1

Graphs and Their Meaning

This appendix introduces graphing in economics. Graphs help illustrate and simplify the economic theories and models presented throughout this book. The old saying that "a picture is worth 1000 words" applies to economics; graphs are the way that economists "picture" relationships between economic variables.

You must master the basics of graphing if these "pictures" are to be of any help to you. This appendix explains how to achieve that mastery. It shows you how to construct a graph from a table with data of two variables, such as income and consumption.

Economists usually, but not always, place the **independent variable** (income) on the horizontal axis and the **dependent variable** (consumption) on the vertical axis of the graph. Once the data points are plotted and a line is drawn to connect the plotted points, you can determine whether there is a **direct** or an **inverse relationship** between the variables. Identifying direct and inverse relationships between variables is an essential skill used repeatedly in this book.

Information from data in graphs and tables can be written in an equation. This work involves determining the **slope** and **intercept** from a straight line in a graph or data in a table. Using values for the slope and intercept, you can write a **linear equation** that will enable you to calculate what the dependent variable would be for a given level of the independent variable.

Some graphs used in the book are *nonlinear*. With **nonlinear curves,** the slope of the line is no longer constant throughout but varies as one moves along the curve. This slope can be estimated at a point by determining the slope of a straight line that is drawn tangent to the curve at that point. Similar calculations can be made for other points to see how the slope changes along the curve.

■ **APPENDIX CHECKLIST**

When you have studied this appendix you should be able to

☐ Explain why economists use graphs.
☐ Construct a graph of two variables using the numerical data from a table.
☐ Make a table with two variables from data on a graph.
☐ Distinguish between a direct and an inverse relationship when given data on two variables.
☐ Identify dependent and independent variables in economic examples and graphs.
☐ Describe how economists use the other-things-equal assumption (*ceteris paribus*) in graphing two variables.

☐ Calculate the slope of a straight line between two points when given the tabular data, and indicate whether the slope is positive or negative.
☐ Describe how slopes are affected by the choice of the units of measurement for either variable.
☐ Explain how slopes are related to marginal analysis.
☐ Graph infinite or zero slopes and explain their meaning.
☐ Determine the vertical intercept for a straight line in a graph with two variables.
☐ Write a linear equation using the slope of a line and the vertical intercept; when given a value for the independent variable, determine a value for the dependent variable.
☐ Estimate the slope of a nonlinear curve at a point using a straight line that is tangent to the curve at that point.

■ **APPENDIX OUTLINE**

1. Graphs illustrate the relationship between variables and give economists and students another way, in addition to verbal explanation, of understanding economic phenomena. Graphs are aids in describing economic theories and models.

2. The construction of a simple graph involves plotting the numerical data of two variables from a table.

    a. Each graph has a **horizontal axis** and a **vertical axis** that can be labeled for each variable and then scaled for the range of the data point that will be measured on the axis.

    b. Data points are plotted on the graph by drawing straight lines from the scaled points on the two axes to the place on the graph where the straight lines intersect.

    c. A line or curve can then be drawn to connect the points plotted on the graph. If the graph is a straight line, it is *linear*. (It is acceptable and typical to call these straight lines "curves.")

3. A graph provides information about relationships between variables.

    a. An upward-sloping line to the right on a graph indicates that there is a positive or *direct relationship* between two variables: an increase in one is associated with an increase in the other; a decrease in one is associated with a decrease in the other.

    b. A downward-sloping line to the right means that there is a negative or *inverse relationship* between the two variables: an increase in one is associated with a decrease in the other; a decrease in one is associated with an increase in the other.

4. Economists are often concerned with determining cause and effect in economic events.

a. A *dependent variable* changes (increases or decreases) because of a change in another variable.

b. An *independent variable* produces or "causes" the change in the dependent variable.

c. In a graph, mathematicians place an independent variable on the horizontal axis and a dependent variable on the vertical axis; economists are more arbitrary in the placement of the dependent or independent variable on an axis.

5. Economic graphs are simplifications of economic relationships. When graphs are plotted, usually an implicit assumption is made that all other factors are being held constant. This "other-things-equal" or *ceteris paribus* assumption is used to simplify the analysis so the study can focus on the two variables of interest.

6. The *slope of a straight line* in a two-variable graph is the ratio of the vertical change to the horizontal change between two points.

a. A *positive* slope indicates that the relationship between the two variables is *direct*.

b. A *negative* slope indicates that there is an *inverse* relationship between the two variables.

c. Slopes are affected by the *measurement units* for either variable.

d. Slopes measure *marginal* changes.

e. Slopes can be *infinite* (line parallel to vertical axis) or zero (line parallel to horizontal axis).

7. The *vertical intercept* of a straight line in a two-variable graph is the point where the line intersects the vertical axis of the graph.

8. The slope and intercept of a straight line can be expressed in the form of a *linear equation,* which is written as $y = a + bx$. Once the values for the intercept (a) and the slope (b) are calculated, then given any value of the independent variable (x), the value of the dependent variable (y) can be determined.

9. The slope of a straight line is constant, but the slope of a nonlinear curve changes throughout. To estimate the slope of a *nonlinear curve* at a point, the slope of a straight line *tangent* to the curve at that point is calculated.

■ **HINTS AND TIPS**

1. This appendix will help you understand the graphs and problems presented throughout the book. Do not skip reading the appendix or working on the self-test questions and problems in this *Study Guide*. The time you invest now will pay off in improved understanding in later chapters. Graphing is a basic skill for economic analysis.

2. Positive and negative relationships in graphs often confuse students. To overcome this confusion, draw a two-variable graph with a positive slope and another two-variable graph with a negative slope. In each graph, show what happens to the value of one variable when there is a change in the value of the other variable.

3. A straight line in a two-variable graph can be expressed in an equation. Make sure you know how to interpret each part of the linear equation.

■ **IMPORTANT TERMS**

vertical axis

horizontal axis

direct (positive) relationship

inverse (negative) relationship

dependent variable

independent variable

slope of a straight line

vertical intercept

linear equation

nonlinear curve

tangent

SELF-TEST

■ **FILL-IN QUESTIONS**

1. The relationship between two economic variables can be visualized with the aid of a two-dimensional (graph, matrix) _____, which has (a horizontal, an inverse) _____ axis and a (vertical, direct) _____ axis.

2. Customarily, the (dependent, independent) _____ variable is placed on the horizontal axis and the _____ is placed on the vertical axis. The _____ variable is said to change because of a change in the _____ variable.

3. The vertical and horizontal (scales, ranges) _____ of the graph are calibrated to reflect the _____ of values in the table of data points on which the graph is based.

4. The graph of a straight line that slopes downward to the right indicates that there is (a direct, an inverse) _____ relationship between the two variables. A graph of a straight line that slopes upward to the right tells us that the relationship is (direct, inverse) _____. When the value of one variable increases and the value of the other variable increases, then the relationship is _____; when the value of one increases, while the other decreases, the relationship is _____.

5. When interpreting an economic graph, the "cause" or the "source" is the (dependent, independent) _____ variable and the "effect" or "outcome" is the _____ variable.

6. Other variables, beyond the two in a two-dimensional graph, that might affect the economic relationship are assumed to be (changing, held constant) _____. This assumption is also referred to as the other-things-equal assumption or as (*post hoc, ceteris paribus*) _____.

7. The slope of a straight line between two points is defined as the ratio of the (vertical, horizontal) _____ change to the _____ change.

8. When two variables move in the same direction, the slope will be (negative, positive) _____; when the variables move in opposite directions, the slope will be _____.

9. The slope of a line will be affected by the (units of measurement, vertical intercept) _____.

10. The concept of a slope is important to economists because it reflects the influence of a (marginal, total) _____ change in one variable on another variable.

11. A graph of a line with an infinite slope is (horizontal, vertical) _____, while a graph of a line with a zero slope is _____.

12. The point at which the slope of the line meets the vertical axis is called the vertical (tangent, intercept) _____.

13. We can express the graph of a straight line with a linear equation that can be written as $y = a + bx$.

   a. *a* is the (slope, intercept) _____ and *b* is the _____

   b. *y* is the (dependent, independent) _____ variable and *x* is the _____ variable.
   c. If *a* were 2, *b* were 4, and *x* were 5, then *y* would be _____. If the value of *x* changed to 7, then *y* would be _____. If the value of *x* changed to 3, then *y* would be _____.

14. The slope of a (straight line, nonlinear curve) _____ is constant throughout; the slope of a _____ varies from point to point.

15. An estimate of the slope of a nonlinear curve at a certain point can be made by calculating the slope of a straight line that is (tangent, perpendicular) _____ to the point on the curve.

■ TRUE–FALSE QUESTIONS

Circle T if the statement is true, F if it is false.

1. Economists design graphs to confuse people.   **T   F**

2. If the straight line on a two-variable graph slopes downward to the right, then there is a positive relationship between the two variables.   **T   F**

3. A variable that changes as a consequence of a change in another variable is considered a dependent variable.   **T   F**

4. Economists always put the independent variable on the horizontal axis and the dependent variable on the vertical axis of a two-variable graph.   **T   F**

5. *Ceteris paribus* means that other variables are changing at the same time.   **T   F**

6. In the ratio for the calculation of the slope of a straight line, the vertical change is in the numerator and the horizontal change is in the denominator.   **T   F**

7. If the slope of the linear relationship between consumption and income was .90, then it tells us that for every $1 increase in income there will be a $.90 increase in consumption.   **T   F**

8. The slope of a straight line in a two-variable graph will *not* be affected by the choice of the units for either variable.   **T   F**

9. The slopes of lines measure marginal changes.   **T   F**

10. Assume in a graph that price is on the vertical axis and quantity is on the horizontal axis. The absence of a relationship between price and quantity would be a straight line parallel to the vertical axis.   **T   F**

11. A line with an infinite slope in a two-variable graph is parallel to the horizontal axis.   **T   F**

12. In a two-variable graph, income is graphed on the vertical axis and the quantity of snow is graphed on the horizontal axis. If income was independent of the quantity of snow, then this independence would be represented by a line parallel to the horizontal axis.   **T   F**

13. If a linear equation is $y = 10 + 5x$, the vertical intercept is 5.   **T   F**

14. When a straight line is tangent to a nonlinear curve, then it intersects the curve at a particular point.   **T   F**

15. If the slope of a straight line on a two-variable (x, y) graph were .5 and the vertical intercept were 5, then a value of 10 for x would mean that y is also 10.   **T   F**

16. A slope of −4 for a straight line in a two-variable graph indicates that there is an inverse relationship between the two variables.   **T   F**

17. If x is an independent variable and y is a dependent variable, then a change in y results in a change in x.   **T   F**

18. An upward slope for a straight line that is tangent to a nonlinear curve indicates that the slope of the nonlinear curve at that point is positive.   **T   F**

19. If one pair of x, y points was (13, 10) and the other pair was (8, 20), then the slope of the straight line between the two sets of points in the two-variable graph, with **x** on the horizontal axis and **y** on the vertical axis, would be 2.

T   F

20. When the value of **x** is 2, a value of 10 for **y** would be calculated from a linear equation of **y** = −2 + 6**x**.

T   F

■ MULTIPLE-CHOICE QUESTIONS

Circle the letter that corresponds to the best answer.

1. If an increase in one variable is associated with a decrease in another variable, then we can conclude that the variables are
   (a) nonlinear
   (b) directly related
   (c) inversely related
   (d) positively related

2. The ratio of the vertical change to the horizontal change between two points of a straight line is the
   (a) slope
   (b) vertical intercept
   (c) horizontal intercept
   (d) point of tangency

3. There are two sets of **x**, **y** points on a straight line in a two-variable graph, with **y** on the vertical axis and **x** on the horizontal axis. If one set of points was (0, 5) and the other set (5, 20), the linear equation for the line would be
   (a) **y** = 5**x**
   (b) **y** = 5 + 3**x**
   (c) **y** = 5 + 15**x**
   (d) **y** = 5 + .33**x**

4. In a two-variable graph of data on the price and quantity of a product, economists place
   (a) price on the horizontal axis because it is the independent variable and quantity on the vertical axis because it is the dependent variable
   (b) price on the vertical axis because it is the dependent variable and quantity on the horizontal axis because it is the independent variable
   (c) price on the vertical axis even though it is the independent variable and quantity on the horizontal axis even though it is the dependent variable
   (d) price on the horizontal axis even though it is the dependent variable and quantity on the vertical axis even though it is the independent variable

5. In a two-dimensional graph of the relationship between two economic variables, an assumption is usually made that
   (a) both variables are linear
   (b) both variables are nonlinear
   (c) other variables are held constant
   (d) other variables are permitted to change

6. If the slope of a straight line is zero, then the straight line is
   (a) vertical
   (b) horizontal
   (c) upsloping
   (d) downsloping

Questions 7, 8, 9, and 10 are based on the following four data sets. In each set, the independent variable is in the left column and the dependent variable is in the right column.

(1)		(2)		(3)		(4)	
A	**B**	**C**	**D**	**E**	**F**	**G**	**H**
0	1	0	12	4	5	0	4
3	2	5	8	6	10	1	3
6	3	10	4	8	15	2	2
9	4	15	0	10	20	3	1

7. There is an inverse relationship between the independent and dependent variables in data sets
   (a) 1 and 4
   (b) 2 and 3
   (c) 1 and 3
   (d) 2 and 4

8. The vertical intercept is 4 in data set
   (a) 1
   (b) 2
   (c) 3
   (d) 4

9. The linear equation for data set 1 is
   (a) **B** = 3**A**
   (b) **B** = 1 + 3**A**
   (c) **B** = 1 + .33**A**
   (d) **A** = 1 + .33**B**

10. The linear equation for data set 2 is
   (a) **C** = 12 − 1.25**D**
   (b) **D** = 12 + 1.25**C**
   (c) **D** = 12 − .80**C**
   (d) **C** = 12 − .80**D**

Answer Questions 11, 12, 13, and 14 on the basis of the following diagram.

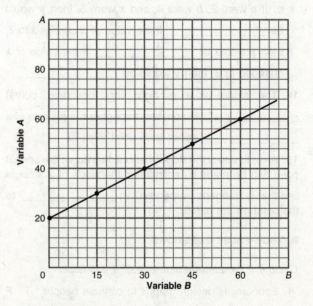

11. The variables **A** and **B** are
   (a) positively related
   (b) negatively related

(c) indirectly related
(d) nonlinear

12. The slope of the line is
(a) .33
(b) .67
(c) 1.50
(d) 3.00

13. The vertical intercept is
(a) 80
(b) 60
(c) 40
(d) 20

14. The linear equation for the slope of the line is
(a) $A = 20 + .33B$
(b) $B = 20 + .33A$
(c) $A = 20 + .67B$
(d) $B = 20 + .67A$

Answer Questions 15, 16, and 17 on the basis of the following diagram.

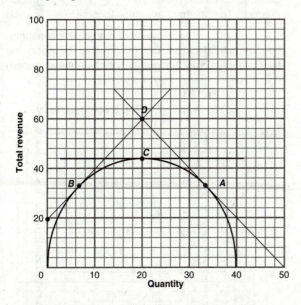

15. The slope of the straight line tangent to the curve at point **A** is
(a) 2
(b) −2
(c) −1.5
(d) −0.5

16. The slope of the straight line tangent to the curve at point **B** is
(a) −2
(b) 2
(c) 3
(d) 0.5

17. The slope of the straight line tangent to the curve at point **C** is
(a) −1
(b) 1
(c) 0
(d) undefined

18. Assume that the relationship between concert ticket prices and attendance is expressed in the equation $P = 25 - 1.25Q$, where P equals ticket price and Q equals concert attendance in thousands of people. On the basis of this equation, it can be said that
(a) more people will attend the concert when the price is high compared to when the price is low
(b) if 12,000 people attended the concert, then the ticket price was $10
(c) if 18,000 people attend the concert, then entry into the concert was free
(d) an increase in ticket price by $5 reduces concert attendance by 1000 people

19. If you know that the equation relating consumption (C) to income (Y) is $C = \$7,500 + .2Y$, then
(a) consumption is inversely related to income
(b) consumption is the independent variable and income is the dependent variable
(c) if income is $15,000, then consumption is $10,500
(d) if consumption is $30,000, then income is $10,000

20. If the dependent variable (vertical axis) changes by 22 units when the independent variable (horizontal axis) changes by 12 units, then the slope of the line is
(a) 0.56
(b) 1.83
(c) 2.00
(d) 3.27

■ **PROBLEMS**

1. Following are three tables for making graphs. On the graphs, plot the economic relationships contained in each table. Be sure to label each axis of the graph and indicate the unit measurement and scale used on each axis.
a. Use the table below to graph national income on the horizontal axis and consumption expenditures on the vertical axis in the graph below; connect the seven points and label the curve "Consumption." The relationship between income and consumption is (a direct, an inverse)

_____ one and the consumption curve is (an

up-, a down-) _____ sloping curve.

0

National income, billions of dollars	Consumption expenditures, billions of dollars
$ 600	$ 600
700	640
800	780
900	870
1000	960
1100	1050
1200	1140

b. Use the next table to graph investment expenditures on the horizontal axis and the rate of interest on the vertical axis on the graph below; connect the seven points and label the curve "Investment." The relationship between the rate of interest and investment expenditures is (a direct, an inverse) _____ one and the investment curve is (an up-, a down-) _____ sloping curve.

Rate of interest, %	Investment expenditures, billions of dollars
8	$ 220
7	280
6	330
5	370
4	400
3	420
2	430

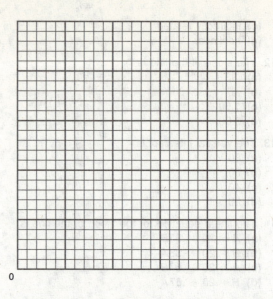

0

c. Use the next table to graph average income on the horizontal axis and milk consumption on the vertical axis on the graph below; connect the seven points.

Average income	Annual per capita milk consumption in gallons
$62,000	11.5
63,000	11.6
64,000	11.7
65,000	11.8
66,000	11.9
67,000	12.0
68,000	12.1

Based on the data, the average income and milk consumption (are, are not) _____ correlated. The higher average income (is, is not) _____ the *cause* of the greater consumption of milk because the relationship between the two variables may be purely (coincidental, planned) _____.

2. This question is based on the following graph.

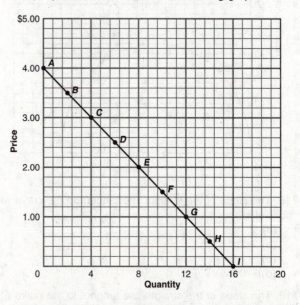

a. Construct a table for points **A–I** from the data shown in the graph.
b. According to economists, price is the (independent, dependent) _____ variable and quantity is the _____ variable.
c. Write a linear equation that summarizes the data.

3. The following three sets of data each show the relationship between an independent variable and a dependent variable. For each set, the independent variable is in the left column and the dependent variable is in the right column.

(1)		(2)		(3)	
A	**B**	**C**	**D**	**E**	**F**
0	10	0	100	0	20
10	30	10	75	50	40
20	50	20	50	100	60
30	70	30	25	150	80
40	90	40	0	200	100

a. Write an equation that summarizes the data for each of the sets (1), (2), and (3).
b. State whether each data set shows a positive or an inverse relationship between the two variables.
c. Plot data sets 1 and 2 on the following graph. Use the same horizontal scale for both sets of independent variables and the same vertical scale for both sets of dependent variables.

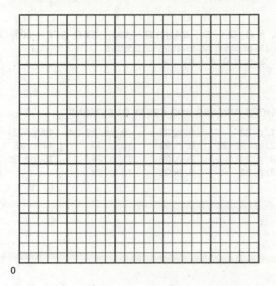

0

4. This problem is based on the following graph.

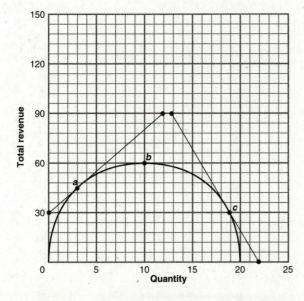

a. The slope of the straight line through point **a** is?
b. The slope of the straight line through point **b** is?
c. The slope of the straight line through point **c** is?

■ SHORT ANSWER AND ESSAY QUESTIONS

1. Why do economists use graphs in their work?

2. Give two examples of a graph that illustrates the relationship between two economic variables.

3. What does the slope tell you about a straight line? How would you interpret a slope of 4? A slope of −2? A slope of .5? A slope of −.25?

4. If the vertical intercept increases in value but the slope of a straight line stays the same, what happens to the graph of the line? If the vertical intercept decreases in value, what will happen to the line?

5. How do you interpret a vertical line on a two-variable graph? How do you interpret a horizontal line?

6. When you know that the price and quantity of a product are inversely related, what does this tell you about the slope of a line where price is on the vertical axis and quantity is on the horizontal axis? What do you know about the slope when the two variables are positively related?

7. Which variable is the dependent and which is the independent in the following economic statement: "A decrease in business taxes had a positive effect on investment spending."

8. How do you tell the difference between a dependent and an independent variable when examining economic relationships?

9. Why is an assumption made that all other variables are held constant when we construct a two-variable graph of the price and quantity of a product?

10. How do mathematicians and economists differ at times in how they construct two-dimensional graphs? Give an example.

11. How is the slope of a straight line in a two-variable graph affected by the choice of the units for either variable? Explain and give an example.

12. What is the relationship between the slopes of lines and marginal analysis?

13. Describe a case in which a straight line in a two-variable graph would have an infinite slope and a case in which the slope of a line would be zero.

14. If you know that the equation relating consumption (C) to income (Y) is $C = 10,000 + 5Y$, then what would consumption be when income is $5000? Construct an income-consumption table for five different levels of income.

15. How do the slopes of a straight line and a nonlinear curve differ? How do you estimate the slope of a nonlinear curve?

ANSWERS

Appendix to Chapter 1 Graphs and Their Meaning

FILL-IN QUESTIONS

1. graph, a horizontal, vertical
2. independent, dependent, dependent, independent
3. scales, ranges

4. an inverse, direct, direct, inverse
5. independent, dependent
6. held constant, *ceteris paribus*
7. vertical, horizontal
8. positive, negative
9. units of measurement
10. marginal
11. vertical, horizontal
12. intercept
13. *a.* intercept, slope; *b.* dependent, independent; *c.* 22, 30, 14
14. straight line, nonlinear curve
15. tangent

TRUE–FALSE QUESTIONS

1. F, p. 22	8. F, p. 24	15. T, p. 25
2. F, p. 23	9. T, p. 24	16. T, p. 24
3. T, p. 23	10. T, pp. 24–25	17. F, p. 23
4. F, p. 23	11. F, pp. 24–25	18. T, pp. 25–26
5. F, pp. 23–24	12. T, pp. 24–25	19. F, p. 25
6. T, p. 24	13. F, p. 25	20. T, p. 25
7. T, p. 24	14. F, pp. 25–26	

MULTIPLE-CHOICE QUESTIONS

1. c, p. 23	8. d, p. 25	15. b, pp. 25–26
2. a, p. 24	9. c, p. 25	16. b, pp. 25–26
3. b, p. 25	10. c, p. 25	17. c, pp. 25–26
4. c, p. 23	11. a, p. 23	18. b, p. 25
5. c, pp. 23–24	12. b, p. 24	19. c, p. 25
6. b, pp. 24–25	13. d, p. 25	20. b, p. 24
7. d, p. 23	14. c, p. 25	

PROBLEMS

1. *a.* a direct, an up-; *b.* an inverse, a down-; *c.* are, is not, coincidental
2. *a. table below*; *b.* independent, dependent; *c.* $P = 4.00 - .25Q$

Point	Price	Quantity
A	$4.00	0
B	3.50	2
C	3.00	4
D	2.50	6
E	2.00	8
F	1.50	10
G	1.00	12
H	.50	14
I	.00	16

3. *a.* (1) $B = 10 + 2A$; (2) $D = 100 - 2.5C$; (3) $F = 20 + .4E$;
b. (1) positive; (2) inverse; (3) positive
4. *a.* 5; *b.* 0; *c.* −10

SHORT ANSWER AND ESSAY QUESTIONS

1. p. 22	5. p. 25	9. pp. 23–24	13. pp. 24–25
2. pp. 22–23	6. p. 24	10. p. 23	14. p. 25
3. p. 24	7. p. 23	11. p. 24	15. pp. 25–26
4. p. 25	8. p. 23	12. p. 24	

CHAPTER 2

The Market System and the Circular Flow

Every economy needs to develop an **economic system** to respond to the economizing problem of limited resources and unlimited wants. The two basic types of systems are the **command system** and the **market system.** In the command system, there is extensive public ownership of resources and the use of central planning for most economic decision making in the economy. In the market system there is extensive private ownership of resources and the use of markets and prices to coordinate and direct economic activity.

A major purpose of Chapter 2 is to explain the major characteristics of the market system because it is the one used in most nations. The first part of this section describes the **ideological** and **institutional** characteristics of the market system. In this system, most of the resources are owned as private property by citizens, who are free to use them as they wish in their own self-interest. Prices and markets express the self-interests of resource owners, consumers, and business firms. Competition regulates self-interest—to prevent the self-interest of any person or any group from working to the disadvantage of the economy and to make self-interests work for the benefit of the entire economy. Government plays an active, but limited, role in a market economy.

Three other characteristics are also found in a market economy. They are the employment of large amounts of **capital goods,** the development of **specialization,** and the **use of money.** Economies use capital goods and engage in specialization because this is a more efficient use of their resources; it results in larger total output and the greater satisfaction of wants. When workers, business firms, and regions within an economy specialize, they become dependent on each other for the goods and services they do not produce for themselves and must engage in trade. Trade is made more convenient by using money as a medium of exchange.

The chapter also explains in detail how the market system works. There are **Five Fundamental Questions** that any economic system must answer in its attempt to use its scarce resources to satisfy its material wants. The five questions or problems are: (1) What goods and services will be produced? (2) How will the goods and services be produced? (3) Who will get the goods and services? (4) How will the system accommodate change? (5) How will the system promote progress?

The explanation of how the market system finds answers to the Five Fundamental Questions is only an approximation—a simplified explanation—of the methods actually employed by the U.S. economy and other market economies. Yet this explanation contains enough realism to be truthful and is general enough to be understandable. If the aims of this chapter are accomplished, you can begin to understand the market system and methods our economy uses to solve the economizing problem presented in Chapter 1.

Although central planning served as a powerful form of economic decision making in command systems such as the Soviet Union and China (before its market reform), it had two serious problems. The first problem was one of **coordination,** which resulted in production bottlenecks and managers and bureaucrats missing production targets. Central planning also created an **incentive problem** because it sent out incorrect and inadequate signals for directing the efficient allocation of an economy's resources and gave workers little reason to work hard. The lack of incentives killed entrepreneurship and stifled innovation and technological advance.

The chapter ends with a description of the **circular flow diagram.** In a market economy, there is a resource market and product market that connect households and businesses. In the diagram, there is a monetary flow of money income, consumption expenditures, revenue, and costs. There also is a flow of resources and goods and services. The model shows that households and businesses have dual roles as buyers and sellers depending on whether they are operating in the product market or resource market.

■ CHECKLIST

When you have studied this chapter you should be able to

☐ Compare and contrast the command system with the market system.
☐ Identify the nine important characteristics of the market system.
☐ Describe the role of private property rights in the market system.
☐ Distinguish between freedom of enterprise and freedom of choice.
☐ Explain why self-interest is a driving force of the market system.
☐ Identify two features of competition in the market system.
☐ Explain the roles of markets and prices in the market system.
☐ Describe how the market system relies on technology and capital.
☐ Discuss how two types of specialization improve efficiency in the market system.

☐ Describe the advantages of money over barter for the exchange of goods and services in the market system.

☐ Describe the size and role of government in the market system.

☐ List the Five Fundamental Questions to answer about the operation of a market economy.

☐ Explain how a market system determines what goods and services will be produced and the role of consumer sovereignty and dollar votes.

☐ Explain how goods and services will be produced in a market system.

☐ Find the least costly combination of resources needed for production when given the technological data and the prices of the resources.

☐ Explain how a market system determines who will get the goods and services it produces.

☐ Describe the guiding function of prices to accommodate change in the market system.

☐ Explain how the market system promotes progress by fostering technological advances and capital accumulation.

☐ State how the "invisible hand" in the market system tends to promote public or social interests.

☐ List three virtues of the market system.

☐ Compare how a command economy coordinates economic activity with how a market economy coordinates economic activity.

☐ Explain the problems with incentives in a command economy.

☐ Draw the circular flow diagram, correctly labeling the two markets and the flows between the two markets.

☐ Define the three main categories of businesses: sole proprietorship, partnership, and corporation.

☐ Describe the role private property plays in helping a market economy find the most productive combination of resources (*Last Word*).

■ **CHAPTER OUTLINE**

1. An *economic system* is a set of institutions and a coordinating mechanism to respond to the economizing problem for an economy.

   a. The *command system* (also called *socialism* or *communism*) is based primarily on extensive public ownership of resources and the use of central planning for most economic decision making. There used to be many examples of command economies (Soviet Union), but today there are few (North Korea, Cuba). Most former socialistic nations have been or are being transformed into capitalistic and market-oriented economies.

   b. The *market system* (*capitalism*) has extensive private ownership of resources and uses markets and prices to coordinate and direct economic activity. In pure (*laissez-faire*) capitalism there is a limited government role in the economy. In a capitalist economy such as the United States, government plays a large role, but the two characteristics of the market system—private property and markets—dominate.

2. The market system has the following nine characteristics.
   a. Private individuals and organizations own and control their property resources by means of the institution of *private property*.

b. These individuals and organizations possess both the *freedom of enterprise* and the *freedom of choice*.

c. These economic units are motivated largely by *self-interest*.

d. *Competition* is based on the independent actions of buyers and sellers. They have the freedom to enter or leave markets. This competition spreads economic power and limits its potential abuse.

e. A *market* is a place, institution, or process where buyers and sellers interact with each other. Markets and prices are used to communicate and coordinate the decisions of buyers and sellers.

f. The market system employs complicated and advanced methods of production, new technology, and large amounts of capital equipment to produce goods and services efficiently.

g. It is a highly specialized economy. Human and geographic *specialization* increase the productive efficiency of the economy. Human specialization is also called *division of labor.* It increases productivity because it allows people to split up work into separate tasks and lets people do the task which they are best at doing. Geographic specialization lets nations produce what they do best and then trade with other nations for what else they want.

h. It uses *money* exclusively to facilitate trade and specialization. Money functions as a *medium of exchange* that is more efficient to use than *barter* for trading goods.

i. Government has an active but limited role.

3. The system of prices and markets and households' and business firms' choices furnish the market economy with answers to *Five Fundamental Questions.*

   a. *What goods and services will be produced?* In a market economy, there is *consumer sovereignty* because consumers are in command and express their wishes for the goods and services through *dollar votes.* The demands of consumers for products and the desires of business firms to maximize their profits determine what and how much of each product is produced and its price.

   b. *How will the goods and services be produced?* The desires of business firms to maximize profits by keeping their costs of production as low as possible guide them to use the most efficient techniques of production and determine their demands for various resources; competition forces them to use the most efficient techniques and ensures that only the most efficient will be able to stay in business.

   c. *Who will get the goods and services?* With resource prices determined, the money income of each household is determined; and with product prices determined, the quantity of goods and services these money incomes will buy is determined.

   d. *How will the system accommodate change?* The market system is able to accommodate itself to changes in consumer tastes, technology, and resource supplies. The desires of business firms for maximum profits and competition lead the economy to make the appropriate adjustments in the way it uses its resources.

e. *How will the system promote progress?* Competition and the desire to increase profits promote better techniques of production and capital accumulation.

(1) The market system encourages technological advance because it can help increase revenue or decrease costs for businesses, thus increasing profits. The use of new technology spreads rapidly because firms must stay innovative or fail. There can also be **creative destruction** where new technology creates market positions of firms adopting the new technology and destroys the market position of firms using the old technology.

(2) Business owners will take their profit income and use it to make more capital goods that improve production and increase profits.

4. Competition in the economy compels firms seeking to promote their own interests to promote (as though led by an *"invisible hand"*) the best interests of society as a whole.

a. Competition results in an allocation of resources appropriate to consumer wants, production by the most efficient means, and the lowest possible prices.

b. Three noteworthy merits of the market system are

(1) The *efficient* use of resources

(2) The *incentive* the system provides for productive activity

(3) The personal *freedom* allowed participants as consumers, producers, workers, or investors

5. The demise of command systems occurred largely because of two basic problems with a centrally planned economy.

a. The *coordination problem* involved the difficulty of coordinating the economy's many interdependent segments and avoiding the chain reaction that would result from a bottleneck in any one of the segments. This coordination problem became even more difficult as the economy grew larger and more complex, and more economic decisions had to be made in the production process. There were also inadequate measures of economic performance to determine the degree of success or failure of enterprises or to give clear signals to the economy.

b. The *incentive problem* arose because in a command economy incentives are ineffective for encouraging economic initiatives and work and for directing the most efficient use of productive resources. In a market economy, profits and losses signal what firms should produce, how they should produce, and how productive resources should be allocated to best meet the wants of a nation. Central planning in the two economies also lacked entrepreneurship and stifled innovation, both of which are important forces for achieving long-term economic growth. Individual workers lacked much motivation to work hard because pay was limited and there were either few consumer goods to buy or they were of low quality.

6. The **circular flow diagram** (or model) is a device used to clarify the relationships between households and businesses in the product and resource markets. It has two types of flows. The monetary flow of money income, consumption expenditures, business revenue, and business costs runs clockwise. The real flow of resources and goods and services runs counterclockwise.

a. *Households* are defined as one or more persons occupying a housing unit.

b. *Businesses* are of three types. A **sole proprietorship** is a business owned and operated by a single person. A **partnership** is a business owned and operated by two or more persons. A **corporation** is a legal entity or structure that operates as a business, so the corporation and not the individual owners are financially responsible for the business's debts and obligations.

c. In the *resource market,* households sell resources (labor, land, capital, and entrepreneurial ability), and in return, they receive money income. Businesses buy these resources, and their resource costs become the money income for households.

d. In the *product market,* businesses sell finished goods and services to households, and in return they receive revenue. Households make consumption expenditures to purchase these goods and services, and they use the money income they obtain from selling their resources to make these consumption expenditures.

7. (*Last Word*). There are tens of billions of ways that resources could be arranged in a market economy, but most combinations would be useless. The reason that a market economy produces the few combinations from the total possible that are productive and serve human goals is because of private property. With it, people have an incentive to make the best use of their resources and find the most rewarding combination.

■ **HINTS AND TIPS**

1. This chapter describes nine characteristics and institutions of a market system. After reading the section, check your understanding by listing the nine points and writing a short explanation of each one.

2. The section on the *Five Fundamental Questions* is both the most important and the most difficult part of the chapter. Detailed answers to the five questions are given in this section of the chapter. If you examine each one individually and in the order in which it is presented, you will more easily understand how the market system works. (Actually, the market system finds the answers simultaneously, but make your learning easier for now by considering them one by one.)

3. Be sure to understand the *importance* and *role* of each of the following in the operation of the market system: (1) the guiding function of prices, (2) the profit motive of business firms, (3) the entry into and exodus of firms from industries, (4) the meaning of competition, and (5) consumer sovereignty.

■ **IMPORTANT TERMS**

economic system	freedom of enterprise
command system	freedom of choice
market system	self-interest
private property	competition

market
specialization
division of labor
medium of exchange
barter
money
consumer sovereignty
dollar votes
creative destruction

"invisible hand"
circular flow diagram
households
businesses
sole proprietorship
partnership
corporation
resource market
product market

SELF-TEST

■ FILL-IN QUESTIONS

1. The institutional arrangements and coordinating mechanisms used to respond to the economic problem are called (*laissez-faire*, an economic system) _____.

2. In a command economy, property resources are primarily (publicly, privately) _____ owned. The coordinating device(s) in this economic system (is central planning, are markets and prices) _____.

3. In capitalism, property resources are primarily (publicly, privately) _____ owned. The means used to direct and coordinate economic activity (is central planning, are markets and prices) _____.

4. The ownership of property resources by private individuals and organizations is the institution of private (resources, property) _____. The freedom of private businesses to obtain resources and use them to produce goods and services is the freedom of (choice, enterprise) _____, while the freedom to dispose of property or money as a person sees fit is the freedom of _____.

5. Self-interest means that each economic unit attempts to do what is best for itself, but this might lead to an abuse of power in a market economy if it were not directed and constrained by (government, competition) _____. Self-interest and selfishness (are, are not) _____ the same thing in a market economy.

6. Broadly defined, competition is present if two conditions prevail; these two conditions are

a. _____

b. _____

7. In a capitalist economy, individual buyers communicate their demands and individual sellers communicate their supplies in the system of (markets, prices) _____, and the outcomes from economic decisions are a set of product and resource _____ that are determined by demand and supply.

8. In market economies, money functions chiefly as a medium of (commerce, exchange) _____. Barter between two individuals will take place only if there is a coincidence of (resources, wants) _____.

9. In a market system, government is active, but is assigned (a limited, an extensive) _____ role.

10. List the Five Fundamental Questions every economy must answer.

a. _____

b. _____

c. _____

d. _____

e. _____

11. Consumers vote with their dollars for the production of a good or service when they (sell, buy) _____ it, and because of this, consumers are said to be (dependent, sovereign) _____ in a market economy. The buying decisions of consumers (restrain, expand) _____ the possible choices of firms over what they produce so they make what is profitable.

12. Firms are interested in obtaining the largest economic profits possible, so they try to produce a product in the (most, least) _____ costly way. The most efficient production techniques depend on the available (income, technology) _____ and the (prices, quotas) _____ of needed resources.

13. The market system determines how the total output of the economy will be distributed among its households by determining the (incomes, expenditures) _____ of each household and by determining the (prices, quality) _____ for each good and service produced.

14. In market economies, change is almost continuous in consumer (preferences, resources) _____, in the supplies of _____, and in technology. To make the appropriate adjustments to these changes, a market economy allows price to perform its (monopoly, guiding) _____ function.

15. The market system fosters technological change. The incentive for a firm to be the first to use a new and improved technique of production or to produce a new and better product is a greater economic (profit, loss) _____, and the incentive for other firms to follow its lead is the avoidance of a _____.

16. Technological advance will require additional (capital, consumer) _____ goods, so the entrepreneur uses profit obtained from the sale of _____ goods to acquire (capital, consumer) _____ goods.

17. A market system promotes (unity, disunity) _____ between private and public interests. Firms and resource suppliers seem to be guided by (a visible, an invisible) _____ hand to allocate the economy's resources efficiently. The two *economic* arguments for a market system are that it promotes (public, efficient) _____ use of resources and that it uses (incentives, government) _____ for directing economic activity. The major *noneconomic* argument for the market system is that it allows for personal (wealth, freedom) _____.

18. Coordination and decision making in a market economy are (centralized, decentralized) _____, but in a command economy they are _____. The market system tends to produce a reasonably (efficient, inefficient) _____ allocation of resources, but in command economies it is _____ and results in production bottlenecks. As a command economy grows over time, the coordination problem becomes (more, less) _____ complex and indicators of economic performance are (adequate, inadequate) _____ for determining the success or failure of economic activities.

19. Another problem with the command economies is that economic incentives are (effective, ineffective) _____ for encouraging work or for giving signals to planners for efficient allocation of resources in the economy. Command economies do not have (production targets, entrepreneurship) _____ that is (are) important for technological advance, and because there was no business competition innovation (fostered, lagged) _____.

20. In the circular flow diagram or model,
   a. Households are buyers and businesses are sellers in (product, resource) _____ markets, and businesses are buyers and households are sellers in _____ markets.
   b. Resources flow from (households, businesses) _____ to be used by _____ to make goods and services.
   c. Consumption expenditures flow as revenue to (households, businesses) _____ for the goods and services purchased by _____.

■ **TRUE–FALSE QUESTIONS**

Circle T if the statement is true, F if it is false.

1. A command economy is characterized by the private ownership of resources and the use of markets and prices to coordinate and direct economic activity. **T F**

2. In a market system, the government owns most of the property resources (land and capital). **T F**

3. Pure capitalism is also called *laissez-faire* capitalism. **T F**

4. Property rights encourage investment, innovation, exchange, maintenance of property, and economic growth. **T F**

5. The freedom of business firms to produce a particular consumer good is always limited by the desires of consumers for that good. **T F**

6. The pursuit of economic self-interest is the same thing as selfishness. **T F**

7. When a market is competitive, the individual sellers of a product are unable to reduce the supply of the product and control its prices. **T F**

8. The market system is an organizing mechanism and also a communication network. **T F**

9. Increasing the amount of specialization in an economy generally leads to the more efficient use of its resources. **T F**

10. One way human specialization can be achieved is through a division of labor in productive activity. **T F**

11. Money is a device for facilitating the exchange of goods and services. **T F**

12. "Coincidence of wants" means that two persons want to acquire the same good or service. **T F**

13. Shells may serve as money if sellers are generally willing to accept them as money. **T F**

14. One of the Five Fundamental Questions is who will control the output. **T F**

15. Industries in which economic profits are earned by the firms in the industry will attract the entry of new firms. **T F**

16. The consumers are sovereign in a market economy and register their economic wants with "dollar votes." **T F**

17. Economic efficiency requires that a given output of a good or service be produced in the least costly way. **T F**

18. If the market price of resource A decreases, firms will tend to employ smaller quantities of resource A. **T F**

19. The incentive that the market system provides to induce technological improvement is the opportunity for economic profits. **T F**

20. Creative destruction is the hypothesis that the creation of new products and production methods simultaneously destroys the market power of existing monopolies and businesses. **T F**

21. The tendency for individuals pursuing their own self-interests to bring about results that are in the best interest of society as a whole is often called the "invisible hand." **T F**

22. A basic economic argument for the market system is that it promotes an efficient use of resources.　　**T　F**

23. A command economy is significantly affected by missed production targets.　　**T　F**

24. Profit is the key indicator of success and failure in a command economy.　　**T　F**

25. In the circular flow model, businesses sell goods and services and buy resources whereas households sell resources and buy goods and services.　　**T　F**

■ **MULTIPLE-CHOICE QUESTIONS**

Circle the letter that corresponds to the best answer.

1. The private ownership of property resources and use of markets and prices to direct and coordinate economic activity is characteristic of
(a) socialism
(b) communism
(c) a market economy
(d) a command economy

2. Which is one of the main characteristics of the market system?
(a) central economic planning
(b) limits on freedom of choice
(c) the right to own private property
(d) an expanded role for government in the economy

3. In the market system, freedom of enterprise means that
(a) government is free to direct the actions of businesses
(b) businesses are free to produce products that consumers want
(c) consumers are free to buy goods and services that they want
(d) resources are distributed freely to businesses that want them

4. The maximization of profit tends to be the driving force in the economic decision making of
(a) workers
(b) consumers
(c) legislators
(d) entrepreneurs

5. How do consumers typically express self-interest?
(a) by minimizing their economic losses
(b) by maximizing their economic profits
(c) by seeking the lowest price for a product
(d) by seeking jobs with the highest wages and benefits

6. Which is a characteristic of competition as economists see it?
(a) a few sellers of all products
(b) the widespread diffusion of economic power
(c) a small number of buyers in product markets
(d) the relatively difficult entry into and exit from industries by producers

7. To decide how to use its scarce resources to satisfy economic wants, a market economy primarily relies on
(a) prices
(b) planning

(c) monopoly power
(d) production targets

8. The market system is a method of
(a) making economic decisions by central planning
(b) communicating and coordinating economic decisions
(c) promoting specialization, but not division of labor
(d) allocating money, but not economic profits or losses

9. When workers specialize in various tasks to produce a commodity, the situation is referred to as
(a) division of labor
(b) freedom of choice
(c) capital accumulation
(d) a coincidence of wants

10. In what way does human specialization contribute to an economy's output?
(a) It is a process of creative destruction.
(b) It serves as consumer sovereignty.
(c) It acts like an "invisible hand."
(d) It fosters learning by doing.

11. Which is a prerequisite of specialization?
(a) market restraints on freedom
(b) having a convenient means of exchanging goods
(c) letting government create a plan for the economy
(d) deciding who will get the goods and services in an economy

12. In the market system, the role of government is best described as
(a) limited
(b) extensive
(c) significant
(d) nonexistent

13. Which would necessarily result, sooner or later, from a decrease in consumer demand for a product?
(a) a decrease in the profits of firms in the industry
(b) an increase in the output of the industry
(c) an increase in the supply of the product
(d) an increase in the prices of resources employed by the firms in the industry

14. The demand for resources is
(a) increased when the price of resources falls
(b) most influenced by the size of government in a capitalist economy
(c) derived from the demand for the products made with the resources
(d) decreased when the product that the resources produce becomes popular

Answer Questions 15, 16, and 17 on the basis of the following information.

Suppose 50 units of product X can be produced by employing just labor and capital according to the four techniques (A, B, C, and D) shown below. Assume the prices of labor and capital are $5 and $4, respectively.

	A	B	C	D
Labor	1	2	3	4
Capital	5	3	2	1

15. Which technique is economically most efficient in producing product X?
(a) A
(b) B
(c) C
(d) D

16. If the price of product X is $1, the firm will realize
(a) an economic profit of $28
(b) an economic profit of $27
(c) an economic profit of $26
(d) an economic profit of $25

17. Now assume that the price of labor falls to $3 and the price of capital rises to $5. Which technique is economically most efficient in producing product X?
(a) A
(b) B
(c) C
(d) D

18. Which is the primary factor determining the share of the total output of the economy received by a household?
(a) the tastes of the household
(b) the medium of exchange used by the household
(c) the prices at which the household sells its resources
(d) ethical considerations in the operation of a market economy

19. If an increase in the demand for a product and a rise in its price cause an increase in the quantity supplied, price is successfully performing its
(a) guiding function
(b) circular flow role
(c) division-of-labor role
(d) medium-of-exchange function

20. In the market system, if one firm introduces a new and better method of production that enhances the firm's economic profits, other firms will be forced to adopt the new method to
(a) increase circular flow
(b) follow rules for capital accumulation
(c) avoid economic losses or bankruptcy
(d) specialize and divide the labor in an efficient way

21. The advent of personal computers and word processing software that eliminated the market for electric typewriters would be an example of
(a) specialization
(b) derived demand
(c) the "invisible hand"
(d) creative destruction

22. The chief economic virtue of the competitive market system is that it
(a) allows extensive personal freedom
(b) promotes the efficient use of resources
(c) provides an equitable distribution of income
(d) eliminates the need for decision making

23. In the system of central planning, the outputs of some industries became the inputs for other industries, but a failure of one industry to meet its production target would cause
(a) widespread unemployment

(b) inflation in wholesale and retail prices
(c) profit declines and potential bankruptcy of firms
(d) a chain reaction of production problems and bottlenecks

24. The two kinds of markets found in the circular flow model are
(a) real and money markets
(b) real and socialist markets
(c) money and command markets
(d) product and resource markets

25. In the circular flow model, businesses
(a) buy products and resources
(b) sell products and resources
(c) buy products and sell resources
(d) sell products and buy resources

■ **PROBLEMS**

1. Use the appropriate number to match the terms with the phrases below.

1. **invisible hand**	4. **consumer sovereignty**
2. **coincidence of wants**	5. **creative destruction**
3. **division of labor**	6. **specialization**

a. Using the resources of an individual, a firm, a region, or a nation to produce one (or a few) goods and services. _____

b. The tendency of firms and resource suppliers seeking to further their own self-interest while also promoting the interests of society in a market economy. _____

c. The situation where new products and production methods eliminate the market position of firms doing business using existing products or older production methods. _____

d. Splitting the work required to produce a product into a number of different tasks that are performed by different workers. _____

e. A situation in which the product the first trader wants to sell is the same as the product the second trader wants to buy, and the product the second trader wants to sell is the same as the product the first trader wants to buy. _____

f. Determination by consumers of the types and quantities of goods and services that will be produced in a market economy. _____

2. Assume that a firm can produce product A, product B, *or* product C with the resources it currently employs. These resources cost the firm a total of $50 per week. Assume, for the purposes of the problem, that the firm's employment of resources cannot be changed. Their market prices, and the quantities of A, B, and C these resources will produce per week, are given in the table below. Compute the firm's profit when it produces A, B, or C, and enter these profits in the table.

Product	Market Price	Output	Economic Profit
A	$7.00	8	$____
B	4.50	10	____
C	.25	240	____

a. Which product will the firm produce?

_____

b. If the price of A rose to $8, the firm would

_____

(Hint: You will have to recompute the firm's profit from the production of A.)

c. If the firm were producing A and selling it at a price of $8, what would tend to happen to the number of firms producing A?

_____

3. Suppose that a firm can produce 100 units of product X by combining labor, land, capital, and entrepreneurial ability using three different methods. If it can hire labor at $2 per unit, land at $3 per unit, capital at $5 per unit, and entrepreneurship at $10 per unit, and if the amounts of the resources required by the three methods of producing 100 units of product X are as indicated in the table, answer the following questions.

	Method		
Resource	**1**	**2**	**3**
Labor	8	13	10
Land	4	3	3
Capital	4	2	4
Entrepreneurship	1	1	1

a. Which method is the least expensive way of producing 100 units of X? _____

b. If X sells for 70 cents per unit, what is the economic profit of the firm? $ _____

c. If the price of labor should rise from $2 to $3 per unit and if the price of X is 70 cents,

(1) the firm's use of

labor would change from _____ to _____

land would change from _____ to _____

capital would change from _____ to _____
entrepreneurship would not change
(2) The firm's economic profit would change from

$_____ to $_____

4. In the circular flow diagram below, the upper pair of flows (**a** and **b**) represents the resource market and the lower pair (**c** and **d**) the product market.

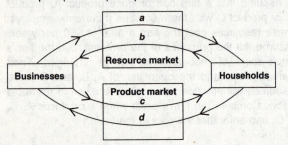

Supply labels or explanations for each of the four flows:

a. _____

b. _____

c. _____

d. _____

■ SHORT ANSWER AND ESSAY QUESTIONS

1. The command system and the market system differ in two important ways. Compare and contrast the two economic systems.

2. Explain the major characteristics—institutions and assumptions—embodied in a market system.

3. What do each of the following seek if they pursue their own self-interest: consumers, resource owners, and business firms?

4. Explain what economists mean by competition. For a market to be competitive, why is it important that there be buyers and sellers and easy entry and exit?

5. How does an economy benefit from specialization and the division of labor?

6. Give an example of how specialization can benefit two separate and diversely endowed geographic regions.

7. What is money? What important function does it perform? Explain how money performs this function and how it overcomes the disadvantages associated with barter.

8. In what way do the desires of entrepreneurs to obtain economic profits and avoid losses make consumer sovereignty effective?

9. Why is the ability of firms to enter industries that are prosperous important to the effective functioning of competition?

10. Explain how an increase in the consumer demand for a product will result in more of the product being produced and more resources being allocated to its production.

11. Describe the production factor for businesses that determines what combinations of resources and technologies will be used to produce goods and services.

12. Who will get the output from a market economy? Explain.

13. How can the market system adapt to change? How is it done?

14. How do prices communicate information and guide and direct production in a market economy?

15. Explain how the market system provides a strong incentive for technological advance and creative destruction.

16. Describe how capital accumulation works. Who "votes" for the production of capital goods? Why do they "vote" for capital goods production? Where do they obtain the dollars needed to cast these "votes"?

17. "An invisible hand operates to identify private and public interests." What are private interests and what is the public interest? What is it that leads the economy to operate as if it were directed by an invisible hand?

18. Describe three virtues of the market system.

19. Explain the two major economic problems with command economies and why market economies avoid such problems.

20. In the circular flow model, what are the two markets? Define households and describe the three basic forms of businesses. What roles do households play and what roles do businesses play in each market?

ANSWERS

Chapter 2 The Market System and the Circular Flow

FILL-IN QUESTIONS

1. an economic system
2. publicly, is central planning
3. privately, are markets and prices
4. property, enterprise, choice
5. competition, are not
6. *a.* independently acting buyers and sellers operating in markets; *b.* freedom of buyers and sellers to enter or leave these markets
7. markets, prices
8. exchange, wants
9. a limited
10. *a.* What goods and services will be produced? *b.* How will the goods and services be produced? *c.* Who will get the goods and services? *d.* How will the system accommodate change? *e.* How will the system promote progress?
11. buy, sovereign, restrain
12. least, technology, prices
13. incomes, prices
14. preferences, resources, guiding
15. profit, loss
16. capital, consumer, capital
17. unity, an invisible, efficient, incentives, freedom
18. decentralized, centralized, efficient, inefficient, more, inadequate
19. ineffective, entrepreneurship, lagged
20. *a.* product, resource; *b.* households, businesses; *c.* businesses, households

TRUE–FALSE QUESTIONS

1. F, p. 30	**10.** T, p. 33	**19.** T, p. 37
2. F, p. 30	**11.** T, pp. 33–34	**20.** T, p. 37
3. T, p. 30	**12.** F, p. 33	**21.** T, p. 38
4. T, pp. 30–31	**13.** T, p. 33	**22.** T, p. 38
5. T, p. 31	**14.** F, p. 34	**23.** T, pp. 38–39
6. F, pp. 31–32	**15.** T, pp. 34–35	**24.** F, pp. 38–39
7. T, p. 32	**16.** T, p. 35	**25.** T, pp. 40–41
8. T, p. 32	**17.** T, pp. 35–36	
9. T, p. 33	**18.** F, p. 36	

MULTIPLE-CHOICE QUESTIONS

1. c, pp. 30–32	**10.** d, p. 33	**19.** a, p. 37
2. c, pp. 30–31	**11.** b, p. 33	**20.** c, p. 37
3. b, p. 31	**12.** a, p. 34	**21.** d, p. 37
4. d, pp. 31–32	**13.** a, p. 35	**22.** b, p. 38
5. c, p. 31	**14.** c, p. 35	**23.** d, pp. 38–39
6. b, p. 32	**15.** b, p. 36	**24.** d, pp. 40–41
7. a, p. 32	**16.** a, p. 36	**25.** d, pp. 40–41
8. b, p. 32	**17.** d, p. 36	
9. a, p. 33	**18.** c, pp. 36–37	

PROBLEMS

1. *a.* 6; *b.* 1; *c.* 5; *d.* 3; *e.* 2; *f.* 4
2. $6, −$5, $10; *a.* C; *b.* produce A and have an economic profit of $14; *c.* it would increase
3. *a.* method 2; *b.* 15; *c.* (1) 13, 8; 3, 4; 2, 4; (2) 15, 4
4. *a.* money income payments (wages, rent, interest, and profit); *b.* services or resources (land, labor, capital, and entrepreneurial ability); *c.* goods and services; *d.* expenditures for goods and services

SHORT ANSWER AND ESSAY QUESTIONS

1. p. 30	**8.** p. 35	**15.** p. 37
2. pp. 30–34	**9.** p. 35	**16.** pp. 37–38
3. pp. 31–32	**10.** pp. 35–36	**17.** p. 38
4. p. 32	**11.** p. 36	**18.** p. 38
5. p. 33	**12.** pp. 36–37	**19.** pp. 38–40
6. p. 33	**13.** p. 37	**20.** pp. 40–41
7. pp. 33–34	**14.** p. 37	

CHAPTER 3

Demand, Supply, and Market Equilibrium

Chapter 3 introduces you to the most fundamental tools of economic analysis: demand and supply. Demand and supply are simply "boxes" or categories into which all the forces and factors that affect the price and the quantity of a good bought and sold in a competitive market are placed. Demand and supply determine price and quantity exchanged. It is necessary to understand *why* and *how* they do this.

Many students never learn to define demand and supply. They never learn (1) what an increase or decrease in demand or supply means, (2) the important distinctions between "demand" and "quantity demanded" and between "supply" and "quantity supplied," and (3) the equally important distinctions between a change in demand and a change in quantity demanded and between a change in supply and a change in quantity supplied.

Having learned these, however, it is no great trick to comprehend the so-called laws of demand and supply. The equilibrium price—that is, the price that will tend to prevail in the market as long as demand and supply do not change—is simply the price at which **quantity demanded** and **quantity supplied** are equal. The quantity bought and sold in the market (the equilibrium quantity) is the quantity demanded and supplied at the equilibrium price. If you can determine the equilibrium price and quantity under one set of demand and supply conditions, you can determine them under any other set.

This chapter includes a brief examination of the factors that determine demand and supply and the ways in which changes in these determinants will affect and cause changes in demand and supply. A graphic method is used in this analysis to illustrate demand and supply, equilibrium price and quantity, changes in demand and supply, and the resulting changes in equilibrium price and quantity. The **demand curve** and the **supply curve** are graphic representations of the same data contained in the schedules of demand and supply. The application section at the end of the chapter explains government-set prices. When the government sets a legal price in a competitive market, it creates a **price ceiling** or **price floor.** This prevents supply and demand from determining the equilibrium price and quantity of a product that will be provided by a competitive market. As you will learn, the economic consequence of a price ceiling is that it will result in a persistent shortage of the product. An example of a price ceiling would be price controls on apartment rents. A price floor will result in a persistent surplus of a product, and the example given is price supports for an agricultural product. You will use demand and supply over and over. It will turn out to be as important to you in economics as jet propulsion is to the pilot of an airplane: You can't get off the ground without it.

■ CHECKLIST

When you have studied this chapter you should be able to

☐ Explain the economic meaning of markets.

☐ Define demand and state the law of demand.

☐ Give three explanations for the inverse relationship between price and quantity demanded.

☐ Graph the demand curve when you are given a demand schedule.

☐ Explain the difference between individual demand and market demand.

☐ List the five major determinants of demand and explain how each one shifts the demand curve.

☐ Explain how changes in income affect the demand for normal goods and inferior goods.

☐ Explain how changes in the prices of a substitute good or a complementary good affect the demand for a product.

☐ Distinguish between change in demand and change in the quantity demanded.

☐ Define supply and state the law of supply.

☐ Graph the supply curve when given a supply schedule.

☐ Explain the difference between individual supply and market supply.

☐ List the major determinants of supply and explain how each shifts the supply curve.

☐ Distinguish between changes in supply and changes in the quantity supplied.

☐ Describe how the equilibrium price and quantity are determined in a competitive market.

☐ Define surplus and shortage.

☐ Determine when you are given the demand for and the supply of a good, the equilibrium price and the equilibrium quantity.

☐ Explain the meaning of the rationing function of prices.

☐ Distinguish between productive efficiency and allocative efficiency.

☐ Predict the effects of changes in demand on equilibrium price and quantity.

☐ Predict the effects of changes in supply on equilibrium price and quantity.

☐ Predict the effects of changes in both demand and supply on equilibrium price and quantity.

☐ Explain the economic effects of a government-set price ceiling on product price and quantity in a competitive market.

☐ Describe the economic consequences of a government-set price floor on product price and quantity.

■ **CHAPTER OUTLINE**

1. A market is any institution or mechanism that brings together buyers ("demanders") and sellers ("suppliers") of a particular good or service. This chapter assumes that markets are highly competitive.

2. *Demand* is a schedule of prices and the quantities that buyers would purchase at each of these prices during a selected period of time.

    a. The *law of demand* states that there is an inverse or negative relationship between price and quantity demanded. Other things equal, as price increases, buyers will purchase fewer quantities, and as price decreases they will purchase more quantities. There are three explanations for the law of demand:

    (1) *Diminishing marginal utility:* After a point, consumers get less satisfaction or benefit from consuming more and more units.

    (2) *Income effect:* A higher price for a good decreases the purchasing power of consumers' incomes so they can't buy as much of the good.

    (3) *Substitution effect:* A higher price for a good encourages consumers to search for cheaper substitutes and thus buy less of it.

    b. The *demand curve* has a downward slope and is a graphic representation of the law of demand.

    c. Market demand for a good is a sum of all the demands of all consumers of that good at each price. Although price has the most important influence on quantity demanded, other factors can influence demand. The factors, called *determinants of demand,* are consumer tastes (preferences), the number of buyers in the market, consumers' income, the prices of related goods, and consumer expectations.

    d. An increase or decrease in the entire demand schedule and the demand curve (a change in demand) results from a change in one or more of the determinants of demand. For a particular good,

    (1) an increase in *consumer tastes or preferences* increases its demand;

    (2) an increase in *the number of buyers* increases its demand;

    (3) *consumers' income* increases its demand if it is a *normal good* (one where income and demand are positively related), but an increase in consumers' income decreases its demand if it is an *inferior good* (one where income and demand are negatively related);

    (4) an increase in *the price of a related good* will increase its demand if the related good is a *substitute good* (one that can be used in place of another) but an increase in the price of a related good will decrease its demand if the related good is a *complementary good* (one that is used with another good).

    (5) an increase in *consumer expectations* of a future price increase or a future rise in income increases its current demand.

    e. A *change in demand* means that the entire demand curve or schedule has changed because of a change in one of the above determinants of demand, but a *change in the quantity demanded* means that there has been a movement along an existing demand curve or schedule because of a change in price.

3. *Supply* is a schedule of prices and the quantities that sellers will sell at each of these prices during some period of time.

    a. The *law of supply* shows a positive relationship between price and quantity supplied. Other things equal, as the price of the good increases, more quantities will be offered for sale, and as the price of the good decreases, fewer quantities will be offered for sale.

    b. The *supply curve* is a graphic representation of supply and the law of supply; it has an upward slope indicating the positive relationship between price and quantity supplied.

    c. The market supply of a good is the sum of the supplies of all sellers or producers of the good at each price.

    d. Although price has the most important influence on the quantity supplied, other factors can also influence supply. The factors, called *determinants of supply,* are changes in (1) resource prices; (2) technology; (3) taxes and subsidies; (4) prices of other good; (5) price expectation; and (6) the number of sellers in a market.

    e. A *change in supply* is an increase or decrease in the entire supply schedule and the supply curve. It is the result of a change in one or more of the determinants of supply that affect the cost of production. For a particular product,

    (1) a decrease in *resource prices* increases its supply;

    (2) an improvement in technology increases its supply;

    (3) a decrease in *taxes* or an increase in *subsidies* increases its supply;

    (4) a decrease in *the price of another good* that could be produced leads to an increase in its supply;

    (5) an increase in *producer expectations* of higher prices for the good may increase or decrease its supply.

    (6) an increase in the number of sellers or suppliers is likely to increase its supply.

    f. A *change in supply* means that the entire supply curve or schedule has changed because of a change in one of the above determinants of supply, but a *change in the quantity supplied* means that there has been a movement along an existing supply curve or schedule because of a change in price.

4. The *equilibrium price* (or *market-clearing price*) of a product is that price at which quantity demanded and quantity supplied are equal. The quantity exchanged in the market (the *equilibrium quantity*) is equal to the quantity demanded and supplied at the equilibrium price.

    a. If the price of a product is above the market equilibrium price, there will be a *surplus* or *excess supply*. In this case, the quantity demanded is less than the quantity supplied at that price.

b. If the price of a product is below the market equilibrium price, there will be a **shortage** or *excess demand*. In this case, the quantity demanded is greater than the quantity supplied at that price.

c. The rationing function of prices is the elimination of surpluses and shortages of a product.

d. Competitive markets produce **productive efficiency,** in which the goods and services society desires are being produced in the least costly way. They also create **allocative efficiency,** in which resources are devoted to the production of goods and services society most highly values.

e. Changes in supply and demand result in changes in the equilibrium price and quantity. The simplest cases are ones where demand changes and supply remains constant, or where supply changes and demand remains constant. More complex cases involve simultaneous changes in supply and demand.

(1) *Demand changes.* An increase in demand, with supply remaining the same, will increase the equilibrium price and quantity; a decrease in demand with supply remaining the same will decrease the equilibrium price and quantity.

(2) *Supply changes.* An increase in supply, with demand staying the same, will decrease the equilibrium price and increase the equilibrium quantity; a decrease in supply, with demand staying the same, will increase the equilibrium price and decrease the equilibrium quantity.

(3) *Complex cases.* These four cases involve changes in demand *and* supply: both increase; both decrease; one increases and one decreases; and, one decreases and one increases. For the possible effects on the equilibrium price and quantity in the four complex cases, see #4 in the "Hints and Tips" section.

5. Supply and demand analysis has many important applications to government-set prices.

a. A **price ceiling** set by government prevents price from performing its rationing function in a market system. It creates a shortage (quantity demanded is greater than the quantity supplied) at the government-set price.

(1) Another rationing method must be found, so government often steps in and establishes one. But all rationing systems have problems because they exclude someone.

(2) A government-set price creates an illegal *black market* for those who want to buy and sell above the government-set price.

(3) One example of a legal price ceiling that creates a shortage would be rent control established in some cities to restrain the rental price of apartments.

b. A **price floor** is a minimum price set by government for the sale of a product or resource. It creates a surplus (quantity supplied is greater than the quantity demanded) at the fixed price. The surplus may induce the government to increase demand or decrease supply to eliminate the surplus. The use of price floors has often been applied to agricultural products such as wheat.

6. (*Last Word*). The supply and demand analysis can be used to understand the shortage of organ transplants. The demand curve for such organs is down-sloping and the supply is fixed (vertical) and left of the zero price on the demand curve. Transplanted organs have a zero price. At that price the quantity demanded is much greater than the quantity supplied, creating a shortage that is rationed with a waiting list. A competitive market for organs would increase the price of organs and then make them more available for transplant (make the supply curve up-sloping), but there are moral and cost objections to this change.

■ HINTS AND TIPS

1. This chapter is the most important one in the book. Make sure you spend extra time on it and master the material. If you do, your long-term payoff will be a much easier understanding of the applications in later chapters.

2. One mistake students often make is to confuse **change in demand** with **change in quantity demanded.** A change in demand causes the entire demand curve to *shift*, whereas a change in quantity demanded is simply a *movement* along an existing demand curve.

3. It is strongly recommended that you draw supply and demand graphs as you work on supply and demand problems so you can see a picture of what happens when demand shifts, supply shifts, or both demand and supply shift.

4. Make a chart and related graphs that show the eight possible outcomes from changes in demand and supply. Figure 3.7 in the text illustrates the *four single shift* outcomes:

(1) **D increase: P ↑, Q ↑**   (3) **S increase: P ↓, Q ↑**
(2) **D decrease: P ↓, Q ↓**   (4) **S decrease: P ↑, Q ↓**

Four shift combinations are described in Table 3.3 of the text. Make a figure to illustrate each combination.

(1) **S ↑, D ↓: P ↓, Q ?**   (3) **S ↑, D ↑: P ?, Q ↓**
(2) **S ↓, D ↑: P ↑, Q ?**   (4) **S ↓, D ↓: P ?, Q ↓**

5. Make sure you understand the "other-things-equal" assumption described in the Consider This box on salsa and coffee beans (p. 61). It will help you understand why the law of demand is not violated even if the price and quantity of a product increase over time.

6. Practice always helps in understanding graphs. Without looking at the textbook, draw a supply and demand graph with a **price ceiling** below the equilibrium price and show the resulting shortage in the market for a product. Then, draw a supply and demand graph with a **price floor** above the equilibrium price and show the resulting surplus. Explain to yourself what the graphs show. Check your graphs and your explanations by referring to textbook Figures 3.8 and 3.9 and the related explanations.

■ IMPORTANT TERMS

demand	income effect
demand schedule	substitution effect
law of demand	demand curve
diminishing marginal utility	determinants of demand

normal goods

inferior goods

substitute good

complementary good

change in demand

change in quantity
  demanded

supply

supply schedule

law of supply

supply curve

determinants of supply

change in supply

change in quantity
  supplied

equilibrium price

equilibrium quantity

surplus

shortage

productive efficiency

allocative efficiency

price ceiling

price floor

SELF-TEST

■ FILL-IN QUESTIONS

1. A market is the institution or mechanism that brings together buyers or (demanders, suppliers) _____ and sellers or _____ of a particular good or service.

2. The relationship between price and quantity in the demand schedule is (a direct, an inverse) _____ relationship; in the supply schedule the relationship is _____ one.

3. The added satisfaction or pleasure a consumer obtains from additional units of a product decreases as the consumer's consumption of the product increases. This phenomenon is called diminishing marginal (equilibrium, utility) _____.

4. A consumer tends to buy more of a product as its price falls because

    a. The purchasing power of the consumer is increased and the consumer tends to buy more of this product (and of other products); this is called the (income, substitution) _____ effect.

    b. The product becomes less expensive relative to similar products and the consumer tends to buy more of the original product and less of the similar products, which is called the _____ effect.

5. When demand or supply is graphed, price is placed on the (horizontal, vertical) _____ axis and quantity on the _____ axis.

6. The change from an individual to a market demand schedule involves (adding, multiplying) _____ the quantities demanded by each consumer at the various possible (incomes, prices) _____.

7. When the price of one product and the demand for another product are directly related, the two products are called (substitutes, complements) _____; how-

ever, when the price of one product and the demand for another product are inversely related, the two products are called _____.

8. When a consumer demand schedule or curve is drawn up, it is assumed that five factors that determine demand are fixed and constant. These five determinants of consumer demand are

    a. _____

    b. _____

    c. _____

    d. _____

    e. _____

9. A decrease in demand means that consumers will buy (larger, smaller) _____ quantities at every price, or will pay (more, less) _____ for the same quantities.

10. A change in income or in the price of another product will result in a change in the (demand for, quantity demanded of) _____ the given product, while a change in the price of the given product will result in a change in the _____ the given product.

11. An increase in supply means that producers will make and be willing to sell (larger, smaller) _____ quantities at every price, or will accept (more, less) _____ for the same quantities.

12. A change in resource prices or the prices of other goods that could be produced will result in a change in the (supply, quantity supplied) _____ of the given product, but a change in the price of the given product will result in a change in the _____.

13. The fundamental factors that determine the supply of any commodity in the product market are

    a. _____

    b. _____

    c. _____

    d. _____

    e. _____

    f. _____

14. The equilibrium price of a product is the price at which quantity demanded is (greater than, equal to) _____ quantity supplied, and there (is, is not) _____ a surplus or a shortage at that price.

15. If quantity demanded is greater than quantity supplied, price is (above, below) _____ the equilibrium price; and the (shortage, surplus) _____ will cause the price to (rise, fall) _____. If quantity demanded is less than the quantity supplied, price is (above, below) _____ the equilibrium price, and the (shortage, surplus) _____ will cause the price to (rise, fall) _____.

16. In the spaces next to **a–h**, indicate the effect [*increase* (+), *decrease* (−), or *indeterminate* (?)] on equilibrium price (**P**) and equilibrium quantity (**Q**) of each of these changes in demand and/or supply.

                                      P   **Q**

  a. Increase in demand, supply constant   ____ ____

  b. Increase in supply, demand constant   ____ ____

  c. Decrease in demand, supply constant   ____ ____

  d. Decrease in supply, demand constant   ____ ____

  e. Increase in demand, increase in supply ____ ____

  f. Increase in demand, decrease in supply ____ ____

  g. Decrease in demand, decrease in supply ____ ____

  h. Decrease in demand, increase in supply ____ ____

17. If supply and demand establish a price for a good so that there is no shortage or surplus of the product, then price is successfully performing its (utility, rationing) _____ function. The price that is set is a market-(changing, clearing) _____ price.

18. A competitive market produces two types of efficiency: goods and services will be produced in the least costly way, so there will be (allocative, productive) _____ efficiency; and resources are devoted to the production of the mix of goods and services society most wants, or there is _____ efficiency.

19. A price ceiling is the (minimum, maximum) _____ legal price a seller may charge for a product or service, whereas a price floor is the _____ legal price set by government.

20. If a price ceiling is below the market equilibrium price, a (surplus, shortage) _____ will arise in a competitive market, and if a price floor is above the market equilibrium price, a (surplus, shortage) _____ will arise in a competitive market.

■ **TRUE–FALSE QUESTIONS**

Circle T if the statement is true, F if it is false.

1. A market is any arrangement that brings together the buyers and sellers of a particular good or service. **T F**

2. Demand is the amount of a good or service that a buyer will purchase at a particular price. **T F**

3. The law of demand states that as price increases, other things being equal, the quantity of the product demanded increases. **T F**

4. The law of diminishing marginal utility is one explanation of why there is an inverse relationship between price and quantity demanded. **T F**

5. The substitution effect suggests that, at a lower price, you have the incentive to substitute the more expensive product for similar products which are relatively less expensive. **T F**

6. There is no difference between individual demand schedules and the market demand schedule for a product. **T F**

7. In graphing supply and demand schedules, supply is put on the horizontal axis and demand on the vertical axis. **T F**

8. If price falls, there will be an increase in demand. **T F**

9. If consumer tastes or preferences for a product decrease, the demand for the product will tend to decrease. **T F**

10. An increase in income will tend to increase the demand for a product. **T F**

11. When two products are substitute goods, the price of one and the demand for the other will tend to move in the same direction. **T F**

12. If two goods are complementary, an increase in the price of one will tend to increase the demand for the other. **T F**

13. A change in the quantity demanded means that there has been a change in demand. **T F**

14. Supply is a schedule that shows the amounts of a product a producer can make in a limited time period. **T F**

15. An increase in resource prices will tend to decrease supply. **T F**

16. A government subsidy for the production of a product will tend to decrease supply. **T F**

17. An increase in the prices of other goods that could be made by producers will tend to decrease the supply of the current good that the producer is making. **T F**

18. A change in supply means that there is a movement along an existing supply curve. **T F**

19. A surplus indicates that the quantity demanded is less than the quantity supplied at that price. **T F**

20. If the market price of a product is below its equilibrium price, the market price will tend to rise because demand will decrease and supply will increase. **T F**

21. The rationing function of prices is the elimination of shortages and surpluses. **T F**

22. Allocative efficiency means that goods and services are being produced by society in the least costly way. **T F**

23. If the supply of a product increases and demand decreases, the equilibrium price and quantity will increase. **T F**

24. If the demand for a product increases and the supply of the product decreases, the equilibrium price will increase and equilibrium quantity will be indeterminate.

T F

25. A price ceiling set by government below the competitive market price of a product will result in a surplus.

T F

■ MULTIPLE-CHOICE QUESTIONS

Circle the letter that corresponds to the best answer.

1. A schedule that shows the various amounts of a product consumers are willing and able to purchase at each price in a series of possible prices during a specified period of time is called
   (a) supply
   (b) demand
   (c) quantity supplied
   (d) quantity demanded

2. The reason for the law of demand can best be explained in terms of
   (a) supply
   (b) complementary goods
   (c) the rationing function of prices
   (d) diminishing marginal utility

3. Assume that the price of video game players falls. What will most likely happen to the equilibrium price and quantity of video games, assuming this market is competitive?
   (a) Price will increase; quantity will decrease.
   (b) Price will decrease; quantity will increase.
   (c) Price will decrease; quantity will decrease.
   (d) Price will increase; quantity will increase.

4. Given the following individuals' demand schedules for product X, and assuming these are the only three consumers of X, which set of prices and output levels below will be on the market demand curve for this product?

	Consumer 1	Consumer 2	Consumer 3
Price X	Q_{dx}	Q_{dx}	Q_{dx}
$5	1	2	0
4	2	4	0
3	3	6	1
2	4	8	2
1	5	10	3

   (a) ($5, 2); ($1, 10)
   (b) ($5, 3); ($1, 18)
   (c) ($4, 6); ($2, 12)
   (d) ($4, 0); ($1, 3)

5. Which change will decrease the demand for a product?
   (a) a favorable change in consumer tastes
   (b) an increase in the price of a substitute good
   (c) a decrease in the price of a complementary good
   (d) a decrease in the number of buyers

6. The income of a consumer decreases and the consumer's demand for a particular good increases. It can be concluded that the good is
   (a) normal
   (b) inferior

(c) a substitute
(d) a complement

7. Which of the following could cause a decrease in consumer demand for product X?
   (a) a decrease in consumer income
   (b) an increase in the prices of goods that are good substitutes for product X
   (c) an increase in the price that consumers expect will prevail for product X in the future
   (d) a decrease in the supply of product X

8. If two goods are substitutes for each other, an increase in the price of one will necessarily
   (a) decrease the demand for the other
   (b) increase the demand for the other
   (c) decrease the quantity demanded of the other
   (d) increase the quantity demanded of the other

9. If two products, A and B, are complements, then
   (a) an increase in the price of A will decrease the demand for B
   (b) an increase in the price of A will increase the demand for B
   (c) an increase in the price of A will have no significant effect on the price of B
   (d) a decrease in the price of A will decrease the demand for B

10. If two products, X and Y, are independent goods, then
   (a) an increase in the price of X will significantly increase the demand for Y
   (b) an increase in the price of Y will significantly increase the demand for X
   (c) an increase in the price of Y will have no significant effect on the demand for X
   (d) a decrease in the price of X will significantly increase the demand for Y

11. The law of supply states that, other things being constant, as price increases
   (a) supply increases
   (b) supply decreases
   (c) quantity supplied increases
   (d) quantity supplied decreases

12. If the supply curve moves from S_1 to S_2 on the graph below, there has been

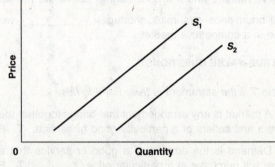

   (a) an increase in supply
   (b) a decrease in supply
   (c) an increase in quantity supplied
   (d) a decrease in quantity supplied

13. A decrease in the supply of a product would most likely be caused by
  (a) an increase in business taxes
  (b) an increase in consumer incomes
  (c) a decrease in resource costs for production
  (d) a decrease in the price of a complementary good

14. If the quantity supplied of a product is greater than the quantity demanded for a product, then
  (a) there is a shortage of the product
  (b) there is a surplus of the product
  (c) the product is a normal good
  (d) the product is an inferior good

15. If the price of a product is below the equilibrium price, the result will be
  (a) a surplus of the good
  (b) a shortage of the good
  (c) a decrease in the supply of the good
  (d) an increase in the demand for the good

16. Which would be the best example of allocative efficiency? When society devoted resources to the production of
  (a) slide rules instead of handheld calculators
  (b) horse-drawn carriages instead of automobiles
  (c) computers with word processors instead of typewriters
  (d) long-playing records instead of compact discs

Answer Questions 17, 18, and 19 on the basis of the data in the following table. Consider the following supply and demand schedules for bushels of corn.

Price	Quantity demanded	Quantity supplied
$20	395	200
22	375	250
24	350	290
26	320	320
28	280	345
30	235	365

17. The equilibrium price in this market is
  (a) $22
  (b) $24
  (c) $26
  (d) $28

18. An increase in the cost of labor lowers the quantity supplied by 65 bushels at each price. The new equilibrium price would be
  (a) $22
  (b) $24
  (c) $26
  (d) $28

19. If the quantity demanded at each price increases by 130 bushels, then the new equilibrium quantity will be
  (a) 290
  (b) 320
  (c) 345
  (d) 365

20. A decrease in supply and a decrease in demand will
  (a) increase price and decrease the quantity exchanged
  (b) decrease price and increase the quantity exchanged
  (c) increase price and affect the quantity exchanged in an indeterminate way
  (d) affect price in an indeterminate way and decrease the quantity exchanged

21. An increase in demand and a decrease in supply will
  (a) increase price and increase the quantity exchanged
  (b) decrease price and decrease the quantity exchanged
  (c) increase price and the effect upon quantity exchanged will be indeterminate
  (d) decrease price and the effect upon quantity exchanged will be indeterminate

22. An increase in supply and an increase in demand will
  (a) increase price and increase the quantity exchanged
  (b) decrease price and increase the quantity exchanged
  (c) affect price in an indeterminate way and decrease the quantity exchanged
  (d) affect price in an indeterminate way and increase the quantity exchanged

23. A cold spell in Florida devastates the orange crop. As a result, California oranges command a higher price. Which of the following statements best explains the situation?
  (a) The supply of Florida oranges decreases, causing the supply of California oranges to increase and their price to increase.
  (b) The supply of Florida oranges decreases, causing their price to increase and the demand for California oranges to increase.
  (c) The supply of Florida oranges decreases, causing the supply of California oranges to decrease and their price to increase.
  (d) The demand for Florida oranges decreases, causing a greater demand for California oranges and an increase in their price.

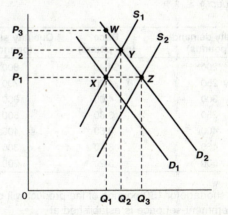

Answer Questions 24, 25, 26, and 27 based on the following graph showing the market supply and demand for a product.

24. Assume that the market is initially in equilibrium where D_1 and S_1 intersect. If there is an increase in the number of buyers, then the new equilibrium would most likely be at point
  (a) *W*
  (b) *X*

(c) **Y**
(d) **Z**

25. Assume that the equilibrium price and quantity in the market are P_2 and Q_2. Which factor would cause the equilibrium price and quantity to shift to P_1 and Q_3?
 (a) an increase in product price
 (b) an increase in demand
 (c) an increase in supply
 (d) a decrease in quantity

26. What would cause a shift in the equilibrium price and quantity from point **Z** to point **X**?
 (a) a decrease in production costs and more favorable consumer tastes for the product
 (b) an increase in the number of suppliers and an increase in consumer incomes
 (c) an increase in production costs and a decrease in consumer incomes
 (d) an improvement in production technology and a decrease in the price of a substitute good

27. Assume that the market is initially in equilibrium where D_1 and S_1 intersect. If consumer incomes increased and the technology for making the product improved, then new equilibrium would most likely be at
 (a) P_1 and Q_1
 (b) P_2 and Q_2
 (c) P_1 and Q_3
 (d) P_3 and Q_1

28. A maximum price set by the government that is designed to help consumers is a
 (a) price ceiling
 (b) price floor
 (c) shortage
 (d) surplus

Questions 29 and 30 relate to the following table that shows a hypothetical supply and demand schedule for a product.

Quantity demanded (pounds)	Price (per pound)	Quantity supplied (pounds)
200	$4.40	800
250	4.20	700
300	4.00	600
350	3.80	500
400	3.60	400
450	3.40	300
500	3.20	200

29. A shortage of 150 pounds of the product will occur if a government-set price is established at
 (a) $3.20
 (b) $3.40
 (c) $3.80
 (d) $4.00

30. If a price floor set by the government is established at $4.20, there will be a
 (a) surplus of 300 pounds
 (b) shortage of 300 pounds

(c) surplus of 450 pounds
(d) shortage of 450 pounds

■ **PROBLEMS**

1. Using the demand schedule below, plot the demand curve on the graph below the schedule. Label the axes and indicate for each axis the units being used to measure price and quantity.

Price	Quantity demanded 1000 bushels of soybeans
$7.20	10
7.00	15
6.80	20
6.60	25
6.40	30
6.20	35

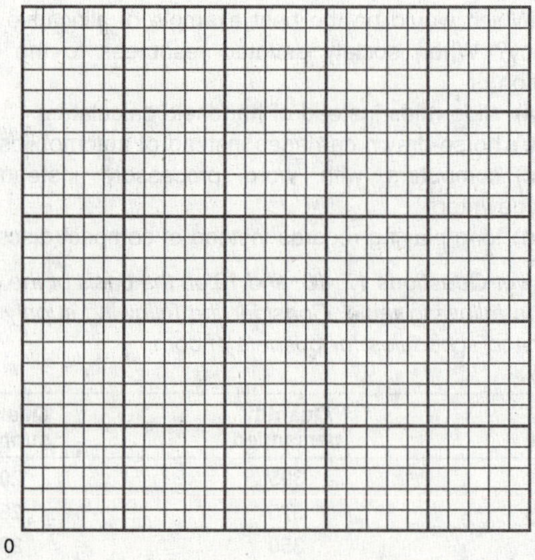

0

a. Plot the following supply schedule on the same graph.

Price	Quantity demanded 1000 bushels of soybeans
$7.20	40
7.00	35
6.80	30
6.60	25
6.40	20
6.20	15

b. The equilibrium price of soybeans will be $_____.
c. How many thousand bushels of soybeans will be exchanged at this price? _____

d. Indicate clearly on the graph the equilibrium price and quantity by drawing lines from the intersection of the supply and demand curves to the price and quantity axes.
e. If the federal government supported a price of $7.00 per bushel there would be a (shortage, surplus)

_____ of _____ bushels of soybeans.

2. The demand schedules of three individuals (Ellie, Sam, and Lynn) for loaves of bread are shown in the following table. Assuming there are only three buyers of bread, determine and graph the total or market demand schedule for bread.

	Quantity demanded, loaves of bread			
Price	Ellie	Sam	Lynn	Total
$1.50	1	4	0	_____
1.40	3	5	1	_____
1.30	6	6	5	_____
1.20	10	7	10	_____
1.10	15	8	16	_____

3. Following is a demand schedule for bushels of apples. In columns 3 and 4 insert any new figures for quantity that represent in column 3 an increase in demand and in column 4 a decrease in demand.

(1) Price	(2) Quantity demanded	(3) Demand increases	(4) Demand decreases
$6.00	400	_____	_____
5.90	500	_____	_____
5.80	600	_____	_____
5.70	700	_____	_____
5.60	800	_____	_____
5.50	900	_____	_____

4. Assume that O'Rourke has, when his income is $100 per week, the demand schedule for good A shown in columns 1 and 2 of the following table and the demand schedule for good B shown in columns 4 and 5. Assume that the prices of A and B are $.80 and $5, respectively.

Demand for A (per week)			Demand for B (per week)		
(1) Price	(2) Quantity demanded	(3) Quantity demanded	(4) Price	(5) Quantity demanded	(6) Quantity demanded
$.90	10	0	$5.00	4	7
.85	20	10	4.50	5	8
.80	30	20	4.00	6	9
.75	40	30	3.50	7	10
.70	50	40	3.00	8	11
.65	60	50	2.50	9	12
.60	70	60	2.00	10	13

a. How much A will O'Rourke buy? _____

How much B?_____

b. Suppose that as a consequence of a $10 increase in O'Rourke's weekly income, the quantities demanded of A become those shown in column 3 and the quantities demanded of B become those shown in column 6.

(1) How much A will he now buy? _____

How much B? _____

(2) Good A is (normal, inferior) _____.

(3) Good B is _____.

5. The market demand for good X is shown in columns 1 and 2 of the following table. Assume the price of X to be $2 and constant.

(1) Price	(2) Quantity demanded	(3) Quantity demanded	(4) Quantity demanded
$2.40	1600	1500	1700
2.30	1650	1550	1750
2.20	1750	1650	1850
2.10	1900	1800	2000
2.00	2100	2000	2200
1.90	2350	2250	2450
1.80	2650	2550	2750

a. If, as the price of good Y rises from $1.25 to $1.35, the quantities demanded of good X become those shown in column 3, it can be concluded that X and Y are (substitute, complementary) _____ goods.

b. If, as the price of good Y rises from $1.25 to $1.35, the quantities of good X become those shown in column 4, it can be concluded that X and Y are _____ goods.

6. The existing demand and supply schedules are given in columns 1, 2, and 3 of the following table.

Demand and Supply Schedules			New Demand and Supply Schedules		
(1) Price	(2) Quantity demanded	(3) Quantity supplied	(4) Price	(5) Quantity demanded	(6) Quantity supplied
$5.00	10	50	$5.00	_____	_____
4.00	20	40	4.00	_____	_____
3.00	30	30	3.00	_____	_____
2.00	40	20	2.00	_____	_____
1.00	50	10	1.00	_____	_____

a. Now the demand *increases* by 10 units at each price and supply *decreases* by 10 units. Enter the new amounts for quantity demanded and quantity supplied in columns 5 and 6.

b. What was the old equilibrium price? _____

What will be the new equilibrium price? _____

c. What was the old equilibrium quantity? _____

What will be the new equilibrium quantity? _____

7. In a local market for hamburger on a given date, each of 300 identical sellers of hamburger has the following supply schedule.

(1) Price	(2) Quantity supplied— one seller, lbs	(3) Quantity supplied— all sellers, lbs
$2.05	150	_____
2.00	110	_____
1.95	75	_____
1.90	45	_____
1.85	20	_____
1.80	0	_____

a. In column 3 construct the market supply schedule for hamburger.

b. Following is the market demand schedule for hamburger on the same date and in the same local market as that given above.

Price	Quantity demanded, lbs
$2.05	28,000
2.00	31,000
1.95	36,000
1.90	42,000
1.85	49,000
1.80	57,000

If the federal government sets a price on hamburger of $1.90 a pound, the result would be a (shortage, surplus) _____ of _____ pounds of hamburger in this market.

8. Each of the following events would tend to increase or decrease either the demand for or the supply of electronic games and, as a result, will increase or decrease the price of these games. In the first blank indicate the effect on demand or supply (increase, decrease); in the second blank, indicate the effect on price (increase, decrease). Assume that the market for electronic games is a competitive one.

a. It becomes known by consumers that there is going to be a major sale on these games one month from now.

_____; _____

b. The workers in the electronic games industry receive a $3 an hour wage increase. _____;

_____

c. It is announced by a respected research institute that children who play electronic games also improve their grades in school. _____;

_____

d. Because of an increase in productivity, the amount of labor necessary to produce a game decreases.

_____; _____

e. The consumers who play these games believe that a shortage of the games is developing in the economy.

_____; _____

f. The federal government imposes a $5 tax per game on the manufacturers of the electronic games.

_____; _____

■ **SHORT ANSWER AND ESSAY QUESTIONS**

1. Define demand and the law of demand.

2. Use the diminishing marginal utility concept to explain why the quantity demanded of a product will tend to rise when the price of the product falls.

3. In past decades, the price of coffee in the United States rose significantly as a result of bad weather in coffee-producing regions. Use the income effect and the substitution effect concepts to explain why the quantity of coffee demanded in the United States significantly decreased.

4. What is the difference between individual demand and market demand? What is the relationship between these two types of demand?

5. Explain the difference between an increase in demand and an increase in the quantity demanded.

6. What are the factors that cause a change in demand? Use supply and demand graphs to illustrate what happens to price and quantity when demand increases.

7. How are inferior and normal (or superior) goods defined? What is the relationship between these goods and changes in income?

8. Why does the effect of a change in the price of related goods depend on whether a good is a substitute or complement? What are substitutes and complements?

9. A newspaper reports that "blue jeans have become even more popular and are now the standard clothing that people wear for both play and work." How will this change affect the demand for blue jeans? What will happen to the price and quantity of blue jeans sold in the market? Explain and use a supply and demand graph to illustrate your answer.

10. Compare and contrast the supply schedule with the demand schedule.

11. Supply does not remain constant for long because the factors that determine supply change. What are these factors? How do changes in them affect supply?

12. Explain the difference between an increase in supply and an increase in the quantity supplied.

13. Describe and illustrate with a supply and demand graph the effect of an increase in supply on price and quantity. Do the same for a decrease in supply.

14. The U.S. Congress passes a law that raises the excise tax on gasoline by $1 per gallon. What effect will this change have on the demand and supply of gasoline? What will happen to gasoline prices and quantity? Explain and use a supply and demand graph to illustrate your answer.

15. Given the demand for and the supply of a commodity, what price will be the equilibrium price of this commodity? Explain why this price will tend to prevail in the market and why higher (lower) prices, if they do exist temporarily, will tend to fall (rise).

16. What is the relationship between the price of a product and a shortage of the product? What is the relationship between the price of a product and a surplus of the product?

17. Explain why competition implies both productive efficiency and allocative efficiency.

18. Analyze the following quotation and explain the fallacies contained in it: "An increase in demand will cause price to rise; with a rise in price, supply will increase and the increase in supply will push price down. Therefore, an increase in demand results in little change in price because supply will increase also."

19. What are the consequences of a price ceiling for a product if it is set below the equilibrium price? Illustrate your answer with a graph.

20. What are the economic problems with price floors? How have they been used by government?

ANSWERS

Chapter 3 Demand, Supply, and Market Equilibrium

FILL-IN QUESTIONS

1. demanders, suppliers
2. an inverse, a direct
3. utility
4. *a.* income; *b.* substitution
5. vertical, horizontal
6. adding, prices
7. substitutes, complements
8. *a.* the tastes or preferences of consumers; *b.* the number of consumers in the market; *c.* the money income of consumers; *d.* the prices of related goods; *e.* consumer expectations with respect to future prices and income (any order for *a–e*)
9. smaller, less
10. demand for, quantity demanded of
11. larger, less
12. supply, quantity supplied
13. *a.* the technology of production; *b.* resource prices; *c.* taxes and subsidies; *d.* prices of other goods; *e.* producer expectations of price; *f.* the number of sellers in the market (any order for *a–f*)
14. equal to, is not
15. below, shortage, rise, above, surplus, fall
16. *a.* +, +; *b.* −, +; *c.* −, −; *d.* +, −; *e.* ?, +; *f.* +, ?; *g.* ?, −; *h.* −, ?
17. rationing, clearing
18. productive, allocative
19. maximum, minimum
20. shortage, surplus

TRUE–FALSE QUESTIONS

1. T, p. 48	10. T, pp. 51–52	19. T, pp. 56–57
2. F, p. 48	11. T, p. 52	20. F, pp. 57–58
3. F, p. 49	12. F, p. 52	21. T, p. 58
4. T, p. 49	13. F, p. 53	22. F, pp. 58–59
5. F, p. 49	14. F, p. 53	23. F, pp. 59–60
6. F, pp. 49–50	15. T, pp. 54–55	24. T, pp. 59–60
7. F, pp. 48–49	16. F, p. 55	25. F, p. 61
8. F, pp. 50–51	17. T, p. 55	
9. T, p. 51	18. F, pp. 54–56	

MULTIPLE-CHOICE QUESTIONS

1. b, p. 48	11. c, p. 53	21. c, pp. 59–60
2. d, p. 49	12. a, pp. 53–55	22. d, pp. 59–60
3. d, pp. 56–58	13. a, pp. 54–55	23. b, pp. 59–60
4. b, p. 50	14. b, pp. 56–57	24. c, pp. 59–60
5. d, pp. 51–52	15. b, pp. 56–57	25. c, pp. 59–60
6. b, pp. 51–52	16. c, pp. 58–59	26. c, pp. 59–60
7. a, pp. 51–52	17. c, pp. 56–57	27. c, pp. 59–60
8. b, p. 52	18. d, pp. 54–57	28. a, p. 61
9. a, p. 52	19. d, pp. 56–57	29. b, p. 61
10. c, p. 52	20. d, pp. 59–60	30. c, pp. 63–64

PROBLEMS

1. *a.* graph; *b.* 6.60; *c.* 25,000; *d.* graph; *e.* surplus, 20,000
2. Total: 5, 9, 17, 27, 39
3. Each quantity in column 3 is greater than in column 2, and each quantity in column 4 is less than in column 2.
4. *a.* 30, 4; *b.* (1) 20, 7; (2) inferior; (3) normal (superior)
5. *a.* complementary; *b.* substitute
6. *a.* column 5 (quantity demanded): 20, 30, 40, 50, 60; column 6 (quantity supplied): 40, 30, 20, 10, 0; *b.* $3.00, $4.00; *c.* 30, 30
7. *a.* 45,000; 33,000; 22,500; 13,500; 6,000; 0; *b.* shortage, 28,500
8. *a.* decrease demand, decrease price; *b.* decrease supply, increase price; *c.* increase demand, increase price; *d.* increase supply, decrease price; *e.* increase demand, increase price; *f.* decrease supply, increase price

SHORT ANSWER AND ESSAY QUESTIONS

1. pp. 48–49	8. p. 52	15. pp. 56–59
2. p. 49	9. pp. 50–51	16. pp. 56–586
3. p. 49	10. pp. 48–49, 53	17. pp. 58–59
4. p. 50	11. pp. 54–56	18. pp. 59–60
5. p. 53	12. pp. 54–56	19. pp. 61–63
6. p. 52	13. pp. 59–60	20. pp. 63–64
7. pp. 51–52	14. pp. 59–60	

APPENDIX TO CHAPTER 3

Additional Examples of Supply and Demand

The first section of the appendix gives more examples of the effects of **changes in supply and demand** on price and quantity. You first will read about simple changes in which either the demand curve changes or the supply curve changes, but not both. These simple changes result in predictable effects on the price and quantity of a product, such as lettuce or a foreign currency such as the euro. Then you are given examples of complex changes, using pink salmon, gasoline, and sushi. In these cases, there is a simultaneous shift in supply and demand. Here the effect of changes in supply and demand on price and quantity will be less certain and will depend on the direction and extent of the changes.

The appendix then extends your understanding of what happens in markets if **pre-set prices** are above or below the equilibrium price. You have already learned that when the government intervenes in a competitive market and sets the price below equilibrium (a price ceiling), it creates a shortage of a product. Similarly, when government sets a price above the equilibrium price (a price floor), it will result in a surplus. As you will learn, shortages and surpluses can also occur in competitive markets when sellers set the price in advance of sales and that pre-set price turns out to be below or above the equilibrium or actual price. The examples given in the text are ticket prices for sporting events that are priced too low or too high by the sellers, resulting in shortages and surpluses.

Supply and demand analysis is one of the most important means for improving your understanding of the economic world. If you master its use, it will help you explain many events and outcomes in everyday life. This appendix helps you achieve that mastery and understanding.

■ APPENDIX CHECKLIST

When you have studied this appendix you should be able to

☐ Explain and graph the effect of a decrease in the supply of a product (lettuce) on its equilibrium price and quantity.
☐ Define the main characteristics of the foreign exchange market.
☐ Describe and graph the effect of an increase in the demand for a foreign currency (the euro) on its equilibrium price and quantity.
☐ Distinguish between the appreciation and depreciation of a currency.
☐ Discuss and graph the effects of an increase in the supply of and a decrease in demand for a product (pink salmon) on its equilibrium price and quantity.

☐ Predict and graph the effects of a decrease in the supply of and an increase in the demand for a product (gasoline) on its equilibrium price and quantity.
☐ Explain and graph the effects of an equal increase in the supply of and demand for a product (sushi) on its equilibrium price and quantity.
☐ Discuss and graph how a seller price for a service (Olympic figure skating finals) that is set below the equilibrium price will result in a shortage.
☐ Describe and graph how a seller price for a service (Olympic curling preliminaries) that is set above the equilibrium price will result in a surplus.

■ APPENDIX OUTLINE

1. **Changes in supply and demand** result in changes in the equilibrium price and quantity. The simplest cases are ones where demand changes and supply remain constant, or where supply changes and demand remain constant. More complex cases involve simultaneous changes in supply and demand.
  a. *Supply increase.* In a competitive market for lettuce, if a severe freeze destroys a portion of the lettuce crop, then the supply of lettuce will decrease. The decrease in the supply of lettuce, with demand remaining the same, will increase the equilibrium price and decrease the equilibrium quantity.
  b. *Demand increase.* In a competitive market for euros, an increase in the demand for euros because of the rising popularity of European goods, with supply remaining the same, will increase the equilibrium price and quantity of euros.
  (1) The **foreign exchange market** is where foreign currencies, such as the European euro and U.S. dollar, are traded for each other. The equilibrium prices for foreign currencies are called **exchange rates** and represent how much of each currency can be exchanged for another currency. In the dollar–euro market, the dollar price of a euro would be on the vertical axis and the quantity of euro would be on the horizontal axis. The intersection of the up-sloping supply of euro curve and down-sloping demand for euro curve would determine the dollar price of a euro.
  (2) If U.S. demand for European goods increased, then more euros will be needed to pay for these imported goods, and so the demand for euros would increase. This change increases the dollar price of euros, which

means that the U.S. dollar has **depreciated** relative to the euro and that the euro has **appreciated** relative to the dollar.

c. *Supply increase and demand decrease.* Over the years, improved fishing techniques and technology contributed to an increase in the supply of pink salmon. Also, an increase in consumer incomes and a lowering of the price of substitute fish contributed to reducing the demand for pink salmon. As a result the price of pink salmon fell. The equilibrium quantity could have increased, decreased, or stayed the same. In this case, the increase in supply was greater than the decrease in demand, so the equilibrium quantity increased.

d. *Demand increase and supply decrease.* An increase in the price of oil, a resource used to produce gasoline, resulted in a decrease in the supply of gasoline. At the same time, rising incomes and a stronger economy created a greater demand for gasoline. This decrease in supply and increase in demand increased the equilibrium price. The equilibrium quantity could have increased, decreased, or stayed the same. In this case, the decrease in supply was less than the increase in demand, so the equilibrium quantity increased.

e. *Demand increase and supply increase.* An increase in the taste for sushi among U.S. consumers resulted in an increase in the demand for this product. At the same time, there was an increase in the number of sushi bars and other food outlets that provide sushi, thus increasing its supply. This increase in both demand and supply increased the equilibrium quantity of sushi. The equilibrium price could have increased, decreased, or stayed the same. In this case, the increase in demand was the same as the increase in supply, so the equilibrium price remained the same.

2. Pre-set prices that the seller establishes below or above the equilibrium price can produce shortages and surpluses. If a price is set below the equilibrium price by a seller, then at that pre-set price the quantity demanded is greater than the quantity supplied, resulting in a **shortage.** If a price is set above the equilibrium price by a seller, then at that pre-set price the quantity demanded is less than the quantity supplied, resulting in a **surplus.**

a. The shortage is typical of the market for tickets to more popular sporting events such as Olympic figure skating finals. The shortage of tickets at the pre-set price creates a secondary market (*black market*) for tickets in which buyers bid for tickets held by the initial purchaser. The ticket scalping drives up the price of tickets.

b. The surplus is typical of the market for tickets to less popular sporting events such as Olympic curling preliminaries at which there are many empty seats.

■ HINTS AND TIPS

1. This appendix offers applications and extensions of Chapter 3 in the textbook, so check your understanding of the corresponding text and appendix sections: (a) Review the Chapter 3 section on "Changes in Supply, Demand, and Equilibrium" before reading the Web appendix section on "Changes in Supply and Demand"; and (b) review the text Chapter 3 section on "Application: Government-Set Prices" before reading the appendix section on "Pre-Set Prices."

2. Correct terminology is important for mastering supply and demand analysis. You must remember the distinction between a change in demand and a change in quantity demanded or a change in supply and a change in quantity supplied. Consider the case of a single shift in demand with supply staying the same. As the demand curve increases along the existing supply curve, it increases the quantity supplied, but it does not increase supply (which would be a shift in the entire supply curve).

SELF-TEST

■ FILL-IN QUESTIONS

1. A decrease in the supply of lettuce will result in an equilibrium price that (increases, decreases) _____ and an equilibrium quantity that _____ .

2. In the foreign exchange market for euros that are priced in U.S. dollars, an increase in the demand for euros (increases, decreases) _____ the U.S. dollar price of a euro and _____ the equilibrium quantity of euros. This change means that the value of the euro (appreciates, depreciates) _____ relative to the U.S. dollar and that the value of the U.S. dollar _____ relative to the euro.

3. An increase in the price of corn resulted in an increase in the (demand for, supply of) _____ farmland in the corn belt and a decrease in the _____ corn-fed beef.

4. An increase in the supply of pink salmon that is greater than the decrease in the demand for pink salmon will result in an equilibrium price that (increases, decreases, stays the same) _____ and an equilibrium quantity that _____ .

5. An increase in the demand for gasoline that is greater than the decrease in the supply of gasoline will result in an equilibrium price that (increases, decreases, stays the same) _____ and an equilibrium quantity that _____ .

6. A large increase in the price of gasoline is most likely to (increase, decrease) _____ the demand for low-gas-mileage SUVs and trucks and _____ the demand for high-gas-mileage hybrid cars.

7. An increase in the demand for sushi that is equal to the increase in the supply of sushi will result in an equilibrium price that (increases, decreases, stays the same) _____ and an equilibrium quantity that _____.

8. If government sets a legal price for a product, a shortage would arise from a price (ceiling, floor) _____ and a surplus would arise from a price _____.

9. If a pre-set price is set by the seller below the equilibrium price it will create a (surplus, shortage) _____, but if a pre-set price is set by the seller above the equilibrium price it will create a _____.

10. A market for tickets to popular sporting events in which buyers bid for tickets held by initial purchasers is referred to as a (primary, secondary) _____ market. In these markets, ticket (destruction, scalping) _____ occurs.

■ TRUE–FALSE QUESTIONS

Circle T if the statement is true, F if it is false.

1. An increase in the supply of lettuce decreases its equilibrium price and increases its equilibrium quantity. **T   F**

2. A decrease in the demand for tomatoes increases the equilibrium price and decreases the equilibrium quantity. **T   F**

3. When demand for euros increases because the United States imports more European goods, then the U.S. dollar price of the euro will increase and the euro has appreciated in value. **T   F**

4. In the market for pink salmon, the reason that the equilibrium quantity increased was that the increase in supply was greater than the decrease in demand. **T   F**

5. In a market for beef, the equilibrium price will increase when the increase in supply is greater than the increase in demand. **T   F**

6. In the market for sushi, an equal increase in supply and demand will increase the equilibrium price, but have no effect on the equilibrium quantity. **T   F**

7. In a market for flat-screen TVs, an increase in supply that is greater than the increase in demand will result in a lower equilibrium price. **T   F**

8. If a seller pre-sets a price that turns out to be below the actual equilibrium price, a shortage will develop in the market. **T   F**

9. Ticket scalping often occurs in markets where there is a surplus of tickets. **T   F**

10. If a sporting event is not sold out, this indicates that the ticket prices for the event were pre-set above the actual equilibrium price. **T   F**

■ MULTIPLE-CHOICE QUESTIONS

Circle the letter that corresponds to the best answer.

1. Bad weather in coffee-producing regions of the world devastated the coffee crop. As a result, coffee prices increased worldwide. Which of the following statements best explains the situation?
(a) The demand for coffee increased.
(b) The supply of coffee decreased.
(c) The demand for coffee increased and the supply of coffee increased.
(d) The demand for coffee decreased and the supply of coffee decreased.

2. Assume that the supply of tomatoes in a competitive market increases. What will most likely happen to the equilibrium price and quantity of tomatoes?
(a) Price will increase; quantity will decrease
(b) Price will decrease; quantity will increase
(c) Price will decrease; quantity will decrease
(d) Price will increase; quantity will increase

3. Assume that the demand for security services increases in a competitive market. What will most likely happen to the equilibrium price and quantity of security services?
(a) price will increase; quantity will decrease
(b) price will decrease; quantity will increase
(c) price will decrease; quantity will decrease
(d) price will increase; quantity will increase

4. A decrease in the demand for beef is more than offset by an increase in its supply. As a result the equilibrium price will
(a) increase and the equilibrium quantity will decrease
(b) increase and the equilibrium quantity will increase
(c) decrease and the equilibrium quantity will decrease
(d) decrease and the equilibrium quantity will increase

5. A decrease in the supply of oil is more than offset by an increase in its demand. As a result, the equilibrium price will
(a) increase and the equilibrium quantity will decrease
(b) increase and the equilibrium quantity will increase
(c) decrease and the equilibrium quantity will decrease
(d) decrease and the equilibrium quantity will increase

6. An increase in the demand for lumber that is less than the increase in the supply of lumber will
(a) increase the equilibrium price and quantity of lumber
(b) decrease the equilibrium price and quantity of lumber
(c) increase the equilibrium price and decrease the equilibrium quantity of lumber
(d) decrease the equilibrium price and increase the equilibrium quantity of lumber

7. What will happen to the equilibrium quantity and price of a product in a competitive market when there is an equal increase in demand and supply?
(a) equilibrium quantity and price will both increase
(b) equilibrium quantity and price will both decrease
(c) equilibrium quantity will increase and equilibrium price will stay the same
(d) equilibrium quantity will stay the same and equilibrium price will increase

8. What will happen to the equilibrium quantity and price of a product in a competitive market when the decrease in demand exactly offsets the increase in supply?
(a) equilibrium quantity will increase and equilibrium price will decrease
(b) equilibrium quantity will decrease and equilibrium price will increase
(c) equilibrium quantity will increase and equilibrium price will stay the same
(d) equilibrium quantity will stay the same and equilibrium price will decrease

9. Which of the following is a correct statement?
(a) price ceilings increase supply
(b) price ceilings create shortages
(c) price floors create shortages
(d) price floors increase demand

10. If a seller sets a price for a product that turns out to be below the equilibrium price, then there will be a
(a) shortage of the product
(b) surplus of the product
(c) price floor for a product
(d) zero price for the product

11. A surplus means that
(a) demand for a product is greater than the supply
(b) supply of the product is greater than the demand
(c) quantity demanded is less than the quantity supplied at that price
(d) quantity demanded is greater than the quantity supplied at that price

Answer Questions 12, 13, and 14 based on the following graph showing the market supply and demand for a product.

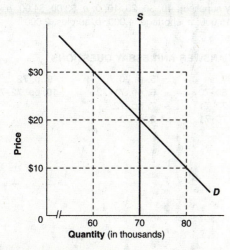

12. Given this market, if a seller pre-sets the price at $10, then this action results in a
(a) surplus of 10,000 units
(b) surplus of 80,000 units
(c) shortage of 10,000 units
(d) shortage of 80,000 units

13. Given this market, if a seller pre-sets the price at $30, then this action results in a
(a) surplus of 10,000 units
(b) surplus of 60,000 units

(c) surplus of 70,000 units
(d) shortage of 10,000 units

14. What price will eliminate a surplus or shortage in this market?
(a) $0
(b) $10
(c) $20
(d) $30

15. A market for tickets in which buyers bid for tickets held by initial purchasers rather than the original seller is a
(a) primary market
(b) secondary market
(c) pre-set market
(d) surplus market

■ PROBLEMS

1. The existing demand and supply schedules are given in columns 1, 2, and 3 of the following table.

Demand and Supply Schedules			New Demand and Supply Schedules		
(1) Price	(2) Quantity demanded	(3) Quantity supplied	(4) Price	(5) Quantity demanded	(6) Quantity supplied
$5.00	10	50	$5.00	___	___
4.00	20	40	4.00	___	___
3.00	30	30	3.00	___	___
2.00	40	20	2.00	___	___
1.00	50	10	1.00	___	___

Now the demand *increases* by 10 units at each price and supply *decreases* by 10 units. Enter the new amounts for quantity demanded and quantity supplied in columns 5 and 6.

a. What was the old equilibrium price? _____
What will be the new equilibrium price? _____

b. What was the old equilibrium quantity? _____
What will be the new equilibrium quantity? _____

2. The demand and supply schedules for a certain product are those given in the following table. Answer the related questions.

Quantity demanded	Price	Quantity supplied
12,000	$10	18,000
13,000	9	17,000
14,000	8	16,000
15,000	7	15,000
16,000	6	14,000
17,000	5	13,000
18,000	4	12,000

The equilibrium price of the product is $ _____
and the equilibrium quantity is _____.

a. If a seller established a pre-set price of $5 on this product, there would be a (shortage, surplus) _____ of _____ units.

b. If a seller established a pre-set price of $8, there would be a (shortage, surplus) _____ of _____ units.

■ **SHORT ANSWER AND ESSAY QUESTIONS**

1. Explain, using a supply and demand graph, how a freeze in a vegetable crop will affect the equilibrium price and quantity.

2. Use the foreign exchange market for euros to explain how an increase in the demand for euros affects its value relative to the U.S. dollar and the equilibrium quantity of euros exchanged in this market. In this case, which currency, the euro or the U.S. dollar, has appreciated or depreciated?

3. When there are single shifts in the supply or demand curve, you can predict the effects on both equilibrium price and quantity. When there are simultaneous shifts in demand and supply, you can make only one prediction of the effects with any certainty. Why?

4. You observe that the equilibrium price has decreased and the equilibrium quantity has increased. What supply and demand conditions would best explain this outcome?

5. If increase in the demand for gasoline outweighs the decrease in the supply of gasoline, what is the most likely effect on the equilibrium price and quantity? Explain and show your answer with a graph.

6. You observe that the equilibrium quantity has increased but the equilibrium price has stayed the same. What supply and demand conditions would best explain this outcome?

7. What are price ceilings and price floors and how are they related to pre-set prices?

8. What are the consequences if a seller sets a price below the actual equilibrium price?

9. Why do secondary markets arise? Give examples of such markets.

10. Explain, using a supply and demand graph, the situation that arises when there are many unsold tickets to a sporting event. Why does this occur?

ANSWERS

Appendix to Chapter 3 Additional Examples of Supply and Demand

FILL-IN QUESTIONS

1. increases, decreases
2. increases, increases, appreciates, depreciates
3. demand for, supply of
4. decreases, increases
5. increases, increases
6. decrease, increase
7. stays the same, increases
8. ceiling, floor
9. shortage, surplus
10. secondary, scalping

TRUE–FALSE QUESTIONS

1. T, p. 69	**5.** F, p. 70	**9.** F, p. 72
2. F, p. 69	**6.** F, pp. 71–72	**10.** T, pp. 72–73
3. T, pp. 69–70	**7.** T, pp. 71–72	
4. T, p. 70	**8.** T, p. 72	

MULTIPLE-CHOICE QUESTIONS

1. b, p. 69	**6.** d, p. 71	**11.** c, p. 72
2. b, p. 69	**7.** c, pp. 71–72	**12.** c, pp. 72–73
3. d, pp. 69–70	**8.** d, pp. 71–72	**13.** a, pp. 72–73
4. d, p. 70	**9.** b, pp. 72–73	**14.** c, pp. 72–73
5. b, p. 71	**10.** a, p. 72	**15.** b, p. 72

PROBLEMS

1. column 5 (quantity demanded): 20, 30, 40, 50, 60; column 6 (quantity supplied): 40, 30, 20, 10, 0; *a.* $3.00, $4.00; *b.* 30, 30
2. $7, 15,000; *a.* shortage, 4,000; *b.* surplus, 2,000

SHORT ANSWER AND ESSAY QUESTIONS

1. p. 69	**5.** p. 70	**9.** p. 72
2. pp. 69–70	**6.** pp. 71–72	**10.** pp. 72–73
3. pp. 70–71	**7.** pp. 72	
4. pp. 70–71	**8.** p. 72	

CHAPTER 4

Elasticity

Chapter 4 is basically a continuation of Chapter 3. The previous chapter provided a basic understanding of supply and demand. Now the economic principles, problems, and policies to be studied require a more detailed discussion of **elasticity** and how it relates to supply and demand.

The concept of **price elasticity of demand** is of great importance for studying the material found in the remainder of the text. You must understand (1) what price elasticity measures; (2) how the price-elasticity formula is applied to measure the price elasticity of demand; (3) the difference between price elastic, price inelastic, and unit elastic; (4) how total revenue varies by the type of price elasticity of demand; (5) the meaning of perfect price elasticity and of perfect price inelasticity of demand; (6) the four major determinants of price elasticity of demand; and (7) the practical application of the concept to many economic issues.

When you have become thoroughly acquainted with the concept of price elasticity of demand, you will find that you have very little trouble understanding the **price elasticity of supply.** The transition requires no more than the substitution of the words "quantity supplied" for the words "quantity demanded." You should concentrate your attention on the meaning of price elasticity of supply and how it is affected by time. Several examples are provided to show how it affects the prices of many products.

The chapter also introduces you to two other elasticity concepts. The **cross elasticity of demand** measures the sensitivity of a change in the quantity demanded for one product due to a change in the price of another product. This concept is especially important in identifying whether two goods are substitutes to each other, complements to each other, or independent of each other. The **income elasticity of demand** assesses the change in the quantity demanded of a product resulting from a change in consumer incomes. It is useful for categorizing goods as normal or inferior. For normal goods, as income increases, the demand for them increases, whereas for inferior goods as income increases, the demand for them decreases.

So elasticity as presented in this chapter is all about the responsiveness of changes in quantity to a change in price or income. Understanding this concept will be useful for answering many questions about demand and supply.

■ CHECKLIST

When you have studied this chapter you should be able to

☐ Describe the concept of the price elasticity of demand.

☐ Compute the coefficient for the price when given the demand data.

☐ State the midpoint formula for price elasticity of demand and explain how it refines the original formula for price elasticity.

☐ State two reasons why the formula for price elasticity of demand uses percentages rather than absolute amounts in measuring consumer responsiveness.

☐ Explain the meaning of elastic, inelastic, and unit elastic as they relate to demand.

☐ Describe the concepts of perfectly elastic demand and perfectly inelastic demand and illustrate them with graphs.

☐ Apply the total-revenue test to determine whether demand is elastic, inelastic, or unit-elastic.

☐ Describe the relationship between price elasticity of demand and the price range for most demand curves.

☐ Explain why the slope of the demand curve is not a sound basis for judging price elasticity.

☐ Illustrate graphically the relationship between price elasticity of demand and total revenue.

☐ List the four major determinants of the price elasticity of demand, and explain how each determinant affects price elasticity.

☐ Describe several applications of the concept of price elasticity of demand.

☐ Describe the concept of the price elasticity of supply.

☐ Compute the coefficient for the price elasticity of supply when given the relevant data.

☐ Explain the effect of three time periods (market period, short run, and long run) on price elasticity of supply.

☐ Describe several applications of price elasticity of supply.

☐ Describe the concept of the cross elasticity of demand.

☐ Compute the coefficient for the cross elasticity of demand when given relevant data.

☐ Use the cross elasticity of demand to categorize substitute goods, complementary goods, and independent goods.

☐ Give applications of cross elasticity of demand.

☐ Describe the concepts of the income elasticity of demand.

☐ Compute the coefficient for the income elasticity of demand when given relevant data.

☐ Use the income elasticity of demand to categorize goods as normal or inferior.

☐ Provide some insights using the concept of income elasticity.

☐ Use the concept of elasticity of demand to explain why different consumers pay different prices (*Last Word*).

■ CHAPTER OUTLINE

1. **Price elasticity of demand** is a measure of the responsiveness or sensitivity of quantity demanded to changes in the price of a product. When quantity demanded is relatively responsive to a price change, demand is said to be **elastic**. When quantity demanded is relatively unresponsive to a price change, demand is said to be **inelastic**.

   a. The degree of elasticity can be measured by using a formula to compute the elasticity coefficient. $E_d =$ percentage change in quantity demanded of product X *divided by* the percentage change in the price of product X.

   (1) A **midpoint formula** calculates price elasticity across a price and quantity range to overcome the problem of selecting the reference points for the price range and the quantity range. In this formula, the *average* of the two quantities and the *average* of the two prices are used as reference points. This formula can be done in three steps: (a) calculate the change in quantity divided by the average of the two quantities; (b) calculate the change in price divided by the average of the two prices; (c) divide the quantity result from (a) by the price result from (b). For example, if the price falls from $5 to $4 while the quantity demanded rises from 10 units to 20 units, then using the midpoint formula, the price elasticity of demand is: (a) $[10 - 20]$ divided by $[(10 + 20)/2] = .67$; (b) $[(5 - 4)$ divided by $[(5 + 4)/2] = .22$; (c) thus .67 divided by .22 means that E_d is approximately equal to 3.

   (2) Economists use percentages rather than absolute amounts in measuring responsiveness because with absolute amounts the choice of units or scale can arbitrarily affect the perception of responsiveness.

   (3) The price elasticity of demand coefficient is a negative number (has a minus sign) because price and quantity demanded are inversely related. Economists ignore the minus sign in front of the coefficient and focus their attention on its absolute value.

   b. The coefficient of price elasticity has several interpretations.

   (1) **Elastic demand** occurs when the percentage change in quantity demanded is greater than the percentage change in price. The elasticity coefficient is greater than 1.

   (2) **Inelastic demand** occurs when the percentage change in quantity demanded is less than the percentage change in price. The elasticity coefficient is less than 1.

   (3) **Unit elasticity** occurs when the percentage change in quantity demanded is equal to the percentage change in price. The elasticity coefficient is equal to 1.

   (4) **Perfectly inelastic demand** means that a change in price results in no change in quantity demanded of a product, whereas **perfectly elastic demand** means that a small change in price causes buyers to purchase all they desire of a product.

   c. **Total revenue (TR)** changes when price changes. The **total-revenue test** shows that when demand is

   (1) *elastic,* a decrease in price will increase total revenue and an increase in price will decrease total revenue.

   (2) *inelastic,* a decrease in price will decrease total revenue and an increase in price will increase total revenue.

   (3) *unit-elastic,* an increase or decrease in price will not affect total revenue.

   d. Note several points about the graph of a linear demand curve and price elasticity of demand.

   (1) It is not the same at all prices. Demand is typically elastic at higher prices and inelastic at lower prices.

   (2) It cannot be judged from the slope of the demand curve.

   e. The relationship between price elasticity of demand and total revenue can be shown by graphing the demand curve and the total-revenue curve, one above the other. In this case, the horizontal axis for each graph uses the same quantity scale. The vertical axis for demand represents price. The vertical axis for the total-revenue graph measures total revenue.

   (1) When demand is price elastic, as price declines and quantity increases along the demand curve, total revenue increases in the total-revenue graph.

   (2) Conversely, when demand is price inelastic, as price declines and quantity increases along the demand curve, total revenue decreases.

   (3) When demand is unit-elastic, as price and quantity change along the demand curve, total revenue remains the same.

   f. The price elasticity of demand for a product depends on four determinants.

   (1) The number of good substitutes for the product. The more substitute products that are available for a product, the greater the price elasticity of demand for the product.

   (2) Its relative importance in the consumer's budget. The higher the price of product relative to consumers' incomes, the greater the price elasticity of demand.

   (3) Whether it is a necessity or a luxury. Luxuries typically have a greater price elasticity of demand than necessities.

   (4) The period of time under consideration. The longer the time period, the greater the elasticity of demand for a product.

   g. Price elasticity of demand has practical applications to public policy and business decisions. The concept is relevant to bumper crops in agriculture, excise taxes, and the decriminalization of illegal drugs.

2. **Price elasticity of supply** is a measure of the sensitivity of quantity supplied to changes in the price of a product. Both the general formula and the midpoint formula for price elasticity of supply are similar to those for the price elasticity of demand, but "quantity supplied" replaces "quantity demanded." This means that the price elasticity of supply is the percentage change in quantity supplied of a product divided by its percentage change in the price of the product. There is a midpoint formula that is an average of quantities and prices and is used for calculating the elasticity of supply across quantity or price ranges. The price elasticity of supply depends primarily on the

amount of time sellers have to adjust to a price change. The easier and faster suppliers can respond to changes in price, the greater the price elasticity of supply.

a. In the ***market period,*** there is too little time for producers to change output in response to a change in price. As a consequence supply is perfectly inelastic. Graphically, this means that the supply curve is vertical at that market level of output.

b. In the ***short run,*** producers have less flexibility to change output in response to a change in price because they have fixed inputs that they cannot change. They have only a limited control over the range in which they can vary their output. As a consequence, supply is *price inelastic* in the short run.

c. In the ***long run,*** producers can make adjustments to all inputs to vary production. As a consequence, supply is *price elastic* in the long run. There is no total-revenue test for price elasticity of supply because price and total revenue move in the same direction regardless of the degree of price elasticity of supply.

d. Price elasticity of supply has many practical applications for explaining price volatility. The concept is relevant to the pricing of antiques and gold, for which the supply is perfectly inelastic.

3. Two other elasticity concepts are important.

a. The ***cross elasticity of demand*** measures the degree to which the quantity demanded of one product is affected by a change in the price of another product. Cross elasticities of demand are

(1) positive for products that are substitutes;

(2) negative for products that are complements; and

(3) zero or near zero for products that are unrelated or independent.

b. The ***income elasticity of demand*** measures the effect of a change in income on the quantity demanded of a product. Income elasticities of demand are

(1) positive for normal or superior products, which means that more of them are demanded as income rises; and

(2) negative for inferior products, which means that less of them are demanded as income rises.

4. (*Last Word*). There are many examples of dual or multiple pricing of products. The main reason for the differences is differences in the price elasticity of demand among groups. Business travelers have a more inelastic demand for travel than leisure travelers and thus can be charged more for an airline ticket. Prices for children are often lower than prices for adults for the same service (for example, movie tickets or restaurant meals) because children have more elastic demand for the service. Low-income groups have a more elastic demand for higher education than high-income groups, so high-income groups are charged the full tuition price and lower-income groups get more financial aid to offset the tuition price.

■ **HINTS AND TIPS**

1. This chapter is an extension of the material presented in Chapter 3. Be sure you thoroughly read and study Chapter 3 again before you read and do the self-test exercises for this chapter.

2. You should **not judge** the price elasticity of demand based on the slope of the demand curve unless it is horizontal (*perfectly elastic*) or vertical (*perfectly inelastic*). Remember that elasticity varies from elastic to inelastic along a down-sloping, linear demand curve. The price elasticity equals 1 at the midpoint of a down-sloping linear demand curve.

3. Master the **total-revenue test** for assessing the price elasticity of demand (review Table 4.2). For many problems, the total-revenue test is easier to use than the midpoint formula for identifying the type of elasticity (elastic, inelastic, unit), and the test has many practical applications.

4. Do not just memorize the elasticity formulas in this chapter. Instead, work on understanding what they mean and how they are used for economic decisions. The elasticity formulas simply measure the *responsiveness* of a percentage change in *quantity* to a percentage change in some other characteristic (price or income). The elasticity formulas each have a similar structure: A percentage change in some type of *quantity* (demanded, supplied) is divided by a percentage change in the other variable. The price elasticity of demand measures the responsiveness of a percentage change in *quantity demanded* for a product to a percentage change in its *price*. The cross elasticity of demand measures the percentage change in the *quantity demanded of product X* to a percentage change in the *price of product Y*. The income elasticity of demand is the percentage change in *quantity demanded* for a product to a percentage change in *income*. The price elasticity of supply is the percentage change in the *quantity supplied* of a product to a percentage change in its price.

■ **IMPORTANT TERMS**

price elasticity of demand	total-revenue test
midpoint formula	price elasticity of supply
elastic demand	market period
inelastic demand	short run
unit elasticity	long run
perfectly inelastic demand	cross elasticity of demand
perfectly elastic demand	income elasticity of
total revenue	demand

SELF-TEST

■ **FILL-IN QUESTIONS**

1. If a relatively large change in price results in a relatively small change in quantity demanded, demand is (elastic, inelastic) _____. If a relatively small change in price results in a relatively large change in quantity demanded, demand is (elastic, inelastic) _____.

2. The midpoint formula for the price elasticity of demand uses the (total, average) _____ of the two quantities as a reference point in calculating the percentage change in quantity and the (total, average) _____ of the two prices as a reference point in calculating the percentage change in price.

3. The price elasticity formula is based on (absolute amounts, percentages) _____ because it avoids the problems caused by the arbitrary choice of units and permits meaningful comparisons of consumer (responsiveness, incomes) _____ to changes in the prices of different products.

4. If a change in price causes no change in quantity demanded, demand is perfectly (elastic, inelastic) _____ and the demand curve is (horizontal, vertical) _____. If an extremely small change in price causes an extremely large change in quantity demanded, demand is perfectly (elastic, inelastic) _____ and the demand curve is (horizontal, vertical) _____.

5. Two characteristics of the price elasticity of a linear demand curve are that elasticity (is constant, varies) _____ over the different price ranges, and that the slope is (a sound, an unsound) _____ basis for judging its elasticity.

6. Assume that the price of a product declines in cases a, b, and c.
    a. When demand is inelastic, the loss of revenue due to the lower price is (less, greater) _____ than the gain in revenue due to the greater quantity demanded.
    b. When demand is elastic, the loss of revenue due to the lower price is (less, greater) _____ than the gain in revenue due to the greater quantity demanded.
    c. When demand is unit-elastic, the loss of revenue due to the lower price (exceeds, is equal to) _____ the gain in revenue due to the greater quantity demanded.

7. Complete the following summary table.

If demand is	The elasticity coefficient is	If price rises, total revenue will	If price falls, total revenue will
Elastic	____	____	____
Inelastic	____	____	____
Unit-elastic	____	____	____

8. What are the four most important determinants of the price elasticity of demand?
    a. _____
    b. _____
    c. _____
    d. _____

9. The price elasticity of demand will tend to be greater when the number of substitute goods that are available for the product is (larger, smaller) _____.

10. The price elasticity of demand will tend to be greater when the price of the product relative to consumers' income is (lower, higher) _____.

11. The price elasticity of demand will tend to be greater when a product is considered to be a (necessity, luxury) _____.

12. The price elasticity of demand will tend to be greater when the time period under consideration for a change in quantity is (shorter, longer) _____.

13. The demand for most farm products is highly (elastic, inelastic) _____, which means that large crop yields will most likely (increase, decrease) _____ the total revenue of farmers. Governments often tax products such as liquor, gasoline, and cigarettes because the price elasticity of the demand is (elastic, inelastic) _____. A higher tax on such products will (increase, decrease) _____ tax revenue.

14. The price elasticity of supply measures the percentage change in (price, quantity supplied) _____ divided by the percentage change in _____. The most important factor affecting the price elasticity of supply is (revenue, time) _____. It is easier to shift resources to alternative uses when there is (more, less) _____ time.

15. In the market period, the price elasticity of supply will be perfectly (elastic, inelastic) _____ and the supply curve will be (horizontal, vertical) _____. Typically, in the short run the price elasticity of supply is (more, less) _____ elastic but in the long run the price elasticity of supply is _____ elastic.

16. There is a total-revenue test for the elasticity of (demand, supply) _____. There is no total-revenue test for the elasticity of (demand, supply) _____ because regardless of the degree of elasticity, price and total revenue are (directly, indirectly) _____ related.

17. The measure of the sensitivity of the consumption of one product given a change in the price of another product is the (cross, income) _____ elasticity of demand, while the measure of the responsiveness of consumer purchases to changes in income is the _____ elasticity of demand.

18. When the cross elasticity of demand is positive, two products are (complements, substitutes) _____, but when the cross elasticity of demand is negative, they are _____.

19. When a percentage change in the price of one product has no effect on another product, then the cross elasticity of demand will be (zero, one) _____ and the two products would be classified as being (dependent, independent) _____.

20. If consumers increase purchases of a product as consumer incomes increase, then a good is classified as (inferior, normal) _____, but if consumers decrease purchases of a product as consumer incomes increase, then a good is classified as _____.

■ **TRUE–FALSE QUESTIONS**

Circle T if the statement is true, F if it is false.

1. If the percentage change in price is greater than the percentage change in quantity demanded, the price elasticity coefficient is greater than 1. **T F**

2. If the quantity demanded for a product increases from 100 to 150 units when the price decreases from $14 to $10, using the midpoint formula, the price elasticity of demand for this product in this price range is 1.2. **T F**

3. A product with a price elasticity of demand equal to 1.5 is described as price inelastic. **T F**

4. If the price of a product increases from $5 to $6 and the quantity demanded decreases from 45 to 25, then according to the total-revenue test, the product is price inelastic in this price range. **T F**

5. Total revenue will not change when price changes if the price elasticity of demand is unitary. **T F**

6. When the absolute value of the price elasticity co-efficient is greater than 1 and the price of the product decreases, then the total revenue will increase. **T F**

7. The flatness or steepness of a demand curve is based on absolute changes in price and quantity, while elasticity is based on relative or percentage changes in price and quantity. **T F**

8. Demand tends to be inelastic at higher prices and elastic at lower prices along a down-sloping linear demand curve. **T F**

9. Price elasticity of demand and the slope of the demand curve are two different things. **T F**

10. In general, the larger the number of substitute goods that are available, the less the price elasticity of demand. **T F**

11. Other things equal, the higher the price of a good relative to consumers' incomes, the greater the price elasticity of demand. **T F**

12. Other things equal, the higher the price of a good relative to the longer the time period the purchase is considered, the greater the price elasticity of demand. **T F**

13. The more that a good is considered to be a "luxury" rather than a "necessity," the less is the price elasticity of demand. **T F**

14. The demand for most agricultural products is price inelastic. Consequently, an increase in supply will reduce the total income of producers of agricultural products. **T F**

15. A state government seeking to increase its excise-tax revenues is more likely to increase the tax rate on restaurant meals than on gasoline. **T F**

16. The degree of price elasticity of supply depends on how easily and quickly producers can shift resources between alternative uses. **T F**

17. If an increase in product price results in no change in the quantity supplied, supply is perfectly elastic. **T F**

18. The market period is a time so short that producers cannot respond to a change in demand and price. **T F**

19. The price elasticity of supply will tend to be more elastic in the long run. **T F**

20. There is a total revenue test for the elasticity of supply. **T F**

21. Cross elasticity of demand is measured by the percentage change in quantity demanded over the percentage change in income. **T F**

22. For a substitute product, the coefficient of the cross elasticity of demand is positive. **T F**

23. Two products are considered to be independent or unrelated when the cross elasticity of demand is zero. **T F**

24. The degree to which consumers respond to a change in their incomes by buying more or less of a particular product is measured by the income elasticity of demand. **T F**

25. Inferior goods have a positive income elasticity of demand. **T F**

■ **MULTIPLE-CHOICE QUESTIONS**

Circle the letter that corresponds to the best answer.

1. If, when the price of a product rises from $1.50 to $2, the quantity demanded of the product decreases from 1000 to 900, the price elasticity of demand coefficient, using the midpoint formula, is.
 (a) 3.00
 (b) 2.71
 (c) 0.37
 (d) 0.33

2. If a 1% fall in the price of a product causes the quantity demanded of the product to increase by 2%, demand is
  (a) inelastic
  (b) elastic
  (c) unit-elastic
  (d) perfectly elastic

3. In the following diagram, D_1 is a

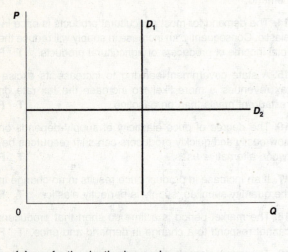

  (a) perfectly elastic demand curve
  (b) perfectly inelastic demand curve
  (c) unit-elastic demand curve
  (d) a long-run demand curve

4. Compared to the lower-right portion, the upper-left portion of most demand curves tends to be
  (a) more inelastic
  (b) more elastic
  (c) unit-elastic
  (d) perfectly inelastic

5. In which range of the demand schedule is demand price inelastic?

Price	Quantity demanded
$11	50
9	100
7	200
5	300
3	400

  (a) $11 − $9
  (b) $9 − $7
  (c) $7 − $5
  (d) $5 − $3

6. If a business increased the price of its product from $7 to $8 when the price elasticity of demand was inelastic, then
  (a) total revenues decreased
  (b) total revenues increased

  (c) total revenues remained unchanged
  (d) total revenues were perfectly inelastic

7. You are the sales manager for a pizza company and have been informed that the price elasticity of demand for your most popular pizza is greater than 1. To increase total revenues, you should.
  (a) increase the price of the pizza
  (b) decrease the price of the pizza
  (c) hold pizza prices constant
  (d) decrease demand for your pizza

8. Assume Amanda Herman finds that her total spending on compact discs remains the same after the price of compact discs falls, other things equal. Which of the following is true about Amanda's demand for compact discs with this price change?.
  (a) It is unit price elastic.
  (b) It is perfectly price elastic.
  (c) It is perfectly price inelastic.
  (d) It increased in response to the price change.

Questions 9, 10, and 11 are based on the following graph.

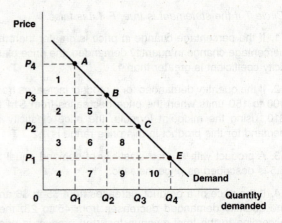

9. If price is P_3, then total revenue is measured by the area
  (a) $0P_3CQ_3$
  (b) $0P_3BQ_2$
  (c) $0P_3BQ_3$
  (d) $0P_3CQ_2$

10. If price falls from P_2 to P_1, then in this price range demand is
  (a) relatively inelastic because the loss in total revenue (areas 3 + 6 + 8) is greater than the gain in total revenue (area 10)
  (b) relatively elastic because the loss in total revenue (areas 3 + 6 + 8) is greater than the gain in total revenue (area 10)
  (c) relatively inelastic because the loss in total revenue (area 10) is less than the gain in total revenue (areas 3 + 6 + 8)
  (d) relatively inelastic because the loss in total revenue (areas 4 + 7 + 9 + 10) is greater than the gain in total revenue (areas 3 + 6 + 8)

11. As price falls from P_4 to P_3, you know that demand is
(a) elastic because total revenue decreased from $0P_4AQ_1$ to $0P_3BQ_2$
(b) inelastic because total revenue decreased from $0P_3BQ_2$ to $0P_4AQ_1$
(c) elastic because total revenue increased from $0P_4AQ_1$ to $0P_3BQ_2$
(d) inelastic because total revenue decreased from $0P_4AQ_1$ to $0P_3BQ_2$

12. Which is characteristic of a product whose demand is elastic?
(a) The price elasticity coefficient is less than 1.
(b) Total revenue decreases if price decreases.
(c) Buyers are relatively insensitive to price changes.
(d) The percentage change in quantity is greater than the percentage change in price.

13. The demand for Nike basketball shoes is more price elastic than the demand for basketball shoes as a whole. This is best explained by the fact that
(a) Nike basketball shoes are a luxury good, not a necessity
(b) Nike basketball shoes are the best made and widely advertised
(c) there are more complements for Nike basketball shoes than for basketball shoes as a whole
(d) there are more substitutes for Nike basketball shoes than for basketball shoes as a whole

14. Which is characteristic of a good whose demand is inelastic?
(a) There are a large number of good substitutes for the good for consumers.
(b) The buyer spends a small percentage of total income on the good.
(c) The good is regarded by consumers as a luxury.
(d) The period of time for which demand is given is relatively long.

15. From a time perspective, the demand for most products is
(a) less elastic in the short run and unit-elastic in the long run
(b) less elastic in the long run and unit-elastic in the short run
(c) more elastic in the short run than in the long run
(d) more elastic in the long run than in the short run

16. If a 5% fall in the price of a commodity causes quantity supplied to decrease by 8%, supply is
(a) inelastic
(b) unit-elastic
(c) elastic
(d) perfectly inelastic

17. In the following diagram, what is the price elasticity of supply between points **A** and **C** (using the midpoint formula)?.

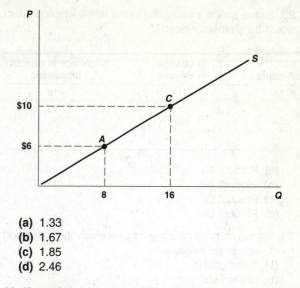

(a) 1.33
(b) 1.67
(c) 1.85
(d) 2.46

18. If supply is inelastic and demand decreases, the total revenue of sellers will
(a) increase
(b) decrease
(c) decrease only if demand is elastic
(d) increase only if demand is inelastic

19. The chief determinant of the price elasticity of supply of a product is
(a) the number of good substitutes the product has
(b) the length of time sellers have to adjust to a change in price
(c) whether the product is a luxury or a necessity
(d) whether the product is a durable or a nondurable good

20. A study shows that the coefficient of the cross elasticity of Coke and Sprite is negative. This information indicates that Coke and Sprite are
(a) normal goods
(b) complementary goods
(c) substitute goods
(d) independent goods

21. If a 5% increase in the price of one good results in a decrease of 2% in the quantity demanded of another good, then it can be concluded that the two goods are
(a) complements
(b) substitutes
(c) independent
(d) normal

22. Most goods can be classified as *normal* goods rather than inferior goods. The definition of a normal good means that
(a) the percentage change in consumer income is greater than the percentage change in price of the normal good
(b) the percentage change in quantity demanded of the normal good is greater than the percentage change in consumer income
(c) as consumer income increases, consumer purchases of a normal good increase
(d) the income elasticity of demand is negative

23. Based on the information in the table, which product would be an inferior good?

Product	% change in income	% change in quantity demanded
A	−10	+10
B	+10	+10
C	+5	+5
D	−5	−5

(a) Product A
(b) Product B
(c) Product C
(d) Product D

24. For which product is the income elasticity of demand most likely to be negative?
(a) automobiles
(b) bus tickets
(c) computers
(d) tennis rackets

25. During a recession, the quantity demanded for which product is likely to be most affected by the decline in consumer incomes?
(a) the buying of ketchup
(b) purchases of toothpaste
(c) the sales of toilet paper
(d) meals bought at restaurants

■ **PROBLEMS**

1. Complete the following table, using the demand data given, by computing total revenue at each of the seven prices and the six price elasticity coefficients between each of the seven prices, and indicate whether demand is elastic, inelastic, or unit-elastic between each of the seven prices.

Price	Quantity demanded	Total revenue	Elasticity coefficient	Character of demand
$1.00	300	_____		
.90	400	_____	_____	_____
.80	500	_____	_____	_____
..70	600	_____	_____	_____
.60	700	_____	_____	_____
.50	800	_____	_____	_____
.40	900	_____	_____	_____

2. Use the data from the table for this problem. On the *first* of the two following graphs, plot the demand curve (price and quantity demanded) and indicate the elastic, inelastic, and unit-elastic portions of the demand curve. On the *second* graph, plot the total revenue on the vertical axis and the quantity demanded on the horizontal axis. (*Note:* The scale for quantity demanded that you plot on the horizontal axis of each graph should be the same.)

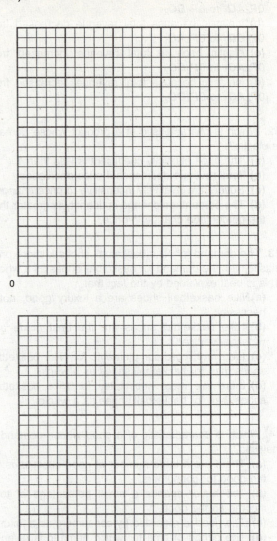

0

0

a. As price decreases from $1.00 to $0.70, demand is (elastic, inelastic, unit-elastic) _____ and total revenue (increases, decreases, remains the same) _____.

b. As price decreases from $0.70 to $0.60, demand is (elastic, inelastic, unit-elastic) _____ and total revenue (increases, decreases, remains the same) _____.

c. As price decreases from $0.60 to $0.40, demand is (elastic, inelastic, unit-elastic) _____ and total revenue (increases, decreases, remains the same) _____.

3. Using the supply data in the following schedule, complete the table by computing the six price elasticity of supply coefficients between each of the seven prices, and indicate whether supply is elastic, inelastic, or unit-elastic.

Price	Quantity demanded	Elasticity coefficient	Character of supply
$1.00	800		
.90	700	_____	_____
.80	600	_____	_____
.70	500	_____	_____
.60	400	_____	_____
.50	300	_____	_____
.40	200	_____	_____

4. The following graph shows three different supply curves (S_1, S_2, and S_3) for a product bought and sold in a competitive market.

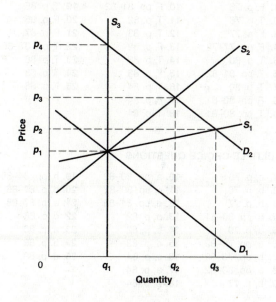

a. The supply curve for the

(1) market period is the one labeled _____.

(2) short run is the one labeled _____.

(3) long run is the one labeled _____.

b. No matter what the period of time under consideration, if the demand for the product were D_1, the equilibrium price of the product would be _____

and the equilibrium quantity would be _____.

(1) If demand were to increase to D_2 in the market period the equilibrium price would increase to

_____ and the equilibrium quantity would be

_____.

(2) In the short run the price of the product would

increase to _____ and the quantity would increase to _____.

(3) In the long run the price of the product would be

_____ and the quantity would be _____.

c. The longer the period of time allowed to sellers

to adjust their outputs the (more, less) _____ elastic is the supply of the product.

d. The more elastic the supply of a product, the

(greater, less) _____ the effect on equilibrium

price and the _____ the effect on equilibrium quantity of an increase in demand.

5. For the following three cases, use a midpoint formula to calculate the coefficient for the cross elasticity of demand and identify the relationship between the two goods (complement, substitute, or independent).

a. The quantity demanded for good A increases from 300 to 400 as the price of good B increases from $1 to $2.

Coefficient: _____ Relationship: _____

b. The quantity demanded for good J decreases from 2000 to 1500 as the price of good K increases from $10 to $15.

Coefficient: _____ Relationship: _____

c. The quantity demanded for good X increases from 100 to 101 units as the price of good Y increases from $8 to $15.

Coefficient: _____ Relationship: _____

6. Use the information in the following table to identify the income characteristic of each product A–E using the following labels: **N** = normal (or superior), **I** = inferior.

Product	% change in income	% change in quantity demanded	Income type (N or I)
A	10	10	_____
B	1	15	_____
C	5	−12	_____
D	5	−2	_____
E	10	1	_____

■ **SHORT ANSWER AND ESSAY QUESTIONS**

1. Define and explain the price elasticity of demand in terms of the relationship between the relative (percentage) change in quantity demanded and the relative (percentage) change in price. Use the elasticity coefficient in your explanation.

2. What is meant by perfectly elastic demand? By perfectly inelastic demand? What does the demand curve look like when demand is perfectly elastic and when it is perfectly inelastic?.

3. Demand seldom has the same elasticity at all prices. What is the relationship between the price of most products and the price elasticity of demand for them?

4. What is the relationship—if there is one—between the price elasticity of demand and the slope of the demand curve?

5. When the price of a product declines, the quantity demanded of it increases. When demand is elastic, total revenue is greater at the lower price, but when demand is inelastic, total revenue is smaller. Explain why total revenue will sometimes increase and why it will sometimes decrease.

6. Explain the effect of the number of substitutes on the price elasticity of demand.

7. Why does the price elasticity of demand differ based on the price of a good as a proportion of household income? Give examples.

8. Is the quantity demanded for necessities more or less responsive to a change in price? Explain using examples.

9. What role does time play in affecting the elasticity of demand?

10. How do opponents of the decriminalization of illegal drugs use elasticity to make their arguments?

11. Explain what determines the price elasticity of supply of an economic good or service.

12. Why is there no total-revenue test for the elasticity of supply?

13. Discuss the supply and demand conditions for antiques. Why are antique prices so high?

14. Use the concepts of the elasticity of supply to explain the volatility of gold prices.

15. How can goods be classified as complementary, substitute, or independent? On what basis is this judgment made?

16. Explain why knowledge of the cross elasticity of demand is important to business.

17. Give an example showing how the government implicitly uses the idea of cross elasticity of demand in its policy-making.

18. Discuss the relationship between the quantity demand for a product and how that quantity responds to a change in income.

19. Supply definitions of a normal good and an inferior good. Illustrate each definition with an example.

20. What is an example of insights that income elasticity of demand coefficients provide about recessions?

ANSWERS

Chapter 4 Elasticity

FILL-IN QUESTIONS

1. inelastic, elastic
2. average, average
3. percentages, responsiveness
4. inelastic, vertical, elastic, horizontal
5. varies, an unsound
6. a. greater; b. less; c. is equal to
7. Elastic: greater than 1, decrease, increase; Inelastic: less than 1, increase, decrease; Unit-elastic: equal to 1, remain constant, remain constant

8. a. The number of good substitute products; b. The relative importance of the product in the total budget of the buyer; c. Whether the good is a necessity or a luxury; d. The period of time in which demand is being considered (any order a–d)
9. larger
10. higher
11. luxury
12. longer
13. inelastic, decrease, inelastic, increase
14. quantity supplied, price, time, more
15. inelastic, vertical, less, more
16. demand, supply, directly
17. cross, income
18. substitutes, complements
19. zero, independent
20. normal, inferior

TRUE-FALSE QUESTIONS

1. F, p. 76	10. F, pp. 81–82	19. T, p. 85
2. T, p. 76	11. T, p. 82	20. F, p. 85
3. F, p. 77	12. T, p. 83	21. F, p. 87
4. F, pp. 77–78	13. F, p. 82	22. T, pp. 87–88
5. T, p. 80	14. T, p. 83	23. T, p. 88
6. T, pp. 81–82	15. F, p. 83	24. T, p. 88
7. T, p. 80	16. T, p. 84	25. F, p. 88
8. F, pp. 80–81	17. F, p. 84	
9. T, pp. 80–81	18. T, p. 84	

MULTIPLE-CHOICE QUESTIONS

1. c, p. 76	10. a, pp. 80–82	19. b, pp. 84–85
2. b, p. 76	11. c, pp. 80–82	20. b, p. 87–88
3. b, p. 77	12. d, pp. 81–82	21. a, p. 87–88
4. b, pp. 80–81	13. d, p. 82	22. c, p. 88
5. d, p. 79	14. b, p. 82	23. a, p. 88
6. b, pp. 78–82	15. d, p. 83	24. b, p. 88
7. b, pp. 78–82	16. c, p. 84	25. d, p. 89
8. a, pp. 80–82	17. a, p. 84	
9. b, p. 77	18. b, p. 84	

PROBLEMS

1. Total revenue: $300, 360, 400, 420, 420, 400, 360; Elasticity coefficient: 2.71, 1.89, 1.36, 1, 0.73, 0.53; Character of demand: elastic, elastic, elastic, unit-elastic, inelastic, inelastic.
2. a. elastic, increases; b. unit-elastic, remains the same; c. inelastic, decreases.
3. Elasticity coefficient: 1.27, 1.31, 1.36, 1.44, 1.57, 1.8; Character of supply: elastic, elastic, elastic, elastic, elastic, elastic
4. a. (1) S_3; (2) S_2; (3) S_1; b. p_1, q_1, (1) p_4, q_1; (2) p_3, q_2; (3) p_2, q_3; c. more; d. less, greater
5. a. .43, substitute; b. −.71, complement; c. .02, independent
6. N, N, I, I, N

SHORT ANSWER AND ESSAY QUESTIONS

1. p. 76	8. p. 82	15. pp. 87–88
2. pp. 77–78	9. p. 83	16. p. 88
3. pp. 77–78	10. p. 83	17. p. 88
4. pp. 78–82	11. p. 84	18. p. 88
5. pp. 78–82	12. p. 85	19. p. 88
6. pp. 81–82	13. pp. 85–86	20. p. 89
7. p. 82	14. pp. 86–87	

Market Failures: Public Goods and Externalities

This chapter is another extension of supply and demand analysis that you learned about in Chapter 3. In that chapter, the assumption was made that competitive markets were highly efficient and allocated scare resources to their most valued use from society's perspective. Sometimes, however, competitive markets are inefficient with the allocation of society's scarce resources, and therefore competitive markets can end up overproducing, underproducing, or not producing some products. These market inefficiencies are referred to as **market failures,** which are presented as two types in the first major section of the chapter. **Demand-side market failures** arise when demand curves do not take into account the full willingness of consumers to pay for a product. **Supply-side market failures** occur when supply curves do not incorporate the full cost of producing a product.

To better understand these failures, this first major section of the chapter also presents some new concepts that should enhance your understanding of **economic efficiency** because of the focus on the efficient allocation of resources. This extension requires an explanation of **consumer surplus** and **producer surplus.** Consumer surplus is the difference between the maximum price consumers are willing to pay for a product and the actual price. Producer surplus is the difference between the minimum price producers are willing to accept for a product and the actual price. The chapter also revisits the concept of **allocative efficiency** and explains that it is achieved when the combination of consumer and producer surplus is at a maximum.

Government often intervenes in the private economy to correct the market inefficiencies and provide **public goods,** as you will learn in the second major section of the chapter. A private good is characterized by rivalry and excludability, but a public good is characterized by nonrivalry and nonexcludability. These differences mean that the demand curve and supply curve for a public good will differ from those of a private good. You are shown how the demand curve for a public good is constructed and how the optimal allocation of a public good is determined. The demand and supply curves for a public good are related to the collective marginal benefit and cost of providing the good. Governments sometimes use **cost-benefit analysis** to determine if they should undertake some specific action or project. This analysis requires the government to estimate the marginal costs and the marginal benefits of the project, and it can be used to decide when such projects should be expanded, contracted, or eliminated.

The third major topic of the chapter is **externalities,** situations in market transactions that create negative or positive spillovers to third parties that are not involved in the buying or selling transactions. Government may intervene in the market economy to reduce inefficiencies associated with negative externalities or engage in activities that capture more of the benefits from positive externalities. Government often uses direct controls (legislation) and taxes to limit or correct negative externalities. It uses subsidies for consumers or producers to realize more of the benefits from positive externalities. In some cases, where the positive externalities are large, the government may provide the product to people without charge or at a minimal fee. This discussion of government intervention, however, needs to be modified by the Coase theorem, which shows that individual bargaining can be used to settle some externality problems.

To correct for the negative externalities associated with pollution, government can create a market for externality rights that results in an **optimal reduction of an externality,** and this cost-benefit approach will be more effective and efficient than simply banning pollution emissions through legislation. All of this analysis has direct application to the problem of CO_2 emissions and government policies as discussed in the Last Word.

The final brief section of the chapter places government's role in the economy in context. While in theory there may be justification for government intervention in some cases to correct for externalities, in practice finding policies or solutions is subject to a political process that can result in inefficient outcomes.

■ **CHECKLIST**

When you have studied this chapter you should be able to

☐ Describe the concept of market failure in competitive markets.
☐ Distinguish between a demand-side market failure and a supply-side market failure.
☐ Define consumer surplus and give a graphical example.
☐ Define producer surplus and give a graphical example.
☐ Use consumer surplus and producer surplus to explain how efficiency is achieved in a competitive market.
☐ List the three conditions for achieving allocative efficiency at a quantity level in a competitive market.
☐ Use a supply and demand graph to illustrate efficiency losses (or deadweight losses).

☐ Use the two concepts of rivalry and excludability to describe a private good.

☐ Use the two concepts of nonrivalry and nonexcludability to describe a public good.

☐ Calculate the demand for a public good when given tabular data.

☐ Explain how marginal benefit is reflected in the demand for a public good.

☐ Describe the relationship between marginal cost and the supply of a public good.

☐ Identify on a graph where there is an overallocation, an underallocation, and an optimal quantity of a public good.

☐ Use cost-benefit analysis to determine how many resources a government should allocate to a project.

☐ Discuss the concept of quasi-public goods and why government often provides them.

☐ Describe negative externalities and give an example.

☐ Describe positive externalities and give an example.

☐ Use supply and demand graphs to illustrate how negative externalities and positive externalities affect the allocation of resources.

☐ Discuss two means government uses to achieve economic efficiency when there are negative externalities.

☐ Describe how some externality problems can be solved through individual bargaining based on the Coase theorem.

☐ Describe three government options to correct for the underallocation of resources when positive externalities are large and diffuse.

☐ Explain and illustrate with a graph a rule for determining society's optimal reduction of a negative externality.

☐ Determine the price a government agency should charge in a market for externality rights (e.g., cap-and-trade program for air pollution), when given the data for analysis.

☐ Compare the advantages of a market for externality rights with the policy of direct government controls.

☐ Explain the qualifications to government's role in the economy and the potential for government failure.

☐ Discuss the economics issues involved in the use of a carbon tax and cap-and-trade program (*Last Word*).

■ **CHAPTER OUTLINE**

1. **Market failures** can occur when competitive markets do not allocate the scarce resources to their most valued or best use. These market failures can be of two types.

   a. **Demand-side market failures** arise when the consumers' full willingness to pay for a good or service is not fully captured in the demand for the good or service. For example, people will not have much incentive to pay to view outdoor fireworks because they can usually still view the fireworks without paying.

   b. **Supply-side market failures** often result from a situation where a business firm does not have to pay the full cost of producing a product. For example, a power plant that uses coal may not have to pay completely for the emissions it discharges into the atmosphere as part of the cost of producing electricity.

   c. When markets are economically efficient, the demand curve in the market must include the full willingness of consumers to pay for the product and the supply curve must capture the full cost of producing the product.

   d. **Consumer surplus** is the difference between the maximum price consumers are willing to pay for a product and the actual (equilibrium) price paid. Graphically, it is the triangular area bounded by the portion of the vertical axis between the equilibrium price and the demand curve intersection, the portion of the demand curve above the equilibrium price, and the horizontal line at the equilibrium price from the vertical axis to the demand curve. Price and consumer surplus are inversely (negatively) related: Higher prices reduce it and lower prices increase it.

   e. **Producer surplus** is the difference between the minimum price producers are willing to accept for a product and the actual (equilibrium) price received. Graphically, it is the triangular area bounded by the portion of the vertical axis between the equilibrium price and the supply curve intersection, the portion of the supply curve below the equilibrium price, and the horizontal line at the equilibrium price from the vertical axis to the supply curve. Price and producer surplus are directly (positively) related: Higher prices increase it and lower prices decrease it.

   f. The equilibrium quantity shown by the intersection of demand and supply curves reflects *economic efficiency.*

   (1) **Productive efficiency** is achieved because production costs are minimized at each quantity level of output.

   (2) **Allocative efficiency** is achieved at the equilibrium quantity of output because three conditions are satisfied: (a) marginal benefit equals marginal cost; (b) maximum willingness to pay equals minimum acceptable price; and, (c) the combination of the consumer and producer surplus is at a maximum.

   g. If quantity is less than or greater than the equilibrium quantity or most efficient level, there are **efficiency losses** (or **deadweight losses**) to buyers and sellers. The efficiency losses reduce the maximum possible size of the combined consumer and producer surplus.

2. When market failures arise because a demand curve for a product fails to reflect consumers' willingness to pay, then a public good that has net benefits for society fails to be produced.

   a. A **private good,** such as a soft drink, is characterized by rivalry and excludability. **Rivalry** means that consumption of the product by a buyer eliminates the possibility of consumption of that product by another person. If, for example, one person buys and drinks a soft drink, it is not possible for another person to drink or consume it. **Excludability** refers to the ability of the seller to exclude a person from consuming the product if the person does not pay for it. In our example, if a person does not pay for the soft drink, the seller can prevent or exclude the person from obtaining or consuming the soft drink.

   b. A **public good,** such as national defense or street lighting, is characterized by nonrivalry and nonexcludability. **Nonrivalry** means that once a public good is consumed by one person, it is still available for consumption by another person. In the case of street lighting, even if one person enjoys the benefits from having streets illuminated (consumes it), that situation does not diminish or reduce the benefit of the lighting for another person. **Nonexcludability** means that those individuals who do not pay for the public good can still obtain the benefits from the public good. For street lighting, once it is provided to one person, other persons will benefit from having it available even if they do not pay for it. These two characteristics create a **free-rider problem** where once a producer provides a public good everyone including nonpayers can receive the benefits.

c. The **optimal quantity of a public good** can be evaluated using demand and supply analysis.

(1) The **demand for a public good** is determined by summing the prices that people are willing to pay collectively for the last unit of the public good at each possible quantity demanded, whereas the demand for a private good is determined by summing the quantities demanded at each possible price. The demand curve for a public good is down-sloping because of the law of diminishing marginal utility.

(2) The **supply curve of a public good** is up-sloping because of the law of diminishing returns. The provision of additional units of the public good reflects increasing marginal costs.

(3) The optimal allocation of a public good is determined by the intersection of the supply and demand curves. If the marginal benefit (MB) is greater than the marginal cost (MC) of the public good, there is an underallocation of a public good. If MB is less than MC, there is an overallocation of the public good. Only when the MB = MC is there an optimal allocation of the public good.

d. Government uses **cost-benefit analysis** to decide if it should use resources for a project and to determine the total quantity of resources it should devote to a project. The **marginal cost = marginal benefit rule** is used to make the decision. Additional resources should be devoted to a project only so long as the marginal benefits to society from the project exceed society's marginal costs. In this case, the total benefits minus the total costs (net benefits) are at a maximum amount.

e. Government also provides **quasi-public goods** that have large external benefits. Although these goods (such as education or highways) can be provided by the private market because people can be excluded from obtaining them if they do not pay for them, if left to be provided by the private market, these goods will be underproduced or underconsumed. Government provides access to these quasi-public goods at a reduced cost to encourage their production or consumption and increase the external benefits for society.

f. Government reallocates resources from the private economy (consumption and investment) to produce public and quasi-public goods. This reallocation is achieved by levying taxes on the private economy and using the tax revenues to produce these public and quasi-public goods, thereby changing the composition of the economy's total output.

3. An **externality** is a spillover from a market transaction to a third party that did not purchase the product. The spillover to the third party can be either positive or negative depending on the conditions.

a. **Negative externalities** occur when the cost for the product does not reflect the full cost of producing it from society's perspective, and therefore a third party who is not part of the private transaction winds up bearing some of the production cost. For example, if a corporation pollutes the environment while making a product and neither the corporation nor the consumer of the product pays for the cost of that pollution, then the pollution cost is an external cost that is borne by third parties, who are the other members of society adversely affected by the pollution. Negative externalities cause supply-side market failures. All the costs associated with the product are not reflected in the supply curve, and therefore, the producer's supply curve lies to the right of the full-cost supply curve. This situation results in an *overallocation* of resources to the production of a product and an efficiency loss.

b. **Positive externalities** are outcomes that benefit third parties without these parties paying for the benefits. Health immunizations and education are examples of services that have external benefits to others who do not pay for the services. Positive externalities cause demand-side market failures. All the benefits from the production of the product are not fully reflected in the demand curve, and therefore, the demand curve lies to the left of the full-benefits demand curve. This situation results in an *underallocation* of resources to the production of a product and an efficiency loss.

c. Government can intervene in the private market to increase economic efficiency when there are substantial external costs or benefits from the production of a product.

(1) *Direct controls* use legislation to ban or limit the activities that produce a negative externality. In the ideal case, these direct controls raise the cost of production so that it reflects the full cost, thus shifting the original supply curve to the left and reducing equilibrium output. Examples of such direct controls include federal legislation for clean air or clean water.

(2) *Taxes* can be imposed as another way to reduce or limit negative externalities. Such taxes raise the cost of production, thereby shifting the original supply curve leftward and reducing equilibrium output. Some negative externalities get resolved through private bargaining if the externalities are not widespread and the negotiating costs can be kept low.

(3) *Subsides and government provision* are options that can be used when there are positive externalities from a product. External benefits can be encouraged by subsidizing consumers to purchase a product or by subsidizing producers to make them, such as is done with certain types of health immunizations. When the positive externalities are large, it may make sense from an economic efficiency perspective for the government to provide the product at no cost to the consumer.

d. (Consider This). As shown by Ronald Coase in the *Coase Theorem,* some negative or positive externality situations can be addressed through individual or private bargaining and without government intervention.

e. In most cases, the *optimal reduction of an externality* is not zero from society's perspective and there is a price to be paid. This condition means that society must consider the marginal benefit and marginal cost of reducing a negative externality.

(1) The equilibrium occurs where the marginal cost to society from reducing the negative externality is just equal to the marginal benefit from reducing the negative externality (MB = MC).

(2) Over time, shifts in the marginal-cost and marginal-benefit curves change the optimal level of externality reduction.

(3) When positive externalities are extremely large, government may decide to provide the good or service.

4. Market failures can be used to justify government interventions in the private economy to encourage or discourage the production and consumption of particular products and increase economic efficiency. However, the expanded economic role of government to correct market failure is conducted in the context of politics. This political process can lead to imperfect and inefficient outcomes.

5. (*Last Word*). There are market-based approaches to externality problems that establish property rights where none existed before. A cap-and-trade program creates a market for property rights to a negative externality. In this program, the government sets a limit for the amount of CO_2 emissions permitted in a region (a cap) and allocates pollution permits to firms in the region based on their typical amount of output and emissions. Then if a firm wanted to expand its output and emissions, it would have to purchase pollution permits from other firms (trade) that wanted to reduce their output and emissions or did not use their limit. A firm would only expand production if the marginal benefit of the additional output was greater than the marginal cost of buying the additional pollution permits. One major problem, however, with this system is the difficulty of monitoring CO_2 emissions by firms and ensuring compliance with permits. As an alternative, many economists have proposed a tax on the use of carbon-based resources such as coal or oil. This alternative would raise the cost of using carbon resources that contribute to pollution and reduce the enforcement costs.

■ HINTS AND TIPS

1. The term "surplus" in this chapter should not be confused with its previous use related to pre-set prices and price floors. What the consumer surplus refers to is the extra utility or satisfaction that consumers get when they do not have to pay the price they were willing to pay and actually pay the lower equilibrium price. The producer surplus arises when producers receive an equilibrium price that is above the minimum price that they consider acceptable to selling the product.

2. Make sure you understand the difference between the demand for public and private goods. The **demand for a private good** is determined by adding the quantities demanded at each possible price. The **demand for a public good** is determined by adding the prices people collectively are willing to pay for the last unit of the public good at each possible quantity demanded.

3. Table 5.5 is important because it summarizes the private actions and government policies taken to correct for negative or positive externalities. The government can influence the allocation of resources in a private market by taking actions that increase or decrease demand or supply.

■ IMPORTANT TERMS

market failures	public goods
demand-side market failures	nonrivalry
supply-side market failures	nonexcludability
consumer surplus	free-rider problem
producer surplus	cost-benefit analysis
efficiency losses (or deadweight losses)	quasi-public goods
private goods	externality
rivalry	Coase theorem
excludability	optimal reduction of an externality

SELF-TEST

■ FILL-IN QUESTIONS

1. When it is impossible to charge consumers what they are willing to pay for a product, the situation that arises is a market failure on the (supply side, demand side) _____, but when a firm does not have to pay the full cost of producing its output, it often leads to a market failure on the _____.

2. A consumer surplus is the difference between the actual price and the (minimum, maximum) _____ price a consumer is (or consumers are) willing to pay for a product. In most markets, consumers individually or collectively gain more total utility or satisfaction when the actual or equilibrium price they have to pay for a product is (less, more) _____ than what they would have been willing to pay to obtain the product. Consumer surplus and price are (positively, negatively) _____ related. This means that higher prices (increase, decrease) _____ consumer surplus and lower prices _____ it.

3. A producer surplus is the difference between the actual or equilibrium price and the (minimum, maximum)

_____ acceptable price a producer is (or producers are) willing to accept in exchange for a product. In most markets, sellers individually or collectively benefit when they sell their product at an actual or equilibrium price that is (less, more) _____ than what they would have been willing to receive in exchange for the product. Producer surplus and price are (positively, negatively) _____ related. This means that higher prices (increase, decrease) _____ producer surplus and lower prices _____ it.

4. When competition forces producers to use the best techniques and combinations of resources to make a product, then (allocative, productive) _____ efficiency is being achieved. When the correct or optimal quantity of output of a product is being produced relative to the other goods and services, then _____ efficiency is being achieved.

5. Allocative efficiency occurs at quantity levels where marginal benefit is (greater than, less than, equal to) _____ marginal cost, maximum willingness to pay by consumers is _____ the minimum acceptable price for producers, and the combined consumer and producer surplus is at a (minimum, maximum) _____.

6. When there is overproduction of a product, there are efficiency (gains, losses) _____ and when there is underproduction there are efficiency _____. In both cases, the combined consumer and producer surplus is (greater than, less than) _____ the maximum that would occur at the efficient quantity of output.

7. Rivalry means that when one person buys and consumes a product, it (is, is not) _____ available for purchase and consumption by another person. Excludability means that the seller (can, cannot) _____ keep people who do not pay for the product from obtaining its benefits. Rivalry and excludability apply to (private, public) _____ goods.

8. One characteristic of a public good is (rivalry, nonrivalry) _____ and the other characteristic of a public good is (excludability, nonexcludability) _____. A private firm will not find it profitable to produce a public good because there is a (free-rider, principal–agent) _____ problem because once the good is provided, everyone, including those who do not pay for it, can obtain the benefits.

9. With a private good, to compute the market demand you add together the (prices people are willing to pay, quantities demanded) _____ at each possible (price, quantity demanded) _____. With a public good, to compute the collective demand you add together the (prices people are willing to pay, quantities demanded) _____ for the last unit of the public good at each possible (price, quantity demanded) _____.

10. The demand curve slopes downward for a public good because of the law of diminishing marginal (returns, utility) _____; the supply curve for a public good is upsloping because of the law of diminishing _____. The demand curve for a public good is, in essence, a marginal-(benefit, cost) _____ curve; the supply curve for a public good reflects rising marginal _____. The optimal quantity of a public good will be shown by the intersection of the collective demand and supply curves, which means that marginal (benefit, cost) _____ of the last unit equals that unit's marginal _____.

11. In applying cost-benefit analysis, government should use more resources in the production of public goods if the marginal (cost, benefit) _____ from the additional public goods exceeds the marginal _____ that results from having fewer private goods. This rule will determine which plan from a cost-benefit analysis will result in the (maximum, minimum) _____ net benefit to society.

12. To reallocate resources from the production of private goods to the production of public and quasi-public goods, government reduces the demand for private goods by (taxing, subsidizing) _____ consumers and then uses the (profits, tax revenue) _____ to buy public or quasi-public goods.

13. There is a negative externality whenever some of the costs of producing a product spill over to people other than the immediate (seller, buyer) _____ and there is a positive externality when some of the benefits from consuming a product spill over to people other than the immediate _____.

14. When there is a negative externality firms do not pay the full cost of production and therefore their supply curves will increase or shift more to the (left, right) _____ than would be the case if firms paid the full cost of production. When there is a positive externality, consumers do not capture the full benefits of the product and therefore the demand curves will decrease or shift more to the (right, left) _____ than would be the case if all the benefits were captured by the buyers of the product.

15. When there are negative externalities in competitive markets, the result is an (over, under) _____ allocation of resources to the production of the good or service. When there are positive externalities, the result is an (over, under) _____ allocation of resources to the production of the good or service.

16. Government may use direct controls to reduce negative externalities by passing legislation that restricts business activity. When direct controls are imposed, the cost

of production will (increase, decrease) _____,

the supply curve will (increase, decrease) _____,

and output will _____.

17. Government also can place taxes on specific products to reduce negative externalities. With these excise taxes, the costs of production will (increase, decrease)

_____, the supply curve will _____, and

output will _____.

18. The government may correct for the underallocation

of resources where (negative, positive) _____ ex-

ternalities are large and diffuse. This objective can be

achieved by (taxing, subsidizing) _____ buyers or

producers and through government (provision, consump-

tion) _____ of a good or service.

19. In the case of positive externalities, the government can give a subsidy to consumers that will increase

the (supply, demand) _____ for a product or it

can give a subsidy to businesses that will increase the

_____ for the product. In either case, the output

of the product will (increase, decrease) _____.

20. Reducing negative externalities comes at a "price" to society, and therefore society must decide how much of

a decrease it wants to (buy, sell) "_____." Further

abatement of a negative externality increases economic efficiency if the marginal cost is (greater than, equal to,

less than) _____ the marginal benefit, but it is eco-

nomically inefficient if the marginal benefit is _____ the marginal cost. The optimal reduction of a negative externality occurs where the society's marginal benefit is

(greater than, equal to, less than) _____ society's

marginal cost.

■ **TRUE–FALSE QUESTIONS**

Circle T if the statement is true, F if it is false.

1. Demand-side market failures arise when demand curves do not reflect consumers' full willingness to pay for a product. **T F**

2. If demand and supply reflected all the benefits and costs of producing a product, there would be economic efficiency in the production of the product. **T F**

3. Consumer surplus is the difference between the minimum and maximum price a consumer is willing to pay for a good. **T F**

4. Consumer surplus is a utility surplus that reflects a gain in total utility or satisfaction. **T F**

5. Consumer surplus and price are directly or positively related. **T F**

6. Producer surplus is the difference between the actual price a producer receives for a product and the minimum price the producer would have been willing to accept for the product. **T F**

7. The higher the actual price, the less the amount of producer surplus. **T F**

8. Efficiency losses are increases in the combined consumer and producer surplus. **T F**

9. Private goods are characterized by rivalry and excludability and public goods are characterized by nonrivalry and nonexcludability. **T F**

10. When determining the collective demand for a public good, you add the prices people are willing to pay for the last unit of the public good at each possible quantity demanded. **T F**

11. When the marginal benefit of a public good exceeds the marginal cost, there will be an overallocation of resources to that public good use. **T F**

12. The optimal allocation of a public good is determined by the rule that marginal cost (MC) equals marginal revenue (MR). **T F**

13. An externality is a cost or benefit accruing to an individual or group—a third party—which is external to the market transaction. **T F**

14. In a competitive product market and in the absence of negative externalities, the supply curve reflects the costs of producing the product. **T F**

15. If demand and supply reflected all the benefits and costs of a product, the equilibrium output of a competitive market would be identical with its optimal output. **T F**

16. There is an underallocation of resources to the production of a commodity when negative externalities are present. **T F**

17. One way for government to correct for a negative externality from the production of a product is to increase the demand for the product. **T F**

18. When negative externalities are involved in the production of a product, more resources are allocated to the production of that product and more of the product is produced than is optimal or most efficient. **T F**

19. The Coase theorem suggests that government intervention is required whenever there are negative or positive externalities. **T F**

20. Taxes that are imposed on businesses that create an externality will lower the marginal cost of production and increase supply. **T F**

21. Subsidizing the firms producing goods that provide positive externalities will usually result in a better allocation of resources. **T F**

22. If a society has marginal costs of $10 for pollution abatement and the marginal benefit of pollution abatement is $8, to achieve an optimal amount of the pollution the society should increase the amount of pollution abatement. **T F**

23. Changes in technology or changes in society's attitudes toward pollution can affect the optimal amount of pollution abatement. **T F**

24. One solution to the negative externalities caused by pollution is to create a market for pollution rights in which the negative externalities from pollution are turned into private costs. **T F**

25. Political pressure can make it difficult to find and implement an economically efficient solution to an externality problem. **T F**

■ MULTIPLE-CHOICE QUESTIONS

Circle the letter that corresponds to the best answer.

1. Katie is willing to pay $50 for a product and Tom is willing to pay $40. The actual price that they have to pay is $30. What is the amount of the consumer surplus for Katie and Tom combined?
   (a) $30
   (b) $40
   (c) $50
   (d) $60

2. Given the demand curve, the consumer surplus is
   (a) increased by higher prices and decreased by lower prices
   (b) decreased by higher prices and increased by lower prices
   (c) increased by higher prices, but not affected by lower prices
   (d) decreased by lower prices, but not affected by higher prices

3. The difference between the actual price that a producer receives (or producers receive) and the minimum acceptable price is producer
   (a) cost
   (b) wealth
   (c) surplus
   (d) investment

4. The minimum acceptable price for a product that Juan is willing to receive is $20. It is $15 for Carlos. The actual price they receive is $25. What is the amount of the producer surplus for Juan and Carlos combined?
   (a) $10
   (b) $15
   (c) $20
   (d) $25

5. When the combined consumer and producer surplus is at a maximum for a product,
   (a) the quantity supplied is greater than the quantity demanded
   (b) the market finds alternative ways to ration the product
   (c) the market is allocatively efficient
   (d) the product is a nonpriced good

6. When the output is greater than the optimal level of output for a product there are efficiency
   (a) gains from the underproduction of the product
   (b) losses from the underproduction of the product
   (c) gains from the overproduction of the product
   (d) losses from the overproduction of the product

7. How do public goods differ from private goods? Public goods are characterized by
   (a) rivalry and excludability
   (b) rivalry and nonexcludability
   (c) nonrivalry and excludability
   (d) nonrivalry and nonexcludability

8. There is a free-rider problem when people
   (a) are willing to pay for what they want
   (b) are not willing to pay for what they want
   (c) benefit from a good without paying for its cost
   (d) want to buy more than is available for purchase in the market

Answer Questions 9, 10, 11, and 12 on the basis of the following information for a public good. P_1 and P_2 represent the prices individuals 1 and 2, the only two people in the society, are willing to pay for the last unit of a public good. P_c represents the price (or collective willingness to pay) for a public good, and Q_s represents the quantity supplied of the public good at those prices.

Q_d	P_1	P_2	P_c	Q_s
1	$4	$5	$9	5
2	3	4	7	4
3	2	3	5	3
4	1	2	3	2
5	0	1	1	1

9. What amount is this society willing to pay for the first unit of the public good?
   (a) $10
   (b) $9
   (c) $8
   (d) $7

10. What amount is this society willing to pay for the third unit of the public good?
   (a) $5
   (b) $6
   (c) $7
   (d) $8

11. Given the supply curve Q_s, the optimal price and quantity of the public good in this society will be
   (a) $9 and 5 units
   (b) $5 and 3 units
   (c) $5 and 4 units
   (d) $3 and 2 units

12. If this good were a private good instead of a public good, the total quantity demanded at the $4 price would be
   (a) 3 units
   (b) 4 units
   (c) 5 units
   (d) 6 units

Answer Questions 13, 14, and 15 for a public good on the basis of the following graph.

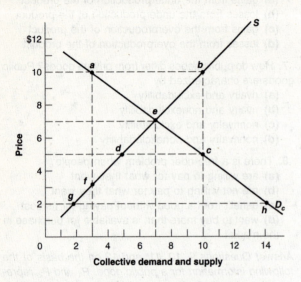

Collective demand and supply

13. Where the marginal benefits equal the collective marginal costs is represented by point
  (a) *b*
  (b) *c*
  (c) *d*
  (d) *e*

14. Which line segment would indicate the amount by which the marginal benefit of this public good is less than the marginal cost?
  (a) *ab*
  (b) *bc*
  (c) *fa*
  (d) *gh*

15. If 3 units of this public good are produced, the marginal
  (a) cost of $10 is greater than the marginal benefit of $3
  (b) cost of $10 is greater than the marginal benefit of $5
  (c) benefit of $10 is greater than the marginal cost of $5
  (d) benefit of $10 is greater than the marginal cost of $3

16. Assume that a government is considering a new antipollution program and may choose to include in this program any number of four different projects. The marginal cost and the marginal benefits of each of the four projects are given in the table below.

Project	Marginal cost	Marginal benefit
#1	$ 2 million	$ 5 million
#2	5 million	7 million
#3	10 million	9 million
#4	20 million	15 million

What total amount should this government spend on the antipollution program?
  (a) $2 million
  (b) $7 million
  (c) $17 million
  (d) $37 million

17. When the production and consumption of a product entail negative externalities, a competitive product market results in a(n)
  (a) underallocation of resources to the product
  (b) overallocation of resources to the product
  (c) optimal allocation of resources to the product
  (d) higher price for the product

18. A positive externality in the production of some product will result in
  (a) overproduction
  (b) underproduction
  (c) the optimal level of production if consumers are price takers
  (d) the optimal level of production if consumers are utility maximizers

Use the following graph which shows the supply and demand for a product to answer Questions 19, 20, and 21.

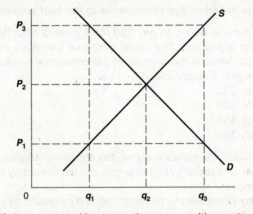

19. If there are neither negative nor positive externalities, the output that results in the optimal allocation of resources to the production of this product is
  (a) q_1
  (b) q_2
  (c) q_3
  (d) 0

20. If the market for a product was in equilibrium at output level q_2 but the optimal level of output for society was at q_1, the government could correct for this
  (a) negative externality with a subsidy to consumers
  (b) negative externality with a subsidy to producers
  (c) positive externality with a subsidy to producers
  (d) negative externality with a tax on producers

21. If the market for a product was in equilibrium at output level q_2 but the optimal level of output for society was at q_3, the government could correct for this
  (a) overallocation of resources by direct controls on consumers
  (b) underallocation of resources through taxes on producers
  (c) overallocation of resources through a market for externality rights
  (d) underallocation of resources through subsidies to producers

22. How does government try to capture more of the benefits for society when there is a positive externality?

(a) by taxing consumers
(b) by taxing producers
(c) by subsidizing producers
(d) by ignoring the free-rider problem

Use the following table to answer Questions 23, 24, and 25. The data in the table show the marginal costs and marginal benefits to a city for five different levels of pollution abatement.

Quantity of pollution abatement	Marginal cost	Marginal benefit
500 tons	$500,000	$100,000
400 tons	300,000	150,000
300 tons	200,000	200,000
200 tons	100,000	300,000
100 tons	50,000	400,000

23. If the city seeks an optimal reduction of the externality, it will select how many tons of pollution abatement?
(a) 100
(b) 300
(c) 400
(d) 500

24. If the marginal benefit of pollution abatement increased by $150,000 at each level because of the community's desire to attract more firms, the optimal level of pollution abatement in tons would be
(a) 200
(b) 300
(c) 400
(d) 500

25. What would cause the optimal level of pollution abatement to be 200 tons?
(a) technological improvement in production that decreases marginal costs by $150,000 at each level
(b) an increase in the health risk from this pollution that increases marginal benefits by $200,000 at each level
(c) the need to replace old pollution monitoring equipment with new equipment that increases marginal costs by $200,000 at each level
(d) reduction in the public demand for pollution control that decreases marginal benefits by $100,000 at each level

■ **PROBLEMS**

1. Given the following information, calculate the consumer surplus for each individual A to F.

(1)	(2)	(3)	(4)
Person	Maximum price willing to pay	Actual price (equilibrium price)	Consumer surplus
A	$25	$12	_____
B	23	12	_____
C	18	12	_____
D	16	12	_____
E	13	12	_____
F	12	12	_____

2. Given the following information, calculate the producer surplus for each producer A to F.

(1)	(2)	(3)	(4)
Producers	Minimum acceptable price	Actual price (equilibrium price)	Producer surplus
A	$4	$12	_____
B	5	12	_____
C	7	12	_____
D	9	12	_____
E	10	12	_____
F	12	12	_____

3. Answer this question based on the following graph showing the market supply and demand for a product. Assume that the output level is Q_1.

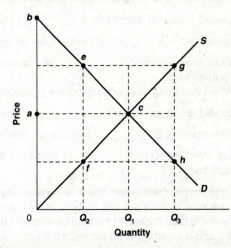

a. The area of consumer surplus would be shown by the area _____.
b. The area of producer surplus would be shown by the area _____.
c. The area that maximizes the combined consumer and producer surplus is _____.
d. If the output level is now Q_2, then there are efficiency losses shown by area _____.
e. If the output level is now Q_3, then there are efficiency losses shown by area _____.

4. Data on two individuals' preferences for a public good are reflected in the following table. P_1 and P_2 represent the prices individuals 1 and 2, the only two people in the society, are willing to pay for the last unit of the public good.

Quantity	P_1	P_2
1	$6	$6
2	5	5
3	4	4
4	3	3
5	2	2
6	1	1

a. Complete the table below showing the collective demand for the public good in this society.

Q_d	Price	Q_s
1	_____	7
2	_____	6
3	_____	6
4	_____	4
5	_____	3
6	_____	2

b. Given the supply schedule for this public good as shown by the Q_s column, the optimal quantity of this public good is _____ units and the optimal price is $_____.

c. When 3 units of this public good are produced, the perceived marginal benefit is $_____ and the marginal cost is $_____; there will be an (overallocation, underallocation) _____ of resources to this public good.

d. When 6 units of this public good are produced, the perceived marginal benefit is $_____ and the marginal cost is $_____; there is an (underallocation, overallocation) _____ of resources to this public good.

5. Imagine that a state government is considering constructing a new highway to link its two largest cities. Its estimate of the total costs and the total benefits of building 2-, 4-, 6-, and 8-lane highways between the two cities are shown in the table below. (All figures are in millions of dollars.)

Project	Total cost	Marginal cost	Total benefit	Marginal benefit
No highway	$ 0		$ 0	
2-lane highway	500	$_____	650	$_____
4-lane highway	680	_____	750	_____
6-lane highway	760	_____	800	_____
8-lane highway	860	_____	825	_____

a. Compute the marginal cost and the marginal benefit of the 2-, 4-, 6-, and 8-lane highways.

b. Will it benefit the state to allocate resources to construct a highway? _____

c. If the state builds a highway,

(1) it should be a _____-lane highway.

(2) the total cost will be $ _____ million.

(3) the total benefit will be $ _____ million.

(4) the *net* benefit will be $ _____ million.

6. The following graph shows the demand and supply curves for a product bought and sold in a competitive market.

a. Assume that there are no negative or positive externalities associated with the production of this product. The optimal level of output would be (Q_1, Q_2, Q_3) _____.

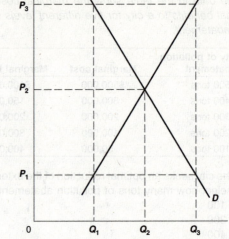

b. Assume that there are negative externalities associated with the cost of production of this product that are not reflected in the optimal output. In this case, the supply curve will shift to the (right, left) _____ and equilibrium level of output would most likely be (Q_1, Q_2, Q_3) _____. There would be an (under, over) _____ allocation of resources to the production of this product. To return to the optimal level of output, government would most likely (tax, subsidize) _____ the producers, which would (decrease, increase) _____ the supply of the product and return the supply curve to its original position at the optimal level of output.

c. Assume that there are positive externalities associated with the production of this product. In this case, the demand curve will shift to the (right, left) _____ and the new equilibrium level of output would most likely be (Q_1, Q_2, Q_3) _____. There would be an (under, over) _____ allocation of resources to the production of this product. To bring about the production of the optimal output for this product, government might (tax, subsidize) _____ the consumers of this product, which would (increase, decrease) _____ the demand of the product and return the demand curve to its original position at the optimal level of output.

7. Assume the atmosphere of a large metropolitan area is able to reabsorb 1500 tons of pollutants per year. The following schedule shows the price polluters would be willing to pay for the right to dispose of 1 ton of pollutants per year and the total quantity of pollutants they would wish to dispose of at each price.

Price (per ton of pollut- ant) rights	Total quantity of pollutant rights demanded (tons)
$ 0	4000
1000	3500
2000	3000
3000	2500
4000	2000
5000	1500
6000	1000
7000	500

a. If there were no emission fee, polluters would put

_____ tons of pollutants in the air each

year, and this quantity of pollutants would exceed the

ability of nature to reabsorb them by _____

tons.

b. To reduce pollution to the capacity of the atmosphere to recycle pollutants, an emission fee of

$_____ per ton should be set.

c. Were this emission fee set, the total emission fees

set would be $_____.

d. Were the quantity of pollution rights demanded at each price to increase by 500 tons, the emis-

sion fee could be increased by $_____

and total emission fees collected would increase by

$_____.

■ **SHORT ANSWER AND ESSAY QUESTIONS**

1. Explain the difference between demand-side market failures and supply-side market failures. Give several examples of each one.

2. How is the consumer surplus related to utility or satisfaction? Explain, using a supply and demand graph.

3. Define, using a supply and demand graph, the meaning of producer surplus.

4. Use consumer and producer surplus to describe efficiency losses in a competitive market. Provide a supply and demand graph to show such losses.

5. Distinguish between a private and a public good. Include in your answer an explanation of rivalry, excludability, and the free-rider problem.

6. Contrast how you construct the demand curve for a public good with the procedure for constructing the demand curve for a private good using individual demand schedules.

7. Explain the relationship between the marginal cost and benefit of a public good when there is an underallocation, an overallocation, and an optimal allocation of resources for the provision of the public good.

8. Describe benefit–cost analysis, and state the rules used to make decisions from marginal and total perspectives.

9. Why are quasi-public goods provided by government even if they could be produce by the private sector?

10. How are resources reallocated from the private economy to produce public or quasi-public goods?

11. What are externalities? Give examples of positive externalities and negative externalities.

12. How does the existence of negative externalities affect the allocation of resources and the prices of products?

13. Describe what happens in a market in terms of demand, supply, output, and price when there are positive externalities associated with a product.

14. What two basic actions can government take to correct for negative externalities in a market?

15. How can government respond to situations in which there are positive externalities associated with a product and it wants to increase output?

16. Explain why the "Fable of the Bee" is a good reminder that it is a fallacy to assume that government must always get involved to remedy externalities.

17. What rule can society use to determine the optimal level of pollution abatement?

18. How does time change answers about the optimal level of pollution abatement?

19. Discuss the economic issues involved in the use of a cap-and-trade program and the use of a carbon tax to reduce or mitigate the adverse effects from carbon dioxide emissions.

20. Why is it difficult for government to correct for externalities through the political process?

ANSWERS

Chapter 5 Market Failures: Public Goods and Externalities

FILL-IN QUESTIONS

1. demand side, supply side
2. maximum, less, negatively, decrease, increase
3. minimum, more, positively, increase, decrease
4. productive, allocative
5. equal to, equal to, maximum
6. losses, losses, less than
7. is not, can, private
8. nonrivalry, nonexcludability, free-rider
9. quantities demanded, price, prices, quantity demanded
10. utility, returns, benefit, cost, benefit, cost (*either order for last two*)
11. benefit, cost, maximum
12. taxing, tax revenue
13. seller, buyer
14. right, left
15. over, under
16. increase, decrease, decrease
17. increase, decrease, decrease
18. positive, subsidizing, provision
19. demand, supply increase
20. buy, less than, less than, equal to

TRUE-FALSE QUESTIONS

1. T, p. 93	**10.** T, pp. 101–102	**19.** F, p. 106
2. T, p. 93	**11.** F, p. 102	**20.** F, p. 107
3. F, pp. 93–94	**12.** F, pp. 103–104	**21.** T, pp. 107–108
4. T, p. 94	**13.** T, pp. 104–105	**22.** F, pp. 108–109
5. F, p. 94	**14.** T, p.105	**23.** T, p. 109
6. T, p. 95	**15.** T, pp. 105–106	**24.** T, p. 110
7. F, pp. 95–96	**16.** F, pp. 105–106	**25.** T, p. 112
8. F, pp. 98–99	**17.** F, pp. 106–107	
9. T, pp. 99–100	**18.** T, pp. 105–106	

MULTIPLE-CHOICE QUESTIONS

1. a, pp. 95–96	**10.** a, pp. 101–102	**19.** b, pp. 104–105
2. b, pp. 94–95	**11.** b, pp. 101–102	**20.** d, pp. 105–107
3. c, p. 95	**12.** a, pp. 101–102	**21.** d, pp. 105–107
4. b, pp. 94–95	**13.** d, p. 102	**22.** c, p.107
5. c, pp. 96–97	**14.** b, p. 102	**23.** b, pp. 108–109
6. d, pp. 98–99	**15.** d, p. 102	**24.** c, pp. 108–109
7. d, pp. 99–100	**16.** b, pp. 102–103	**25.** c, pp. 108–109
8. c, p. 100	**17.** b, p. 105	
9. b, pp. 101–102	**18.** b, p. 105	

PROBLEMS

1. 13, 11, 6, 4, 1, 0

2. 8, 7, 5, 3, 2, 0

3. *a.* abc; *b.* 0ac; *c.* 0bc; *d.* efc; *e.* ghc

4. *a.* $12, 10, 8, 6, 4, 2; *b.* 4, 6; *c.* 8, 4, underallocation; *d.* 2, 10, overallocation

5. *a.* Marginal cost: $500, $180, $80, $100; Marginal benefit: $650, $100, $50, $25; *b.* yes; *c.* (1) 2, (2) $500, (3) $650, (4) $150

6. *a.* Q_2; *b.* right, Q_3, over, tax, decrease; *c.* left, Q_1, under, subsidize, increase

7. *a.* 4000, 2500; *b.* 5000; *c.* 7,500,000; *d.* 1000, 1,500,000

SHORT ANSWER AND ESSAY QUESTIONS

1. p. 93	**8.** pp. 102–103	**15.** pp. 107–108
2. pp. 94–95	**9.** p. 104	**16.** p. 106
3. pp. 95–96	**10.** p. 104	**17.** pp. 108–109
4. pp. 96–99	**11.** pp. 104–105	**18.** p. 109
5. pp. 99–100.	**12.** p. 105	**19.** p. 110
6. pp. 101–102	**13.** pp. 105–106	**20.** pp. 109, 111
7. pp. 101–102	**14.** pp. 106–107	

CHAPTER 6

Consumer Behavior

Previous chapters explained that consumers typically buy more of a product as its price decreases and less of a product as its price increases. Chapter 6 looks behind this law of demand to explain why consumers behave this way. It also explains factors that influence consumer decisions when they act in less rational ways and are confronted with good or bad decisions.

The chapter first explains the **law of diminishing marginal utility** and uses it to explain why the demand curve slopes downward. This explanation is based on the concept of marginal utility. In this view, the additional satisfaction (or marginal utility) that a consumer obtains from the consumption of each additional unit of a product will tend to decline; therefore a consumer will have an incentive to purchase additional units of a product only if its price falls. (Another explanation of the law of demand that is more complete, but more complex, is based on indifference curves and is presented in the appendix to this chapter.)

Most of this chapter presents the **marginal-utility** view of consumer behavior. This explanation requires that you first understand the concepts and assumptions on which this theory of consumer behavior rests, and second, do some rigorous reasoning using these concepts and assumptions. It is an exercise in logic, but be sure that you follow the reasoning. To help you, the text provides several numerical examples for you to follow.

No one believes that consumers actually perform these mental gymnastics before they spend their incomes or make purchases. But we study the marginal-utility approach to consumer behavior because the consumers behave as if they made their purchases on the basis of very fine calculations. Thus, this approach explains what we do in fact observe and makes it possible for us to predict with a good deal of precision how consumers will react to changes in their incomes and the prices of products.

The final section of the chapter describes how the theory of consumer behavior can be used to explain many economic events in the real world. The five applications discussed are the takeover by iPods of the market for recorded music, the water–diamond paradox, the value of time in consumption, the reasons for increased consumer purchases of medical care, and the economic effects of cash and noncash gifts. Be sure you understand how consumer theory is used to explain these five phenomena.

The chapter also offers insights about consumer behavior from the field of **behavioral economics.** Here you will learn about **prospect theory** and how it can be used to explain situations in which consumers are presented with good or bad choices and may be less rational in their decision making than has been assumed in previous theory. This interesting section of the chapter presents the concepts of loss aversion, framing effects, anchoring, mental accounting, and the endowment effect. Each concept is illustrated with a practical example showing how it changes the evaluations of gains and losses by consumers.

■ CHECKLIST

When you have studied this chapter you should be able to

☐ Describe the law of diminishing marginal utility.

☐ Define utility, marginal utility, and total utility.

☐ Explain the relationship of the law of diminishing marginal utility to demand.

☐ List four dimensions of the typical consumer's situation.

☐ State the utility-maximizing rule.

☐ Use the utility-maximizing rule to determine how consumers would spend their fixed incomes when given the utility and price data.

☐ Explain how a consumer decides between an optimal solution and an inferior solution to a utility-maximization problem.

☐ Give an algebraic restatement of the utility-maximizing rule based on an example using two products, A and B.

☐ Derive a consumer's demand schedule for a product from utility, income, and price data.

☐ Explain how the income and substitution effects affect utility maximization and the deriving of the product demand curve.

☐ Use consumer theory to explain the popularity of iPods.

☐ Describe the diamond–water paradox in terms of the theory of consumer behavior.

☐ Generalize the theory of consumer behavior to account for the economic value of time.

☐ Discuss how the method of payments affects consumer purchases of medical care.

☐ Describe the economic trade-offs between cash and noncash gifts.

☐ State three facts about how people deal with good and bad situations that form the basis for prospect theory.

☐ Explain why a manufacturer will keep the price constant for a product while shrinking its size when input costs rise.

☐ Describe how framing effects influence consumers' perceptions of product purchases.

☐ Discuss the role of anchoring in affecting later consumer decisions or purchases.

☐ Give an example of how mental accounting influences the buying of a warranty.

☐ Use the endowment effect to explain why people put different valuations on what they own or would like to own.

☐ Describe two "nudges" based on behavioral economics that were used to influence consumer decisions (*Last Word*).

■ **CHAPTER OUTLINE**

1. The *law of diminishing marginal utility* can be used to explain why the demand curve slopes downward.

    a. *Utility* is subjective and difficult to quantify. For the purposes of this chapter it will be assumed that utility is the satisfaction or pleasure a person gets from consuming a product. It will be measured in hypothetical units called *utils.*

    b. *Total utility* is the total amount of satisfaction that a consumer obtains from consuming a product. *Marginal utility* is the extra satisfaction that a consumer obtains from consuming an additional or extra unit of a product. The principle that the marginal utility of a product falls as a consumer uses (consumes) additional units of a product is the law of diminishing marginal utility. There is a relationship between total and marginal utility. As shown in text Figure 6.1, total utility increases, but at a decreasing rate until it reaches a maximum and then declines. Marginal utility decreases as total utility increases. When total utility reaches a maximum, marginal utility is zero. When total utility declines, marginal utility is negative.

    c. The law of diminishing marginal utility explains why the demand curve for a product slopes downward. As more and more of a product is consumed, each additional unit consumed provides less satisfaction. The consumer will only buy more of a product if the price falls.

2. The law of diminishing marginal utility is also the basis of the **theory of consumer behavior** that explains how consumers will spend their incomes for particular goods and services.

    a. In the simple case, it is assumed that the typical consumer engages in *rational behavior,* knows marginal-utility schedules for the various goods available (has preferences), has a limited money income to spend (a *budget constraint*), and must pay a price to acquire each of the goods that yield utility.

    b. Given these assumptions, the consumer maximizes the total utility obtained when the marginal utility of the last dollar spent on each product is the same for all products (the *utility-maximizing rule*). When the consumer follows this rule, he or she has achieved *consumer equilibrium* and has no incentive to change expenditures.

    c. A numerical example is used to illustrate the rule using two products, A and B, and assuming that all money income is spent on one of the two products. In making the decision, the rational consumer must compare the extra or marginal utility from each product with its added cost (as measured by its price). Thus, marginal utility is compared on a per dollar basis.

    d. The allocation rule states that consumers will maximize their satisfaction when they allocate their money income so that the last dollar spent on each product yields the same marginal utility. In the two-product case, this can be stated algebraically as

$$\frac{\text{Marginal utility of A}}{\text{Price of A}} = \frac{\text{Marginal utility of B}}{\text{Price of B}}$$

Total utility is a maximum when the marginal utility of the last unit of a product purchased divided by its price is the same for all products.

3. The utility-maximizing rule can be applied to determine the amount of the product the consumer will purchase at different prices with income, tastes, and the prices of other products remaining constant.

    a. The numerical example that is used is based on one price for a product. If the price of the product falls, it is possible to use the utility-maximizing rule to determine how much more of the product the consumer will purchase. Based on this exercise it is possible to show the inverse relationship between price and quantity demanded as shown by a demand curve.

    b. Utility maximization also can be understood in terms of the *income effect* and the *substitution effect* to explain the law of demand. As the price of a product drops, a consumer increases the amounts purchased to restore equilibrium following the utility-maximizing rule. The change can be viewed as the consumer substituting more of the now less expensive product for another product and having more real income to spend.

4. Five of the many **applications** and **extensions** of consumer theory for the real world are discussed in this chapter.

    a. iPods have gained popularity among consumers relative to portable CD players because many consumers have concluded that iPods have a higher ratio of marginal utility to price than the ratio for portable CD players.

    b. Diamonds are high in price, but of limited usefulness, while water is low in price, but essential for life. This diamond–water paradox is explained by distinguishing between marginal and total utility. Water is low in price because it is generally in plentiful supply and thus has low marginal utility. Diamonds are high in price because they are relatively scarce and thus have high marginal utility. Water, however, is considered more useful than diamonds because it has much greater total utility.

    c. The facts that consumption takes time and time is a scarce resource can be included in the marginal-utility theory. The full price of any consumer good or service is equal to its market price plus the value of time taken to consume it (i.e., the income the consumer could have earned had he or she used that time for work).

    d. Expenditures on medical care have increased because of its financing through insurance. The consumer does not pay the full price of medical care services and thus has an incentive to consume more than if the consumer paid the full price.

e. Cash gifts tend to be more efficient for consumers because they are more likely to match consumer preferences and increase the total utility compared to non-cash gifts that restrict consumer choice.

5. *Behavioral economics* combines insights from economics, psychology, and neuroscience to understand decision making when people are not always rational, deliberate, or unemotional. *Prospect theory* is a part of behavioral economics that takes into account decision making when outcomes are bad or good. It is based on three facts or insights: people judge good and bad things relative to their current situation or the *status quo;* people experience both diminishing marginal utility for gains and diminishing marginal disutility for losses; and people are *loss adverse,* which means that losses are experienced more intensely than gains.

a. Consumers often fixate on a price increase rather than other product characteristics when assessing a loss. For example, if the costs of inputs increase for a product, businesses can respond by raising its price or by reducing its size. Businesses may not increase price but shrink size because they know consumers view price increases more adversely than a size reduction.

b. *Framing effects* can affect perceptions of gains or losses. New information changes the mental frame people use for evaluating whether outcomes are good or bad. For example, getting a 10-percent wage increase would typically be considered good, but not if the person found out that everyone else working in a business received a 15-percent wage increase.

c. *Anchoring* produces situations where irrelevant information affects people's perceptions of the status quo and decisions. For example, students who recently received a high grade on a test might be more likely to purchase a product such as candy bars because their assessment of the product is influenced by the positive feedback from the test.

d. Consumers may not look at their consumption options simultaneously, but rather use *mental accounting* to separate items and consider them in isolation. For example, people would be less likely to purchase a warranty for a TV if they did not separate the TV purchase from the warranty purchase, thus recognizing that a TV is not likely to break and future income will cover a loss.

e. The *endowment effect* refers to situations where people place greater value on items they possess or own than identical items they might want to purchase. For example, people who value coffee mugs at $10 each might sell them for a higher price (say $15 each) if they were given possession of the mugs and wanted to sell them.

6. (*Last Word*). Studies in behavioral economics offer suggestions to "nudge" people to make better economic and financial decisions. For example, enrollments in retirement plans are higher when people are enrolled and then given the option to opt out than if they are not enrolled and given the option to opt in. Also, people are more likely to reduce their electricity usage when given positive or negative feedback about how their behavior compares with other similar users.

■ HINTS AND TIPS

1. Utility is simply an abstraction useful for explaining consumer behavior. Do not become overly concerned with the precise measurement of utility or satisfaction. What you should focus on is the relative comparison of the additional satisfaction (marginal utility) from a dollar spent on one good to the additional satisfaction obtained from a dollar spent on another good. The choice of producing more additional utility satisfaction from one good than the other will maximize consumer satisfaction. Thus, you just need to know which good won the contest, not the final score (how much additional utility was added).

2. Master the difference between marginal utility and total utility. Once you think you understand the difference, use the concepts to explain to someone the diamond–water paradox at the end of the chapter.

3. The utility-maximization model provides insights about the income and substitution effects that occur with a change in price. For most products, a price decrease gives consumers more income to spend on that product and other products, so the quantity demanded for that product increases. The three steps in the logic for a typical product A are (1) $P_A\downarrow$, (2) income$\uparrow$, and (3) $Q_{dA}\uparrow$. A price decrease also makes product A more attractive to buy relative to its substitutes, so the demand for these substitutes decreases and the quantity demanded for product A increases. Again, there are three steps in the logic: (1) $P_A\downarrow$, (2) demand for substitutes$\downarrow$, and (3) $Q_{dA}\uparrow$. In both cases, the end result is the same: $Q_{dA}\uparrow$. Practice your understanding by showing the logic for an increase in the price of product A.

4. Prospect theory offers interesting explanations for some economic decisions and outcomes. To gain mastery of the different terms used throughout this section, think of one aspect of the theory (loss aversion, framing effects, anchoring, mental accounting, and the endowment effect) and a related example to explain it.

■ IMPORTANT TERMS

law of diminishing marginal utility	substitution effect
utility	behavioral economics
total utility	prospect theory
marginal utility	status quo
rational behavior	loss averse
budget constraint	framing effects
utility-maximizing rule	anchoring
consumer equilibrium	mental accounting
income effect	endowment effect

SELF-TEST

■ FILL-IN QUESTIONS

1. Utility is (an objective, a subjective) _____ concept and is not the same thing as usefulness. The overall satisfaction a consumer gets from consuming a good or service is (marginal, total) _____ utility, but the extra or additional satisfaction that a consumer gets from a good or service is (marginal, total) _____ utility.

2. A graph of total utility and marginal utility shows that when total utility is increasing, marginal utility is (positive, negative) _____, and when total utility is at a maximum, marginal utility is at (a maximum, zero, a minimum) _____.

3. The law of diminishing marginal utility states that marginal utility will (increase, decrease) _____ as a consumer increases the quantity consumed of a product. This law explains why the (demand, supply) _____ curve slopes downward.

4. The marginal-utility theory of consumer behavior assumes that the consumer is (wealthy, rational) _____ and has certain (preferences, discounts) _____ for various goods. A consumer cannot buy every good and service desired because income is (subsidized, limited) _____ and goods and services are scarce in relation to the demand for them; thus they have (prices, quantities) _____ attached to them.

5. When the consumer is maximizing the utility the consumer's income will obtain, the ratio of the marginal utility of the (first, last) _____ unit purchased of a product to its price is (the same, greater than) _____ for all the products bought.

6. If the marginal utility of the last dollar spent on one product is greater than the marginal utility of the last dollar spent on another product, the consumer should (increase, decrease) _____ purchases of the first and _____ purchases of the second product.

7. Assume there are only two products, X and Y, that a consumer can purchase with a fixed income. The consumer is maximizing utility algebraically when:

a. _____ **b.** _____

c. _____ = **d.** _____

8. In deriving a consumer's demand for a particular product, the two factors (other than the preferences or tastes of the consumer) that are held constant are

a. _____

b. _____

9. The utility-maximizing rule and the demand curve are logically (consistent, inconsistent) _____. Because marginal utility declines, a lower price is needed to get the consumer to buy (less, more) _____ of a particular product.

10. A fall in the price of a product tends to (increase, decrease) _____ a consumer's real income, and a rise in its price tends to _____ real income. This is called the (substitution, income) _____ effect.

11. When the price of a product increases, the product becomes relatively (more, less) _____ expensive than it was and the prices of other products become relatively (higher, lower) _____ than they were; the consumer will therefore buy (less, more) _____ of the product in question and _____ of the other products. This is called the (substitution, income) _____ effect.

12. When consumer preferences changed from portable CD players to iPods, and the prices of iPods (increased, decreased) _____ significantly, this led to (increased, decreased) _____ purchases of iPods.

13. Water is low in price because its (total, marginal) _____ utility is low, while diamonds are high in price because their _____ utility is high. Water, however, is more useful than diamonds because the (total, marginal) _____ utility of water is much greater than the _____ utility of diamonds.

14. The theory of consumer behavior has been generalized to account for (supply, time) _____. This is a valuable economic resource because it is (limited, unlimited) _____. Its value is (greater than, equal to) _____ the income that can be earned with it. The full price to the consumer of any product is, therefore, the market (time, price) _____ plus the value of the consumption _____.

15. With health insurance coverage, the price consumers pay for health care services is less than the "true" value or opportunity (benefit, cost) _____. The lower price to consumers encourages them to consume (more, less) _____ health care services.

16. Comparing food consumption at an all-you-can-eat buffet with a pay-per-item cafeteria would show that people eat (less, more) _____ at the buffet because the marginal utility of an extra food is (positive, zero) _____ while its price is _____.

17. Noncash gifts are (less, more) _____ preferred than cash gifts because they yield (less, more) _____ total utility to consumers.

18. Prospect theory suggests that people judge good and bad things relative to the (status quo, future) _____. People experience diminishing marginal utility for (losses, gains) _____ and diminishing marginal disutility for _____. People are loss adverse and experience losses (less, more) _____ intensely than they do gains.

19. Changes in people's preferences that are caused by new information that changes their perspectives on whether there are gains or losses are referred to as (framing, endowment) _____ effects whereas the tendency that people have to put a higher valuation on anything they currently possess than identical items they do not own is a(n) _____ effect.

20. When consumers consider purchasing a warranty for a large consumer product such as a TV in isolation without thinking about the other options or aspects of the purchase, they are using mental (accounting, economics) _____ that often can lead to (overpayment, underpayment) _____ for the warranty protection.

■ **TRUE–FALSE QUESTIONS**

Circle T if the statement is true, F if it is false.

1. Utility is the benefit or satisfaction a person receives from consuming a good or service. **T F**

2. Utility and usefulness are not synonymous. **T F**

3. Marginal utility is the change in total utility from consuming one more unit of a product. **T F**

4. Because utility cannot actually be measured, the marginal-utility theory cannot really explain how consumers will behave. **T F**

5. The law of diminishing marginal utility indicates that gains in satisfaction become smaller as successive units of a specific product are consumed. **T F**

6. A consumer's demand curve for a product is downsloping because total utility decreases as more of the product is consumed. **T F**

7. If total utility is increasing, then marginal utility is positive and may be either increasing or decreasing. **T F**

8. The theory of consumer behavior assumes that consumers act rationally to get the most from their money. **T F**

9. All consumers are subject to budget constraints. **T F**

10. To find a consumer's demand for a product, the price of the product is varied while tastes, income, and the prices of other products remain unchanged. **T F**

11. The theory of consumer behavior assumes that consumers attempt to maximize marginal utility. **T F**

12. If the marginal utility per dollar spent on product A is greater than the marginal utility per dollar spent on product B, then to maximize utility, the consumer should purchase less of A and more of B. **T F**

13. When consumers are maximizing total utility, the marginal utilities of the last unit of every product they buy are identical. **T F**

14. The marginal utility of product X is 15 and its price is $5, while the marginal utility of product Y is 10 and its price is $2. The utility-maximizing rule suggests that there should be *less* consumption of product Y. **T F**

15. In most cases, a change in incomes will cause a change in the portfolio of goods and services purchased by consumers. **T F**

16. An increase in the real income of a consumer will result from an increase in the price of a product the consumer is buying. **T F**

17. The income and substitution effects will induce the consumer to buy less of normal good Z when the price of Z increases. **T F**

18. A fall in the price of iPods will decrease the demand for iTunes. **T F**

19. The diamond–water paradox is explained by the fact that the total utility derived from water is low while the total utility derived from diamonds is high. **T F**

20. If a consumer can earn $10 an hour and it takes 2 hours to consume a product, the value of the time required for the consumption of the product is $5. **T F**

21. One reason for the increased use of health care services is that consumers pay only part of the full price of the services. **T F**

22. People tend to eat more at an "all-you-can-eat buffet" because the "price" of additional items is zero but the marginal utility for these items is likely to be positive. **T F**

23. Noncash gifts add more to total utility than cash gifts. **T F**

24. If the price of a consumer product rather than its size is the status quo for assessing losses, then when input costs rise, a business is more likely to increase the price of the product rather than reduce its size to help pay for these additional costs. **T F**

25. When people's decisions are influenced by irrelevant information that they recently considered, this phenomenon is referred to in behavior economics as anchoring. **T F**

■ **MULTIPLE-CHOICE QUESTIONS**

Circle the letter that corresponds to the best answer.

1. Utility as defined in this chapter refers to the
   (a) usefulness of a purchased product
   (b) value of the money a consumer spends on a good
   (c) satisfaction or pleasure from consuming a good
   (d) extra income a consumer gets from buying a good at a lower price

2. Which best expresses the law of diminishing marginal utility?
   (a) The more a person consumes of a product, the smaller becomes the utility that he receives from its consumption.
   (b) The more a person consumes of a product, the smaller becomes the additional utility that she receives as a result of consuming an additional unit of the product.
   (c) The less a person consumes of a product, the smaller becomes the utility that she receives from its consumption.
   (d) The less a person consumes of a product, the smaller becomes the additional utility that he receives as a result of consuming an additional unit of the product.

3. Summing the marginal utilities of each unit consumed will determine total
   (a) cost
   (b) revenue
   (c) utility
   (d) consumption

The following table shows a hypothetical total utility schedule for a consumer of chocolate candy bars. Use the table to answer Questions 4, 5, and 6.

Number consumed	Total utility
0	0
1	9
2	19
3	27
4	35
5	42
6	42
7	40

4. This consumer begins to experience diminishing marginal utility when he consumes the
   (a) first candy bar
   (b) second candy bar
   (c) third candy bar
   (d) fourth candy bar

5. Marginal utility becomes negative with the consumption of the
   (a) fourth candy bar
   (b) fifth candy bar
   (c) sixth candy bar
   (d) seventh candy bar

6. Based on the data, you can conclude that the
   (a) marginal utility of the fourth unit is 6
   (b) marginal utility of the second unit is 27
   (c) total utility of 5 units is 42
   (d) total utility of 3 units is 55

7. After eating eight chocolate chip cookies, you are offered a ninth cookie. You turn down the cookie. Your refusal indicates that the
   (a) marginal utility for chocolate chip cookies is negative
   (b) total utility for chocolate chip cookies is negative
   (c) marginal utility is positive for the eighth and negative for the ninth cookie
   (d) total utility was zero because you ate one cookie and refused the other

8. Which is a dimension or assumption of the marginal-utility theory of consumer behavior?
   (a) The consumer has a small income.
   (b) The consumer is rational.
   (c) Goods and services are free.
   (d) Goods and services yield continually increasing amounts of marginal utility as the consumer buys more of them.

9. A consumer is making purchases of products A and B such that the marginal utility of product A is 20 and the marginal utility of product B is 30. The price of product A is $10 and the price of product B is $20. The utility-maximizing rule suggests that this consumer should
   (a) increase consumption of product B and decrease consumption of product A
   (b) increase consumption of product B and increase consumption of product A
   (c) increase consumption of product A and decrease consumption of product B
   (d) make no change in consumption of A or B

10. Suppose that the prices of A and B are $3 and $2, respectively, that the consumer is spending her entire income and buying 4 units of A and 6 units of B, and that the marginal utility of both the fourth unit of A and the sixth unit of B is 6. It can be concluded that the consumer should buy
   (a) more of both A and B
   (b) more of A and less of B
   (c) less of A and more of B
   (d) less of both A and B

11. Robert Woods is maximizing his satisfaction consuming two goods, X and Y. If the marginal utility of X is half that of Y, what is the price of X if the price of Y is $1.00?
   (a) $0.50
   (b) $1.00
   (c) $1.50
   (d) $2.00

Answer Questions 12, 13, and 14 based on the following table showing the marginal-utility schedules for goods X and Y for a hypothetical consumer. The price of good X is $1 and the price of good Y is $2. The income of the consumer is $9.

Good X		Good Y	
Quantity	MU	Quantity	MU
1	8	1	10
2	7	2	8
3	6	3	6
4	5	4	4
5	4	5	3
6	3	6	2
7	2	7	1

12. To maximize utility, the consumer will buy
(a) 7X and 1Y
(b) 5X and 2Y
(c) 3X and 3Y
(d) 1X and 4Y

13. When the consumer purchases the utility-maximizing combination of goods X and Y, total utility will be
(a) 36
(b) 45
(c) 48
(d) 52

14. Suppose that the consumer's income increased from $9 to $12. What would be the utility-maximizing combination of goods X and Y?
(a) 5X and 2Y
(b) 6X and 3Y
(c) 2X and 5Y
(d) 4X and 4Y

15. A decrease in the price of product Z will
(a) increase the marginal utility per dollar spent on Z
(b) decrease the marginal utility per dollar spent on Z
(c) decrease the total utility per dollar spent on Z
(d) cause no change in the marginal utility per dollar spent on Z

Answer Questions 16, 17, 18, and 19 on the basis of the following total utility data for products A and B. Assume that the prices of A and B are $6 and $8, respectively, and that consumer income is $36.

Units of A	Total utility	Units of B	Total utility
1	18	1	32
2	30	2	56
3	38	3	72
4	42	4	80
5	44	5	84

16. What is the level of total utility for the consumer in equilibrium?
(a) 86
(b) 102
(c) 108
(d) 120

17. How many units of the two products will the consumer buy?
(a) 1 of A and 4 of B
(b) 2 of A and 2 of B
(c) 2 of A and 3 of B
(d) 3 of A and 4 of B

18. If the price of A decreases to $4, then the utility-maximizing combination of the two products is
(a) 2 of A and 2 of B
(b) 2 of A and 3 of B
(c) 3 of A and 3 of B
(d) 4 of A and 4 of B

19. Which of the following represents the demand curve for A?

(a)		(b)		(c)		(d)	
P	Q_d	P	Q_d	P	Q_d	P	Q_d
$6	1	$6	2	$6	2	$6	2
4	4	4	5	4	3	4	4

20. Kristin Hansen buys only two goods, food and clothing. Both are normal goods for Kristin. Suppose the price of food decreases. Kristin's consumption of clothing will
(a) decrease due to the income effect
(b) increase due to the income effect
(c) increase due to the substitution effect
(d) not change due to the substitution effect

21. The reason the substitution effect works to encourage a consumer to buy more of a product when its price decreases is because
(a) the real income of the consumer has been increased
(b) the real income of the consumer has been decreased
(c) the product is now relatively less expensive than it was
(d) other products are now relatively less expensive than they were

22. The price of water is substantially less than the price of diamonds because
(a) the marginal utility of a diamond is significantly less than the marginal utility of a gallon of water
(b) the marginal utility of a diamond is significantly greater than the marginal utility of a gallon of water
(c) the total utility of diamonds is greater than the total utility of water
(d) diamonds have a low marginal utility

23. A consumer has two basic choices: rent a movie for $4.00 and spend 2 hours of time watching it or spend $15 for dinner at a restaurant that takes 1 hour of time. If the marginal utilities of the movie and the dinner are the same, and the consumer values time at $15 an hour, the rational consumer will most likely
(a) rent more movies and buy fewer restaurant dinners
(b) buy more restaurant dinners and rent fewer movies
(c) buy fewer restaurant dinners and rent fewer movies
(d) make no change in the consumption of both

24. Compared to cash gifts, noncash gifts are preferred
(a) more because they decrease total utility
(b) more because they increase total utility
(c) less because they increase total utility
(d) less because they decrease total utility

25. According to prospect theory, for gains or losses near the status quo
(a) gains and losses are experienced more intensely
(b) gains and losses are experienced less intensely
(c) losses are experienced more intensely while gains are experienced less intensely
(d) losses are experienced less intensely while gains are experienced more intensely

■ PROBLEMS

1. Assume that Harriet Palmer finds only three goods, A, B, and C, for sale and that the amounts of utility that their consumption will yield her are as shown in the table below. Compute the marginal utilities for successive units of A, B, and C and enter them in the appropriate columns.

	Good A			Good B			Good C	
Quantity	Total utility	Marginal utility	Quantity	Total utility	Marginal utility	Quantity	Total utility	Marginal utility
1	21	_____	1	7	_____	1	23	_____
2	41	_____	2	13	_____	2	40	_____
3	59	_____	3	18	_____	3	52	_____
4	74	_____	4	22	_____	4	60	_____
5	85	_____	5	25	_____	5	65	_____
6	91	_____	6	27	_____	6	68	_____
7	91	_____	7	28.2	_____	7	70	_____

2. Using the marginal-utility data for goods A, B, and C that you obtained in problem 1, assume that the prices of A, B, and C are $5, $1, and $4, respectively, and that Palmer has an income of $37 to spend.

a. Complete the table below by computing the *marginal utility per dollar* for successive units of A, B, and C.

	Good A		Good B		Good C
Quantity	Marginal utility per dollar	Quantity	Marginal utility per dollar	Quantity	Marginal utility per dollar
1	_____	1	_____	1	_____
2	_____	2	_____	2	_____
3	_____	3	_____	3	_____
4	_____	4	_____	4	_____
5	_____	5	_____	5	_____
6	_____	6	_____	6	_____
7	_____	7	_____	7	_____

b. Palmer would *not* buy 4 units of A, 1 unit of B, and 4 units of C because _____.

c. Palmer would *not* buy 6 units of A, 7 units of B, and 4 units of C because _____.

d. When Palmer is maximizing her utility, she will buy _____ units of A, _____ units of B, _____ units of C; her total utility will be _____, and the marginal utility of the last dollar spent on each good will be _____.

e. If Palmer's income increased by $1, she would spend it on good _____, assuming she can buy fractions of a unit of a good, because _____.

3. Sam Thompson has an income of $36 to spend each week. The only two goods he is interested in purchasing are H and J. The marginal-utility schedules for these two goods are shown in the table below.

The price of J does not change from week to week and is $4. The marginal utility per dollar from J is also shown in the table. But the price of H varies from one week to the next. The marginal utilities per dollar from H when the prices of H are $6, $4, $3, $2, and $1.50 are shown in the table.

	Good H						Good J	
Quantity	MU	MU/$6	MU/$4	MU/$3	MU/$2	MU/$1.50	MU	MU/$4
1	45	7.5	11.25	15	22.5	30	40	10
2	30	5	7.5	20	15	20	36	9
3	20	3.33	5	6.67	10	13.33	32	8
4	15	2.5	3.75	5	7.5	10	28	7
5	12	2	3	4	6	8	24	6
6	10	1.67	2.5	3.33	5	6.67	20	5
7	9	1.5	2.25	3	4.5	6	16	4
8	7.5	1.25	1.88	2.5	3.75	5	12	3

a. Complete the table below to show how much of H Thompson will buy each week at each of the five possible prices of H.

Price of H	Quantity of H demanded
$6.00	_____
4.00	_____
3.00	_____
2.00	_____
1.50	_____

b. What is the table you completed in part **a** called?

_____

4. Assume that a consumer can purchase only two goods: R (recreation) and M (material goods). The market price of R is $2 and the market price of M is $1. The consumer spends all her income in such a way that the marginal utility of the last unit of R she buys is 12 and the marginal utility of the last unit of M she buys is 6.

a. If we ignore the time it takes to consume R and M, is the consumer maximizing the total utility she obtains from the two goods? _____

b. Suppose it takes 4 hours to consume each unit of R, 1 hour to consume each unit of M, and the consumer can earn $2 an hour when she works.

(1) The full price of a unit of R is $_____.

(2) The full price of a unit of M is $_____.

c. If we take into account the full price of each of the commodities, is the consumer maximizing her total utility? _____ How do you know this? _____

d. If the consumer is not maximizing her utility, should she increase her consumption of R or of M? _____

Why should she do this? _____

e. Will she use more or less of her time for consuming R? _____

5. Match one of the terms from behavioral economics to an example using the appropriate number.

1. status quo   4. loss aversion

2. endowment effect   5. framing effects

3. mental accounting 6. anchoring

a. You always buy a warranty for every major consumer product you purchase regardless of whether a product is highly reliable or whether you can afford to take the loss if something should happen. _____

b. You like the number 99. Whenever you see a product sold for $0.99 you will often buy it even if you have no practical or valid use for the product. _____

c. You buy some stock in a drug company, but then the price drops sharply because one of the major drugs it sells is found to have bad side effects. You think you should sell the stock but don't want to lose money on what you purchased. _____

d. You tend to judge your gains or losses relative to your current situation. _____

e. You go to the store and purchase a gas grill and get 5 percent off, and think you got a good deal. You then talk with your neighbor who purchased the same gas grill and received 15 percent off and think you did not get a good deal. _____

f. You buy a new GPS device for $50 and start using it. Then you happen to meet a friend who sees your device and wants to buy it from you on the spot. You think about it and say fine, but state an asking price of $75. _____

■ SHORT ANSWER AND ESSAY QUESTIONS

1. Define the law of diminishing marginal utility and give an example of it in practice.

2. How does the subjective nature of utility limit the practical usefulness of the marginal-utility theory of consumer behavior?

3. Define total utility and marginal utility. What is the relationship between total utility and marginal utility?

4. What is the law of diminishing marginal utility?

5. What essential assumptions are made about consumers and the nature of goods and services in developing the marginal-utility theory of consumer behavior?

6. When is the consumer in equilibrium and maximizing total utility? Explain why any deviation from this equilibrium will decrease the consumer's total utility.

7. Why must the amounts of extra utility derived from differently priced goods mean that marginal utility must be put on a per-dollar-spent basis? Give an example.

8. How can saving be incorporated into the utility-maximizing analysis?

9. Give and explain an algebraic restatement of the utility-maximizing rule.

10. Using the marginal-utility theory of consumer behavior, explain how an individual's demand schedule for a particular consumer good can be obtained.

11. Why does the demand schedule that is based on the marginal-utility theory almost invariably result in an inverse or negative relationship between price and quantity demanded?

12. What insights does the utility-maximization model provide about the income and substitution effects from a price decline?

13. What aspects of the theory of consumer behavior explain why consumers started buying iPods in larger numbers instead of portable CD players in the past decade?

14. Why does water have a lower price than diamonds despite the fact that water is more useful than diamonds?

15. Explain how a consumer might determine the value of his or her time. How does the value of time affect the full price the consumer pays for a good or service?

16. What does taking time into account explain that the traditional approach to consumer behavior does not explain?

17. How does the way that we pay for goods and services affect the quantity purchased? Explain using medical care as an example.

18. Why are noncash gifts less preferred than cash gifts?

19. Explain what three "facts" about how people deal with goods and bads form the basis for prospect theory.

20. Discuss how anchoring can be used to explain the amount set for minimum payments on credit card bills.

ANSWERS

Chapter 6 Consumer Behavior

FILL-IN QUESTIONS

1. subjective, total, marginal
2. positive, zero
3. decrease, demand
4. rational, preferences, limited, prices
5. last, the same
6. increase, decrease
7. *a.* MU of product *X*; *b.* MU of product *Y*; *c.* price of *X*; *d.* price of *Y*
8. *a.* the income of the consumer; *b.* the prices of other products
9. consistent, more
10. increase, decrease, income
11. more, lower, less, more, substitution
12. decreased, increased
13. marginal, marginal, total, total
14. time, limited, equal to, price, time
15. cost, more
16. more, positive, zero
17. less, less
18. status quo, gains, losses, more
19. framing, endowment
20. accounting, overpayment

TRUE–FALSE QUESTIONS

1. T, p. 117
2. T, p. 117
3. T, pp. 117–119
4. F, pp. 117–119
5. T, p. 117
6. F, p. 119
7. T, pp. 117–119
8. T, pp. 119–120
9. T, pp. 119–120
10. T, pp. 119–120
11. F, pp. 119–120
12. F, p. 120
13. F, pp. 120–121
14. F, pp. 120–121
15. T, pp. 122–123
16. F, pp. 122–123
17. T, pp. 122–123
18. F, pp. 122–123
19. F, p. 124
20. F, pp. 124–125
21. T, p. 125
22. T, p. 125
23. F, p. 125
24. F, pp. 126–127
25. T, p. 127

MULTIPLE-CHOICE QUESTIONS

1. c, p. 117
2. b, p. 117
3. c, pp. 117–119
4. c, pp. 117–119
5. d, pp. 117–119
6. c, pp. 117–119
7. c, pp. 117–119
8. b, pp. 119–120
9. c, pp. 120–121
10. c, pp. 120–121
11. a, pp. 120–121
12. b, pp. 121–122
13. c, pp. 121–122
14. b, pp. 121–122
15. a, pp. 121–122
16. b, pp. 117–119
17. c, pp. 118–119
18. c, pp. 117–119
19. c, p. 122
20. b, pp. 122–123
21. c, pp. 122–123
22. b, p. 124
23. b, pp. 124–125
24. d, p. 125
25. c, pp. 125–126

PROBLEMS

1. marginal utility of good A: 21, 20, 18, 15, 11, 6, 0; marginal utility of good B: 7, 6, 5, 4, 3, 2, 1.2; marginal utility of good C: 23, 17, 12, 8, 5, 3, 2
2. *a.* marginal utility per dollar of good A: 4.2, 4, 3.6, 3, 2.2, 1.2, 0; marginal utility per dollar of good B: 7, 6, 5, 4, 3, 2, 1.2; marginal utility of good C: 5.75, 4.25, 3, 2, 1.25, .75, .5; *b.* the marginal utility per dollar spent on good B (7) is greater than the marginal utility per dollar spent on good A (3), and the latter is greater than the marginal utility per dollar spent on good C (2); *c.* she would be spending more than her $37 income; *d.* 4, 5, 3, 151, 3; *e.* A, she would obtain the greatest marginal utility for her dollar (2.2)
3. *a.* 2, 3, 4, 6, 8; *b.* the demand schedule (for good H)
4. *a.* yes; *b.* (1) 10, (2) 3; *c.* no, the marginal utility to price ratios are not the same for the two goods; *d.* of M, because its MU/P ratio is greater; *e.* less
5. *a.* 3; *b.* 6; *c.* 4; *d.* 1; *e.* 5; *f.* 2

SHORT ANSWER AND ESSAY QUESTIONS

1. p. 119
2. p. 119
3. p. 119
4. pp. 119–121
5. p. 119
6. pp. 119–120
7. p. 119
8. pp. 120–121
9. p. 120
10. pp. 120–121
11. pp. 121–122
12. p. 122
13. p. 122
14. pp. 122–123
15. pp. 123–124
16. p. 124
17. p. 125
18. p. 125
19. pp. 125–126
20. p. 127

Indifference Curve Analysis

This brief appendix contains another explanation of or approach to the theory of consumer behavior. It is based on *ordinal utility* (the rank-ordering of consumer preferences) rather than *cardinal utility* (the precise measurement of utility). For this explanation you are introduced first to the **budget line** and then to the **indifference curve.** These two geometrical concepts are then combined to explain when a consumer is purchasing the combination of two products that maximizes the satisfaction obtainable with his or her income. The last step is to vary the price of one of the products to find the consumer's demand (schedule or curve) for the product.

■ APPENDIX CHECKLIST

When you have studied this appendix you should be able to

☐ Distinguish between cardinal utility and ordinal utility.
☐ Describe the concept of a budget line and its characteristics.
☐ Explain how to measure the slope of a budget line and determine the location of the budget line.
☐ Describe the concept of an indifference curve.
☐ State two characteristics of indifference curves.
☐ Explain the meaning of an indifference map.
☐ Given an indifference map, determine which indifference curves bring more or less total utility to consumers.
☐ Use indifference curves to identify which combination of two products maximizes the total utility of consumers.
☐ Derive a consumer's demand for a product using indifference curve analysis.
☐ Compare and contrast the marginal-utility and the indifference curve analyses of consumer behavior.

■ APPENDIX OUTLINE

1. Indifference curve analysis is based on ordinal utility in which consumer preferences are rank-ordered, but not measured. By contrast, the utility-maximization analysis and rule presented in Chapter 6 is based on cardinal utility, or the precise measurement of utility or satisfaction.

2. A **budget line** shows graphically the different combinations of two products a consumer can purchase with a particular money income. A budget line has a negative slope.
    a. An increase in the money income of the consumer will shift the budget line to the right without affecting its slope. A decrease in money income will shift the budget line to the left.

    b. An increase in the prices of both products shifts the budget line to the left. A decrease in the prices of both products shifts the budget line to the right. An increase (decrease) in the price of the product, the quantity of which is measured horizontally (the price of the other product remaining constant), pivots the budget line around a fixed point on the vertical axis in a clockwise (counterclockwise) direction.

3. An *indifference curve* shows graphically the different combinations of two products that bring a consumer the same total utility.
    a. An indifference curve is down-sloping. If the utility is to remain the same when the quantity of one product increases, the quantity of the other product must decrease.
    b. An indifference curve is also convex to the origin. The more a consumer has of one product, the smaller the quantity of a second product he or she is willing to give up to obtain an additional unit of the first product. The slope of an indifference curve is the **marginal rate of substitution** (MRS), the rate at which the consumer will substitute one product for another to remain equally satisfied.

4. The consumer has an indifference curve for every level of total utility or satisfaction. The nearer a curve is to the origin in this **indifference map,** the smaller is the utility of the combinations on that curve. The further a curve is from the origin, the larger is the utility of the combinations on that curve.

5. The consumer is in an **equilibrium position** and purchasing the combination of two products that brings the maximum utility to her or him when the budget line is tangent to the highest attainable indifference curve.

6. In the marginal-utility approach to consumer behavior, it is assumed that utility is cardinal and it is measurable. In the indifference-curve approach, utility is ordinal and rank-ordered. It need only be assumed that a consumer can say whether a combination of products has more utility than, less utility than, or the same amount of utility as another combination.

7. The demand (schedule or curve) for one of the products is derived by varying the price of that product and shifting the budget line, holding the price of the other product and the consumer's income constant, and finding the quantity of the product the consumer will purchase at each price when in equilibrium.

■ HINTS AND TIPS

1. This appendix simplifies the analysis by limiting consumer choice to just two goods. The **budget line** shows the consumer what it is possible to purchase in the two-good world, given an income. Make sure that you understand what a budget line is. To test your understanding, practice with different income levels and prices. For example, assume you had an income of $100 to spend for two goods (A and B). Good A costs $10 and Good B costs $5. Draw a budget line to show the possible combinations of A and B that you could purchase.

2. Indifference curves and the marginal rate of substitution are perhaps the most difficult concepts to understand in this appendix. Remember that the points on the curve show the possible combinations of two goods for which the consumer is *indifferent,* and thus does not care what combination is chosen. The **marginal rate of substitution** is the rate at which the consumer gives up units of one good for units of another along the indifference curve. This rate will change (diminish) as the consumer moves down an indifference curve because the consumer is less willing to *substitute* one good for the other.

■ IMPORTANT TERMS

budget line

indifference map

indifference curve

equilibrium position

marginal rate of
  substitution (MRS)

SELF-TEST

■ FILL-IN QUESTIONS

1. A schedule or curve that shows the various combinations of two products a consumer can buy with a specific (income, feature) _____ is called (a budget, an indifference) _____ line.

2. Given two products, X and Y, and a graph with the quantities of X measured horizontally and the quantities of Y measured vertically, the budget line has a slope equal to the ratio of the _____ to the _____.

3. When a consumer's income increases, the budget line shifts to the (left, right) _____, while a decrease in income shifts the budget line to the _____.

4. Given two products, A and B, and a budget line graph with the quantities of A measured horizontally and the quantities of B measured vertically, an increase in the price of A will fan the budget line (outward, inward) _____, and a decrease in the price of A will fan the budget line _____ around a fixed point on the (A, B) _____ axis.

5. (A demand, An indifference) _____ curve shows the various combinations of two products that give a consumer the same total satisfaction or total (cost, utility) _____.

6. An indifference curve slopes (upward, downward) _____ and is (concave, convex) _____ to the origin.

7. The slope of the indifference curve at each point measures the (marginal, total) _____ rate of substitution of the combination represented by that point.

8. The more a consumer has of the first product than the second product, the (greater, smaller) _____ is the quantity of the first product the consumer will give up to obtain an additional unit of the second product. As a result, the marginal rate of substitution (MRS) of the first for the second product (increases, decreases) _____ as a consumer moves from left to right (downward) along an indifference curve.

9. A set of indifference curves reflects different levels of (marginal, total) _____ utility and is called an indifference (plan, map) _____.

10. The farther from the origin an indifference curve lies, the (greater, smaller) _____ the total utility obtained from the combinations of products on that curve.

11. A consumer obtains the greatest attainable total utility or satisfaction when he or she purchases that combination of two products at which his or her budget line is (tangent to, greater than) _____ an indifference curve. At this point the consumer's marginal rate of substitution is equal to the (slope, axis) _____ of the budget line.

12. Were a consumer to purchase a combination of two products that lie on her budget line and at which her budget line is steeper than the indifference curve intersecting that point, she could increase her satisfaction by trading (down, up) _____ her budget line.

13. The marginal-utility approach to consumer behavior requires that we assume utility is (cardinal, ordinal) _____, or numerically measurable; the indifference-curve approach assumes the utility is _____, and that preferences are ranked.

14. When quantities of product X are measured along the horizontal axis, a decrease in the price of X

    a. fans the budget line (inward, outward) _____ and to the (right, left) _____;

    b. puts the consumer, when in equilibrium, on a (higher, lower) _____ indifference curve; and

    c. normally induces the consumer to purchase (more, less) _____ of product X.

15. Using indifference curves and different budget lines to determine how much of a particular product an individual consumer will purchase at different prices makes it possible to derive that consumer's (supply, demand)

_____ curve or schedule for that product.

■ TRUE–FALSE QUESTIONS

Circle T if the statement is true, F if it is false.

1. The budget line shows all combinations of two products that the consumer can purchase, given money income and the prices of the products. **T F**

2. The slope of the budget line when quantities of Alpha are measured horizontally and quantities of Beta are measured vertically is equal to the price of Beta divided by the price of Alpha. **T F**

3. A consumer is unable to purchase any of the combinations of two products which lie below (or to the left) of the consumer's budget line. **T F**

4. An increase in the money income of a consumer shifts the budget line to the right. **T F**

5. If a consumer moves from one combination (or point) on an indifference curve to another combination (or point) on the same curve, the total utility obtained by the consumer does not change. **T F**

6. An indifference curve is concave to the origin. **T F**

7. The marginal rate of substitution shows the rate, at the margin, at which the consumer is prepared to substitute one good for the other so as to remain equally satisfied. **T F**

8. The closer to the origin an indifference curve lies, the smaller the total utility a consumer obtains from the combinations of products on that indifference curve. **T F**

9. On an indifference map, the further from the origin, the lower the level of utility associated with each indifference curve. **T F**

10. There can be an intersection of consumer indifference curves. **T F**

11. A consumer maximizes total utility when she or he purchases the combination of the two products at which her or his budget line crosses an indifference curve. **T F**

12. On an indifference map, the consumer's equilibrium position will be where the slope of the highest attainable indifference curve equals the slope of the budget line. **T F**

13. It is assumed in the marginal-utility approach to consumer behavior that utility is cardinal, or numerically measurable. **T F**

14. In both the marginal-utility and indifference curve approaches to consumer behavior, it is assumed that a consumer is able to say whether the total utility obtained from combination A is greater than, equal to, or less than the total utility obtained from combination B. **T F**

15. A decrease in the price of a product normally enables a consumer to reach a higher indifference curve. **T F**

■ MULTIPLE-CHOICE QUESTIONS

Circle the letter that corresponds to the best answer.

1. Suppose a consumer has an income of $8, the price of **R** is $1, and the price of **S** is $0.50. Which of the following combinations is on the consumer's budget line?
 (a) 8R and 1S
 (b) 7R and 1S
 (c) 6R and 6S
 (d) 5R and 6S

2. If a consumer has an income of $100, the price of **U** is $10, and the price of **V** is $20, the maximum quantity of **U** the consumer is able to purchase is
 (a) 5
 (b) 10
 (c) 20
 (d) 30

3. When the income of a consumer is $20, the price of **T** is $5, the price of **Z** is $2, and the quantity of **T** is measured horizontally, the slope of the budget line is
 (a) 0.4
 (b) 2.5
 (c) 4
 (d) 10

4. Assume that everything else remains the same, but there is a decrease in a consumer's money income. The most likely effect is
 (a) an inward shift in the indifference curves because the consumer can now satisfy fewer wants
 (b) an inward shift in the budget line because the consumer can now purchase less of both products
 (c) an increase in the marginal rate of substitution
 (d) no change in the equilibrium of the consumer

5. An indifference curve is a curve that shows the different combinations of two products that
 (a) give a consumer equal marginal utilities
 (b) give a consumer equal total utilities
 (c) cost a consumer equal amounts
 (d) have the same prices

6. In the following schedule for an indifference curve, how much of **G** is the consumer willing to give up to obtain the third unit of **H**?
 (a) 3
 (b) 4
 (c) 5
 (d) 6

Quantity of G	Quantity of H
18	1
12	2
7	3
3	4
0	5

7. The slope of the indifference curve measures the
(a) slope of the budget line
(b) total utility of a good
(c) space on an indifference map
(d) marginal rate of substitution

8. The marginal rate of substitution
(a) may rise or fall, depending on the slope of the budget line
(b) rises as you move downward along an indifference curve
(c) falls as you move downward along an indifference curve
(d) remains the same along a budget line

9. Which of the following is characteristic of indifference curves?
(a) They are concave to the origin.
(b) They are convex to the origin.
(c) Curves closer to the origin have the highest level of total utility.
(d) Curves closer to the origin have the highest level of marginal utility.

10. To derive the demand curve of a product, the price of the product is varied. For the indifference curve analysis, the
(a) budget line is held constant
(b) money income of the consumer changes
(c) tastes and preferences of the consumer are held constant
(d) prices of other products the consumer might purchase change

Questions 11, 12, 13, and 14 are based on the diagram below.

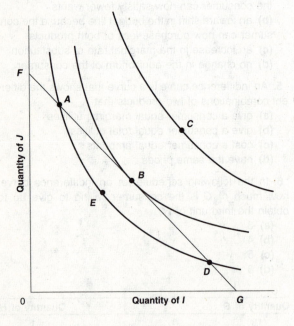

11. The budget line is best represented by line
(a) *AB*
(b) *AD*
(c) *FG*
(d) *DG*

12. Which combination of goods *I* and *J* will the consumer purchase?
(a) *A*
(b) *B*
(c) *C*
(d) *E*

13. Suppose the price of good *I* increases. The budget line will shift
(a) inward around a point on the *J* axis
(b) outward around a point on the *J* axis
(c) inward around a point on the *I* axis
(d) outward around a point on the *I* axis

14. If the consumer chooses the combination of goods *I* and *J* represented by point *E*, then the consumer could
(a) obtain more goods with the available money income
(b) not obtain more goods with the available money income
(c) shift the budget line outward so that it is tangent with point *C*
(d) shift the budget line inward so that it is tangent with point *E*

15. In indifference curve analysis, the consumer will be in equilibrium at the point where the
(a) indifference curve is concave to the origin
(b) budget line crosses the vertical axis
(c) two indifference curves intersect and are tangent to the budget line
(d) budget line is tangent to an indifference curve

16. If a consumer is initially in equilibrium, a decrease in money income will
(a) move the consumer to a new equilibrium on a lower indifference curve
(b) move the consumer to a new equilibrium on a higher indifference curve
(c) make the slope of the consumer's indifference curves steeper
(d) have no effect on the equilibrium position

Questions 17, 18, 19, and 20 are based on the following graph.

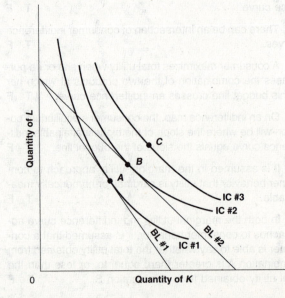

17. If the budget line shifts from **BL #1** to **BL #2**, it is because the price of
    (a) *K* increased
    (b) *K* decreased
    (c) *L* increased
    (d) *L* decreased

18. If the budget line shifts from **BL #2** to **BL #1**, it is because the price of
    (a) *K* increased
    (b) *K* decreased
    (c) *L* increased
    (d) *L* decreased

19. When the budget line shifts from **BL #2** to **BL #1**, the consumer will buy
    (a) more of *K* and *L*
    (b) less of *K* and *L*
    (c) more of *K* and less of *L*
    (d) less of *K* and more of *L*

20. Point *C* on indifference curve **IC #3** can be an attainable combination of products *K* and *L* if
    (a) the price of *K* increases
    (b) the price of *L* increases
    (c) money income increases
    (d) money income decreases

■ **PROBLEMS**

1. Following are the schedules for three indifference curves.

Indifference schedule 1		Indifference schedule 2		Indifference schedule 3	
A	**B**	**A**	**B**	**A**	**B**
1	28	0	36	0	45
2	21	1	28	1	36
3	15	2	21	2	28
4	10	3	15	3	21
5	6	4	11	4	15
6	3	5	7	5	10
7	1	6	4	6	6
	0	7	1	7	3
			0	8	1
				9	0

a. On the following graph measure quantities of *A* along the horizontal axis (from 0 to 9) and quantities of *B* along the vertical axis (from 0 to 45).
(1) Plot the 8 combinations of *A* and *B* from indifference schedule 1 and draw through the 8 points a curve which is in no place a straight line. Label this curve **IC #1**.
(2) Do the same for the 9 points in indifference schedule 2 and label it **IC #2**.
(3) Repeat the process for the 10 points in indifference schedule 3 and label the curve **IC #3**.
b. Assume the price of *A* is $12, the price of *B* is $2.40, and a consumer has an income of $72.

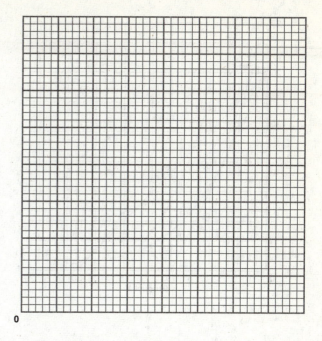

0

(1) Complete the following table to show the quantities of *A* and *B* this consumer is able to purchase.

A	B
0	___
1	___
2	___
3	___
4	___
5	___
6	___

(2) Plot this budget line on the graph you completed in part **a**.

(3) This budget line has a slope equal to _____.
c. To obtain the greatest satisfaction or utility from his income of $72 this consumer will

(1) purchase _____ units of *A* and _____ of *B*;

(2) and spend _____ $ on *A* and $ _____ on *B*.

2. Following is a graph with three indifference curves and three budget lines. This consumer has an income of $100, and the price of *Y* remains constant at $5.
a. When the price of *X* is $10, the consumer's budget line is **BL #1** and the consumer

(1) purchases _____ *X* and _____ *Y*;

(2) and spends $ _____ on *X* and $ _____ on *Y*.
b. If the price of X is $6.67, 2/3 the budget line is **BL #2** and the consumer

(1) purchases _____ *X* and _____ *Y*;

(2) 2 and spends $ _____ for *X* and $ for

_____ *Y*.

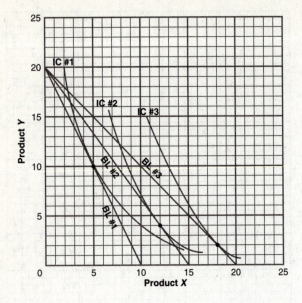

1. Why is the slope of the budget line negative?

2. How will each of the following events affect the budget line?
- **a.** a decrease in the money income of the consumer
- **b.** an increase in the prices of both products
- **c.** a decrease in the price of one of the products

3. Explain why the budget line can be called "objective" and an indifference curve "subjective."

4. What is the relationship between an indifference curve and total utility? Between an indifference map and total utility?

5. Why is the slope of an indifference curve negative and convex to the origin?

6. You are given two products, alpha and beta. Why will the utility-maximizing combination of the two products be the one lying on the highest attainable indifference curve?

7. Suppose a consumer purchases a combination of two products that is on her budget line but the budget line is not tangent to an indifference curve at that point. Of which product should the consumer buy more, and of which should she buy less? Why?

8. What is the important difference between the marginal-utility theory and the indifference-curve theory of consumer demand in terms of how utility is considered or measured?

9. Explain how the indifference map of a consumer and the budget line are utilized to derive the consumer's demand for one of the products. In deriving demand, what is varied and what is held constant?

10. How does a change in the price of one product shift the budget line and determine a new equilibrium point? Explain and illustrate with a graph.

c. And when the price of **X** is $5, the consumer has budget line **BL #3** and

(1) buys _____ **X** and _____ **Y**; and

(2) spends $_____ on **X** and $ _____on **Y**.

d. On the following graph, plot the quantities of **X** demanded at the three prices.

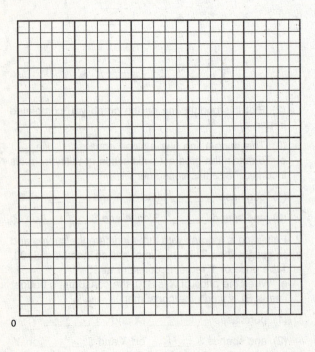

a. Between $10 and $5 this consumer's demand for

X is (elastic, inelastic) _____, and for him products **X** and **Y** are (substitutes, complements) _____.

ANSWERS

Appendix to Chapter 6 Indifference Curve Analysis

FILL-IN QUESTIONS

1. income, a budget
2. price of X, price of Y
3. right, left
4. inward, outward, B
5. An indifference, utility
6. downward, convex
7. marginal
8. greater, decreases
9. total, map
10. greater
11. tangent, slope
12. up
13. cardinal, ordinal
14. a. outward, right; b. higher; c. more
15. demand

TRUE–FALSE QUESTIONS

1. T, pp. 133–134   **6.** F, pp. 134–135   **11.** F, p. 136
2. F, pp. 133–134   **7.** T, p. 135   **12.** T, p. 136
3. F, pp. 133–134   **8.** T, pp. 135–136   **13.** T, p. 136
4. T, p. 134   **9.** F, pp. 135–136   **14.** T, p. 136
5. T, p. 134   **10.** F, p. 135   **15.** T, pp. 136–137

MULTIPLE-CHOICE QUESTIONS

1. d, pp. 133–134   **8.** c, pp. 134–135   **15.** d, p. 136
2. b, pp. 133–134   **9.** b, p. 135   **16.** a, pp. 134, 136
3. b, pp. 133–134   **10.** c, pp. 134–135   **17.** b, pp. 137–138
4. b, p. 134   **11.** c, pp. 135–136   **18.** a, pp. 137–138
5. b, p. 134   **12.** b, pp. 135–136   **19.** b, pp. 137–138
6. c, p. 134   **13.** a, p. 136   **20.** c, pp. 134, 136
7. d, pp. 134–135   **14.** a, pp. 135–136

PROBLEMS

1. *a.* graph; *b.* (1) 30, 25, 20, 15, 10, 5, 0, (2) graph, (3) −5;
c. (1) 3, 15, (2) 36, 36
2. *a.* (1) 5, 10, (2) 50, 50; *b.* (1) 12, 4, (2) 80, 20; *c.* (1) 18, 2,
(2) 90, 10; *d.* graph; *e.* elastic, substitutes

SHORT ANSWER AND ESSAY QUESTIONS

1. pp. 133–134   **5.** pp. 134–135   **9.** pp. 137–138
2. p. 134   **6.** p. 136   **10.** pp. 137–138
3. pp. 133–134   **7.** p. 136
4. pp. 134–135   **8.** pp. 136–137

CHAPTER 7

Businesses and the Costs of Production

Previous chapters discussed consumer behavior and product demand. This chapter switches to producer behavior and business firms. It explains how a firm's **costs of production** change as the firm's output changes, in the short run and in the long run.

This chapter begins with a definition of cost and profit. You should be somewhat familiar with these terms because they were first introduced in Chapters 1 and 2. The explanation is now more detailed. Several definitions of cost and profit are given in the chapter, so you must know the distinctions if you are to understand the true meaning of **economic cost** and **economic profit.**

The second and third sections of the chapter focus on **short-run** variable relationships and production costs for the firm. You are first introduced to the important **law of diminishing returns,** which defines the relationship between the quantity of resources used by the firm and the output the firm produces in the short run. The chapter discussion then shifts to costs because resource prices are associated with the fixed and variable resources the typical firm uses to produce its output. The three basic types of short-run costs—total, average, and marginal—vary for the firm as the quantity of resources and output changes. The chapter describes the relationship among the various cost curves and how they are shaped by the law of diminishing returns.

The fourth section of the chapter looks at production costs in the **long run.** All resources, and also production costs, are variable in the long run. You will learn that the long-run cost curve for the typical firm is based on the short-run cost curves for firms of different sizes. In the long run, firms can experience **economies of scale** and **diseconomies of scale** that will shape the long-run cost curve for the firm. The chapter concludes with several practical applications of the concept of scale economies.

It is important that you master this material on the costs of production because it sets the foundation for understanding the price and output decisions of a firm operating under different market structures that you will be reading about in the next three chapters.

■ CHECKLIST

When you have studied this chapter you should be able to

☐ Define economic cost in terms of opportunity cost.
☐ Distinguish between an explicit cost and an implicit cost.
☐ Define accounting profit in terms of revenue and costs.

☐ Describe how normal profit is measured.
☐ Define economic profit in terms of revenue and costs.
☐ Distinguish between the short run and the long run in production.
☐ Define total product, marginal product, and average product.
☐ State the law of diminishing returns and explain its rationale.
☐ Compute marginal product and average product to illustrate the law of diminishing returns when you are given the necessary data.
☐ Describe the relationship between marginal product and average product.
☐ Define fixed costs, variable costs, and total cost.
☐ Define average fixed cost, average variable cost, and average total cost.
☐ Explain how average product is related to average variable cost.
☐ Define marginal cost.
☐ Explain how marginal product is related to marginal cost.
☐ Compute and graph average fixed cost, average variable cost, average total cost, and marginal cost when given total-cost data.
☐ Describe the relation of marginal cost to average variable cost and average total cost.
☐ Explain why short-run cost curves shift.
☐ Illustrate the difference between short-run average total cost curves for a firm at different outputs and its long-run average total cost curve.
☐ Describe various possible long-run average total cost curves.
☐ Define and list reasons for the economies and diseconomies of scale.
☐ Explain the concept of minimum efficient scale and its relation to industry structure.
☐ Give examples of short-run costs, economies of scale, and minimum efficient scale in the real world.
☐ Explain why sunk costs are irrelevant in decision making (*Last Word*).

■ CHAPTER OUTLINE

1. Resources are scarce and are used to produce many different products. The **economic cost** of using resources to produce a product is an opportunity cost: the value or worth of the resources in their best alternative use.

   a. Economic costs can be explicit or implicit. **Explicit costs** are the monetary payments that a firm makes to obtain resources from nonowners of the firm. *Implicit costs* are the monetary payments that would have been paid for self-owned or self-employed resources if they had been used in their next best alternative outside the firm. Both types of costs are opportunity costs because the use of the resources for this use means that they are not available for use in the next best alternative use.

   b. *Accounting profit* is the difference between a firm's total sales revenue and its total explicit costs. *Normal profit* is an implicit cost and is the typical or normal amount of accounting profit that an entrepreneur would have received for working at other firms of this type and supplying entrepreneurial resources.

   c. *Economic profit* is the revenue a firm receives in excess of all its explicit and implicit economic costs. These economic costs are opportunity costs that measure the value of the forgone use of the resources. Included in the implicit costs is a normal profit which represents the entrepreneur's forgone income. The firm's accounting profit will be greater than its economic costs because accounting profit is the total of its sales revenue minus its explicit costs.

   d. A distinction is made between the *short run* and the *long run.* The firm's economic costs vary as the firm's output changes. These costs depend on whether the firm is able to make short-run or long-run changes in its resource use. In the short run, the firm's plant is a fixed resource, but in the long run it is a variable resource. So, in the short run the firm cannot change the size of its plant and can vary its output only by changing the quantities of the variable resources it employs.

2. There are *short-run* relationships between inputs and outputs in the production process.

   a. Several product terms need to be defined to show these relationships. *Total product (TP)* is the total quantity of output produced. *Marginal product (MP)* is the change made in total product from a change in a variable resource input. *Average product (AP),* or productivity, is the total product per unit of resource input.

   b. The *law of diminishing returns* determines the manner in which the costs of the firm change as it changes its output in the short run. As more units of a variable resource are added to a fixed resource, beyond some point the marginal product from each additional unit of a variable resource will decline.

   (1) There are three phases reflected in a graph of the total product and marginal product curves: increasing, decreasing, and negative marginal returns.

   (2) When total product is increasing at an increasing rate, marginal product is rising; when total product is increasing at a decreasing rate, marginal product is falling; and when total product declines, marginal product is negative.

   (3) When marginal product is greater than average product, average product rises, and when marginal product is less than average product, average product falls.

3. When input, output, and price information is available, it is possible to calculate **short-run production costs.**

   a. The *total cost* is the sum of the firm's fixed costs and variable costs. As output increases,
   (1) *fixed costs* do not change;
   (2) at first, the *variable costs* increase at a decreasing rate, and then increase at an increasing rate;
   (3) and at first total costs increase at a decreasing rate and then increase at an increasing rate.

   b. **Average costs** consist of *average fixed costs (AFC), average variable costs (AVC),* and *average total costs (ATC).* They are equal, respectively, to the firm's fixed, variable, and total costs divided by its output. As output increases,
   (1) average fixed cost decreases
   (2) at first, average variable cost decreases and then increases
   (3) and at first, average total cost also decreases and then increases

   c. *Marginal cost (MC)* is the extra cost incurred in producing one additional unit of output.
   (1) Because the marginal product of the variable resource increases and then decreases (as more of the variable resource is employed to increase output), marginal cost decreases and then increases as output increases.
   (2) At the output at which average variable cost is a minimum, average variable cost and marginal cost are equal, and at the output at which average total cost is a minimum, average total cost and marginal cost are equal.
   (3) On a graph, marginal cost will always intersect average variable cost at its minimum point and marginal cost will always intersect average total cost at its minimum point. These intersections will always have marginal cost approaching average variable cost and average total cost from below.
   d. Changes in either resource prices or technology will cause the cost curves to shift.

4. In the long run, all the resources employed by the firm are variable resources. **Long-run production costs** are all variable costs.

   a. As the firm expands its output by increasing the size of its plant, average total cost tends to fall at first because of the *economies of scale,* but as this expansion continues, sooner or later, average total cost begins to rise because of the *diseconomies of scale.*

   b. The long-run average total cost curve shows the least average total cost at which any output can be produced after the firm has had time to make all changes in its plant size. Graphically, it is made up of all the points of tangency of the unlimited number of short-run average total cost curves.

   c. The economies and diseconomies of scale encountered in the production of different goods are important factors influencing the structure and competitiveness of various industries.

   (1) *Economies of scale* (a decline in long-run average total costs) arise because of labor specialization, managerial specialization, efficient capital, and other factors such as spreading the start-up, advertising, or development costs over an increasing level of output.

(2) *Dieconomies of scale* arise primarily from the problems of efficiently managing and coordinating the firm's operations as it becomes a large-scale producer.

(3) *Constant returns to scale* are the range of output where long-run average total cost does not change.

d. Economies and diseconomies of scale can determine the structure in an industry. *Minimum efficient scale (MES)* is the smallest level of output at which a firm can minimize long-run average costs. This concept explains why relatively large and small firms could co-exist in an industry and be viable when there is an extended range of constant returns to scale.

(1) In some industries the long-run average cost curve will decline over a range of output. Given consumer demand, efficient production will be achieved only with a small number of large firms.

(2) If economies of scale extend beyond the market size, the conditions for a *natural monopoly* are produced, which is a rare situation where unit costs are minimized by having a single firm produce a product.

(3) If there are few economies of scale, then there is minimum efficient size at a low level of output and there are many firms in an industry.

5. There are several applications and illustrations of short-run costs, economies of scale, and minimum efficient cost.

a. A rise in the price of gasoline raises short-run cost curves (AVC, MC, ATC) for businesses that use gasoline as an input for trucks and vehicles used to produce a product.

b. Economies of scale can be seen in successful start-up firms such as Intel, Microsoft, or Starbucks.

c. Economies of scale are also exhibited in the Verson stamping machine that makes millions of auto parts per year.

d. As the number of newspaper readers has fallen due to the shift of readership to the Internet, the average fixed cost of producing a newspaper has risen. In response, some newspapers have raised their prices, thus further reducing the number of readers. This situation creates a back (few readers) and forth (rising newspaper prices) problem that has the potential to bankrupt many newspapers.

e. Economies of scale are extensive in aircraft production, but modest in concrete mixing, which achieves minimum efficient scale at a low level of output. As a consequence, there are few aircraft factories and many concrete mixing companies.

6. (*Last Word*). Sunk costs are irrelevant to economic decision making because they are already incurred and cannot be recovered. Sunk costs are the result of making a past decision, not a current decision. A current decision is made on the basis of evaluating marginal costs and marginal benefits. If the marginal costs are less than the marginal benefits, the action will be taken.

■ HINTS AND TIPS

1. Many **cost** terms and **profit** terms are described in this chapter. Make yourself a glossary so that you can distinguish among them. You need to know what each one

means if you are to master the material in the chapter. If you try to learn them in the order in which you encounter them, you will have little difficulty because the later terms build on the earlier ones.

2. Make sure you know the difference between **marginal** and **average** relationships in this chapter. Marginal product (MP) shows the *change* in total output associated with each additional input. Average product (AP) is simply the output per unit of resource input. Marginal cost (MC) shows the change in total cost associated with producing another unit of output. Average cost shows the per-unit cost of producing a level of output.

3. Practice drawing the different sets of **cost curves** used in this chapter: (1) short-run total cost curves, (2) short-run average and marginal cost curves, and (3) long-run cost curves. Also, explain to yourself the relationship between the curves in each set that you draw.

4. In addition to learning *how* the costs of the firm vary as its output varies, be sure to understand *why* the costs vary the way they do. In this connection note that the behavior of short-run costs is the result of the law of diminishing returns and that the behavior of long-run costs is the consequence of economies and diseconomies of scale.

■ IMPORTANT TERMS

economic cost	fixed costs
explicit costs	variable costs
implicit costs	average fixed cost (AFC)
accounting profit	average variable cost (AVC)
normal profit	average total cost (ATC)
economic profit	marginal cost (MC)
short run	economies of scale
long run	diseconomies of scale
total product (TP)	constant returns to scale
marginal product (MP)	minimum efficient scale (MES)
average product (AP)	
law of diminishing returns	natural monopoly
total cost (TC)	

SELF-TEST

■ FILL-IN QUESTIONS

1. The value or worth of any resource in its best alternative use is called the (out-of-pocket, opportunity) _____ cost of that resource.

2. The economic cost of producing a product is the amount of money or income the firm must pay or provide to (government, resource suppliers) _____ to attract land, labor, and capital goods away from alternative uses in the economy. The monetary payments for resources used for production are (explicit, implicit) _____ costs, and the self-owned or self-employed resources used by the firm are _____ costs.

3. Accounting profit is equal to the firm's total revenue less its (explicit, implicit) _____ costs. Normal profit is an (explicit, implicit) _____ cost because it represents the forgone income that the entrepreneur could have earned working at another firm. Economic profit is equal to the firm's total (costs, revenues) _____ minus all its economic _____, both explicit and implicit.

4. In the short run the firm can change its output by changing the quantity of the (fixed, variable) _____ resources it employs, but it cannot change the quantity of the _____ resources. This means that the firm's plant capacity is fixed in the (short, long) _____ run and variable in the _____ run.

5. The law of diminishing returns is that as successive units of a (fixed, variable) _____ resource are added to a _____ resource, beyond some point the (total, marginal) _____ product of the former resource will decrease. The law assumes that all units of input are of (equal, unequal) _____ quality.

6. If the total product increases at an increasing rate, the marginal product is (rising, falling) _____. If it increases at a decreasing rate, the marginal product is (positive, negative, zero) _____, but (rising, falling) _____.

7. If total product is at a maximum, the marginal product is (positive, negative, zero) _____, but if it decreases, the marginal product is _____.

8. If the marginal product of any input exceeds its average product, the average product is (rising, falling) _____, but if it is less than its average product, the average product is _____. If the marginal product is equal to its average product, the average product is at a (minimum, maximum) _____.

9. Those costs that in total do not vary with changes in output are (fixed, variable) _____ costs, but those costs that in total change with the level of output are _____ costs. The sum of fixed and variable costs at each level of output is (marginal, total) _____ cost.

10. The law of diminishing returns explains why a firm's average variable, average total, and marginal cost may at first tend to (increase, decrease) _____ but ultimately _____ as the output of the firm increases.

11. Marginal cost is the increase in (average, total) _____ variable cost or _____ cost that occurs when the firm increases its output by one unit.

12. If marginal cost is less than average variable cost, average variable cost will be (rising, falling, constant) _____, but if average variable cost is less than marginal cost, average variable cost will be _____.

13. Assume that labor is the only variable input in the short run and that the wage rate paid to labor is constant.
   a. When the marginal product of labor is rising, the marginal cost of producing a product is (rising, falling) _____.
   b. When the average variable cost of producing a product is falling, the average product of labor is (rising, falling) _____.
   c. At the output at which marginal cost is at a minimum, the marginal product of labor is at a (minimum, maximum) _____.
   d. At the output at which the average product of labor is at a maximum, the average variable cost of producing the product is at a (minimum, maximum) _____.
   e. At the output at which the average variable cost is at a minimum, average variable cost and (marginal, total) _____ cost are equal and average product and _____ product are equal.

14. Changes in either resource prices or technology will cause cost curves to (shift, remain unchanged) _____. If average fixed costs increase, then the average fixed costs curve will (shift up, shift down, remain unchanged) _____ and the average total cost curve will _____, but the average variable cost curve will _____ and the marginal cost curve will (shift up, shift down, remain unchanged) _____.

15. If average variable costs increase, then the average variable cost curve will (shift up, shift down, remain unchanged) _____ and the average total cost curve will _____, and the marginal cost curve will (shift up, shift down, remain unchanged) _____, but the average fixed cost curve would _____.

16. The short-run costs of a firm are fixed and variable costs, but in the long run all costs are (fixed, variable) _____. The long-run average total cost of producing a product is equal to the lowest of the short-run costs of producing that product after the firm has had all the time it requires to make the appropriate adjustments in the size of its (workforce, plant) _____.

17. List the three important sources of economies of scale:

a. _____

b. _____

c. _____

18. When the firm experiences diseconomies of scale, it has (higher, lower) _____ average total costs as output increases. Where diseconomies of scale are operative, an increase in all inputs will cause a (greater, less) _____-than-proportionate increase in output. The factor that gives rise to large diseconomies of scale is managerial (specialization, difficulties) _____.

19. The smallest level of output at which a firm can minimize long-run average costs is (maximum, minimum) _____ efficient scale. Relatively large and small firms could coexist in an industry and be equally viable when there is an extended range of (increasing, decreasing, constant) _____ returns to scale.

20. In some industries, the long-run average cost curve will (increase, decrease) _____ over a long range of output and efficient production will be achieved with only a few (small, large) _____ firms. The conditions for a natural monopoly are created when (economies, diseconomies) _____ of scale extend beyond the market's size so that unit costs are minimized by having a single firm produce a product.

■ TRUE–FALSE QUESTIONS

Circle T if the statement is true, F if it is false.

1. The economic costs of a firm are the explicit or implicit costs for resources used for production by the firm.   **T F**

2. Economic profit is an explicit cost, while normal profit is an implicit cost.   **T F**

3. In the short run the size (or capacity) of a firm's plant is fixed.   **T F**

4. The resources employed by a firm are all variable in the long run and all fixed in the short run.   **T F**

5. The law of diminishing returns states that as successive amounts of a variable resource are added to a fixed resource, beyond some point total output will diminish.   **T F**

6. An assumption of the law of diminishing returns is that all units of variable inputs are of equal quality.   **T F**

7. When total product is increasing at a decreasing rate, marginal product is positive and increasing.   **T F**

8. When average product is falling, marginal product is greater than average product.   **T F**

9. When marginal product is negative, total production (or output) is decreasing.   **T F**

10. The larger the output of a firm, the smaller the fixed cost of the firm.   **T F**

11. The law of diminishing returns explains why increases in variable costs associated with each 1-unit increase in output become greater and greater after a certain point.   **T F**

12. Fixed costs can be controlled or altered in the short run.   **T F**

13. Total cost is the sum of fixed and variable costs at each level of output.   **T F**

14. Marginal cost is the change in fixed cost divided by the change in output.   **T F**

15. The marginal cost curve intersects the average total cost (ATC) curve at the ATC curve's minimum point.   **T F**

16. If the fixed cost of a firm increases from one year to the next (because the premium it must pay for the insurance on the buildings it owns has been increased) while its variable cost schedule remains unchanged, its marginal cost schedule also will remain unchanged.   **T F**

17. Marginal cost is equal to average variable cost at the output at which average variable cost is at a minimum.   **T F**

18. When the marginal product of a variable resource increases, the marginal cost of producing the product will decrease, and when marginal product decreases, marginal cost will increase.   **T F**

19. If the price of a variable input should increase, the average variable cost, average total cost, and marginal cost curves would all shift upward, but the position of the average fixed cost curve would remain unchanged.   **T F**

20. One explanation why the long-run average total cost curve of a firm rises after some level of output has been reached is the law of diminishing returns.   **T F**

21. If a firm increases all its inputs by 20% and its output increases by 30%, the firm is experiencing economies of scale.   **T F**

22. The primary cause of diseconomies of scale is increased specialization of labor.   **T F**

23. If a firm has constant returns to scale in the long run, the *total* cost of producing its product does not change when it expands or contracts its output.   **T F**

24. Minimum efficient scale occurs at the largest level of output at which a firm can minimize long-run average costs.   **T F**

25. One reason many daily newspapers are going bankrupt is that their average fixed costs are rising because more people are getting their news from the Internet and there are fewer subscribers to newspapers.   **T F**

■ **MULTIPLE-CHOICE QUESTIONS**

Circle the letter that corresponds to the best answer.

1. Suppose that a firm produces 100,000 units a year and sells them all for $5 each. The explicit costs of production are $350,000 and the implicit costs of production are $100,000. The firm has an accounting profit of
(a) $200,000 and an economic profit of $25,000
(b) $150,000 and an economic profit of $50,000
(c) $125,000 and an economic profit of $75,000
(d) $100,000 and an economic profit of $50,000

2. Economic profit for a firm is defined as the total revenue of the firm minus its
(a) accounting profit
(b) normal profit
(c) implicit costs
(d) economic costs

3. Which would best describe the short run for a firm as defined by economists?
(a) The plant capacity for a firm is variable.
(b) The plant capacity for a firm is fixed.
(c) There are diseconomies of scale.
(d) There are economies of scale.

4. Which is most likely to be a long-run adjustment for a firm that manufactures golf carts on an assembly line basis?
(a) an increase in the amount of steel the firm buys
(b) a reduction in the number of shifts of workers from three to two
(c) a change in the production managers of the assembly line
(d) a change from the production of golf carts to motorcycles

5. The change in total product divided by the change in resource input defines
(a) total cost
(b) average cost
(c) average product
(d) marginal product

Use the following table to answer Questions 6 and 7. Assume that the only variable resource used to produce output is labor.

Amount of labor	Amount of output
1	3
2	8
3	12
4	15
5	17
6	18

6. The marginal product of the fourth unit of labor is
(a) 2 units of output
(b) 3 units of output
(c) 4 units of output
(d) 15 units of output

7. When the firm hires four units of labor the average product of labor is
(a) 3 units of output
(b) 3.75 units of output
(c) 4.25 units of output
(d) 15 units of output

8. Because the marginal product of a variable resource initially increases and later decreases as a firm increases its output,
(a) average variable cost decreases at first and then increases
(b) average fixed cost declines as the output of the firm expands
(c) variable cost at first increases by increasing amounts and then increases by decreasing amounts
(d) marginal cost at first increases and then decreases

9. Because the marginal product of a resource at first increases and then decreases as the output of the firm increases,
(a) average fixed cost declines as the output of the firm increases
(b) average variable cost at first increases and then decreases
(c) variable cost at first increases by increasing amounts and then increases by decreasing amounts
(d) total cost at first increases by decreasing amounts and then increases by increasing amounts

For Questions 10, 11, and 12, use the data given in the following table. The fixed cost of the firm is $500, and the firm's total variable cost is indicated in the table.

Output	Total variable cost
1	$ 200
2	360
3	500
4	700
5	1000
6	1800

10. The average variable cost of the firm when 4 units of output are produced is
(a) $175
(b) $200
(c) $300
(d) $700

11. The average total cost of the firm when 4 units of output are being produced is
(a) $175
(b) $200
(c) $300
(d) $700

12. The marginal cost of the sixth unit of output is
(a) $200
(b) $300
(c) $700
(d) $800

13. Marginal cost and average variable cost are equal at the output at which
(a) marginal cost is a minimum
(b) marginal product is a maximum
(c) average product is a maximum
(d) average variable cost is a maximum

14. Average variable cost may be either increasing or decreasing when
(a) marginal cost is decreasing
(b) marginal product is increasing
(c) average fixed cost is decreasing
(d) average total cost is increasing

15. Why does the short-run marginal cost curve eventually increase for the typical firm?
(a) diseconomies of scale
(b) minimum efficient scale
(c) the law of diminishing returns
(d) economic profit eventually decreases

16. If the price of labor or some other variable resource increased, the
(a) AVC curve would shift downward
(b) AFC curve would shift upward
(c) AFC curve would shift downward
(d) MC curve would shift upward

Questions 17, 18, 19, and 20 are based on the following figure.

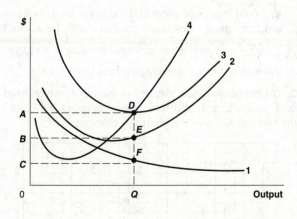

17. In the figure, curves **1, 3,** and **4,** respectively, represent
(a) average variable cost, marginal cost, and average total cost
(b) average total cost, average variable cost, and marginal cost
(c) average fixed cost, average total cost, and marginal cost
(d) marginal cost, average total cost, and average variable cost

18. At output level **Q**, the average fixed cost is measured by the vertical distance represented by
(a) **DE**
(b) **DF**
(c) **DQ**
(d) **EF**

19. As output increases beyond the level represented by **Q**,
(a) marginal product is rising
(b) marginal product is falling
(c) total fixed costs are rising
(d) total costs are falling

20. If the firm is producing at output level **Q**, then the total variable costs of production are represented by area
(a) 0**QFC**
(b) 0**QEB**
(c) 0**QDC**
(d) **CFEB**

21. At an output of 10,000 units per year, a firm's total variable costs are $50,000 and its average fixed costs are $2. The total costs per year for the firm are
(a) $50,000
(b) $60,000
(c) $70,000
(d) $80,000

22. A firm has total fixed costs of $4,000 a year. The average variable cost is $3.00 for 2000 units of output. At this level of output, its average total costs are
(a) $2.50
(b) $3.00
(c) $4.50
(d) $5.00

23. If you know that total fixed cost is $100, total variable cost is $300, and total product is 4 units, then
(a) marginal cost is $50
(b) average fixed cost is $45
(c) average total cost is $125
(d) average variable cost is $75

24. If the short-run average variable costs of production for a firm are falling, then this indicates that
(a) average variable costs are above average fixed costs
(b) marginal costs are below average variable costs
(c) average fixed costs are constant
(d) total costs are falling

Answer Questions 25 and 26 using the following table. Three short-run cost schedules are given for three plants of different sizes that a firm might build in the long run.

Plant 1		Plant 2		Plant 3	
Output	ATC	Output	ATC	Output	ATC
10	$10	10	$15	10	$20
20	9	20	10	20	15
30	8	30	7	30	10
40	9	40	10	40	8
50	10	50	14	50	9

25. What is the long-run average cost of producing 40 units of output?
(a) $7
(b) $8
(c) $9
(d) $10

26. At what output is long-run average cost at a minimum?
   (a) 20
   (b) 30
   (c) 40
   (d) 50

27. If the long-run average total cost curve for a firm is down-sloping, then it indicates that there
   (a) is a minimum efficient scale
   (b) are constant returns to scale
   (c) are diseconomies of scale
   (d) are economies of scale

28. Which factor contributes to economies of scale?
   (a) less efficient use of capital goods
   (b) less division of labor and specialization
   (c) greater specialization in management of a firm
   (d) greater difficulty controlling the operations of a firm

29. A firm is encountering constant returns to scale when it increases all of its inputs by 20% and its output increases by
   (a) 10%
   (b) 15%
   (c) 20%
   (d) 25%

30. If economies of scale are limited and diseconomies appear quickly in an industry, then minimum efficient scale occurs at a
   (a) high level of output, and there will be a few firms
   (b) high level of output, and there will be many firms
   (c) low level of output, and there will be few firms
   (d) low level of output, and there will be many firms

■ PROBLEMS

1. On the following graph, sketch the way in which the average product and the marginal product of a resource change as the firm increases its employment of that resource.

2. The table shows the total production of a firm as the quantity of labor employed increases. The quantities of all other resources employed remain constant.
   a. Compute the marginal products of the first through the eighth units of labor and enter them in the table.

Units of labor	Total production	Marginal product of labor	Average product of labor
0	0		0
1	80	_____	_____
2	200	_____	_____
3	330	_____	_____
4	400	_____	_____
5	450	_____	_____
6	480	_____	_____
7	490	_____	_____
8	480	_____	_____

b. Now compute the average products of the various quantities of labor and enter them in the table.
c. There are increasing returns to labor from the first through the _____ units of labor and decreasing returns from the _____ through the eighth units.
d. When total production is increasing, marginal product is (positive, negative) _____ and when total production is decreasing, marginal product is _____ .
e. When marginal product is greater than average product, then average product will (rise, fall) _____ , and when marginal product is less than average product, the average product will _____ .

3. On the graph below sketch the manner in which fixed cost, variable cost, and total cost change as the output the firm produces in the short run changes.

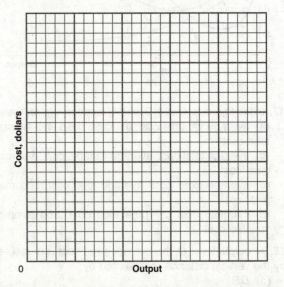

4. Assume that a firm has a plant of fixed size and that it can vary its output only by varying the amount of labor it employs. The table below shows the relationships among

Quantity of labor employed	Total ouput	Marginal product of labor	Average product of labor	Total cost	Marginal cost	Average variable cost
0	0	—	—	$_____	—	—
1	5	5	5	_____	$_____	$_____
2	11	6	5.50	_____	_____	_____
3	18	7	6	_____	_____	_____
4	24	6	6	_____	_____	_____
5	29	5	5.80	_____	_____	_____
6	33	4	5.50	_____	_____	_____
7	36	3	5.14	_____	_____	_____
8	38	2	4.75	_____	_____	_____
9	39	1	4.33	_____	_____	_____
10	39	0	3.90	_____	_____	_____

the amount of labor employed, the output of the firm, the marginal product of labor, and the average product of labor.

a. Assume each unit of labor costs the firm $10. Compute the total cost of labor for each quantity of labor the firm might employ, and enter these figures in the table.

b. Now determine the marginal cost of the firm's product as the firm increases its output. Divide the increase in total labor cost by the *increase* in total output to find the marginal cost. Enter these figures in the table.

c. When the marginal product of labor
(1) increases, the marginal cost of the firm's product

(increases, decreases) _____.
(2) decreases, the marginal cost of the firm's product

_____.

d. If labor is the only variable input, the total labor cost and total variable cost are equal. Find the average variable cost of the firm's product (by dividing the total labor cost by total output) and enter these figures in the table.

e. When the average product of labor
(1) increases, the average variable cost (increases,

decreases) _____.

(2) decreases, the average variable cost _____.

5. The law of diminishing returns causes a firm's average variable, average total, and marginal cost to decrease at first and then to increase as the output of the firm increases.

Sketch these three cost curves on the following graph in such a way that their proper relationship to each other is shown.

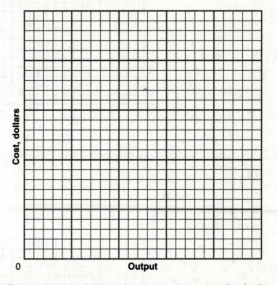

6. The table that follows is a schedule of a firm's fixed cost and variable cost.

a. Complete the table by computing total cost, average fixed cost, average total cost, and marginal cost.

b. On the graph at the top of the next page, plot and label fixed cost, variable cost, and total cost.

c. On the graph at the bottom of the next page, plot average fixed cost, average variable cost, average total cost, and marginal cost. Label the four curves.

Output	Total fixed cost	Total variable cost	Total cost	Average fixed cost	Average variable cost	Average total cost	Marginal cost
0	$200	$ 0	$_____				
1	200	50	_____	$_____	$50.00	$_____	$_____
2	200	90	_____	_____	45.00	_____	_____
3	200	120	_____	_____	40.00	_____	_____
4	200	160	_____	_____	40.00	_____	_____
5	200	220	_____	_____	44.00	_____	_____
6	200	300	_____	_____	50.00	_____	_____
7	200	400	_____	_____	57.14	_____	_____
8	200	520	_____	_____	65.00	_____	_____
9	200	670	_____	_____	74.44	_____	_____
10	200	900	_____	_____	90.00	_____	_____

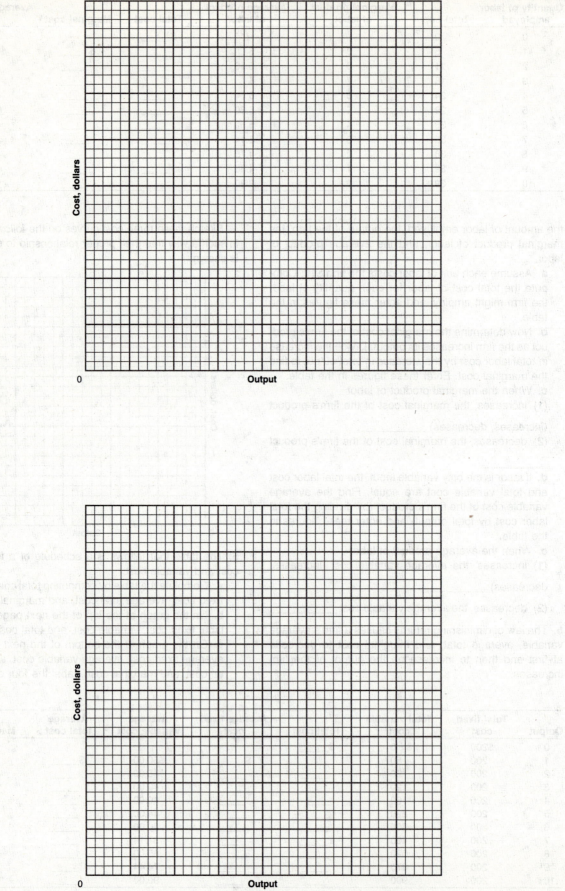

7. Following are the short-run average cost curves of producing a product with three different sizes of plants, Plant 1, Plant 2, and Plant 3. Draw the firm's long-run average cost on this graph.

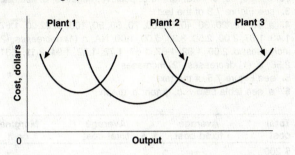

8. Following are the short-run average total cost schedules for three plants of different sizes that a firm might build to produce its product. Assume that these are the only possible sizes of plants that the firm might build.

Plant size A		Plant size B		Plant size C	
Output	ATC	Output	ATC	Output	ATC
10	$ 7	10	$17	10	$53
20	6	20	13	20	44
30	5	30	9	30	35
40	4	40	6	40	27
50	5	50	4	50	20
60	7	60	3	60	14
70	10	70	4	70	11
80	14	80	5	80	8
90	19	90	7	90	6
100	25	100	10	100	5
110	32	110	16	110	7
120	40	120	25	120	10

a. Complete the long-run average cost schedule for the firm in the following table.

Output	Average cost	Output	Average cost
10	$_____	70	$_____
20	_____	80	_____
30	_____	90	_____
40	_____	100	_____
50	_____	110	_____
60	_____	120	_____

b. For outputs between

(1) _____ and _____, the firm should build Plant A.

(2) _____ and _____, the firm should build Plant B.

(3) _____ and _____, the firm should build Plant C.

■ **SHORT ANSWER AND ESSAY QUESTIONS**

1. Explain the meaning of the opportunity cost of producing a product and the difference between an explicit cost and an implicit cost. How would you determine the implicit money cost of a resource?

2. What is the difference between normal profit and economic profit? Why is the former an economic cost? How do you define accounting profit?

3. What type of adjustments can a firm make in the long run that it cannot make in the short run? What adjustments can it make in the short run? How long is the short run?

4. Why is the distinction between the short run and the long run important?

5. State precisely the law of diminishing returns. Exactly what is it that diminishes, and why does it diminish?

6. Distinguish between a fixed cost and a variable cost.

7. Why are short-run total costs partly fixed and partly variable costs, and why are long-run costs entirely variable?

8. Why do short-run variable costs increase at first by decreasing amounts and later increase by increasing amounts?

9. How does the behavior of short-run variable costs influence the behavior of short-run total costs?

10. Describe the ways in which short-run average fixed cost, average variable cost, average total cost, and marginal cost vary as the output of the firm increases.

11. What are the connections between marginal product and marginal cost, and between average product and average variable cost? How will marginal cost behave as marginal product decreases and increases? How will average variable cost change as average product rises and falls?

12. What are the precise relationships between marginal cost and minimum average variable cost, and between marginal cost and minimum average total cost? Why are these relationships necessarily true?

13. What happens to the average total cost, average variable cost, average fixed cost, and marginal cost curves when the price of a variable input increases or decreases? Describe what other factor can cause short-run cost curves to shift.

14. What does the long-run average cost curve of a firm show? What relationship is there between long-run average cost and the short-run average total cost schedules of the different-sized plants which a firm might build?

15. Why is the long-run average cost curve of a firm U-shaped?

16. What is meant by economies of scale and by diseconomies of scale?

17. What are factors that contribute to economies of scale?

18. What causes diseconomies of scale?

19. What is minimum efficient scale? How can this concept, combined with economies and diseconomies of scale, be used to describe the number and size of firms in an industry?

20. Describe real examples of short-run costs, economies of scale, and minimum efficient scale.

ANSWERS

Chapter 7 Businesses and the Costs of Production

FILL-IN QUESTIONS

1. opportunity
2. resource suppliers, explicit, implicit
3. explicit, implicit, revenues, costs
4. variable, fixed, short, long
5. variable, fixed, marginal, equal
6. rising, positive, falling
7. zero, negative
8. rising, falling, maximum
9. fixed, variable, total
10. decrease, increase
11. total, total
12. falling, rising
13. *a.* falling; *b.* rising; *c.* maximum; *d.* minimum; *e.* marginal, marginal
14. shift, shift up, shift up, remain unchanged, remain unchanged
15. shift up, shift up, shift up, remain unchanged
16. variable, plant
17. *a.* labor specialization; *b.* managerial specialization; *c.* more efficient use
18. higher, less, difficulties
19. minimum, constant
20. decrease, large, economies

TRUE–FALSE QUESTIONS

1. T, p. 141	**10.** F, p. 147	**19.** T, pp. 151–152
2. F, pp.141–143	**11.** T, pp. 147–148	**20.** F, pp. 152–153
3. T, p. 143	**12.** F, pp. 147–149	**21.** T, pp. 153–154
4. F, p. 143	**13.** T, p. 148	**22.** F, p. 156
5. F, p. 144	**14.** F, pp. 149–150	**23.** F, p. 156
6. T, pp. 144–145	**15.** T, pp. 149–150	**24.** F, pp. 156–157
7. F, pp. 145–147	**16.** T, pp. 150–151	**25.** T, p. 158
8. F, pp. 145–147	**17.** T, pp. 150–151	
9. T, pp. 145–147	**18.** T, pp. 150–151	

MULTIPLE-CHOICE QUESTIONS

1. b, pp. 141–143	**11.** c, p. 149	**21.** c, pp. 148–149
2. d, pp. 142–143	**12.** d, pp. 149–150	**22.** d, pp. 148–149
3. b, p. 143	**13.** c, pp. 150–151	**23.** d, pp. 148–149
4. d, p. 143	**14.** c, pp. 150–151	**24.** b, pp. 149–152
5. d, p. 144	**15.** c, p. 150	**25.** b, pp. 152–153
6. b, p. 144	**16.** d, pp. 150–151	**26.** b, pp. 153–154
7. b, p. 144	**17.** c, p. 151	**27.** d, pp. 152–154
8. a, pp. 149–151	**18.** a, p. 151	**28.** c, pp. 154–156
9. d, pp. 149–151	**19.** b, pp. 150–152	**29.** c, p. 156
10. a, p. 149	**20.** b, pp. 148–149	**30.** d, p. 156

PROBLEMS

1. see Figure 7.2(b) of the text
2. *a.* 80, 120, 130, 70, 50, 30, 10, −10; *b.* 80, 100, 110, 100, 90, 80, 70, 60; *c.* third, fourth; *d.* positive, negative; *e.* rise, fall
3. see Figure 7.3 of the text
4. *a.* $0, 10, 20, 30, 40, 50, 60, 70, 80, 90, 100; *b.* $2.00, 1.67, 1.43, 1.67, 2.00, 2.50, 3.33, 5.00, 1.00, NA; *c.* (1) decreases, (2) increases; *d.* 2.00, 1.82, 1.67, 1.67, 1.72, 1.82, 1.94, 2.11, 2.31, 2.56; *e.* (1) decreases, (2) increases
5. see Figure 7.5 of the text
6. *a.* see table below; *b.* graph; *c.* graph

Total cost	Average fixed cost	Average total cost	Marginal cost
$ 200	—	—	—
250	$200.00	$250.00	$ 50
290	100.00	145.00	40
320	66.67	106.67	30
360	50.00	90.00	40
420	40.00	84.00	60
500	33.33	83.33	80
600	28.57	85.71	100
720	25.00	90.00	120
870	22.22	96.67	150
1100	20.00	110.00	230

7. see Figures 7.7 and 7.8 of the text
8. *a.* $7.00, 6.00, 5.00, 4.00, 4.00, 3.00, 4.00, 5.00, 6.00, 5.00, 7.00, 10.00; *b.* (1) 10, 40, (2) 50, 80, (3) 90, 120

SHORT ANSWER AND ESSAY QUESTIONS

1. p. 141	**8.** pp. 148–152	**15.** pp. 153–154
2. pp. 141–143	**9.** pp. 148–149	**16.** pp. 153–156
3. p. 143	**10.** pp. 148–152	**17.** pp. 153–156
4. p. 143	**11.** pp. 149–152	**18.** p. 156
5. pp. 144–146	**12.** pp. 149–152	**19.** pp. 156–157
6. pp. 147–148	**13.** pp. 152–153	**20.** pp. 157–159
7. pp. 147, 151	**14.** pp. 153–154	

CHAPTER 8

Pure Competition in the Short Run

Chapter 8 is the first of four chapters that bring together the previous discussion of demand and production costs. These chapters examine demand and production costs in four different market structures: pure competition, monopoly, oligopoly, and monopolistic competition. This chapter focuses exclusively on the market structure for pure competition, which is characterized by (1) a large number of firms, (2) the selling of a standardized product, (3) firms that are price takers rather than price makers, and (4) ease of entry into and exit from the industry.

The main section of the chapter describes profit maximization for the purely competitive firm in the **short run.** In the short run the firm has a fixed plant and adjusts its output through changes in the amount of variable resources it uses. Although two approaches to profit maximization are presented, the one given the greatest emphasis is the **marginal revenue–marginal cost** approach. You will learn the rule that a firm maximizes profit or minimizes losses by producing the output level at which marginal revenue equals marginal cost. Finding this equality provides the answers to the three central questions each firm has to answer: (1) Should we produce? (2) If so, how much output? (3) What profit (or loss) will be realized?

Answers to these questions also give insights about the **short-run supply curve** for the individual firm. The firm will find it profitable to produce at any output level where marginal revenue is greater than marginal costs. The firm also will produce in the short run, but it will experience losses if marginal revenue is less than marginal costs and greater than the minimum of average total cost. You will be shown how to construct the short-run supply curve for the purely competitive firm, given price and output data. The market supply curve for the industry is the sum of all supply curves for individual firms.

This chapter limits the discussion of pure competition to the short run where there are fixed costs and the size of plants producing the output do not change. In the next chapter you will learn about pure competition in the long run, where all costs are variable and firms are free to change plant size. In the long run, there is also ease of entry and exit from the industry that can change the level of output and market prices.

You must understand the purely competitive model because it is the efficiency standard or norm for evaluating different market structures. You will be using it often for comparison with the pure monopoly model in Chapter 10 and with the models for monopolistic competition and oligopoly in Chapter 11. Understanding pure competition in the short run is a start to developing this evaluation perspective and sets the basis for comprehending pure competition in the long run as presented in the next chapter.

■ **CHECKLIST**

When you have studied this chapter you should be able to

☐ List the five characteristics of each of the four basic market models.

☐ Give examples of industries related to the four basic market models.

☐ Describe four major features of pure competition.

☐ Explain why a purely competitive firm is a price taker.

☐ Describe the elasticity of the demand curve for a purely competitive firm.

☐ Distinguish between average revenue, total revenue, and marginal revenue.

☐ Explain the relationship between average revenue, marginal revenue, and price in pure competition.

☐ Compute average, total, and marginal revenues when given a demand schedule faced by a purely competitive firm.

☐ Use the total-revenue and total-cost approaches to determine the output that a purely competitive firm will produce in the short run in the profit-maximizing case when given the necessary data.

☐ Draw a total revenue and total cost graph illustrating the break-even points and the level of output producing maximum economic profit.

☐ State characteristics of the MR = MC rule.

☐ Use the marginal-revenue and marginal-cost approach to determine the output that a purely competitive firm will produce in the short run in the three different cases: profit-maximizing, loss-minimizing, and shutdown.

☐ Draw a graph with average cost, marginal cost, marginal revenue, and price illustrating output and the area of profit in the profit-maximizing case and the area of loss in the loss-minimizing case.

☐ Discuss the reasons why a firm will shut down in the short run and not produce any output.

☐ Find the firm's short-run supply curve when you are given the firm's short-run cost schedules.

☐ Explain the links among the law of diminishing returns, production costs, and product supply in the short run.

☐ Graph a shift in the firm's short-run supply curve and cite factors that cause the curve to increase or decrease.

☐ Find the industry's short-run supply curve (or schedule) when you are given the typical firm's short-run cost schedules.

☐ Determine, under short-run conditions, the price at which the product will sell, the output of the industry, and the output of the individual firm.

☐ Discuss why shutting down a business in the short run makes economic sense and may be temporary (*Last Word*).

■ CHAPTER OUTLINE

1. The price a firm charges for the good or service it produces and its output of that product depend not only on the demand for and the cost of producing it, but on the characteristics of the market (industry) in which it sells the product. The *four market models* are *pure competition, pure monopoly, monopolistic competition,* and *oligopoly.* These models are defined by the number of firms, whether the product is standardized or differentiated, the firm's control over price, the conditions for entry into the industry, and degree of nonprice competition (see Table 8.1 in text). Compared with *pure competition,* the other three market models are considered different forms of *imperfect competition.*

2. This chapter examines *pure competition,* in which a very large number of independent firms, no one of which is able to influence market price by itself, sell a standardized product in a market where firms are free to enter and to leave in the long run. Although pure competition is rare in practice, it is the standard against which the *efficiency* of the economy and other market models can be compared.

3. *Demand* as seen by the purely competitive firm is unique because a firm selling its product cannot influence the price at which the product sells, and therefore is a *price taker.*

  a. The demand for its product is perfectly elastic.

  b. There are three types of revenue. *Average revenue* is the amount of revenue per unit of output. *Total revenue* is calculated as the price times the quantity a firm can produce. *Marginal revenue* is the change in total revenue from selling one more unit. Average revenue (or price) and marginal revenue are equal and constant at the fixed (equilibrium) market price ($AR = P = MR$). Total revenue increases at a constant rate as the firm increases its output.

  c. The demand (average revenue) and marginal revenue curves faced by the firm are horizontal and identical at the market price. The total revenue curve has a constant positive slope.

4. The purely competitive firm operating in the *short run* is a price taker that can maximize profits (or minimize losses) only by changing its level of output. Two approaches can be used to determine the optimal level of output for the firm.

  a. The *total revenue–total cost* approach to profit maximization sets the level of output at that quantity where the difference between total revenue and total cost is greatest. An output at which total revenue covers total costs (including a normal profit) is a *break-even point.*

  b. The *marginal revenue–marginal cost* approach to profit maximization basically sets the level of output at the quantity where marginal revenue (or price) equals marginal cost. There are three possible cases to consider when using this approach.

  (1) The firm uses the *MR = MC rule* to evaluate profit maximization. The firm will produce that level of output where the marginal revenue from each additional unit produced is equal to the marginal cost of each additional unit produced. The rule is an accurate guide to profit maximization for the four basic types of firms. For the purely competitive firm, however, the rule can be restated as $P = MC$.

  (2) The firm will *maximize profits* when MR = MC at an output level where price is greater than average total cost.

  (3) The firm will *minimize losses* when MR = MC at an output level where price is greater than the minimum average variable cost (but less than average total cost).

  (4) The firm will *shut down* when MR = MC at an output level where price is less than average variable cost.

5. There is a close relationship between marginal cost and the *short-run supply curve* for the purely competitive firm and industry.

  a. The short-run supply curve for the purely competitive firm is the portion of the marginal cost curve that lies above average variable cost.

  b. There are links among the law of diminishing returns, production costs, and product supply. The law of diminishing returns suggests that marginal costs will increase as output expands. The firm must receive more revenue (get higher prices for its products) if it is to expand output.

  c. Changes in variable inputs will change the marginal cost or supply curve for the purely competitive firm. For example, an improvement in technology that increases productivity will decrease the marginal cost curve (shift it downward).

  d. The *short-run supply curve of the industry* (which is the sum of the supply curves of the individual firms) and the total demand for the product determine the short-run equilibrium price and equilibrium output of the industry. Firms in the industry may be either prosperous or unprosperous in the short run.

6. (*Last Word*). If a firm finds that the revenue it earns from the output it produces and sells does not even cover its fixed costs, then the firm will shut down. In many cases in the real world, the shutdown is temporary and part of business conditions firms may face. For example, oil wells are shut down if the price of oil does not cover the fixed costs of oil production. Seasonal resorts shut down over the off-season months because there are not enough paying customers to cover the fixed costs. During recessions, businesses shut down factories because product demand and revenue are insufficient to cover fixed costs. Shutdowns are more common than typically thought and are often temporary until economic conditions and revenues expand to cover the fixed costs.

■ HINTS AND TIPS

1. The purely competitive model is extremely important for you to master even if examples of it in the real world are rare. The model is the standard against which the other market models—pure monopoly, monopolistic competition, and oligopoly—will be compared for effects on economic efficiency. Spend extra time learning the material in this chapter so you can make model comparisons in later chapters.

2. Make sure that you understand why a purely competitive firm is a **price "taker"** and not a price "maker." The purely competitive firm has no influence over the price of its product and can only make decisions about the level of output.

3. Construct a table for explaining how the purely competitive firm maximizes profits or minimizes losses in the short run. Ask yourself the three questions in the table: (1) Should the firm produce? (2) What quantity should be produced to maximize profits? (3) Will production result in economic profit? Answer the questions using a marginal revenue–marginal cost approach. Check your answers against those presented in the text Table 8.3.

■ IMPORTANT TERMS

pure competition	average revenue
pure monopoly	total revenue
monopolistic competition	marginal revenue
oligopoly	break-even point
imperfect competition	MR = MC rule
price taker	short-run supply curve

SELF-TEST

■ FILL-IN QUESTIONS

1. The four market models examined in this and the next three chapters are

a. _____
b. _____
c. _____
d. _____

2. The four market models differ in terms of the (age, number) _____ of firms in the industry, whether the product is (a consumer good, standardized) _____ or (a producer good, differentiated) _____, and how easy or difficult it is for new firms to (enter, leave) _____ the industry.

3. What are the four specific conditions that characterize pure competition?

a. _____
b. _____
c. _____
d. _____

4. The individual firm in a purely competitive industry is a price (maker, taker) _____ and finds that the demand for its product is perfectly (elastic, inelastic) _____. The demand curve for the individual firm is graphed as a (vertical, horizontal) _____ line.

5. The price per unit to the seller is (marginal, total, average) _____ revenue; price multiplied by the quantity the firm can sell is _____ revenue; and the extra revenue that results from selling one more unit of output is _____ revenue.

6. In pure competition, as an individual firm increases output, the product price (rises, falls, is constant) _____. Marginal revenue is (less than, greater than, equal to) _____ product price and average revenue is _____ product price.

7. The purely competitive firm's demand schedule is a (cost, revenue) _____ schedule. Demand is equal to (marginal, total) _____ revenue and is equal to (average, total) _____ revenue.

8. There are two ways to determine the level of output at which the competitive firm will realize maximum (loss, profit) _____ or minimum _____. One method is to compare total revenue with (total, marginal) _____ cost and the other way is to compare marginal revenue with _____ cost.

9. Economic profit is total revenue (plus, minus) _____ total cost. If the firm is making only a normal profit, total revenue is (greater than, equal to) _____ total cost. This output level is called the (profit, break-even) _____ point by economists. A firm will produce a level of output where the difference between total revenue and total cost is at a (minimum, maximum) _____.

10. The rule for profit maximization is that marginal revenue (MR) is (less than, equal to, greater than) _____ marginal cost (MC), and in the case of pure competition this rule can be restated as price is _____ marginal cost; but this rule implies that price is _____ minimum average variable cost.

11. In a graph with marginal and average cost curves, the way to calculate economic profit is to take the difference between average total cost and (price, output) _____ and multiply it by _____.

12. If a purely competitive firm produces any output at all, it will produce that output at which its profit is at a (maximum, minimum) _____ or its loss is at a _____. Or, said another way, the firm will produce output at which marginal cost is (equal to, greater than) _____ marginal revenue.

13. In the short run, a firm will be willing to produce its output at an economic loss if the price which it receives is less than its average (fixed, variable, total) _____ cost but greater than its average _____ cost.

14. In the short run, a firm will choose to shut down and not produce output if the price which it receives is less than its average (fixed, variable, total) _____ cost.

15. In the short run, the individual firm's supply curve in pure competition is that portion of the firm's (total, marginal) _____ cost curve which lies (above, below) _____ the average variable cost curve. The break-even point for a firm is where price equals average (total, variable) _____ cost.

16. Because of the law of diminishing returns, marginal costs eventually (fall, rise) _____ as more units of output are produced, and to be motivated to produce more units of output at higher marginal costs, the price of the product must _____.

17. An increase in the price of variable inputs such as worker wages will shift the marginal-cost or short-run supply curve of the individual firm (upward, downward) _____ while a decrease in the price of variable input or an improvement in technology will shift this curve _____.

18. The short-run market supply curve is the (average, sum) _____ of the (short-run, long-run) _____ supply curves of all firms in the industry.

19. In the short run in a purely competitive industry, the equilibrium price is the price at which quantity demanded is (greater than, equal to, less than) _____ quantity supplied, and the equilibrium quantity is the quantity at which quantity demanded is _____ quantity supplied at the equilibrium price.

20. Product price is a given fact to the (firm, industry) _____ but the supply plans of the _____ as a group of firms are a basic determinant of product price.

■ TRUE–FALSE QUESTIONS

Circle T if the statement is true, F if it is false.

1. The structures of the markets in which business firms sell their products in the U.S. economy are very similar.   **T F**

2. There are significant obstacles to entry in a purely competitive industry.   **T F**

3. In a purely competitive industry individual firms do not have control over the price of their product.   **T F**

4. Imperfectly competitive markets are defined as all markets except those that are purely competitive.   **T F**

5. One reason for studying the pure competition model is that most industries are purely competitive.   **T F**

6. The purely competitive firm views an average revenue schedule as identical to its marginal revenue schedule.   **T F**

7. The demand curves for an individual firm in a purely competitive industry are perfectly inelastic.   **T F**

8. Price and average revenue are the same in pure competition.   **T F**

9. Total revenue for each sales level is found by multiplying price by the quantity the firm can sell at that price.   **T F**

10. Marginal revenue is the change in average revenue that results from selling one more unit of output.   **T F**

11. In pure competition, price is equal to marginal revenue and also equal to average revenue.   **T F**

12. Under purely competitive conditions, the product price charged by the firm increases as output increases.   **T F**

13. The purely competitive firm can maximize its economic profit (or minimize its loss) only by adjusting its output.   **T F**

14. Economic profit is the difference between total revenue and average revenue.   **T F**

15. The break-even point means that the firm is realizing normal profits, but not economic profits.   **T F**

16. A purely competitive firm that wishes to produce and not close down will maximize profits or minimize losses at that output at which marginal costs and marginal revenue are equal.   **T F**

17. Assuming that the purely competitive firm chooses to produce and not close down, to maximize profits or minimize losses it should produce at that point where price equals average cost.   **T F**

18. If a purely competitive firm is producing output less than its profit-maximizing output, marginal revenue is greater than marginal cost.   **T F**

19. If, at the profit-maximizing level of output for the purely competitive firm, price exceeds the minimum average variable cost but is less than average total cost, the firm will make a profit.   **T F**

20. A purely competitive firm will produce in the short run the output at which marginal cost and marginal revenue are equal provided that the price of the product is greater than its average variable cost of production.   **T F**

21. The short-run supply curve of the purely competitive firm is the segment of the firm's short-run marginal cost curve that lies above the firm's average variable cost curve.   **T F**

22. The short-run supply curve of a purely competitive firm tends to slope upward from left to right because of the law of diminishing returns. **T F**

23. An increase in the price of a variable input will shift the marginal cost or short-run supply curve downward. **T F**

24. An improvement in technology that raises productivity will shift the marginal cost or short-run supply curve downward. **T F**

25. Product price is a given fact to the individual competitive firm, but the supply plans of all competitive firms as a group are a basic determinant of product price. **T F**

■ **MULTIPLE-CHOICE QUESTIONS**

Circle the letter that corresponds to the best answer.

1. For which market model are there a very large number of firms?
 (a) monopolistic competition
 (b) oligopoly
 (c) pure monopoly
 (d) pure competition

2. In which market model is the individual seller of a product a price taker?
 (a) pure competition
 (b) pure monopoly
 (c) monopolistic competition
 (d) oligopoly

3. Which industry comes *closest* to being purely competitive?
 (a) agriculture
 (b) retail trade
 (c) electricity
 (d) automobile

4. In a purely competitive industry,
 (a) each existing firm will engage in various forms of nonprice competition
 (b) new firms are free to enter and existing firms are able to leave the industry very easily
 (c) individual firms have a price policy
 (d) each firm produces a differentiated (nonstandardized) product

5. The demand schedule or curve confronted by the individual purely competitive firm is
 (a) perfectly inelastic
 (b) inelastic but not perfectly inelastic
 (c) perfectly elastic
 (d) elastic but not perfectly elastic

6. Total revenue for producing 10 units of output is $6. Total revenue for producing 11 units of output is $8. Given this information, the
 (a) average revenue for producing 11 units is $2.
 (b) average revenue for producing 11 units is $8.
 (c) marginal revenue for producing the 11th unit is $2.
 (d) marginal revenue for producing the 11th unit is $8.

7. In pure competition, product price is
 (a) greater than marginal revenue
 (b) equal to marginal revenue
 (c) equal to total revenue
 (d) greater than total revenue

8. Suppose that when 2000 units of output are produced, the marginal cost of the 2001st unit is $5. This amount is equal to the minimum of average total cost, and marginal cost is rising. If the optimal level of output in the short run is 2500 units, then at that level,
 (a) marginal cost is greater than $5 and marginal cost is less than average total cost
 (b) marginal cost is greater than $5 and marginal cost is greater than average total cost
 (c) marginal cost is less than $5 and marginal cost is greater than average total cost
 (d) marginal cost is equal to $5 and marginal cost is equal to average total cost

9. The Zebra, Inc., is selling in a purely competitive market. Its output is 250 units, which sell for $2 each. At this level of output, marginal cost is $2 and average variable cost is $2.25. The firm should
 (a) produce zero units of output
 (b) decrease output to 200 units
 (c) continue to produce 250 units
 (d) increase output to maximize profits

Questions 10, 11, 12, and 13 are based on the following graph.

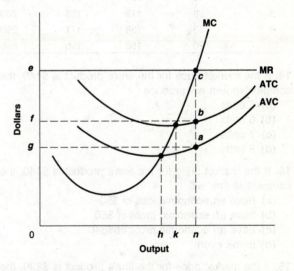

10. If the firm is producing at output level 0*n*, the rectangular area *fecb* is
 (a) total variable cost
 (b) total fixed costs
 (c) total revenue
 (d) total economic profit

11. At the profit-maximizing output, average fixed cost is
 (a) *ab*
 (b) *ac*
 (c) *na*
 (d) *nb*

12. At the profit-maximizing output, the total variable costs are equal to the area
(a) 0*fbn*
(b) 0*ecn*
(c) 0*gan*
(d) *gfba*

13. The demand curve for this firm is equal to
(a) **MR,** and the supply curve is the portion of the **MC** curve where output is greater than level *n*
(b) **MR,** and the supply curve is the portion of the **MC** curve where output is greater than level *k*
(c) **MR,** and the supply curve is the portion of the **MC** curve where output is greater than level *h*
(d) **MR,** and the supply curve is the portion of the **ATC** curve where output is greater than level *k*

Answer Questions 14 through 20 on the basis of the following cost data for a firm that is selling in a purely competitive market.

Output	AFC	AVC	ATC	MC
0				
1	$300	$100	$400	$100
2	150	75	225	50
3	100	70	170	60
4	75	73	148	80
5	60	80	140	110
6	50	90	140	140
7	43	103	146	180
8	38	119	156	230
9	33	138	171	290
10	30	160	190	360

14. If the market price for the firm's product is $140, the competitive firm will produce
(a) 5 units
(b) 6 units
(c) 7 units
(d) 8 units

15. If the market price for the firm's product is $140, the competitive firm will
(a) have an economic loss of $50
(b) have an economic profit of $50
(c) have an economic profit of $840
(d) break even

16. If the market price for the firm's product is $290, the competitive firm will produce
(a) 7 units
(b) 8 units
(c) 9 units
(d) 10 units

17. If the market price for the firm's product is $290, the competitive firm will produce an economic profit of
(a) $1071
(b) $1368
(c) $1539
(d) $2610

18. If the product price is $179, the *per-unit* economic profit at the profit-maximizing output is
(a) $15
(b) $23
(c) $33
(d) $39

19. If the market price for the firm's product is $60, the competitive firm will produce
(a) 0 units
(b) 1 units
(c) 2 units
(d) 3 units

20. For this firm, the total fixed costs are
(a) $100
(b) $200
(c) $300
(d) $400

Assume there are 100 identical firms in this industry and total or market demand is as shown.

Price	Quantity demanded
$360	600
290	700
230	800
180	900
140	1000
110	1100
80	1200

21. The equilibrium price will be
(a) $140
(b) $180
(c) $230
(d) $290

22. The individual firm's short-run supply curve is that part of its marginal cost curve lying above its
(a) average total cost curve
(b) average variable cost curve
(c) average fixed cost curve
(d) average revenue curve

23. Which statement is true of a purely competitive industry in short-run equilibrium?
(a) Price is equal to average total cost.
(b) Total quantity demanded is equal to total quantity supplied.
(c) Profits in the industry are equal to zero.
(d) Output is equal to the output at which average total cost is a minimum.

24. Because of the law of diminishing marginal returns, marginal costs eventually
(a) fall as fewer units of output are produced, thus higher prices are required to motivate producers to supply less
(b) fall as fewer units of output are produced, thus higher prices are required to motivate producers to supply more

(c) rise as more units of output are produced, thus lower prices are required to motivate producers to supply less

(d) rise as more units of output are produced, thus higher prices are required to motivate producers to supply more

25. If other factors are held constant, an increase in wages for a purely competitive firm would result in a shift

(a) downward in the marginal cost curve

(b) downward in the average fixed cost curve

(c) upward in the marginal cost curve

(d) upward in the average fixed cost curve

■ PROBLEMS

1. Using the following set of terms, complete the following table by inserting the appropriate letter or letters in the blanks.

a. one	**h.** considerable
b. few	**i.** very easy
c. many	**j.** blocked
d. a very large number	**k.** fairly easy
e. standardized	**l.** fairly difficult
f. differentiated	**m.** none
g. some	**n.** unique

Market characteristics	Market model			
	Pure competition	Monopolistic competition	Oligopoly	Pure monopoly
Number of firms	____	____	____	____
Type of product	____	____	____	____
Control over price	____	____	____	____
Conditions of entry	____	____	____	____
Nonprice competition	____	____	____	____

2. Following is the demand schedule facing the individual firm.

Price	Quantity demanded	Average revenue	Total revenue	Marginal revenue
$10	0	$____	$____	—
10	1	____	____	$____
10	2	____	____	____
10	3	____	____	____
10	4	____	____	____
10	5	____	____	____
10	6	____	____	____

a. Complete the table by computing average revenue, total revenue, and marginal revenue.

b. Is this firm operating in a market that is purely competitive? _____ How can you tell? _____

_____

c. The coefficient of the price elasticity of demand is the same between every pair of quantities demanded.

What is it? _____

d. What relationship exists between average revenue and marginal revenue? _____

_____

e. On the graph below, plot the demand schedule, average revenue, total revenue, and marginal revenue; label each curve.

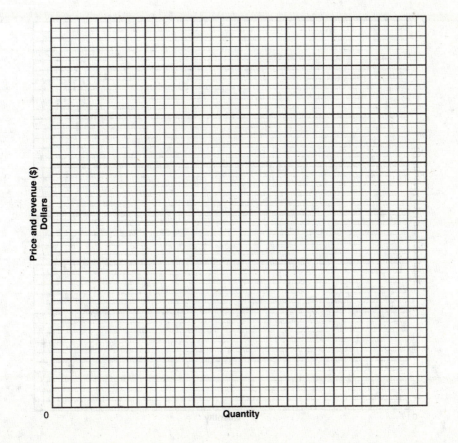

f. The demand, average revenue, and marginal revenue curves are all _____ lines at a price of $_____ across all quantities.

g. The total revenue curve is an up-sloping line with a _____ slope because marginal revenue is _____.

3. Assume that a purely competitive firm has the following schedule of costs.

Output	TFC	TVC	TC
0	$300	$ 0	$ 300
1	300	100	400
2	300	150	450
3	300	210	510
4	300	290	590
5	300	400	700
6	300	540	840
7	300	720	1020
8	300	950	1250
9	300	1240	1540
10	300	1600	1900

a. Complete the following table to show the total revenue and total profit of the firm at each level of output the firm might produce. Assume the market price is $200.

	Market price = $200	
Output	Revenue	Profit
0	$_____	$_____
1	_____	_____
2	_____	_____
3	_____	_____
4	_____	_____
5	_____	_____
6	_____	_____
7	_____	_____
8	_____	_____
9	_____	_____
10	_____	_____

b. At a price of $200, the firm would produce an output of _____ units and earn a profit of $_____.

c. Plot the cost data for total variable cost and total cost on the graph below. Then plot the total revenue when the price is $200. For this price, indicate the level of output and the economic profit or loss on the graph.

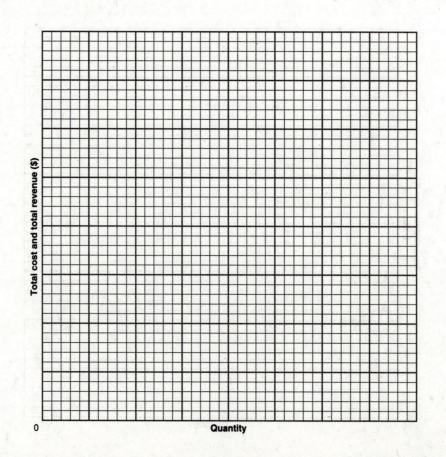

4. Now assume that the same purely competitive firm has the following schedule of average and marginal costs.

Output	AFC	AVC	ATC	MC
0				
1	$300	$100	$400	$100
2	150	75	225	50
3	100	70	170	60
4	75	73	148	80
5	60	80	140	110
6	50	90	140	140
7	43	103	146	180
8	38	119	156	230
9	33	138	171	290
10	30	160	190	360

a. At a price of $55, the firm would produce _____ units of output. At a price of $120, the firm would produce _____ units of output. At a price of $200, the firm would produce _____ units of output. At the $200 price compare your answers to those you gave in problem 3.

b. The *per-unit* economic profit (or loss) is calculated by subtracting _____ at a particular level of output from the product price. This *per-unit* economic profit is then multiplied by the number of units of _____ to determine the economic profit for the competitive firm.

(1) At the product price of $200, the average total costs are $_____, so *per-unit* economic profit is $_____. Multiplying this amount by the number of units of output results in an economic profit of $_____.

(2) At the product price of $120, the average total costs are $_____, so *per-unit* economic losses are $_____. Multiplying this amount by the number of units of output results in an economic loss of $_____.

c. Plot the data for average and marginal cost in the graph at bottom of the page. Then plot each marginal revenue when the price is $55, $120, and $200. For each price, indicate the level of output and the economic profit or loss on the graph.

5. Use the average and marginal cost data in problem 4 in your work on problem 5.

a. In the following table, complete the supply schedule for the competitive firm and state what the economic profit will be at each price.

Price	Quantity supplied	Profit
$360	_____	$_____
290	_____	_____
230	_____	_____
180	_____	_____
140	_____	_____
110	_____	_____
80	_____	_____
60	_____	_____

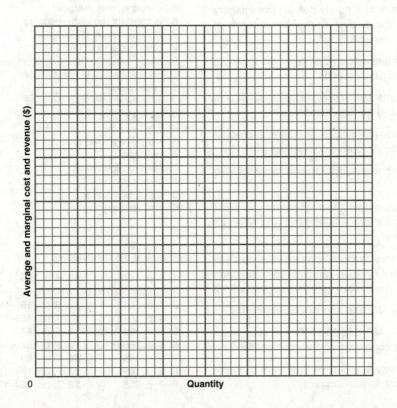

Average and marginal cost and revenue ($)

0   Quantity

b. If there are 100 firms in the industry and all have the same cost schedule,

(1) Complete the market supply schedule in the following table.

Quantity demanded	Price	Quantity supplied
400	$360	_____
500	290	_____
600	230	_____
700	180	_____
800	140	_____
900	110	_____
1000	80	_____

(2) Using the demand schedule given in (1):

(a) What will the market price of the product be?

$_____

(b) What quantity will the individual firm produce?

_____

(c) How large will the firm's profit be? $_____

■ **SHORT ANSWER AND ESSAY QUESTIONS**

1. What are the four market models (or situations) that economists employ, and what are the major characteristics of each type of market?

2. Describe in detail four characteristics of pure competition.

3. If pure competition is so rare in practice, why are students of economics asked to study it?

4. Explain how the firm in a purely competitive industry sees the demand for the product it produces in terms of the price elasticity of demand.

5. Describe the differences between average revenue, total revenue, and marginal revenue.

6. What happens to total average, revenue, and marginal revenue as the output of the firm increases?

7. Why is price equal to marginal revenue and also equal to average revenue for the purely competitive firm?

8. Describe the total revenue–total cost approach to profit maximization.

9. In the total revenue–total cost approach to profit maximization, what is the break-even point and how is it related to normal profit?

10. Compare and contrast the total revenue–total cost approach with the marginal revenue–marginal cost approach to profit maximization. Are the two approaches consistent?

11. Explain the MR = MC rule and its characteristics.

12. Why do the MC = MR rule and MC = P rule mean the same thing under conditions of pure competition?

13. Why does the purely competitive firm want to maximize total profit but not its per-unit profit?

14. Use an equation to calculate the area of economic profit and draw marginal and average graphs to show the area.

15. Why is a firm willing to produce at a loss in the short run if the loss is no greater than the fixed costs of the firm?

16. In the MR = MC approach, under which conditions will the firm shut down production? Supply a graph of the shutdown case.

17. Use the price equals marginal cost rule to describe the firm's short-run supply curve.

18. Explain the links between the law of diminishing returns, production costs, and product supply in the short run.

19. Explain how the short-run supply of an individual firm and of the purely competitive industry is each determined.

20. What determines the equilibrium price and output of a purely competitive industry in the short run? Will economic profits in the industry be positive or negative?

ANSWERS

Chapter 8 Pure Competition in the Short Run

FILL-IN QUESTIONS

1. *a.* pure competition; *b.* pure monopoly; *c.* monopolistic competition; *d.* oligopoly (any order *a–d*)
2. number, standardized, differentiated, enter
3. *a.* a large number of sellers; *b.* a standardized product; *c.* firms are price takers; *d.* free entry and exit of firms
4. taker, elastic, horizontal
5. average, total, marginal
6. is constant, equal to, equal to
7. revenue, marginal, average
8. profit, loss, total, marginal
9. minus, equal to, break-even, maximum
10. equal to, equal to, greater than
11. price, output
12. maximum, minimum, equal to
13. total, variable
14. fixed
15. marginal, above, total
16. rise, rise
17. upward, downward
18. sum, short-run
19. equal to, equal to
20. firm, industry

TRUE–FALSE QUESTIONS

1. F, p. 164	**10.** F, p. 165	**19.** F, p. 171
2. F, pp. 164–165	**11.** T, pp. 165–166	**20.** T, pp. 171–172
3. T, p. 165	**12.** F, pp. 165–167	**21.** T, pp. 173–174
4. T, p. 164	**13.** T, pp. 166–167	**22.** T, p. 175
5. F, p. 164	**14.** F, p. 167	**23.** F, p. 175
6. T, p. 165	**15.** T, p. 167	**24.** T, p. 175
7. T, p. 165	**16.** T, p. 169	**25.** T, p. 176
8. T, p. 165	**17.** F, pp. 169–171	
9. T, p. 165	**18.** T, pp. 169–171	

MULTIPLE-CHOICE QUESTIONS

1. d, p. 164   **10.** d, pp. 169–171   **19.** a, pp. 171–171
2. a, p. 164   **11.** a, pp. 169–171   **20.** c, pp. 169–171
3. a, p. 164   **12.** c, pp. 169–171   **21.** c, pp. 175–176
4. b, p. 165   **13.** c, pp. 173–174   **22.** b, pp. 175–176
5. c, p. 165   **14.** b, pp. 169–171   **23.** b, p. 175
6. c, p. 165   **15.** d, pp. 169-171   **24.** d, p. 175
7. b, p. 165   **16.** c, pp. 169–171   **25.** c, p. 175
8. b, pp. 169–171   **17.** a, pp. 169-171
9. a, pp. 169–171   **18.** d, pp. 169–171

PROBLEMS

1. Number of firms: d, a, c, b; Type of product: e, n, f, e, or f; Control over price: m, h, g, g; Conditions of entry: i, j, k, l; Non-price competition: m, g, h, g, or h

2. *a.* Average revenue: all are $10.00; Total revenue: $0, 10.00, 20.00, 30.00, 40.00, 50.00, 60.00; Marginal revenue: all are $10.00; *b.* yes, because price (average revenue) is constant and equal to marginal revenue; *c.* infinity; *d.* they are equal; *e.* see Figure 8.1 of the text for an example; *f.* horizontal, $10; *g.* constant, constant

3. *a.* see following table; *b.* 7, 380; *c.* see Figure 8.2 of the text for an example

Output	Market price = $200	
	Revenue	Profit
0	$ 0	$ −300
1	200	−200
2	400	−50
3	600	90
4	800	210
5	1000	300
6	1200	360
7	1400	380
8	1600	350
9	1800	260
10	2000	100

4. *a.* 0, 5, 7 (last answer is the same as 3b); *b.* average total cost, output; (1) $146, ($200 − $146 = $54), ($54 × 7 = $378), (2) $140, ($120 − $140 = −$20), (−$20 × 5 = −$100); *c.* see Figure 8.3 of the text for an example

5. *a.* see following table; *b.* (1) Quantity supplied: 1000, 900, 800, 700, 600, 500, 400, (2) (*a*) 180, (*b*) 7, (*c*) 238

Price	Quantity supplied	Profit
$360	10	$1700
290	9	1071
230	8	592
180	7	238
140	6	0
110	5	−150
80	4	−272
60	0	−300

SHORT ANSWER AND ESSAY QUESTIONS

1. p. 164   **8.** pp. 166–167   **15.** pp.171–172
2. pp. 164–165   **9.** p. 167   **16.** pp. 171–172
3. p. 165   **10.** pp. 166–171   **17.** pp. 173–175
4. p. 165   **11.** pp. 169   **18.** p. 175
5. pp. 165–166   **12.** p. 169   **19.** p. 175
6. pp. 165–167   **13.** pp. 169–171   **20.** p.175–176
7. p. 165   **14.** pp. 169–171

CHAPTER 9

Pure Competition in the Long Run

This chapter discusses what happens to competitive firms in the long run as equilibrium conditions change. Over time, new firms will enter an industry that is making economic profits. As a result, product supply will increase and the price of the product will fall, thereby eroding economic profits until firms earns just a normal profit. Also, when an industry is realizing economic losses, then over time firms will exit the industry. As a consequence, product supply will decrease and the product price will increase to eliminate the economic losses and restore a normal profit for firms.

In this chapter too you will learn that the shape of the **long-run supply curve** is directly affected by the resource cost characteristics of the industry. Three possible shapes of the long-run supply curve are described and discussed: a constant-cost industry with a horizontal long-run supply curve, an increasing-cost industry with an up-sloping long-run supply curve, and a decreasing-cost industry with a down-sloping long-run supply curve.

In the long run, pure competition produces almost ideal conditions for **economic efficiency.** These ideal conditions and their qualifications are discussed in the chapter. Pure competition results in products produced in the least costly way, and thus it is *productively efficient.* Pure competition also allocates resources to firms so that they produce the products most wanted by society, and therefore it is *allocatively efficient.* You will find out that these two efficiency conditions can be expressed in the triple equality: price (and marginal revenue) = marginal cost = minimum of average total cost.

The last section of the chapter discusses competition in a broader context. It describes the role of entrepreneurs and how they can change industries and bring innovation and technological advance. Competition has transformative effects that are both creative (think new products) and at the same time destructive (think of bankrupt firms). Although this **creative destruction** has net positive benefits for society, it is not without costs.

■ **CHECKLIST**

When you have studied this chapter you should be able to

☐ Explain the role played by the entry and exit of firms in a purely competitive industry in achieving equilibrium in the long run.
☐ Specify three assumptions used in the chapter to reduce the complexity of the long-run analysis in pure competition.

☐ Describe the basic goal for long-run adjustments in pure competition.
☐ Explain using graphs what happens to price, profit, and output for the firm and the industry in pure competition when firms enter the industry because there are economic profits.
☐ Explain using graphs what happens to price, profit, and output for the firm and the industry in pure competition when firms exit the industry when there are economic losses.
☐ Describe the characteristics of the long-run supply curve in a constant-cost industry.
☐ State a rationale for the long-run supply curve in an increasing-cost industry.
☐ Illustrate the shape of the long-run supply curve in a decreasing-cost industry.
☐ Demonstrate with a graph the efficiency characteristics of firms and the market after long-run adjustments in pure competition.
☐ Describe the rationale and requirements for productive efficiency in pure competition.
☐ State the conditions for achieving allocative efficiency in pure competition.
☐ Explain the significance of MR (= P) = MC = minimum ATC.
☐ Describe how allocative efficiency maximizes the combined consumer and producer surplus.
☐ Discuss how pure competition makes dynamic adjustments.
☐ Describe how the "invisible hand" works in competitive markets.
☐ Explain the role of the entrepreneur and innovation in pure competition.
☐ Discuss and give examples of how creative destruction transforms industries.
☐ Explain how a fall in the price of drugs increases the consumer surplus and society experiences efficiency gains (*Last Word*).

■ **CHAPTER OUTLINE**

1. This chapter focuses on how the entry and exit of firms leads to long-run equilibrium in a purely competitive industry.
   a. Three assumptions are made in the chapter to simplify the analysis, but none of them affect the conclusions presented in the chapter: the only long-run adjustment is the entry and exit of firm; all firms in the

industry have identical costs; and the industry is a constant-cost industry.

b. The basic conclusion that is explained by the chapter is that when all long-run adjustments have been made, the price of a product will be equal to the minimum average total cost (**P = minimum ATC**) and output will occur at this level. The conclusion arises from the fact that firms want to earn profits and want to avoid losses and also the fact that firms are free to enter or exit an industry.

c. In long-run equilibrium, purely competitive firms in the industry will neither earn economic profits nor suffer economic losses.

(1) If economic profits are being received in the industry in the short run, firms will enter the industry in the long run (attracted by the profits), increase total supply, and thereby force price down to the minimum average total cost, leaving only a normal profit.

(2) If losses are being suffered in the industry in the short run, firms will leave the industry in the long run (seeking to avoid losses), reduce total supply, and thereby force price up to the minimum average total cost, leaving only a normal profit.

d. Each industry has a **long-run supply curve.** If an industry is a **constant-cost industry,** the entry of new firms will not affect the average-total-cost schedules or cost curves of firms in the industry. An increase in demand will result in no increase in the long-run equilibrium price, and the industry will be able to supply larger outputs at a constant price. Graphically, the long-run supply curve in a constant-cost industry is horizontal at the minimum of the average-total-cost curve, indicating that firms make only normal profits, but not economic profits.

e. If an industry is an **increasing-cost industry,** the entry of new firms will raise the average-total-cost schedules or curves of firms in the industry. An increase in demand will result in an increase in the long-run equilibrium price, and the industry will be able to supply larger outputs only at higher prices. Graphically, the long-run supply curve in an increasing-cost industry is up-sloping at the minimum of the average-total-cost curve, indicating that firms make only normal profits but not economic profits.

f. If an industry is a **decreasing-cost industry,** the entry of new firms will lower the average-total-cost schedules or curves of firms in the industry. An increase in demand will result in a decrease in the long-run equilibrium price, and the industry will be able to supply larger outputs only at lower prices. Graphically, the long-run supply curve in a decreasing-cost industry is down-sloping at the minimum of the average-total-cost curve, indicating that firms make only normal profits, but not economic profits.

2. In the long run, **competition** and **efficiency** compel the purely competitive firm to produce that output at a price at which marginal revenue, average cost, and marginal cost are equal and average total cost is a minimum. An economy in which all industries are purely competitive makes efficient use of its resources.

a. **Productive efficiency** requires that each good be produced in the least costly way. In the long run, competition forces firms to produce at the point of minimum average total cost and to charge a price which is just equal to those costs. Buyers benefit most from this efficiency when they are charged a price just equal to minimum average total cost (**P = minimum ATC**).

b. **Allocative efficiency** means that resources are distributed among firms such that a mix of products is produced that is most desired by society. The price of any product is society's measure of its perceived marginal benefit from consumption of the product. The marginal cost measures the relative value of the resources that were used to produce the product. Pure competition is allocatively efficient because P equals MC (**P = MC**), or society's perceived marginal benefit from the consumption of the product just equals the opportunity cost of the resources used to produce the product. When $P > $ MC, there is an *underallocation* of resources to the production of a product. When $P < $ MC, and price is less than marginal cost, there is an *overallocation* of resources to the production of a product.

c. Pure competition is allocatively efficient because it maximizes the combined consumer surplus and producer surplus. The **consumer surplus** is the difference between the maximum prices that consumers are willing to pay for a product and the market price of that product. The **producer surplus** is the difference between the minimum prices that producers are willing to accept for a product and the market price of the product. In long-run equilibrium, the maximum willingness to pay for the last unit of a product is equal to the minimum acceptable price for that unit.

d. Dynamic adjustments will occur automatically in pure competition from changes in demand, changes in resource supplies, or changes in technology. These adjustments will restore allocative efficiency. For example, if demand for a product increases, the price of the product will increase ($P > $ MC). This situation means there is an underallocation of resources to the production of the product. It will create temporary economic profits for firms in the industry. The economic profits will attract new firms to the industry to supply output. This increased supply will result in a decline in price until the equilibrium of $P = $ MC is restored.

e. The "invisible hand" is at work in a competitive market system by organizing the private interests of producers that will help achieve society's interest in the efficient allocation and use of scarce resources.

3. So far the assumption has been that firms in an industry have identical cost curves. This condition implies that the only change to a purely competitive industry comes from the entry or exit of firms and there is no technological change or innovation. From a broader perspective, however, industries are changed by competition. Entrepreneurs will try to earn more than the normal profit earned in pure competition either by lowering the cost of production with new production methods or by developing new products for which they are the unique producers. These actions, however, will eventually stimulate competition from other firms that adopt the new production methods or develop competing products, so that in the long run with competition the above normal profit will not persist.

  a. Competition has transformative effects for firms and industries through a process described by economist Joseph Schumpeter as **creative destruction**. Firms are "creative" in the sense that they develop new production methods and new products. In the long run, these new products and methods cause "destruction" in the sense that firms go bankrupt and workers lose their jobs in dying industries. There are net benefits to society from this transformative process arising from competition, but there are costs imposed on particular industries and their workers. There are many examples of creative destruction throughout economic history (the railroads displacing barges and canals) and in more recent times (e-mail undermining the use of regular mail).

4. (*Last Word*). The competitive model predicts that when there are new entrants into a previously monopolized market, prices will fall, output will increase, and efficiency will improve. Such is the case in the drug market when a drug patent expires and the drug can be produced as a generic. Generic drugs are cheaper for consumers. The decline in price for these drugs compared with the patented versions boosts output and increases the consumer surplus.

■ **HINTS AND TIPS**

1. The average purely competitive firm in long-run equilibrium will not make economic profits. Find out why by following the graphical analysis in Figures 9.1 and 9.2.

2. The triple equality of MR (= P) = MC = minimum ATC is the most important equation in the chapter because it allows you to judge the allocative and productive efficiency of a purely competitive economy. Check your understanding of this triple equality by explaining what happens to productive efficiency when $P >$ minimum ATC, or to allocative efficiency when $P <$ MC or $P >$ MC.

■ **IMPORTANT TERMS**

long-run supply curve	productive efficiency
constant-cost industry	allocative efficiency
increasing-cost industry	consumer surplus
decreasing-cost industry	producer surplus

SELF-TEST

■ **FILL-IN QUESTIONS**

1. The entry and exit of firms in a purely competitive market can only occur in the (short run, long run) _____. In the short run, the industry is composed of a specific number of firms, each with a plant size

that is (fixed, variable) _____, but in the long run the number of firms is _____.

2. State three assumptions about profit maximization in the long run to keep the analysis simple in this chapter.

  a. _____

  b. _____

  c. _____

3. After all long-run adjustments are made in a purely competitive industry, product price will be equal to, and production will occur at, each firm's minimum average (variable, total) _____ cost because firms (shut down production, seek profits) _____ and firms are free to (enter or exit, raise prices or lower prices) _____ in an industry.

4. An industry will be in long-run equilibrium when firms are earning (normal, economic) _____ profits, which means that the firms are earning what they could be earning elsewhere in the economy and there (is, is not) _____ an incentive for change.

5. When a purely competitive industry is in long-run equilibrium, the price that the individual firm is paid for its product is equal to (total, marginal) _____ revenue and its _____ cost. Also in this case the long-run average total cost for the firm is at a (maximum, minimum) _____.

6. New firms will enter an industry In the long run if the existing firms in the industry are earning (accounting, economic) _____ profits. As new firms enter, the market supply of the product will (decrease, increase) _____ and this change will _____ the market price until it is equal to minimum long-run average total cost.

7. Existing firms will leave an industry in the long run if they are realizing economic (profits, losses) _____. As firms leave the industry, the market supply of the product will (decrease, increase) _____ and this change will _____ the market price until it is equal to minimum long-run average total cost.

8. If the entry of new firms into an industry does not change the costs of all firms in the industry, the industry is said to be (a constant-, an increasing-, a decreasing-) _____ cost industry. Its long-run supply curve is (horizontal, down-sloping, up-sloping) _____.

9. If the entry of new firms into an industry raises costs of all firms in the industry, the industry is said to be (a constant-, an increasing-, a decreasing-) _____ cost industry. Its long-run supply curve is (horizontal, down-sloping, up-sloping) _____.

10. If the entry of new firms into an industry lowers costs of all firms in the industry, the industry is said to be (a constant-, an increasing-, a decreasing-) _____ cost industry. Its long-run supply curve is (horizontal, down-sloping, up-sloping) _____.

11. The purely competitive economy achieves productive efficiency in the long run because price and average (variable, total) _____ cost are equal and the latter is at a (maximum, minimum) _____.

12. In the long run the purely competitive economy is allocatively efficient because price and (total, marginal) _____ cost are equal and it implies that resources will be allocated according to the "tastes and preferences" of (producers, consumers) _____.

13. Another way to think about allocative efficiency is that it occurs because, at the equilibrium level of output, the marginal benefit to consumers, as reflected by points on the (supply, demand) _____ curve, equal marginal cost for producers, as reflected by the points on the _____ curve.

14. Consumer surplus is the difference between the (minimum, maximum) _____ prices that consumers are willing to pay for a product and the market price of that product whereas producer surplus is the difference between the _____ prices that producers are willing to accept for a product and the market price of a product. At the long-run equilibrium level of output, the (minimum, maximum) _____ willingness to pay for the last unit is just equal to the _____ acceptable price for that unit so that the combined consumer and producer surplus is at a _____.

15. One of the attributes of purely competitive markets is their ability to restore (surplus, efficiency) _____ when disrupted by changes in the economy. If the demand for a product increases, this change will (increase, decrease) _____ price so that it is greater than marginal cost. This situation in turn will (increase, decrease) _____ profits and give incentive to expand supply so that price will _____ and return to an equilibrium where price is equal to marginal cost.

16. The "invisible hand" also operates in a competitive market system because it (maximizes, minimizes) _____ the profits of individual producers and at the same time the system creates a pattern of resource allocation that _____ consumer satisfaction.

17. The model of pure competition used in this chapter assumed that all firms in the industry had the same cost curves and production technology, so as a result, firms entering an industry just duplicate the production methods of other firms, so there (is, is no) _____ innovation and there _____ dynamism. Entries and exits of firms in pure competition will ensure that every firm will make the same (normal, economic) _____ profit in the long run.

18. An entrepreneur will improve production methods to earn more than a(n) (normal, economic) _____ profit typically earned by firms in pure competition. A successful new method of production will reduce the firm's cost, and if revenues stay the same, the firm will earn a(n) (normal, economic) _____ profit for a while; but if other firms copy those production methods and increase production eventually there will be return to a(n) _____ profit typically earned by firms.

19. A second strategy for an entrepreneur trying to earn more than a (normal, economic) _____ profit typically earned by firms in pure competition would be to develop a new product that is popular with consumers. If the product is successful, then the firm will be able to earn a(n) _____ profit for a while; but, when other firms develop similar products, then eventually there will be a return to a(n) _____ profit typically earned by firms.

20. The dynamism and change arising from competition and the search for economic profit is often referred to as creative (construction, destruction) _____, where the creative part leads to new products and lower-cost production methods and the _____ part leads to the loss of jobs and bankruptcy of businesses.

■ TRUE–FALSE QUESTIONS

Circle T if the statement is true, F if it is false.

1. In the long run in pure competition, economic profits will attract new firms to enter an industry, while economic losses will cause existing firms to leave an industry. **T F**

2. The long-run equilibrium for firms in pure competition is for marginal revenue to equal marginal cost (MR = MC) and for price to equal the minimum of average total cost. **T F**

3. When there is long-run equilibrium in pure competition, the normal profit is zero for the existing firms. **T F**

4. The existence of economic profits in an industry will attract new firms to enter an industry. **T F**

5. When new firms enter a purely competitive industry it will lead to an increase in market demand. **T F**

6. As new firms enter a purely competitive industry with economic profits, product price for the typical firm will decrease until eventually price equals marginal cost at the minimum of average total cost. **T F**

7. When there are economic losses in a purely competitive industry, some of the existing firms will exit the industry. **T F**

8. When firms in a purely competitive industry are earning profits that are less than normal, the supply of the product will eventually decrease.   **T F**

9. As firms experiencing economic losses exit a purely competitive industry, product price for the typical firm will decrease until eventually price equals marginal cost and the minimum of average total cost.   **T F**

10. In a constant-cost industry in pure competition, an expansion of the industry will increase resource prices.   **T F**

11. The long-run supply curve for a constant-cost industry in pure competition is horizontal.   **T F**

12. In an increasing-cost industry in pure competition, an expansion of the industry will increase resource prices.   **T F**

13. The long-run supply curve for an increasing-cost industry in pure competition is downsloping.   **T F**

14. In a decreasing-cost industry in pure competition, an expansion of the industry will decrease resource prices.   **T F**

15. The long-run supply curve for a decreasing-cost industry in pure competition is vertical.   **T F**

16. Assuming a constant- or increasing-cost industry, the final long-run equilibrium positions of all firms have the same basic efficiency characteristics: $P > MC > ATC$.   **T F**

17. Under conditions of pure competition, firms achieve productive efficiency by producing in the least costly way.   **T F**

18. In the long run, pure competition forces firm to produce at the minimum average total cost of production and to charge a price that is just consistent with the cost.   **T F**

19. In a purely competitive market, product price measures the marginal benefit, or additional satisfaction, that society obtains from producing additional units of the product.   **T F**

20. In pure competition, allocative efficiency is achieved when product price is greater than marginal cost.   **T F**

21. Pure competition minimizes the combined consumer and producer surplus.   **T F**

22. A major attribute of pure competition is the ability to restore productive and allocative efficiency when it is disrupted by changes in the economy.   **T F**

23. The "invisible hand" of the competitive market system organizes the private interests of producers in a way that complements society's interest in the efficient use of scarce resources.   **T F**

24. With pure competition any advantage that innovative firms gain by either lowering production costs or by introducing new products will not persist over time.   **T F**

25. Creative destruction is the concept that the creation of new products and new production methods are beneficial for society, but that it also leads to the destruction of jobs, businesses, and even industries.   **T F**

■ **MULTIPLE-CHOICE QUESTIONS**

Circle the letter that corresponds to the best answer.

1. Pure competition in the long run in an industry is most affected by
(a) the fixed costs of firms
(b) the normal profit of firms
(c) the entry and exit of firms
(d) the identical costs of firms

2. For a purely competitive firm in long-run equilibrium,
(a) MR = MC = minimum ATC
(b) MR = MC = maximum ATC
(c) $P > MR > ATC$
(d) MR > MC

3. Assume that the market for wheat is purely competitive. Currently, firms growing wheat are experiencing economic losses. In the long run, we can expect this market's
(a) supply curve to increase
(b) demand curve to increase
(c) supply curve to decrease
(d) demand curve to decrease

Use the two graphs below to answer questions 4, 5, 6, and 7. Graph A represents a typical firm in a purely competitive industry. Graph B represents the supply and demand conditions in that industry. Assume that the marginal cost curve is an up-sloping curve that intersects ATC at its minimum.

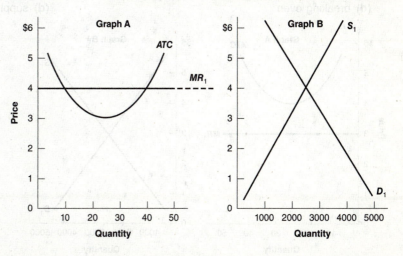

4. If the price of the product in this industry is $4, the typical firm in this industry is
(a) earning a normal profit
(b) earning an economic profit
(c) realizing an economic loss
(d) breaking even

5. Given the economic conditions shown in the graphs, what is most likely to occur in graph B?
(a) Firms will exit the industry and the demand curve will shift to the left.
(b) Firms will enter the industry and the supply curve will shift to the right.
(c) Firms will exit the industry and the supply curve will shift to the right.
(d) Firms will enter the industry and the demand curve will shift to the right.

6. As this industry moves toward long-run equilibrium, the market price will
(a) increase and the marginal revenue for the firm will decrease
(b) decrease and the marginal revenue for the firm will increase
(c) decrease and the marginal revenue for the firm will decrease
(d) increase and the marginal revenue for the firm will increase

7. Long-run equilibrium will be restored in this industry when
(a) product price and marginal revenue fall to $3
(b) product price and marginal revenue fall to $2
(c) product price and marginal revenue rise to $5
(d) product price and marginal revenue remain at $4

Use the two graphs below to answer questions 8, 9, 10, and 11. Graph A represents a typical firm in a purely competitive industry. Graph B represents the supply and demand conditions in that industry. Assume that the marginal cost curve is an up-sloping curve that intersects ATC at its minimum.

8. If the price of the product in this industry is $3, the typical firm in this industry is
(a) earning a normal profit
(b) earning an economic profit
(c) realizing an economic loss
(d) breaking even

9. Given the economic conditions shown in the graphs, what is most likely to occur?
(a) Demand will increase as firms will exit the industry.
(b) Supply will increase as firms enter the industry.
(c) Supply will decrease as firms exit the industry.
(d) Demand will decrease as firms exit the industry.

10. As this industry moves to long-run equilibrium, the market price will
(a) increase and the marginal revenue for the firm will decrease
(b) decrease and the marginal revenue for the firm will increase
(c) decrease and the marginal revenue for the firm will decrease
(d) increase and the marginal revenue for the firm will increase

11. Long-run equilibrium will be restored in this industry when
(a) product price and marginal revenue fall to $2
(b) product price and marginal revenue rise to $5
(c) product price and marginal revenue rise to $4
(d) product price and marginal revenue remain at $3

12. The long-run supply curve under pure competition will be
(a) down-sloping in an increasing-cost industry and up-sloping in a decreasing-cost industry
(b) horizontal in a constant-cost industry and up-sloping in a decreasing-cost industry
(c) horizontal in a constant-cost industry and up-sloping in an increasing-cost industry
(d) up-sloping in an increasing-cost industry and vertical in a constant-cost industry

13. The long-run supply curve in a constant-cost industry will be
(a) perfectly elastic
(b) perfectly inelastic
(c) unit-elastic
(d) income elastic

14. In a decreasing-cost industry, the long-run
(a) demand curve would be perfectly inelastic
(b) demand curve would be perfectly elastic
(c) supply curve would be up-sloping
(d) supply curve would be down-sloping

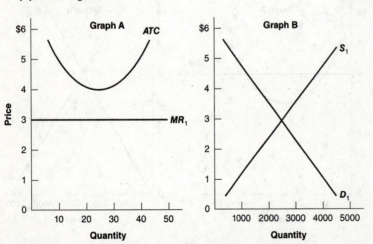

15. Increasing-cost industries find that their costs rise as a consequence of an increased demand for their product because of
(a) the diseconomies of scale
(b) diminishing returns
(c) higher resource prices
(d) a decreased supply of the product

16. When a purely competitive industry is in long-run equilibrium, which statement is true?
(a) Firms in the industry are earning normal profits.
(b) Price and long-run average total cost are not equal to each other.
(c) Marginal cost is at its minimum level.
(d) Marginal cost is equal to total revenue.

17. Which triple identity results in the most efficient use of resources?
(a) $P = MC = $ minimum ATC
(b) $P = AR = MR$
(c) $P = MR = $ minimum MC
(d) $TR = MC = MR$

18. An economy is producing the goods most wanted by society when, for each and every good, its
(a) price and average cost are equal
(b) price and marginal cost are equal
(c) marginal revenue and marginal cost are equal
(d) price and marginal revenue are equal

Answer questions 19, 20, 21, and 22 on the basis of the following supply and demand graph.

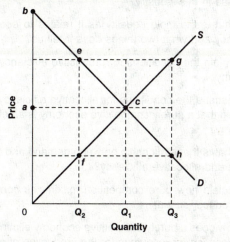

19. The area of consumer surplus would be shown by the area
(a) 0*bc*
(b) 0*ac*
(c) *abc*
(d) *cef*

20. The area of producer surplus would be shown by the area
(a) 0*bc*
(b) 0*ac*
(c) *abc*
(d) *cgh*

21. The area that maximizes the combined consumer surplus and producer surplus would be shown by the area
(a) 0*bc*
(b) 0*ac*

(c) *abc*
(d) *efgh*

22. Allocative efficiency occurs at Q_1 because marginal benefit, reflected in points on the
(a) demand curve equal price as reflected by the points on the supply curve
(b) supply curve equal marginal cost as reflected by the points on the demand curve
(c) demand curve equal marginal cost as reflected by the points on the supply curve
(d) supply curve equal minimum average cost as reflected by the points on the supply curve

23. If there is an increase in demand for a product in a purely competitive industry, it results in a dynamic adjustment in which there is an industry
(a) contraction that will end when the price of the product is greater than its marginal cost
(b) contraction that will end when the price of the product is equal to its marginal cost
(c) expansion that will end when the price of the product is greater than its marginal cost
(d) expansion that will end when the price of the product is equal to its marginal cost

24. The idea of the "invisible hand" operating in the competitive market system means that
(a) there is a unity of private and social interests that promotes efficiency
(b) the industries in this system are described as decreasing-cost industries
(c) there is an overallocation of resources to the production of goods and services
(d) productive efficiency is more important than allocative efficiency

25. The elimination of the market positions of firms and their products by new firms with new products and innovative ways of doing business would be most closely associated with the concept of
(a) consumer surplus
(b) producer surplus
(c) creative destruction
(d) an increasing-cost industry

■ **PROBLEMS**

1. If the average total costs assumed for the individual firm below were long-run average total costs and if the industry were a constant-cost industry,

Output	ATC	MC
1	$400	$100
2	225	50
3	170	60
4	148	80
5	140	110
6	140	140
7	146	180
8	156	230
9	171	290
10	190	360

a. what would be the market price of the product in the long run? $ _____

b. what output would each firm produce when the industry was in long-run equilibrium? _____

c. approximately how many firms would there be in the industry in the long run, given the present demand for the product as shown in the table below?

_____

Quantity demanded	Price	Quantity supplied
400	$360	1000
500	290	900
600	230	800
700	180	700
800	140	600
900	110	500
1000	80	400

d. if the following table were the market demand schedule for the product, how many firms would there be in the long run in the industry? _____

Price	Quantity demanded
$360	500
290	600
230	700
180	800
140	900
110	1000
80	1100

2. On the following graph, draw a long-run supply curve of
   a. a constant-cost industry
   b. an increasing-cost industry
   c. a decreasing-cost industry

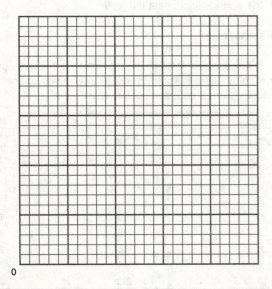

0

SHORT ANSWER AND ESSAY QUESTIONS

1. What are the important distinctions between the short run and the long run and between equilibrium in the short run and in the long run in a competitive industry?

2. When is the purely competitive industry in long-run equilibrium? What forces the purely competitive firm into this position?

3. Assume that a firm is in a purely competitive industry. Assume that the demand for the product increases and it increases the product price. Describe what happens over time to industry supply and product price. What happens to the firm's profit? What will the economic conditions be when long-run equilibrium is restored?

4. Assume that a firm is in a purely competitive industry. Assume that the demand for the product decreases and it decreases the product price. Describe what happens over time to industry supply and product price. What happens to the firm's profits? What will the economic conditions be when long-run equilibrium is restored?

5. What is a constant-cost industry? Explain what happens in this industry when demand increases or decreases.

6. What is an increasing-cost industry? Why will costs increase in this industry?

7. What is a decreasing-cost industry? Why will costs decrease in this industry?

8. What is the triple equality as it relates to economic efficiency and what two things does it tell us?

9. Explain the conditions for productive efficiency in an economy.

10. Describe the conditions for allocative efficiency. Why is it said that a purely competitive economy is an efficient economy?

11. What is the relationship between demand and supply curves and allocative efficiency?

12. Explain how pure competition maximizes consumer and producer surpluses.

13. How does a purely competitive economy eliminate an overallocation for resources for the production of a product and correct for an underallocation?

14. Explain how dynamic adjustments are made in pure competition as a result of changes in demand for a product or the supply of a resource.

15. In what way does an "invisible hand" work to ensure an efficient allocation of society's scare resources?

16. Describe how entrepreneurs affect profits by improving production methods. What happens in the long run to these changes in pure competition?

17. What role does innovation play in fostering competition? Explain what occurs in the long run to new products or innovations that create economic profit.

18. Why is running a company a hard business?

19. Describe the concept of creative destruction. How does it create and how does it destroy?

20. Give examples of creative destruction activity in the past and in recent years.

ANSWERS

Chapter 9 Pure Competition in the Long Run

FILL-IN QUESTIONS

1. long run, fixed, variable
2. *a.* only entry and exits affects long-run adjustments; *b.* firms in the industry have identical costs; *c.* the industry is a constant-cost industry
3. total, seek profit, enter or exit
4. normal, is not
5. economic, increase, decrease
6. marginal, marginal, minimum
7. losses, decrease, increase
8. a constant-, horizontal
9. an increasing-, up-sloping
10. a decreasing-, down-sloping
11. total, minimum
12. marginal, consumers
13. demand, supply
14. maximum, minimum, maximum, minimum, maximum
15. efficiency, increase, increase, decrease
16. maximizes, maximizes
17. is no, is no, normal
18. normal, economic, normal
19. normal, economic, normal
20. destruction, destruction

TRUE–FALSE QUESTIONS

1. T, p. 182	**10.** F, p. 184	**19.** T, p. 188
2. T, p. 182	**11.** T, p. 184	**20.** F, p. 188
3. F, p. 182	**12.** T, p. 185	**21.** F, pp. 188–189
4. T, p. 182	**13.** F, p. 185	**22.** T, p. 189
5. F, pp. 182–183	**14.** T, pp. 185–186	**23.** T, p. 189
6. T, pp. 182–183	**15.** F, pp. 185–186	**24.** T, p. 190
7. T, pp. 183–184	**16.** F, pp. 186–187	**25.** T, pp. 190–191
8. T, p. 183	**17.** T, pp. 186–187	
9. F, pp. 182–183	**18.** T, p. 187	

MULTIPLE-CHOICE QUESTIONS

1. c, p. 182	**10.** d, pp. 183–184	**19.** c, pp. 188–189
2. a, pp. 182, 186	**11.** c, p. 183	**20.** b, pp. 188–189
3. c, pp. 183–184	**12.** c, pp. 184–186	**21.** a, pp. 188–189
4. b, p. 183	**13.** a, p. 184	**22.** c, p. 189
5. b, p. 183	**14.** d, pp. 185–186	**23.** d, p. 189
6. c, p. 183	**15.** c, p. 185	**24.** a, p. 189
7. a, p. 183	**16.** a, p. 182	**25.** c, pp. 190, 192
8. c, pp. 183–184	**17.** a, p. 186	
9. c, pp. 183–184	**18.** b, p. 188	

PROBLEMS

1. *a.* 140; *b.* 6; *c.* 133 = 800 [the total quantity demanded at $140 divided by 6 (the output of each firm)]; *d.* 150 = 900 divided by 6
2. *a.* The curve is a horizontal line (see Figure 9.3 in the text); *b.* the curve slopes upward (see Figure 9.4 in the text); *c.* the curve slopes downward (see Figure 9.5 in the text)

SHORT ANSWER AND ESSAY QUESTIONS

1. pp. 181–182	**8.** p. 186	**15.** p. 189
2. p. 182	**9.** p. 187	**16.** pp. 189–190
3. pp. 182–183	**10.** p. 188	**17.** p. 190
4. pp. 182–183	**11.** p. 188	**18.** p. 190
5. pp. 184–185	**12.** pp. 188–189	**19.** pp. 190, 192
6. pp. 184–185	**13.** pp. 188–189	**20.** pp. 190, 192
7. p. 185	**14.** p. 189	

CHAPTER 10

Pure Monopoly

This chapter looks at the other end of the spectrum and examines pure monopoly, a market structure in which there is a **single seller.** Like pure competition, pure monopoly is rarely found in the U.S. economy, but it is still important. Many government-owned or government-regulated public utilities (electricity, water, natural gas, or cable television) are close to being pure monopolies, and other business firms are near monopolies because they have a large share of a market. Monopolies play a key role in the allocation of resources and the production of goods and services in the economy.

It is possible for a single seller or pure monopolist to dominate an industry if firms are prevented in some way from entering the industry. Factors that restrict firms from entering an industry are referred to as **barriers to entry.** The second section of this chapter is devoted to a description of the more important types of these barriers, such as economies of scale, patents and licenses, control of essential resources, and strategies for product pricing.

The chapter answers certain questions about the pure monopolist, such as what output the firm will produce, what price it will charge, and the amount of profit for the firm. In answering these questions and in comparing pure competition and pure monopoly, note the following:

1. Both the competitive and monopoly firm try to maximize profits by producing the output at which marginal cost and marginal revenue are equal (**MR = MC**).

2. The individual firm in a perfectly competitive industry sees a perfectly price elastic demand for its product at the going market price because it is but one of many firms in the industry, but the monopolist sees a market demand schedule that is less than perfectly price elastic because the **monopolist is the industry.** The purely competitive firm has *only* an output policy and is a price taker, but the monopolist is able to determine the price at which it will sell its product and is a price maker.

3. When demand is perfectly price elastic, price is equal to marginal revenue and is constant, but when demand is less than perfectly price elastic, marginal revenue is less than price and both decrease as the output of the firm increases.

4. Because entry is blocked in the long run, firms cannot enter a monopolistic industry to compete away profits as they can under conditions of pure competition.

This chapter has three other goals that deserve your study time and careful attention. One goal is to evaluate **economic efficiency** under pure monopoly. Here the purely competitive industry that you read about in Chapters 8 and 9 serves as the standard for comparison. You will learn that unlike the purely competitive industry, pure monopoly does not result in allocative efficiency. Although the inefficiencies of monopoly are offset or reduced by economies of scale and technological progress, they are reinforced by the presence of X-inefficiency and rent-seeking behavior.

The second goal is to discuss the possible pricing strategies of the pure monopolist. The monopolist may be able to set multiple prices for the same product even when the price differences are not justified by cost differences, a situation called **price discrimination.** This type of pricing power works only under certain conditions, and when it is effective it results in higher profits for the monopolist and also greater output.

The pricing power and inefficiency of the pure monopoly have made it a target for **regulation.** Therefore, the last section of the chapter explains the economic choices a regulatory agency faces when it must determine the maximum price that a public utility will be allowed to charge for its product. Here you will learn about the **socially optimum price** and the **fair-return price** and their effects on efficiency and profits. You will also discover the difficult economic dilemma regulatory officials face as they decide what prices they should permit a monopolist to charge.

■ **CHECKLIST**

When you have studied this chapter you should be able to

☐ Define pure monopoly based on five characteristics.
☐ Give several examples of monopoly and explain its importance.
☐ List and explain four potential barriers that would prevent or deter the entry of new firms into an industry.
☐ Define a natural monopoly using an average total cost curve.
☐ Compare the demand curve for the pure monopolist with that of the purely competitive firm.
☐ Compute marginal revenue when you are given the demand for the monopolist's product.
☐ Explain the relationship between the price a monopolist charges and the marginal revenue from the sale of an additional unit of the product.
☐ Explain why the monopolist is a price maker.
☐ Use elasticity to explain the region of the demand curve where the monopolist produces.

☐ State the rule that explains what output the monopolist will produce and the price that will be charged.

☐ Determine the profit-maximizing output and price for the pure monopolist when you are given the demand and cost data.

☐ Explain why there is no supply curve for the pure monopolist.

☐ Counter two popular misconceptions about the price charged and the profit target in pure monopoly.

☐ Explain why monopolists can experience losses.

☐ Compare the economic effects of pure monopoly in terms of price, output, efficiency, and income distribution with a purely competitive industry producing the same product.

☐ Discuss the cost complications caused by economies of scale, X-inefficiency, rent-seeking behavior, and technological advance for pure monopoly and a purely competitive industry.

☐ Describe three general policy options for dealing with the economic inefficiency of monopoly.

☐ Define and give examples of price discrimination.

☐ List three conditions that are necessary for price discrimination.

☐ Explain the economic consequences of price discrimination.

☐ Use graphical analysis to identify the socially optimal price and the fair-return price for the regulated monopoly.

☐ Explain the dilemma of regulation based on a graphical analysis of a regulated monopoly.

☐ Discuss the market forces that made De Beers change its monopoly behavior and end its attempts to control the diamond market (*Last Word*).

■ **CHAPTER OUTLINE**

1. *Pure monopoly* is a market structure in which a single firm sells a product for which there are no close substitutes. These characteristics make the monopoly firm a *price maker* rather than a price taker, as was the case for the purely competitive firm. Entry into the industry is blocked, and there can be nonprice competition through advertising to influence the demand for the product.

    a. Examples of monopolies typically include regulated public utilities such as firms providing electricity, natural gas, local telephone service, and cable television, but they can also be unregulated, such as the De Beers diamond syndicate.

    b. The study of monopoly is useful for understanding the economic effects of other market structures—oligopoly and monopolistic competition—where there is some degree of monopoly power.

2. Pure monopoly can exist in the long run only if potential competitors find there are *barriers* that prevent their entry into the industry. There are four major **barriers to entry** that can prevent or severely restrict entry into an industry.

    a. *Economies of scale* can reduce production costs in the long run so that one producer can supply a range of output at a minimum total cost. If other producers try to enter the industry, extensive financing would be

required and they may not be able to produce output at a lower cost than the monopolist. The conditions for a *natural monopoly* arise in the extreme case in which the market demand curve cuts the long-run ATC curve where they are still declining. One firm can supply the market demand at a minimum cost.

    b. Government creates legal restrictions through issuing patents and licenses. *Patents* give the inventor the exclusive right to use or allow others to use the invention. *Licenses* give a firm the exclusive right to provide a good or service.

    c. The ownership or control of essential resources can effectively block entry into an industry.

    d. Pricing and other strategic practices, such as price cuts, advertising campaigns, and producing excess capacity, can deter entry into an industry by making entry very costly for a firm.

3. The *demand curve* of the pure monopolist is down-sloping because the monopolist is the industry. By contrast, the purely competitive firm has a horizontal (perfectly price elastic) demand curve because it is only one of many small firms in an industry. There are several implications of the down-sloping shape of the monopolist's demand curve.

    a. The monopolist can increase sales only by lowering product price; thus price will exceed marginal revenue ($P > $ **MR**) for every unit of output but the first.

    b. The monopolist will have a pricing policy, and is a *price maker;* the purely competitive firm has no price policy and is a price taker.

    c. The monopolist will avoid setting price in the inelastic segment of its demand curve because total revenue will be decreasing and marginal revenue will be negative; price will be set in the *elastic* portion of the demand curve.

4. The *output* and *price determination* of the profit-maximizing pure monopolist entails several considerations.

    a. Monopoly power in the sale of a product does not necessarily affect the prices that the monopolist pays for resources or the costs of production; an assumption is made in this chapter that the monopolist hires resources in a competitive market and uses the same technology as competitive firms.

    b. The monopolist produces that output at which marginal cost and marginal revenue are equal (**MR = MC**) and charges a price at which this profit-maximizing output can be sold.

    c. The monopolist has **no supply curve** because there is no unique relationship between price and quantity supplied; price and quantity supplied will change when demand and marginal revenue change. By contrast, a purely competitive firm has a supply curve that is the portion of the marginal cost curve above average variable cost, and there is a unique relationship between price and quantity supplied.

    d. Two popular misconceptions about monopolists are that they charge as high a price as possible and that they seek maximum profit per unit of output.

    e. The monopolist is **not guaranteed a profit** and can experience losses because of weak demand for a product or high costs of production.

5. Pure monopoly has significant *economic effects* on the economy when compared to outcomes that would be produced in a purely competitive market.

a. The pure monopolist charges a *higher price* and *produces less output* than would be produced by a purely competitive industry. Pure monopoly is **not productively efficient** because price is greater than the minimum of average cost. It is **not allocatively efficient** because price is greater than marginal cost.

b. Monopoly transfers income from consumers to the owners of the monopoly because these consumers pay a higher price for the product than they otherwise would have to pay if the product was produced by a purely competitive firm with a similar cost structure.

c. A pure monopolist in an industry may produce output at a lower or higher average cost than would be the case for a purely competitive industry producing the same product. The costs of production may differ between the two industries for four reasons.

(1) **Economies of scale** in the production of the product allow the pure monopolist to produce it at a lower long-run average cost than a large number of small pure competitors. In the extreme, a firm may be a **natural monopoly** that can supply the market demand at the lowest average cost. There can also be other factors such as **simultaneous consumption** (a product's ability to satisfy a large number of consumers at the same time) and **network effects** (increases in the value of the product for users as the number of users increase) that create extensive economies of scale for firms, especially those firms involved in information technology.

(2) If a pure monopolist is more susceptible to **X-inefficiency** (having an output level that is higher than the lowest possible cost of producing it) than firms in a purely competitive industry, then long-run average costs at every level of output for the monopolist are higher than those purely competitive firms.

(3) **Rent-seeking** expenditures in the form of legal fees, lobbying, and public-relations expenses to obtain or maintain a position as a monopoly add nothing to output, but do increase monopoly costs.

(4) Monopoly is not likely to contribute to technological advance because there is little incentive for the monopolist to produce a more advanced product. The threat of potential competition, however, may stimulate research and more technological advance, but the purpose of this effort is often to restrict or block entry into the industry.

d. Monopoly causes problems for an economy because of higher prices and restricted output. Monopoly, however, is relatively rare. Technological advance and the development of substitute products can also undermine a monopoly. The policy options for dealing with the economic inefficiency of monopoly include the use of antitrust laws and the breakup of firms, the regulation of price, output, and profits of the monopolist, and simply ignoring the monopoly because its position cannot be sustained.

6. To increase profits a pure monopolist may engage in **price discrimination** by charging different prices to different buyers of the same product (when the price differences do not represent differences in the costs of producing the product).

a. To discriminate, the seller must have some monopoly power, be capable of separating buyers into groups with different price elasticities of demand, and be able to prevent the resale of the product from one group to another group.

b. Price discrimination is common in the U.S. economy. Airlines charge different fares to different passengers for the same flight. Movie theaters vary prices for the same product based on time of day or age. Discount coupons allow firms to charge different prices to different customers for the purchase of the same product.

c. Graphical analysis can be used to show price discrimination to different groups of buyers. The monopolist maximizes its total profit by dividing the market in the segmented groups based on the differences in elasticity of demand. It then produces and sells that output in each market where **MR = MC**. It charges a higher price to customers with a less elastic demand and a lower price to customers with a more elastic demand.

7. Monopolies are often **regulated** by government to reduce the misallocation of resources and control prices.

a. One goal of regulation is to get the monopolist to be allocatively efficient. A regulated price determined by the intersection of the marginal cost and demand curve is the **socially optimal price,** or where $P = MC$. This price becomes the marginal revenue for the monopolist and gives the monopolist an incentive to increase output until marginal revenue equals marginal cost.

b. The socially optimal price, however, may force the firm to produce at a loss if the price is set below average total costs. The government regulator, therefore, may set the price at a level determined by the intersection of the average total cost and demand schedules to allow the monopolist a **fair-return price** or where $P = ATC$. In this case the monopolist covers its cost of production and earns a normal profit, but not an economic profit.

c. The dilemma of regulation is that the socially optimal price may cause losses for the monopolist, and a fair-return price may result in a less efficient allocation of resources. Also, fair-return price regulation can be complex to conduct in the real world.

8. (*Last Word*). The price and output decisions of the original De Beers firm fit the monopoly model. It controlled a large supply of diamonds and was able to sell a limited quantity to yield price that was in excess of production costs, and thus obtain monopoly profits. Several factors undercut the monopoly power of De Beers. New discoveries increased supply and previous agreements to sell diamonds exclusively to De Beers were terminated. The firm could no longer control price by manipulating supply and placed more emphasis on increasing demand to maintain price.

■ HINTS AND TIPS

1. Make sure you understand **how pure monopoly differs from pure competition.** Here are key distinctions: (a) The monopolist's demand curve is down-sloping, not horizontal as in pure competition; (b) the monopolist's marginal revenue is less than price (or average revenue) for each level of output except the first, whereas in pure competition marginal revenue equals price; (c) the monopoly firm is a price maker, not a price taker as in pure competition; (d) *the firm is the industry* in monopoly, but not in pure competition; (e) there is the potential for long-run economic profits in pure monopoly, but purely competitive firms will only break even in the long run; and (f) there is no supply curve for a pure monopoly, but there is one for the purely competitive firm.

2. A key similarity between a profit-maximizing pure monopolist and a purely competitive firm is that both types of firms will produce up to that output level at which marginal revenue equals marginal cost (**MR = MC**).

3. Figure 10.3 helps explain why the profit-maximizing monopolist will always want to select some price and quantity combination in the **elastic** and not in the **inelastic** portion of the demand curve. In the inelastic portion, total revenue declines and marginal revenue is negative.

4. Drawing the marginal revenue curve for a monopolist with a linear demand curve is easy if you remember that the marginal revenue curve will always be a straight line that intersects the quantity axis at half of the level of output as the demand curve. (See Figure 10.3.)

5. Spend extra time studying Figure 10.8 and reading the related discussion. It will help you see how **price discrimination** results in more profits, a greater output, and a higher price for some consumers and lower prices for other consumers.

■ IMPORTANT TERMS

pure monopoly	rent-seeking behavior
barriers to entry	price discrimination
simultaneous consumption	socially optimal price
network effects	fair-return price
X-inefficiency	

SELF-TEST

■ FILL-IN QUESTIONS

1. Pure monopoly is an industry in which a single firm is the sole producer of a product for which there are no close (substitutes, complements) _____ and into which entry in the long run is effectively (open, blocked) _____.

2. The closest example of pure monopoly would be government-regulated (nonprofit organizations, public utilities) _____ that provide water, electricity, or natural gas. There are also "near monopolies," such as private businesses that might account for (40, 80) _____% of a particular market, or businesses in a geographic region that are the (multiple, sole) _____ suppliers of a good or service.

3. If there are substantial economies of scale in the production of a product, a small-scale firm will find it difficult to enter into and survive in an industry because its average costs will be (greater, less) _____ than those of established firms, and a firm will find it (easy, difficult) _____ to start out on a large scale because it will be nearly impossible to acquire the needed financing.

4. Legal barriers to entry by government include granting an inventor the exclusive right to produce a product for 20 years, or a (license, patent) _____, and limiting entry into an industry or occupation through its issuing of a _____.

5. Other barriers to entry include the ownership of essential (markets, resources) _____ and strategic changes in product (price, regulation) _____.

6. The demand schedule confronting the pure monopolist is (perfectly elastic, down-sloping) _____. This means that marginal revenue is (greater, less) _____ than average revenue (or price) and that both marginal revenue and average revenue (increase, decrease) _____ as output increases.

7. When demand is price elastic, a decrease in price will (increase, decrease) _____ total revenue, but when demand is price inelastic, a decrease in price will _____ total revenue. The demand curve for the purely competitive firm is (horizontal, down-sloping) _____, but it is _____ for the monopolist. The profit-maximizing monopolist will want to set price in the price (elastic, inelastic) _____ portion of its demand curve.

8. The supply curve for a purely competitive firm is the portion of the (average variable cost, marginal cost) _____ curve that lies above the _____ curve. The supply curve for the monopolist (is the same, does not exist) _____.

9. When the economic profit of a monopolist is at a maximum, (marginal, average) _____ revenue equals _____ cost and price is (greater, less) _____ than marginal cost.

10. Two common misconceptions about pure monopoly are that it charges the (lowest, highest) _____ price possible and seeks the maximum (normal, per-unit) _____ profit.

11. The pure monopolist (is, is not) _____ guaranteed an economic profit; in fact, the pure monopolist can experience economic losses in the (short run, long run) _____ because of (strong, weak) _____ demand for the monopoly product.

12. The monopolist will typically charge a (lower, higher) _____ price and produce (less, more) _____ output and is (less, more) _____ efficient than if the product was produced in a purely competitive industry.

  a. The monopolist is inefficient *productively* because the average (variable, total) _____ cost of producing a product is not at a (maximum, minimum) _____.

  b. It is inefficient *allocatively* because (marginal revenue, price) _____ is not equal to (marginal, total) _____ cost.

  c. A monopoly will charge a (lower, higher) _____ price than would a purely competitive firm with same costs, and as a result consumers pay a _____ price and this income gets transferred as revenue to the owners of the monopoly.

13. Resources can be said to be more efficiently allocated by pure competition than by pure monopoly only if the purely competitive firms and the monopoly have the same (costs, revenues) _____, and they will not be the same if the monopolist

  a. by virtue of being a large firm enjoys (economies, diseconomies) _____ of scale not available to a pure competitor;

  b. is more susceptible to X-(efficiency, inefficiency) _____ than pure competitors;

  c. may need to make (liability, rent-seeking) _____ expenditures to obtain or maintain monopoly privileges granted by government; and

  d. reduces costs through adopting (higher prices, new technology) _____.

14. The incidence of pure monopoly is relatively (rare, common) _____ because eventually new developments in technology (strengthen, weaken) _____ monopoly power or (substitute, complementary) _____ products are developed.

15. Three general policy options to reduce the economic (losses, inefficiency) _____ of a monopoly are to file charges against it through (liability, antitrust) _____ laws, have government regulate it if it is a (conglomerate, natural monopoly) _____, or ignore it if it is unsustainable.

16. Price discrimination occurs whenever a product is sold at different (markets, prices) _____, and these differences are not equal to the differences in the (revenue from, cost of) _____ producing the product.

17. Price discrimination is possible when the following three conditions exist:

  a. _____

  b. _____

  c. _____

18. One economic consequence of a monopolist's use of price discrimination is (an increase, a decrease) _____ in profits.

19. If the monopolist were regulated and a socially optimal price for the product were sought, the price would be set equal to (marginal, average total) _____ cost. Such a legal price would achieve (productive, allocative) _____ efficiency but might result in losses for the monopolist.

20. If a regulated monopolist is allowed to earn a fair return, the price the government regulators let the monopolist charge for the price would be set equal to (marginal, average total) _____ cost. Such a regulated price falls short of (allocative, productive) _____ efficiency, but it is an improvement over the unregulated case in terms of price and output.

■ **TRUE–FALSE QUESTIONS**

Circle T if the statement is true, F if it is false.

1. The pure monopolist produces a product for which there are no close substitutes. **T   F**

2. The weaker the barriers to entry into an industry, the more competition there will be in the industry, other things equal. **T   F**

3. In pure monopoly, there are strong barriers to entry. **T   F**

4. A monopolist may create an entry barrier by price cutting or substantially increasing the advertising of its product. **T   F**

5. The monopolist can increase the sales of its product if it charges a lower price. **T   F**

6. As a monopolist increases its output, it finds that its total revenue at first decreases, and that after some output level is reached, its total revenue begins to increase. **T   F**

7. A purely competitive firm is a price taker but a monopolist is a price maker. **T F**

8. A monopolist will avoid setting a price in the *inelastic* segment of the demand curve and prefer to set the price in the e*lastic* segment. **T F**

9. The monopolist determines the profit-maximizing output by producing that output at which marginal cost and marginal revenue are equal and sets the product price equal to marginal cost and marginal revenue at that output. **T F**

10. The supply curve for a monopolist is the up-sloping portion of the marginal cost curve that lies above the average variable cost. **T F**

11. A monopolist will charge the highest price it can get. **T F**

12. A monopolist seeks maximum total profits, not maximum unit profits. **T F**

13. Pure monopoly guarantees economic profits. **T F**

14. Resources are misallocated by monopoly because price is not equal to marginal cost. **T F**

15. One of the economic effects of monopoly is the transfer of income from consumers to the owners of the monopoly. **T F**

16. When there are substantial economies of scale in the production of a product, the monopolist may charge a price that is lower than the price that would prevail if the product were produced by a purely competitive industry. **T F**

17. The purely competitive firm is more likely to be affected by X-inefficiency than a monopolist. **T F**

18. Rent-seeking expenditures that monopolists make to obtain or maintain monopoly privilege have no effect on the firm's costs. **T F**

19. The general view of economists is that a pure monopoly is efficient because it has strong incentives to be technologically progressive. **T F**

20. One general policy option for a monopoly that creates substantial economic inefficiency and is long lasting is to directly regulate its prices and operation. **T F**

21. Price discrimination occurs when a given product is sold at more than one price and these price differences are not justified by cost differences. **T F**

22. A discriminating monopolist who can segment its market based on elasticity of demand will charge a higher price to the customers with a less elastic demand and a lower price to customers with a more elastic demand. **T F**

23. The regulated utility is likely to make an economic profit when price is set to achieve the most efficient allocation of resources ($P = $ **MC**). **T F**

24. A fair-return price for a regulated utility would have price set to equal average total cost. **T F**

25. The dilemma of monopoly regulation is that the production by a monopolist of an output that causes no misallocation of resources may force the monopolist to suffer an economic loss. **T F**

■ **MULTIPLE-CHOICE QUESTIONS**

Circle the letter that corresponds to the best answer.

1. Which would be defining characteristics of pure monopoly?
   (a) The firm does no advertising and it sells a standardized product.
   (b) No close substitutes for the product exist and there is one seller.
   (c) The firm can easily enter into or exit from the industry and profits are guaranteed.
   (d) The firm holds a patent and is technologically progressive.

2. A barrier to entry that significantly contributes to the establishment of a monopoly would be
   (a) economies of scale
   (b) price-taking behavior
   (c) technological progress
   (d) X-inefficiency

3. The demand curve for the pure monopolist is
   (a) perfectly price elastic
   (b) perfectly price inelastic
   (c) down-sloping
   (d) up-sloping

4. Which is true with respect to the demand data confronting a monopolist?
   (a) Marginal revenue is greater than average revenue.
   (b) Marginal revenue decreases as average revenue decreases.
   (c) Demand is perfectly price elastic.
   (d) Average revenue (or price) increases as the output of the firm increases.

5. When the monopolist is maximizing total profits or minimizing losses,
   (a) total revenue is greater than total cost
   (b) average revenue is greater than average total cost
   (c) average revenue is greater than marginal cost
   (d) average total cost is less than marginal cost

6. At which combination of price and marginal revenue is the price elasticity of demand less than 1?
   (a) Price equals $102, marginal revenue equals $42.
   (b) Price equals $92, marginal revenue equals $22.
   (c) Price equals $82, marginal revenue equals $2.
   (d) Price equals $72, marginal revenue equals −$18.

7. The region of demand in which the monopolist will choose a price-output combination will be the
   (a) elastic one because total revenue will increase as price declines and output increases
   (b) inelastic one because total revenue will increase as price declines and output increases

(c) elastic one because total revenue will decrease as price declines and output increases

(d) inelastic one because total revenue will decrease as price declines and output increases

8. At present output a monopolist determines that its marginal cost is $18 and its marginal revenue is $21. The monopolist will maximize profits or minimize losses by

(a) increasing price while keeping output constant

(b) decreasing price and increasing output

(c) decreasing both price and output

(d) increasing both price and output

Answer Questions 9, 10, and 11 based on the demand and cost data for a pure monopolist given in the following table.

Quantity demanded	Price	Total cost
0	$700	$ 300
1	650	400
2	600	450
3	550	510
4	500	590
5	450	700
6	400	840
7	350	1020
8	300	1250
9	250	1540
10	200	1900

9. The profit-maximizing output and price for this monopolist would be

(a) 5 units and $450

(b) 6 units and $400

(c) 7 units and $350

(d) 8 units and $300

10. The profit-maximizing price for this monopolist would be

(a) $300 price

(b) $350 price

(c) $400 price

(d) $450 price

11. At the profit-maximizing price and output, the amount of profit for the monopolist would be

(a) $1410

(b) $1430

(c) $1550

(d) $1560

12. The supply curve for a pure monopolist

(a) is the portion of the marginal cost curve that lies above the average variable cost curve

(b) is perfectly price elastic at the market price

(c) is up-sloping

(d) does not exist

13. The analysis of monopoly indicates that the monopolist

(a) will charge the highest price it can get

(b) will seek to maximize total profits

(c) is guaranteed an economic profit

(d) is only interested in normal profit

14. When compared with the purely competitive industry with identical costs of production, a monopolist will charge a

(a) higher price and produce more output

(b) lower price and produce more output

(c) lower price and produce less output

(d) higher price and produce less output

15. At an equilibrium level of output, a monopolist is *not* productively efficient because

(a) the average total cost of producing the product is not at a minimum

(b) the marginal cost of producing the last unit is equal to its price

(c) it is earning a profit

(d) average revenue is less than the cost of producing an extra unit of output

16. A product's ability to satisfy a large number of consumers at the same time is called

(a) network effects

(b) X-inefficiency

(c) economies of scale

(d) simultaneous consumption

17. Which will tend to increase the inefficiencies of the monopoly producer?

(a) price-taking behavior

(b) rent-seeking behavior

(c) economies of scale

(d) technological progress

18. Which is one of the conditions that must be met before a seller finds that price discrimination is workable?

(a) The demand for the product is perfectly elastic.

(b) The seller must be able to segment the market.

(c) The buyer must be able to resell the product.

(d) The product must be a service.

19. A monopolist can segment two groups of buyers of its product based on elasticity of demand. Assume that ATC remains constant. The monopolist will maximize profit by charging

(a) the highest price to all customers

(b) the lowest price to all customers

(c) a higher price to customers with an elastic demand and a lower price to customers with an inelastic demand

(d) a lower price to customers with an elastic demand and a higher price to customers with an inelastic demand

Answer Questions 20, 21, and 22 based on the demand and cost data for a pure monopolist given in the following table.

Output	Price	Total cost
0	$1000	$ 500
1	600	520
2	500	580
3	400	700
4	300	1000
5	200	1500

20. The profit-maximizing output and price for this monopolist would be
(a) 1 and $100
(b) 2 and $200
(c) 3 and $400
(d) 4 and $300

21. At the profit-maximizing price and output, the amount of profit for the monopolist would be
(a) $200
(b) $340
(c) $420
(d) $500

22. If the monopolist were forced to produce the socially optimal output by the imposition of a government-set price, the regulated price would have to be
(a) $200
(b) $300
(c) $400
(d) $500

23. A monopolist who is limited by the imposition of a government-set or regulated price to a fair return would sell the product at a price equal to
(a) average total cost
(b) average variable cost
(c) marginal cost
(d) average fixed cost

Questions 24 and 25 are based on the following graph.

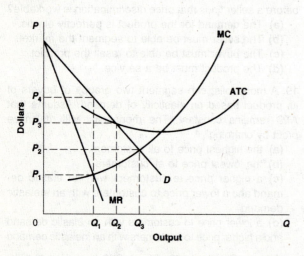

24. The price and output combination for the unregulated profit-maximizing monopoly compared with the socially optimal price and output combination for the regulated monopoly would be, respectively,
(a) P_4 and Q_1 versus P_3 and Q_2
(b) P_4 and Q_1 versus P_2 and Q_3
(c) P_3 and Q_2 versus P_4 and Q_1
(d) P_2 and Q_3 versus P_3 and Q_2

25. The dilemma of regulation that compares the fair-return price and output with the socially optimal price and output would be, respectively,

(a) P_4 and Q_1 versus P_3 and Q_2
(b) P_4 and Q_1 versus P_2 and Q_3
(c) P_3 and Q_2 versus P_4 and Q_1
(d) P_2 and Q_3 versus P_3 and Q_2

■ **PROBLEMS**

1. The demand schedule for the product produced by a monopolist is given in the following table.

Quantity demanded	Price	Total revenue	Marginal revenue	Price elasticity
0	$700	$____		
1	650	____	$____	____
2	600	____	____	____
3	550	____	____	____
4	500	____	____	____
5	450	____	____	____
6	400	____	____	____
7	350	____	____	____
8	300	____	____	____
9	250	____	____	____
10	200	____	____	____
11	150	____	____	____
12	100	____	____	____
13	50	____	____	____
14	0	____	____	____

a. Complete the table by computing total revenue, marginal revenue, and the price elasticity of demand (use midpoints formula).
b. The relationships in the table indicate that
(1) total revenue rises from $0 to a maximum of

$_____ as price falls from $700 to $_____, and as price falls to $0, total revenue falls from its maximum to $_____;
(2) the relationship between price and total revenue suggests that demand is price (elastic, inelastic)

_____ when quantity demanded is between 0 and 7 units of output, but that demand is price (elastic,

inelastic) _____ when quantity demanded is between 8 units and 14 units;
(3) when demand is price elastic and total revenue rises from $0 to a maximum, marginal revenue is

(negative, positive) _____, but when demand is price inelastic and total revenue falls from its

maximum, marginal revenue is _____.
c. Use the data in the previous table and the following graph to plot and graph the demand curve and the marginal revenue curve for the monopolist. Indicate the portion of the demand curve that is price elastic and the portion that is price inelastic.

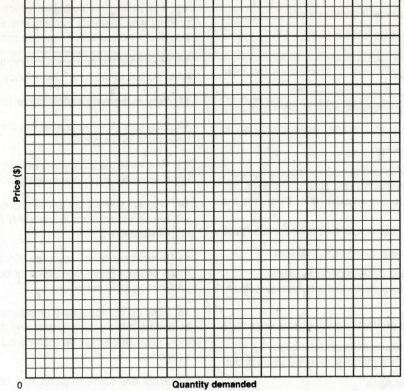

Price ($)

0   Quantity demanded

2. The following table shows demand and cost data for a pure monopolist.

Quantity demanded	Price	Total revenue	Marginal revenue	Total cost	Marginal cost
0	$17	$_____		$10	
1	16	_____	$_____	18	$_____
2	15	_____	_____	23	_____
3	14	_____	_____	25	_____
4	13	_____	_____	27	_____
5	12	_____	_____	28	_____
6	11	_____	_____	32	_____
7	10	_____	_____	40	_____
8	9	_____	_____	50	_____
9	8	_____	_____	64	_____
10	7	_____	_____	80	_____

a. Complete the table by filling in the columns for total revenue, marginal revenue, and marginal cost.
b. Answer the next three questions using the data you calculated in the table.
(1) What output will the monopolist produce?

_____

(2) What price will the monopolist charge?

_____

(3) What total profit will the monopolist receive at the profit-maximizing level of output? _____

3. In the following table are cost and demand data for a pure monopolist.

Quantity demanded	Price	Marginal revenue	Average cost	Marginal cost
0	$17.50			
1	16.00	$16.00	$24.00	$24.00
2	14.50	13.00	15.00	6.00
3	13.00	10.00	11.67	5.00
4	11.50	7.00	10.50	7.00
5	10.00	4.00	10.00	8.00
6	8.50	1.00	9.75	8.50
7	7.00	−2.00	9.64	9.00
8	5.50	−5.00	9.34	9.25
9	4.00	−8.00	9.36	9.50

a. An unregulated monopolist would produce _____ units of this product, sell it at a price of $ _____, and receive a total profit of $_____.
b. If this monopolist were regulated and the maximum price it could charge were set equal to marginal cost, it would produce _____ units of a product, sell it at a price of $ _____, and receive a total profit of $_____. Such regulation would either _____ the firm or require that the regulating (bankrupt, subsidize) government _____ the firm.

c. If the monopolist were regulated and allowed to charge a fair-return price, it would produce _____ units of product, charge a price of $_____, and receive a profit of $_____.

d. From which situation—*a*, *b*, or *c*—does the most efficient allocation of resources result? _____ From which situation does the least efficient allocation result? _____ In practice, government would probably select situation _____.

4. Identify whether the following long-run conditions apply to a firm under pure monopoly (**M**), pure competition (**C**), or both. Put the appropriate letter(s) (**M** or **C**) next to the condition.

a. There is the potential for long-run profits because price is greater than or equal to average total cost. _____

b. The firm's demand curve is perfectly elastic. _____

c. The firm maximizes profits at the output level where MC = MR. _____

d. The firm exhibits productive efficiency because price is equal to the minimum average total cost. _____

e. Price is greater than marginal revenue for each output level except the first. _____

f. There is an optimal allocation of resources because price is equal to marginal cost. _____

■ **SHORT ANSWER AND ESSAY QUESTIONS**

1. What is pure monopoly? Define its characteristics.

2. Give examples of monopoly. How might a professional sports team be considered a monopoly when there are other such teams in the nation?

3. Why are the economies of scale a barrier to entry?

4. Why are most natural monopolies also public utilities? What does government hope to achieve by granting exclusive franchises to and regulating such natural monopolies?

5. How do patents and licenses create barriers to entry? Cite examples.

6. How can the monopolist use changes in price and other strategic actions to maintain a monopoly position?

7. Compare the pure monopolist and the individual pure competitor with respect to: (a) the demand schedule; (b) the marginal revenue schedule; (c) the relationship between marginal revenue and average revenue; (d) price policy, and (e) the ability to administer (or set) price.

8. Explain why marginal revenue is always less than average revenue (price) when demand is less than perfectly elastic.

9. Suppose a pure monopolist discovered it was producing and selling an output at which the demand for its product was inelastic. Explain why a decrease in its output would increase its economic profits.

10. How does the profit-maximizing monopolist determine what output to produce? What price will it charge?

11. Why is there no supply curve for a monopoly?

12. Why does the monopolist not charge the highest possible price for its product?

13. Why does the monopolist not set the price for its product in such a way that average profit is a maximum?

14. Why are some monopolies unprofitable? Explain what will happen to the firm in the short run and the long run in this situation.

15. In what sense are resource allocation and production more efficient under conditions of pure competition than under monopoly conditions?

16. How do monopolies allegedly affect the distribution of income in the economy and why do monopolies seemingly have this effect on income distribution in the U.S. economy?

17. What are some reasons why costs might differ between a monopoly and purely competitive firms operating in the same industry? Give at least four possible reasons.

18. Explain how economies of scale offset some of the economic inefficiencies of a monopoly. Evaluate the importance of this factor in reducing a monopolist's cost.

19. What is X-inefficiency? How does it affect the cost of production for the monopolist?

20. A monopolist will often engage in rent-seeking behavior. Explain what this means and how it changes a monopolist's cost.

21. Evaluate this statement from an economic perspective: "A pure monopoly has great incentive to discover and use new technology."

22. What is meant by price discrimination? Define it. What conditions must be met before it is workable?

23. Explain how a monopolist who can segment its market based on elasticity determines the price to charge for each unit of the product sold (or to charge each group of buyers).

24. How does price discrimination affect the profits and the output of the monopolist? How does it affect consumers?

25. Explain what public-utility regulatory agencies attempt to do to eliminate the misallocation of resources that results from monopoly. Describe the dilemma of regulation for these agencies and explain why a fair-return policy only reduces but does not eliminate misallocation.

ANSWERS

Chapter 10 Pure Monopoly

FILL-IN QUESTIONS

1. substitutes, blocked
2. public utilities, 80, sole
3. greater, difficult
4. patent, license
5. resources, price
6. down-sloping, less, decrease
7. increase, decrease, horizontal, down-sloping, elastic
8. marginal cost, average variable cost, does not exist
9. marginal, marginal, greater
10. highest, per-unit
11. is not, short run, weak
12. higher, less, less; *a.* total, minimum; *b.* price, marginal; *c.* higher, higher
13. costs; *a.* economies; *b.* inefficiency; *c.* rent-seeking; *d.* new technology
14. rare, weaken, substitute
15. inefficiency, antitrust, natural monopoly
16. prices, cost of
17. *a.* the seller has some monopoly power; *b.* the seller is able to separate buyers into groups that have different elasticities of demand for the product; *c.* the original buyers cannot resell the product
18. an increase
19. marginal, allocative
20. average total, allocative

TRUE–FALSE QUESTIONS

1. T, p.195
2. T, p. 195
3. T, p. 195
4. T, pp. 196–197
5. T, pp. 197–198
6. F, pp. 198–199
7. T, pp. 199–200
8. T, p. 200
9. F, pp. 200–201
10. F, pp. 201–202
11. F, p. 202
12. T, p. 202
13. F, pp. 202–203
14. T, pp. 203–204
15. T, p. 204
16. T, p. 205
17. F, p. 205
18. F, pp. 205–206
19. F, p. 206
20. T, pp. 206–207
21. T, pp. 207–208
22. T, pp. 207–208
23. F, pp. 209–210
24. T, pp. 210–211
25. T, p. 211

MULTIPLE-CHOICE QUESTIONS

1. b, p. 195
2. a, p. 196
3. c, pp. 197–198
4. b, pp. 198–199
5. c, pp. 198–199
6. d, pp. 198–199
7. a, p. 200
8. b, pp. 200–201
9. b, pp. 200–201
10. c, pp. 200–201
11. d, pp. 200–201
12. d, pp. 201–202
13. b, p. 202
14. d, pp. 203–204
15. a, pp. 203–204
16. d, p. 205
17. b, pp. 205–206
18. b, pp. 207–208
19. d, pp. 208–209
20. c, pp. 203–204
21. d, pp. 203–204
22. b, p. 210
23. a, pp. 210–211
24. b, pp. 202–203, 210
25. d, p. 211

PROBLEMS

1. *a.* Total revenue: $0, 650, 1200, 1650, 2000, 2250, 2400, 2450, 2400, 2250, 2000, 1650, 1200, 650, 0; Marginal revenue: $650, 550, 450, 350, 250, 150, 50, −50, −150, −250, −350, −450, −550, −650; Price elasticity: 27, 8.33, 4.60, 3.00, 2.11, 1.55, 1.15, .87, .65, .47, .33, .22, .12, .04; *b.* (1) $2450, $350, 0, (2) elastic, inelastic, (3) positive, negative; *c.* see Figure 10.3a in the text as an example
2. *a.* Total revenue: $0, 16, 30, 42, 52, 60, 66, 70, 72, 72, 70; Marginal revenue: $16, 14, 12, 10, 8, 6, 4, 2, 0, −2; Marginal cost: $8, 5, 2, 2, 1, 4, 8, 10, 14, 16; *b.* (1) 6, (2) $11, (3) $34 (TR of $66 minus TC of $32)
3. *a.* 4, 11.50, 4.00; *b.* 6, 8.50, −7.50, bankrupt, subsidize; *c.* 5, 10.00, zero; *d.* b, a, c
4. *a.* M; *b.* C; *c.* C, M; *d.* C; *e.* M; *f.* C

SHORT ANSWER AND ESSAY QUESTIONS

1. p. 195
2. p. 195
3. p. 196
4. p. 197
5. pp. 196–197
6. p. 197
7. pp. 197–200
8. pp. 198–199
9. p. 200
10. pp. 200–201
11. pp. 201–202
12. p. 202
13. p. 202
14. pp. 202–203
15. pp. 203–204
16. p. 204
17. pp. 204–206
18. p. 205
19. p. 205
20. pp. 205–206
21. p. 206
22. pp. 207–208
23. p. 207
24. pp. 208–209
25. pp. 209–211

Monopolistic Competition and Oligopoly

This chapter examines two market structures, monopolistic competition and oligopoly, that fall between the extremes of pure competition and pure monopoly. Both structures are important because they offer descriptions of firms and industries typically found in the U.S. economy.

Monopolistically competitive firms are prevalent because most retail establishments, such as clothing stores and restaurants, fall into the monopolistically competitive category. In such industries, there are a relatively large number of firms, so no one has a large market share, they sell differentiated products, and each has limited pricing power.

Economists use **four-firm concentration ratios** and the **Herfindahl index** to measure the degree of firm dominance of an industry and to determine whether an industry is monopolistically competitive or oligopolistic.

The first part of the chapter focuses on the **demand curve** for the monopolistically competitive firm. This demand curve differs from those found in pure competition and pure monopoly. As the individual firm changes the character of its product, or changes product promotion, both the costs of the firm and the demand for its product will change.

The **price–output** analysis of the monopolistic competitor is relatively simple. In the short run, this analysis is identical with the analysis of the price–output decision of a pure monopolist. Only in the long run does the competitive element make itself apparent: The entry of firms forces the price a firm charges to fall. This price, however, is not equal either to minimum average cost or to marginal cost; consequently, monopolistic competition can be said to be less efficient than pure competition.

This chapter also discusses **product variety** under monopolistic competition. A part of the competitive effort of individual firms is devoted to product differentiation, product development, and advertising. Each firm has three things to manipulate—price, product, and advertising—in maximizing profits. Although monopolistic competition has been characterized as inefficient, some of the positive benefits of product variety may offset some of the inefficiencies of this market structure.

The concept of **oligopoly** is fairly easy to grasp: a few firms that are mutually interdependent dominate the market for a product. The underlying causes of oligopoly are economies of scales and barriers to entry. More difficult to grasp is oligopoly behavior. **Game theory** helps explain what is meant by mutual interdependence and why it exists in an oligopoly. It also explains why specific conclusions cannot be drawn about the price and output decisions of individual firms. Oligopolists are loath to engage in price competition because of **mutual interdependence,** and frequently resort to **collusion** to set prices and sometimes use nonprice competition to determine market share. Collusion does not give firms complete protection from competition because there are incentives to cheat on agreements.

There is no standard model of oligopoly because of the diversity of markets and the uncertainty caused by mutual interdependence among firms. **Three oligopoly models,** however, cover the range of most market situations. The **kinked-demand curve** explains why, in the absence of collusion, oligopolists will not raise or lower their prices even when their costs change. This model does not explain what price oligopolists will set; it only explains why prices will be relatively inflexible.

The second model examines how oligopolists resort to **collusion** to set price. The collusion can be **overt,** as in a cartel agreement, or the collusion can be **covert,** as in a secret agreement. The OPEC oil cartel is a classic example of covert collusion. Obstacles, such as cheating on price, make collusive agreements difficult to establish and maintain.

The third model of oligopoly is **price leadership.** In some industries a dominant firm serves as the price leader for other firms. There is no overt collusion, only unwritten, informal (tacit) understandings about price and competition among firms. This model explains why there are infrequent price changes, why the lead firm makes price and output announcements for other firms to follow, and why low pricing is used to prevent new entry. Such covert collusion, however, can be undermined by price wars.

The next-to-last section of the chapter looks at **advertising** in oligopoly. Product development and advertising are often the means of competition in oligopoly. Drawing conclusions about the effects of advertising, however, is difficult. Reasonable arguments can be made that advertising is both beneficial and costly for consumers and about whether advertising helps or hurts economic efficiency.

Compared with pure competition, oligopoly does not result in allocative or productive efficiency. Nevertheless, the qualifications noted at the end of the chapter may offset some of oligopoly's shortcomings.

■ CHECKLIST

When you have studied this chapter you should be able to

☐ Describe monopolistic competition in terms of the number of sellers, type of product, entry and exit conditions, and advertising.

☐ Cite three consequences from having relatively large numbers of sellers in monopolistic competition.

☐ Describe five aspects of differentiated products in monopolistic competition.

☐ Describe the entry and exit conditions in monopolistic competition.

☐ State the role of advertising and nonprice competition in monopolistic competition.

☐ Define four-firm concentration ratio and use it to describe whether industries are monopolistically competitive or oligopolistic.

☐ Define the Herfindahl index and use it to assess influence of dominant firms in different types of industries.

☐ Compare the firm's demand curve under monopolistic competition with firms' demand curves in pure competition and pure monopoly.

☐ Determine the output of and the price charged by a monopolistic competitor in the short run when given cost and demand data.

☐ Explain why the price charged by a monopolistic competitor will in the long run tend to equal average cost and result in only a normal profit.

☐ Cite two real-world complications that may affect the outcome for monopolistically competitive firms in the long run.

☐ Show graphically how the typical firm in monopolistic competition achieves neither productive nor allocative efficiency and how excess capacity occurs.

☐ Discuss the effects of product variety in monopolistic competition.

☐ Explain why monopolistic competition is more complex in practice.

☐ Define oligopoly in terms of the number of producers, type of product, control over price, and interdependence.

☐ Explain how entry barriers and mergers contribute to the existence of oligopolies.

☐ Use game theory to explain three characteristics of oligopoly behavior.

☐ Cite two reasons why there is no standard model of oligopoly.

☐ Use the kinked-demand theory to explain the tendency for prices to be inflexible in a noncollusive model oligopoly.

☐ Describe the price and output conditions for a cartel or collusive pricing model of oligopoly.

☐ Give real examples of overt and covert collusion.

☐ State six obstacles to collusion.

☐ Describe the price leadership model of oligopoly and its outcomes.

☐ Explain why advertising is often heavily used in oligopoly.

☐ Cite the potential positive and negative effects of advertising.

☐ Compare economic efficiency in oligopoly to other market structures.

☐ Describe the major demand and supply factors over the years that turned the beer industry into an oligopoly (*Last Word*).

■ **CHAPTER OUTLINE**

1. *Monopolistic competition* has several defining characteristics.

   a. The *relatively large number of sellers* means that each has a small market share, there is no collusion,

and firms take actions that are independent of each other.

   b. Monopolistic competition exhibits *product differentiation.* This differentiation occurs through differences in attributes or features of products; services to customers; location and accessibility; brand names and packaging; and some control over price.

   c. *Entry* into the industry or *exit* is relatively easy.

   d. There is *nonprice competition* in the form of product differentiation and advertising.

   e. Monopolistically competitive firms are common, and examples include asphalt paving, quick printing, saw mills, retail bakeries, clothing stores, restaurants, and grocery stores (see Table 11.1). (An explanation of how all industries are classified based on market type or market power is provided in section 5g of this chapter outline.)

2. Given the products produced in a monopolistically competitive industry and the amounts of promotional activity, it is possible to analyze the *price and output decisions* of a firm.

   a. The *demand curve* confronting each firm will be highly but not perfectly price elastic because each firm has many competitors who produce close but not perfect substitutes for the product it produces.

   (1) Comparing the demand curve for the monopolistic competitor to other market structures suggests that it is not perfectly elastic, as is the case with the pure competitor, but it is also more elastic than the demand curve of the pure monopolist.

   (2) The degree of elasticity, however, for each monopolistic competitor will depend on the number of rivals and the extent of product differentiation.

   b. In the *short run* the individual firm will produce the output at which marginal cost and marginal revenue are equal and charge the price at which the output can be sold; either economic profits or losses may result in the short run.

   c. In the *long run* the entry and exodus of firms will tend to change the demand for the product of the individual firm in such a way that economic profits are eliminated and there are only normal profits. (Price and average costs are made equal to each other.)

3. Monopolistic competition among firms producing a given product and engaged in a given amount of promotional activity results in *less economic efficiency and more excess capacity* than does pure competition.

   a. The average cost of each firm is equal in the long run to its price. The industry *does not achieve allocative efficiency* because output is smaller than the output at which marginal cost and price are equal. The industry *does not achieve productive efficiency* because the output is less than the output at which average cost is a minimum.

   b. *Excess capacity* results because firms produce less output than at the minimum of average total cost. In monopolistic competition, many firms operate below optimal capacity.

4. Each monopolistically competitive firm attempts to differentiate its product and advertise it to increase the firm's profit. These activities give rise to **nonprice competition** among firms.

    a. The benefit of product variety is that firms offer consumers a wide range of types, style, brands, and quality variants of a product. Products can also be improved. The expanded range of consumer choice from product differentiation and improvement may offset some of the economic inefficiency (excess capacity problem) of monopolistic competition.

    b. Monopolistic competition is more complex than the simple model presented in the chapter because the firm must constantly juggle three factors—price, product characteristics, and advertising—in seeking to maximize profits.

5. **Oligopoly** is frequently encountered in the U.S. economy.

    a. It is composed of a few firms that dominate an industry.

    b. It can be a **homogeneous oligopoly** that produces standardized industrial products such as steel, or a **differentiated oligopoly** that produces different types of consumer products such as automobiles.

    c. Firms have control over price, and thus are price makers. Oligopolistic firms engage in **strategic behavior,** which means they take into account the actions of other firms in making their decisions. **Mutual interdependence** exists because firms must consider the reaction of rivals to any change in price, output, product characteristic, or advertising.

    d. Barriers to entry, such as economies of scale or ownership, control over raw materials, patents, and pricing strategies, can explain the existence of oligopoly.

    e. Some industries have become oligopolistic not from internal growth but from external factors such as mergers.

    f. Most large industries are oligopolistic. They include ones such as primary copper, electric light bulbs, petrochemicals, motor vehicles, tires, and breakfast cereals (see Table 11.2).

    g. The degree of concentration or market power in an industry is measured in several ways. A **four-firm concentration ratio** gives the percentage of an industry's total sales provided by the four largest firms. If the ratio is very small, the industry is competitive. If the ratio is less than 40 percent, but not very small, the industry is considered monopolistically competitive. If the ratio is 40 percent or greater, the industry is classified as oligopolistic. There are, however, shortcomings with concentration ratios:

    (1) The ratio may understate concentration if markets are more local than national because the ratio is based on national data.

    (2) The ratio may overstate concentration because definitions of industries can be somewhat arbitrary and there may be substantial **interindustry competition.**

    (3) The ratio may overstate concentration if there is **import competition** because the ratio does not account for world trade.

    (4) The ratio may understate concentration if there is a dominant firm or firms among the firms in an industry. The **Herfindahl index** addresses the dominant firm problem because it accounts for the market share of each firm. It is the sum of the squared percentage market shares of all firms in the industry. This formula gives a greater weight in the index to larger firms in an industry.

6. Insight into the pricing behavior of oligopolists can be gained by thinking of the oligopoly as a game of strategy. This **game-theory model** leads to three conclusions.

    a. Firms in an oligopolistic industry are mutually interdependent and must consider the actions of rivals when they make price decisions.

    b. Oligopoly often leads to overt or covert collusion among the firms to fix prices or to coordinate pricing because competition among oligopolists results in low prices and profits; collusion helps maintain higher prices and profits.

    c. Collusion creates incentives to cheat among oligopolists by lowering prices or increasing production to obtain more profit.

7. Economic analysis of oligopoly is difficult because of the diversity among the firms and complications resulting from mutual interdependence. Nevertheless, two important characteristics of oligopoly are inflexible prices and simultaneous price changes by firms. An analysis of three oligopoly models helps explain the pricing practices of oligopolists.

    a. In the **kinked-demand model** there is no collusion. Each firm believes that if it lowers its price its rivals will lower their prices, but if it raises its price its rivals *will not* increase their prices. Therefore, the firm is reluctant to change its price for fear of reducing its profits. The model has two shortcomings: it does not explain how the going price gets set; prices are not as rigid as the model implies.

    b. Mutual interdependence indicates there is **collusion** among oligopoly firms to maintain or increase profits.

    (1) Firms that collude tend to set their prices and joint output at the same level a pure monopolist would set them.

    (2) Collusion may be overt, as in a **cartel** agreement. The OPEC cartel is an example of effective overt collusion.

    (3) Collusion may be covert whereby agreements or unwritten, informal (tacit) understandings between firms set price or market share. Examples of such collusion have included bid rigging on milk prices for schools or fixing worldwide prices for a livestock feed additive.

    (4) At least six obstacles make it difficult for firms to collude or maintain collusive arrangements: difference in demand and cost among firms, the number of firms in the arrangement, incentives to cheat, changing economic conditions, potential for entry by other firms, and legal restrictions and penalties.

    c. **Price leadership** is a form of covert collusion in which one firm initiates price changes and the other firms in the industry follow the lead. Three price leadership tactics have been observed.

(1) Price adjustments tend to be made infrequently, only when cost and demand conditions change to a significant degree.

(2) The price leader announces the price change in various ways, through speeches, announcements, or other such activities.

(3) The price set may not maximize short-run profits for the industry, especially if the industry wants to prevent entry by other firms.

(4) Price leadership can break down and result in a **price war.** Eventually the wars end, and a price leader re-emerges.

8. Oligopolistic firms often avoid price competition but engage in **product development and advertising** for two reasons: Price cuts are easily duplicated, but nonprice competition is more unique; and firms have more financial resources for advertising and product development.

   a. The potential positive effects of advertising include providing low-cost information to consumers that reduces search time and monopoly power, thus enhancing economic efficiency.

   b. The potential negative effects of advertising include manipulating consumers to pay higher prices, serving as a barrier to entry into an industry, and offsetting campaigns that raise product costs and prices.

9. The **efficiency of oligopoly** is difficult to evaluate.

   a. Many economists think that oligopoly price and output characteristics are similar to those of monopoly. Oligopoly firms set output where price exceeds marginal cost and the minimum of average total cost. Oligopoly is allocatively inefficient (P > **MC**) and productively inefficient (P > minimum **ATC**).

   b. This view must be qualified because of increased foreign competition to oligopolistic firms, the use of limit pricing that sets prices at less than the profit-maximizing price, and the technological advances arising from this market structure.

10. (*Last Word*). In 1947, there were over 400 independent brewers in the United States, but today the two major brewers account for 76 percent of the market. One reason for this change is that demand changed. Preferences shifted from stronger-flavored beers to lighter, dryer products. Consumption also shifted from taverns to homes, which results in different packaging. On the supply side, technology changed to produce significant economies of scale that now are barriers to entry. Mergers have occurred, but they are not the fundamental cause of increased concentration. Advertising and product differentiation have also been important in the growth of some firms.

■ HINTS AND TIPS

1. Review the four basic market models in Table 8.1 so that you see how monopolistic competition and oligopoly compare with the other market models on five characteristics.

2. The same **MC = MR** rule for maximizing profits or minimizing losses for the firm from previous chapters is now used to determine output and price in monopolistic competition and in certain oligopoly models. If you understood how the rule applied under pure competition and pure monopoly, you should have no trouble applying it here.

3. Make sure you know how to interpret Figure 11.1 because it is an important graph. It illustrates why a representative firm in monopolistic competition just breaks even in the long run and earns just a normal rather than an economic profit. It also shows how economic inefficiency in monopolistic competition produces excess capacity.

4. Where is the kink in the kinked-demand model? To find out, practice drawing the model. Then use Figure 11.4 to check your answer. Explain to yourself what each line means in the graph.

5. Price and output determinations under collusive oligopoly or a cartel are essentially the same as those for pure monopoly.

■ IMPORTANT TERMS

monopolistic competition	strategic behavior
product differentiation	mutual interdependence
nonprice competition	interindustry competition
four-firm concentration ratio	import competition
Herfindahl index	game theory
excess capacity	collusion
oligopoly	kinked-demand curve
homogeneous oligopoly	price war
differentiated oligopoly	cartel
	price leadership

SELF-TEST

■ FILL-IN QUESTIONS

1. In a monopolistically competitive market, there are a relatively (large, small) _____ number of producers who sell (standardized, differentiated) _____ products. Entry into such a market is relatively (difficult, easy) _____. The number of firms means that each one has a (large, small) _____ market share, the firms (do, do not) _____ collude, and they operate in (an independent, a dependent) _____ manner.

2. Identify the different aspects of production differentiation in monopolistic competition:

   a. _____

   b. _____

   c. _____

   d. _____

   e. _____

3. In the *short run* for a monopolistically competitive firm,

a. the demand curve will be (more, less) _____ elastic than that facing a monopolist and _____ elastic than that facing a pure competitor;

b. the elasticity of this demand curve will depend on

(1) _____ and

(2) _____; and

c. it will produce the output level where marginal cost is (less than, equal to, greater than) _____ marginal revenue.

4. In the *long run* for a monopolistically competitive industry,

a. the *entry* of new firms will (increase, decrease) _____ the demand for the product produced by each firm in the industry and _____ the elasticity of that demand; and

b. the price charged by the individual firm will tend to equal (average, marginal) _____ cost, its economic profits will tend to be (positive, zero) _____, and its average cost will be (greater, less) _____ than the minimum average cost of producing and promoting the product.

5. Although representative firms in monopolistic competition tend to earn (economic, normal) _____ profits in the long run, there can be complications that may result in firms earning _____ profits in the long run. Some firms may achieve a degree of product differentiation that (can, cannot) _____ be duplicated by other firms. There may be (collusion, barriers to entry) _____ that prevent penetration of the market by other firms.

6. In monopolistic competition, price is (less than, equal to, greater than) _____ marginal cost, and so the market structure (does, does not) _____ yield allocative efficiency. Also, average total cost is (less than, equal to, greater than) _____ the minimum of average total cost, and so the market structure (does, does not) _____ result in (allocative, productive) _____ efficiency.

7. In the long run, the monopolistic competitor tries to earn economic profits by using (price, nonprice) _____ competition in the form of product differentiation and advertising. This results in a trade-off between a choice of more consumer goods and services and (more, less) _____ economic efficiency.

8. The more complex model of monopolistic competition suggests that in seeking to maximize profits, each firm juggles the factors of (losses, price) _____, changes in (collusion, product) _____, and decisions about

(controls, advertising) _____ until the firm feels no further change in the variables will result in greater profit.

9. The percentage of the total industry sales accounted for by the top four firms in an industry is known as a four-firm (Herfindahl index, concentration ratio) _____, whereas summing the squared percentage market shares of each firm in the industry is the way to calculate the _____.

10. In an oligopoly (many, a few) _____ large firms produce either a differentiated or a (heterogeneous, homogeneous) _____ product, and entry into such an industry is (easy, difficult) _____. The oligopolistic firm is a price (maker, taker) _____ and there is mutual (independence, interdependence) _____ among firms in an industry. The existence of oligopoly can be explained by (exit, entry) _____ barriers and by (markets, mergers) _____.

11. The basics of the pricing behavior of oligopolists can be understood from a (game, advertising) _____ theory perspective. Oligopoly consists of a few firms that are mutually (funded, interdependent) _____. This means that when setting the price of its product, each producer (does, does not) _____ consider the reaction of its rivals. The monopolist (does, does not) _____ face this problem because it has no rivals, and the pure competitor, or monopolistic competitor, _____ face the problem because it has many rivals.

12. It is difficult to use formal economic analysis to explain the prices and outputs of oligopolists because oligopoly encompasses (diverse, similar) _____ market situation(s), and when firms are mutually interdependent, each firm is (certain, uncertain) _____ about how its rivals will react when it changes the price of its product. Despite the analytical problems, oligopoly prices tend to be (flexible, inflexible) _____ and oligopolists tend to change their prices (independently, together) _____.

13. The noncolluding oligopolist has a kinked-demand curve that

a. is highly (elastic, inelastic) _____ at prices above the current or going price and tends to be only slightly _____ or (elastic, inelastic) _____ below that price.

b. is drawn on the assumption that if the oligopolist raises its price its rivals (will, will not) _____ raise their prices or if it lowers its price its rivals _____ lower their prices.

c. has an associated marginal (cost, revenue) _____ curve with a gap, such that small changes in the marginal _____ curve do not change the price the oligopolist will charge.

14. A situation in which firms in an industry reach an agreement to fix prices, divide up the market, or otherwise restrict competition among themselves is called (concentration, collusion) _____. In this case, the prices they set and their combined output tend to be the same as that found with pure (competition, monopoly) _____.

15. A formal written agreement among sellers in which the price and the total output of the product and each seller's share of the market are specified is a (cartel, duopoly) _____. It is a form of (covert, overt) _____ collusion, whereas tacit understandings among firms to divide up a market would be _____ collusion.

16. Six obstacles to collusion among oligopolists are

    a. _____

    b. _____

    c. _____

    d. _____

    e. _____

    f. _____

17. When one firm in an oligopoly is almost always the first to change its price and the other firms change their prices after the first firm has changed its price, the oligopoly model is called the (price war, price leadership) _____ model. The tactics of this model include (infrequent, frequent) _____ price changes, announcements of such price changes, and (limit, no limit) _____ pricing. One event that can undermine this practice is (price leadership, price wars) _____.

18. There tends to be very little (price, nonprice) _____ competition among oligopolists and a great deal of _____ competition such as product development and advertising used to determine each firm's share of the market.

    a. The positive view of advertising contends that it is (efficient, inefficient) _____ because it provides important information that (increases, reduces) _____ search costs, and information about competing goods _____ monopoly power.

    b. The negative view of advertising suggests that it is (inefficient, efficient) _____ because the advertising campaigns are (offsetting, reinforcing) _____, the creation of brand loyalty serves as a barrier to (entry, exit) _____, and consumers

are persuaded to pay (lower, higher) _____ prices than they would have paid otherwise.

19. Although it is difficult to evaluate the economic efficiency of oligopoly, when comparisons are made to pure competition, the conclusion drawn is that oligopoly (is, is not) _____ allocatively efficient and (is, is not) _____ productively efficient. The price and output behavior of the oligopolist is more likely to be similar to that found under (competition, monopoly) _____.

20. The view that oligopoly is inefficient in the short run needs to be qualified because of the effects of (decreased, increased) _____ foreign competition that make pricing more competitive, policies to restrict entry into an industry that keep consumer prices (high, low) _____, and profits that are used to fund (more, less) _____ research and development that produces improved products.

■ **TRUE–FALSE QUESTIONS**

Circle T if the statement is true, F if it is false.

1. Monopolistic competitors have no control over the price of their products. **T F**

2. The firm's reputation for servicing or exchanging its product is a form of product differentiation under monopolistic competition. **T F**

3. Entry is relatively easy in pure competition, but there are significant barriers to entry in monopolistic competition. **T F**

4. The smaller the number of firms in an industry and the greater the extent of product differentiation, the greater will be the elasticity of the individual seller's demand curve. **T F**

5. The demand curve of the monopolistic competitor is likely to be less elastic than the demand curve of the pure monopolist. **T F**

6. In the short run, firms that are monopolistically competitive may earn economic profits or incur losses. **T F**

7. The long-run equilibrium position in monopolistic competition would be where price is equal to marginal cost. **T F**

8. Representative firms in a monopolistically competitive market earn economic profits in the long run. **T F**

9. One reason why monopolistic competition is economically inefficient is that the average cost of producing the product is greater than the minimum average cost at which the product could be produced. **T F**

10. The more product variety offered to consumers by a monopolistically competitive industry, the less excess capacity there will be in that industry. **T F**

11. Successful product improvement by one firm has little or no effect on other firms under monopolistic competition.   **T   F**

12. The products produced by the firms in an oligopolistic industry may be either homogeneous or differentiated.   **T   F**

13. Oligopolistic industries contain a few large firms that act independently of one another.   **T   F**

14. Concentration ratios include adjustments for inter-industry competition in measuring concentration in an industry.   **T   F**

15. The Herfindahl index is the sum of the market shares of all firms in the industry.   **T   F**

16. Game theory analysis of oligopolist behavior suggests that oligopolists will not find any benefit in collusion.   **T   F**

17. One shortcoming of kinked-demand analysis is that it does not explain how the going oligopoly price was established in the first place.   **T   F**

18. Collusion occurs when firms in an industry reach an overt or covert agreement to fix prices, divide or share the market, and in some way restrict competition among the firms.   **T   F**

19. A cartel is usually a written agreement among firms which sets the price of the product and determines each firm's share of the market.   **T   F**

20. Secret price concessions and other forms of cheating will strengthen collusion.   **T   F**

21. The practice of price leadership is almost always based on a formal written or oral agreement.   **T   F**

22. Limit pricing is the leadership tactic of limiting price increases to a certain percentage of the basic price of a product.   **T   F**

23. Those contending that advertising contributes to monopoly power argue that the advertising by established firms creates barriers to the entry of new firms into an industry.   **T   F**

24. Oligopolies are allocatively and productively efficient when compared with the standard set in pure competition.   **T   F**

25. Increased competition from foreign firms in oligopolistic industries has stimulated more competitive pricing in those industries.   **T   F**

■ MULTIPLE-CHOICE QUESTIONS

Circle the letter that corresponds to the best answer.

1. Which would be most characteristic of monopolistic competition?
 (a) collusion among firms
 (b) firms selling a homogeneous product
 (c) a relatively large number of firms
 (d) difficult entry into and exit from the industry

2. The concern that monopolistically competitive firms express about product attributes, services to customers, or brand names are aspects of
 (a) allocative efficiency in the industry
 (b) collusion in the industry
 (c) product differentiation
 (d) concentration ratios

3. The demand curve a monopolistically competitive firm faces is
 (a) perfectly elastic
 (b) perfectly inelastic
 (c) highly, but not perfectly inelastic
 (d) highly, but not perfectly elastic

4. In the short run, a typical monopolistically competitive firm will earn
 (a) only a normal profit
 (b) only an economic profit
 (c) only an economic or normal profit
 (d) an economic or normal profit or suffer an economic loss

5. A monopolistically competitive firm is producing at an output level in the short run where average total cost is $3.50, price is $3.00, marginal revenue is $1.50, and marginal cost is $1.50. This firm is operating
 (a) with an economic loss in the short run
 (b) with an economic profit in the short run
 (c) at the break-even level of output in the short run
 (d) at an inefficient level of output in the short run

6. If firms enter a monopolistically competitive industry, we would expect the typical firm's demand curve to
 (a) increase and the firm's price to increase
 (b) decrease and the firm's price to decrease
 (c) remain the same but the firm's price to increase
 (d) remain the same and the firm's price to remain the same

Answer Questions 7, 8, 9, and 10 on the basis of the following diagram for a monopolistically competitive firm in short-run equilibrium.

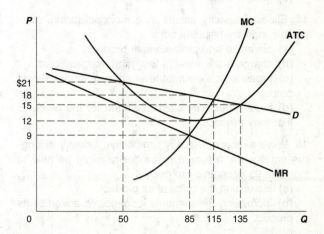

7. The firm's profit-maximizing price will be
(a) $9
(b) $12
(c) $15
(d) $18

8. The equilibrium output for this firm will be
(a) 50
(b) 85
(c) 115
(d) 135

9. This firm will earn an economic profit of
(a) $510
(b) $765
(c) $1021
(d) $1170

10. If firms enter this industry in the long run,
(a) demand will decrease
(b) demand will increase
(c) the marginal revenue curve will shift upward
(d) economic profits will increase

11. Given a representative firm in a typical monopolistically competitive industry, in the long run
(a) the firm will produce that output at which marginal cost and price are equal
(b) the elasticity of demand for the firm's product will be less than it was in the short run
(c) the number of competitors the firm faces will be greater than it was in the short run
(d) the economic profits being earned by the firm will tend to equal zero

12. *Productive* efficiency is not achieved in monopolistic competition because production occurs where
(a) MR is greater than MC
(b) MR is less than MC
(c) ATC is greater than minimum ATC
(d) ATC is less than MR and greater than MC

13. The *underallocation* of resources in monopolistic competition means that at the profit-maximizing level of output, price is
(a) greater than MC
(b) less than MC
(c) less than MR
(d) greater than minimum ATC

14. Excess capacity occurs in a monopolistically competitive industry because firms
(a) advertise and promote their product
(b) charge a price that is less than marginal cost
(c) produce at an output level short of the least-cost output
(d) have a perfectly elastic demand for the products that they produce

15. Were a monopolistically competitive industry in long-run equilibrium, a firm in that industry might be able to increase its economic profits by
(a) increasing the price of its product
(b) increasing the amounts it spends to advertise its product

(c) decreasing the price of its product
(d) decreasing the output of its product

16. Which would be most characteristic of oligopoly?
(a) easy entry into the industry
(b) a few large producers
(c) product standardization
(d) no control over price

17. Mutual interdependence means that
(a) each firm produces a product similar but not identical to the products produced by its rivals
(b) each firm produces a product identical to the products produced by its rivals
(c) each firm must consider the reactions of its rivals when it determines its price policy
(d) each firm faces a perfectly elastic demand for its product

18. One major problem with concentration ratios is that they fail to take into account
(a) the national market for products
(b) competition from imported products
(c) excess capacity in production
(d) mutual interdependence

19. Industry A is composed of four large firms that hold market shares of 40, 30, 20, and 10. The Herfindahl index for this industry is
(a) 100
(b) 1000
(c) 3000
(d) 4500

Questions 20, 21, and 22 are based on the following pay-off matrix for a duopoly in which the numbers indicate the profit in thousands of dollars for a high-price or a low-price strategy.

		Firm A Strategy	
		High-price	**Low-price**
Firm B Strategy	**High-price**	A = $425 B = $425	A = $525 B = $275
	Low-price	A = $275 B = $525	A = $300 B = $300

20. If both firms collude to maximize joint profits, the total profits for the two firms will be
(a) $400,000
(b) $800,000
(c) $850,000
(d) $950,000

21. Assume that Firm B adopts a low-price strategy while Firm A maintains a high-price strategy. Compared to the results from a high-price strategy for both firms, Firm B will now
(a) lose $150,000 in profit and Firm A will gain $150,000 in profit

(b) gain $100,000 in profit and Firm A will lose $150,000 in profit

(c) gain $150,000 in profit and Firm A will lose $100,000 in profit

(d) gain $525,000 in profit and Firm A will lose $275,000 in profit

22. If both firms operate independently and do not collude, the most likely profit is
(a) $300,000 for Firm A and $300,000 for Firm B
(b) $525,000 for Firm A and $275,000 for Firm B
(c) $275,000 for Firm A and $525,000 for Firm B
(d) $425,000 for Firm A and $425,000 for Firm B

23. If an individual oligopolist's demand curve is kinked, it is necessarily
(a) perfectly elastic at the going price
(b) less elastic above the going price than below it
(c) more elastic above the going price than below it
(d) of unitary elasticity at the going price

Use the following diagram to answer Question 24.

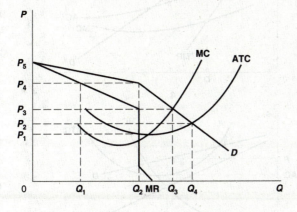

24. The profit-maximizing price and output for this oligopolistic firm is
(a) P_5 and Q_2
(b) P_4 and Q_2
(c) P_3 and Q_3
(d) P_2 and Q_4

25. What is the situation called whenever firms in an industry reach an agreement to fix prices, divide up the market, or otherwise restrict competition?
(a) interindustry competition
(b) incentive to cheat
(c) price leadership
(d) collusion

26. When oligopolists collude the results are generally
(a) greater output and higher price
(b) greater output and lower price
(c) smaller output and lower price
(d) smaller output and higher price

27. To be successful, collusion requires that oligopolists be able to
(a) keep prices and profits as low as possible
(b) block or restrict the entry of new producers

(c) reduce legal obstacles that protect market power
(d) keep the domestic economy from experiencing high inflation

28. Which is a typical tactic that has been used by the price leader in the price leadership model of oligopoly?
(a) limit pricing
(b) frequent price changes
(c) starting a price war with competitors
(d) giving no announcement of a price change

29. Market shares in oligopoly are typically determined on the basis of
(a) product development and advertising
(b) covert collusion and cartels
(c) tacit understandings
(d) joint profit maximization

30. Many economists think that relative to pure competition, oligopoly is
(a) allocatively efficient, but not productively efficient
(b) productively efficient, but not allocatively efficient
(c) both allocatively and productively efficient
(d) neither allocatively nor productively efficient

■ **PROBLEMS**

1. Assume that the short-run cost and demand data given in the following table confront a monopolistic competitor selling a given product and engaged in a given amount of product promotion.

Output	Total cost	Marginal cost	Quantity demanded	Price	Marginal revenue
0	$ 50		0	$120	
1	80	$_____	1	110	$_____
2	90	_____	2	100	_____
3	110	_____	3	90	_____
4	140	_____	4	80	_____
5	180	_____	5	70	_____
6	230	_____	6	60	_____
7	290	_____	7	50	_____
8	360	_____	8	40	_____
9	440	_____	9	30	_____
10	530	_____	10	20	_____

a. Compute the marginal cost and marginal revenue of each unit of output and enter these figures in the table.

b. In the short run the firm will (1) produce _____ units of output, (2) sell its output at a price of $_____, and (3) have a total economic profit of $_____.

c. In the long run, (1) the demand for the firm's product will _____, (2) until the price of the product equals _____, and (3) the total economic profits of the firm are _____.

2. Match the following descriptions to the six graphs below. Indicate on each graph the area of economic profit or loss or state if the firm is just making normal profits.

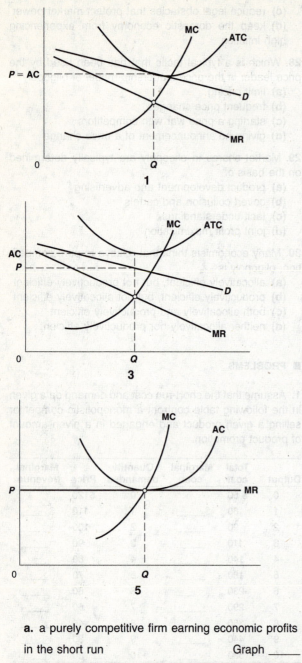

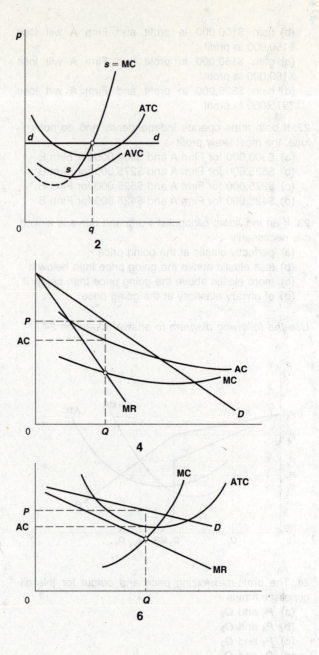

a. a purely competitive firm earning economic profits
in the short run   Graph _____

b. a purely competitive firm in long-run equilibrium
                                                    Graph _____

c. a natural monopoly   Graph _____

d. a monopolistically competitive firm earning economic profits in the short run   Graph _____

e. a monopolistically competitive firm experiencing
economic losses in the short run   Graph _____

f. a monopolistically competitive firm in long-run equilibrium   Graph _____

3. Consider the following payoff matrix in which the numbers indicate the profit in millions of dollars for a duopoly based on either a high-price or a low-price strategy.

		Firm X Strategy	
		High-price	Low-price
Firm Y Strategy	**High-price**	X = $200 Y = $200	X = $250 Y = $ 50
	Low-price	X = $ 50 Y = $250	X = $ 50 Y = $ 50

a. Situation 1: Each firm chooses a high-price strategy. **Result:** Each firm will earn $_____ million in profit for a total of $_____ million for the two firms.

b. Situation 2: Firm X chooses a low-price strategy while Firm Y maintains a high-price strategy. **Result:** Firm X will earn $_____ million and Firm Y will earn $_____ million. Compared to Situation 1, Firm X has an incentive to cut prices because it will earn $_____ million more in profit and Firm Y will earn $_____ million less in profit. Together, the firms will earn $_____ million in profit, which is $_____ million less than in Situation 1.

c. *Situation 3:* Firm Y chooses a low-price strategy while Firm X maintains a high-price strategy. *Result:* Compared to Situation 1, Firm Y has an incentive to cut prices because it will earn $_____ million and Firm X will earn $_____. Compared to Situation 1, Firm Y will earn $_____ million more in profit and Firm X will earn $_____ million less in profit. Together, the firms will earn $_____ million in profit, which is $_____ less than in Situation 1.

d. *Situation 4:* Each firm chooses a low-price strategy.

Result: Each firm will earn $_____ million in profit for a total of $_____ million for the two firms. This total is $_____ less than in Situation 1.

e. *Conclusions:*

(1) The two firms have a strong incentive to collude and adopt the high-price strategy because there is the potential for $_____ million more in profit for the two firms than with a low-price strategy (Situation 4), or the potential for $_____ million more for the two firms than with a mixed-price strategy (Situations 2 or 3).

(2) There is also a strong incentive for each firm to cheat on the agreement and adopt a low-price strategy when the other firm maintains a high-price strategy because this situation will produce $_____ million more in profit for the cheating firm compared to its honoring a collusive agreement for a high-price strategy.

4. The kinked-demand schedule which an oligopolist believes confronts the firm is presented in the following table.

Price	Quantity demanded	Total revenue	Marginal revenue per unit
$2.90	100	$_____	
2.80	200	_____	$_____
2.70	300	_____	_____
2.60	400	_____	_____
2.50	500	_____	_____
2.40	525	_____	_____
2.30	550	_____	_____
2.20	575	_____	_____
2.10	600	_____	_____

a. Compute the oligopolist's total revenue at each of the nine prices and enter these figures in the table.
b. Also compute marginal revenue *for each unit* between the nine prices and enter these figures in the table.
c. What is the current, or going, price for the oligopolist's product? $_____ How much is it selling? _____
d. On the graph below plot the oligopolist's demand curve and marginal revenue curve. Connect the demand points and the marginal revenue points with as straight a line as possible. (Be sure to plot the marginal revenue figures at the average of the two quantities involved, that is, at 150, 250, 350, 450, 512.5, 537.5, 562.5, and 587.5.)

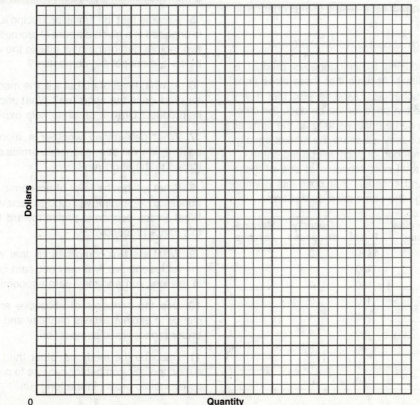

Dollars

0   Quantity

e. Assume that the marginal cost schedule of the oligopolist is given in columns 1 and 2 of the following table. Plot the marginal cost curve on the graph on which demand and marginal revenue were plotted.

(1) Output	(2) MC	(3) MC'	(4) MC"
150	$1.40	$1.90	$.40
250	1.30	1.80	.30
350	1.40	1.90	.40
450	1.50	2.00	.50
512.5	1.60	2.10	.60
537.5	1.70	2.20	.70
562.5	1.80	2.30	.80
587.5	1.90	2.40	.90

(1) Given demand and marginal cost, what price should the oligopolist charge to maximize profits? $_____ How many units of product will it sell at this price? _____

(2) If the marginal cost schedule changed from that shown in columns 1 and 2 to that shown in columns 1 and 3, what price should it charge? $_____ What level of output will it produce? _____ How have profits changed as a result of the change in costs? _____ Plot the new marginal cost curve on the graph.

(3) If the marginal-cost curve schedule changed from that shown in columns 1 and 2 to that shown in columns 1 and 4, what price should it charge? $_____ What level of output will it produce? _____ How have profits changed as a result of the change in costs? _____ Plot the new marginal cost curve on the graph.

5. An oligopoly producing a homogeneous product is composed of three firms. Assume that these three firms have identical cost schedules. Assume also that if any one of these firms sets a price for the product, the other two firms charge the same price. As long as the firms all charge the same price they will share the market equally, and the quantity demanded of each will be the same.

Following is the total cost schedule of one of these firms and the demand schedule that confronts it when the other firms charge the same price as this firm.

Output	Total cost	Marginal cost	Price	Quantity demanded	Marginal revenue
0	$ 0		$140	0	
1	30	$_____	130	1	$_____
2	50	_____	120	2	_____
3	80	_____	110	3	_____
4	120	_____	100	4	_____
5	170	_____	90	5	_____
6	230	_____	80	6	_____
7	300	_____	70	7	_____
8	380	_____	60	8	_____

a. Complete the marginal cost and marginal revenue schedules facing the firm.

b. What price would this firm set if it wished to maximize its profits? $_____

c. How much would

(1) it sell at this price? _____

(2) its profits be at this price? $_____

d. What would be the industry's

(1) total output at this price? _____

(2) joint profits at this price? $_____

e. Is there any other price this firm can set, assuming that the other two firms charge the same price, that would result in a greater joint profit for them? _____

f. If these three firms colluded in order to maximize their joint profit, what price would they charge? $_____

■ **SHORT ANSWER AND ESSAY QUESTIONS**

1. What are the three characteristics of monopolistic competition?

2. What is meant by product differentiation? By what methods can products be differentiated?

3. How does product differentiation affect the kind of competition and the degree of monopoly in monopolistic competition?

4. Describe the elasticity of the demand curve faced by a monopolistically competitive firm in the short run.

5. Assume that the firm is producing a given product and is engaged in a given amount of promotional activity. What two factors determine how elastic the demand curve will be for a monopolistic competitor?

6. At what level of output will the monopolistic competitor produce in the short run? What price will it charge for its product? Draw a graph to help explain your answer.

7. What determines whether a monopolistically competitive firm will earn economic profits or suffer economic losses in the short run?

8. What will be the level of economic profit that the monopolistic competitor will tend to receive in the long run? What forces economic profits toward this level? Why is this just a *tendency*?

9. What are two complications that would explain why the representative firm may not earn only a normal profit in the long run and may earn economic profits?

10. Use the concepts of allocative and productive efficiency to explain excess capacity and the level of prices under monopolistic competition.

11. Describe the methods, other than price cutting, that a monopolistic competitor can use to protect and increase its economic profits in the long run.

12. Explain how product variety and improvement may offset the economic inefficiency associated with monopolistic competition.

13. What are the essential characteristics of an oligopoly? How does oligopoly differ from pure competition, pure monopoly, and monopolistic competition?

14. Explain how the concentration ratio in a particular industry is computed. What is the relationship between this ratio and fewness? What are the shortcomings of the concentration ratio as a measure of the extent of competition in an industry?

15. What is the Herfindahl index? How can it be used to correct problems with concentration ratios?

16. How can game theory be used to explain strategic behavior under oligopoly? What do mutual interdependence and collusion mean with respect to oligopoly?

17. Why is it difficult to use one standard model to explain the prices charged by and the outputs of oligopolists?

18. How can the kinked-demand curve be used to explain why oligopoly prices are relatively inflexible?

19. Suppose a few firms produce a homogeneous product, have identical cost curves, and charge the same price (act as a cartel). Compare the results in terms of price, combined output, and joint profits with those from a pure monopoly producing the same market output.

20. Why do oligopolists find it advantageous to collude? What are the obstacles to collusion?

21. What is the price leadership model, and what leadership tactics do oligopolistic firms use?

22. Why do oligopolists engage in little price competition and in extensive product development and advertising?

23. How is it possible for consumers to get a lower price on a product with advertising than they would in its absence?

24. Explain how the advertising efforts of firms may be offsetting and lead to higher prices for consumers.

25. Evaluate the economic efficiency of the oligopoly market structure. What qualifications should be noted for the evaluation?

ANSWERS

Chapter 11 Monopolistic Competition and Oligopoly

FILL-IN QUESTIONS

1. large, differentiated, easy, small, do not, an independent
2. *a.* product attributes; *b.* services; *c.* location; *d.* brand names and packaging; *e.* some control over price
3. *a.* more, less; *b.* (1) number of rivals the firm has, (2) the degree of product differentiation; *c.* equal to
4. *a.* decrease, increase; *b.* average, zero, greater
5. normal, economic, cannot, barriers to entry
6. greater than, does not, greater than, does not, productive
7. nonprice, more
8. price, product, advertising
9. concentration ratio, Herfindahl index
10. a few, homogeneous, difficult, maker, interdependence, entry, mergers
11. game, interdependent, does, does not, does not
12. diverse, uncertain, inflexible, together
13. *a.* elastic, elastic, inelastic; *b.* will not, will; *c.* revenue, cost
14. collusion, monopoly
15. cartel, overt, covert
16. *a.* demand and cost differences; *b.* a large number of firms; *c.* cheating (secret price cutting); *d.* a recession; *e.* potential entry; *f.* legal obstacles (antitrust laws) (any order for *a–f*)
17. price leadership, infrequent, limit, price wars
18. price, nonprice; *a.* efficient, reduces, reduces; *b.* inefficient, offsetting, entry, higher
19. is not, is not, monopoly
20. increased, low, more

TRUE–FALSE QUESTIONS

1. F, pp. 217–218	**10.** F, pp. 222–223	**19.** T, pp. 230–232
2. T, p. 217	**11.** F, p. 223	**20.** F, p. 232
3. F, p. 218	**12.** T, p. 224	**21.** F, p. 233
4. F, pp. 219–220	**13.** F, p. 223	**22.** F, p. 233
5. F, pp. 219–220	**14.** F, p. 225	**23.** T, pp. 234–235
6. T, pp. 219–221	**15.** F, p. 226	**24.** F, p. 235
7. F, pp. 220–221	**16.** F, pp. 226–227	**25.** T, p. 235
8. F, p. 221	**17.** T, pp. 228–230	
9. T, pp. 221–222	**18.** T, pp. 230–232	

MULTIPLE-CHOICE QUESTIONS

1. c, p. 217	**11.** d, pp. 219–220	**21.** b, p. 226
2. c, pp. 217–218	**12.** c, pp. 221–222	**22.** a, pp. 226
3. d, pp. 219–220	**13.** a, pp. 221–222	**23.** c, pp. 228–230
4. d, pp. 219–220	**14.** c, p. 222	**24.** b, pp. 228–230
5. a, pp. 219–220	**15.** b, pp. 222–223	**25.** d, pp. 230–231
6. b, p. 221	**16.** b, p. 223	**26.** d, pp. 230–231
7. d, pp. 219–220	**17.** c, p. 224	**27.** b, p. 233
8. b, pp. 219–220	**18.** b, p. 225	**28.** a, p. 233
9. a, pp. 219–220	**19.** c, p. 226	**29.** a, pp. 234–235
10. a, pp. 220–221	**20.** c, p. 226	**30.** d, p. 235

PROBLEMS

1. *a.* Marginal cost: $30, 10, 20, 30, 40, 50, 60, 70, 80, 90, Marginal revenue: $110, 90, 70, 50, 30, 10, −10, −30, −50, −70; *b.* (1) 4, (2) $80, (3) $180; *c.* (1) decrease, (2) average cost, (3) equal to zero
2. *a.* 2; *b.* 5; *c.* 4; *d.* 6; *e.* 3; *f.* 1
3. *a.* 200, 400; *b.* 250, 50, 50, 150, 300, 100; *c.* 250, 50, 50, 150, 300, 100; *d.* 50, 100, 300; *e.* (1) 300, 100, (2) 50
4. *a.* Total revenue: 290, 560, 810, 1,040, 1,250, 1,260, 1,265, 1,265, 1,260; *b.* Marginal revenue: 2.70, 2.50, 2.30, 2.10, 0.40, 0.20, 0, −0.20; *c.* 2.50, 500; *d.* graph; *e.* (1) 2.50, 500, (2) 2.50, 500, they have decreased, (3) 2.50, 500, they have increased
5. *a.* Marginal cost: $30, 20, 30, 40, 50, 60, 70, 80; Marginal revenue: $130, 110, 90, 70, 50, 30, 10, −10; *b.* $90; *c.* (1) 5, (2) $280; *d.* (1) 15, (2) $840; *e.* no; *f.* $90

SHORT ANSWER AND ESSAY QUESTIONS

Additional Game Theory Applications

This appendix provides some additional applications of oligopoly based on game theory and behavior. The first section of the appendix discusses strategies and equilibrium for games that occur just one time between two rivals. Here you will learn about the **Nash equilibrium,** which is an outcome from which neither rival wants to deviate because each firm sees its strategy as optimal given the strategy of its rival. The second section introduces the ideas of a **credible threat** and an **empty threat** and evaluates how each will affect Nash equilibrium. The third section turns to **repeated games,** which are games played more than once, and explains how strategies are influenced by the thought that there will be reciprocity from a rival, or less direct or intense competition. The final section turns to the topic of **sequential games,** in which the outcome depends on **first-mover advantage** and the ability to preclude entry by rivals.

■ APPENDIX CHECKLIST

When you have studied this appendix you should be able to

☐ Describe a one-time game and simultaneous game.
☐ Define positive-sum game, zero-sum game, and negative-sum game.
☐ Give an example of a dominant strategy in a game.
☐ Define the Nash equilibrium for a one-time game.
☐ Explain how a credible threat affects the Nash equilibrium.
☐ Explain how an empty threat affects the Nash equilibrium.
☐ Describe a repeated game and the effect of a reciprocity strategy on game outcomes.
☐ Supply an example of a sequential game.
☐ Explain how first-mover advantages in a sequential game affect decisions by rivals and entry into markets.

■ APPENDIX OUTLINE

1. In a **one-time game,** two firms (rivals) select their optimal strategies in a single time period without considering subsequent time periods. If both firms make their strategies at the same time, it is also a **simultaneous game.**

    a. If the net outcome from such one-time and simultaneous games is positive, it is a **positive-sum game.** If the net outcome is negative, it a **negative-sum game.** If the net outcome is zero, it is a **zero-sum game.**

    b. If one option in a game is better for a firm than any alternative option in a game regardless of the choice made by another firm, the better option is a **dominant strategy.** Not all games have a dominant strategy, however.

    c. The dominant strategy for each firm determines the game's **Nash equilibrium.** It is the outcome from which neither firm wants to deviate because it is optimal given the strategic choice made by the other firm.

2. If there is a **credible threat** in a single-period and simultaneous game, then it can cause the firms to abandon the Nash equilibrium. The credible threat can occur if one firm is believed to have the power to dictate the decision of another firm and thus the firms collude. It is, however, difficult to enforce such a threat and if it is not credible, it is an **empty threat.** In this case, the Nash equilibrium will hold.

3. A **repeated game** is not a one-time event, but occurs more often or somewhat regularly. In this situation, the optimal strategy for a firm may be to limit competition with the other firm, if the other firm reciprocates by limiting its competition. Thus reciprocity strategies, and whether they will be used, are important for determining outcomes in repeated games.

4. A **sequential game** is one in which the final outcome may depend on which firm makes the first move because the first-mover may be able to establish the Nash equilibrium. A real-world example would be a large store such as Walmart that, by making a first-mover decision to enter a market, prevents other large firms from also entering the same market because it would not be profitable.

■ HINTS AND TIPS

1. This appendix extends your understanding of game theory and strategic behavior described in Chapter 11. Before you start the appendix, make sure you master how the profit-payoff matrix works for two-firm oligopolies as in the example shown in Figure 11.3. A similar matrix is used to illustrate each two-firm game discussed in this appendix.

2. There is nothing complicated about the content of this appendix, but it does introduce subtle distinctions in the definitions and conditions for games that you will need to learn as shown in the following list of important terms.

■ IMPORTANT TERMS

one-time game

simultaneous games

positive-sum games

zero-sum games

negative-sum games

dominant strategy

Nash equilibrium

credible threat

empty threat

repeated games

sequential games

first-mover advantage

SELF-TEST

■ FILL-IN QUESTIONS

1. If firms select their optimal strategies in a single time period, it is a (one-time, repeated) _____ game, but if firms select their optimal strategies based on a situation that is recurring, it is a _____ game.

2. Outcomes from games can be used to categorize games: if there is an "I win and you lose" outcome, it is a (positive, zero, negative) _____-sum game; if there is a "win-win" outcome, it is a _____-sum game; and, if there is a "lose-lose" outcome, it is a _____-sum game.

3. A strategic choice for a firm that is better than any other option is a (subordinate, dominant) _____ strategy.

4. In a two-firm game, the dominant strategy for each firm determines the (Crowe, Nash) _____ equilibrium.

5. At such an equilibrium, both firms consider their current strategy as optimal and (do, do not) _____ want to deviate from it; so such an equilibrium is (stable, unstable) _____.

6. If a firm is capable or likely to use coercion to force a desired decision on a rival firm, the threat is (credible, empty) _____, but if the firm cannot use coercion to force a desired decision, the threat is _____.

7. If a threat is credible, firms will (deviate, not deviate) _____ from the Nash equilibrium and seek greater profits, but if a threat is empty, threatening firms will _____ from the Nash equilibrium and be unable to seek greater profits.

8. In a repeated game, if one firm avoids taking advantage of another firm because the firm knows the other firm will take advantage of it in a subsequent game, then there is likely to be a (monopolistic, reciprocity) _____ strategy enacted by the firms that can (harm, improve) _____ the outcomes from such games.

9. If one firm moves first and commits to a strategy and the other firm must then respond, it is a (repeated, sequential) _____ game.

10. In a sequential game involving two large, but similar retailers, the first-mover retailer may have the opportunity to (establish, destroy) _____ a Nash equilibrium and it may make it (profitable, unprofitable) _____ for the other retailer to enter the market.

■ TRUE–FALSE QUESTIONS

Circle T if the statement is true, F if it is false.

1. Games can either be one-time games or repeated games. **T F**

2. Negative-sum games feature an "I win and you lose" outcome. **T F**

3. Decisions in games may be made simultaneously, but not sequentially. **T F**

4. When two firms are playing a strategic game, a firm has a dominant strategy if one option leads to a better result than all other options no matter what the other firm does. **T F**

5. The Nash equilibrium is an outcome from which neither firm wants to deviate because both firms see their current strategy as optimal given the selected strategy of the other firm. **T F**

6. A Nash equilibrium is unstable and changing. **T F**

7. An empty threat in a two-firm game will change outcomes and the Nash equilibrium. **T F**

8. Reciprocity means that one firm avoids taking advantage of the other firm because it knows that the other firm can take advantage of it in subsequent games. **T F**

9. Reciprocity makes outcomes worse for firms participating in repeated games. **T F**

10. If there is a first-mover advantage for two rival firms seeking to enter a market, it may be possible for the first-mover firm to preempt entry by the other firm. **T F**

■ MULTIPLE-CHOICE QUESTIONS

Circle the letter that corresponds to the best answer.

1. If one firm's gain equals another firm's loss it is a
   (a) negative-sum game
   (b) zero-sum game
   (c) repeated game
   (d) sequential game

*Questions 2, 3, and 4 are based on the following payoff matrix for a single-period, two-firm game for firms **Rig** and **Dig**. The numbers in the matrix indicate the profit in* millions of dollars for a national or regional strategy. The profit outcome cells are **A**, **B**, **C**, and **D**.

		Rig Strategy	
		National	Regional
Dig Strategy	National	(A) Rig = $24 / Dig = $24	(B) Rig = $12 / Dig = $42
	Regional	(C) Rig = $42 / Dig = $12	(D) Rig = $36 / Dig = $36

2. Which strategies are the dominant ones for Rig and Dig?

(a) national for Rig and regional for Dig
(b) regional for Rig and national for Dig
(c) national for Rig and national for Dig
(d) regional for Rig and regional for Dig

3. The Nash equilibrium will be represented by which cell showing the set of profit outcomes for the two firms?

(a) A
(b) B
(c) C
(d) D

4. If Dig can make a credible threat that determines the strategy for Rig, then which combinations of strategies will be selected?

(a) national for Rig and regional for Dig
(b) regional for Rig and national for Dig
(c) national for Rig and national for Dig
(d) regional for Rig and regional for Dig

5. If Dig makes a threat, but it is an empty threat that is not believable for Rig, then which cell shows the set of profit outcomes for the two firms?

(a) A
(b) B
(c) C
(d) D

6. In a repeated game among two firms, if the optimal strategy for one firm is to cooperate with the other firm and restrain competition in the expectation that the other firm will do the same, then the firm is using a

(a) dominant strategy
(b) reciprocity strategy
(c) credible threat strategy
(d) empty threat strategy

7. If one firm make the first move and then the other firm responds, it would be a

(a) zero-sum game
(b) negative-sum game
(c) simultaneous game
(d) sequential game

*Questions 8, 9, and 10 are based on the following payoff matrix for a single-period, two-firm game for the two major aircraft makers, **Fly** and **Sky**. The numbers in the matrix*

indicate the profit in billions of dollars if a firm builds or does not build a new aircraft to compete with the other firm. The profit outcome cells are **A**, **B**, **C**, and **D**.

		Fly Strategy	
		Build	Don't build
Sky Strategy	Build	(A) Fly = $12 / Sky = $12	(B) Fly = $ 0 / Sky = $15
	Don't build	(C) Fly = $15 / Sky = $ 0	(D) Fly = $ 0 / Sky = $ 0

8. What will be the total amount of profit or losses for both firms if both firms decide simultaneously to build a new aircraft?

(a) $0
(b) $15 billion
(c) −$12 million
(d) −$24 million

9. Which pair of cells contains the possible Nash equilibrium?

(a) A and B
(b) B and C
(c) C and D
(d) A and D

10. If Sky makes the first move and builds an aircraft then

(a) Sky will earn $15 billion and Fly will earn $0
(b) Sky will lose $12 billion and Fly will lose $12 billion
(c) Sky will earn $15 billion and Fly will earn $15 billion
(d) Neither firm will make a profit, but neither firm will suffer a loss

■ **PROBLEMS**

*For problems 1 to 4 use the following payoff matrix for two retail firms, **Top** and **Pop**, in a single-period, one-time game. The numbers in each cell (**A**, **B**, **C**, or **D**) indicate the profit in millions of dollars based on whether they adopt a high-price or a low-price strategy.*

		Top Strategy	
		High-price	Low-price
Pop Strategy	High-price	(A) Top = $30 / Pop = $30	(B) Top = $15 / Pop = $60
	Low-price	(C) Top = $60 / Pop = $15	(D) Top = $45 / Pop = $45

1. Determine the dominant strategy for Pop.

a. If Top adopts a high-price strategy, then Pop will be better off if it chooses a high-price strategy because it can earn $_____ million. By contrast, if Pop had used a low-price strategy in this case, it only would earn $_____ million in profit.

b. If Top adopts a low-price strategy, then Pop will be better off if it chooses a high-price strategy because it can earn $_____ million. By contrast, if Pop used a low-price strategy in this case, it only would earn $_____ million in profit.

c. Regardless of whether Top adopts a high-price or low-price strategy, Pop will be better off it if adopts a high-price strategy because it can earn either $_____ million or $_____ million. A high-price strategy is the dominant strategy for Pop.

2. Determine the dominant strategy for Pop.
   a. If Pop adopts a high-price strategy, then Top will be better off if it chooses a high-price strategy because it can earn $_____ million. By contrast, if Top used a low-price strategy in this case, it only would earn $_____ million in profit.
   b. If Pop adopts a low-price strategy, then Top will still be better off if it chooses a high-price strategy because it can earn $_____ million. By contrast, if Top used a low-price strategy in this case, it only would earn $_____ million in profit.
   c. Regardless of whether Pop adopts a high-price or low-price strategy, Top will be better off it if adopts a high-price strategy because it can earn either $_____ million or $_____ million. A high-price strategy is the dominant strategy for Top.

3. Identify the Nash equilibrium.
   a. Each firm will adopt a _____-price strategy because such a strategy is dominant over all other choices for each firm. The Nash equilibrium will be in cell _____.
   b. At the Nash equilibrium each firm will earn $_____ million.

4. Identify the effects of credible and empty threats.
   a. If Pop chooses a low-price strategy and makes a credible threat to get Top to adopt a low-price strategy, then both firms will abandon the Nash equilibrium at cell _____ and move to cell _____ in the profit-payoff matrix. Pop will earn a profit of $_____ million.
   b. If Pop chooses a low-price strategy and makes a threat to get Top to adopt a low-price strategy, but Pop cannot enforce that threat or it is not believable, then the Nash equilibrium will be at cell _____. The profit for each firm will be $_____.

5. Determine outcomes from repeated games and reciprocity.

*Use the following payoff matrix for two shoe firms, **Skip** and **Jump**, which are involved in a two-period game. The numbers in each cell (**A**, **B**, **C**, or **D**) indicate the profit in millions of dollars based on whether they adopt more*

advertising or less advertising for the introduction of a new shoe. Assume that in period 1, Jump introduces a new shoe, Clog, and it adopts an advertising strategy of placing more ads to sell the new shoe.

Period 1: Jump introduces a new shoe, Clog

		Skip Strategy	
		More-ads	**Fewer-ads**
Jump Strategy	**More-ads**	(A) Skip = $20 / Jump = $20	(B) Skip = $16 / Jump = $32
	Fewer-ads	(C) Skip = $32 / Jump = $16	(D) Skip = $24 / Jump = $24

a. If, in response, Skip counters by placing more ads, the amount of profit for each firm will be $_____ million. The profit outcomes for both firms will be at cell _____.

b. But if, in response, Skip adopts a fewer-ads strategy in hopes that Jump will do the same when Skip launches its new shoe, then Skip will earn $_____ million in profit. The profit outcomes for both firms will be at cell _____.

Now assume that in period 2 Skip launches its new shoe, Fleet, and adopts a more-ads strategy.

Period 2: Skip introduces a new shoe, Fleet

		Skip Strategy	
		More-ads	**Fewer-ads**
Jump Strategy	**More-ads**	(A) Skip = $22 / Jump = $22	(B) Skip = $20 / Jump = $28
	Fewer-ads	(C) Skip = $30 / Jump = $20	(D) Skip = $26 / Jump = $26

c. If, in response, Jump counters by placing more ads, the amount of profit earned by each firm will be $_____ million. The profit outcomes for both firms will be at cell _____.

d. But if, in response, Jump cooperates and adopts a reciprocity strategy of fewer ads, Jump will earn $_____ million. The profit outcomes for both firms will be at cell _____.

e. By cooperating and showing reciprocity to each other, the firms will earn more total profit. In period 1, Jump will earn $_____ million and in period 2 Jump will earn $_____ million, for a total of $_____ million. In period 1, Skip will earn $_____ million and in period 2 Skip will earn $_____ million for a total of $_____ million.

f. Had there been no cooperation or reciprocity, each firm would have earned $_____ million in the first period and $_____ million in the second period, for a total of $_____ million.

■ SHORT ANSWER AND ESSAY QUESTIONS

1. What are the differences between positive-sum, negative-sum, and zero-sum games?

2. How can decisions in games be either simultaneous or sequential? Give examples of each type.

3. Explain what is meant by a dominant strategy in a one-period game involving two rival firms.

4. Define the Nash equilibrium. Is it stable or unstable?

5. How does the use of credible threats or empty threats from firms affect outcomes and the Nash equilibrium in one-period games?

6. Give examples of real-world companies for which repeated games apply.

7. What strategies might two dominant firms use in repeated games to increase profits over what might be achieved with competitive strategies?

8. Explain how the first mover might have an advantage in a sequential game. Does such an advantage always produce a positive outcome?

9. Why might there be two outcomes that could create the Nash equilibrium in sequential games with first-mover advantages?

10. Supply some real-world examples of firms that have used first-mover advantages to saturate markets or preempt entry by rivals.

ANSWERS

Appendix to Chapter 11: Additional Game Theory Applications

FILL-IN QUESTIONS

1. one-time, repeated
2. zero, positive, negative
3. dominant
4. Nash
5. do not, stable
6. credible, empty
7. deviate, not deviate
8. reciprocity, improve
9. sequential
10. establish, unprofitable

TRUE–FALSE QUESTIONS

1. T, pp. 241–242	**5.** T, p. 241	**9.** F, p. 243
2. F, p. 241	**6.** F, p. 241	**10.** T, pp. 243–244
3. F, pp. 241, 243	**7.** F, p. 242	
4. T, p. 241	**8.** T, p. 242	

MULTIPLE-CHOICE QUESTIONS

1. b, p. 241	**5.** a, p. 242	**9.** b, pp. 243–244
2. c, p. 241	**6.** b, p. 242	**10.** a, pp. 243–244
3. a, p. 241	**7.** d, p. 243	
4. d, pp. 241–242	**8.** d, pp. 243–244	

PROBLEMS

1. *a.* 30, 15; *b.* 60, 45; *c.* 30, 60
2. *a.* 30, 15; *b.* 60, 45; *c.* 30, 60
3. *a.* high, A; *b.* 30
4. *a.* A, D, 45; *b.* A, 30
5. *a.* 20, A; *b.* 16, B; *c.* 22, A; *d.* 20, C; *e.* 32, 20, 52, 16, 46, 46; *f.* 20, 22, 42

SHORT ANSWER AND ESSAY QUESTIONS

1. p. 242	**5.** pp. 242–243	**9.** p. 244
2. pp. 242, 244	**6.** p. 242	**10.** p. 244
3. p. 242	**7.** p. 243	
4. p. 242	**8.** pp. 243–244	

Technology, R&D, and Efficiency

Note: The bonus web chapter is available at: www.mcconnell19e.com.

A market economy is not static but subject to change over time. One dynamic force affecting an economy and industries is **technological advance.** This advance occurs over a very long time and allows firms to introduce new products and adopt new methods of production.

The chapter begins by discussing the three-step process that constitutes technological advance: **invention, innovation,** and **diffusion.** Here the text describes many real-world examples of how technological change has affected firms and industries. You will also find out that research and development (R&D) expenditures by firms and government play an integral role in directly supporting this technological advance. The traditional view of economists was that technological advance was something external to the economy, but most contemporary economists think that technological advance is integral to capitalism and arises from intense rivalry among firms.

Entrepreneurs and other innovators play a major role in encouraging innovation and technological change. Entrepreneurs typically form small companies—**start-ups**—to create and introduce new products and production techniques. In this activity entrepreneurs assume personal financial risk, but if they are successful, they can be highly rewarded in the marketplace. There also are innovators within existing firms who can use R&D work to develop new products. University and government research also can contribute output that can be useful for fostering technological advance.

A major section of this chapter analyzes how the firm determines the **optimal amount of R&D spending.** The decision is made by equating marginal benefit with marginal cost. The marginal cost is measured by the interest-rate cost of funds that the firm borrows or obtains from other sources to finance its R&D expenditures. The expected rate of return from the last dollar spent on R&D is the measure of marginal benefit. You should remember that the outcomes from R&D spending are only expected, not guaranteed, for the firm.

Technological changes can increase a firm's profit in two ways. Recall that profit is simply the difference between total revenue and total cost. **Product innovation** can increase revenues because people buy more products from the innovative firm. These increased revenues will increase profits, assuming that costs stay the same. **Process innovation** also can increase profits by reducing costs. This type of innovation leads to better methods

for producing a product and decreases the average total cost for the firm.

One problem with technological advance is that it encourages **imitation.** Successful innovative firms often are emulated by others. This imitation problem can be especially threatening to innovative, smaller firms because the dominant firms in the industry can challenge them. A firm, however, has some advantages in taking the lead in innovation because there are protections and rewards. Legal protections include patents, copyrights, and trademarks; other advantages are early brand-name recognition or the potential for a profitable buyout.

You spent the past three chapters learning about the differences in the four market structures. Now you may be wondering whether one market structure is better suited than another for encouraging technological progress. The answer is clearly mixed because each structure has its strengths and shortcomings. The **inverted-U theory of R&D** gives you an even better framework for figuring out the optimal industry structure for R&D.

The chapter ends by returning to the issue of **economic efficiency,** a topic discussed throughout the text. Technological advance has a double benefit because it enhances both productive efficiency and allocative efficiency. Productive efficiency increases from process innovation that reduces production costs. Allocative efficiency increases because product innovation gives consumers more choice and gives society a more desired mix of products. The efficiency results are not automatic, and the outcome may depend on whether innovation strengthens or weakens monopoly power.

■ CHECKLIST

When you have studied this chapter you should be able to

☐ Define technological advance.

☐ Describe each of the three steps in technological advance.

☐ Explain the role of research and development (R&D) in technological advance.

☐ Contrast the traditional with the modern view of technological advance.

☐ Distinguish between entrepreneurs and other innovators and between start-ups and innovation in existing firms.

☐ Explain how innovators are rewarded for anticipating the future.

☐ Describe the role that universities and government play in fostering technological advance.

☐ Identify five means for financing R&D that are available to firms.

☐ Describe and give a rationale for the interest-rate cost-of-funds curve and the expected-rate-of-return curve.

☐ Show graphically with an example how the optimal level of R&D expenditures is determined.

☐ State three important points from the analysis of optimal R&D expenditures.

☐ Explain how product innovation can increase profits by increasing revenues.

☐ Describe how process innovation can increase profits by reducing costs.

☐ Explain the imitation problem for firms.

☐ Identify six protections for or advantages to being the first to develop a new product or process.

☐ Evaluate which of the four market structures is best suited to technological advance.

☐ Explain the inverted-U theory of R&D and its implications for technological progress.

☐ Describe how technological advance enhances both productive and allocative efficiency.

☐ Explain how innovation may lead to creative destruction and describe the criticisms of this view.

☐ Describe how technological advance is reflected in the development of the modern computer and emergence of the Internet (*Last Word*).

■ **CHAPTER OUTLINE**

1. *Technological advance* involves the development of new and improved products and new and improved ways of producing and distributing the products. The technological change occurs in the *very long run.* It is a three-step process of invention, innovation, and diffusion.

   a. *Invention* is the most basic part of technological advance and involves the discovery of a product or process. Governments encourage invention by granting the inventor a *patent,* which is an exclusive right to sell a product for a period of time.

   b. *Innovation* is the first successful commercial use of a new product or method or the creation of a new form of business. There are two major types: *product innovation,* which involves new and improved products or services, and *process innovation,* which involves new and improved production or distribution methods. Innovation is an important factor in competition because it can enable a firm to leapfrog competitors by making their products or methods obsolete.

   c. *Diffusion* is the spread of an innovation through imitation or copying. New and existing firms copy or imitate successful innovation of other firms to profit from new opportunities or to protect their profits.

   d. In business, research and development (R&D) includes work and expenditures directed toward invention, innovation, and diffusion. Government also supports R&D through defense expenditures and the funding of other activities.

   e. The traditional view of technological advance was that it was external to the economy. It was viewed as a random force to which the economy adjusted and it

depended on the advance of science. The modern view is that it is internal to capitalism. Intense rivalry among individuals and firms motivates them to seek and exploit new or expand existing opportunities for profit. Entrepreneurs and other innovators are the drivers of technological advance.

2. The *entrepreneur* is an initiator, innovator, and risk bearer. Other innovators are key people involved in the pursuit of innovation but who do not bear personal financial risk.

   a. Entrepreneurs often form small new companies called *start-ups,* which are firms that create and introduce a new product or production technique.

   b. Innovators are found within existing corporations. R&D work in major corporations has resulted in technological improvements, often by splitting off units to form innovative firms.

   c. Innovators attempt to anticipate future needs. Product innovation and development are creative activities with both nonmonetary and monetary rewards. More resources for further innovation by entrepreneurs often come from past successes. Successful businesses that meet consumer wants are given the opportunity to produce goods and services for the market.

   d. New scientific knowledge is important to technological advance. Entrepreneurs study the scientific results from university and government laboratories to find those with commercial applicability.

3. The *optimal amount of R&D* expenditures for the firm depends on the marginal benefit and marginal cost of R&D activity. To earn the greatest profit, the firm will expand an activity until its marginal benefit equals its marginal cost.

   a. Several sources are available for financing firms' R&D activities: bank loans, bonds, retained earnings, *venture capital,* or personal savings. A firm's marginal cost of these funds is an interest rate i.

   b. A firm's marginal benefit of R&D is its expected profit (or return) from the last dollar spent on R&D.

   c. The *optimal amount of R&D* in marginal-cost and marginal-benefit analysis is the point where the *interest-rate cost-of-funds* (marginal-cost) *curve* and the *expected-rate-of-return* (marginal-benefit) *curve* intersect. This analysis leads to three important points. First, R&D expenditures can be justified only if the expected return equals or exceeds the cost of financing R&D. Second, the firm expects positive outcomes from R&D, but the results are not guaranteed. Third, firms adjust R&D spending when expected rates of return change on various projects.

4. A firm's profit can be increased through *innovation* in two ways.

   a. The firm can increase revenues through *product innovation.* From a utility perspective, consumers will purchase a new product only if it increases total utility from their limited incomes. The purchases of the product by consumers increase the firm's revenues. Note three other points.

   (1) Consumer acceptance of a new product depends on both its marginal utility and price.

(2) Many new products are not successful, so the firm fails to realize the expected return in these instances.

(3) Most product innovations are small or incremental improvements to existing products, not major changes.

b. *Process innovation,* the introduction of better ways to make products, is another way to increase profit and obtain a positive return on R&D expenditures. It results in a shift upward in the firm's total product curve and a shift downward in the firm's average total cost curve, which increases the firm's profit.

5. The *imitation problem* is that the rivals of a firm may copy or emulate the firm's product or process and thus decrease the profit from the innovator's R&D effort. When a dominant firm quickly imitates the successful new product of smaller competitors with the goal of becoming the second firm to adopt the innovation, it is using a *fast-second strategy.*

    a. Taking the lead in innovation offers the firm several protections and potential advantages from being first to produce a product.

    (1) Patents limit imitation and protect profits over time.

    (2) Copyrights and trademarks reduce direct copying and increase the incentives for product innovation.

    (3) Brand names may provide a major marketing asset.

    (4) Trade secrets and learning by doing give firms advantages.

    (5) The time lags between innovation and diffusion give innovators time to make substantial economic profits.

    (6) There is the potential purchase of the innovating firm by a larger firm at a high price.

6. Certain market structures may foster *technological advance.*

    a. Each *market structure* has strengths and limitations.

    (1) *Pure competition:* Strong competition gives firms the reason to innovate, but the expected rate of return on R&D may be low or negative for a pure competitor.

    (2) *Monopolistic competition:* These firms have a strong profit incentive to develop and differentiate products, but they have limited ability to obtain inexpensive R&D financing. It is also difficult for these firms to extract large profits because the barriers to entry are relatively low.

    (3) *Oligopoly:* Although the size of these firms makes them capable of promoting technological progress, there is little reason for them to introduce costly new technology and new products when they earn large economic profits without doing it.

    (4) *Pure monopoly:* This type of firm has little incentive to engage in R&D because its high profit is protected by high barriers to entry.

    b. *Inverted-U theory of R&D* suggests that R&D effort is weak in industries with very low concentration (pure competition) and very high concentration (pure monopoly). The optimal industry structure for R&D is one in which expected returns on R&D spending are high and funds are readily available and inexpensive to finance. This generally occurs in industries with a few firms that are absolutely and relatively large, but the concentration ratio is not so high as to limit strong competition by smaller firms.

    c. General support for the inverted-U theory of R&D comes from industry studies. The optimal market structure for technological advance appears to be an industry with a mix of large oligopolistic firms (a 40 to 60% concentration ratio) and several highly innovative smaller firms. The technical characteristics of an industry, however, may be a more important factor influencing R&D than its market structure.

7. Technological advance enhances *economic efficiency.*

    a. *Process innovation* improves productive efficiency by increasing the productivity of inputs and reducing average total costs.

    b. *Product innovation* enhances allocative efficiency by giving society a more preferred mixture of goods and services.

    (1) The efficiency gain from innovation, however, can be reduced if patents and the advantages of being first lead to monopoly power.

    (2) Monopoly power can be reduced or destroyed by innovation because it provides competition where there was none.

    c. Innovation may foster *creative destruction,* whereby the creation of new products and production methods simultaneously destroys the monopoly positions of firms protecting existing products and methods. This view is expressed by Joseph Schumpeter, and there are many examples of it in business history. Another view suggests that creative destruction is not inevitable or automatic. In general, innovation improves economic efficiency, but in some cases it can increase monopoly power.

8. (*Last Word*). The history of the development of the modern computer and the Internet are examples of technological advance. This Last Word chronicles the developments and changes from 1945 to 2007.

■ HINTS AND TIPS

1. The section of the chapter on a firm's **optimal amount of R&D** uses marginal-cost and marginal-benefit analysis similar to what you saw in previous chapters. In this case, the interest rate or expected return is graphed on the vertical axis and the amount of R&D spending on the horizontal axis. The only difference from previous MB–MC graphs is that the marginal cost in this example is assumed to be constant at the given interest rate. *It is graphed as a horizontal line.* The expected-rate-of-return curve is downsloping because there are fewer opportunities for R&D expenditures with higher expected rates of return than at lower expected rates of return.

2. The explanation for how new products gain acceptance by consumers is based on the marginal utility theory that you learned about in Chapter 6. Be sure to review the text discussion of Table 6.1 before reading about the example in Table 11W.1.

3. When new processes are developed, they can increase a firm's total product curve and decrease a firm's average total cost curve. Review the section in Chapter 7, "Shifts of the Cost Curves," to understand these points.

■ IMPORTANT TERMS

technological advance

very long run

invention

patent

innovation

product innovation

process innovation

diffusion

start-ups

venture capital

interest-rate cost-of-funds curve

expected-rate-of-return curve

optimal amount of R&D

imitation problem

fast-second strategy

inverted-U theory of R&D

SELF-TEST

■ FILL-IN QUESTIONS

1. Technological advance is a three-step process of

a. _____

b. _____

c. _____

2. The first discovery of a product or process is (innovation, invention) _____, whereas the first commercial introduction of a new product or process is _____; patent protection is available for (invention, innovation) _____ but not _____. The spread of an innovation through imitation or copying is (trademarking, diffusion) _____.

3. The development of new or improved products is (process, product) _____ innovation; the development of new or improved production or distribution methods is _____ innovation.

4. The traditional view of technological advance was that it was (internal, external) _____ to the economy, but the modern view is that technological advance is _____. In the modern view, technological advance arises from (scientific progress, rivalry among firms) _____, but the traditional view holds that it arises from _____ that is largely (internal, external) _____ to the market system.

5. The individual who is an initiator, innovator, and risk bearer who combines resources in unique ways to produce new goods and services is called an (entrepreneur, intrapreneur) _____, but an individual who promotes entrepreneurship within existing corporations is called an _____. Entrepreneurs tend to form (large, small) _____ companies called start-ups, and if they are successful they will receive _____ monetary rewards.

6. Past successes often give entrepreneurs access to (more, less) _____ resources for further innovation because the market economy (punishes, rewards) _____ those businesses that meet consumer wants.

7. To earn the greatest profit from R&D spending, the firm should expand the activity until its marginal benefit is (greater than, less than, equal to) _____ its marginal cost, but a firm should cut back its R&D if its marginal benefit is _____ its marginal cost.

8. Five ways a firm can obtain funding to finance R&D spending are

a. _____

b. _____

c. _____

d. _____

e. _____

9. Product innovation will tend to increase a firm's profit by increasing the (costs, revenues) _____ of the firm; process innovation will tend to increase a firm's profit by reducing the (costs, revenues) _____ of the firm.

10. Consumer acceptance of a new product depends on its marginal utility (and, or) _____ its price. The expected return that motivates product innovation (is, is not) _____ always realized. Most product innovations are (major, minor) _____ improvements to existing products.

11. Process innovation results in a shift (downward, upward) _____ in the firm's total product curve and a shift _____ in the firm's average-total-cost curve, which in turn (increases, decreases) _____ the firm's profit.

12. The imitation problem occurs when rivals of a firm copy or emulate the firm's product or process and thus (increase, decrease) _____ the innovator's profit from the R&D effort. When a dominant firm quickly imitates the successful new product of smaller competitors with the goal of becoming the second firm to adopt the innovation, it is using a (second-best, fast-second) _____ strategy.

13. An example of legal protection for taking the lead in innovation would be (copyrights, trade secrets) _____, but a nonlegal advantage might come from (patents, learning by doing) _____.

14. In regard to R&D, purely competitive firms tend to be (less, more) _____ complacent than monopolists, but the expected rate of return for a pure competitor may be (high, low) _____, and they (may, may not) _____ be able to finance R&D.

15. Monopolistically competitive firms have a (weak, strong) _____ profit incentive to develop and differentiate products, but they have (extensive, limited) _____ ability to obtain inexpensive R&D financing, and it is (difficult, easy) _____ for these firms to extract large profits because the barriers to entry are relatively (high, low) _____.

16. The size of oligopolistic firms makes them (capable, incapable) _____ of promoting technological advance, but there is (much, little) _____ reason for them to introduce costly new technology and new products when they earn (small, large) _____ economic profit without doing it.

17. Pure monopoly has a (strong, weak) _____ incentive to engage in R&D because its high profit is protected by (low, high) _____ barriers to entry. This type of firm views R&D spending as (an offensive, a defensive) _____ move to protect the monopoly from new products that would undercut its monopoly position.

18. Inverted-U theory suggests that R&D effort is at best (strong, weak) _____ in industries with very low and very high concentrations. The optimal industry structure for R&D is one in which expected returns on R&D spending are (low, high) _____ and funds are readily available and inexpensive to finance R&D. This generally occurs in industries with (many, a few) _____ firms that are absolutely and relatively large, but the concentration ratio is not so high as to limit strong competition by smaller firms.

19. Technological advance increases the productivity of inputs, and by reducing average total costs it enhances (allocative, productive) _____ efficiency; when it gives society a more preferred mixture of goods and services it enhances _____ efficiency. The efficiency gain from innovation can be (increased, decreased) _____ if patents and the advantages of being first lead to monopoly power, but it can be _____ if innovation provides competition where there was none.

20. Innovation may foster creative destruction, where the (destruction, creation) _____ of new products and production methods simultaneously leads to the _____ of the monopoly positions of firms

committed to existing products and methods. Another view, however, suggests that creative destruction (is, is not) _____ automatic. In general, innovation improves economic efficiency, but in some cases it can increase monopoly power.

■ TRUE–FALSE QUESTIONS

Circle T if the statement is true, F if it is false.

1. Technological advance consists of new and improved goods and services and new and improved production or distribution processes.   **T   F**

2. In economists' models, technological advance occurs in the short run, not the long run.   **T   F**

3. Invention is the first successful commercial introduction of a new product.   **T   F**

4. Firms channel a majority of their R&D expenditures to innovation and imitation rather than to basic scientific research.   **T   F**

5. Historically, most economists viewed technological advance as a predictable and internal force to which the economy adjusted.   **T   F**

6. The modern view of economists is that capitalism is the driving force of technological advance and such advance occurs in response to profit incentives within the economy.   **T   F**

7. The entrepreneur is an innovator but not a risk bearer.   **T   F**

8. Start-ups are small companies focused on creating and introducing a new product or using a new production or distribution technique.   **T   F**

9. The only innovators are entrepreneurs.   **T   F**

10. The market entrusts the production of goods and services to businesses that have consistently succeeded in fulfilling consumer wants.   **T   F**

11. Research and development rarely occur outside the labs of major corporations.   **T   F**

12. When entrepreneurs use personal savings to finance the R&D for a new venture, the marginal cost of financing is zero.   **T   F**

13. The optimal amount of R&D spending for the firm occurs where its expected return is greater than its interest-rate cost-of-funds to finance it.   **T   F**

14. Most firms are guaranteed a profitable outcome when making an R&D expenditure because the decisions are carefully evaluated.   **T   F**

15. A new product succeeds when it provides consumers with higher marginal utility per dollar spent than do existing products.   **T   F**

16. Most product innovations consist of major changes to existing products and are not incremental improvements.   **T   F**

17. Process innovation increases the firm's total product, lowers its average total cost, and increases its profit.   **T   F**

18. Imitation poses no problems for innovators because there are patent and trademark protections for their innovations.   **T   F**

19. A fast-second strategy involves letting the dominant firm set the price of the product and then smaller firms quickly undercutting that price.   **T   F**

20. Pure competition is the best market structure for encouraging R&D and innovation.   **T   F**

21. One major shortcoming of monopolistic competition in promoting technological progress is its limited ability to secure inexpensive financing for R&D.   **T   F**

22. The inverted-U theory of R&D suggests that R&D effort is strongest in very low-concentration industries and weakest in very high-concentration industries. **T   F**

23. The technical and scientific characteristics of an industry may be more important than its structure in determining R&D spending and innovation.   **T   F**

24. Technological advance enhances productive efficiency but not allocative efficiency.   **T   F**

25. Creative destruction is the process the inventor goes through in developing new products and innovations. **T   F**

■ MULTIPLE-CHOICE QUESTIONS

Circle the letter that corresponds to the best answer.

1. The period in which technology can change and in which firms can introduce entirely new products is the
   (a) short run
   (b) very short run
   (c) long run
   (d) very long run

2. Technological progress is a three-step process of
   (a) creation, pricing, and marketing
   (b) invention, innovation, and diffusion
   (c) manufacturing, venturing, and promotion
   (d) start-ups, imitation, and creative destruction

3. The first discovery of a product or process through the use of imagination, ingenious thinking, and experimentation and the first proof that it will work is
   (a) process innovation
   (b) product innovation
   (c) creative destruction
   (d) invention

4. An exclusive right to sell any new and useful process, machine, or product for a set number of years is called a
   (a) trademark
   (b) copyright
   (c) patent
   (d) brand

5. Innovation is a major factor in competition because it can
   (a) be patented to protect the investment of the developers
   (b) enable firms to make competitors' products obsolete
   (c) guarantee the monopoly position of innovative firms
   (d) reduce research and development costs for firms

6. What idea is best illustrated by the example of McDonald's successfully introducing the fast-food hamburger and then that idea being adopted by other firms such as Burger King and Wendy's?
   (a) start-ups
   (b) diffusion
   (c) invention
   (d) fast-second strategy

7. About what percentage of GDP in the United States is spent on research and development?
   (a) 2.8%
   (b) 7.6%
   (c) 10.6%
   (d) 21.2%

8. The modern view of technological advance is that it is
   (a) rooted in the independent advancement of science
   (b) best stimulated through government R&D spending
   (c) a result of intense rivalry among individuals and firms
   (d) a random outside force to which the economy adjusts

9. The major difference between entrepreneurs and other innovators is
   (a) innovators work in teams, but entrepreneurs do not
   (b) innovators manage start-ups, but entrepreneurs do not
   (c) entrepreneurs bear personal financial risk, but innovators do not
   (d) entrepreneurs invent new products and processes, but innovators do not

10. Past successes in developing products often mean that entrepreneurs and innovative firms
   (a) have access to more private resources for further innovation
   (b) have access to less private resources for further innovation
   (c) have access to more public support for further innovation
   (d) experience no change in the availability of private or public resources for further innovation

Questions 11, 12, and 13 are based on the following table showing the expected rate of return, R&D spending, and interest-rate cost of funds for a hypothetical firm.

Expected rate of return (%)	R&D (millions of $)	Interest-rate cost of funds (%)
15	20	9
13	40	9
11	60	9
9	80	9
7	100	9

11. In a supply and demand graph, the interest-rate cost-of-funds curve would be a(n)
  (a) vertical line at 9%
  (b) horizontal line at 9%
  (c) upsloping line over the 15 to 7% range
  (d) downsloping line over the 15 to 7% range

12. The optimal amount of R&D would be
  (a) $40 million
  (b) $60 million
  (c) $80 million
  (d) $100 million

13. If the interest-rate cost-of-funds curve rose to 13%, the optimal amount of R&D spending would be
  (a) $40 million
  (b) $60 million
  (c) $80 million
  (d) $100 million

14. Product innovation tends to increase the profits of firms primarily by
  (a) decreasing the firm's average costs
  (b) increasing the firm's total revenue
  (c) decreasing marginal utility per dollar spent
  (d) increasing the success of R&D spending

15. Consumers will buy a new product only if
  (a) it has a lower marginal utility per dollar spent than another product
  (b) there is a substantial budget for promotion and marketing
  (c) it can be sold at a lower price than that for a competing product
  (d) it increases the total utility they obtain from their limited income

16. Process innovation produces a(n)
  (a) downward shift in the total-product curve and an upward shift in the average-cost curve
  (b) upward shift in the total-product curve and a downward shift in the average-cost curve
  (c) upward shift in both the total-product and average-cost curves
  (d) downward shift in both the total-product and average-cost curves

17. Some dominant firms in an industry use a fast-second strategy that involves
  (a) developing two products to compete with rivals
  (b) cutting the development time for the introduction of a new product
  (c) moving quickly to buy the second largest firm in the industry to gain larger market share
  (d) letting smaller firms initiate new products and then quickly imitating the success

18. One legal protection for taking the lead in innovation is
  (a) venture capital
  (b) trademarks
  (c) trade secrets
  (d) mergers

19. One major advantage of being the first to develop a product is the
  (a) use of the fast-second strategy
  (b) increase in retained earnings
  (c) lower interest-rate costs of funds
  (d) potential for profitable buyouts

20. Which firm has a strong incentive for product development and differentiation?
  (a) a monopolistically competitive firm
  (b) a purely competitive firm
  (c) an oligopolistic firm
  (d) a pure monopoly

21. In which market structure is there the least incentive to engage in R&D?
  (a) a monopolistically competitive firm
  (b) a purely competitive firm
  (c) an oligopolistic firm
  (d) a pure monopoly

22. The inverted-U theory of R&D suggests that R&D effort is at best weak in
  (a) low-concentration industries only
  (b) high-concentration industries only
  (c) low- and high-concentration industries
  (d) low- to middle-concentration industries

23. The optimal market structure for technological advance seems to be an industry in which there
  (a) are many purely competitive firms
  (b) are monopolists closely regulated by government
  (c) is a mix of large oligopolistic firms with several small and highly innovative firms
  (d) is a mix of monopolistically competitive firms and a few large monopolists in industries with high capital costs

24. Technological advance as embodied in process innovation typically
  (a) decreases allocative efficiency
  (b) increases allocative efficiency
  (c) decreases productive efficiency
  (d) increases productive efficiency

25. Which statement would best describe the concept of creative destruction as used by economist Joseph Schumpeter?
  (a) Innovation would lead to monopoly power and thus destroy the economy.
  (b) The creation of new products and production methods would destroy the market for existing products.
  (c) Invention would create new products, but diffusion would destroy many potentially good ideas.
  (d) Firms are being creative with learning by doing, but this spirit is destroyed by the inability of firms to finance R&D expenditures.

■ **PROBLEMS**

1. Match the terms with the phrases using the appropriate number.
  1. invention **2.** innovation **3.** diffusion

a. Imitation of the Chrysler Corporation's Jeep Grand Cherokee with sport utility vehicles developed by other auto companies _____

b. The first working model of the microchip _____

c. Computers and word processing software that eliminated the need for typewriters _____

d. Adoption of Alamo's offer of unlimited mileage by other major car rental companies _____

e. The creation of the first electric light bulb _____

f. Development of iPhones by Apple _____

2. Use the following table that shows the rate of return and R&D spending for a hypothetical firm.

Expected rate of return (%)	R&D (millions of $)
24	3
20	6
16	8
12	12
9	15
6	18
3	21

a. Assume the interest-rate cost of funds is 12%. The optimal amount of R&D expenditures will be $_____ million. At this amount, the marginal cost of R&D spending is _____% and the marginal benefit (the expected rate of return) is _____%.

b. Graph the expected-rate-of-return and the interest-rate cost-of-fund curves of R&D spending in the graph below. Be sure to label the axes.

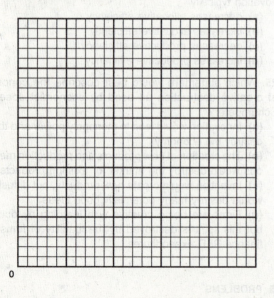

c. Now assume that the interest-rate cost of funds falls to 6%. The optimal amount of spending will be $_____ million. For this amount of R&D spending,

the marginal cost of R&D spending is _____% and the marginal benefit (expected rate of return) is _____%.

d. Show on the graph how the interest-rate cost-of-funds curve changed in the answer that you gave for **b**.

3. Following are two average-total-cost schedules for a firm. The first schedule (ATC$_1$) shows the cost of producing the product at five levels of output before a new innovation. The second schedule (ATC$_2$) shows the average total cost at the five output levels after the innovation.

Output	Before ATC$_1$	After ATC$_2$
10	$30	$27
20	25	18
30	18	14
40	22	19
50	28	26

a. Plot the average-cost curves for the schedules on the following graph.

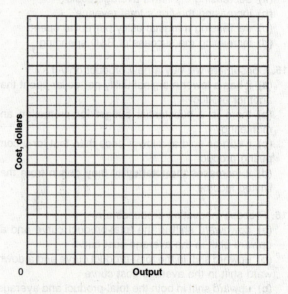

b. What was the reduction in average total cost at each of the five levels of output as a result of the innovation?

10_____, 20_____, 30_____, 40_____, 50_____.

c. If the product price is $20 per unit and the firm was producing at 30 units of output, the profit for the firm before the innovation was $_____. At this level of output, the profit after the innovation was $_____.

■ **SHORT ANSWER AND ESSAY QUESTIONS**

1. Give a definition of technological advance. According to economists, what role does time play in the definition?

2. Explain and give examples of invention. What does government do to protect it?

3. How does innovation differ from invention and diffusion? How does innovation affect competition among firms?

4. Compare and contrast the modern view of technological advance with the traditional view.

5. In what ways do entrepreneurs differ from other innovators? In what types of business does each tend to work? How have the characteristics of entrepreneurs changed over time?

6. What does it mean that "innovators try to anticipate the future"? What are the economic consequences of this effort?

7. Why do entrepreneurs and other innovators actively study the scientific output of universities and government laboratories?

8. What are the many different sources of funding to finance firms' R&D expenditures? If an entrepreneur uses personal funds, is there a cost for financing?

9. Explain how the firm decides on the optimal amount of research and development. Use a marginal-cost and marginal-benefit graph in your explanation.

10. Why might many R&D expenditures be affordable but not worthwhile? Are outcomes from R&D guaranteed?

11. Describe how a firm's revenues and profits are increased through product innovation. Why does consumer acceptance of a new product depend on both its marginal utility and price?

12. Explain how process innovation reduces cost and increases profits. Illustrate the point graphically using a total-product and average-cost curve graph.

13. Describe the fast-second strategy and give an example of it.

14. What is the imitation problem resulting from technological advance?

15. Describe the legal protections and potential advantages of taking the lead in innovation.

16. Compare and contrast the suitability of different market structures for fostering technological advance.

17. Explain the basic conclusions from inverted-U theory of R&D. What will be the optimal market structure for technological progress?

18. How does technological advance enhance economic efficiency? Distinguish between its effects on productive efficiency and allocative efficiency.

19. How might innovation create or reduce monopoly power? Why might both effects be possible?

20. Explain the idea of creative destruction as championed by Joseph Schumpeter. What are the objections to that idea?

ANSWERS

Chapter 11 Web Technology, R&D, and Efficiency

FILL-IN QUESTIONS

1. *a.* invention; *b.* innovation; *c.* diffusion
2. invention, innovation, invention, innovation, diffusion
3. product, process
4. external, internal, rivalry among firms, scientific progress, external
5. entrepreneur, intrapreneur, small, large
6. more, rewards
7. equal to, less than
8. *a.* bank loans; *b.* bonds; *c.* retained earnings; *d.* venture capital; *e.* personal savings (any order *a–e*)
9. revenues, costs
10. and, is not, minor
11. upward, downward, increases
12. decrease, fast-second
13. copyrights, learning by doing
14. less, low, may not
15. strong, limited, difficult, low
16. capable, little, large
17. weak, high, a defensive
18. weak, high, a few
19. productive, allocative, decreased, increased
20. creation, destruction, is not

Note: Page numbers for True–False, Multiple Choice, and Short Answer and Essay Questions refer to Bonus Web Chapter 11.

TRUE–FALSE QUESTIONS

1. T, pp. 1–2
2. F, p. 2
3. F, p. 2
4. T, p. 3
5. F, pp. 3–4
6. T, pp. 3–4
7. F, p. 4
8. T, p. 4
9. F, p. 4
10. T, p. 5
11. F, p. 5
12. F, p. 6
13. F, pp. 7–8
14. F, p. 8
15. T, p. 9
16. F, p. 9
17. T, pp. 9–10
18. F, p. 10
19. F, p. 10
20. F, p. 13
21. T, p. 13
22. F, p. 14
23. T, pp. 14–15
24. F, p. 15
25. F, p. 15

MULTIPLE-CHOICE QUESTIONS

1. d, p. 2
2. b, pp. 2–3
3. d, p. 2
4. c, p. 2
5. b, p. 2
6. b, pp. 2–3
7. a, p. 3
8. c, pp. 3–4
9. c, p. 4
10. a, pp. 4–5
11. b, p. 6
12. c, pp. 7–8
13. a, pp. 7–8
14. b, pp. 8–9
15. d, pp. 8–9
16. b, pp. 9–10
17. d, p. 10
18. b, p. 11
19. d, pp. 11–12
20. a, pp. 13–14
21. d, p. 14
22. c, p. 14
23. c, pp. 14–15
24. d, p. 15
25. b, p. 15

PROBLEMS

1. *a.* 3; *b.* 1; *c.* 2; *d.* 3; *e.* 1; *f.* 2
2. *a.* 12, 12, 12; *b.* similar to Figure 11 W.4 in the text; *c.* 18, 6, 6; *d. horizontal* interest-rate-cost-of-funds curve will drop from 12 to 6%
3. *a.* Put output on the horizontal axis, and put average cost on the vertical axis. Plot the set of points. Connect the set with lines; *b.* 3, 7, 4, 3, 2; *c.* Before: TR is $600 (30 × $20), TC is $540 (30 × $18), profit is $60; After: TR is $600, TC is $420 (30 × $14), profit is $180

SHORT ANSWER AND ESSAY QUESTIONS

1. pp. 1–2	8. pp. 5–6	15. pp. 10–12
2. p. 2	9. pp. 7–8	16. pp. 13–14
3. pp. 2–3	10. p. 8	17. p. 14
4. pp. 3–4	11. pp. 8–9	18. p. 15
5. p. 4	12. pp. 9–10	19. p. 15
6. pp. 4–5	13. p. 10	20. pp. 15–17
7. p. 5	14. p. 10	

CHAPTER 12

The Demand for Resources

This chapter is the first of three that examine the market for economic resources such as labor, capital, land, and natural resources. In resource markets the demanders are the employers of the resources and the suppliers are the owners of the resources. As you already know, the demand for and the supply of a resource will determine the resource price and the quantities in a competitive market.

Chapter 12 focuses on the demand or employer side of the resource market. It offers a general explanation of what determines demand for any resource. Chapters 13 and 14 discuss the characteristics of the market for particular resources—labor, capital, land, or entrepreneurial ability—and present the supply side of the resource market.

The **resource market is important** for several reasons, as you will learn in the first section of the chapter. Resource prices determine what resource owners (or households) receive in exchange for supplying their resources, and thus they determine the incomes of households. Prices allocate resources to their most efficient uses and encourage the least costly methods of production in our economy. Many public policy issues also involve resource pricing, such as setting a minimum wage.

The next section of the chapter focuses on the **marginal productivity theory of resource demand.** When a firm wishes to maximize its profits, it produces that output at which marginal revenue and marginal cost are equal. But how much of each resource does the firm hire if it wishes to maximize its profits? You will learn that the firm hires that amount of each resource up to the point that the marginal revenue product and the marginal resource cost of that resource are equal (MRP = MRC).

There is another similarity between the output and the resource markets for the firm. Recall that the competitive firm's supply curve is a portion of its marginal-cost curve. The purely competitive firm's demand curve for a resource is a portion of its marginal-revenue-product curve. Just as cost is the important determinant of supply, the revenue derived from the use of a resource is the important factor determining the demand for that resource in a competitive market for resources.

The next major section of the chapter presents the **determinants of resource demand.** Three major ones are discussed—changes in product demand, productivity, and the prices of other resources. The last one is the most complicated because you must consider whether the other resources are substitutes or complements and also the underlying factors affecting them.

This chapter has a section on the **elasticity of resource demand,** which is no different from the elasticity

concept you learned about in Chapter 6. In this case, it is the relation of the percentage change in quantity demanded of the resource to a percentage change in the price of the resource. As you will discover, three factors that affect elasticity are the availability of other substitute resources, the elasticity of product demand, and the ratio of resource cost to total cost.

Most of the chapter examines the situation in which there is only one variable resource. The next-to-last section of the chapter, however, offers a general perspective on the **combination of resources** the firm will choose to use when multiple inputs are used and all inputs are variable. Two rules are presented. The least-cost rule states that the firm will minimize costs when the last dollar spent on each resource results in the same marginal product. The profit-maximizing rule means that in a competitive market the firm will maximize its profits when each resource is used so that its marginal product is equal to its price. The second rule is equally important because a firm that employs the quantity of resources that maximizes its profits also produces the output that maximizes its profits and is thus producing at the least cost.

The marginal productivity theory of resource demand is not without criticism, as you will learn in the last section of the chapter. If resource prices reflect marginal productivity, then this relationship can produce income inequality in society. In addition, market imperfection may skew the distribution of income.

■ **CHECKLIST**

When you have studied this chapter you should be able to

☐ Present four reasons for studying resource pricing.
☐ Explain why the demand for an economic resource is a derived demand.
☐ Define the marginal revenue product and relate it to the productivity and price of a resource.
☐ Determine the marginal-revenue-product schedule of a resource for a product sold in a purely competitive market, when given the data.
☐ Define the marginal resource cost.
☐ State the rule used by a profit-maximizing firm to determine how much of a resource it will employ.
☐ Apply the MRP = MRC rule to determine the quantity of a resource a firm will hire, when you are given the necessary data.
☐ Explain why the marginal-revenue-product schedule of a resource is the firm's demand for the resource.

161

☐ Find the marginal-revenue-product schedule of a resource for a product sold in an imperfectly competitive market, when given the data.

☐ Derive the market demand for a resource.

☐ List the three factors which would change a firm's demand for a resource.

☐ Predict the effect on resource demand of an increase or decrease in one of its three determinants.

☐ Give trends on the occupations with the fastest growth in jobs both in percentage terms and in absolute numbers.

☐ State three determinants of the price elasticity of resource demand.

☐ Describe how a change in each determinant would change the price elasticity of demand for a resource.

☐ State the rule used by a firm for determining the least-cost combination of resources.

☐ Use the least-cost rule to find the least-cost combination of resources for production, when given data.

☐ State the rule used by a profit-maximizing firm to determine the quantity of each of several resources to employ.

☐ Apply the profit-maximizing rule to determine the quantity of each resource a firm will hire, when given the data.

☐ Explain the marginal productivity theory of income distribution.

☐ Give two criticisms of the marginal productivity theory of income distribution.

☐ Explain using the least-cost rule why ATMs have replaced tellers (*Last Word*).

■ CHAPTER OUTLINE

1. The study of what determines the prices of resources *is important* because resource prices influence the size of individual incomes and the resulting distribution of income. They allocate scarce resources and affect the way in which firms combine resources in production. Resource pricing also raises policy and ethical issues about income distribution.

2. The marginal productivity theory of resource demand assumes that the firm is a "price taker" or "wage taker" in the resource market.

 a. The demand for a single resource is a *derived demand* that depends on the demand for the goods and services it can produce.

 b. Because resource demand is a derived demand, it depends on two factors: the marginal productivity of the resource and the market price of the good or service it is used to produce.

 (1) *Marginal revenue product (MRP)* is the change in total revenue divided by a one-unit change in resource quantity.

 (2) It combines two factors—the *marginal product* (the additional output from each additional unit of resource) of a resource and the market price of the product it produces—into a single useful tool.

 c. *Marginal resource cost (MRC)* is the change in total resource cost divided by a one-unit change in resource quantity. A firm will hire resources until the marginal revenue product of the resource is equal to its marginal resource cost (**MRP = MRC**).

 d. The firm's marginal-revenue-product schedule for a resource is that firm's demand schedule for the resource.

 e. If a firm sells its output in an *imperfectly competitive product market,* the more the firm sells, the lower the price of the product becomes. This causes the firm's marginal-revenue-product (resource demand) schedule to be less elastic than it would be if the firm sold its output in a purely competitive market.

 f. The market (or total) demand for a resource is the horizontal summation of the demand schedules of all firms using the resource.

3. The **determinants of resource demand** are changes in the demand for the product produced, changes in the productivity of the resource, and changes in the prices of other resources.

 a. A change in the demand for a product produced by a resource will change the demand of a firm for labor in the same direction.

 b. A change in the productivity of a resource will change the demand of a firm for the resource in the same direction.

 c. A change in the price of a

 (1) *substitute resource* will change the demand for a resource in the same direction if the **substitution effect** outweighs the **output effect** and in the opposite direction if the output effect outweighs the substitution effect

 (2) *complementary resource* will change the demand for a resource in the opposite direction

 d. Changes in the demand for labor have significant effects on employment growth in occupations, both in percentage and absolute terms. Projections (2008–2018) are reported for the fastest growing occupations (e.g., biomedical engineers; network systems and data communication analysts; home health aides) and the most rapidly declining occupations (e.g., textile machine operators; sewing machine operators; postal service workers; lathe operators).

4. The price **elasticity of resource demand** measures the sensitivity of resource quantity to changes in resource prices.

 a. Three factors affect the price elasticity of resource demand:

 (1) the ease of substitution of other resources: the greater the substitutability of other resources, the more elastic the resource demand

 (2) the elasticity of the demand for the product that the resource produces: the more elastic the product demand, the more elastic the resource demand

 (3) the ratio of labor cost to total cost: the greater the ratio of labor cost to total cost, the greater the price elasticity of demand for labor.

5. Firms often employ more than one resource in producing a product.

 a. The firm employing resources in purely competitive markets is hiring resources in the **least-cost combination of resources** when the ratio of the marginal product of a resource to its price is the same for all the resources the firm hires.

b. The firm is hiring resources in the *profit-maximizing combination of resources* if it hires resources in a purely competitive market when the marginal revenue product of each resource is equal to the price of that resource.

c. A numerical example illustrates the least-cost and profit-maximizing rules for a firm that employs resources in purely competitive markets.

6. The *marginal productivity theory of income distribution* seems to result in an equitable distribution of income because each unit of a resource receives a payment equal to its marginal contribution to the firm's revenue. The theory has at least two serious faults.

a. The distribution of income will be unequal because resources are unequally distributed among individuals in the economy.

b. The income of those who supply resources will not be based on their marginal productivities if there is monopsony or monopoly in the resource markets of the economy.

7. (*Last Word*). ATMs have eliminated many human teller positions over the past few decades as explained by the resource theory presented in this chapter. The least-cost combination of resources rule implies that firms will change inputs in response to technological change or changes in input prices. If the marginal product of an ATM divided by its price is greater than the marginal product of a human teller divided by its price, then more ATMs will be used in the banking sector.

■ **HINTS AND TIPS**

1. The list of important terms for Chapter 12 is relatively short, but included in the list are two very important concepts—**marginal revenue product** and **marginal resource cost**—which you must grasp if you are to understand how much of a resource a firm will hire. These two concepts are similar to, but not identical with, the marginal-revenue and marginal-cost concepts used in the study of product markets and in the explanation of the quantity of output a firm will produce.

2. Marginal revenue and marginal cost are, respectively, the change in the firm's total revenue and the change in the firm's total cost when it produces and sells an additional unit of *output*. Marginal revenue product and marginal resource cost are, respectively, the change in the firm's total revenue and the change in the firm's total cost when it hires an additional unit of *input*. Note that the two new concepts deal with changes in revenue and costs as a consequence of hiring more of a *resource*.

3. The marginal revenue product (MRP) of a resource is simply the marginal product of the resource (MP) times the price of the product that the resource produces (*P*), or MRP = MP × *P*. Under pure competition, MP changes, but *P* is constant as more resources are added to production. Under imperfect competition, both MP and *P* change as more resources are added, and thus each variable (MP and *P*) affects MRP. Compare the data in Tables 12.1 and 12.2 in the textbook to see this difference.

4. Make sure you understand the rule **MRP = MRC.** A firm will hire one more unit of a resource only so long as the resource adds more to the firm's revenues than it does to its costs. If MRP > MRC, the firm will hire more resources. If MRP < MRC, the firm will cut back on resource use.

5. It can be difficult to figure out what effect a change in the price of a substitute resource (capital) will have on the demand for another resource (labor). It is easy to understand why the demand for labor might decrease if the price of capital decreases because cheaper capital would be substituted for labor. It is harder to explain why the opposite might be true. That insight requires an understanding of both the **substitution effect** and the **output effect.** Find out how one effect may offset the other.

6. The **profit-maximizing rule** for a combination of resources may seem difficult, but it is relatively simple. Just remember that the price of any resource must be equal to its marginal revenue product, and thus *the ratio must always equal 1.*

■ **IIMPORTANT TERMS**

derived demand

marginal product

marginal revenue product (MRP)

marginal resource cost (MRC)

MRP = MRC rule

substitution effect

output effect

elasticity of resource demand

least-cost combination of resources

profit-maximizing combination of resources

marginal productivity theory of income distribution

SELF-TEST

■ **FILL-IN QUESTIONS**

1. Resource prices allocate (revenues, resources) _____ and are one factor that determines household (incomes, costs) _____ and business _____.

2. The demand for a resource is a (constant, derived) _____ demand that depends on the (productivity, cost) of the resource and the (cost, price) _____ of the product made from the resource.

3. A firm will find it profitable to hire units of a resource up to the quantity at which the marginal revenue (cost, product) _____ equals the marginal resource _____.

4. If the firm hires the resource in a purely competitive market, the marginal resource (cost, product) _____ will be (greater than, less than, equal to) _____ the price of the resource.

5. A firm's demand schedule for a resource is the firm's marginal revenue (cost, product) _____ schedule for that resource because both indicate the quantities of the resource the firm will employ at various resource (costs, prices) _____.

6. A producer in an imperfectly competitive market finds that the more of a resource it employs, the (higher, lower) _____ becomes the price at which it can sell its product. As a consequence, the (supply, demand) _____ schedule for the resource is (more, less) _____ elastic than it would be if the output were sold in a purely competitive market.

7. Adding the quantity demanded for the resource at each and every price for each firm using the resource gives the market (supply, demand) _____ curve for the resource.

8. The demand for a resource will change if the (demand, supply) _____ of the product the resource produces changes, if the (productivity, price) _____ of the resource changes, or if the (price, elasticity) _____ of other resources change.

9. If the demand for a product increases, then the demand for the resource that produces that product will (increase, decrease) _____. Conversely, if the demand for a product decreases, then the demand for the resource that produces that product will _____.

10. When the productivity of a resource falls, the demand for the resource (rises, falls) _____, but when the productivity of a resource rises, the demand for the resource _____.

11. The output of the firm being constant, a decrease in the price of resource A will induce the firm to hire (more, less) _____ of resource A and _____ of other resources; this is called the (substitution, output) _____ effect. But if the decrease in the price of A results in lower total costs and an increase in output, the firm may hire (more, less) _____ of both resources; this is called the (substitution, output) _____ effect.

12. A decrease in the price of a complementary resource will cause the demand for labor to (increase, decrease) _____, but an increase in the price of a complementary resource will cause the demand for labor to _____.

13. The three determinants of the price elasticity of demand for a resource are the ease with which other resources can be (substitutes, complements) _____

for it, the price elasticity of (supply, demand) _____ for the product the resource produces, and the ratio of resource (demand, cost) _____ to total (demand, cost) _____.

14. If the marginal product of labor declines slowly when added to a fixed stock of capital, the demand curve for labor (MRP) will decline (rapidly, slowly) _____ and will tend to be highly (elastic, inelastic) _____.

15. The greater the substitutability of other resources for a resource, the (greater, less) _____ will be the elasticity of demand for a resource.

16. Suppose a firm employs resources in purely competitive markets. If the firm wishes to produce any given amount of its output in the least costly way, the ratio of the marginal (cost, product) _____ of each resource to its (demand, price) _____ must be the same for all resources.

17. A firm that hires resources in purely competitive markets is employing the combination of resources that will result in maximum profits for the firm when the marginal (revenue product, resource cost) _____ of every resource is equal to its (demand, price) _____.

18. If the marginal revenue product of a resource is equal to the price of that resource, the marginal revenue product divided by its price is equal to (1, infinity) _____.

19. In the marginal productivity theory, the distribution of income is an equitable one because each unit of each resource is paid an amount equal to its (total, marginal) _____ contribution to the firm's (revenues, costs) _____.

20. The marginal productivity theory rests on the assumption of (competitive, imperfect) _____ markets. In the real world, there are many labor markets with imperfections because of employer pricing or monopoly power, so wage rates and other resource prices (do, do not) _____ perfectly measure contributions to domestic output.

■ **TRUE–FALSE QUESTIONS**

Circle T if the statement is true, F if it is false.

1. In the resource markets of the economy, resources are demanded by business firms and supplied by households.   **T F**

2. The prices of resources are an important factor in the determination of resource allocation.   **T F**

3. The demand for a resource is a derived demand based on the demand for the product it produces.   **T F**

4. A resource that is highly productive will always be in great demand. **T F**

5. A firm's demand schedule for a resource is the firm's marginal-revenue-product schedule for the resource. **T F**

6. It will be profitable for a firm to hire additional units of labor resources up to the point where the marginal revenue product of labor is equal to its marginal resource cost. **T F**

7. A firm with one worker can produce 30 units of a product that sells for $4 a unit, but the same firm with two workers can produce 70 units of that product. The marginal revenue product of the second worker is $400. **T F**

8. The competitive firm's marginal revenue product of labor will fall as output expands because marginal product diminishes and product price falls. **T F**

9. A producer's demand schedule for a resource will be more elastic if the firm sells its product in a purely competitive market than it would be if it sold the product in an imperfectly competitive market. **T F**

10. The market demand for a particular resource is the sum of the individual demands of all firms that employ that resource. **T F**

11. An increase in the price of a resource will cause the demand for the resource to decrease. **T F**

12. The demand curve for labor will increase when the demand for (and price of) the product produced by that labor increases. **T F**

13. There is an inverse relationship between the productivity of labor and the demand for labor. **T F**

14. The demand for a resource will be increased with improvements in its quality. **T F**

15. When two resources are substitutes for each other, both the substitution effect and the output effect of a decrease in the price of one of these resources operate to increase the quantity of the other resource employed by the firm. **T F**

16. The output effect of an increase in the price of a resource increases the quantity demanded of that resource. **T F**

17. If two resources are complementary, an increase in the price of one will reduce the demand for the other. **T F**

18. Price declines for computer equipment have had stronger output effects than substitution effects, increasing the demand for computer software engineers and specialists. **T F**

19. The greater the substitutability of other resources, the less will be the elasticity of demand for a particular resource. **T F**

20. The greater the elasticity of product demand, the greater the elasticity of resource demand. **T F**

21. The demand for labor will be less elastic when labor is a smaller proportion of the total cost of producing a product. **T F**

Use the following information as the basis for answering Questions 22 and 23. The marginal revenue product and price of resource A are $12 and a constant $2, respectively, and the marginal revenue product and price of resource B are $25 and a constant $5, respectively. The firm sells its product at a constant price of $1.

22. The firm should decrease the amount of A and increase the amount of B it employs if it wishes to decrease its total cost without affecting its total output. **T F**

23. If the firm wishes to maximize its profits, it should increase its employment of both A and B until their marginal revenue products fall to $2 and $5, respectively. **T F**

24. The marginal productivity theory of income distribution results in an equitable distribution if resource markets are competitive. **T F**

25. The marginal productivity theory rests on the assumption of imperfectly competitive markets. **T F**

■ **MULTIPLE-CHOICE QUESTIONS**

Circle the letter that corresponds to the best answer.

1. The prices paid for resources affect
(a) the money incomes of households in the economy
(b) the allocation of resources among different firms and industries in the economy
(c) the quantities of different resources employed to produce a particular product
(d) all of the above

2. In a competitive resource market, the firm employing a resource such as labor is a
(a) price maker
(b) cost maker
(c) wage taker
(d) revenue taker

3. The demand for a resource is *derived* from the
(a) demand for the products it helps produce
(b) price of the resource
(c) supply of the resource
(d) income of the firm selling the resource

4. The law of diminishing returns explains why
(a) the MRP of an input in a purely competitive market decreases as a firm increases the quantity of an employed resource
(b) the MRC of an input in a purely competitive market decreases as a firm increases the quantity of an employed resource
(c) resource demand is a derived demand
(d) there are substitution and output effects for resources

Answer Questions 5, 6, and 7 on the basis of the information in the following table for a purely competitive market.

Number of workers	Total product	Product price ($)
0	0	4
1	16	4
2	26	4
3	34	4
4	40	4
5	44	4

5. At a wage rate of $15, the firm will choose to employ
 (a) 2 workers
 (b) 3 workers
 (c) 4 workers
 (d) 5 workers

6. At a wage rate of $30, the firm will choose to employ
 (a) 2 workers
 (b) 3 workers
 (c) 4 workers
 (d) 5 workers

7. If the product price increases to a constant $8, then at a wage rate of $30, the firm will choose to employ
 (a) 2 workers
 (b) 3 workers
 (c) 4 workers
 (d) 5 workers

Use the following total-product and marginal-product schedules for a resource to answer Questions 8, 9, 10, and 11. Assume that the quantities of other resources the firm employs remain constant.

Units of resource	Total product	Marginal product
0	0	—
1	8	8
2	14	6
3	18	4
4	21	3
5	23	2

8. If the product the firm produces sells for a constant $3 per unit, the marginal revenue product of the fourth unit of the resource is
 (a) $3
 (b) $6
 (c) $9
 (d) $12

9. If the firm's product sells for a constant $3 per unit and the price of the resource is a constant $15, the firm will employ how many units of the resource?
 (a) 2
 (b) 3
 (c) 4
 (d) 5

10. If the firm can sell 14 units of output at a price of $1 per unit and 18 units of output at a price of $0.90 per unit,

the marginal revenue product of the third unit of the resource would be
 (a) $4
 (b) $3.60
 (c) $2.20
 (d) $0.40

11. If the firm can sell 8 units at a price of $1.50, 14 units at a price of $1.00, 18 units at a price of $0.90, 21 units at a price of $0.70, and 23 units at a price of $0.50, then the firm is
 (a) maximizing profits at a product price of $0.50
 (b) minimizing its costs at a product price of $1.00
 (c) selling in an imperfectly competitive market
 (d) selling in a purely competitive market

12. As a firm that sells its product in an imperfectly competitive market increases the quantity of a resource it employs, the marginal revenue product of that resource falls because
 (a) the price paid by the firm for the resource falls
 (b) the marginal product of the resource falls
 (c) the price at which the firm sells its product falls
 (d) both the marginal product and the price at which the firm sells its product fall

13. Which would increase a firm's demand for a particular resource?
 (a) an increase in the prices of complementary resources used by the firm
 (b) a decrease in the demand for the firm's product
 (c) an increase in the productivity of the resource
 (d) an increase in the price of the particular resource

14. The substitution effect indicates that a firm will use
 (a) more of an input whose relative price has decreased
 (b) more of an input whose relative price has increased
 (c) less of an input whose relative price has decreased
 (d) less of an input whose relative price has remained constant

15. Suppose resource A and resource B are substitutes and the price of A increases. If the output effect is greater than the substitution effect,
 (a) the quantity of A employed by the firm will increase and the quantity of B employed will decrease
 (b) the quantities of both A and B employed by the firm will decrease
 (c) the quantities of both A and B employed by the firm will increase
 (d) the quantity of A employed will decrease and the quantity of B employed will increase

16. Two resource inputs, capital and labor, are complementary and used in fixed proportions. A decrease in the price of capital will
 (a) increase the demand for labor
 (b) decrease the demand for labor
 (c) decrease the quantity demanded for labor
 (d) have no effect because the relationship is fixed

17. Which would result in an increase in the elasticity of demand for a particular resource?
(a) an increase in the demand for the resource
(b) a decrease in the elasticity of demand for the product that the resource helps to produce
(c) an increase in the percentage of the firm's total costs accounted for by the resource
(d) a decrease in the ease of resource substitutability for the particular resource

18. The demand for labor would most likely become more inelastic as a result of
(a) an increase in the elasticity of the demand for the product that the labor produces
(b) an increase in the time for employers to make technological changes or purchase new equipment
(c) a decrease in the proportion of labor costs to total costs
(d) a decrease in the demand for the product

19. A firm is allocating its expenditures for resources in a way that will result in the least total cost of producing any given output when the
(a) amount the firm spends on each resource is the same
(b) marginal revenue product of each resource is the same
(c) marginal product of each resource is the same
(d) marginal product per dollar spent on the last unit of each resource is the same

20. A business is employing inputs such that the marginal product of labor is 20 and the marginal product of capital is 45. The price of labor is $10 and the price of capital is $15. If the business wants to minimize costs while keeping output constant, then it should
(a) use more labor and less capital
(b) use less labor and less capital
(c) use less labor and more capital
(d) make no change in resource use

21. Assume that a computer disk manufacturer is employing resources so that the MRP of the last unit hired for resource X is $240 and the MRP of the last unit hired for resource Y is $150. The price of resource X is $80 and the price of resource Y is $50. To maximize profit the firm should
(a) hire more of resource X and less of resource Y
(b) hire less of resource X and more of resource Y
(c) hire less of both resource X and resource Y
(d) hire more of both resource X and resource Y

22. Which does not suggest that a firm that hires resources in a purely competitive market is maximizing its profits?
(a) The marginal revenue product of every resource is equal to 1.
(b) The marginal revenue product of every resource is equal to its price.
(c) The ratio of the marginal revenue product of every resource to its price is equal to 1.
(d) The ratio of the price of every resource to its marginal revenue product is equal to 1.

23. Assume that a purely competitive firm uses two resources—labor (L) and capital (C)—to produce a product. In which situation would the firm be maximizing profit?

	MRP_L	MRP_C	P_L	P_C
(a)	10	20	30	40
(b)	10	20	10	20
(c)	15	15	10	10
(d)	30	40	10	5

24. In the marginal productivity theory of income distribution, when all markets are purely competitive, each unit of each resource receives a money payment equal to
(a) its marginal product
(b) its marginal revenue product
(c) the needs of the resource owner
(d) the payments received by each of the units of the other resources in the economy

25. A major criticism of the marginal productivity theory of income distribution is that
(a) the demand for labor resources is price elastic
(b) labor markets are often subject to imperfect competition
(c) the theory suggests that there will be equality in incomes
(d) purely competitive firms are only interested in profit maximization

■ **PROBLEMS**

1. The table below shows the total production a firm will be able to obtain if it employs varying amounts of resource A while the amounts of the other resources the firm employs remain constant.

Quantity of resource A employed	Total product	Marginal product of A	Total revenue	Marginal revenue product of A
0	0		$_____	
1	12	_____	_____	$_____
2	22	_____	_____	_____
3	30	_____	_____	_____
4	36	_____	_____	_____
5	40	_____	_____	_____
6	42	_____	_____	_____
7	43	_____	_____	_____

a. Compute the marginal product of each of the seven units of resource **A** and enter these figures in the table.

b. Assume the product the firm produces sells in the market for $1.50 per unit. Compute the total revenue of the firm at each of the eight levels of output and the marginal revenue product of each of the seven units of resource **A**. Enter these figures in the table below.

c. On the basis of your computations, complete the firm's demand schedule for resource **A** by indicating in the following table how many units of resource **A** the firm would employ at the given prices.

Price of A	Quantity of A demanded
$21.00	_____
18.00	_____
15.00	_____
12.00	_____
9.00	_____
6.00	_____
3.00	_____
1.50	_____

2. In the table below are the marginal product data for resource **B**. Assume that the quantities of other resources employed by the firm remain constant.

a. Compute the total product (output) of the firm for each of the seven quantities of resource **B** employed and enter these figures in the table.

b. Assume that the firm sells its output in an imperfectly competitive market and that the prices at which it can sell its product are those given in the table. Compute and enter in the table:

(1) the total revenue for each of the seven quantities of **B** employed.

(2) the marginal revenue product of each of the seven units of resource **B**.

c. How many units of **B** would the firm employ if the market price of **B** were

(1) $25? _____

(2) $20? _____

(3) $15? _____

(4) $9? _____

(5) $5? _____

(6) $1? _____

3. Use the following total-product schedule as a resource to answer questions **a**, **b**, and **c**. Assume that the quantities of other resources the firm employs remain constant.

Units of resource	Total product
0	0
1	15
2	28
3	38
4	43
5	46

a. If the firm's product sells for a constant $2 per unit, what is the marginal revenue product of the second unit of the resource? _____

b. If the firm's product sells for a constant $2 and the price of the resource is $10, how many units of the resource will the firm employ? _____

c. If the firm can sell 15 units of output at a price of $2.00 and 28 units of output at a price of $1.50, what is the marginal revenue product of the second unit of the resource? _____

4. In the space to the right of each of the following changes, indicate whether the change would tend to increase (+) or decrease (−) a firm's demand for a particular resource.

a. An increase in the demand for the firm's product _____

b. A decrease in the price of the firm's output _____

c. An increase in the productivity of the resource _____

d. An increase in the price of a substitute resource when the output effect is greater than the substitution effect _____

e. A decrease in the price of a complementary resource _____

f. A decrease in the price of a substitute resource when the substitution effect is greater than the output effect _____

Quantity of resource B employed	Marginal product of B	Total product	Product price	Total revenue	Marginal revenue product of B
0	—	0		$0.00	—
1	22	_____	$1.00	_____	_____
2	21	_____	.90	_____	_____
3	19	_____	.80	_____	_____
4	16	_____	.70	_____	_____
5	12	_____	.60	_____	_____
6	7	_____	.50	_____	_____
7	1	_____	.40	_____	_____

Quantity of resource C employed	Marginal product of C	Marginal revenue product of C	Quantity of resource D employed	Marginal product of D	Marginal revenue product of D
1	10	$5.00	1	21	$10.50
2	8	4.00	2	18	9.00
3	6	3.00	3	15	7.50
4	5	2.50	4	12	6.00
5	4	2.00	5	9	4.50
6	3	1.50	6	6	3.00
7	2	1.00	7	3	1.50

5. The table above shows the marginal-product and marginal-revenue-product schedules for resource **C** and resource **D**. Both resources are variable and are employed in purely competitive markets. The price of **C** is $2 and the price of **D** is $3. (Assume that the productivity of each resource is independent of the quantity of the other.)

a. The least-cost combination of **C** and **D** that would enable the firm to produce

(1) units of its product is _____ **C** and _____ **D**.

(2) 99 units of its product is _____ **C** and _____ **D**.

b. The profit-maximizing combination of **C** and **D** is

_____ **C** and _____ **D**.

c. When the firm employs the profit-maximizing combination of **C** and **D**, it is also employing **C** and **D** in

the least-cost combination because _____

equals _____.

d. Examination of the figures in the table reveals that

the firm sells its product in a _____ com-

petitive market at a price of $_____.

e. Employing the profit-maximizing combination of **C** and **D**, the firm's

(1) total output is _____.

(2) total revenue is $_____.

(3) total cost is $_____.

(4) total profit is $_____.

■ **SHORT ANSWER AND ESSAY QUESTIONS**

1. Give four reasons why it is important to study resource pricing.

2. How does the demand for a product differ from the demand for a resource? Explain why the demand for a resource is a derived demand.

3. What two factors determine the strength of the demand for a resource?

4. Explain why firms that wish to maximize their profits follow the MRP = MRC rule.

5. What effects do marginal product and marginal price have on a firm's resource demand curve under pure competition and under imperfect competition?

6. Why is the demand schedule for a resource less elastic when the firm sells its product in an imperfectly competitive market than when it sells it in a purely competitive market?

7. How do you derive the market demand for a resource?

8. Identify and describe three factors that will cause the demand for a resource to increase or decrease. Give examples of how each factor influences changes in demand.

9. What is the difference between the substitution effect and the output effect?

10. If the price of capital falls, what will happen to the demand for labor if capital and labor are substitutes in production? Describe what happens when the substitution effect outweighs the output effect and when the output effect outweighs the substitution effect. What can you conclude?

11. Why does a change in the price of a complementary resource cause the demand for labor to change in the opposite direction?

12. Describe trends in occupational employment data. Give examples of jobs with the greatest projected growth and decline.

13. What are the three factors that determine the elasticity of demand for a resource?

14. Use an example to explain what happens to elasticity when substitutability for a resource is greater rather than lesser.

15. How can the ratio of labor cost to the total cost influence how producers react to changes in the price of labor?

16. Assume that a firm employs resources in purely competitive markets. How does the firm know that it is spending money on resources in such a way that it can produce a given output for the least total cost?

17. Why is minimizing cost not sufficient for maximizing profit for a firm?

18. When is a firm that employs resources in purely competitive markets using these resources in amounts that will maximize the profits of the firm?

19. What is the marginal productivity theory of income distribution? What ethical proposition must be accepted if this distribution is to be fair and equitable?

20. What are the two major shortcomings of the marginal productivity theory of income distribution?

ANSWERS

Chapter 12 The Demand for Resources

FILL-IN QUESTIONS

1. resources, incomes, costs
2. derived, productivity, price
3. product, cost
4. cost, equal to
5. product, prices
6. lower, demand, less
7. demand
8. demand, productivity, price
9. increase, decrease
10. falls, rises
11. more, less, substitution, more, output
12. increase, decrease
13. substitutes, demand, cost, cost
14. slowly, elastic
15. greater
16. product, price
17. revenue product, price
18. 1
19. marginal, revenues
20. competitive, do not

TRUE–FALSE QUESTIONS

1. T, p. 248	10. T, pp. 252–253	19. F, pp. 256–257
2. T, p. 249	11. F, p. 253	20. T, pp. 256–257
3. T, p. 249	12. T, p. 253	21. T, pp. 256–257
4. F, pp. 249–250	13. F, pp. 253–254	22. F, pp. 259–260
5. T, p. 250	14. T, pp. 253–254	23. T, pp. 258–259
6. T, p. 250	15. F, p. 254	24. F, pp. 260–261
7. F, p. 250	16. F, p. 254	25. F, pp. 260–262
8. F, p. 250	17. T, pp. 254–255	
9. T, pp. 250–252	18. T, pp. 254–255	

MULTIPLE-CHOICE QUESTIONS

1. d, p. 249	10. c, pp. 250–251	19. d, p. 258
2. c, p. 249	11. c, pp. 250–251	20. c, pp. 259–260
3. a, p. 249	12. d, pp. 251–252	21. d, p. 260
4. a, pp. 249–250	13. c, pp. 253–254	22. a, p. 260
5. d, pp. 250–251	14. a, p. 254	23. b, pp. 259–260
6. b, pp. 250–251	15. b, p. 254	24. b, pp. 260–261
7. d, pp. 250–251	16. a, pp. 254–255	25. b, pp. 260–261
8. c, pp. 250–251	17. c, pp. 256–257	
9. a, pp. 250–251	18. c, pp. 256–257	

PROBLEMS

1. *a.* Marginal product of A: 12, 10, 8, 6, 4, 2, 1; *b.* Total revenue: 0, 18.00, 33.00, 45.00, 54.00, 60.00, 63.00, 64.50; Marginal revenue product of A: 18.00, 15.00, 12.00, 9.00, 6.00, 3.00, 1.50; *c.* 0, 1, 2, 3, 4, 5, 6, 7
2. *a.* Total product: 22, 43, 62, 78, 90, 97, 98; *b.* (1) Total revenue: 22.00, 38.70, 49.60, 54.60, 54.00, 48.50, 39.20, (2) Marginal revenue product of B: 22.00, 16.70, 10.90, 5.00, −0.60, −5.50, −9.30; *c.* (1) 0, (2) 1, (3) 2, (4) 3, (5) 4, (6) 4
3. *a.* $26. The second worker increases TP by 13 units (13 × $2 = $26); *b.* 4 units. The marginal product of the fourth resource is 5 units of output (5 × $2 = $10). Thus MRP = $10 and MRC = $10 when the fourth resource is employed; *c.* $12. The total revenue from 1 unit is $30.00 (15 × $2.00). The total revenue with 2 units is $42 (28 × $1.50). The difference is the MR of the second unit.
4. *a.* +; *b.* −; *c.* +; *d.* −; *e.* +; *f.* −
5. *a.* (1) 1, 3, (2) 3, 5; *b.* 5, 6; *c.* the marginal product of **C** divided by its price, the marginal product of **D** divided by its price; *d.* purely, $.50; *e.* (1) 114, (2) $57, (3) $28, (4) $29

SHORT ANSWER AND ESSAY QUESTIONS

1. p. 249	8. pp. 253–255	15. p. 257
2. p. 249	9. p. 254	16. p. 258
3. pp. 249–250	10. p. 254	17. p. 258
4. p. 250	11. pp. 254–255	18. pp. 258–260
5. pp. 250–252	12. pp. 255–256	19. pp. 260–262
6. pp. 251–252	13. pp. 256–257	20. pp. 260–262
7. pp. 252–253	14. p. 257	

CHAPTER 13

Wage Determination

The preceding chapter explained the demand for any resource in a competitive resource market. Chapter 13 uses demand and supply analysis to describe what determines the quantity of a particular resource—**labor**—and the price paid for it—**wages**—in different markets.

The chapter begins by defining terms and briefly discussing the general level of wages in the United States and other advanced economies. You will learn about the role that productivity plays in explaining the long-run growth of real wages and the increased demand for labor over time.

In a product market, the degree of competition significantly influences how prices are determined and what output is produced. In a labor resource market, the degree of competition directly affects the determination of **wage rates** and the level of employment. The main purpose of the chapter is to explain how wage rates and the quantity of labor are determined in labor markets varying in competitiveness.

Six labor markets are discussed in the chapter: (1) the **purely competitive** market, in which the number of employers is large and labor is nonunionized; (2) the **monopsony** market, in which a single employer hires labor under competitive (nonunion) conditions; (3) a market in which a union controls the supply of labor, the number of employers is large, and the union attempts to increase the total demand for labor; (4) a similar market in which the union attempts to reduce the total supply of labor; (5) another similar market in which the union attempts to obtain a wage rate that is above the competitive-equilibrium level by threatening to strike; and (6) the **bilateral monopoly** market, in which a single employer faces a labor supply controlled by a single union.

What is important for you to learn is how the characteristics of each labor market affect wage rates and employment. In the purely competitive or monopsony labor market, there is no union. The determination of the wage rate and employment will be quite definite, although different for each market. In the next four types of labor markets, **unions** control the supply of labor, and thus the outcomes for wage rates and employment will be less definite. If the demand for labor is competitive, the wage rate and the amount of employment will depend on how successful the union is in increasing the demand for labor, restricting the supply of labor, or setting a wage rate that employers will accept. If there is both a union and one employer (a bilateral monopoly), wages and employment will fall within certain limits, but exactly where will depend on the bargaining power of the union or the employer.

Three other issues are discussed in the last three sections of the chapter. First, for many years the Federal government has set a legal **minimum wage** for labor. The chapter uses supply and demand analysis to make the case for and against the minimum wage and then discusses its real-world effects. Second, wage rates are not homogeneous and differ across workers and occupations. The chapter presents important reasons why these **wage differentials** exist. Third, there is a **principal–agent problem** in most types of employment that may lead to shirking on the job. Different pay schemes have been devised to tie workers' pay to performance in an effort to overcome this problem. Each of these issues should be of direct interest to you and deepen your understanding about how labor markets work.

■ **CHECKLIST**

When you have studied this chapter you should be able to

☐ Define wages (or the wage rate).

☐ Distinguish between nominal and real wages.

☐ List five reasons for high productivity in the United States and other advanced economies.

☐ Describe the long-run relationship between real wages and productivity in the United States.

☐ Evaluate the importance of the two factors contributing to the long-run trend of growth in U.S. real wages.

☐ Define the three characteristics of a purely competitive labor market.

☐ Use demand and supply graphs to explain wage rates and the equilibrium level of employment in a purely competitive labor market.

☐ Define the three characteristics of a labor market monopsony and compare it with a purely competitive labor market.

☐ Explain why the marginal resource cost exceeds the wage rate in monopsony.

☐ Use demand and supply graphs to explain wage rates and the equilibrium level of employment in the monopsony model.

☐ Give examples of monopsony power.

☐ List three types of union models.

☐ Identify two strategies of labor unions to increase the demand for labor and their effects on wage rates and employment.

☐ Explain and illustrate graphically the effects of actions taken by craft unions to decrease the supply of labor on wages and the employment of workers.

☐ Explain and illustrate graphically how the organization of workers by an industrial union in a previously competitive labor market would affect the wage rate and the employment level.

☐ Describe the effect of unions on wage increases and union employment.

☐ Use a graph to explain why the equilibrium wage rate and employment level are indeterminate when a labor market is a bilateral monopoly and to predict the range for the wage rate.

☐ Present the case for and the case against a legally established minimum wage.

☐ Use supply and demand analysis to explain wage differentials.

☐ Connect wage differentials to marginal revenue productivity.

☐ Give two reasons why noncompeting groups of workers earn different wages.

☐ Explain why some wage differentials are due to compensatory differences in the nonmonetary aspects of jobs.

☐ Cite four types of labor market imperfections that contribute to wage differentials.

☐ Describe the principal–agent problem in worker pay and performance.

☐ Describe four pay schemes employers use to prevent shirking or to tie worker pay to performance.

☐ Explain the negative side effects of pay-for-performance schemes.

☐ Evaluate from an economic perspective the issue of whether chief executive officers (CEOs) of corporations are overpaid (*Last Word*).

■ **CHAPTER OUTLINE**

1. A **wage** (or the **wage rate**) is the price paid per unit of time for any type of labor. Earnings are equal to the wage multiplied by the amount of time worked. Wages can be measured either in nominal or real terms. A **real wage** is adjusted for the effects of inflation. It reflects the quantity of goods and services a worker can purchase with a **nominal wage.**

2. The **general level of real wages** in the United States and other advanced economies is high because the demand for labor has been large relative to the supply of labor.
   a. The demand for labor in the United States and advanced economies has been strong because labor is highly productive for several reasons: substantial quantities of capital goods and natural resources; technological advancement; improvements in labor quality; and other intangible factors (management techniques, business environment, and size of the domestic market).
   b. The real hourly wage rate and output per hour of labor are closely and directly related to each other, and real income per worker can increase only at the same rate as output per worker (productivity).
   c. The long-run trend shows that real wages have increased because increases in the demand for labor

over time have been greater than increases in the supply of labor in the United States.

3. In a **purely competitive labor market** many firms compete in hiring a specific type of labor and there are many qualified workers with identical skills who independently supply this labor. Both firms and workers are "wage takers" who do not influence the price of labor.
   a. The market *demand curve* for labor is a horizontal summation of the demand curves for individual firms.
   b. The market *supply curve* slopes upward, indicating that a higher wage will entice more workers to supply their labor.
   c. The *wage rate* for labor in this market is determined by the interaction of the market demand for and the supply of that labor. For the individual firm, the supply of labor is perfectly elastic at this wage rate (so the marginal labor cost is equal to the wage rate). The firm will hire the amount of labor at which its marginal revenue product of labor is equal to its marginal labor cost.

4. In a **monopsony** market for labor, there is only one buyer of a particular kind of labor, the labor is relatively immobile, and the hiring firm is a "wage maker" (the wage rate a firm pays varies with the number of workers it employs).
   a. The supply curve is up-sloping and indicates that the firm (the single buyer of labor) must pay higher wages to attract more workers.
   b. A monopsonistic firm's marginal labor costs are greater than the wage rates it must pay to obtain various amounts of labor because once it offers a higher wage to one worker, it must offer the same wage to all workers.
   c. The firm hires the amount of labor at which marginal labor cost and the marginal revenue product of labor are equal. Both the wage rate and the level of employment are less than they would be under purely competitive conditions in labor markets.
   (1) Note that if the firm employs resources in imperfectly competitive markets, it is hiring resources in the least-cost combination when the ratio of the marginal product of a resource to its marginal resource cost is the same for all resources.
   (2) It is hiring resources in the most profitable combination when the marginal revenue product of each resource is equal to its marginal resource cost.
   d. Monopsony power can be found in such situations as small cities where there are one or two firms that hire most of the workers of a particular type in a region or in professional sports franchises that have exclusive rights to obtain the service of professional athletes.

5. In labor markets in which **labor unions** represent workers, the unions attempt to raise wages in three ways.
   a. The union can increase *the demand for labor* by increasing the demand for the products the union workers produce through political lobbying. They also can increase demand by increasing the prices of resources that are substitutes for the labor provided by the mem-

bers of the union or by reducing the price of a complementary resource.

b. With *exclusive unionism,* a *craft union* will seek to increase wages by reducing the supply of labor. *Occupational licensing* is another means of restricting the supply of a particular type of labor.

c. With *inclusive unionism* an industrial union will try to increase wages by forcing employers to pay wages in excess of the equilibrium rate that would prevail in a purely competitive labor market.

d. Labor unions are aware that their actions to increase wage rates may also increase the unemployment of their members, which tends to limit the demands for higher wages.

6. A *bilateral monopoly* is a labor market with a monopsony (single buyer of labor) and an inclusive union (single seller of labor).

a. In this situation, the wage rate depends, within certain limits, on the relative bargaining power of the union and of the employer.

b. This model may be desirable because the monopoly power on the buy side is offset by the monopoly power on the sell side. The resulting wage rate may be close to levels found in purely competitive markets.

7. The *minimum wage* is a price floor that has been used to set a minimum price for unskilled labor.

a. Critics argue that it increases wage rates and reduces the employment of workers. It is a poor policy for reducing household poverty because the benefits largely go to teenagers who do not need the assistance.

b. Defenders think that in a monopsonistic market, it can increase the wage rate and employment. A minimum wage also may increase productivity, thus increasing the demand for labor and reducing labor turnover.

c. The evidence is mixed. In theory, a higher wage should reduce employment, but in practice the negative effects on employment may be minor or nil. The minimum wage, however, is not a strong antipoverty policy, despite its popular appeal in this respect.

8. *Wage differentials* are found across many occupations. They are often explained by the forces of demand and supply.

a. The strength of the demand for workers in an occupation, given the supply of workers, is due largely to the productivity of workers and the revenues they generate for the firm (or *marginal revenue productivity*).

b. One major reason for wage differentials is that workers are not homogeneous and can be thought of as falling into many *noncompeting groups.* The wages for each group differ because of

(1) differences in the abilities or skills possessed by workers, the number of workers in each group, and the demand for those abilities or skills in the labor market

(2) the stock of knowledge and skills people have, called *human capital.* Investment in human capital by workers through education and training can lead to higher future wages.

c. A second reason for wage differentials is that jobs vary in difficulty and attractiveness, so there are *compensating differences.* Higher wages may be necessary to compensate for less desirable nonmonetary aspects of some jobs.

d. A third reason for wage differentials is market imperfections. These arise from a lack of job information, geographic immobilities, union or government restraints, and discrimination.

9. Wage payments in labor markets are often more complex in practice and are often designed to make a connection between *worker pay and performance.*

a. A principal–agent problem arises when the interests of agents (workers) diverge from the interests of the principals (firms). For example, shirking on the job can occur if workers give less than the desired level of performance for pay received.

b. Firms can try to reduce shirking by monitoring worker activity, but this monitoring is costly; therefore, *incentive pay plans* are adopted by firms to tie worker compensation more closely to performance. Among the various incentive schemes are

(1) piece rate payments, commissions, royalties, bonuses, and profit sharing plans

(2) efficiency wages that pay workers above-market wages to get greater effort.

c. Sometimes the "solutions" to principal–agent problems lead to negative results. Commissions may cause employees to pad bills; changes in work rules may demoralize workers.

10. (*Last Word*). The basic argument for why CEOs are highly paid is related to market conditions. On the supply side, there is a restrictive supply of corporate talent to provide leadership and direction. On the demand side, there is a high demand for individuals who have the qualities necessary to make the major managerial decisions and lead corporations. These market conditions of limited supply and high demand explain the high salaries. In addition, becoming a CEO has the elements of a game or tournament. The fact that there is a prize for winning will encourage intense competition and increase productivity. Critics of CEO payment think corporate boards that set CEO pay are too controlled by the CEO and these board members overvalue CEO work.

■ **HINTS AND TIPS**

1. The reason why the market supply curve for labor rises in competitive markets is based on an economic concept from Chapter 2 that you may want to review. To obtain more workers, firms must increase wages to cover the **opportunity cost** of workers' time spent on other alternatives (other employment, household work, or leisure).

2. In monopsony, the marginal resource cost exceeds the wage rate (and the marginal-resource-cost curve lies above the supply curve of labor). The relationship is difficult to understand, so you should pay careful attention to the discussion of Table 13.2 and Figure 13.4.

3. To illustrate the differences in the three union models presented in this chapter, draw supply and demand graphs of each model.

4. The chapter presents the positive economic explanations for the differences in wages between occupations. Remember that whether these wage differentials are "fair" is a normative question. (See Chapter 1 for the positive and normative distinction.)

■ **IMPORTANT TERMS**

wage rate	bilateral monopoly
real wage	minimum wage
nominal wage	wage differentials
purely competitive labor market	marginal revenue productivity
monopsony	noncompeting groups
exclusive unionism	human capital
occupational licensing	compensating differences
inclusive unionism	incentive pay plan

SELF-TEST

■ **FILL-IN QUESTIONS**

1. The price paid for labor per unit of time is the (piece, wage) _____ rate. The earnings of labor are equal to the _____ rate (divided, multiplied) _____ by the amount of time worked. The amount of money received per hour or day by a worker is the (nominal, real) _____ wage, while the purchasing power of that money is the _____ wage.

2. The general level of wages is high in the United States and other advanced economies because the demand for labor in these economies is (weak, strong) _____ relative to the supply of labor. United States labor tends to be highly productive, among other reasons, because it has access to relatively large amounts of (consumer, capital) _____ goods, plentiful (financial, natural) _____ resources, a high-quality (service sector, labor force) _____, and superior (wages, technology) _____. There is a close (short-run, long-run) _____ relationship between output per labor hour and real hourly wages in the United States.

3. In a purely competitive labor market,
   a. the supply curve slopes upward from left to right because it is necessary for employers to pay (higher, lower) _____ wages to attract workers from alternative employment. The market supply curve rises because it is an (average cost, opportunity cost) _____ curve.

b. the demand is the sum of the marginal (revenue product, resource cost) _____ schedules of all firms hiring this type of labor.
   c. the wage rate will equal the rate at which the total quantity of labor demanded is (less than, equal to, greater than) _____ the total quantity of labor supplied.

4. Insofar as an individual firm hiring labor in a purely competitive market is concerned, the supply of labor is perfectly (elastic, inelastic) _____ because the individual firm is unable to affect the wage rate it must pay. The firm will hire that quantity of labor at which the wage rate, or marginal labor cost, is (less than, equal to, greater than) _____ the marginal revenue product.

5. A monopsonist employing labor in a market that is competitive on the supply side will hire that amount of labor at which the marginal revenue product is (less than, equal to, greater than) _____ marginal labor cost. In such a market, the marginal labor cost is (less, greater) _____ than the wage rate, so the employer will pay a wage rate that is _____ than both the marginal revenue product of labor and the marginal labor cost.

6. A monopsonist facing a competitive supply of labor
   a. is employing the combination of resources that enables it to produce any given output in the least costly way when the marginal product of every resource (divided, multiplied) _____ by its marginal resource cost is the same for all resources.
   b. is employing the combination of resources that maximizes its profits when the marginal revenue product of every resource is (equal to, greater than) _____ its marginal resource cost or when the marginal revenue product of each resource (divided, multiplied) _____ by its marginal resource cost is equal to (infinity, 1) _____.

7. When compared with a competitive labor market, a market dominated by a monopsonist results in (higher, lower) _____ wage rates and in (more, less) _____ employment.

8. The basic objective of labor unions is to increase wages, and they attempt to accomplish this goal either by increasing the (demand for, supply of) _____ labor, restricting the _____ labor, or imposing (a below, an above) _____-equilibrium wage rate on employers.

9. Labor unions can increase the demand for the services of their members by increasing the (demand for, supply of) _____ the products they produce, by (increasing, decreasing) _____ the prices of resources that are substitutes for the services supplied by their members, and by (increasing, decreasing)

_____ the price of a complementary resource used to produce a product.

10. Restricting the supply of labor to increase wages is the general policy of (exclusive, inclusive) _____ unionism, and imposing above-equilibrium wage rates is the strategy used in _____ unionism. An example of exclusive unionism is (an industrial, a craft) _____ union, while an example of inclusive unionism would be _____ union.

11. If unions are successful in increasing wages, employment in the industry will (increase, decrease) _____, but this effect on members may lead unions to _____ their wage demands. Unions, however, will not worry too much about the effect on employment from the higher wage rates if the economy is growing or if the demand for labor is relatively (elastic, inelastic) _____.

12. In a labor market that is a bilateral monopoly, the monopsonist will try to pay a wage (less, greater) _____ than the marginal revenue product of labor; the union will ask for some wage _____ than the competitive and monopsonist equilibrium wage. Within these limits, the (wage rate, elasticity) _____ of labor will depend on the relative bargaining strength of the union and the monopsonist.

13. Critics of the minimum wage contend that in purely competitive labor markets, the effect of imposing such a wage is to (increase, decrease) _____ the wage rate and to _____ employment. Defenders of the minimum wage argue that such labor markets are monopsonistic, so the effect is to (increase, decrease) _____ the wage rate and to _____ employment. The evidence suggests that the employment and antipoverty effects from increasing the minimum wage are (positive, uncertain) _____.

14. Actual wage rates received by different workers tend to differ because workers (are, are not) _____ homogeneous, jobs (vary, do not vary) _____ in attractiveness, and labor markets may be (perfect, imperfect) _____.

15. The total labor force is composed of a number of (competing, noncompeting) _____ groups of workers. Wages differ among these groups as a consequence of differences in (ability, wealth) _____ and because of different investments in (the stock market, human capital) _____.

16. Within each of these noncompeting groups, some workers receive higher wages than others to compensate these workers for the less desirable (monetary, nonmon-etary) _____ aspects of a job. These wage differentials are called (monopsony, compensating) _____ differences.

17. Workers performing identical jobs often receive different wages due to market imperfections such as lack of information about (investment, job) _____ opportunities, geographic (mobility, immobility) _____, union or government (subsidies, restraints) _____, and (taxes, discrimination) _____.

18. Firms, or parties, who hire others to achieve their objectives may be regarded as (agents, principals) _____, while workers, or parties, who are hired to advance firms' interests can be regarded as the firms' _____. The objective of a firm is to maximize (wages, profits) _____ and workers are hired to help a firm achieve that objective in return for _____, but when the interests of a firm and the workers diverge, a principal–agent problem is created.

19. An example of this type of problem is a situation in which workers provide less than the agreed amount of work effort on the job, which is called (licensure, shirking) _____. To prevent this situation, firms can closely monitor job (pay, performance) _____, but this is costly; therefore, many firms offer different incentive _____ plans.

20. Examples of such pay-for-performance schemes include (efficiency, piece) _____ rate payments, commissions and royalties, bonuses and profit sharing, and _____ wages, which means that workers are paid above-equilibrium wages to encourage greater work effort. Such plans must be designed with care because of possible (positive, negative) _____ side effects.

■ TRUE–FALSE QUESTIONS

Circle T if the statement is true, F if it is false.

1. If you received a 5% increase in your nominal wage and the price level increased by 3%, then your real wage has increased by 8%. **T F**

2. The general level of wages is high in the United States and other advanced economies because the supply of labor is large relative to the demand for it. **T F**

3. One reason for the high productivity of labor in the United States and other advanced economies is access to large amounts of capital equipment. **T F**

4. Real hourly compensation per worker can increase only at about the same rate as output per worker. **T F**

5. In a purely competitive labor market, there are few qualified workers who supply labor and few firms who employ labor. **T F**

6. If an individual firm employs labor in a purely competitive market, it finds that its marginal labor cost is equal to the wage rate in that market.   **T   F**

7. Given a purely competitive employer's demand for labor, a lower wage will result in more workers being hired.   **T   F**

8. Both monopsonists and firms hiring labor in purely competitive markets hire labor up to the quantity at which the marginal revenue product of labor and marginal labor cost are equal.   **T   F**

9. Political lobbying for special projects or legislation is used by unions to increase the demand for labor.   **T   F**

10. One strategy unions use to bolster the demand for union workers is to lobby against a higher minimum wage for nonunion workers.   **T   F**

11. Restricting the supply of labor is a means of increasing wage rates more commonly used by craft unions than by industrial unions.   **T   F**

12. Occupational licensing is a means of increasing the supply of specific kinds of labor.   **T   F**

13. Unions that seek to organize all available or potential workers in an industry are called craft unions.   **T   F**

14. The imposition of an above-equilibrium wage rate will cause employment to fall off more when the demand for labor is inelastic than it will when the demand is elastic.   **T   F**

15. Union members are paid wage rates that on the average are greater by about 15% than the wage rates paid to nonunion members.   **T   F**

16. The actions of both exclusive and inclusive unions that raise the wage rates paid to them by competitive employers of labor also cause, other things remaining constant, an increase in the employment of their members.   **T   F**

17. In a bilateral monopoly, the negotiated wage will be below the competitive equilibrium wage in that labor market.   **T   F**

18. If a labor market is purely competitive, the imposition of an effective minimum wage will increase the wage rate paid and decrease employment in that market.   **T   F**

19. If an effective minimum wage is imposed on a monopsonist, the wage rate paid by the firm will increase and the number of workers employed by it may also increase.   **T   F**

20. The strength of labor demand differs greatly among occupations due to differences in how much each occupation contributes to its employer's revenue.   **T   F**

21. Actual wage rates received in different labor markets tend to differ because the demands for particular types of labor relative to their supplies differ.   **T   F**

22. Wage differentials that are used to compensate workers for unpleasant aspects of a job are called efficiency wages.   **T   F**

23. Market imperfections that impede workers from moving from lower- to higher-paying jobs help explain wage differentials.   **T   F**

24. Shirking is an example of a principal–agent problem.   **T   F**

25. There are examples of solutions that have been implemented to solve principal–agent problems that produce negative results.   **T   F**

■ **MULTIPLE-CHOICE QUESTIONS**

Circle the letter that corresponds to the best answer.

1. Real wages would decline if the
(a) prices of goods and services rose more rapidly than nominal-wage rates
(b) prices of goods and services rose less rapidly than nominal-wage rates
(c) prices of goods and services and wage rates both rose
(d) prices of goods and services and wage rates both fell

2. The basic explanation for high real wages in the United States and other industrially advanced economies is that the
(a) price levels in these nations have increased at a faster rate than nominal wages
(b) governments in these nations have imposed effective minimum wage laws to improve the conditions of labor
(c) demand for labor in these nations is quite large relative to the supply of labor
(d) supply of labor in these nations is quite large relative to the demand for labor

3. A characteristic of a purely competitive labor market would be
(a) firms hiring different types of labor
(b) workers supplying labor under a union contract
(c) wage taker behavior by the firms
(d) price maker behavior by the firms

4. The supply curve for labor in a purely competitive market is up-sloping because the
(a) opportunity costs for workers rise
(b) marginal resource cost is constant
(c) wage rate paid to workers falls
(d) marginal revenue product rises

5. The individual firm that hires labor under purely competitive conditions faces a supply curve for labor that
(a) is perfectly inelastic
(b) is of unitary elasticity
(c) is perfectly elastic
(d) slopes upward from left to right

6. Which is a characteristic of a monopsonist?
(a) The type of labor is relatively mobile.
(b) The supply curve is the marginal resource cost curve.

(c) There are many buyers of a particular kind of labor.
(d) The wage rate it must pay workers varies directly with the number of workers it employs.

7. A monopsonist pays a wage rate that is
(a) greater than the marginal revenue product of labor
(b) equal to the marginal revenue product of labor
(c) equal to the firm's marginal labor cost
(d) less than the marginal revenue product of labor

8. If a firm employs resources in imperfectly competitive markets, to maximize its profits the marginal revenue product of each resource must equal
(a) its marginal product
(b) its marginal resource cost
(c) its price
(d) 1

9. Compared with a purely competitive labor market, a monopsonistic market will result in
(a) higher wage rates and a higher level of employment
(b) higher wage rates and a lower level of employment
(c) lower wage rates and a higher level of employment
(d) lower wage rates and a lower level of employment

10. The monopsonistic labor market for nurses that would be found in a smaller city with two hospitals would lead to
(a) lower starting salaries
(b) higher starting salaries
(c) more employment opportunities
(d) greater demand for nursing services

11. One way that unions can increase the demand for their labor is to
(a) Increase the supply of their labor
(b) decrease in the productivity of their labor
(c) demand an above-equilibrium wage rate
(d) increase the demand for products they help produce

12. Occupational licensing laws have the economic effect of
(a) increasing the demand for labor
(b) decreasing the supply of labor
(c) strengthening the bargaining position of an industrial union
(d) weakening the bargaining position of a craft union

13. Industrial unions typically attempt to increase wage rates by
(a) imposing an above-equilibrium wage rate on employers
(b) decreasing the demand for labor
(c) increasing the supply of labor
(d) forming a bilateral monopoly

14. Which of the following is a significant trade-off that unions face?
(a) Actions by inclusive unions on wages undermine actions by exclusive unions.
(b) When unions obtain higher wage rates it reduces the number of union workers employed.
(c) An increase in the price of a substitute labor resource will decrease the employment of union workers.
(d) A decrease in the price of a complementary resource will decrease the employment of union workers.

Answer Questions 15, 16, and 17 using the data in the following table.

Wage rate	Quantity of labor supplied	Marginal labor cost	Marginal revenue product of labor
$10	0	—	—
11	100	$11	$17
12	200	13	16
13	300	15	15
14	400	17	14
15	500	19	13
16	600	21	12

15. If the firm employing labor were a monopsonist, the wage rate and the quantity of labor employed would be, respectively,
(a) $14 and 300
(b) $13 and 400
(c) $14 and 400
(d) $13 and 300

16. But if the market for this labor were purely competitive, the wage rate and the quantity of labor employed would be, respectively,
(a) $14 and 300
(b) $13 and 400
(c) $14 and 400
(d) $13 and 300

17. If the firm employing labor were a monopsonist and the workers were represented by an industrial union, the wage rate would be
(a) between $13 and $14
(b) between $13 and $15
(c) between $14 and $15
(d) below $13 or above $15

*Answer Questions 18, 19, 20, and 21 on the basis of the following labor market diagram, where **D** is the demand curve for labor, **S** is the supply curve for labor, and **MRC** is the marginal resource (labor) cost.*

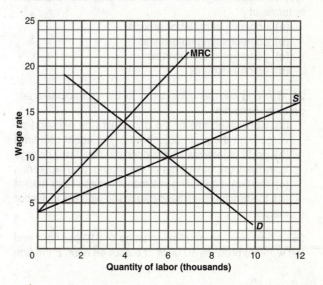

18. If this were a purely competitive labor market, the number of workers hired and the wage rate in equilibrium would be
   (a) 4000 and $14
   (b) 4000 and $8
   (c) 6000 and $10
   (d) 8000 and $12

19. If this were a monopsonistic labor market, the number of workers hired and the wage rate in equilibrium would be
   (a) 4000 and $14
   (b) 4000 and $8
   (c) 6000 and $10
   (d) 8000 and $12

20. Suppose an inclusive union seeks to maximize the employment of workers with the monopsonist. If successful, the number of workers employed and the wage rate would be
   (a) 4000 and $14
   (b) 6000 and $12
   (c) 6000 and $10
   (d) 8000 and $12

21. If the market were characterized as a bilateral monopoly, the number of workers hired and the wage rate in equilibrium would be
   (a) 6000 and $10
   (b) 4000 and $14
   (c) 4000 and $8
   (d) indeterminate

22. The major reason that major league baseball players receive an average salary of over $1 million a year and teachers receive an average salary of about $40,000 a year can best be explained in terms of
   (a) noncompeting labor groups
   (b) compensating differences
   (c) lack of job information
   (d) discrimination

23. The fact that unskilled construction workers typically receive higher wages than bank clerks is best explained in terms of
   (a) noncompeting labor groups
   (b) compensating differences
   (c) geographic immobilities
   (d) union restraints

24. Shirking can be considered to be a principal–agent problem because
   (a) work objectives of the principals (the workers) diverge from the profit objectives of the agent (the firm)
   (b) profit objectives of the principal (the firm) diverge from the work objectives of the agents (the workers)
   (c) the firm is operating in a monopsonistic labor market
   (d) the firm pays efficiency wages to workers in a labor market

25. A firm pays an equilibrium wage of $10 per hour and the workers produce 10 units of output an hour. If the firm

adopts an efficiency wage and it is successful, then the wage rate for these workers will
   (a) rise and output will fall
   (b) fall and output will rise
   (c) rise and output will rise
   (d) fall and output will fall

■ **PROBLEMS**

1. Suppose a single firm has for a particular type of labor the marginal-revenue-product schedule given in the following table.

Number of units of labor	MRP of labor
1	$15
2	14
3	13
4	12
5	11
6	10
7	9
8	8

a. Assume there are 100 firms with the same marginal-revenue-product schedules for this particular type of labor. Compute the total or market demand for this labor by completing column 1 in the following table.

(1) Quantity of labor demanded	(2) Wage rate	(3) Quantity of labor supplied
_____	$15	850
_____	14	800
_____	13	750
_____	12	700
_____	11	650
_____	10	600
_____	9	550
_____	8	500

b. Using the supply schedule for labor given in columns 2 and 3,

(1) what will be the equilibrium wage rate? $_____

(2) what will be the total amount of labor hired in the market? _____

c. The individual firm will

(1) have a marginal labor cost of $_____.

(2) employ _____ units of labor.

(3) pay a wage of $_____.

d. On the following graph, plot the market demand and supply curves for labor and indicate the equilibrium wage rate and the total quantity of labor employed.

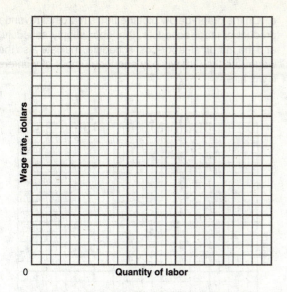

(1) Number of labor units	(2) MRP of labor	(3) Wage rate	(4) Total labor cost	(5) Marginal labor cost
0		$ 2	$_____	
1	$36	4	_____	$_____
2	32	6	_____	_____
3	28	8	_____	_____
4	24	10	_____	_____
5	20	12	_____	_____
6	16	14	_____	_____
7	12	16	_____	_____
8	8	18	_____	_____

a. Compute the firm's total labor costs at each level of employment and the marginal labor cost of each unit of labor, and enter these figures in columns 4 and 5.

b. The firm will

(1) hire _____ units of labor.

(2) pay a wage of $_____.

(3) have a marginal revenue product for labor of

$_____ for the last unit of labor employed.

c. Plot the marginal revenue product of labor, the supply curve for labor, and the marginal-labor-cost curve on the following graph and indicate the quantity of labor the firm will employ and the wage it will pay.

e. On the following graph, plot the individual firm's demand curve for labor, the supply curve for labor, and the marginal-labor-cost curve which confronts the individual firm, and indicate the quantity of labor the firm will hire and the wage it will pay.

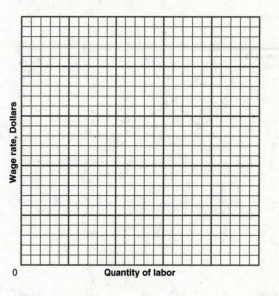

d. If this firm's labor market were competitive, there would

be at least _____ units hired at a wage of at least

$_____.

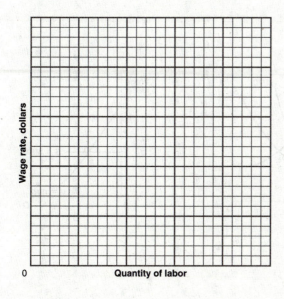

f. The imposition of a $12 minimum wage rate would change the total amount of labor hired in this market

to _____.

2. In the following table, assume a monopsonist has the marginal-revenue-product schedule for a particular type of labor given in columns 1 and 2 and that the supply schedule for labor is that given in columns 1 and 3.

3. Assume that the employees of the monopsonist in problem 2 organize a strong industrial union. The union demands a wage rate of $16 for its members, and the monopsonist decides to pay this wage because a strike would be too costly.

   a. In the following table, compute the supply schedule for labor that now confronts the monopsonist by completing column 2.

(1) Number of labor units	(2) Wage rate	(3) Total labor cost	(4) Marginal labor cost
0	$____	$____	
1	____	____	$____
2	____	____	____
3	____	____	____
4	____	____	____
5	____	____	____
6	____	____	____
7	____	____	____
8	____	____	____

   b. Compute the total labor cost and the marginal labor cost at each level of employment and enter these figures in columns 3 and 4.

   c. The firm will hire_____ units of labor, pay a wage of $_____, and pay total wages of $_____.
   d. As a result of unionization, the wage rate has _____, the level of employment has_____, and the earnings of labor have_____.

   e. On the graph below plot the firm's marginal revenue product of labor schedule, the labor supply schedule, and the marginal-labor-cost schedule. Indicate also the wage rate the firm will pay and the number of workers it will hire.

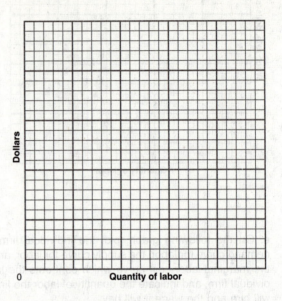

4. Match the following descriptions to one of the six graphs below.

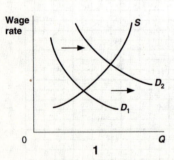

1

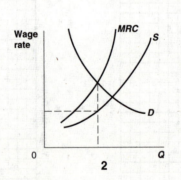

2

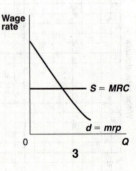

3

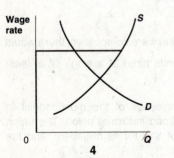

4

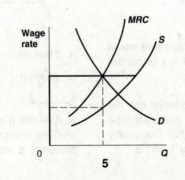

5

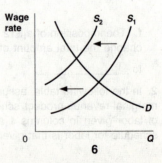

6

a. A bilateral monopoly Graph _____

b. The supply and demand for labor for a purely competitive firm Graph _____

c. The labor strategy used by a craft union to raise wages Graph _____

d. A monopsonistic labor market Graph _____

e. The strategy used by an industrial union to raise wages above a competitive level Graph _____

f. A strategy used by a union to get people to buy union-made products Graph _____

■ **SHORT ANSWER AND ESSAY QUESTIONS**

1. What is meant by the term *wages?* What is the difference between real wages and nominal wages?

2. How does the level of wages in the United States compare with that in other nations?

3. Explain why the productivity of the U.S. labor force has increased to its present high level.

4. Why has the level of real wages continued to increase even though the supply of labor has continually increased?

5. In the competitive model, what determines the market demand for labor and the wage rate? What kind of supply situation do all firms as a group confront? What kind of supply situation does the individual firm confront? Why?

6. In the monopsony model, what determines employment and the wage rate? What kind of supply situation does the monopsonist face? Why? How do the wage rate paid and the level of employment compare with what would result if the market were competitive?

7. In what sense is a worker who is hired by a monopsonist "exploited" and one who is employed in a competitive labor market "justly" rewarded? Why do monopsonists wish to restrict employment?

8. When supply is less than perfectly elastic, marginal labor cost is greater than the wage rate. Why?

9. What political methods do labor unions use to try to increase the wages their members receive? Give examples.

10. When labor unions attempt to restrict the supply of labor to increase wage rates, what devices do they use to do this for the economy as a whole, and what means do they use to restrict the supply of a given type of worker?

11. How do industrial unions attempt to increase wage rates, and what effect does this method of increasing wages have on employment in the industry affected?

12. Both exclusive and inclusive unions are able to raise the wage rates their members receive. Why might unions limit or temper their demands for higher wages? What two factors determine the extent to which they will or will not reduce their demands for higher wages?

13. Have U.S. unions been successful in raising the wages of their members? Evaluate the evidence on wages and employment effects.

14. What is bilateral monopoly? What determines wage rates in a labor market of this type?

15. Using supply and demand graphs, describe the effect of minimum wage laws on wage rates and employment in (a) purely competitive labor markets and (b) monopsony labor markets.

16. Offer an evaluation of the employment and antipoverty effects of the minimum wage based on past and current evidence.

17. What is meant by the term "noncompeting" groups in a labor market? What two factors tend to explain wage differentials in noncompeting groups?

18. How are wages used to equalize differences in the characteristics of jobs? Give examples.

19. Describe four types of imperfections in labor markets. Discuss how these imperfections contribute to wage differentials.

20. Explain what is meant by the principal–agent problem, and relate it to shirking. What are the different pay incentive plans that correct for shirking on the job? How does profit sharing reduce shirking? What is the reason for efficiency wages?

ANSWERS

Chapter 13 Wage Determination

FILL-IN QUESTIONS

1. wage, wage, multiplied, nominal, real
2. strong, capital, natural, labor force, technology, long-run
3. *a.* higher, opportunity cost; *b.* revenue product; *c.* equal to
4. elastic, equal to
5. equal to, greater, less
6. *a.* divided; *b.* equal to, divided, 1
7. lower, less
8. demand for, supply of, an above
9. demand for, increasing, decreasing
10. exclusive, inclusive, a craft, an industrial
11. decrease, decrease, inelastic
12. less, greater, wage rate
13. increase, decrease, increase, increase, uncertain
14. are not, vary, imperfect
15. noncompeting, ability, human capital
16. nonmonetary, compensating
17. job, immobility, restraints, discrimination
18. principals, agents, profits, wages
19. shirking, performance, pay
20. piece, efficiency, negative

TRUE–FALSE QUESTIONS

1. F, p. 267
2. F, p. 267
3. T, pp. 267–268
4. T, pp. 268–269
5. F, p. 269
6. T, pp. 269–271
7. T, pp. 269–271
8. T, pp. 271–273
9. T, pp. 273–274
10. F, pp. 273–274

11. T, p. 274
12. F, p. 274
13. F, pp. 274–275
14. F, pp. 274–275
15. T, p. 275
16. F, pp. 274–275
17. F, pp. 275–276
18. T, pp. 276–277

19. T, pp. 276–277
20. T, pp. 278–279
21. T, p. 280
22. F, p. 282
23. T, pp. 280–281
24. T, p. 281
25. T, pp. 281–282

3. *a.* Wage rate: 16.00, 16.00, 16.00, 16.00, 16.00, 16.00, 16.00, 16.00, 16.00; *b.* Total labor cost: 0, 16.00, 32.00, 48.00, 64.00, 80.00, 96.00, 112.00, 128.00; Marginal labor cost: 16.00, 16.00, 16.00, 16.00, 16.00, 16.00, 16.00, 16.00; *c.* (1) 6, (2) 16.00, (3) 96.00; *d.* increased, increased, increased; *e.* graph (similar to Figure 13.8)
4. *a.* 5; *b.* 3; *c.* 6; *d.* 2; *e.* 4; *f.* 1

MULTIPLE-CHOICE QUESTIONS

1. a, p. 267
2. c, p. 267
3. c, p. 269
4. a, p. 269
5. c, pp. 269–271
6. d, p. 271
7. d, pp. 272–273
8. b, pp. 272–273
9. d, pp. 271–273
10. a, p. 273
11. d, pp. 273–274
12. b, p. 274
13. a, p. 274–275

14. b, p. 275
15. d, pp. 271–273
16. c, pp. 269–271
17. b, pp. 275–276
18. c, pp. 269–271
19. b, pp. 271–273
20. c, pp. 275–276
21. d, pp. 274–275
22. a, p. 279
23. b, pp. 279–280
24. b, pp. 281–282
25. c, p. 282

SHORT ANSWER AND ESSAY QUESTIONS

1. p. 267
2. p. 267
3. pp. 267–268
4. pp. 268–269
5. pp. 269–271
6. pp. 271–273
7. pp. 271–273
8. pp. 271–272
9. pp. 273–274
10. p. 274

11. pp. 274–275
12. pp. 274–275
13. p. 275
14. pp. 275–276
15. pp. 276–277
16. pp. 276–277
17. p. 279
18. pp. 279–280
19. pp. 280–281
20. pp. 281–282

PROBLEMS

1. *a.* Quantity of labor demanded: 100, 200, 300, 400, 500, 600, 700, 800; *b.* (1) 10.00, (2) 600; *c.* (1) 10.00, (2) 6, (3) 10.00; *d.* graph; *e.* graph; *f.* 400
2. *a.* Total labor cost: 0, 4.00, 12.00, 24.00, 40.00, 60.00, 84.00, 112.00, 144.00, Marginal labor cost: 4.00, 8.00, 12.00, 16.00, 20.00, 24.00, 28.00, 32.00; *b.* (1) 5, (2) 12.00, (3) 20.00; *c.* graph; *d.* 6, 14.00

Labor Unions and Their Impacts

This appendix provides some additional information about American **labor unions,** collective bargaining, and union impacts. The labor union is an important economic institution in the U.S. economy. About 15.3 million workers covering about 12.3 percent of the labor force belong to unions. Unions typically focus on specific economic objectives such as improving pay, hours, and working conditions. Union members are more likely to work in government or to be employed in transportation, construction, manufacturing, and mining industries. In spite of its importance, unionism has been on the decline since the mid-1950s.

In Chapter 13 you learned how unions directly and indirectly seek to influence wage rates. The impact of the union on its own membership, on employers, and on the economy is more than just a matter of wages; it involves a contract between a union and an employer. This appendix discusses **collective bargaining** to give you some insights about the union goals and other issues over which employers and employees bargain. Another important idea discussed is that labor-management relations involve more than the periodic signing of a contract; they also involve the day-to-day relations between the union and the employer and the new issues not settled in the contract but which must be resolved under the general provisions of the contract.

The appendix elaborates on the **economic effects of unions** on the economy. Unions improve their members' wage rates relative to the wage rates for nonunionized workers. The effects of unions on output and efficiency, however, are more negative for three reasons that you will learn about in the chapter, although there is one factor that in the long run may offset some of these negative effects.

■ APPENDIX CHECKLIST

When you have studied this appendix you should be able to

☐ Identify the number and percentage of union members and the major union organizations.
☐ Describe the characteristics of workers belonging to unions.
☐ State how unions have declined since the mid-1950s.
☐ Present two reasons to explain unionism's decline.
☐ Explain the four basic areas covered by work agreements in collective bargaining.

☐ Describe the bargaining process and major labor relations law.
☐ Draw conclusions about the effects of unions on the wages of workers.
☐ Identify three negative effects unions might have on output and efficiency.
☐ Use a supply and demand model to show how a union might lead to a misallocation of labor resources and reduced output.
☐ Explain the potentially positive effect that unions might have on output and efficiency in the long run because of lower rate of worker turnover.

■ APPENDIX OUTLINE

1. About 15.3 million workers in the United States belong to *unions*, and they account for only about 12.3 percent of wage and salary workers. Over half (8 million) of these workers are members of unions affiliated with the **American Federation of Labor and Congress of Industrial Organizations** (AFL-CIO). About 6 million workers are members of a loose federation of seven unions called **Change to Win** that include Service Workers and Teamsters. The rest of the union members belong to **independent unions** that are not affiliated with the other major organizations.

Occupation and industry are important factors that explain who belongs to unions. The **unionization rate** is high in government and in the transportation, construction, manufacturing, and mining industries. Men, African-Americans, and those living in urban areas are more likely to be union members.

2. Union membership has declined since the mid-1950s, when about 25 percent of the workforce was unionized. Two complementary hypotheses explain the decline. One reason for the decline is that changes in the structure of the economy and the labor force have limited the expansion of union membership. A second reason for the decline is that the opposition of management to unions increased because union firms were thought to be less profitable than nonunion firms. The policies management used against unions decreased union membership.

3. *Collective bargaining* between labor and management results in work agreements that take many different forms, but usually cover four basic areas: union status and managerial prerogatives; wages and hours; seniority and job protection; and grievance procedures.

a. Union status can be of several types. In a **closed shop,** a worker must be a member of the union before being hired or must become one. In a **union shop,** employers can hire nonunion members but they must become one within a certain period. An **agency shop** requires that nonunion members pay union dues or make a donation to charity similar to the amount of the dues. Twenty-two states prohibit union or agency shops through **right-to-work laws.** In an **open shop,** an employer can hire either union or nonunion members and nonunion members do not have to pay dues. Contracts also typically contain clauses that give management prerogatives over certain work and business practices.

b. Wages (and fringe benefits) and hours of work are the main focus of collective bargaining agreements. Such wage and hour negotiations are influenced by what other workers are being paid, the profitability of the firm, cost of living concerns, and increase in labor productivity.

c. Unions typically are concerned about giving preference for promotion based on the seniority of workers. Unions also may seek job protection for their workers by limiting businesses' discretion to shift work abroad, change production locations, or use nonunion labor.

d. Grievance procedures are specified in labor contracts to help resolve disputes with management over changes in work assignment and other matters affecting workers.

4. The bargaining process on a new contract typically occurs in the 60-day period before the end of the existing contract. After the deadline, a union can **strike,** or there can be a **lockout** by the firm. Most contract agreements are compromises; strikes, lockouts, and violence are rare. The **National Labor Relations Act** specifies legal and illegal practices in collective bargaining, and the **National Labor Relations Board** is authorized to investigate unfair labor practices.

5. Labor unions have economic effects. The most direct effect is that unions typically increase the wages of their members relative to the wages of nonunion members (the wage advantage averages 15 percent). Whether unions increase output and efficiency is more complicated, but the overall effect appears negative.

a. Decreased output and efficiency result from featherbedding and establishing work rules that increase the cost of production.

b. Unions reduce output when they conduct strikes and work stoppages.

c. There are efficiency losses from the misallocation of labor to union and nonunion jobs because of the union wage advantage.

d. One long-run factor that may offset some of these negative effects of unions on output and efficiency is that unions may reduce the turnover or quit rate of workers. Unions offer a collective **voice mechanism** to help correct work problems before workers think they have to express their **exit mechanism** by quitting a job. Reducing the turnover rate may help businesses benefit from their investment in worker training and the experience of workers.

■ **HINTS AND TIPS**

1. This appendix deals with unionism, which can provoke emotional reactions. Make sure you remember the distinction between *positive* and *normative* economics made in Chapter 1. The purpose of the appendix is to analyze and explain the economics of unions (*what is*), and not the ideal world (*what ought to be*).

2. In Figure 2 of the textbook's appendix, the wage rate is plotted on the vertical axis and the quantity of labor is on the horizontal axis. The graph shows how unionization of a labor market affects the wage rate, employment, and domestic output. Make sure you do problem 2 in this Study Guide appendix to help you master this material.

■ **IMPORTANT TERMS**

American Federation of Labor and Congress of Industrial Organizations (AFL-CIO)

Change to Win

independent unions

unionization rate

collective bargaining

closed shop

union shop

agency shop

right-to-work laws

open shop

strike

lockout

National Labor Relations Act (NLRA)

National Labor Relations Board (NLRB)

voice mechanism

exit mechanism

SELF-TEST

■ **FILL-IN QUESTIONS**

1. About (15.3, 32.4) _____ million workers belong to labor unions in the United States. This number represents about (12.3, 28.9) _____% of wage and salary workers.

2. The unionization rate is relatively (low, high) _____ among workers in government, transportation, construction, and manufacturing, and it is _____ among protective service workers, machine operators, and craft workers. Men are (more, less) _____ likely to be union members than women; African-Americans are _____ likely to be union members than whites; and those in urban areas are _____ likely to be union members than those workers in other locations.

3. Since the mid-1950s, union membership as a percentage of the labor force has (increased, decreased) _____ since 1980, the number of unionized workers has _____.

4. Two reasons can be used to explain the changes in the size of union membership. The (structural-change, managerial-opposition) _____ reason suggests that conditions unfavorable to the expansion of unions have occurred in the economy and labor; the _____ reason suggests that union growth has been deterred by the policies of firms to limit or dissuade workers from joining unions.

5. A typical work agreement between a union and an employer covers the following four basic areas:

a. _____

b. _____

c. _____

d. _____

6. Collective bargaining typically begins about (20, 60) _____ days before a labor contract is set to expire. If the contract demands from workers are not met satisfactorily by the employer, a labor union may authorize a (lockout, strike) _____ that results in a work stoppage, but employers can put pressure on workers to settle the contract by engaging in a _____ that prevents workers from returning to work.

7. Federal labor laws set the framework for bargaining, strikes, and lockout through the National Labor Relations (Act, Board) _____ and the organization that is responsible for investigating charges of unfair labor practices is the National Labor Relations _____.

8. Unionization of workers in the U.S. economy has (increased, decreased) _____ the wage rates of union members relative to the wage rates of nonunion workers, with the wage premium being about (15, 25) _____ percent.

9. Unions have a negative effect on output and efficiency in the economy to the extent that they engage in (collective bargaining, featherbedding) _____ and impose burdensome (exit mechanisms, work rules) _____ on their employers, or impose (above, below) _____-equilibrium wage rates on employers that lead to misallocation of labor resources.

10. In the long run, unions can have a positive effect on output and efficiency in the economy because unions can (increase, decrease) _____ labor turnover.

■ TRUE–FALSE QUESTIONS

Circle T if the statement is true, F if it is false.

1. Most union members in the U.S. belong to independent unions not affiliated with the AFL-CIO.　　**T　F**

2. The rate of unionization is relatively high in transportation, construction, and manufacturing industries.　**T　F**

3. Union membership as a percentage of the labor force has been rising since the 1950s.　　　　　　　**T　F**

4. The structural changes in the economy that shift workers from manufacturing employment to service employment is one main reason for the decline in union membership.　　　　　　　　　　　　　**T　F**

5. Collective bargaining between labor and management means no more than deciding on the wage rates employees will receive during the life of the contract.　**T　F**

6. Bargaining, strikes, and lockouts occur within a framework of federal labor laws such as the National Labor Relations Act.　　　　　　　　　　　　**T　F**

7. The wages of union members exceed the wages of nonunion members on the average by more than 40%.　　　　　　　　　　　　　　　　**T　F**

8. Strikes in the U.S. economy result in little lost work time and reductions in total output.　　　**T　F**

9. The loss of output in the U.S. economy resulting from increases in wage rates imposed by unions on employers is relatively large.　　　　　　　　　**T　F**

10. Over time, labor unions reduce worker turnover, which offsets some of the negative effects of union on output and efficiency.　　　　　　　　　　**T　F**

■ MULTIPLE-CHOICE QUESTIONS

Circle the letter that corresponds to the best answer.

1. About what percent of employed wage and salary workers in the United States belong to unions?
   (a) 7.5%
   (b) 12.3%
   (c) 21.3%
   (d) 35.4%

2. The rate of unionization is highest in
   (a) services
   (b) retail trade
   (c) government
   (d) manufacturing

3. If workers at the time they are hired have a choice of joining the union and paying dues or of not joining the union and paying no dues, there exists
   (a) a union shop
   (b) an open shop
   (c) a nonunion shop
   (d) a closed shop

4. A major responsibility of the National Labor Relations Board is to
   (a) enforce right-to-work laws
   (b) keep unions from becoming politically active
   (c) investigate unfair labor practices under labor law
   (d) maintain labor peace between the AFL and CIO

5. Unionization has tended to
(a) increase the wages of union workers and decrease the wages of some nonunion workers
(b) increase the wages of some nonunion workers and decrease wages of union workers
(c) increase the wages of both union and nonunion workers
(d) increase the average level of real wages in the economy

6. The higher wages imposed on employers in a unionized labor market tend to result in
(a) lower wage rates in nonunionized labor markets and a decline in domestic output
(b) lower wage rates in nonunionized labor markets and an expansion in domestic output
(c) higher wage rates in nonunionized labor markets and a decline in domestic output
(d) higher wage rates in nonunionized labor markets and an expansion in domestic output

7. Which tends to decrease or have a negative effect on output and efficiency in the economy?
(a) the seniority system
(b) reduced labor turnover
(c) featherbedding and union-imposed work rules
(d) the shock effect of higher union-imposed wage rates

8. The reallocation of a unit of labor from employment where its MRP is $50,000 to employment where its MRP is $40,000 will
(a) increase the output of the economy by $10,000
(b) increase the output of the economy by $90,000
(c) decrease the output of the economy by $10,000
(d) decrease the output of the economy by $90,000

9. Which tends to increase or have a positive effect on output and efficiency in the economy?
(a) strikes
(b) reduced labor turnover
(c) featherbedding and union-imposed work rules
(d) a decrease in the training programs for workers

10. Unions tend to reduce labor turnover by providing workers with all but one of the following. Which one?
(a) an exit mechanism
(b) a voice mechanism
(c) a collective voice
(d) a wage advantage

■ PROBLEMS

1. Match the union term with the phrase using the appropriate number.

1. lockout   5. open shop
2. union shop   6. agency shop
3. closed shop   7. National Labor Relations Act
4. right-to-work laws   8. collective bargaining

a. Employer can hire union or nonunion workers. _____
b. Acts by states to make compulsory union membership, or the union shop, illegal. _____

c. A worker must be a member of the union before he or she is eligible for employment in the firm. _____
d. First passed as the Wagner Act of 1935 and sets forth the dos and don'ts of union and management-labor practices. _____
e. Requires a worker to pay union dues or donate an equivalent amount to charity. _____
f. A firm forbids its workers from returning to work until a new contract is signed. _____
g. Permits the employer to hire nonunion workers, but provides that these workers must join the union within a specified period or relinquish their jobs. _____
h. The negotiations of labor contracts. _____

2. Suppose there are two identical labor markets in the economy. The supply of workers and the demand for workers in each of these markets are shown in the following table.

Quantity of labor demanded	Wage rate (MRP of labor)	Quantity of labor supplied
1	$100	7
2	90	6
3	80	5
4	70	4
5	60	3
6	50	2
7	40	1

a. In each of the two labor markets the equilibrium wage rate in a competitive labor market would be $_____ and employment would be _____ workers.
b. Now suppose that in the first of these labor markets workers form a union and the union imposes an above-equilibrium wage rate of $90 on employers.
(1) Employment in the unionized labor market will (rise, fall) _____ to _____ workers; and
(2) the output produced by workers employed by the firms in the unionized labor market will (expand, contract) _____ by $_____.
c. If the workers displaced by the unionization of the first labor market all enter and find employment in the second labor market which remains nonunionized and competitive,
(1) the wage rate in the second labor market will (rise, fall) _____ to $_____.
(2) the output produced by the workers employed by firms in the second labor market will (expand, contract) _____ by $_____.
d. While the total employment of labor in the two labor markets has remained constant, the total output produced by the employers in the two labor markets has (expanded, contracted) _____ by $_____.

■ SHORT ANSWER AND ESSAY QUESTIONS

1. Describe the current status of unions in the United States and the major union organization.

2. Who belongs to unions? Answer in terms of the types of industries and occupations and the personal characteristics of workers.

3. What evidence is there that the labor movement in the United States has declined? What are two possible causes of this decline?

4. What are the four basic areas usually covered in collective-bargaining agreements between management and labor?

5. What four arguments does labor (management) use in demanding (resisting) higher wages?

6. Describe the bargaining process in labor negotiations. What are the two aspects of federal labor laws that set the framework for this negotiation?

7. How large is the union wage advantage in the United States? How has the unionization of many labor markets affected the average level of real wages in the U.S. economy?

8. Explain how featherbedding and work rules by unions imposes a negative effect on output and efficiency in the economy.

9. What effect does the unionization of a particular labor market have on the wage rate in that market, wage rates in other labor markets, and the total output of the economy?

10. Explain how unions reduce labor turnover and improve the skills of younger workers.

TRUE–FALSE QUESTIONS

1. F, p. 287
2. T, p. 287
3. F, pp. 287–288
4. T, pp. 287–288
5. F, pp. 288–289
6. T, p. 289
7. F, p. 289
8. T, pp. 289–290
9. F, pp. 290–291
10. T, p. 291

MULTIPLE-CHOICE QUESTIONS

1. b, p. 287
2. c, p. 287
3. b, p. 288
4. c, p. 289
5. a, p. 289
6. a, p. 289
7. c, p. 289
8. c, pp. 290–291
9. b, p. 291
10. a, p. 291

PROBLEMS

1. *a.* 5; *b.* 4; *c.* 3; *d.* 7; *e.* 6; *f.* 1; *g.* 2; *h.* 8
2. *a.* 70, 4; *b.* (1) fall, 2, (2) contract, 150; *c.* (1) fall, 50, (2) expand, 110; *d.* contracted, 40

SHORT ANSWER AND ESSAY QUESTIONS

1. p. 287
2. p. 287
3. pp. 287–288
4. pp. 288–289
5. pp. 288–289
6. p. 289
7. pp. 289–290
8. p. 289
9. pp. 289–291
10. p. 291

ANSWERS

Appendix to Chapter 13 Labor Unions and Their Impacts

FILL-IN QUESTIONS

1. 15.3, 12.3
2. high, high, more, more, more
3. decreased, decreased
4. structural-change, managerial-opposition
5. *a.* the degree of recognition and status accorded the union and the prerogatives of management; *b.* wages and hours; *c.* seniority and job opportunities; *d.* a procedure for settling grievances (any order for *a–d*)
6. 60, strike, lockout
7. Act, Board
8. increased, 15
9. featherbedding, work rules, above
10. decrease

CHAPTER 14

Rent, Interest, and Profit

Chapter 14 concludes the study of the **prices of resources** by examining rent, interest, and profits. There is nothing difficult about this chapter. By now you should understand that the marginal revenue product of a resource determines the demand for that resource. This understanding can be applied to the demand for land and capital. It will be on the supply side of the land market that you will encounter whatever difficulties there are. The **supply of land** is unique because it is **perfectly inelastic:** Changes in rent do not change the quantity of land that will be supplied. Given the quantity of land available, **demand is the sole determinant of economic rent.** Of course land varies in productivity and can be used for different purposes, but these are merely the factors that explain why the rent on all lands is not the same.

Capital, as the economist defines it, means capital goods. Is the rate of interest, then, the price paid for the use of capital goods? No, not quite. Capital is not one kind of good; it is many different kinds. To be able to talk about the price paid for the use of capital goods, there must be a simple way of adding up different kinds of capital goods. The simple way is to measure the quantity of capital goods in terms of money. **Interest** is the price paid for the use of money (or of financial capital) that in turn is used to purchase **capital goods** such as factories, technology, or machines. (Of course, the concept of interest applies to purchases of consumer goods too, but the basic demand and supply model for interest presented in the chapter focuses on capital goods.)

The **demand for and supply of loanable funds** in the economy determines the **interest rate.** In a simplified model, businesses are the primary demanders of loanable funds because they want to use this financial capital to buy capital goods (e.g., equipment, machinery, factories). As with the demand for any good or service, the greater the price of using loanable funds (the interest rate), the smaller the amount of loanable funds that firms will be able and willing to borrow. A business will most likely borrow funds and make an investment in capital goods if the expected rate of return on the investment is greater than the interest rate. Therefore, the lower the interest rate, the greater the opportunities for profitable investments and the greater the amount of loanable funds demanded.

On the supply side, households are the typical suppliers of loanable funds. At a higher rate of interest, households are willing to supply more loanable funds than at lower interest rates because of the weighing of present consumption to future consumption. Most consumers prefer present consumption, but they would be willing to forgo this current use of funds and make them available for loan if there is compensation in the form of interest payments. Thus, the greater the interest rate, the more saving by households, which in turn creates a greater supply of loanable funds.

The intersection of the demand curve and the supply curve for loanable funds determines the equilibrium rate of interest, or the price of loanable funds, and the equilibrium quantity. This relationship is illustrated in Figure 14.2. The demand and supply curves of loanable funds can also shift due to a variety of factors. For example, there could be an increase in the rates of return on investments, which would increase the demand for loanable funds at each and every interest rate; changes in the tax laws could make savings more attractive and this change would increase the supply of loanable funds. Note too that while in the simplified model businesses are the demanders and households the suppliers of loanable funds, in reality these sectors can operate on both sides of the market.

It should be noted that there is a **time-value of money** that is reflected in the rate of interest. Interest is the price that borrowers need to pay lenders for transferring purchasing power from the present to the future. With interest and compounding, a given amount of money today will be equivalent to a larger amount of money in the future. Or conversely, a future amount of money will be equivalent to a smaller amount of money today. Several simple formulas are presented in the chapter to calculate the **present value** and **future value** of money based on different rates of interest.

When it comes to **economic profit,** supply and demand analysis fails the economist. Such a thing as "the quantity of uninsurable risks taken" simply cannot be measured, and consequently, it is impossible to talk about the demand for or the supply of it or other sources of profits. Profit is not a wage payment for a particular type of labor, but rather arises from entrepreneurs developing a new product, using better production methods, or obtaining a monopoly advantage. Profit is important for the economy because it is a reward for doing things that have to be done if there is to be efficient allocation of resources in the economy. The expectation of profit is the lure or the bait that makes entrepreneurs willing to accept the uninsurable risks that result in economic efficiency, innovation, and progress.

The final brief section of Chapter 14 explains what part of the income paid to American resource suppliers goes to workers and what part goes to capitalists—those who provide the economy with land, capital goods, and entrepreneurial ability. You may be surprised to learn that the lion's share—about 80%—of the income paid to American resource suppliers goes to workers today and went to workers at the beginning of the century, and that only about 20% of it goes to the capitalists today or went to them in 1900.

■ **CHECKLIST**

When you have studied this chapter you should be able to

☐ Define economic rent.

☐ Explain why supply of land does not affect economic rent.

☐ Illustrate how changes in demand determine economic rent.

☐ Illustrate graphically how productivity differences affect land rent.

☐ Explain why land rent is a surplus payment.

☐ Contrast the views on private land ownership with the nationalization of land.

☐ Give the rationale for a single tax on land proposed by Henry George.

☐ State four criticisms of the single tax on land.

☐ Define interest and its relation to money.

☐ Explain why money is not a resource.

☐ Describe the relationship between interest rate and interest income.

☐ List four reasons why interest rates differ.

☐ Define the pure rate of interest and state how it is measured.

☐ Describe the loanable funds theory of interest using supply and demand analysis.

☐ Show how the equilibrium rate of interest is established in the loanable funds market using supply and demand analysis.

☐ Explain why the supply of loanable funds curve has a positive slope.

☐ Explain why the demand for loanable funds curve has a negative slope.

☐ List factors that change the supply of or demand for loanable funds.

☐ Distinguish between a change in demand or supply and a change in quantity demanded or supplied as applied to the loanable funds market.

☐ Identify the different sides that participants (households, businesses, or government) take in the demand or supply of loanable funds.

☐ Describe the time-value of money and calculate the present value or future value of an amount of money when given different interest rates.

☐ Explain how the interest rate affects investment spending, total output, the allocation of capital, and research and development (R&D) spending.

☐ Distinguish between nominal and real interest rates.

☐ Use graphical analysis to explain the three effects of usury laws.

☐ Define economic profit and normal profit.

☐ Describe the relationship between entrepreneurship and economic profit.

☐ Distinguish between insurable and uninsurable risks.

☐ List four sources of uninsurable risks.

☐ Explain why profit is compensation for bearing uninsurable risks.

☐ State three sources of economic profit.

☐ Explain how profit rations entrepreneurship.

☐ Discuss how profit and risk are shared with corporate stockholders.

☐ Describe the shares of income paid to American resource suppliers going to labor and capital.

☐ Identify the different factors that affect the calculation of interest rates and the price of credit (*Last Word*).

■ **CHAPTER OUTLINE**

1. *Economic rent* is the price paid for the use of land or natural resources whose supply is perfectly inelastic.

   a. The *supply of land is perfectly inelastic* because it is virtually fixed in the quantity available. Supply has no influence in determining economic rent.

   b. The demand for land is the active determinant of economic rent. As demand increases or decreases, economic rent will increase or decrease given the perfectly inelastic supply of land.

   c. Economic rents on different types of land vary because different plots of land vary in productivity or might have location advantages. The productivity differences create different demands for different types of land.

   d. Economic rent serves no *incentive function* given the fixed supply of land. It is not necessary to increase economic rent to bring forth more quantity, as is the case with other natural resources. Economists, therefore, consider economic rent a surplus payment.

   e. Some have argued land ownership should be nationalized so the government collects and redistributes the rents. Arguments for private ownership of land, however, are based on allocative efficiency. Private landowners have strong incentives to manage the land properly and allocate this resource to its highest and best use. From society's perspective, economic rent may be a surplus payment, but from a landowner's perspective, economic rent is a cost. An individual or firm must pay economic rent to bid the land it wants to use for its production away from alternative uses of the land.

   f. Socialists have argued that land rent is unearned income and that land should be nationalized.

   (1) Henry George, in his 1879 book *Progress and Poverty,* called for a *single tax* on land as the sole source of government tax revenue. He based his argument on the grounds of equity and efficiency. Such a tax would not alter the supply of land because economic rent serves no incentive function.

   (2) Critics of the single tax cite its inadequacy for meeting government needs, the difficulty of identifying the portion of rent in incomes, the conflicting interpretations of unearned income, and adverse equity effects arising from changes in land ownership.

2. *Interest* is the price paid for the use of money. Interest is stated as a percentage of the amount borrowed.

   a. Money is *not* an economic resource because it is not productive. People borrow money at an interest rate and use it to buy capital goods. These capital goods are economic resources that can be used to produce other goods and services.

b. The interest income that people receive is determined by the interest rate on the amount of money loaned.

c. There is a range of interest rates, although it is convenient to speak as if there were one interest rate. These rates differ because of differences in four factors: risk, maturity, loan size, and taxability.

d. When economists talk about "the interest rate," they are referring to the **pure rate of interest,** which is best measured by the interest paid on long-term and risk-less securities, such as 20-year Treasury bonds issued by the U.S. government.

e. The **loanable funds theory of interest** describes how the interest rate is determined by the demand for and supply of loanable funds. The intersection of the demand for and supply of loanable funds determines the equilibrium interest rate and the quantity of funds loaned.

(1) The **supply of loanable funds** is generally provided by households through savings. There is a positive relationship between the interest rate and the quantity of loanable funds supplied. The supply curve, however, may be relatively inelastic and thus not very responsive to changes in the interest rate.

(2) The **demand for loanable funds** typically comes from businesses for investment in capital goods. There is an inverse relationship between the interest rate and the quantity of loanable funds demanded. Lower interest rates provide more profitable investment opportunities; higher interest rates reduce investments.

f. There are some extensions to the simplified model of the loanable funds market.

(1) Financial institutions serve as intermediaries in the supply and demand market for loanable funds.

(2) The supply of funds can change because of changes in factors that affect the thriftiness of households.

(3) The demand for funds can change because of changes in the rate of return on potential investments.

(4) Households and businesses can operate on both sides of the market—as both demanders and suppliers of loanable funds. Government also participates on both sides of the loanable fund market.

g. The **time value of money** is the concept that a specific amount of money is more valuable for an individual or business the sooner it is obtained.

(1) If an amount of money is placed in an interest-bearing account, the amount will become larger in the future because of **compound interest** that accumulates over time. This compound interest is composed of interest paid both on the initial amount of money deposited (the principal) and interest earnings from the principal.

(2) The **future value** of money is the value of money in the future given a current value today. Because of compound interest, the higher the interest rate, the larger is the future value for a specific amount today. By contrast, the **present value** of money is the value of money today for a specific amount that will be received

in the future. With present value, the higher the interest rate, the smaller will be the present value of money today for a specific amount that is to be received in the future.

h. Interest rates play several roles in the economy.

(1) They affect the total output because of the inverse relationship between interest rates and investment spending; government often tries to influence interest rates to achieve its policy goals.

(2) They allocate financial and real capital among competing firms and determine the level and composition of the total output of capital goods.

(3) They change the level and composition of spending on research and development.

(4) These effects are based on changes in the **real interest rate,** which is the rate expressed in inflation-adjusted dollars, not the **nominal interest rate,** which is the rate expressed in current dollars.

i. **Usury laws** specify a maximum interest rate for loans. They were passed to limit borrowing costs, but they can have other effects. First, they may cause a shortage of credit, which is then given only to the most worthy borrowers. Second, borrowers gain from paying less for credit and lenders lose from receiving less interest income. Third, it creates inefficiency in the economy because funds get directed to less-productive investments.

3. **Economic profit,** or **pure profit,** is what is left of the firm's revenue after all its costs, both **explicit costs** and **implicit costs,** have been deducted.

a. Economic profit is a payment for obtaining the resource of entrepreneurship. Entrepreneurs bear the risk of running a business and are *residual claimants* because they only receive revenue after all other claims and expenses of the firm have been paid.

b. There are **insurable risks** for which it is possible to buy insurance and **uninsurable risks** for which it is not possible to buy insurance. Insurable risks can be insured because their frequencies can be predicted with some degree of accuracy, but that is not the case for uninsurable risk.

c. Uninsurable risk comes from four basic sources: changes in general economic conditions, such as downturns in the business cycle; changes in the structure of the economy, such as technology change that adversely affects particular industries; changes in government policy, such as new regulations or taxes that increase business costs or decrease its revenues; and new products or production methods, such as ones that give one firm an economic advantage over other firms.

d. Economic profit can be viewed as the compensation that entrepreneurs receive for bearing the uninsurable risks associated with running a business and as a payment for supplying their entrepreneurship resources to the firm instead of some other firm.

e. Entrepreneurs can earn economic profits in three main ways: creating and selling new products that appeal to consumers; reducing production costs to become the low-cost producer of a product; and developing a monopoly position that can be used to restrict output and raise product price. Entrepreneurs increase allocative efficiency by creating products that people want and they improve productive efficiency by developing production methods to make products in a less costly way. But the third source of profit, monopoly position, results in problems for society because it imposes higher prices on consumers and reduces output, thus contributing to allocative inefficiency. Actions to control monopoly sources of profit are discussed in the antitrust chapter.

f. Profit rations entrepreneurship because it serves as a "price" for obtaining entrepreneurship resources. If this price is below a normal profit, then entrepreneurs may leave an industry and go elsewhere with their abilities and talents to earn a higher profit.

g. Economic profits are widely distributed because of the corporate form of business ownership. Other people who are stockholders in a business also bear the uninsurable risk, but the main driver of profits comes from the entrepreneur who created the profit opportunity in which others people participate. Profit serves several functions in the economy. Profit encourages businesses to innovate, and this innovation contributes to economic growth. Profits (and losses) guide businesses to produce products that people want, to use resources in the ways most desired by society, and to produce products in the least costly way; thus profits give incentive for entrepreneurs and the economy to be allocatively and productively efficient.

4. *Income paid to American resource suppliers* is distributed among wages, rent, interest, and profit. Using a broad definition, the share of this income going to labor is about 80%. The share going to capitalists from rent, interest, and profit is about 20%. These percentages have remained relatively stable since 1900.

5. (*Last Word*). To determine the interest rate paid for the use of credit, compare the interest rate paid to the amount borrowed. The calculation of the interest rate, however, is not that simple. The calculation can be affected by the payback period, the amount of a discount, the number of installments, the number of days in a year used in the calculation, and whether the interest is compounded. Several types of legislation have tried to clarify the explanations of how the interest rate is calculated.

■ HINTS AND TIPS

1. Although this chapter focuses on three resource payments (rent, interest, and profit), the discussion is much simpler and easier to understand than it was for the one resource payment (wages) in the previous chapter. It will help if you think of this chapter as three mini-chapters.

2. Use a supply and demand graph for land to explain to yourself why **land rent is surplus payment.** Draw a vertical (perfectly inelastic) supply curve and a down-sloping demand curve. Identify the price and quantity combination where the two curves intersect. Then draw a new demand curve showing an increase in demand. What happens to price? (It increases.) What happens to quantity? (No

change.) Changes in land rent perform no incentive function for the economy because they bring forth no more supply of land. Land rents are unnecessary (surplus) payments for the economy.

3. The **loanable funds theory of interest** will be easy to understand if you think of it as an application of supply and demand analysis. You need to remember, however, who are the suppliers and who are the demanders of loanable funds. In this simplified model, the *suppliers* of loanable funds are *households* who have a different quantity of savings to make available for loans at different interest rates; the higher the interest rate, the greater the quantity of loanable funds supplied. The *demanders* of loanable funds are *businesses* that want to borrow a quantity of money at each interest rate; the higher the interest rate, the smaller the quantity of loanable funds demanded for investment purposes.

4. It is the expectation of profit and not the certainty of it that drives the entrepreneur. The generation of profit involves risk taking by the entrepreneur. Be sure to distinguish between **insurable risks** and **uninsurable risks.** A major source of profit for the entrepreneur comes from the uninsurable risks that the entrepreneur is willing to assume in an uncertain world.

■ IMPORTANT TERMS

economic rent	nominal interest rate
incentive function	real interest rate
single-tax movement	usury laws
pure rate of interest	explicit costs
loanable funds theory of interest	implicit costs
	economic or pure profit
time-value of money	insurable risks
compound interest	uninsurable risks
future value	normal profit
present value	

SELF-TEST

■ FILL-IN QUESTIONS

1. Economic rent is the price paid for the use of (labor, land) _____ and (capital, natural) _____ resources which are completely (fixed, variable) _____ in supply.

2. The active determinant of economic rent is (demand, supply) _____ and the passive determinant is _____.

3. Rents on different pieces of land are not the same because land differs in (price, productivity) _____. From a business firm's perspective, land rent is a (surplus payment, cost) _____ because land (is a free good, has alternative uses) _____, but from society's perspective, land rent is a _____.

4. Economic rent does not bring forth more supply and serves no (profit, incentive) _____ function. Economists consider economic rent a (tax, surplus) _____ payment that is not necessary to ensure that land is available to the economy.

5. Socialists argue that land rents are (earned, unearned) _____ incomes. Henry George called for a single (price, tax) _____ on land to transfer economic rent to government because it would not affect the amount of land. One criticism of George's proposal is that it would not generate enough (revenue, profit) _____.

6. The price paid for the use of money is (profit, interest) _____. It is typically stated as a (price, percentage) _____ of the amount borrowed. Money (is, is not) _____ an economic resource because money _____ productive.

7. State four reasons why there is a range of interest rates:

a. _____

b. _____

c. _____

d. _____

8. Economists often talk of the (loan, pure) _____ rate of interest. It is approximated by the interest paid on (short-term, long-term) _____ Treasury bonds issued by the U.S. government.

9. Money or financial capital is obtained in the (mutual, loanable) _____ funds market. At the equilibrium rate of interest, the quantity demanded for loanable funds is (greater than, equal to, less than) _____ the quantity supplied of loanable funds.

10. The quantity supplied of loanable funds is (inversely, directly) _____ related to the interest rate while the quantity demanded for loanable funds is _____ related to the interest rate.

11. With a higher interest rate, there are (greater, fewer) _____ opportunities for profitable investment and hence a (larger, smaller) _____ quantity demanded for loanable funds.

12. An increase in the thriftiness of households will result in (an increase, a decrease) _____ in the (supply, demand) _____ of loanable funds. Anything that increases the rate of return on potential

investments will (increase, decrease) _____ the (supply, demand) _____ of loanable funds.

13. The concept that a specific amount of money is more valuable for an individual or business the sooner it is obtained is the (pure rate of interest, time value of money) _____. Interest that is composed of interest paid both on the initial amount of money deposited (the principal) and interest earnings from the principal is (usury, compound) _____ interest. The higher the interest rate, the (larger, smaller) _____ is the future value for a specific amount today, but with a higher interest rate, the _____ will be the present value of money today for a specific amount that is to be received in the future.

14. A higher equilibrium interest rate often (increases, decreases) _____ business borrowing for investment and thus _____ total spending in the economy, whereas a lower equilibrium interest rate (increases, decreases) _____ business borrowing and thus _____ total spending in the economy.

15. The rate of interest expressed in purchasing power, or inflation-adjusted dollars, is the (real, nominal) _____ interest rate, while the rate of interest expressed in dollars of current value is the _____ interest rate.

16. Laws that state the maximum interest rate at which loans can be made are called (antitrust, usury) _____ laws. These laws cause (market, non-market) _____ rationing of credit that favors creditworthy (lenders, borrowers) _____ and leads to (less, more) _____ economic efficiency in the allocation of credit.

17. The difference between total revenue and total costs, which includes both explicit and implicit costs, is (economic, accounting) _____ profit, but the difference between total revenue and explicit costs is _____ profit. The typical accounting profit is known as a (economic, normal) _____ profit and it is the "price" that allocates scarce entrepreneurship resources to different economic activities.

18. Economic profit is a reward for assuming (insurable, uninsurable) _____ risk. Sources of this type of risk include:

a. _____

b. _____

c. _____

d. _____

19. Economic profit over time can arise in three ways, such as creating (old, new) _____ products that are popular, (increasing, reducing) _____ production costs below the costs for a rival. Profits also arise from (pure competition, monopoly) _____, but this source of profit is different because it is not a reward for entrepreneurial risk taking and serves to (increase, decrease) _____ economic efficiency.

20. Defining labor income broadly to include both wages and salaries and proprietors' income, labor's share of the total income paid to American resource suppliers is about (20%, 50%, 80%) _____, while capitalists' share of income is about _____. The share of income going to capitalists has (increased, decreased, remained stable) _____ since 1900.

■ **TRUE–FALSE QUESTIONS**

Circle T if the statement is true, F if it is false.

1. Rent is the price paid for use of capital resources. **T F**

2. The determination of economic rent for land and other natural resources is based on a demand curve that is perfectly inelastic. **T F**

3. Rent is unique because it is not determined by demand and supply. **T F**

4. Rent is a surplus payment because it does not perform an incentive function. **T F**

5. For individual producers, rental payments are surplus payments, but for society they are a cost. **T F**

6. Money is an economic resource and the interest rate is the price paid for this resource. **T F**

7. Other things equal, long-term loans usually command lower rates of interest than do short-term loans. **T F**

8. The pure rate of interest is best approximated by the interest paid on long-term bonds with very low risk, such as 20-year U.S. Treasury bonds. **T F**

9. The quantity of loanable funds supplied is directly related to the interest rate. **T F**

10. The quantity of loanable funds demanded is directly related to the interest rate. **T F**

11. An increase in the demand for loanable funds would tend to increase the interest rate. **T F**

12. An increase in the rate of return on investments would most likely increase the supply of loanable funds **T F**

13. The time value of money is the concept that one U.S. dollar can be converted into more than one U.S. dollar of future value through compound interest. **T F**

14. The higher the rate of interest, the greater will be the future value of a specific amount of money today. **T F**

15. A higher equilibrium interest rate discourages business borrowing for investment, reducing investment and total spending. **T F**

16. Higher equilibrium interest rates encourage businesses to borrow more for investment, other things equal. **T F**

17. If the nominal rate of interest is 6% and the inflation rate is 3%, the real rate of interest is 9%. **T F**

18. Usury laws result in a shortage of loanable funds and nonmarket rationing in credit markets. **T F**

19. Lenders or banks are the main beneficiaries of usury laws. **T F**

20. If the economists' definition of profit were used, total profit in the economy would be greater than would be the case if the accountants' definition were used. **T F**

21. Entrepreneurs are residual claimants of a firm, which means that they only receive whatever residual revenue remains after all other factors of production have been paid. **T F**

22. A change in government policy to impose a new regulation on business is an example of a type of an insurable risk. **T F**

23. Entrepreneurs are rewarded with profit to compensate them for personally assuming the uninsurable risks of running a business. **T F**

24. Economic profit arising from monopoly is more economically desirable than economic profit arising from uncertainty. **T F**

25. Economic profit influences both the level of economic output and the allocation of resources among alternative uses. **T F**

■ **MULTIPLE-CHOICE QUESTIONS**

Circle the letter that corresponds to the best answer.

1. The price paid for a natural resource that is completely fixed in supply is
   (a) profit
   (b) interest
   (c) rent
   (d) a risk payment

2. In total, the supply of land is
   (a) perfectly inelastic
   (b) of unitary elasticity
   (c) perfectly elastic
   (d) elastic but not perfectly elastic

3. The economic rent from land will increase, *ceteris paribus*, whenever the
   (a) price of land decreases
   (b) demand for land increases
   (c) demand for land decreases
   (d) supply curve for land increases

4. When the supply curve for a plot of land lies entirely to the right of the demand curve,

(a) landowners will receive an economic rent
(b) landowners will not receive an economic rent
(c) the interest rate on loans for land will increase
(d) the interest rate on loans for land will decrease

5. Which is true?

(a) The greater the demand for land, the greater the supply of land.
(b) A windfall profits tax on the increases in the profits of petroleum producers was proposed by Henry George.
(c) Individual users of land have to pay a rent to its owner because that land has alternative uses.
(d) The less productive a particular piece of land is, the greater will be the rent its owner is able to earn from it.

6. A major criticism of the single tax on land is that it would

(a) bring in more tax revenues than is necessary to finance all current government spending
(b) not distinguish between payments for the use of land and those for improvements to land
(c) take into account the history of ownership of the land in determining the tax
(d) not tax "unearned" income

7. Which of the following do economists consider a productive economic resource?

(a) money
(b) capital goods
(c) interest
(d) profit

8. Which would tend to result in a lower interest rate for a loan?

(a) the greater the risk involved
(b) the shorter the length of the loan
(c) the smaller the amount of the loan
(d) the greater the monopoly power of the lender

9. What is the most likely reason why a lender would prefer a high-quality municipal bond that pays a 6% rate of interest rather than a high-quality corporate bond paying 8%?

(a) The municipal bond is tax-exempt.
(b) The municipal bond is a long-term investment.
(c) The corporate bond is safer than the municipal bond.
(d) The municipal bond is easier to purchase than a corporate bond.

10. The pure rate of interest is best approximated by the interest paid on

(a) consumer credit cards
(b) tax-exempt municipal bonds
(c) 90-day Treasury bills
(d) 20-year Treasury bonds

11. The up-sloping supply of loanable funds is best explained by the idea that most people prefer

(a) current consumption to future consumption
(b) future consumption to present consumption
(c) saving over consumption
(d) investment over saving

12. Why is the demand for loanable funds down-sloping?

(a) At lower interest rates, fewer investment projects will be profitable to businesses, and hence a small quantity of loanable funds will be demanded.
(b) At lower interest rates, more investment projects will be profitable to businesses, and hence a small quantity of loanable funds will be demanded.
(c) At higher interest rates, more investment projects will be profitable to businesses, and hence a large quantity of loanable funds will be demanded.
(d) At higher interest rates, fewer investment projects will be profitable to businesses, and hence a small quantity of loanable funds will be demanded.

13. In the competitive market for loanable funds, when the quantity of funds demanded exceeds the quantity supplied, then the

(a) interest rate will decrease
(b) interest rate will increase
(c) demand curve will increase
(d) supply curve will decrease

14. A decrease in the productivity of capital goods will, *ceteris paribus*,

(a) increase the supply of loanable funds
(b) decrease the supply of loanable funds
(c) increase the demand for loanable funds
(d) decrease the demand for loanable funds

15. If a person invests $1,000 in an account that pays 5% interest at the end of each year, then after two years what will be the total amount in the account?

(a) $1,050.00
(b) $1,075.25
(c) $1,100.00
(d) $1,102.50

16. If the annual rate of interest were 18% and the rate of return a firm expects to earn annually by building a new plant were 20%, the firm would

(a) not build the new plant
(b) build the new plant
(c) have to toss a coin to decide whether to build the new plant
(d) not be able to determine from these figures whether to build the plant

Questions 17 and 18 refer to the following data.

Expected rate of return	Amount of capital goods investment (in billions)
19%	$220
17	250
15	300
13	360
11	430
9	500

17. If the interest rate is 13%,

(a) $300 billion of investment will be undertaken
(b) $360 billion of investment will be undertaken
(c) $430 billion of investment will be undertaken
(d) $500 billion of investment will be undertaken

18. An increase in the interest rate from 15% to 17% would
(a) increase investment by $40 billion
(b) increase investment by $50 billion
(c) decrease investment by $50 billion
(d) decrease investment by $40 billion

19. Which is the definition of a usury law? It is a law that specifies the
(a) alternative uses of surplus government land
(b) tax rate on interest paid for state and municipal bonds
(c) maximum interest rate at which loans can be made
(d) interest paid on long-term, virtually riskless bonds of the U.S. government

20. Which would be a likely economic effect of a usury law?
(a) There would be an increase in economic efficiency.
(b) There would be a decrease in the rationing of credit.
(c) Creditworthy borrowers would lose and lenders would gain.
(d) Creditworthy borrowers would gain and lenders would lose.

21. The difference between total revenue and all opportunity costs, both explicit and implicit, is
(a) economic profit
(b) accounting profit
(c) monopoly profit
(d) normal profit

22. Economic profit is the compensation for entrepreneurs for
(a) assuming insurable risks for a firm
(b) assuming uninsurable risks for a firm
(c) being the first claimant for the firm's revenue
(d) being the second claimant for the firm's revenue

23. One basic reason why there is economic profit is that
(a) the risks for a firm are insurable
(b) production costs for a firm increase
(c) new popular products are developed by a firm
(d) product markets become more purely competitive

24. Profit from a monopoly position for a firm is obtained because of
(a) the firm assuming insurable risk
(b) the firm assuming uninsurable risk
(c) control over product output and price
(d) control over output, but not product price

25. Since 1900, the share of income paid to American resource suppliers
(a) has increased for capitalists, but decreased for labor
(b) has decreased for capitalists, but increased for labor
(c) has increased for capitalists and for labor
(d) has remained relatively constant for capitalists and labor

■ PROBLEMS

1. Assume that the quantity of a certain type of land available is 300,000 acres and the demand for this land is that given in the following table.

Pure land rent, per acre	Land demanded, acres
$350	100,000
300	200,000
250	300,000
200	400,000
150	500,000
100	600,000
50	700,000

a. The pure rent on this land will be $_____.

b. The total quantity of land rented will be _____ acres.

c. On the following graph, plot the supply and demand curves for this land and indicate the pure rent for land and the quantity of land rented.

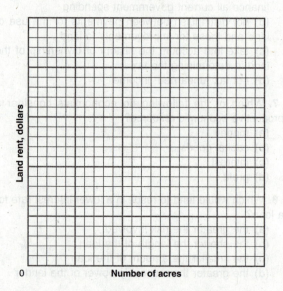

d. If landowners were taxed at a rate of $250 per acre for their land, the pure rent on this land after taxes would be $_____ but the number of acres rented would be _____.

2. The following schedule shows interest rates (column 1), the associated quantity demanded of loanable funds (column 2), and the quantity supplied of loanable funds (column 4) in billions of dollars at those interest rates.

Interest rate (1)	Quantity demanded (2)	(3)	Quantity supplied (4)	(5)
12	50	____	260	____
10	100	____	240	____
8	150	____	220	____
6	200	____	200	____
4	250	____	180	____
2	300	____	160	____

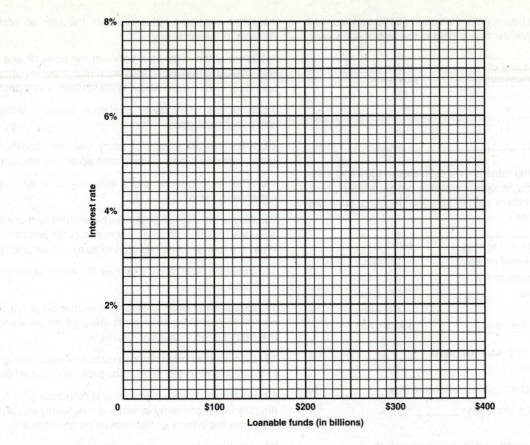

Loanable funds (in billions)

a. Plot the demand and supply schedule on the graph above. (The interest rate is measured along the vertical axis and the quantity demanded or supplied is measured on the horizontal axis.)

(1) The equilibrium interest rate is _____ %. The quantity demanded is $_____ billion and the quantity supplied is $_____ billion.

(2) At an interest rate of 10%, the quantity demanded of loanable funds is $_____ billion and the quantity supplied of loanable funds is $_____ billion.

There is an excess of loanable funds of $_____ billion.

(3) At an interest rate of 4%, the quantity demanded of loanable funds is $_____ billion and the quantity supplied of loanable funds is $_____ billion.

There is a shortage of loanable funds of $_____ billion.

b. If technology improves and the demand for loanable funds increases by $70 billion at each interest rate, then the new equilibrium interest rate will be _____% and the equilibrium quantity of loanable funds will be $_____ billion. Fill in the new demand schedule in column 3 of the table, and plot this new demand curve on the graph.

c. Then, because of changes in the tax laws, households become thriftier by $140 at each interest rate.

The new equilibrium interest rate will be _____% and the new equilibrium quantity of loanable funds will be $_____ billion. Fill in the new supply schedule in column 5 of the table, and plot this new supply curve on the graph.

3. Firms make investment decisions based on the rate of return and the interest rate.

a. In each of the following simple cases, calculate the rate of return on an investment.

(1) You invest in a new machine that costs $2000 but which is expected to increase total revenues by $2075 in 1 year. _____%

(2) You invest in a new piece of equipment that costs $150,000 but which is expected to increase total revenues in 1 year by $160,000. _____%

(3) You invest in a new plant that costs $3 million and which is expected to increase total revenues in 1 year by $3.5 million. _____%

b. Given each of the following interest rates, in which cases (1, 2, and 3) in **3a** would you make an investment?

(1) An interest rate of 5% _____

(2) An interest rate of 8% _____

(3) An interest rate of 15% _____

4. In the table below, enter the value of $100 compounded at 4 percent interest that is paid at the end of each year.

Years of compounding	Value at year's end
1	$_____
2	_____
3	_____
4	_____

5. The following table shows estimated wages and salaries, proprietors' income, corporate profits, interest, rent, and the total income paid to American resource suppliers in a recent year.

Wages and salaries	$5642 billion
Proprietors' income	717 billion
Corporate profits	967 billion
Interest	571 billion
Rent	139 billion
Total income	$8036 billion

a. Wages and salaries were _____% of the total income.

b. Labor's share of the total income was _____% and capital's share was _____%.

■ **SHORT ANSWER AND ESSAY QUESTIONS**

1. Explain what determines the economic rent paid for the use of land. What is unique about the supply of land?

2. Even though land rent is an economic surplus payment, it is also an economic cost for the individual use of land. Why and how can it be both an economic surplus payment and an economic cost?

3. What economic difficulties would be encountered if the government adopted Henry George's single tax proposal as a means of confiscating this surplus? What do the critics think of the concept of a single tax on land?

4. Explain what interest is and why there are many different interest rates at any given time.

5. What is the pure rate of interest? How is it approximated?

6. Explain what determines (a) the amount of loanable funds that households are willing to supply, (b) the amount that businesses wish to demand, and (c) how these desires are resolved in the market for loanable funds.

7. How might a change in productivity affect the interest rate? How might a change in the tax laws affect household savings and the interest rate? What are the implications if the supply curve for loanable funds is highly inelastic?

8. Explain the concept of the time value of money using compound interest, future value, and present value.

9. What is the connection between the rate of return on a capital goods investment and the interest rate? Give examples of possible investment situations.

10. What important functions does the rate of interest perform in the economy?

11. What is the difference between the nominal and the real interest rates? How does each one affect investment spending or decisions about research and development?

12. What are usury laws? Explain in terms of demand and supply analysis.

13. What are the effects of usury laws on allocation of credit, borrowers and lenders, and economic efficiency?

14. What is economic profit and why is it related to entrepreneurship?

15. Why is the distinction between insurable and uninsurable risk important from an economic profit perspective? What are four sources that contribute to uninsurable risk?

16. Describe and give example of three sources of economic profit.

17. Explain why profit arising from monopoly is not economically desirable, while profit arising from uninsurable risk taking is economically desirable.

18. Discuss how profit rations entrepreneurship using the terms economic profit, accounting profit, and normal profit.

19. What role do entrepreneurs and corporate stockholders play in the economy in terms of risk taking and profit? What are the effects of this activity on the economy?

20. What part of the income paid to American resource suppliers is labor's share, and what part is capitalists' share? Have the shares changed much since 1900?

ANSWERS

Chapter 14 Rent, Interest, and Profit

FILL-IN QUESTIONS

1. land, natural, fixed
2. demand, supply
3. productivity, cost, has alternative uses, surplus payment
4. incentive, surplus
5. unearned, tax, revenue
6. interest, percentage, is not, is not
7. *a.* risk; *b.* length of loan; *c.* amount of loan; *d.* tax status of loan (or investment) (any order for *a–d*)
8. pure, long-term
9. loanable, equal to
10. directly, inversely
11. fewer, smaller
12. an increase, supply, increase, demand
13. time value of money, compound, larger, smaller
14. decreases, decreases, increases, increases
15. real, nominal
16. usury, nonmarket, borrowers, less
17. economic, accounting, normal
18. uninsurable; *a.* changes in the general economic environment; *b.* change in the structure of the economy; *c.* changes in government policy; *d.* new product or product methods developed by rival (*any order for a–d*)
19. new, reducing, monopoly, decrease
20. 80%, 20%, remained stable

TRUE–FALSE QUESTIONS

1. F, p. 294	**10.** F, p. 299	**19.** F, p. 303
2. F, p. 294	**11.** T, p. 300	**20.** F, p. 303
3. F, pp. 294–295	**12.** F, pp. 299–300	**21.** T, p. 304
4. T, p. 295	**13.** T, pp. 300–301	**22.** F, p. 304
5. F, pp. 295–296	**14.** T, p. 301	**23.** T, p. 305
6. F, p. 297	**15.** T, p. 302	**24.** F, pp. 305–306
7. F, pp. 297–298	**16.** F, p. 302	**25.** T, pp. 307–308
8. T, p. 298	**17.** F, p. 302	
9. T, pp. 298–299	**18.** T, p. 302	

MULTIPLE-CHOICE QUESTIONS

1. c, p. 294	**10.** d, p. 298	**19.** c, p. 303
2. a, p. 294	**11.** a, pp. 298–299	**20.** d, p. 303
3. b, pp. 294–295	**12.** d, p. 299	**21.** a, p. 304
4. b, pp. 294–295	**13.** b, p. 299	**22.** b, p. 304
5. c, p. 295	**14.** d, p. 300	**23.** c, p. 305
6. b, pp. 296–297	**15.** d, pp. 301–302	**24.** c, pp. 305–306
7. b, p. 297	**16.** b, p. 302	**25.** d, p. 308
8. b, pp. 297–298	**17.** b, p. 302	
9. a, p. 298	**18.** c, p. 302	

PROBLEMS

1. *a.* 250; *b.* 300,000; *c.* graph; *d.* 0, 300,000

2. *a.* (1) 6, 200, 200, (2) 100, 240, 140, (3) 250, 180, 70; *b.* 8, 220; 120, 170, 220, 270, 320, 370; *c.* 4, 320; 400, 380, 360, 340, 320, 300

3. *a.* (1) 3.75; (2) 6.67; (3) 16.67; *b.* (1) 2, 3; (2) 3; (3) 3

4. 104.00, 108.16, 112.49, 116.99

5. *a.* 70; *b.* 79, 21

SHORT ANSWER AND ESSAY QUESTIONS

1. p. 294	**8.** pp. 300–301	**15.** pp. 304–305
2. pp. 295–296	**9.** p. 302	**16.** pp. 305–306
3. pp. 296–297	**10.** p. 302	**17.** pp. 305–306
4. pp. 297–298	**11.** p. 302	**18.** pp. 304, 306
5. p. 298	**12.** p. 303	**19.** pp. 307–308
6. pp. 298–300	**13.** p. 303	**20.** p. 308
7. p. 300	**14.** p. 304	

CHAPTER 15

Natural Resource and Energy Economics

This chapter discusses many issues related to natural resource and energy economics. The material is important because it provides an understanding of why dire predictions for the economy related to energy or resource use turn out to be false. It also shows how resources can be efficiently managed to increase economic output and how such resources can be conserved and sustained over time. The first major section of the chapter investigates two dire predictions. The first one is that **population growth** will overwhelm the economy and thus lead to declining living standards. The second one is that the economy will run out of **supplies of resources** for sustaining economic growth. Neither prediction has turned out to be true for many reasons, as you will learn from the chapter. As nations have grown and living standards have improved, nations have experienced a decline in birthrates such that they are lower than the replacement rate necessary to keep the population from falling over time. Also, the economy is not likely to run out of resource supplies because total demand for resources is starting to decline and the supply of resources to meet the demand is ample and increasing.

The second section of the chapter looks at **energy economics.** Here you will learn that energy demand has leveled off in recent years in developed countries such as the United States. One reason for this change is that there has been a huge increase in energy efficiency. This efficiency keeps improving because of new developments in technology that help make better use of energy inputs. As a consequence, the U.S. economy has been able to increase real output per capita by slightly more than one-third from 1988–2009 while at the same time energy inputs per capita have remained relatively constant.

Another dire prediction addressed in this section of the chapter is that the economy is running out of energy. This prediction is another false one because it fails to take into account the effects of increasing energy prices on the viability of alternative energy sources. In a dynamic economy, as one energy resource becomes scarcer and higher-priced, it creates incentives to find and use other energy resources that will substitute for that energy resource. As energy prices rise, they will provide incentives for greater energy production. The third and remaining sections of the chapter discuss **natural resource economics** and how to manage natural resources for efficient and sustainable use in the economy. One important tool that is used to make resource decisions is the calculation of present value. The ability of policy makers to compare the present value of current

or future uses in the calculation of the net benefits of resources helps them decide how much of a resource to consume today or conserve for the future. This approach provides economic incentives for efficient management and conservation of resources.

There are two basic types of natural resources. **Nonrenewable resources** such as oil, coal, metal ores, or natural gas must be pumped out or mined from the ground before they can be used. The determination of how much to pump or mine in the present or the future again involves the calculation of present value. A simple model is used to show that under the right incentive structure, profit-maximizing firms will extract nonrenewable resources in an efficient manner over time to maximize the net benefits and the profit stream. If, however, there are weak or uncertain property rights, there is a market failure and it leads to more extraction in the present and less conservation such as the case with the mining of conflict diamonds.

The second type of resources is **renewable resources** such as wildlife (elephants), forests, and fisheries. In this case, too, clear and enforceable property rights are important for the optimal and efficient harvesting of such resources, and for the conservation and sustainable use of such resources over time. If property rights are not clear or enforceable, then firms have more of a profit incentive to harvest today and less of an incentive to conserve such resources for the future.

The property rights problem is especially complex when considering the conservation and sustainability of fisheries. For this issue, economists have recommended the limits on the total catch of fish and the use of tradable catch quotas for individual fishers so their fishing is conducted in the least costly way and the fish population remains large enough to reproduce and grow.

■ **CHECKLIST**

When you have studied this chapter you should be able to

☐ Explain Malthus's theory about population and economic growth.

☐ Discuss the trends in living standards and birthrates over time.

☐ Describe the predictions for future population growth.

☐ Identify the two major factors affecting the demand for resources.

☐ Explain the trends in the long-run supply of commodity resources.

☐ Describe the trends in resource consumption per person since the 1950s.

☐ Compare the expected demand for resources to the expected supply of resources.

☐ Discuss why there is cause for optimism about the availability of supply of resources in the future.

☐ Define energy economics.

☐ Explain why the demand for energy resources has not outstripped the supply.

☐ Use electrical power generation as an example to illustrate why energy use has become more efficient.

☐ Define natural resource economics.

☐ Distinguish between renewable and nonrenewable natural resources.

☐ Use present value to evaluate decisions about the optimal use of a limited supply of a nonrenewable resource.

☐ Define user cost of exaction and extraction costs.

☐ Use a graph of user cost and extraction cost to show how a firm will decide how much of a resource to extract in the present or the future.

☐ Use a graph of user cost and extraction cost to show how an increase in expected future profits leads to less extraction.

☐ Explain how market failures lead to excessive present use of a resource and apply it to conflict diamonds.

☐ Explain why property rights are important for conservation of elephants and the management of forests.

☐ Discuss the optimal harvesting of forests.

☐ Describe optimal management of fisheries.

☐ Evaluate alternative government policies to limit catch sizes for fish.

☐ Explain the economic incentives of a policy of TAC and ITQs.

☐ Explain the relationship between environmental quality and economic growth based on GDP per capita (*Last Word*).

■ **CHAPTER OUTLINE**

1. Living standards for the average American today are at least 12 times higher than they were in 1800. The population is larger today and resource use per person is higher. The increasing demand for and concerns about a limited supply of resources have raised questions about whether these high living standards can be sustained.

   a. There are many aspects of *population growth* that have changed over time.

   (1) Thomas Malthus in his "An Essay on the Principle of Population" argued that human living standards could only temporarily rise above subsistence levels. In his view, higher living standards would bring forth more population and the increased population would eventually reduce living standards. The opposite, however, has occurred. Higher living standards have resulted in birthrates that are lower than the *replacement rate* that is necessary to keep a population from declining over time. The majority of the world's population now resides in nations where the *total fertility rate* is less than that needed to keep a nation's population stable over time.

   (2) *Demographers,* the scientists who study human population, find that the world population growth is slowing and turning negative in many nations. Many demographers think that the world's population will only rise to peak at 9 billion people in the next 50 years and then decline rapidly. This possible demographic shift means that there will be a substantial decrease in the demand for resources.

   (3) The world's population increased rapidly from 1800 to the present because of the rapid fall in the death rate due to better medical care and modernization. As living standards begin to rise and the death rate to fall, people still are slow to realize that they need few children to ensure that some of the children will survive to adulthood.

   (4) The overall world population is increasing because countries such as India and Indonesia are still in the transition phase where death rates have fallen, but birthrates are still high. In other nations with rising standards of living and modernization birthrates are falling below the replacement rate. This change is likely to produce a decline in world population during this century.

   (5) Demographers have been surprised by the rapid decline in the fertility rate below the replacement rate in many nations and attribute the change to changing attitudes towards religion, greater labor market opportunities for women outside the household, and the increasing cost of raising children. It appears that the view of children has changed from one of their being an economic asset for families, as was the case in countries with an agricultural economy, to one of their being an economic liability, costly to raise to *adulthood, as is the case in nations that have modernized.*

   b. *Resource consumption per person* has also changed over time.

   (1) Many individuals and groups have made dire predictions about the decline in living standards and explosive population growth that will outstrip the capacity of the economy to supply resources, but the predictions have been wrong. The reasons are twofold. The population growth rate has fallen substantially as living standards have risen around the world. Also, the supply of productive resources has been increasing faster than the demand for resources, thus driving down the price of resources.

   (2) The real cost (inflation adjusted) of buying resource commodities in 2009 was about 60 percent lower than it was in the initial 1845–1850 period. The long-run decline in the prices of these commodities indicates that the supply of such resources has grown faster than the demand for them that arises because of the population increase and rising consumption per person.

   (3) The demand trends are likely to continue into the future. There is likely to be a decline in population this century and resource consumption per person is likely to remain relatively constant or decline. The demand trends and the long-run decline in resource commodity prices indicate that resource supplies have been able to meet growth and exceed demand.

   (4) The decline in resource consumption per person can be seen in data from the United States on total and per capita water use, trash generation, and energy use. In fact, annual per capita energy use in the United

States peaked in 1979 at 360 million **British thermal units** (BTU). (A BTU is the amount of energy required to raise the temperature of 1 pound of water by 1 degree Fahrenheit.)

(5) Resource demand is likely to increase significantly during the next few decades as more countries modernize and begin to consume more energy and other resources per capita. The increasing demand in developing countries will be offset somewhat by the declining demand in richer nations as population growth and resource use per capita decline in these nations. Improvements in technology should also contribute to more efficient resource use.

(6) There will continue to be imbalances in resource availability and demand in certain regions that can cause conflicts and challenges. Water is very scarce in the Middle East and other arid and desert regions of the world. Oil is more plentiful in the Middle East and highly sought in Europe and the United States.

2. *Energy economics* studies how people deal with the fact there are relatively unlimited wants for energy and relatively limited energy resources. This scarcity problem involves changes in demand and supply and applies to all types of energy resources or sources such as oil, coal, natural gas, nuclear power, hydroelectric power, and renewables.

a. In recent years, the demand for energy has leveled off in the United States and developing countries. One reason for this development is that the economy has become increasingly efficient at using energy to produce goods and services. For example, as energy input per capita has remained relatively constant, real GDP per capita rose by 39 percent from 1988 to 2008.

b. The increase in energy efficiency has been part of a long-term trend. From 1950 to 2008, real GDP more than doubled per million BTUs of energy consumed. One factor contributing to this more efficient use of energy has been the availability of better technology over the period.

c. One of the interesting aspects of energy efficiency is that it involves using a mix of energy inputs, some of which are more expensive than others. Electrical power generation provides an illustration of this point. An electric plant faces varying demands for power during the day and night. To meet these varying demands, electric companies will build a large plant that requires a high fixed cost to build, but produces energy at a low price when it is fully operational and meets most of peak consumer demand. To supplement its energy production for peak demand periods, instead of building another large plant, it will build a smaller plant that has a lower fixed cost to build, but produces energy at a higher cost.

d. One concern people have about energy is whether the economy is running out of energy, particularly oil. Economists view this situation rather as one where the economy is running out of *cheap* energy. As is known from basic economics, as the price of oil rises, alternative sources of energy become economically viable. And as technology reduces the cost of producing such alternatives, their prices will fall, bringing forth more energy production. However, there are other concerns about the types of alternative energy sources developed and the degree to which they impose negative externalities on the environment.

3. *Natural resource economics* focuses on maximizing the net benefits from policies or actions taken to extract or harvest a natural resource.

a. The term **net benefits** refers to the difference between the total dollar value of all the benefits of a project and the total dollar value of all the costs. The decision can be a complex one because some of these costs and benefits are incurred in the present and others are incurred in the future.

b. The type of natural resource makes a large difference in the application of this net benefits rule. **Renewable natural resources** include such items as forests, wildlife, rivers, lakes, oceans, the atmosphere, and solar energy. These resources are capable of growing back or renewing themselves, and thus can provide benefits in perpetuity if managed well. **Nonrenewable natural resources** include such items as oil, coal, natural gas, and metal ores that are found in relatively fixed supply.

c. The challenge of natural resource economics is to design incentive structures that maximize the net benefits, and also conserve resources in the present so they are available in the future.

4. Natural resource economists use **present value** to evaluate future possibilities.

a. For example, assume it costs $50 a barrel to pump oil today, but it costs $60 a barrel to pump it in five years. If there is a 5 percent interest rate, it makes more sense to pump oil today because $60 received five years in the future would be worth only $47.01 today [$60/(1 + .05)^5 = $47.01] (see Chapter 14 for more discussion of present value).

b. Present value calculations enable decision makers to compare the net benefits of using a natural resource today with conserving the natural resource for future use. As a result of such net benefit decisions, natural resources will be used more efficiently in the economy either in the present or in the future.

5. *Nonrenewable resources* include oil, coal, and other resources that must be pumped or mined from the ground. A company has the goal of maximizing profits, but this involves maximizing the stream of profits over the extraction period. Every bit of a nonrenewable natural resource that is extracted and sold today has a **user cost** in the form of its not being extracted and sold in the future. Current extraction and use means lower future extraction and use.

a. The decision between present and future extraction can be illustrated with a graph that shows a firm's cost of extraction for mining a resource. The graph shows cost or dollars on the vertical axis and the first-year quantity extracted on the horizontal axis. The **extraction cost (EC)** line will be upsloping because it typically costs more to extract more of the resource in the first year. Where the EC line crosses the horizontal market price line determines the quantity (Q_0) extraction of the resource.

b. But the EC line does not account for all the costs. For each unit extracted today there is a user cost, which is the present value of the profits that the firm would earn if the extraction and sale of each ton of coal were delayed until the second year. When this user cost (UC) is added to the **extraction costs (EC),** it creates a total cost (TC) line that is parallel to the EC line but shifted upward by the amount of the user cost. This TC line crosses the market price line at a lower quantity (Q_1). This result means that a smaller quantity will be extracted than would be the case if only EC is considered.

c. The general point is that the firm will produce a quantity of the resource the first year so long as the first-year profit is greater than the present value of the second-year profit. A firm will not mine all of its resource the first year, but seek to maximize the stream of profits over time.

d. If future profits are expected to increase, then the user cost will increase and thus shift the TC line upward. The higher TC line means that the firm will extract less of the resource today and more of the resource in the future than was the previous case. Thus, given the right institutional structure and incentives, profit-maximizing firms will extract resources efficiently over time to obtain the most net benefits.

e. Firms are willing to reduce current extraction if they have the ability to profit from future extraction and sale of their products. Market failures, however, can lead to excessive present use of resources. If property rights are uncertain, then a firm has less incentive to conserve a resource for future extraction and will increase extraction today. Weak or uncertain property rights reduce the user cost to zero and give more incentive to extract today.

f. One application of where nonrenewable resources will be extracted too quickly if there is no way to profit from conservation is **conflict diamonds** that are mined in war zones. This mining is very wasteful precisely because of the uncertainty over the control of the mine, as the war can change which army controls the mine. The incentive in this case is thus more current extraction, which will result in more difficult and expensive extraction in the future when the war ends and the nation needs the revenue.

6. Profit incentives and property rights affect the extraction or harvesting of **renewable resources,** influencing whether they are preserved and provide a steady stream of profits over time. Property rights need to be structured properly and enforced so there is a strong profit incentive to manage the resource on a sustainable basis and not extract or harvest too much of the resource today.

a. Elephant preservation is a renewable resource that is affected by property rights. In those cases where villages have been given financial incentives to protect the elephant herd because they receive a share of the tourist dollars, herds grow. In those cases in which the state controls the resource, and property rights are not enforced, there is illegal poaching and elephant herds decline.

b. Forests in different countries are managed differently and this explains why forests in some countries are increasing and in other countries there is widespread deforestation. In countries where the forests are increasing, there are clear property rights and they are enforced, so there are good profit incentives to harvest woods on a sustainable basis over time. In countries experiencing deforestation, the property rights are uncertain or not enforced, so there is a strong profit incentive to harvest more trees today because the possibility of future harvesting or profitability is uncertain.

c. Optimal harvesting of trees in a forest involves understanding the growth rate of trees in those cases in which property rights are clear and enforceable. For example, trees may grow at a slow rate during their first 50 years, then growth at a fast rate from 50 to 100 years, and then grow at a slow or zero rate thereafter. A lumber company will have a strong profit incentive to harvest young trees some time during the fast growth period because it will produce the most wood in the least amount of time. Of course the market demand condition and the cost of harvesting will affect the precise year for optimal harvesting that produces the greatest net benefits for the company.

d. A **fishery** is defined as a stock of fish or marine animals that is considered to be a distinct group such as Pacific tuna or Alaskan crab. Oceans are common property resources without ownership. The only property rights come after a fisher catches the fish. In this case, there are strong incentives for the fisher to overfish the ocean to catch more fish before another fisher does so. This overfishing of a fishery can lead to **fishery collapse** when a fish population becomes so depleted that it can no longer reproduce at a sustainable rate. Data from 2007 show that only 2% of the world's fisheries are underexploited, but 80% are fully exploited, overexploited, depleted, or recovering from depletion.

e. Governments have adopted policies to reduce the number of fish caught each year so that fisheries can be prevented from collapsing. Some policies, such as limiting the number of days of fishing or the number of fishing boats, have not worked because the fishers would use bigger boats that would allow them to catch the same number of fish as before but in a fewer number of days and with fewer boats.

(1) One policy that seems to work is to use a **total allowable catch** (TAC) system in which biologists specify the TAC for a fishery. The chief advantage of this system is that it limits the actual amount of the catch so that the uncaught fish will still be able to **sustain** the population. One problem with the TAC is that fishing costs rise because fishers buy bigger boats to catch as many fish as possible before the TAC limit is reached.

(2) Economists like the TAC system, but prefer it to be used with **individual transferable quotas (ITQs)** that also limit the individual catch size by a fisher to a specified quantity. This policy provides disincentives to use bigger boats under a TAC system alone because each fisher has a specified catch limit, and thus it reduces fishing costs. The ITQs issued will also add up to the TAC limit so the fish population can be sustained. It also encourages fishing to be done at the least cost because ITQs are tradable quotas. An ITQ held by a

fisher who is less efficient at fishing can be traded to one who is more efficient at fishing. The overall result is that there will be efficiency gains for society and fishing will be less costly.

7. (*Last Word*). The evidence indicates that economic growth and rising living standards are good for the environment because as nations become wealthier, they tend to spend more on environmental protection and adopt better economic policies to correct environmental problems. A graph with an environmental performance index on the vertical axis and GDP per capita on the horizontal axis shows that nations with a low level of GDP per capita have a low EPI score and nations with a high GDP per capita have a high EPI score. The results indicate that economic growth can promote a healthier environment.

■ **HINTS AND TIPS**

1. This chapter builds on ideas and concepts presented in previous chapters. Make sure you review the concept of present value presented in Chapter 14.

2. It might be easy to get lost in the tables and graphs presented in this chapter and miss the general point. All of the tables and graphs in this chapter are simply used to illustrate trends or general points described in the text. Make sure you find and highlight those general points in the text.

3. One of the great advantages of understanding the material in this chapter is that it is useful for showing that dire predictions about economic catastrophes are wrong. These predictions include population growth undermining living standards, energy resources being exhausted, or the demise of renewable resources. The economic analysis in this chapter shows that the economy and ecosystems are more robust than realized, especially when there are clear and enforceable property rights and good economic incentives for efficient resource use.

■ **IMPORTANT TERMS**

replacement rate
total fertility rate
demographers
British thermal unit (BTU)
net benefits
renewable natural
  resources
nonrenewable natural
  resources

present value
user cost
extraction cost
conflict diamonds
fishery
fishery collapse
total allowable catch (TAC)
individual transferable
  quotas (ITQs)

SELF-TEST

■ **FILL-IN QUESTIONS**

1. Per capita living standards in the United States are at least (2, 12) _____ times higher than they

were for the average American in 1800. This increase in living standards has required using much (larger, smaller) _____ amounts of resources to produce more goods and services.

2. The increase in resource use is the result of two factors: There has been a large (increase, decrease) _____ in resource use per person and there are now (more, less) _____ people consuming resources than in previous periods.

3. Thomas Malthus predicted that higher living standards would tend to lead to (higher, lower) _____ birthrates, but the opposite has occurred because higher living standards have led to _____ birthrates.

4. The majority of the world's population now lives in countries where the total fertility rate is (greater, less) _____ than the replacement rate of (2.1, 3.3) _____ births per woman per lifetime that is necessary to keep a country's population constant over time.

5. The world population growth is slowing and in many countries it is turning (positive, negative) _____. As a result the demand for resources in the future will be (higher, lower) _____ than would be case if population levels continued to increase.

6. Many demographers expect the world's population will reach a maximum of (9, 18) _____ billion people in the next 50 years before beginning to (rise, decline)_____.

7. The expected (rise, decline) _____ in population levels and the fact that per capita resource use has leveled off or (risen, fallen) _____ suggests that the total demand for resources is likely to reach a peak in the relatively near future before (rising, falling) _____ over time.

8. The confidence that resource supplies will be likely to grow faster than resource demands in the future is based on the fact that since 1850 the real (inflation-adjusted) prices of resources have fallen by about (20, 70) _____ percent. This fall in price happened at the same time that total resource use was (increasing, decreasing) _____.

9. In the future, resource supplies should grow (slower, faster) _____ than resource demands because the population is growing _____ and resource use per capita has leveled off or turned negative.

10. Living standards can continue to rise without consuming more energy due to (more, less) _____ efficient technologies for producing energy. Real GDP per capita in the United States increased by slightly more than (one-third, two-thirds) _____ from 1988 to 2009 while annual per capita energy consumption (increased, decreased, remained constant) _____.

11. Differences in (variable, fixed) _____ costs in energy production mean that a wide variety of energy sources are used in the economy even if some sources are (more, less) _____ costly than others.

12. For example, coal-fired electric generating plants that generate large amounts of electricity use a (low-cost, high-cost) _____ energy source, but these plants are _____ to build; other plants that produce small amounts of electricity use _____ fuel sources, but are _____ to build. An investment's proper current price is equal to the sum of the (present, future) _____ values of each of the investment's expected _____ payments.

13. The United States (is, is not) _____ running out of energy such as oil because there are other energy sources that become viable to produce and sell as the price of energy (falls, rises) _____.

14. Natural resources such as forests and wildlife are (nonrenewable, renewable) _____ whereas natural resources such as oil or coal are _____.

15. Renewable and nonrenewable natural resources tend to be overused in the (present, future) _____ unless there are arrangements created that provide resource users with a way to benefit from conservation. Governments can ensure that there are net benefits from conservation by strictly defining and enforcing (civil, property) _____ rights so that resource owners know that if they conserve a resource, they will be able to use it in the (future, present) _____.

16. The optimal level of extraction of a nonrenewable resource over time is based on calculation of a total cost, which is the combination of the cost of not being able to extract it in the future, which is called the (user, extraction) _____ cost, plus the cost of producing the resource, which is called the _____ cost.

17. In a mining situation, if only extraction costs were considered as the total cost, there would be (more, less) _____ of the resource extracted in the present and _____ will be extracted in the future, but if total costs include both the user cost and extraction costs, then _____ will be extracted in the present and _____ will be extracted in the future.

18. It is difficult to encourage conservation in the open ocean because it is difficult to define or enforce (civil, property) _____ rights. This situation means that there is a rush by each fisher to catch as much as possible in the (least, most) _____ amount of time. These actions cause (over-, under-) _____ fishing and the fish population to (expand, collapse) _____.

19. Closer to shore nations can define property rights within the waters they control and set (limits, prices) _____ on the fish caught.

20. A policy that specifies the complete amount that all fishers can catch of a fishery is the (total allowable catch, individual transferable quota) _____ whereas the policy that specifies that amount each fisher can catch is the _____.

■ **TRUE–FALSE QUESTIONS**

Circle T if the statement is true, F if it is false.

1. The average American enjoys a standard of living at least 12 times higher than that of the average American living in 1800.　　　　**T　F**

2. Higher living standards are associated with lower birthrates.　　　　**T　F**

3. The replacement rate is the average number of children that a woman is expected to have during her lifetime.　　　　**T　F**

4. Total fertility rates in many nations are well below the 2.1 rate necessary to keep the population stable over time.　　　　**T　F**

5. Demographers expect the world's population to reach a peak of about 9 billion people or fewer around the middle of this century before beginning to decline.　　　　**T　F**

6. The long-run evidence indicates that the available supply of productive resources to be made into goods and services has been increasing faster than the demand for those resources for at least 150 years.　　　　**T　F**

7. The long-run fall of commodity prices implies that commodity supplies have grown slower than the demand for them.　　　　**T　F**

8. Resource consumption per person has either leveled off or declined in the past decade.　　　　**T　F**

9. A BTU is a measure of trash generation and refers to a biodegradable trash unit.　　　　**T　F**

10. If per capita consumption continues to stay the same or decrease while the population declines, total resource demand will decline.　　　　**T　F**

11. Resource demand is likely to increase substantially for the next few decades as large parts of the world modernize and begin to consume as much per capita as the citizens of rich countries do today. **T F**

12. Since energy is only one input into a production process, often the best energy source to use is sometimes rather expensive, but still the best choice when other costs are taken into account. **T F**

13. In developed countries, per capita energy use has increased significantly in recent years. **T F**

14. Better technology means that more output can be produced with the same amount of energy input, so rising living standards in the future will not necessarily depend on using more energy. **T F**

15. It is highly likely that the United States will run out of energy when the cost of a barrel of oil reaches $250. **T F**

16. Net benefits are the total dollar value of all benefits minus the total dollar value of all costs. **T F**

17. Aquifers are considered to be a nonrenewable resource. **T F**

18. Present value calculation provides a financial incentive to make sure that resources will be conserved for future use whenever doing so will generate higher net benefits than using them in the present. **T F**

19. A mining company's goal of maximizing profits means choosing a strategy that maximizes the stream of profits over the time of extraction. **T F**

20. Extraction cost means that a resource that is extracted and sold today will come at a cost of its not being extracted and sold in the future. **T F**

21. Under the right institutional structure, profit-maximizing firms will extract resources efficiently over time so that each unit of resource will tend to be extracted when the gains from doing so are greatest. **T F**

22. Resources will tend to be extracted too slowly if there is no way to benefit from conservation. **T F**

23. In the case of forests, if property rights are ill-defined or not enforced, resource owners have more incentive to cut trees today and less incentive to conserve trees for future use. **T F**

24. A fishery collapse occurs when a fishery's population is sent into a rapid decline because the fish are being raised and released into the water at too fast a rate. **T F**

25. Where governments can define property rights for fishing, the best system for limiting fishing involves combining total allowable catch (TAC) with individual transferable quota (ITQ) limits for individual fishers. **T F**

■ **MULTIPLE-CHOICE QUESTIONS**

Circle the letter that corresponds to the best answer.

1. Which is a factor that explains why resource use has increased?
(a) fewer people are alive today
(b) living standards have decreased

(c) the cost of resources has increased
(d) consumption per person has increased

2. What is the total fertility rate that is needed to keep the population constant over time?
(a) 1.5 births
(b) 2.1 births
(c) 3.0 births
(d) 3.6 births

3. One major reason why the world's population increased so rapidly from 1800 to the present is because
(a) the total fertility rate was less than the death rate
(b) the total fertility rate was less than the replacement rate
(c) higher living standards contributed to a large increase in the number of births over time
(d) higher living standards improved health care and resulted in a lower death rate

4. One major reason predictions that population growth would outstrip the economy's capacity to support a population turned out to be false is that
(a) the supply of resources increased faster than the demand for them
(b) the demand for resources increased faster than the supply of them
(c) the population growth rate slowed and so did living standards around the world
(d) governments around the world set strict quotas on the total fertility rates

5. Compared with the 1845–1850 period, the real cost of buying commodities today is about
(a) 30 percent higher
(b) 30 percent lower
(c) 60 percent higher
(d) 60 percent lower

6. Which would be a factor that would make the prospects hopeful for overcoming the demand for resources in the future?
(a) Total fertility rates are increasing in many nations.
(b) Total death rates are increasing in many nations.
(c) Resource consumption per person has leveled off in wealthier nations.
(d) Resource consumption per person has leveled off in developing nations such as China and India.

7. Recent trends in water use, energy consumption, and trash generation indicate that the total demand for resources is likely to
(a) increase substantially over time
(b) decrease and then increase substantially over time
(c) trough in the near future before rising as populations grow
(d) peak in the near future before falling as populations decline

8. About what percentage of energy was generated by coal-fired plants in 2008?
(a) 18 percent
(b) 48 percent
(c) 78 percent
(d) 98 percent

9. The main reason the nation will *not* run out of energy is that
   (a) the demand for energy has risen substantially
   (b) the demand for energy has fallen substantially
   (c) the government can control the price of energy and keep it low
   (d) rising energy prices bring forth more supply from alternative sources

10. A forestry company wants to spend $1000 per acre today to plant seedlings that will grow into $125,000 in 100 years. The present value of $125,000 in 100 years at an interest rate of 5 percent is $950.56. The present value results indicate that the company should
   (a) not make the investment because the future is too uncertain
   (b) make the investment because an acre is worth $125,000 today
   (c) make the invest because the benefits are greater then the costs
   (d) not make the investment because the costs are greater than the benefits

Answer Questions 11, 12, 13, 14, and 15 based on the graph below for a firm that mines coal over a two-year period. P is the market price.

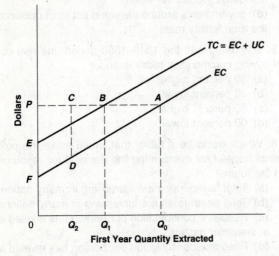

11. User cost is measured by the difference between
   (a) A–B
   (b) E–F
   (c) P–B
   (d) P–F

12. If only extraction cost is considered, then during the first year the firm will extract
   (a) 0
   (b) Q_0
   (c) Q_1
   (d) Q_2

13. If the firm considers both extraction costs and user costs, then during the first year the firm will extract
   (a) 0
   (b) Q_0

(c) Q_1
(d) Q_2

14. The profit that a firm can extract at Q_2 the first year is equal to
   (a) C–D
   (b) E–F
   (c) P–E
   (d) P–F

15. Assume that the firm is producing at Q_1. If user costs increased in the first year because of an increase in expected future profits, this increase will shift the TC line
   (a) down and reduce the quantity extracted to less than Q_1
   (b) down and increase the quantity extracted to more than Q_1
   (c) up and reduce the quantity extracted to less than Q_1
   (d) up and increase the quantity extracted to more than Q_1

16. Conflict diamonds are diamonds that are mined
   (a) under production conditions that use old technology rather than new technology
   (b) under war conditions where there is little incentive to conserve them
   (c) where the government specifies that the diamonds cannot be sold outside the nation
   (d) where the diamond producer is fighting a takeover offer from another company

17. If the property rights to renewable resources are clear and enforced, resource owners will have
   (a) strong incentives to preserve the resources and will harvest them slowly over time
   (b) weak incentives to preserve the resources and will harvest them quickly over time
   (c) strong incentives to turn to government for a subsidy to preserve the resources
   (d) weak incentives to profit from the resources by harvesting them either in the present or the future

18. Which offers the best economic explanation as to why elephant populations have declined in many parts of Africa?
   (a) The prices of ivory tusks and elephant hides have declined.
   (b) Governments spend too much money on defining and enforcing property rights.
   (c) There is less interest in hunting elephants for sport or photographing them.
   (d) There are few economic incentives to provide benefits from preserving elephants.

19. Forestry companies have an incentive
   (a) to harvest the trees early in the growth cycle because of the expense of growing for so many years
   (b) to harvest the trees only after they have fully matured because more profit can be made at that point

(c) not to harvest the trees early in the growth cycle, but cut them down before they are fully mature

(d) not to harvest the trees in middle age, but cut them down either early in the growth cycle or after they have fully matured

20. A stock of fish or other marine animal that can be thought of as a logically distinct group is a
(a) catch
(b) quota
(c) fishery
(d) school

21. In the case of Maine red hake, the annual catch fell from 190.3 million metric tons in 1986 to less than 1 ton per year since 1995. This situation would be an example of
(a) fishery collapse
(b) replacement rate
(c) total fertility rate
(d) total allowable catch

22. Approximately what percentage of the world's fisheries are underexploited?
(a) 0%
(b) 2%
(c) 9%
(d) 18%

23. If a fisher is given the right to catch a specified amount of fish during a period of time and the fisher can trade this right, this would be called
(a) total allowable catch
(b) fish market allocation
(c) exchangeable fishery tariff
(d) individual transferable quota

Answer Questions 24 and 25 based on the following information. The market price of tuna is $10 per ton. It costs fisher Sven $9 a ton to catch tuna and it costs fisher Tammy $6 a ton to catch tuna. Both Sven and Tammy have ITQs to catch 1000 tons of tuna.

24. If Sven agrees to sell his ITQ to Tammy for $2 a ton, then Sven is
(a) better off because he gets $2000 from selling the ITQ and he can earn $2000 in profit from fishing
(b) better off because he gets $2000 from selling the ITQ instead of $1000 if he fished on his own
(c) worse off because he gets paid $2000 for selling the ITQ, but Tammy makes $2000 more in profit from buying his ITQ
(d) worse off because he will get $2000 by selling the ITQ but could have made $9000 in profit

25. If Sven agrees to sell his ITQ to Tammy, then there is a
(a) net cost to society because fishing costs for Sven's 1000 tons are increased by $3000
(b) net cost to society because fishing costs for Sven's 1000 tons are increased by $6000
(c) net benefit to society because fishing costs for Sven's 1000 tons are reduced by $3000
(d) net benefit to society because fishing costs for Sven's 1000 tons are reduced by $9000

■ **PROBLEMS**

1. Assume that a mining company can mine a ton of ore so that it can make a certain profit per ton by selling it in five years or selling it today. The table below shows the value in five years and the present value today and assumes a 5 percent interest rate.

Value in 5 years	Value today
$50	$39.18
60	47.01
70	54.85
80	62.68
90	70.52

a. Given a choice between selling a ton of ore to get $40 profit per barrel today or $60 profit per ton in five years, the mining company will sell the ton of ore for

$_____.

b. Given a choice between selling a ton of ore to get $50 profit per ton today or $60 profit per ton in five years, the mining company will sell the ton of ore for

$_____.

c. Given a choice between selling a ton of ore to get $50 profit per ton today or $70 profit per ton in five years, the mining company will sell the ton of ore for

$_____.

d. Given a choice between selling a ton of ore to get $60 profit per ton today or $70 profit per ton in five years, the mining will sell the ton of ore for $_____.

e. Given a choice between selling a ton of ore to get $70 profit per ton today or $90 profit per ton in five years, the mining company will sell the ton of ore for

$_____.

2. Fisher Harvey can catch tuna for $10 per ton and fisher Jose can catch tuna for $7 per ton. Both Harvey and Jose each have an individual transferable quota to catch 1000 tons of tuna. The market price of tuna is $12 per ton.

a. If both Harvey and Jose catch fish that year, the profit for Harvey will be $_____ and the profit for Jose will be $_____.

b. If next year, Harvey trades his quota for the year to Jose, how much should Harvey be paid for the quota to make more than he can by fishing? At least

$_____.

c. Harvey decides to trade his ITQ for the year to Jose. What will be the reduction in fishing cost to society now that only Jose is doing the fishing?

$_____.

d. If the market price for tuna should rise to $13 a ton, and Harvey still wants to sell his ITQ for the year to Jose, how much should Harvey be paid for the quota to be better off? At least $_____.

e. If the market price for tuna should rise to $15 a ton and Harvey sells his ITQ for the year to Jose, what will be the reduction in fishing costs to society now that only Jose is doing the fishing? $_____.

■ SHORT ANSWER AND ESSAY QUESTIONS

1. Describe the changes in population and living standards since 1800. What implications do these changes have for human beings?

2. Explain how Thomas Malthus viewed population growth and contrast it with what has happened since.

3. Define total fertility rate and replacement rate and use the terms to describe the population prospects for many developed countries.

4. State the predictions about population growth offered by demographers and explain the bases on which they are made.

5. What are likely factors that have contributed to declining birthrates in developing nations?

6. Discuss whether governments are able to increase birthrates in their nations.

7. What has happened to the supply of productive resources relative to the demand for them since the 1850s? What factors account for this development?

8. Will the supply of resources be able to meet the demand for resources in the future? What evidence can you cite to make the case that the supply will meet or exceed the demand?

9. Describe the trends in total and per capita water use, energy consumption, and trash generation in the United States from 1950 to 2008. What do they indicate about resource use?

10. What is energy economics and what does it have to say about energy demand and efficiency?

11. Use the case of electrical power generation to explain why the energy resource inputs that are used are sometimes low-cost and other times high-cost.

12. Make the case that the United States is not running out of oil or energy.

13. What are net benefits, nonrenewable resources, and renewable resources?

14. Explain how present value calculations are used to evaluate future possibilities in the case of renewable resources such as a forest.

15. What is the trade-off in the extraction of nonrenewable resources? How can this trade-off be analyzed in an economic framework?

16. Explain the difference between user cost and extraction costs. How does the addition of user cost to extraction costs affect the quantity extracted in the present compared with the future? What will happen to the quantity extracted in the present compared with profitability increase in the future? Illustrate the change with a graph.

17. Explain how market failures and the lack of property rights affect nonrenewable and renewable resource use. Give an application for nonrenewable resources using conflict diamonds and an application for renewable resources using elephant preservation.

18. Explain what is needed for optimal harvesting of a forest. How do changes in economic incentives and structures affect present and future decisions?

19. Define fisheries and describe their optimal management. Why do fishery collapses occur?

20. Discuss the use of policies for total allowable catch (TAC) and individual transferable quotas (ITQs) for making fishing more efficient and sustainable.

ANSWERS

Chapter 15 Natural Resource and Energy Economics

FILL-IN QUESTIONS

1. 12, larger
2. increase, more
3. higher, lower
4. less, 2.1
5. negative, lower
6. 9, decline
7. decline, fallen, falling
8. 70, increasing
9. slower, slower
10. more, one-third, remained constant
11. fixed, more
12. low-cost, high-cost, high-cost, low-cost, present, future
13. is not, rises
14. renewable, nonrenewable
15. present, property, future
16. user, extraction
17. more, less, less, more
18. property, least, over-, collapse
19. limits
20. total allowable catch, individual transferable quota

TRUE–FALSE QUESTIONS

1. T, p. 313	**10.** T, p. 316	**19.** T, pp. 322–324
2. T, p. 313	**11.** T, p. 317	**20.** F, pp. 322–323
3. F, p. 313	**12.** T, pp. 317–318	**21.** T, pp. 322–324
4. T, p. 313	**13.** F, p. 318	**22.** F, p. 324
5. T, p. 313	**14.** T, p. 318	**23.** T, p. 326
6. T, pp. 314–315	**15.** F, pp. 319–320	**24.** F, pp. 327–328
7. F, p. 315	**16.** T, p. 321	**25.** T, pp. 328–329
8. T, p. 315	**17.** F, p. 321	
9. F, p. 316	**18.** T, pp. 321–322	

MULTIPLE-CHOICE QUESTIONS

1. d, p. 313	**10.** d, pp. 321–322	**19.** c, pp. 326–327
2. b, p. 313	**11.** b, pp. 323–324	**20.** c, p. 327
3. d, pp. 313–314	**12.** b, pp. 323–324	**21.** a, pp. 327–328
4. a, p. 315	**13.** c, pp. 323–324	**22.** b, p. 328
5. d, p. 315	**14.** a, pp. 323–324	**23.** d, p. 329
6. c, p. 315	**15.** c, pp. 323–324	**24.** b, p. 329
7. d, pp. 315–317	**16.** b, p. 325	**25.** c, p. 329
8. b, p. 319	**17.** a, p. 325	
9. d, pp. 319–320	**18.** d, pp. 325–326	

SHORT ANSWER AND ESSAY QUESTIONS

1. pp. 313–314	**8.** pp. 315–317	**15.** pp. 322–324
2. p. 313	**9.** pp. 315–317	**16.** pp. 322–324
3. pp. 313–314	**10.** pp. 317–319	**17.** pp. 324–326
4. pp. 313–314	**11.** pp. 318–319	**18.** pp. 326–327
5. pp. 313–314	**12.** pp. 319–320	**19.** pp. 327–328
6. p. 314	**13.** p. 321	**20.** pp. 328–329
7. pp. 314–315	**14.** pp. 321–322	

PROBLEMS

1. *a.* 60; *b.* 50; *c.* 70; *d.* 70; *e.* 90
2. *a.* 2000, 5000; *b.* 2000; *c.* 2000; *d.* 3000; *e.* 3000

Public Finance: Expenditures and Taxes

Chapter 16 returns to the **circular flow model** first presented in Chapter 2. The model has now been modified to include government along with business and household sectors. This addition changes the real and monetary flows in the model.

The facts of **government finance** in the United States also are presented in Chapter 16. The organization of the discussion is relatively simple. First, the trends for taxes collected and expenditures made by all levels of government—federal, state, and local—are examined. Second, an explanation is given for the major items on which the federal government spends its income, the principal taxes it levies to obtain its income, and the relative importance of these taxes. Third, the chapter looks at the major expenditures and taxes of the state and local governments. Fourth, there is a brief description of the types of employment at the federal, state, and local levels.

Chapter 16 then shifts to the subject of taxation. Here you will learn about the benefit-received and the ability-to-pay principles of taxation. You also will learn about the **regressive, progressive,** and **proportional** classifications for taxes and how most U.S. taxes fit into this classification scheme.

The **tax incidence** and **efficiency loss of a tax** are then discussed in the chapter. Incidence means "who ends up paying the tax." As you will discover, the elasticities of demand and of supply determine how much of the tax will be paid by buyers and how much of it will be paid by sellers. No matter who pays the tax, however, there is an efficiency loss to society from the tax, the size of which also is affected by the elasticities of demand and of supply. With this knowledge, you are now ready to study the probable incidence of five taxes—personal income, corporate income, sales, excise, and property—that are used to raise most of the tax revenue for government in the United States.

The chapter ends with a brief discussion of whether the U.S. tax structure is progressive, regressive, or proportional. As you will learn, the answer varies based on the level of government considered and whether the system is viewed as a whole.

■ CHECKLIST

When you have studied this chapter you should be able to

☐ Draw the circular flow model that includes businesses, households, and government.

☐ Explain the difference between government purchases and transfer payments in terms of their output effects.
☐ State three sources of government revenue.
☐ Describe the relationship between government borrowing and deficit spending.
☐ Identify the four largest categories of federal expenditures.
☐ List the three main sources of federal tax revenues.
☐ Define and explain the differences between marginal and average tax rates.
☐ List the major expenditures and tax revenues of state governments.
☐ Identify the major expenditures and tax revenues of local governments.
☐ Describe the employment of workers in the federal government and state and local governments.
☐ Explain why the level of taxation is a controversial issue.
☐ Distinguish between the ability-to-pay and the benefits-received principles of taxation.
☐ Determine whether a tax is regressive, progressive, or proportional when given the data.
☐ Describe the progressivity or regressivity of the five major taxes used in the United States.
☐ Illustrate the incidence of an excise tax with a supply and demand graph.
☐ Explain how demand and supply elasticities affect tax incidence.
☐ Describe the efficiency loss of a tax with a supply and demand graph.
☐ Explain the effects of demand or supply elasticities on the efficiency loss of a tax.
☐ Evaluate the probable incidence of the personal income, corporate income, sales and excise, and property taxes.
☐ Describe the progressivity of the U.S. tax structure overall and at the federal, state, and local levels.
☐ Explain how the government uses taxes and spending to transfer a large amount of income from those with high incomes to those with low incomes (*Last Word*).

■ CHAPTER OUTLINE

1. A *circular flow model* that was first introduced in Chapter 2 showed business firms and households in the private sector of the economy. In Chapter 16 the public sector is now added. It shows that government purchases public goods from private businesses, collects taxes from and makes transfer payments to these firms, purchases labor services from households, collects taxes from and makes transfer payments to these households, and can alter the distribution of income, reallocate resources, and change the level of economic activity by affecting the real and monetary flows in the diagram.

2. **Government finance** through the taxes it raises and its expenditures is important at the federal, state, and local levels.

   a. Government spending consists of **government purchases** of goods and services and **transfer payments,** which are payments made to people for which no contribution is made by the people in return for them. The two types of spending have different effects on the economy. Government purchases are *exhaustive* because they directly use the economy's resources, while transfers are *nonexhaustive* because they do not absorb resources or create output. Government spending and the tax revenue needed to finance it is about 35 percent of domestic output.

   b. Government revenues come from three sources: taxes, proprietary income, and funds borrowed from the public.

   (1) Government can maintain its spending during an economic downturn by borrowing from the public if tax revenues and proprietary income are insufficient to cover government spending. This borrowing occurs when government sells bonds to the public and pays interest on the use of the funds obtained. This borrowing has an opportunity cost in the form of interest paid to bondholders, and this opportunity cost can be low or high depending on the interest rates and whether private investment gets crowded out by government borrowing. Government spending that is financed by borrowing is *deficit spending.*

3. The expenditures and tax revenues for the federal government are of several types.

   a. *The main sources of federal* expenditures are for pensions and income security (35%), health care (22%), national defense (19%), and interest on the public debt (5%).

   b. The main source of federal tax revenues are personal income taxes (43%), payroll taxes (42%), and corporate income taxes (7%).

   (1) The **personal income tax** is placed on taxable income and is a progressive tax, which means people with higher incomes pay a higher percentage of their income as taxes than do those with lower incomes. The **marginal tax rate** is the rate paid on additional income. The marginal rates rise as taxpayers earn additional income and move into higher income brackets. The **average tax rate** is the total tax paid divided by total taxable income. When marginal tax rates rise, the average tax rate also will rise, although by a smaller rate because the marginal rate applies only to taxable income in a specific income bracket and not to all income as is the average rate. The personal income tax is progressive because the average tax rate rises as income increases.

   (2) **Payroll taxes** are taxes paid on wages and salaries that are used to make contributions to Social Security and Medicare.

   (3) **Corporate income taxes** are taxes levied on the profits of corporations that are paid to the federal government.

   (4) An **excise tax** is paid on a per-unit basis for specific items such as gasoline or tires that are sold (for example: $0.50 per gallon of gasoline). A **sales tax** is a tax on a broad range of items and is charged as a percentage of the amount paid (for example: 7% of a $50 purchase of goods or services). The federal government collects excise taxes, whereas state and local governments rely heavily on the general sales tax.

4. State and local governments have different sources of revenue and spend their funds on different types of public goods.

   a. *State governments* depend largely on sales and excise taxes (47%), and also personal income taxes (35%). They spend their revenues on education (36%), welfare (28%), health care and hospitals (7%), highways (7%), and public safety (4%).

   b. *Local governments* rely heavily on **property taxes** (71%), which are taxes levied on the assessed value of property. They also rely to some extent on sales and excise taxes (17%). Local governments spend much of the revenue on education (44%), welfare, health care, and hospitals (12%), public safety (11%), housing, parks, sewerage (11%), and streets and highways (6%).

5. Local, state, and federal employment provides insights to the different types of services provided by the different levels of government. For example, a large percentage of employment in state and local government is accounted for by elementary and secondary teachers and administrators (41%) with the next largest category being hospital or health care workers (9%). About half of federal employment is for national defense (26%) or the postal service (26%) with the next largest category being hospital and health care (12%). The remainder for each level of government is split among many other types of employment (see Figure 16.6 in the textbook).

6. The financing of public goods and services through taxation also raises an important question about how the **tax burden** is allocated among people. Taxes are controversial because they are levied on a wide variety of goods and services and types of incomes so they have a widespread reach. Whether taxes have positive or negative effects on individuals or the economy and how they should be apportioned among people often depends on personal or philosophical perspectives.

   a. The benefits-received principle and the ability-to-pay principle are widely used to determine how the tax bill should be apportioned among the economy's citizens.

   (1) The **benefits-received principle** suggests that those people who benefit most from public goods should pay for them. This principle is practical to apply to specific purchases such as gasoline (and its excise tax), but it is difficult to assess how much or how little people benefit from public goods of a less specific and broader nature, such as national defense, criminal justice, or education.

(2) The **ability-to-pay principle** states that taxes for the support of public goods should be tied to the incomes and wealth of people or their ability to pay. From a marginal utility perspective, people derive greater value from the first dollar spent than from the last dollar spent. Since those persons with low incomes have fewer dollars to spend, the marginal utility of the last dollar spent and its sacrifice will be greater than such a sacrifice will be for those persons with higher incomes. Taxing those persons with higher incomes more than those persons with lower incomes will help balance the sacrifice. The problem with this reasoning, however, is that there is no scientific way of making utility comparisons to measure someone's ability to pay taxes.

b. Taxes can be classified as progressive, regressive, or proportional according to the way in which the average tax rate changes as incomes change.

(1) With a **progressive tax,** the average tax rate increases as income increases.

(2) With a **regressive tax,** the average tax rate decreases as income increases.

(3) With a **proportional tax,** the average tax rate remains the same as income increases.

(4) In the United States, whether taxes are progressive, regressive, or proportional may depend on the tax and the situation in which it is applied.

(a) The personal income tax tends to be mildly progressive because marginal tax rates rise across income brackets and so does the average tax rate, even after taking into account certain deductions.

(b) The sales tax is regressive with respect to income because those individuals with low incomes are more likely to pay the tax across all their income than are those individuals with high incomes who might save a large portion of their income.

(c) The corporate income tax is proportional, unless the tax in the long run is partially passed to workers through less capital accumulation in lower wages, in which case it is partially regressive.

(d) The payroll tax is regressive because there are limits on the amount of income that is subject to Social Security contributions, thus lowering the average tax rate paid by high-income earners. This tax also does not apply to income derived from nonwage sources such as rents or dividends that often go to high income earners.

(e) Property taxes are regressive because the amount paid tends to be higher as a percentage of income for low-income families than for high income families. Low-income households also spend a large proportion of their incomes on housing. Also property owners of apartments add the tax onto the rents they charge so even renters indirectly pay property taxes.

7. Tax incidence is the degree to which a tax is paid by a person or group. The **efficiency loss of a tax** is the reduction in production and consumption because of the tax. Both concepts are important in discussion of the economics of taxation.

a. The price elasticities of demand and supply determine the incidence of a sales or excise tax.

(1) The payment of the tax will generally be divided between the buyer and the seller. The imposition of a tax on a product decreases the supply of the product and increases its price. The amount of the price increase is the portion of the tax paid by the buyer. The remainder is paid by the seller.

(2) The price elasticities of demand and supply for a product affect the portions paid by buyers and sellers: (a) the more *elastic* the demand, the greater the portion paid by the seller; (b) the more *inelastic* the demand, the smaller the portion paid by the seller; (c) the more *elastic* the supply, the greater the portion paid by the buyer; and (d) the more *inelastic* the supply, the smaller the portion paid by the buyer.

b. An excise tax levied on the sale of a product has economic effects.

(1) The tax generates tax revenue, part of which is paid for by the buyer and part of which is paid for by the seller. The tax revenues are used to provide public goods and services, so there is no loss of well-being for society.

(2) There is an **efficiency loss of a tax.** This loss occurs because the tax raises the product price and leads to a reduction in output, despite the fact that the marginal benefits of that output are greater than the marginal cost. Thus, the consumption and production of the taxed product have been reduced below the optimal level by the tax.

(3) The degree of the efficiency loss of a sales or an excise tax depends on the elasticities of supply and demand. Other things equal, the *greater* the elasticity of supply and demand, the *greater* the efficiency loss of a sales or an excise tax; consequently, the total tax burden to society may not be equal even though the two taxes produce equal tax revenue.

(4) Other tax goals, however, may be more important than minimizing efficiency losses from taxes. These goals may include redistributing income or reducing negative externalities.

8. A tax levied on one person or group of persons may be shifted partially or completely to another person or group; and to the extent that a tax can be shifted or passed on through lower prices paid or higher prices received, its incidence is passed on to others. Table 16.2 in the text summarizes the probable shifting and incidence of the personal income tax, payroll tax, corporate income tax, general sales tax, specific excise taxes, and property taxes.

a. The incidence of the personal income tax is on the individual because the tax cannot easily be shifted to others.

b. Workers bear the full burden of the half of payroll taxes that they pay. The half paid by employers is likely shifted to workers because the employers can offer workers lower before-tax wages.

c. In the short run, the incidence of the corporate income tax falls on stockholders, who receive lower dividends or there is less retained corporate earnings. In the long run, workers may bear some burden of the tax in the form of lower wage growth because the firm has less funds available for investment in human capital (training) or physical capital goods that benefit worker productivity.

d. The incidence of the sales tax is largely paid by consumers in the form of higher prices because they cannot shift the burden to producers. With excise taxes, the consumer might be able to shift the burden if there are substitute goods available for purchase, but if there are goods for which there are few substitutes the burden is not likely to be shifted from buyer to seller.

e. The property tax is generally paid by the property owner and is difficult to shift. Taxes on rented or business property, however, can be shifted from the owner to the renter or tenant in terms of the rental or lease price.

9. Estimates of the progressivity of the tax system depend on the assumed incidence of various taxes and transfer payments made by governments to reduce income inequality in the United States. Overall, the federal tax system is progressive. The state and local tax structures are largely regressive. The progressivity of the federal income tax offsets the regressivity of state and local tax structures, so the overall tax system is progressive.

10. (*Last Word*). The progressivity of the tax system may not have much effect if the tax revenues collected are then spent for public goods and services or transfer payments that go to those with higher incomes rather than those with lower incomes. A recent study by two economists found that the government does use tax revenues collected to make substantial income transfer payments to those with lower incomes rather than to those with higher incomes. The combined tax and transfer system makes income distribution more equal than it would be if just the tax revenues collected are considered.

■ HINTS AND TIPS

1. There are many descriptive statistics about the public sector. Avoid memorizing these statistics. Instead, look for the trends and generalizations that these statistics illustrate about the public sector. For example, the discussion of government finance describes recent trends in government expenditures and taxes and indicates the relative importance of taxes and expenditures at each level of government.

2. Remember that what happens to the **average tax rate** as income increases determines whether a tax is progressive, regressive, or proportional. The average tax rate increases for progressive taxes, decreases for regressive taxes, and remains the same for proportional taxes as income increases.

3. This chapter applies supply, demand, and elasticity concepts to taxation issues. Chapter 4 is worth checking to review your understanding of elasticity. Figure 16.10 and the related discussion in the text are crucially important for understanding the efficiency loss from a tax.

■ IMPORTANT TERMS

government purchases	marginal tax rate
transfer payments	average tax rate
personal income tax	payroll taxes
corporate income tax	regressive tax
sales and excise taxes	proportional tax
property taxes	tax incidence
benefits-received principle	efficiency loss of a tax
ability-to-pay principle	
progressive tax	

SELF-TEST

■ FILL-IN QUESTIONS

1. An examination of government finance reveals that since 1960 government *purchases* of goods and services as a percentage of domestic output have (increased, decreased) _____, and government *transfer payments* as a percentage of domestic output have (increased, decreased) _____.

2. Government purchases of goods and services are (exhaustive, nonexhaustive) _____ because they absorb resources, and government transfer payments are (exhaustive, nonexhaustive) _____ because they do not absorb resources or create output.

3. Funds used to pay for government purchases and transfer payments come from (taxes, savings) _____, proprietary (information, income) _____, and funds that are borrowed by (buying, selling) _____ government bonds to the public.

4. Government spending that is financed by borrowing is referred to as (surplus, deficit) _____ spending because the government revenues from taxes or proprietary income are (less than, equal to) _____ its spending.

5. The largest category of federal expenditures is for (health, national defense, pensions and income security) _____, followed by _____, and then followed by _____.

6. The most important source of revenue for the federal government is the (personal income, payroll) _____ tax followed closely by the _____ tax.

7. Federal income tax rates are progressive, which means that people with (lower, higher) _____ incomes pay a larger percentage of that income as taxes than do persons with _____ incomes. The tax rate paid on an additional unit of income is the (average, marginal) _____ tax rate, while the total tax paid divided by the total taxable income is the _____ tax rate.

8. Many state governments rely primarily on the (property, sales) _____ tax and many local governments rely primarily on the _____ tax. The largest category of spending for both state and local governments is (education, public safety) _____.

9. Over half of state and local government employment is focused on (education, national defense) _____ whereas just over a quarter of Federal government employment is for _____.

10. The tax philosophy that asserts that households and businesses should purchase public goods and services in about the same way private goods and services are bought is the (ability-to-pay, benefits-received) _____ principle of taxation, but the tax philosophy that the tax burden should be based on a person's wealth or income is the _____ principle of taxation.

11. If the average tax rate remains constant as income increases, the tax is (regressive, progressive, proportional) _____. If the average tax rate decreases as income increases, the tax is _____. If the average tax rate increases as income increases, the tax is (regressive, progressive, proportional) _____.

12. In the United States, the personal income tax is (regressive, progressive, proportional) _____, but sales taxes, property taxes, and payroll taxes are _____. If corporate shareholders bear the burden of the corporate income tax, then it is (regressive, progressive, proportional) _____, but in the long run, if part of the tax reduces wage rates or capital formation, then the tax is _____.

13. The degree to which a tax falls on a particular person or group is called the tax (avoidance, incidence) _____. In some cases the tax is shifted from those persons or groups on whom the tax is levied, so they (do, do not) _____ pay the tax or only pay part of it.

14. When an excise tax is placed on a product, the supply curve will (increase, decrease) _____ and the price of the product will _____. The amount the product price rises as a result of the tax is the portion of the tax burden borne by (buyers, sellers) _____, and the difference between the original price and the after-tax price is the portion of the tax burden borne by _____.

15. The incidence of an excise tax primarily depends on the price elasticities of demand and of supply. The buyer's portion of the tax is larger the (more, less) _____ elastic the demand and the _____ elastic the supply. The seller's portion of the tax is larger the (more, less) _____ elastic the demand and the _____ elastic the supply.

16. When an excise tax is levied on a product, the amount of the product produced (increases, decreases) _____ as the supply curve shifts left, and as the price of the product increases, the amount of the product consumed _____. This change in output and consumption creates the efficiency (gain, loss) _____ of the tax, which is also called a deadweight _____.

17. Other things equal, the greater the elasticity of demand, the (greater, less) _____ the efficiency loss of the tax and the greater the elasticity of supply, the _____ the efficiency loss of the tax.

18. The incidence of the personal income tax is on (individuals, businesses) _____. In the short run, the incidence of the corporate income tax falls on (businesses, workers) _____ but in the long run, it also can fall on _____ because such taxes may reduce capital accumulation or lower wage rates.

19. The incidence of the sales tax is generally shifted to the (sellers, buyers) _____ of the product, and with excise taxes, if the demand for a product is inelastic, the tax incidence will be shifted to the _____. In the case of the property tax, the incidence of the tax for owner-occupied housing is borne by (owners, government) _____ and with renter-occupied housing it is borne by (owners, renters) _____. In the case of business property, the tax incidence is shifted to (businesses, consumers) _____.

20. The Federal tax system is generally (progressive, regressive, proportional) _____, state and local tax systems are generally _____, and overall the U.S. tax system is slightly _____, but these conditions depend on the incidence of the taxes.

■ **TRUE–FALSE QUESTIONS**

Circle T if the statement is true, F if it is false.

1. In the circular flow government provides goods and services to households and businesses and obtains net taxes.   **T   F**

2. Proprietary income is revenue the government obtains from government-run or government-sponsored businesses such as public utilities or state lotteries.   **T   F**

3. Government purchases of goods and services are called nonexhaustive expenditures and government transfer payments are called exhaustive expenditures. **T F**

4. Government spending and tax revenues to finance it are about 35 percent of U.S. output. **T F**

5. One way the government obtains revenue for its spending is by selling bonds to the public. **T F**

6. Government spending that is financed by borrowing is often referred to as surplus spending. **T F**

7. The chief source of revenue for the federal government is the corporate income tax. **T F**

8. Property taxes are the largest percentage of the total revenues of local governments. **T F**

9. Just over half of federal government employees work in education. **T F**

10. The chief difficulty in applying the benefits-received principle of taxation is determining who receives the benefit of many of the goods and services that government supplies. **T F**

11. The state and federal taxes on gasoline are examples of taxes levied on the benefits-received principle. **T F**

12. The ability-to-pay principle of taxation states that those with greater incomes should be taxed less, absolutely and relatively, than those with lesser incomes. **T F**

13. A tax is progressive when the average tax rate decreases as income increases. **T F**

14. A general sales tax is considered a proportional tax with respect to income. **T F**

15. A payroll (Social Security) tax is regressive. **T F**

16. When an excise tax is placed on a product bought and sold in a competitive market, the portion of the tax borne by the seller equals the amount of the tax less the rise in the price of product due to the tax. **T F**

17. The more elastic the demand for a good, the greater the portion of an excise tax on the good borne by the seller. **T F**

18. The efficiency loss of an excise tax is the gain in net benefits for the producers from the increase in the price of the product. **T F**

19. The degree of efficiency loss from an excise tax varies from market to market and depends on the elasticities of supply and demand. **T F**

20. Other things equal, the smaller the elasticities of supply and demand, the greater the efficiency loss of a particular tax. **T F**

21. A sales tax is levied on a broad range of consumer goods and services whereas an excise tax is levied on only a particular product. **T F**

22. The evidence on the incidence of the corporate income tax is that this tax is borne by company stockholders or owners in the short run. **T F**

23. The probable incidence of the tax on rented apartment properties is on the landlord, not on the tenant. **T F**

24. The federal income tax system is progressive. **T F**

25. The state and local tax structures are largely regressive. **T F**

■ **MULTIPLE-CHOICE QUESTIONS**

Circle the letter that corresponds to the best answer.

1. In the circular flow model, government provides goods and services and receives net taxes from
(a) colleges and universities
(b) businesses and households
(c) resource and product markets
(d) foreign nations and corporations

2. Which would be an example of a government transfer payment?
(a) taxes
(b) proprietary income
(c) Social Security benefits
(d) spending on national defense

3. Which accounts for the largest percentage of all federal expenditures?
(a) health care
(b) national defense
(c) interest on the public debt
(d) pensions and income security

4. Which is the largest source of the tax revenues of the federal government?
(a) payroll taxes
(b) property taxes
(c) sales and excise taxes
(d) personal income taxes

5. A progressive tax is one where people with
(a) lower incomes pay the same percentage of their income in taxes as people with higher incomes do
(b) lower incomes pay a larger percentage of their income in taxes as people with higher incomes do
(c) higher incomes pay a smaller percentage of their income in taxes than people with lower incomes do
(d) higher incomes pay a larger percentage of their income in taxes than people with lower incomes do

Questions 6 and 7 are based on the tax table given below. [Note: Total tax is for the highest income in that tax bracket.]

Taxable income	Total tax
$ 0	$ 0
30,000	5,000
70,000	15,000
150,000	42,000

6. The marginal tax rate at the $70,000 level of taxable income is
(a) 16.6%
(b) 21.4%

(c) 25.0%
(d) 28.0%

7. The average tax rate at the $150,000 level of taxable income is
(a) 21.4%
(b) 28.0%
(c) 31.5%
(d) 33.8%

8. Which pair represents the chief source of income and the most important type of expenditure of *state* governments?
(a) personal income tax and expenditures for hospitals
(b) personal income tax and expenditures for highways
(c) sales and excise taxes and expenditures for education
(d) sales and excise taxes and expenditures for public safety

9. Which pair represents the chief source of income and the most important type of expenditure of *local* governments?
(a) property tax and expenditures for highways
(b) property tax and expenditures for education
(c) sales and excise taxes and expenditures for public welfare
(d) sales and excise taxes and expenditures for police, fire, safety, and general government

10. Which is true of the ability-to-pay principle as applied in the United States?
(a) It is less widely applied than the benefits-received principle.
(b) Tax incidence is generally taken as the measure of the ability to pay.
(c) Gasoline taxes are based on this principle.
(d) As an individual's income increases, taxes paid increase both absolutely and relatively.

11. Taxing people according to the principle of ability to pay would be most characteristic of
(a) a payroll tax
(b) a value-added tax
(c) a general sales tax
(d) a progressive income tax

12. With a regressive tax, as income
(a) increases, the tax rate remains the same
(b) decreases, the tax rate decreases
(c) increases, the tax rate increases
(d) increases, the tax rate decreases

13. Which tends to be a progressive tax in the United States?
(a) personal income tax
(b) state property tax
(c) sales tax
(d) payroll tax

14. In a competitive market, the portion of an excise tax borne by a buyer is equal to the
(a) amount the price of the product rises as a result of the tax
(b) amount of the tax

(c) amount of the tax less the amount the price of the product rises as a result of the tax
(d) amount of the tax plus the amount the price of the product rises as a result of the tax

15. Which statement is correct?
(a) The more elastic the supply, the greater the portion of an excise tax borne by the seller.
(b) The more elastic the demand, the greater the portion of an excise tax borne by the seller.
(c) The more inelastic the supply, the greater the portion of an excise tax borne by the buyer.
(d) The more inelastic the demand, the greater the portion of an excise tax borne by the seller.

Answer Questions 16, 17, 18, and 19 based on the following graph of an excise tax imposed by government.

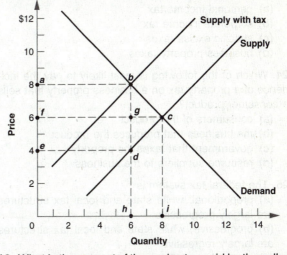

16. What is the amount of the excise tax paid by the seller in terms of price per unit sold?
(a) $1
(b) $2
(c) $3
(d) $4

17. The total amount of the excise tax paid by consumers for all units bought is
(a) $2
(b) $6
(c) $12
(d) $16

18. The tax revenue for government is represented by area
(a) *abde*
(b) *abgf*
(c) *fgde*
(d) *abcde*

19. The efficiency loss of the tax is represented by area
(a) *bgc*
(b) *bdc*
(c) *abcf*
(d) *hbci*

20. The efficiency loss of an excise tax is
(a) greater, the greater the elasticity of supply and demand
(b) greater, the less the elasticity of supply and demand

(c) less, the greater the elasticity of supply and demand
(d) not affected by the elasticity of supply and demand

21. If government imposes a tax on wine to shift the market supply to reduce the amount of resources allocated to wine, then the primary purpose of this tax is to
(a) redistribute income
(b) improve tax progressivity
(c) reduce negative externalities
(d) minimize efficiency losses

22. The probable incidence of a sales tax is borne by
(a) government units that collect the tax
(b) businesses that make the product
(c) businesses that sell the product
(d) consumers who buy the product

23. Which tax is the most difficult to shift to others?
(a) personal income tax
(b) corporate income tax
(c) specific excise taxes
(d) business property taxes

24. Which of the following is most likely to pay the incidence of a property tax on a business property that sells a consumer product?
(a) consumers of the product
(b) the business that produces the product
(c) government that taxes the property
(d) resource suppliers to the business

25. The federal tax system is
(a) proportional, while state and local tax structures are largely progressive
(b) progressive, while state and local tax structures are largely regressive
(c) regressive, while state and local tax structures are largely proportional
(d) proportional, while state and local tax structures are largely regressive

■ **PROBLEMS**

1. The following circular flow diagram includes business firms, households, and the government (the public sector). Also shown are the product and resource markets.

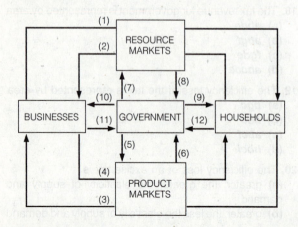

a. Supply a label or an explanation for each of the 12 flows in the model:

(1) _____
(2) _____
(3) _____
(4) _____
(5) _____
(6) _____
(7) _____
(8) _____
(9) _____
(10) _____
(11) _____
(12) _____

b. If government wished to
(1) expand output and employment in the economy, it would increase expenditure flows _____ or _____, decrease net tax flows _____ or _____, or do both;
(2) increase the production of public goods and decrease the production of private goods in the economy, it would increase flows _____ and _____ or _____;
(3) redistribute income from high-income to low-income households, it would (increase, decrease) _____ the net taxes (taxes minus transfers) paid by the former and _____ the net taxes paid by the latter in flow _____.

2. In the following table are several levels of taxable income and hypothetical marginal tax rates for each $1000 increase in income.

Taxable income	Marginal tax rate,%	Tax	Average tax rate,%
$1500		$300	20
2500	22	520	20.8
3500	25	____	
4500	29	____	
5500	34	____	
6500	40	____	

a. At the four income levels compute the tax and the average tax rate.
b. As the marginal tax rate
(1) increases, the average tax rate (increases, decreases, remains constant) _____.
(2) decreases, the average tax rate _____.

c. This tax is (progressive, regressive) _____ because the average tax rate increases as income (decreases, increases) _____.

3. The following table shows the demand and supply schedules for copra in the New Hebrides Islands.

Quantity demanded (pounds)	Price (per pound)	Before-tax quantity supplied (pounds)	After-tax quantity supplied (pounds)
150	$4.60	900	_____
200	4.40	800	_____
250	4.20	700	_____
300	4.00	600	_____
350	3.80	500	_____
400	3.60	400	_____
450	3.40	300	_____
500	3.20	200	_____
550	3.00	100	_____

a. Before a tax is imposed on copra, its equilibrium price is $_____.

b. The government of New Hebrides now imposes an excise tax of $.60 per pound on copra. Complete the after-tax supply schedule in the right-hand column of the table.

c. After the imposition of the tax, the equilibrium price of copra is $_____.

d. Of the $.60 tax, the amount borne by

(1) the buyer is $_____ or _____%.

(2) the seller is $_____ or _____%.

4. On the following graph, draw a perfectly elastic demand curve and a normal up-sloping supply curve for a product. Now impose an excise tax on the product, and draw the new supply curve that would result.

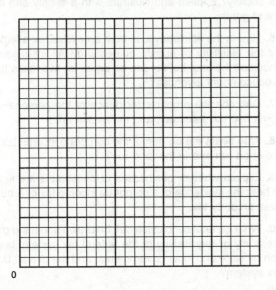

a. As a consequence of the tax, the price of the product has (increased, decreased) _____ by the amount of the tax.

b. It can be concluded that when demand is perfectly elastic, the buyer bears (all, none) _____ of the tax and the seller bears _____ of the tax.

c. Thus the *more* elastic the demand, the (larger, smaller) _____ is the portion of the tax borne by the buyer and the _____ is the portion borne by the seller.

d. But the *less* elastic the demand, the (smaller, larger) _____ is the portion borne by the buyer and the _____ is the portion borne by the seller.

5. In the graph below, draw a perfectly elastic supply curve and a normal down-sloping demand curve. Impose an excise tax on the product, and draw the new supply curve.

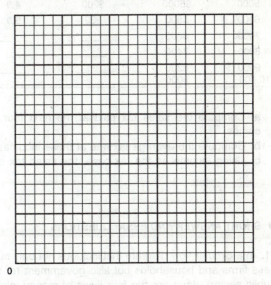

a. As a result of the tax, the price of the product has (increased, decreased) _____ by the amount of the tax.

b. From this it can be concluded that when supply is perfectly elastic, the buyer bears (all, none) _____ of the tax and the seller bears _____ of the tax.

c. Thus the *more* elastic the supply, the (smaller, larger) _____ is the portion of the tax borne by the buyer and the _____ is the portion borne by the seller.

d. But the less elastic the supply, the (smaller, larger) _____ is the portion borne by the buyer and the _____ is the portion borne by the seller.

6. The following table shows five levels of taxable income and the amount that would be paid at each of the five levels under three tax laws: *A*, *B*, and *C*. Compute for each of the three tax laws the average rate of taxation at each of the four remaining income levels. Indicate whether the tax is regressive, proportional, progressive, or some combination thereof.

Income	Tax A			Tax B			Tax C		
	Tax paid	Av. tax rate		Tax paid	Av. tax rate		Tax paid	Av. tax rate	
$ 1500	$ 45.00	3%		$ 30.00	2%		$135.00	9%	
3000	90.00	____		90.00	____		240.00	____	
5000	150.00	____		150.00	____		350.00	____	
7500	225.00	____		187.50	____		450.00	____	
10,000	300.00	____		200.00	____		500.00	____	
Type of tax:	_____			_____			_____		

7. Assume a state government levies a 4% sales tax on all consumption expenditures. Consumption expenditures at six income levels are shown in the following table.

Income	Consumption expenditures	Sales tax paid	Average tax rate, %
$ 5000	$5000	$200	4.0
6000	5800	232	3.9
7000	6600	____	____
8000	7400	____	____
9000	8200	____	____
10,000	9000	____	____

a. Compute the sales tax paid at the next four incomes.
b. Compute the average tax rate at these incomes.
c. Using income as the tax base, the sales tax is a _____ tax.

■ **SHORT ANSWER AND ESSAY QUESTIONS**

1. In a circular flow diagram that includes not only business firms and households but also government (or the public sector), what are the four flows of money into or out of the government sector of the economy? Using this diagram, explain how government redistributes income, reallocates resources from the private to the public sector, and stabilizes the economy.

2. Government expenditures fall into two broad classes: expenditures for goods and services and transfer payments. Explain the difference between these, and give examples of expenditures that fall into each of the two classes.

3. Why would the federal government borrow from the public by selling bonds? What is the opportunity cost of this method of obtaining government revenue? How does this opportunity cost change depending on the economic conditions?

4. What are four major types of federal government revenue and four major types of federal government expenditures?

5. Explain precisely the difference between the marginal tax rate and the average tax rate.

6. On what goods and services are state and local governments most likely to spend their revenues? What are the major sources for the revenues of state and local governments?

7. Describe some of the key differences in the job functions of state and local employees compared with federal employees.

8. What are the two basic philosophies for apportioning the tax burden in the United States? Explain each one.

9. What are the difficulties encountered in putting the two basic tax philosophies into practice?

10. Explain the differences among progressive, regressive, and proportional taxes.

11. Discuss the personal income tax, sales taxes, corporate income tax, payroll tax, and property tax in terms of progressivity, regressivity, or proportionality.

12. Explain the effect the imposition of an excise tax has on the supply of a product that is bought and sold in a competitive market.

13. Illustrate with a supply and demand graph what part of an excise tax is passed on to the buyer and what part is borne by the seller. What determines the division of the tax between the buyer and the seller?

14. What is the relationship between the price elasticity of demand for a commodity and the portion of an excise tax on a commodity borne by the buyer and the seller?

15. How does an excise tax produce an efficiency loss for society? Explain and illustrate with a supply and demand graph.

16. How is the efficiency loss from an excise tax affected by the elasticity of supply or demand? All else equal, shouldn't the total tax burden be equal for two taxes that produce equal revenues?

17. Describe the probable incidence of the personal income tax, the sales tax, and the excise tax.

18. Who bears the burden of the corporate income tax in the short run and in the long run?

19. Explain whether businesses or consumers are likely to bear the incidence of a corporate income tax or a business property tax.

20. What general conclusion can be drawn about the progressivity or regressivity of the federal tax system, taxation by state and local governments, and the overall U.S. tax system?

ANSWERS

Chapter 16 Public Finance: Expenditures and Taxes

FILL-IN QUESTIONS

1. decreased, increased
2. exhaustive, nonexhaustive
3. taxes, income, selling
4. deficit, less than
5. pensions and income security, health, national defense
6. personal income, payroll
7. higher, lower, marginal, average
8. sales, property, education
9. education, national defense
10. benefits-received, ability-to-pay
11. proportional, regressive, progressive
12. progressive, regressive, proportional, regressive
13. incidence, do not
14. decrease, increase, buyers, sellers
15. less, more, more, less
16. decreases, decreases, loss, loss
17. greater, greater
18. individuals, businesses, workers
19. buyers, buyers, owners, renters, consumers
20. progressive, regressive, progressive

TRUE–FALSE QUESTIONS

1. T, pp. 337–338
2. T, p. 338
3. F, p. 338
4. T, p. 338
5. T, p. 339
6. F, p. 339
7. F, pp. 340–341
8. T, pp. 342–343
9. F, pp. 342–343
10. T, p. 344
11. T, p. 344
12. F, pp. 345–346
13. F, p. 345
14. F, p. 345
15. T, pp. 346
16. T, pp. 347–348
17. T, pp. 347–348
18. F, pp. 348–349
19. T, p. 349
20. F, p. 349
21. T, p. 351
22. T, p. 350
23. F, p. 351
24. T, p. 353
25. T, p. 354

MULTIPLE-CHOICE QUESTIONS

1. b, pp. 337–338
2. c, p. 338
3. d, pp. 339–340
4. d, p. 340
5. d, p. 340
6. c, pp. 340–341
7. b, pp. 340–341
8. c, pp. 341–342
9. b, pp. 342–343
10. d, pp. 344–345
11. d, pp. 344–345
12. d, p. 345
13. a, pp. 345–346
14. a, pp. 347–348
15. b, pp. 347–348
16. b, pp. 347–348
17. c, pp. 347–348
18. a, pp. 347–348
19. b, p. 348–349
20. a, pp. 348–349
21. c, pp. 349–350
22. d, p. 350
23. a, pp. 350–351
24. a, p. 351
25. b, p. 353

PROBLEMS

1. *a.* (1) businesses pay costs for resources that become money income for households; (2) households provide resources to businesses; (3) household expenditures become receipts for businesses; (4) businesses provide goods and services to households; (5) government spends money in product market; (6) government receives goods and services from product market; (7) government spends money in resource market; (8) government receives resources from resource market; (9) government provides goods and services to households; (10) government provides goods and services to businesses; (11) businesses pay net taxes to government; (12) households pay net taxes to government; *b.* (1) 5, 7 (either order), 11, 12 (either order); (2) 9, 10, 11 (any order); (3) increase, decrease, 12
2. *a.* tax: $770, 1,060, 1,400, 1,800; average tax rate: 22%, 23.6%, 25.5%, 27.7%; *b.* (1) increases, (2) decreases; *c.* progressive, increases
3. *a.* $3.60; *b.* (reading down) 600, 500, 400, 300, 200, 100, 0, 0, 0; *c.* $4.00; *d.* (1) $.40, 67, (2) $.20, 33
4. *a.* not changed; *b.* none, all; *c.* smaller, larger; *d.* larger, smaller
5. *a.* increased; *b.* all, none; *c.* larger, smaller; *d.* smaller, larger
6. Tax A: 3, 3, 3, 3, proportional; Tax B: 3, 3, 2.5, 2, combination; Tax C: 8, 7, 6, 5, regressive
7. *a.* $264, 296, 328, 360; *b.* 3.8, 3.7, 3.64, 3.6; *c.* regressive

SHORT AND ESSAY QUESTIONS

1. pp. 337–338
2. p. 338
3. p. 339
4. pp. 340–341
5. pp. 340–341
6. pp. 341–342
7. pp. 342–343
8. p. 345
9. pp. 344–345
10. p. 345
11. pp. 345–346
12. pp. 347–348
13. pp. 347–348
14. pp. 347–348
15. pp. 348–349
16. p. 349
17. pp. 350–351
18. p. 350
19. p. 351
20. pp. 350–351

Asymmetric Information, Voting, and Public Choice

One type of market failure is **asymmetric information.** You have probably never thought about the role of information in the functioning of markets, but you will discover how important information is to both buyers and sellers. For example, buyers need some assurance about the measurement standards or quality of products that they purchase, be it gasoline or medical care. The government may intervene in some markets to ensure that this information is made available to buyers.

Inadequate information in markets creates problems for sellers, too. In certain markets, such as insurance, sellers experience a **moral hazard problem** because buyers change their behavior and become less careful, and the change in behavior makes the insurance more costly to sellers. There is also an **adverse-selection problem** in the insurance market because those buyers most likely to benefit (higher-risk buyers) are more likely to purchase the insurance; therefore, this group imposes higher costs on sellers than if the risks were more widely spread among the population. Actions of sellers to screen buyers would mean that fewer people would be covered by insurance and create situations that may lead to the provision of social insurance by government. Government may provide better information about workplace safety or enforce safety standards to address these information problems.

Many public decisions are made by **majority voting,** but this decision-making procedure may distort the true preferences of society. In the first section of the chapter you will find out how majority voting may lead to inefficient outcomes in the provision of public goods. In some choices, the benefits of a public good are greater than the costs, but the majority votes against having it. In other choices, the costs outweigh the benefits, but the provision of the public good is supported by the majority vote. Although actions by interest groups and the use of logrolling may tend to reduce inefficiencies created by majority rule, the final result depends on the circumstances of the decision.

Also note that there is a **paradox of voting** from majority voting. Depending on how a vote or election is arranged, it is possible for majority rule to produce choices that are inconsistent with the ranking of preferences among voters. You should spend time working through the example in the textbook so you understand how opposing outcomes can result from majority rule. You should also learn why the median voters strongly influence the result of a vote or an election when there is majority rule. In fact, the **median-voter model** is very useful for explaining why the middle position on issues is often adopted in public decisions.

The last section of Chapter 17 discusses other reasons for inefficiencies by government. Here you will learn that (1) the **principal–agent problem, special-interest effect,** and **rent seeking** impair public decisions; (2) politicians often have a strong incentive to adopt an economic policy that has clear benefits to voters, but hidden or uncertain costs; (3) public choice is more limited and less flexible than private choice because it entails voting for or accepting a "bundle" of programs, some good and some bad; (4) bureaucratic inefficiencies in the public sector arise from the lack of the economic incentives and competitive pressures found in the private sector; and (5) the characteristics of public corruption. None of the above concepts or topics are presented to make you cynical about the public sector, but rather to help you understand that it is not just markets that are subject to failure. Government too can be an imperfect institution for making economic decisions and allocating resources.

■ **CHECKLIST**

When you have studied this chapter you should be able to

☐ Define asymmetric information as it relates to sellers and buyers.

☐ Describe the problem of inadequate information about sellers in the gasoline market and government response.

☐ Describe the problem of inadequate information about sellers in the medical market for surgeons and government response.

☐ Explain how inadequate information about buyers can cause a moral hazard problem and give an example.

☐ Describe how inadequate information about buyers can create an adverse selection problem and give an example.

☐ Describe how inadequate information about employers can create a workplace problem and how government responds.

☐ Cite examples of how asymmetric information problems are overcome without government intervention.

☐ Explain the purpose of public choice theory and the topics it covers.

☐ Describe how majority voting procedures can produce inefficient outcomes when the vote is "yes."

☐ Describe how majority voting procedures can produce inefficient outcomes when the vote is "no."

☐ Discuss the implications of inefficient outcomes from majority voting.

☐ Describe how interest groups and political logrolling affect the efficiency of voting outcomes.

☐ Describe the paradox of voting and give an example with voting on three goods.

☐ Discuss the median-voter model, its real-world applicability, and two implications.

☐ Explain the term "government failure" and cite examples.

☐ Discuss principal–agent problems in a representative democracy.

☐ Explain the special-interest effect and give an example as it relates to earmarks.

☐ Describe rent-seeking and give an example.

☐ Discuss how clear benefits and hidden costs in political decisions create poor outcomes.

☐ Compare consumer choices in private markets with the limited and bundled choices presented to voters.

☐ Contrast the incentives for economic efficiency in private business with those in public agencies and bureaucracies.

☐ Discuss effects of political corruption on government outcomes.

☐ Discuss how government and markets are imperfect in allocating resources.

☐ Cite examples of pork-barrel politics, limited and bundled choices, earmarks, or bureaucratic inefficiencies (*Last Word*).

■ **CHAPTER OUTLINE**

1. Economic inefficiency from information failures can occur in markets when buyers have inadequate information about sellers and when sellers have inadequate information about buyers. These information failures arise from *asymmetric information*—unequal knowledge that is held by parties to a market transaction.

   a. When information about sellers is incomplete or inaccurate it can create problems for buyers that are costly and result in market failures because the buyers do not have sufficient information to trust the sellers and buy the good or service.

   (1) In the market for gasoline, consumers need accurate information about the amount and quality of gasoline they purchase from sellers, but the cost of obtaining such information can be high. Government will intervene in this market to correct this asymmetric information problem by establishing measurement standards so that consumers have accurate, reliable, and standardized information for making the consumer choices in this market.

   (2) In the market for medical services, it is important that consumers have some assurances about the credentials of physicians, but such information can be difficult and costly for consumers to obtain. Government can respond to the information failures by such actions as testing and licensing of surgeons so that consumers have some assurance that a surgeon is competent.

   b. Inadequate information about buyers can cause problems for sellers of products that are costly and result in market failures because the sellers do not have sufficient information to trust the buyers and thus may not offer the good or service.

   (1) A market may produce less than the optimal amount of goods and services from society's perspective because of a *moral hazard problem,* which results when buyers alter their behavior in a way that increases the costs for sellers. For example, when car insurance is offered, some of the insured may become less cautious in their driving habits than when there was no insurance because they know that if they have an accident, the insurance company will now cover a large portion of the cost of the accident.

   (2) An *adverse-selection problem* occurs in many markets. In the case of insurance, the buyers most likely to need or benefit from insurance are the ones most likely to purchase it. These higher-risk buyers impose higher costs on sellers. Sellers then screen out the higher-risk buyers, but this action reduces the population covered by insurance in the private market. In some cases, government may establish a social insurance system that is designed to cover a much broader group of the population than would be covered by the private insurers, such as with Social Security.

   (3) Market failures occur in resource markets when there is inadequate information about employers (the buyers of labor resource) so that workers know about the health hazards or safety of a workplace. Government can act to correct these problems by publishing health and safety information or by forcing businesses to provide more information about health and safety. The typical approach to this problem has been the enforcement of standards for health and safety on the job.

   c. Government does not always need to intervene in the private market to address information problems. Businesses can adopt policies to correct these problems on their own, and some private firms or other nongovernment organizations can specialize in providing important market information for buyers or sellers.

2. *Public choice theory* involves the economic analysis of government decision making, politics, and voting. It shows that there can be problems with government resulting in government failure, and that by understanding how government functions from an economic perspective it may be possible to reduce or mitigate some of the inefficiency of government.

3. Most decisions about government activity involving such matters as regulation, taxation, or spending are made collectively through *majority voting.* Although the use of majority voting in a representative democracy is a good way to reveal society's preferences, the procedure is not without problems.

   a. Majority voting outcomes can be economically *inefficient* in several ways, although some methods have been developed to overcome these outcomes.

   (1) Voters may vote "no" and reject a public good whose total benefits exceed total costs, resulting in too little of a public good being produced than is wanted by society.

   (2) Voters may vote "yes" and fund a public good whose total costs are greater than the total benefits, resulting in too much of a public good being produced than is wanted by society.

(3) The major problem with majority voting is that it fails to take into account the *strength* of preferences by the individual voter for public goods and therefore the collective decision can result in the underproduction of a public good ("no" vote) or the overproduction of a public good ("yes" vote) and inefficient outcomes in each case.

(4) The formation of interest groups and logrolling work to overcome inefficient outcomes from the political process.

(a) Interest groups can be formed to lobby others to make a certain decision, thus better reflecting the strength of preferences.

(b) There can be the use of political *logrolling,* in which votes are traded to secure a favorable and efficient decision, although the opposite also can occur.

b. The *paradox of voting* suggests that the public through majority voting may not be able to make consistent choices that reflect society's preferences for goods or services.

c. Based on the *median-voter model,* it is suggested that the person or groups holding the middle position on an issue will likely determine the outcome from a majority-rule election. A group of people on one side of a political decision and a group of people on the other side will need to sway the median voter to their side to gain a majority.

(1) The median-voter model has a real-world applicability because public decisions often reflect the median view of voters.

(2) One implication of the median-voter model is that there will continue to be debate and controversy because people who are not in the middle will be dissatisfied with government intervention in the economy and view it as either being too large or too small. A second implication is that people may move to locations where they can become the median voter or to locations more aligned with their political views.

4. *Government failure* refers to those situations where the political process used to make public decisions is inherently weak and the decisions result in an economically inefficient allocation of resources.

a. Representative democracy is subject to a *principal–agent problem* that occurs when there are differences between the positions of the principals (voters) and the actions taken by their agents (elected officials). Once elected, political representatives may pursue their own goals and objectives to suit their personal interests (gaining power or getting re-elected) at the expense of representing the broader interests of their constituents. Another example of a principal–agent problem is found in the business world when the interests of stockholders (principals) differ from the interests of corporate managers (agents).

(1) The weakness of the decision-making process in the public sector and the resulting inefficient allocation of resources are often the result of pressures exerted on Congress and the government bureaucracy by special interests and other groups. There can be a *special-interest effect* in which a small number of people obtain a government program or policy giving them large gains at the expense of a large number of people who individually suffer small losses. This effect is also present in *pork-barrel politics* where a government program will mostly benefit one constituency. An example of pork-barrel politics is *earmarks,* which are specific authorizations for government expenditures to benefit a group or organization in the legislator's district.

(2) *Rent-seeking* behavior is reflected in appeals to government for special benefits or treatment at the taxpayers' or someone's expense. Government can dispense such rents through laws, rules, hiring, and purchases.

b. Those seeking election to public office frequently favor programs whose benefits are clear and immediate and whose costs are uncertain and deferred, even when the benefits are less than the costs. Conversely, they frequently oppose programs whose costs are clear and immediate and whose benefits are uncertain and deferred, even when the benefits are greater than the costs.

c. There are limited and bundled choices in political decisions. When citizens must vote for candidates who represent different but complete programs, the voters are unable to select those parts of a program which they favor and reject the other parts of the program.

d. It is argued that the public sector (unlike the private sector) is inefficient because those employed there are offered no incentive to be efficient; there is no way to measure efficiency in the public sector; and government bureaucrats can join with the special-interest groups to block budget cuts or lobby for increased funding.

e. Government resources and actions also can be misdirected and inefficiently allocated through *political corruption,* where government officials use their offices for personal gain. Political decisions can be influenced by bribery or other types of payments, such as asking people for contributions that are not really voluntary. Political corruption may be relatively limited in the United States compared with many foreign nations.

f. Just as the private or market sector of the economy does not allocate resources perfectly, and there can be market failure, the public sector can be quite inefficient in performing its functions, thus leading to government failure. The imperfections of both the market and government sectors can make it difficult to determine which sector will be more efficient in providing a particular good or service.

5. (*Last Word*). There are many examples of government actions that illustrate pork-barrel politics, limited and bundled choices, or bureaucratic inefficiency. For example, congressional spending bills often contain *earmarks* that authorize funding for home-state projects with a narrow purpose and little national benefit.

■ **HINTS AND TIPS**

1. Problems occur because information in a market is sometimes asymmetric, which means that there is **unequal** information for sellers or buyers about product price, quality, or other product conditions. Use the examples in the text to help you distinguish among the different types of information problems created by sellers or buyers.

2. The main part of the chapter explains **public choice theory,** but this theory has many practical applications to politics. As you read about the reasons for inefficient outcomes from majority voting, the influence of special-interest groups, political logrolling, the median-voter model, rent-seeking behavior, the principal–agent problem, and limited and bundled choices, try to apply the ideas to public issues at the local, state, or federal level. Also ask your instructor for current examples of the ideas from public choice theory.

■ IMPORTANT TERMS

asymmetric information	government failure
moral hazard problem	principal agent problems
adverse-selection problem	collective-action problem
public choice theory	special-interest effect
logrolling	earmarks
paradox of voting	rent-seeking
median-voter model	political corruption

SELF-TEST

■ FILL-IN QUESTIONS

1. Markets can produce failures because of (symmetric, asymmetric) _____ information, which means that knowledge possessed by the parties to a market transaction is (equal, unequal) _____.

2. When information involving sellers is (complete, incomplete) _____ or obtaining such information is (costless, costly) _____, the market will (under, over) _____ allocate resources to the production of that good or service.

3. To correct for information problems in the gasoline market, the government establishes quality (prices, standards) _____. In the medical market, the government protects consumers by (taxing, licensing) _____ physicians.

4. Inadequate information involving buyers can lead to two problems. If a market situation arises whereby buyers alter their behavior after making a purchase and increase the cost to sellers, (an adverse-selection, a moral hazard) _____ problem is created, but if at the time of the purchase buyers withhold information from sellers that would impose a large cost on sellers, _____ problem is created.

5. Another example of information failure occurs in labor markets in which there is incomplete or inadequate information about (productivity, safety) _____. The government will intervene in these situations to enforce (quotas, standards) _____ or provide (health care, information) _____ related to workplace hazards.

6. Private businesses overcome some information problems about the product reliability or quality through (prices, warranties) _____ for products or the (penalizing, franchising) _____ of businesses that make them more uniform. Some businesses and organizations also collect and publish product information that is useful for (sellers, buyers) _____. Despite these actions, there may still be a need for government actions to correct (wage, information) _____ problems and to promote an efficient allocation of society's scarce resources.

7. Many collective decisions are made on the basis of (minority, majority) _____ voting. One problem with this voting system is that it results in (efficient, inefficient) _____ voting outcomes because it fails to incorporate the strength of (individual, majority) _____ preferences.

8. One example of an inefficiency problem with majority voting would be a case where voters defeat a proposal to provide a public good even though the total costs are (less than, greater than) _____ the total benefits, and another example of inefficiency from majority voting would be a case where they adopt a proposal to provide a public good even though the total costs are _____ the total benefits.

9. Some voting problems might be resolved or reversed through the influence of (interest, social) _____ groups or through political (primaries, logrolling) _____.

10. Another problem with this voting system occurs in a situation in which the public may not be able to rank its preferences with consistency; this is called the (fallacy, paradox) _____ of voting.

11. There also are insights into majority voting based on the (motor-voter, median-voter) _____ model, whereby the person holding the (lower, middle, upper) _____ position is likely to determine the outcome of an election.

12. When governments use resources to attempt to solve problems and the employment of these resources (does, does not) _____ result in solutions to these problems, there has been (market, government) _____ failure. This means that there are shortcomings in government that promote economic (efficiency, inefficiency) _____.

13. Representative democracy suffers from a principal–agent problem because the power and authority delegated by one group of people, the (agents, principals) _____, conflicts with the interests of another group responsible for taking action, the _____; in the case of representative democracy, the voters would be the (agents, principals) _____ and the elected officials would be the _____.

14. One reason for inefficient government decisions is due to a special-interest effect whereby a (large, small) _____ number of people benefit from a government program at the expense of a _____ number of persons who individually suffer (large, small) _____ losses. An example of such a special-interest effect would be (logrolling, earmarks) _____ that provide(s) public expenditures for narrow, home-state projects without careful evaluation or competitive bidding.

15. Inefficiencies also can be caused by an appeal to government for special benefits at taxpayers' or someone else's expense that is called (revealed preferences, rent-seeking behavior) _____. One example would be (land rent, tax breaks) _____ that benefit specific corporations.

16. Another reason for the failure is that the benefits from a government program or project are often (clear, hidden) _____ to citizens or groups, but the costs are frequently _____ when legislation is passed or programs are funded.

17. There also can be inefficiencies in government because voters or elected representatives have to accept political choices that are (limited, unlimited) _____ and (bundled, unbundled) _____, which means government legislation forces voters or elected representatives to take bad programs with the good programs.

18. The incentives for economic efficiency tend to be stronger in the (private, public) _____ sector because there is a profit incentive in the _____ sector but not a similar incentive in the (private, public) _____ sector. As a result, there tends to be (more, less) _____ government bureaucracy and _____ efficient use of scarce resources.

19. When government officials abuse their office for personal gain, this action would be considered (rent-seeking, political corruption) _____. An example of it would be a payment by a citizen to a government official to get the official to do his or her job and this payment would be a (earmark, bribe) _____.

20. Although the public sector can experience (market, government) _____ failure, the private sector also can experience _____ failure, and thus both government and markets can be considered (perfect, imperfect) _____ economic institutions.

■ TRUE–FALSE QUESTIONS

Circle T if the statement is true, F if it is false.

1. Asymmetric information is a market failure that occurs when parties to a market transaction possess unequal knowledge.　　　　　　　T　F

2. The inspection of meat products by the federal government for quality is justified on the grounds that it reduces the costs for buyers of obtaining information in the market for meat.　　　　　　　T　F

3. Inadequate information about sellers and their products may lead to an overallocation of resources to those products.　　　　　　　T　F

4. If the provision of government health insurance encourages people to take more health risks, it has created a moral hazard.　　　　　　　T　F

5. If unemployment compensation insurance leads some workers to not look for work, this has created a principal–agent problem.　　　　　　　T　F

6. Adverse-selection problems primarily result when the government begins enforcing standards for safety in the workplace.　　　　　　　T　F

7. Households and businesses have found many effective ways to overcome information difficulties without government intervention.　　　　　　　T　F

8. Public choice theory is the economic analysis of government decision making, politics, and elections.　T　F

9. Majority voting may deliver outcomes that are economically inefficient because it fails to take into account the strength of preferences of the individual voter.　T　F

10. Logrolling will always diminish economic efficiency in government.　　　　　　　T　F

11. The paradox of voting is that majority voting will result in consistent choices that reflect the preferences of the public.　　　　　　　T　F

12. The proposition that the person holding the middle position on an issue will likely determine the outcome of an election is suggested by the median-voter model.　T　F

13. One implication of the median-voter model is that some people may "vote with their feet" by moving into political jurisdictions where the median voter's preferences are closer to their own.　　　　　　　T　F

14. Government failure refers to economically inefficient outcomes caused by shortcomings in the public sector.　　　　　　　T　F

15. Principal–agent problems are conflicts that arise when the interests of the agents differ from the interests of the principals whom the agents are supposed to serve.   **T   F**

16. The special-interest effect will reduce government failures because the pressures exerted on government by one special-interest group are offset by the pressures brought to bear by other special-interest groups.   **T   F**

17. Earmarks refer to government legislation that is the result efficient voting outcomes.   **T   F**

18. The appeal to government for special benefits at taxpayers' or someone else's expense is called rent seeking.   **T   F**

19. An example of rent-seeking would be unions lobbying for government construction jobs for which only union workers qualify.   **T   F**

20. When the costs of programs are hidden and the benefits are clear, vote-seeking politicians tend to reject economically justifiable programs.   **T   F**

21. The limited choice of citizens refers to the inability of individual voters to select the precise bundle of social goods and services that will best satisfy the citizen's wants when he or she must vote for a candidate and the candidate's entire program.   **T   F**

22. Critics of government contend that there is a tendency for government bureaucracy to justify continued employment by finding new problems to solve.   **T   F**

23. Political corruption such as bribery is a frequent and common event in the conduct of government business in the United States.   **T   F**

24. A clear example of political corruption would be when a political candidate accepts a campaign contribution from a special-interest group and then helps pass legislation that the special-interest group supports.   **T   F**

25. When comparing government with markets, government is imperfect, whereas markets are perfect in efficiently allocating resources.   **T   F**

■ MULTIPLE-CHOICE QUESTIONS

Circle the letter that corresponds to the best answer.

1. Inadequate buyer information about sellers and their product can cause market failure in the form of
   (a) an increase in the number of market sellers
   (b) an increase in the number of market buyers
   (c) an overallocation of resources to the product
   (d) an underallocation of resources to the product

2. The establishment of a system of weights and measures by government is designed to correct situations in which there is
   (a) a moral hazard problem
   (b) an adverse-selection problem
   (c) inadequate buyer information about sellers
   (d) inadequate seller information about buyers

3. For what type of profession would the marginal cost to buyers of obtaining information about sellers of professional services be relatively high and not having that information could impose a high cost on the buyer?
   (a) medical surgery
   (b) house painting
   (c) lawn mowing
   (d) golf instruction

4. A situation in which one party to a contract alters his or her behavior after signing the contract in ways that can be costly to the other party would be
   (a) an adverse-selection problem
   (b) a moral hazard problem
   (c) a tragedy of the commons
   (d) a positive externality

5. If Congress adopted an increase in government insurance on bank deposits, this action would create a moral hazard problem because it may
   (a) lead to careful screening of depositors and the source of their funds
   (b) restrict the amount of deposits made by bank customers
   (c) encourage bank officers to make riskier loans
   (d) reduce bank investments in real estate

6. Assume that individuals who are most likely to benefit substantially from an insurance policy decide to buy one and the insurance company does not know this information. This situation would be an example of
   (a) a free-rider problem
   (b) a principal–agent problem
   (c) a moral hazard problem
   (d) an adverse-selection problem

7. Which one of the following situations would most likely create an adverse-selection problem?
   (a) The government sponsoring an insurance program for bank deposits
   (b) A business that conducts random inspections of its franchised restaurants
   (c) An insurance company offering a life insurance policy with no medical exam
   (d) A professional sports organization that offers guaranteed contracts to its players

8. What has been the main approach used by the federal government to improve workplace safety?
   (a) Provide information to workers about the injury records of employers
   (b) Require firms to provide information to workers about workplace hazards
   (c) Establish standards for workplace safety and enforce them with inspections and penalties
   (d) Mandate that employers pay into a special fund to be used to improve workplace safety at businesses

9. Which one of the following would be an example of a service provided by the private sector to overcome information failure for buyers of goods and services?
   (a) issuing licenses to dentists
   (b) regulating prescription drugs

(c) publishing *Consumer Reports*

(d) enforcing a systems of weights

10. Deficiencies in the processes used to make collective decisions of government and economic inefficiencies caused by government are the primary focus of

(a) political corruption

(b) public choice theory

(c) median-voter model

(d) principal–agent problems

Answer questions 11, 12, and 13 using the following information. Assume that only three citizens (A, B, and C) in a society are voting on whether to offer a public good. The government can provide a public good for $1200. If the public good is provided, the three citizens will equally share the tax expense. The benefits of the public good are $800 for voter A, $350 for voter B, and $250 for voter C. Each person votes based only on a benefit-cost evaluation.

11. If the total costs are subtracted from the total benefits, what will the difference be?

(a) −$200

(b) +$200

(c) −$1400

(d) +$1400

12. How will each person vote on this issue?

(a) A-yes, B-yes, and C-yes

(b) A-yes, B-no, and C-no

(c) A-yes, B-yes, and C-no

(d) A-no, B-yes, and C-yes

13. What conclusion can be drawn about the majority voting outcome for this public good proposal?

(a) It is inefficient because the proposal will pass even though there are no net benefits.

(b) It is efficient because the proposal will pass because there are net benefits.

(c) It is inefficient because the proposal will fail even though there are net benefits.

(d) It is efficient because the measure will fail because there are no net benefits.

14. The trading of votes to secure favorable outcomes on decisions that otherwise would be adverse is referred to as

(a) logrolling, and it increases economic efficiency

(b) logrolling, and it may increase or decrease economic efficiency

(c) rent-seeking behavior, and it decreases economic efficiency

(d) rent-seeking behavior, and it may increase or decrease economic efficiency

Answer Questions 15, 16, 17, and 18 on the basis of the following table, which shows the rankings of the public goods by three voters: A, B, and C.

Public good	Voter A	Voter B	Voter C
Dam	1	2	3
School	3	1	2
Road	2	3	1

15. In a choice between a dam and the school

(a) a majority of voters favor the dam

(b) a majority of voters favor the school

(c) a majority of voters favor both the dam and the school

(d) there is no majority of votes for either the dam or the school

16. In a choice between a road and a dam

(a) a majority of voters favor the dam

(b) a majority of voters favor the road

(c) a majority of voters favor both the dam and the road

(d) there is no majority of votes for either the road or the dam

17. In a choice between a school and a road

(a) a majority of voters favor the road

(b) a majority of voters favor the school

(c) a majority of voters favor both the road and the school

(d) there is no majority of votes for either the road or the school

18. What do the rankings in the table indicate about choices made under majority rule? Majority voting in this case

(a) reflects irrational preferences

(b) produces inconsistent choices

(c) produces consistent choices in spite of irrational preferences

(d) results in economically efficient outcomes because they have been influenced by special interests

19. The idea that the person holding the middle position will in a sense determine the outcome of an election is suggested by the

(a) rent-seeking behavior

(b) paradox of voting

(c) median-voter model

(d) special-interest effect

20. Suppose a government committee is composed of three persons (Andy, Barb, and Carla) who each develop a proposal for a new project. Andy's proposal costs $800. Barb's proposal costs $500. Carla's proposal costs $300. According to the median-voter model, which proposal is most likely to be adopted?

(a) Andy's

(b) Barb's

(c) Carla's

(d) either Andy's or Carla's

21. When elected officials decide to pursue their personal interests at the expense of the voters who elected them the conflict is an example of

(a) the paradox of voting

(b) the median-voter model

(c) a principal–agent problem

(d) a moral hazard problem

22. Actions that groups take to seek government legislation that puts tariffs on foreign products to limit foreign

competition or that gives tax breaks to specific corporations would best be an example of
  (a) how the median-voter model works
  (b) how political choices are bundled
  (c) rent-seeking behavior
  (d) the paradox of voting

23. According to public choice theory, politicians tend to favor programs with
  (a) clear benefits and immediate costs
  (b) clear benefits and deferred costs
  (c) uncertain benefits and clear costs
  (d) uncertain benefits and deferred costs

24. One type of government failure that involves the unlawful misdirection of government resources or actions that arise when government officials use their offices for personal gain is
  (a) logrolling
  (b) rent seeking
  (c) pork barrel politics
  (d) political corruption

25. It is difficult to determine whether provision for a particular good or service should be assigned to the private or public sector of the economy because the
  (a) institutions in both sectors function efficiently
  (b) markets function efficiently and the agencies of government perform imperfectly
  (c) markets are faulty and government agencies function with much greater efficiency
  (d) institutions in both sectors are imperfect

■ **PROBLEMS**

1. Assume that only three citizens (Dan, Ellie, and Frank) in a society are voting on whether to offer a public good. The government can provide a public good for $2400. If the public good is provided, the three citizens will equally share the tax expense. The benefits of the public good are $400 for Dan, $900 for Ellie, and $900 for Frank. Each person votes based only on a benefit-cost evaluation.

  a. List who will vote for and who will vote against the proposal _____

  b. What are the total benefits and total costs of the proposal? _____

  c. Is the majority voting outcome efficient? Explain

  _____

2. This problem is based on the following table, which shows the preference rankings (1 = most preferred) of the public goods by three voters: Xena, Yvonne, and Zoey.

Public good	Xena	Yvonne	Zoey
New fire truck	1	2	3
New police car	3	1	2
New ambulance	2	3	1

  a. In the choice between a new fire truck and new police car, the majority will favor a _____?

  b. In a choice between a new ambulance and a new fire truck, the majority will favor a _____?

  c. In the choice between a new police car and a new ambulance, the majority will favor a _____?

  d. What do the rankings in the table indicate about choices made under majority rule? _____

  _____?

3. Following is a list of a few chapter terms. Next is a series of brief statements. Match each term with the appropriate statement by placing the appropriate number of the term after each statement.

  1. Median-voter model
  2. paradox of voting
  3. principal–agent problem
  4. moral hazard problem
  5. adverse-selection problem

  a. Medical malpractice insurance increases the amount of malpractice _____

  b. Proposition that the persons holding the middle position on an issue will determine the voter outcome _____

  c. There is a conflict between interests of politicians and the voters they represent _____

  d. People who are most likely to need insurance payouts are those who are most likely to buy the insurance _____

  e. Paired-choice voting by majority rule fails to provide a consistent ranking of society's preferences for public goods and services _____

■ **SHORT ANSWER AND ESSAY QUESTIONS**

  1. What is the meaning of the term asymmetric information? How does it create a market failure?

  2. Describe how inadequate buyer information about sellers creates market problems for buyers in the gasoline market.

  3. Why do surgeons need to be licensed? What economic problem is being addressed by licensing such professionals?

  4. Explain how inadequate seller information about buyers can create a moral hazard problem. Give some examples of the application of this problem.

  5. How can the market for insurance result in an adverse-selection problem? What actions might government take to correct this information problem?

  6. In what way does workplace safety become an information problem? How might this problem be resolved by government or businesses?

  7. How have households and businesses found other ways to overcome information problems without government intervention?

  8. What is the relationship between majority voting and the efficiency of outcomes from an election? Give an example of a "yes" vote that would be considered an inefficient outcome and a "no" vote that would be considered an inefficient outcome.

9. How do special-interest groups influence the efficiency of voting outcomes?

10. What is political logrolling? Use an example of it to explain how it can either increase or decrease the efficiency of voting outcome.

11. Why is there a paradox with majority voting? Do the outcomes from majority voting suggest that voters are irrational in their preferences?

12. Describe how median voters influence the election results and debates over public issues. What are two important implications of the median-voter model?

13. Discuss the principal–agent problem as it applies to representative democracy.

14. How are efficient public decisions impaired by the special-interest effect?

15. Describe and give examples of rent-seeking that influence or direct government policies.

16. Why do politicians tend to favor government programs that have immediate and clear-cut benefits and vague or deferred costs?

17. Explain the problem of limited choice and bundled goods in government decision making as regards what public goods to provide.

18. Describe the differences in incentive in private markets and government and how they affect government efficiency.

19. Discuss the issue of political corruption by describing how it occurs, differences among nations, and whether political contributions from special-interest groups should be considered a form of it.

20. It is generally agreed that "national defense must lie in the public sector while wheat production can best be accomplished in the private sector." Why is there no agreement on where many other goods or services should be produced?

ANSWERS

Chapter 17 Asymmetric Information, Voting, and Public Choice

FILL-IN QUESTIONS

1. asymmetric, unequal
2. incomplete, costly, under
3. standards, licensing
4. a moral hazard, an adverse-selection
5. safety, standards, information
6. warranties, franchising, buyers, information
7. majority, inefficient, individual
8. less than, greater than
9. interest, logrolling
10. paradox
11. median-voter, middle
12. does not, government, inefficiency
13. principals, agents, principals, agents
14. small, large, small, earmarks
15. rent-seeking behavior, tax breaks
16. clear, hidden
17. limited, bundled
18. private, private, public, more, less
19. political corruption, bribe
20. government, market, imperfect

TRUE–FALSE QUESTIONS

1. T, p. 358	10. F, p. 363	19. T, p. 367
2. T, p. 358	11. F, pp. 363–364	20. F, p. 367
3. F, p. 358	12. T, p. 364	21. T, pp. 367–368
4. T, p. 359	13. T, p. 365	22. T, p. 368
5. F, p. 359	14. T, p. 365	23. F, p. 368
6. F, p. 359–360	15. T, pp. 365–366	24. F, pp. 368–369
7. T, p. 361	16. F, p. 366	25. F, p. 369
8. T, p. 361	17. F, p. 366–367	
9. T, p. 362	18. T, p. 367	

MULTIPLE-CHOICE QUESTIONS

1. d, p. 358	10. b, p. 361	19. c, p. 364
2. c, p. 358	11. b, p. 362	20. b, pp. 364–365
3. a, pp. 358–359	12. b, p. 362	21. c, pp. 365–366
4. b, p. 359	13. c, p. 362	22. c, p. 367
5. c, p. 359	14. b, p. 363	23. b, p. 367
6. d, pp. 359–360	15. b, pp. 363–364	24. d, p. 368
7. c, pp. 359, 361	16. a, pp. 363–364	25. d, p. 369
8. c, pp. 360–361	17. a, pp. 363–364	
9. c, p. 361	18. b, pp. 363–364	

PROBLEMS

1. *a. for:* Ellie, Frank; *against:* Dan; *b.* total benefits are $2200 ($400 + $900 + $900), total cost is $2400, *c.* No. The majority (Ellie and Frank) vote in favor of proposal, but the total costs are greater than the benefits.
2. *a.* police car; *b.* fire truck; *c.* ambulance; *d.* majority voting produces inconsistent outcome.
3. *a.* 4; *b.* 1; *c.* 3; *d.* 5; *e.* 3

SHORT ANSWER AND ESSAY QUESTIONS

1. p. 358	8. p. 362	15. p. 367
2. p. 358	9. p. 363	16. p. 367
3. pp. 358–359	10. p. 363	17. p. 367–368
4. p. 359	11. pp. 363–364	18. p. 368
5. pp. 359–360	12. pp. 365–365	19. pp. 368–369
6. pp. 360–361	13. pp. 365–366	20. p. 369
7. p. 361	14. p. 366	

CHAPTER 18

Antitrust Policy and Regulation

Chapter 18 examines issues related to antitrust policy and the regulation of markets and society. These issues are important for you to study because they affect prices, economic efficiency, and economic welfare.

Over the years the federal government has taken action to curb or limit the growth of monopolies in the United States through the passage of **antitrust laws** and the establishment of regulatory agencies. The Sherman Act of 1890 was the first major antitrust law. It was followed by other antitrust legislation and the creation of regulatory agencies and commissions.

The chapter discusses major antitrust issues and evaluates the effectiveness of **antitrust policy.** Several issues of interpretation address whether businesses should be judged for antitrust violations on the basis of monopoly behavior or structure and what should be the definition of the market. You will learn about the two conflicting perspectives on the enforcement of antitrust laws—activist and laissez-faire. The effectiveness of antitrust policy is also evaluated in the chapter based on such factors as the degree of the monopoly control, mergers, price fixing, price discrimination, and tying contracts.

Industrial regulation focuses on the control of natural monopolies so that they produce economic outcomes that benefit society. It is based on the public interest theory of regulation. This regulation by agencies and commissions has several problems of which you should be aware. One problem is that some of the regulated industries may not be natural monopolies at all and would be competitive industries if they were left unregulated. From this problem comes the legal cartel theory of regulation: Many industries want to be regulated so that competition among the firms will be reduced and the profits will increase.

Beginning in the 1970s, many industries in the United States underwent **deregulation.** These included the airline, trucking, banking, railroad, natural gas, television broadcasting, and telecommunications industries. The results generally show that this deregulation was beneficial for consumers and the efficiency of the economy. A more recent experience with deregulation occurred in the market for electricity. The outcomes from this experiment in deregulation have been less certain because of pricing problems in California.

Beginning in the early 1960s, new agencies and commissions began to engage in **social regulation** that differed from the regulation of the prices, services, and output provided by specific industries. This regulation focused on production conditions, product attributes, and production effects on society. This regulation increases product prices and indirectly reduces worker productivity, but supporters argue that the social benefits over time will exceed the costs. Critics contend that it is costly, is often poorly conceived, and has negative secondary effects. The debate over the optimal level of social regulation is not easily resolved because the costs and benefits are difficult to measure. You should spend time understanding both sides of the issue.

■ **CHECKLIST**

When you have studied this chapter you should be able to

☐ State the purpose of antitrust policy.

☐ Discuss the historical background and rationale for antitrust laws and regulatory agencies.

☐ Describe the major provisions of the Sherman Act, Clayton Act, Federal Trade Commission Act, Wheeler-Lea Act, and Celler-Kefauver Act.

☐ Contrast the monopoly behavior view with the monopoly structure view using two landmark Supreme Court decisions.

☐ Explain the importance of the relevant market definition in the interpretation of antitrust laws.

☐ Compare and contrast the active antitrust perspective with the laissez-faire perspective.

☐ Describe the enforcement and application of antitrust laws to monopoly.

☐ Distinguish among horizontal, vertical, and conglomerate mergers.

☐ Discuss the difference in the enforcement of antitrust laws by merger type.

☐ Explain the concept of the Herfindahl index and its application to merger guidelines.

☐ Describe antitrust policy toward price fixing and price discrimination.

☐ Discuss the antitrust issue in tying contracts.

☐ Define a natural monopoly and cite two ways government controls natural monopolies.

☐ Explain the public interest theory of regulation.

☐ Describe two problems with industrial regulation by government agencies and commissions.

☐ Explain the legal cartel theory of regulation.

☐ Discuss the outcomes from deregulation of selected U.S. industries since the 1970s.

☐ State three distinguishing features of social regulation.

☐ Make a case for social regulation in terms of benefits and costs.

☐ Present a case against social regulation in terms of benefits and costs.

☐ Offer two economic reminders about social regulation.

☐ Explain the charges, findings, and rulings in the Microsoft antitrust case (*Last Word*).

■ **CHAPTER OUTLINE**

1. The basic purposes of *antitrust policy* are to restrict monopoly power, promote competition, and achieve allocative efficiency.

   a. Following the Civil War, the expansion of the U.S. economy brought with it the creation of trusts (or monopolies) in many industries. The economic problem with monopolies is that they produce less output and charge higher prices than would be the case if their industries were more competitive. To control them, government has passed antitrust laws and created regulatory agencies.

   b. The *Sherman Act* of 1890 was the first antitrust legislation. It made restraint of trade and monopolization criminal offenses.

   c. The *Clayton Act* of 1914 outlawed price discrimination not based on cost, *tying contracts,* mergers that lessened competition, and *interlocking directorates.*

   d. The *Federal Trade Commission Act* of 1914 established the *Federal Trade Commission* to investigate unfair practices that might lead to the development of monopoly power. It can issue *cease-and-desist orders* for cases involving unfair competition. In 1938 this act was amended by the *Wheeler-Lea Act* to prohibit deceptive practices (including false and misleading advertising and misrepresentation of products).

   e. The *Celler-Kefauver Act* of 1950 plugged a loophole in the Clayton Act and prohibited mergers that might lead to a substantial reduction in competition.

2. The effectiveness of antitrust laws in preventing monopoly and maintaining competition has depended on judicial interpretation of the laws and enforcement of these laws by federal agencies.

   a. Two issues arise in the judicial interpretation of the antitrust laws.

   (1) Should a firm be judged on the basis of its monopoly structure or behavior? In the *Standard Oil case* of 1911, the U.S Supreme Court found the company guilty of monopolizing the petroleum industry. The *U.S. Steel case* of 1920, which also came before the Supreme Court, applied the *rule of reason* and said that a firm should be judged on the basis of its *behavior.* The *Alcoa case* of 1945 judged a firm on the basis of its *structure* (large control of a market). The courts and most economists now use the rule of reason that bases antitrust action on market behavior, not structure.

   (2) Should a broad or narrow definition of the market in which firms sell their products be used to judge monopoly power? In the 1956 *DuPont cellophane case,* the court ruled that DuPont did not monopolize the industry because there were other types of packaging materials that could be used.

   b. There are differences in political philosophies about whether antitrust enforcement should be more or less strictly enforced. The active antitrust perspective calls for enforcement of antitrust laws to stop illegal business activity, prevent anticompetitive mergers, and counter monopoly practices. The laissez-faire perspective contends that enforcement is largely unnecessary because market forces will control monopoly behavior and undermine monopoly positions.

   c. A question can be raised about whether the antitrust laws have been effective regarding monopoly, mergers, price fixing, price discrimination, and tying contracts.

   (1) For existing market structures, enforcement of antitrust laws has been lenient in general if the expansion of market share by a monopolistic firm is reasonable. The Sherman Act, however, has still been invoked in several high profile cases in which anticompetitive practices were alleged (*Microsoft case*). The European Union also generally has been more aggressive in prosecuting monopolies.

   (2) For *horizontal, vertical,* or *conglomerate mergers,* the application of the laws usually varies by the type of merger and the particulars of a case. Merger guidelines are based on the Herfindahl index (the sum of the squared values of market shares within an industry), but other factors, such as economies of scale, degree of foreign competition, and ease of entry, are considered.

   (3) Prohibitions against price fixing are strictly enforced. These activities are viewed as *per se violations,* so even the attempt, and not the actual outcome, will bring legal action and penalties.

   (4) Price discrimination is rarely challenged on antitrust grounds because in most cases it benefits consumers, but the practice can be challenged if the purpose is to reduce competition or block entry into a business.

   (5) The laws against tying contracts that require a buyer to purchase other products or take certain actions as a condition of a sale have been strictly enforced.

   (6) Overall, antitrust laws have not been very effective in breaking up monopolies or in preventing the growth of large oligopolies that have developed legally and because of market conditions. The laws have been effective against abusive or predatory monopolies. They have also been effective in blocking anticompetitive mergers, preventing price fixing, and restricting the use of tying contracts.

3. *Industrial regulation* occurs in some industries for economic reasons.

   a. A *natural monopoly* exists if a single producer can provide a good or service for the entire market at a lower average cost (because of economies of scale) than several producers, making competition uneconomical. To achieve better economic outcomes from this situation, government may opt for public ownership of the business or public (industrial) regulation. The latter option is based on the *public interest theory of regulation* that calls for controlling the economic decisions of the monopoly producers to achieve lower costs and greater output benefits for the public.

   b. The effectiveness of the regulation of business firms by regulatory agencies has been criticized for two main reasons.

   (1) Regulation increases costs and leads to an inefficient allocation of resources and higher prices.

ANTITRUST POLICY AND REGULATION **237**

(2) Regulated monopolies get perpetuated over time and would be more competitive firms if they were not regulated. Regulatory agencies contribute to the problem by protecting these industries, and these actions hurt the public and consumers.

   c. The *legal cartel theory of regulation* holds that potentially competitive industries often want and support the regulation of their industries to increase their profits by limiting competition among firms. The government regulatory agency in essence creates a government-sponsored cartel in an industry.

4. Since the 1970s there has been *deregulation* of many industries in the United States: airline, trucking, banking, railroad, natural gas, electricity, television broadcasting, and communications. The overall consensus among economists is that deregulation has produced large net benefits because it has resulted in lower prices, lower costs of production, and increased output. It has also allowed for greater technological advances in many industries. There is less certainty about the positive outcomes from deregulation in electricity markets because of pricing problems in California and illegal manipulations of electricity supplies by some business firms.

5. *Social regulation* has developed since the 1960s and resulted in the creation of additional regulatory agencies that focus on production conditions, product qualities, and production effects on society.

   a. Social regulation differs in three ways from industrial regulation: broader coverage of industries; more intrusion into the day-to-day production process; and rapid expansion into many areas.

   b. Discussions about social regulation involve deciding whether there is an optimal level of such regulation. The costs and benefits are difficult to measure, so ideology often influences the debate over the proper amount of this regulation.

   c. Supporters of social regulation contend it is needed to fight serious problems such as job and auto safety, environment pollution, product defects, and discrimination. Although such regulation is costly, the social benefits would exceed the costs over time, if they could be easily measured. Defenders point to many specific benefits resulting from such regulation.

   d. Critics argue that this social regulation is inefficient because the regulations are poorly drawn and targeted. The rules and regulations are also often made based on limited and inadequate information. In addition, there are unintended secondary effects from the regulation that boost product costs. Regulatory agencies tend to attract "overzealous" workers who dislike the market system and advocate government intervention as the only solution.

   e. Two reminders are needed in the debate over social regulation.

   (1) Supporters need to remember that there is no "free lunch," and that social regulation increases product prices, may slow product innovation, and may lessen competition.

   (2) Defenders need to remember that the market system has flaws that sometimes need to be addressed by government through social regulation and that by doing so, government creates continuing support of the operation of the market system.

6. (*Last Word*). In 1998, Microsoft was charged with violating Section 2 of the Sherman Act by using business practices that maintained its Windows software monopoly. Microsoft denied the charges and argued that technological advances made any monopoly highly transitory. The ruling from the federal district court divided the company into two firms, one for software applications and the other for the Windows operating system. The breakup ruling was overturned on appeal, but it still affirmed that Microsoft used illegal business practices to maintain its monopoly. Microsoft was prevented from using these anticompetitive practices in the future. A behavior remedy for antitrust violations was used rather than a structural (breakup) remedy in this case.

■ **HINTS AND TIPS**

1. The first section of the chapter discusses several federal antitrust laws. After looking at this section, many students ask, "Am I expected to know these laws?" Yes, you should have an understanding of these laws. A related question asked is, "Why should I know them?" To examine a current economic issue, you need to know how the problem arose, what actions have been taken over time to solve it, and what the outcomes are. Many of these major antitrust laws are enforced to some degree today and may affect a business for which you may work.

2. The **Herfindahl index** was first introduced in Chapter 11. Reread that material if you cannot remember what the index is. In Chapter 18 you will learn how the index is used for merger guidelines.

3. This chapter discusses controversies about many topics—antitrust policy, industrial regulation, deregulation, and social regulation. To help understand these controversies, make a table showing the pro and con positions for each issue. See problem 4 for an example.

■ **IMPORTANT TERMS**

antitrust policy	DuPont cellophane case
Sherman Act	Microsoft case
Clayton Act	horizontal merger
tying contracts	vertical merger
interlocking directorate	conglomerate merger
Federal Trade Commission Act	per se violations
cease-and-desist order	industrial regulation
Wheeler-Lea Act	natural monopoly
Celler-Kefauver Act	public interest theory of regulation
Standard Oil case	legal cartel theory of regulation
U.S. Steel case	social regulation
rule of reason	
Alcoa case	

SELF-TEST

■ FILL-IN QUESTIONS

1. Laws and government actions designed to prevent monopoly and promote competition are referred to as (industrial regulation, antitrust policy) _____. Action taken to control a firm's prices within selected industries is referred to as (social, industrial) _____ regulation whereas establishing the conditions under which goods are produced, monitoring the physical characteristics of products, and reducing the negative effects of production fall under the category of _____ regulation.

2. The two techniques of federal control that have been adopted as substitutes for, or to maintain competition in, markets are

a. _____

b. _____

3. Antitrust legislation in 1890 that made it illegal to monopolize or restrain trade between the states or between nations was the (Clayton, Sherman) _____ Act. Legislation passed in 1914 that prohibited such practices as price discrimination, acquisition of the stock of corporations to reduce competition, tying contracts, and interlocking directorates was the (Clayton, Sherman) _____ Act.

4. The 1914 act that had set up an agency to investigate unfair competitive practices, hold public hearings on such complaints, and issue cease-and-desist orders was the (Clayton, Federal Trade Commission) _____ Act.

5. The 1938 antitrust act that had the effect of prohibiting false and misleading advertising was the (Celler-Kefauver, Wheeler-Lea) _____ Act, while the act that plugged a loophole in the Clayton Act by banning the acquisition of assets of one firm by another when it would lessen competition was the _____ Act.

6. When the judicial courts used the rule of reason to evaluate industrial concentration by U.S. Steel in 1920, they were judging the firm on the basis of its market (behavior, structure) _____, but when the courts made a decision to break up Alcoa in 1945, they were judging the firm on the basis of its market _____. Since 1945, the courts have returned to evaluating a firm on the basis of its market (behavior, structure) _____.

7. One major issue of interpretation in antitrust law is the definition of a market. The firm's market share will appear small if the courts define a market (narrowly, broadly) _____, but the firm's market share will appear large if the courts define a market share _____. In 1956, the courts ruled that although DuPont sold nearly all the cellophane produced in the United States, it (did, did not) _____ dominate the market for flexible packaging materials.

8. The active antitrust perspective is that antitrust laws need to be (strictly, loosely) _____ enforced to promote (monopoly, competition) _____ in business. The laissez-faire perspective contends that enforcement is largely (necessary, unnecessary) _____ because monopoly power and control can be countered by (government, markets) _____.

9. A merger between two competitors selling similar products in the same market is a (vertical, horizontal, conglomerate) _____ merger; a _____ merger occurs among firms at different stages in the production process of the same industry; a _____ merger results when a firm in one industry is purchased by a firm in an unrelated industry.

10. The (Sherman, Herfindahl) _____ index is used as a guideline for mergers. An industry of only four firms, each with a 25 percent market share, has an index score of (2500, 10,000) _____ but if the industry was a pure monopoly with only one firm its index score would be _____.

11. If a firm attempted to fix prices, even if the attempt were not effective, it would be an example of a (tying contract, per se violation) _____ under antitrust laws; if a producer will only sell a desired product on condition that the buyer acquire other products, this is an example of a _____ under antitrust laws. In both cases, the laws are (loosely, strictly) _____ enforced.

12. Most economists conclude that, overall, U.S. antitrust policy (has, has not) _____ been effective in achieving its goal of promoting competition and efficiency and that the application of antitrust laws _____ been effective against predatory and abusive monopoly.

13. A natural monopoly exists when a single firm is able to supply the entire market at a (higher, lower) _____ average cost than a number of competing firms. In the United States, many of these natural monopolies are controlled by (business cartels, regulatory commissions) _____.

14. The two major criticisms of regulation of industries by a government agency or commission are

a. The regulated firms have no incentive to lower their costs because the commission will then require them to (raise, lower) _____ their prices, and because the prices they are allowed to charge are based on the value of their capital equipment, firms tend to make uneconomical substitutions of (labor, capital) _____ for _____.

b. Regulation has been applied to industries that (are, are not) _____ natural monopolies, which in the absence of regulation would be more competitive.

15. The public interest theory of regulation assumes that the objective of regulating an industry is to (encourage, discourage) _____ the abuses of monopoly power. An alternative theory assumes firms wish to be regulated because it enables them to form, and the regulatory commission helps them to create, a profitable and legal (conglomerate, cartel) _____.

16. The available evidence indicates that deregulation of many industries that began in the 1970s generally resulted in (decreased, increased) _____ prices because _____ competition among firms led to _____ costs and _____ output.

17. The Food and Drug Administration would be an example of a federal regulatory commission engaged in (social, industrial) _____ regulation and the Federal Communications Commission would be an example of an agency engaged in _____ regulation.

18. Compared with industrial regulation, social regulation applies to (more, fewer) _____ firms, affects day-to-day production to a (greater, lesser) _____ extent, and has expanded more (rapidly, slowly) _____.

19. It should be remembered by supporters of social regulation that there is "no free lunch" because it can (increase, decrease) _____ product prices and _____ worker productivity, and it also may _____ the rate of innovation.

20. It should be remembered by critics of social regulation that it can be (anti-, pro-) _____ capitalist because when such social problems in the market are addressed, the public support for the market system is (increased, decreased) _____.

■ TRUE–FALSE QUESTIONS

Circle T if the statement is true, F if it is false.

1. The basic purposes of antitrust policy are to prevent monopolization, promote competition, and achieve allocative efficiency. **T F**

2. The issue of antitrust arose from the emergence of trusts and monopolies in the U.S. economy in the two decades before the U.S. Civil War. **T F**

3. The economic problem with monopolists is that they charge a lower price and produce more output than if their industries were competitive. **T F**

4. The Clayton Act declares that price discrimination, tying contracts, stock acquisitions between corporations, and interlocking directorates are illegal when their effect is to reduce competition. **T F**

5. The Federal Trade Commission is in charge of stimulating more international trade between domestic and foreign producers. **T F**

6. The Celler-Kefauver Act of 1950 prohibits one firm from acquiring the assets of another firm when the result is to lessen competition. **T F**

7. In 1920 the courts applied the rule of reason to the U.S. Steel Corporation and decided that the corporation possessed monopoly power and had unreasonably restrained trade. **T F**

8. Those who believe an industry should be judged on the basis of its structure contend that any industry with a monopolistic structure must behave like a monopolist. **T F**

9. The courts broadly defined the market for cellophane in the DuPont cellophane case of 1956. **T F**

10. There is only one perspective on the enforcement of antitrust laws, and it calls for strict enforcement of all laws. **T F**

11. A horizontal merger is a merger between firms at different stages of the production process. **T F**

12. The Herfindahl index is the sum of the squared values of the market shares within an industry. **T F**

13. To gain a conviction under *per se violations,* the party making the charge must show that the conspiracy to fix prices actually succeeded or caused damage. **T F**

14. There is substantial evidence that antitrust policy has *not* been effective in identifying and prosecuting price fixing by businesses. **T F**

15. Industrial regulation pertains to regulation of the conditions under which products are made, the impact of products on society, and the physical qualities of the products. **T F**

16. Public ownership rather than public regulation has been the primary means used in the United States to ensure that the behavior of natural monopolists is socially acceptable. **T F**

17. The rationale underlying the public interest theory of regulation of natural monopolies is to allow the consumers of their goods or services to benefit from the economies of scale. **T F**

18. Regulated firms, because the prices they are allowed to charge enable them to earn a "fair" return over their costs, have a strong incentive to reduce their costs. **T F**

19. From the perspective of the legal cartel theory of regulation, some industries want to be regulated by government. **T F**

20. Deregulation of industries since the 1970s has resulted in large gains in economic efficiency for the U.S. economy.   **T F**

21. The marginal costs and benefits of social regulation are easy to measure for determining the optimal level of such regulation.   **T F**

22. Those who favor social regulation believe that the expenditures on it are needed to obtain a hospitable, sustainable, and just society.   **T F**

23. Critics of social regulation argue that its marginal costs exceed its marginal benefits.   **T F**

24. The likely effect of social regulation is that it lowers product prices, raises worker productivity, and increases product innovation.   **T F**

25. Social regulation can contribute to public support for a market system by addressing production and consumption problems arising from the system.   **T F**

■ **MULTIPLE-CHOICE QUESTIONS**

Circle the letter that corresponds to the best answer.

1. Which term describes the laws and government actions designed to prevent monopoly and promote competition?
  (a) industrial regulation
  (b) social regulation
  (c) legal cartel policy
  (d) antitrust policy

2. Which law stated that contracts and conspiracies in restraint of trade, monopolies, attempts to monopolize, and conspiracies to monopolize are illegal?
  (a) Sherman Act
  (b) Clayton Act
  (c) Federal Trade Commission Act
  (d) Wheeler-Lea Act

3. Which act specifically outlawed tying contracts and interlocking directorates?
  (a) Sherman Act
  (b) Clayton Act
  (c) Federal Trade Commission Act
  (d) Wheeler-Lea Act

4. Which act has given the Federal Trade Commission the task of preventing false and misleading advertising and the misrepresentation of products?
  (a) Sherman Act
  (b) Clayton Act
  (c) Federal Trade Commission Act
  (d) Wheeler-Lea Act

5. Which act banned the acquisition of a firm's assets by a competing firm when the acquisition would tend to reduce competition?
  (a) Celler-Kefauver Act
  (b) Wheeler-Lea Act
  (c) Clayton Act
  (d) Federal Trade Commission Act

6. The argument that an industry that is highly concentrated will behave like a monopolist and the Alcoa court case of 1945 would both provide support for the case that the application of antitrust laws should be based on industry
  (a) behavior
  (b) structure
  (c) efficiency
  (d) rule of reason

7. If the market is defined broadly to include a wide range of somewhat similar products, then
  (a) firms in the industry will be able to behave as monopolists
  (b) firms in the industry will follow the rule of reason
  (c) a firm's market share will appear large
  (d) a firm's market share will appear small

8. Which perspective holds that the enforcement of antitrust laws is largely unnecessary, especially as related to monopoly, because market forces will counter monopoly?
  (a) concentration perspective
  (b) active antitrust perspective
  (c) relevant market perspective
  (d) laissez-faire perspective

9. The merger of a firm in one industry with a firm in an unrelated industry is called a
  (a) horizontal merger
  (b) vertical merger
  (c) secondary merger
  (d) conglomerate merger

10. Which is most likely to be the focus of antitrust law scrutiny and enforcement?
  (a) a publicly regulated utility
  (b) a conglomerate merger
  (c) a vertical merger
  (d) a horizontal merger

11. An industry has four firms, each with a market share of 25%. There is no foreign competition, entry into the industry is difficult, and no firm is on the verge of bankruptcy. If two of the firms in the industry sought to merge, this action would most likely be opposed by the government because the new Herfindahl index for the industry would be
  (a) 2000 and the merger would increase the index by 1000
  (b) 2500 and the merger would increase the index by 1000
  (c) 3750 and the merger would increase the index by 1250
  (d) 5000 and the merger would increase the index by 1250

12. When the government or another party making a charge can show that there was a conspiracy to fix prices, even if the conspiracy did not succeed, this would be an example of
  (a) a tying contract
  (b) a per se violation
  (c) the rule of reason
  (d) the legal cartel theory

13. Antitrust laws have been most effective in
(a) breaking up monopolies
(b) prosecuting price fixing in business
(c) expanding industrial concentration
(d) blocking entry of foreign competition in domestic markets

14. If a movie distributor forced theaters to "buy" projection rights to a full package of films as a condition of showing a blockbuster movie, then this would be an example of
(a) price fixing
(b) a tying contract
(c) a per se violation
(d) an interlocking directorate

15. An example of a government organization involved primarily in industrial regulation would be the
(a) Federal Communications Commission
(b) Food and Drug Administration
(c) Occupational Safety and Health Administration
(d) Environmental Protection Agency

16. Legislation designed to regulate natural monopolies would be based on which theory of regulation?
(a) cartel
(b) public interest
(c) rule of reason
(d) public ownership

17. Those who oppose the regulation of industry by regulatory agencies contend that
(a) many of the regulated industries are natural monopolies
(b) the regulatory agencies may favor industry because they are often staffed by former industry executives
(c) regulation contributes to an increase in the number of mergers in industries
(d) regulation helps moderate costs and improves efficiency in the production of a good or service produced by the regulated industry

18. The legal cartel theory of regulation
(a) would allow the forces of demand and supply to determine the rates (prices) of the good or service
(b) would attempt to protect the public from abuses of monopoly power
(c) assumes that the regulated industry wishes to be regulated
(d) assumes that both the demand for and supply of the good or service produced by the regulated industry are perfectly inelastic

19. Deregulation of previously regulated industries in the United States has resulted in
(a) higher prices, higher costs, and decreased output
(b) higher prices and costs, but increased output
(c) lower prices and costs, but decreased output
(d) lower prices, lower costs, and increased output

20. Which is a concern of social regulation?
(a) the prices charged for goods
(b) the service provided to the public
(c) the conditions under which goods are manufactured
(d) the impact on business profits from the production of goods

21. A major difference between industrial regulation and social regulation is that social regulation
(a) covers fewer industries across the economy
(b) has expanded slowly and waned in recent years
(c) is targeted at the prices charged, the costs of production, and amount of profit
(d) focuses on product design, employment conditions, and the production process

22. Which government organization is primarily engaged in social regulation?
(a) the Federal Trade Commission
(b) the Interstate Commerce Commission
(c) the Environmental Protection Agency
(d) the Federal Energy Regulatory Commission

23. Supporters of social regulation contend that
(a) there is a pressing need to reduce the number of mergers in U.S. business
(b) the presence of natural monopoly requires strong regulatory action by government
(c) the social benefits will exceed the social costs
(d) there are no social costs associated with it

24. A criticism of social regulation by its opponents is that it
(a) is a strong procapitalist force
(b) will decrease the rate of innovation in the economy
(c) will increase the amount of price fixing among businesses
(d) will require too long a time to achieve its objectives

25. The captions for two reminders for proponents and opponents of social regulation are
(a) "there is no free lunch" and "less government is not always better than more"
(b) "the rule of reason will prevail" and "restraint of trade will not be tolerated by government"
(c) "the public interest will win over the powerful" and the "legal cartel will be broken by government"
(d) "demand the lowest price" and "protect the greatest number"

■ **PROBLEMS**

1. Following is a list of federal laws. Next is a series of provisions found in federal laws. Match each law with the appropriate provision by placing the appropriate capital letter after each provision.

A. Sherman Act   D. Wheeler-Lea Act
B. Clayton Act   E. Celler-Kefauver Act
C. Federal Trade
   Commission Act

a. Established a commission to investigate and prevent unfair methods of competition _____

b. Made monopoly and restraint of trade illegal and criminal _____

c. Prohibited the acquisition of the assets of a firm by another firm when such an acquisition would lessen competition _____

d. Had the effect of prohibiting false and misleading advertising and the misrepresentation of products

_____

e. Clarified the Sherman Act and outlawed specific techniques or devices used to create monopolies and restrain trade

_____

2. Indicate with the letter **L** for leniently and the letter **S** for strictly how the antitrust laws tend to be applied to each of the following.

a. Vertical mergers in which each of the merging firms sells a small portion of the total output of its industry _____

b. Price fixing by a firm in an industry _____

c. Conglomerate mergers _____

d. Existing market structures in which no firm sells 60% or more of the total output of its industry _____

e. Horizontal mergers in which the merged firms would sell a large portion of the total output of their industry and no firm is on the verge of bankruptcy _____

f. Action by firms in an industry to divide up sales

_____

g. Horizontal mergers where one of the firms is on the verge of bankruptcy _____

3. The following table contains data on five different industries and the market shares for each firm in the industry. Assume that there is no foreign competition, entry into the industry is difficult, and no firm in each industry is on the verge of bankruptcy.

	Market share of firms in industry						Herfindahl index
Industry	1	2	3	4	5	6	
A	35	25	15	11	10	4	_____
B	30	25	25	20	—	—	_____
C	20	20	20	15	15	10	_____
D	60	25	15	—	—	—	_____
E	22	21	20	18	12	7	_____

a. In the last column, calculate the Herfindahl index.
b. The industry with the most concentration is Industry

_____, and the industry with the least monopoly power is Industry _____.

c. If the *sixth* firm in Industry A sought to merge with the *fifth* firm in that industry, then the government (would, would not) _____ be likely to challenge the merger. The Herfindahl index for this industry is

_____, which is higher than the merger guideline of _____ points used by the government, but the merger increases the index by only _____ points.
d. If the *fourth* firm in Industry B sought to merge with the *third* firm in that industry, then the government (would, would not) _____ be likely to challenge the

merger. The Herfindahl index for this industry is

_____, which is higher than the merger guideline of the government, and the merger increases the index

by _____ points.
e. A *conglomerate* merger between the *fourth* firm in Industry C and the *fourth* firm in Industry E (would, would not) _____ likely be challenged by the government. The Herfindahl index would (increase, remain

the same) _____ with this merger.
f. If a *vertical* merger between the *first* firm in Industry B with the *first* firm in Industry D lessened competition in each industry, then the merger (would, would not)

_____ likely be challenged by the government, but

the merger _____ likely be challenged if it did not lessen competition in each industry.

4. Social regulation has had its critics and defenders. In the blank spaces in the following table, indicate the effect that critics and defenders thought social regulation would have on each characteristic. Mark an **I** for increase and **D** for decrease. If the text states nothing about this effect, mark an **N**.

	Critics	Defenders
a. Prices	_____	_____
b. Output	_____	_____
c. Competition	_____	_____
d. Product innovation	_____	_____
e. Net benefits to society	_____	_____

■ **SHORT ANSWER AND ESSAY QUESTIONS**

1. Explain the basic differences between antitrust policy, industrial regulation, and social regulation.

2. What are the historical background to and the main provisions of the Sherman Act?

3. The Clayton Act and the Federal Trade Commission Act amended or elaborated on the provisions of the Sherman Act, and both aimed at preventing rather than punishing monopoly. What were the chief provisions of each act, and how did they attempt to prevent monopoly? In what two ways is the FTC Act important?

4. What loophole in the Clayton Act did the Celler-Kefauver Act plug in 1950, and how did it alter the coverage of the antitrust laws with respect to mergers?

5. Contrast the two different approaches to court interpretation of antitrust laws that are illustrated by the decisions of the courts in the U.S. Steel and Alcoa cases.

6. Why is defining the market an important issue in the application of the antitrust laws? How did the courts define the market in the case brought against DuPont for monopolizing the market for cellophane?

7. Discuss two perspectives on strict enforcement of antitrust laws.

8. How have the antitrust laws been applied in the past and in recent years to monopoly in the United States and by the European Union? Give examples.

9. Explain the difference between horizontal, vertical, and conglomerate mergers. Give an example of each type.

10. What is the Herfindahl index and how is it used as a guideline for mergers?

11. What are per se violations? Give examples of recent price-fixing investigations and court cases.

12. What is a natural monopoly? What two alternative ways can a natural monopoly be used to ensure that it behaves in a socially acceptable fashion?

13. Explain how public interest regulation can lead to increased costs and economic inefficiency as it is practiced by U.S. commissions and agencies.

14. Discuss the issue involved in regulation that perpetuates a natural monopoly after the conditions for it have evaporated. Give examples.

15. What is the legal cartel theory of regulation? Contrast it with the public interest theory of regulation.

16. Why were a number of industries in the U.S. economy deregulated beginning in the 1970s? What have been the economic effects of deregulation?

17. How does social regulation differ from industrial (or public) regulation? Describe three major differences.

18. Can the optimal level of social regulation be determined? Explain.

19. What are the major arguments for and against social regulation?

20. What two reminders does economic analysis provide for supports and opponents of social regulation?

ANSWERS

Chapter 18 Antitrust Policy and Regulation

FILL-IN QUESTIONS

1. antitrust policy, industrial, social
2. *a.* establishing regulatory agencies; *b.* passing antitrust laws (either order for *a* and *b*)
3. Sherman, Clayton
4. Federal Trade Commission
5. Wheeler-Lea, Celler-Kefauver
6. behavior, structure, behavior
7. broadly, narrowly, did not
8. strictly, competition, unnecessary, markets
9. horizontal, vertical, conglomerate
10. Herfindahl, 2500, 10,000
11. per se violation, tying contract, strictly
12. has, has
13. lower, regulatory commissions
14. *a.* lower, capital, labor; *b.* are not
15. discourage, cartel
16. decreased, increased, decreased, increased
17. social, industrial
18. more, greater, rapidly
19. increase, decrease, decrease
20. pro-, increased

TRUE–FALSE QUESTIONS

1. T, p. 375	**10.** F, p. 378	**19.** T, pp. 382–383
2. F, p. 375	**11.** F, p. 379	**20.** T, pp. 383–384
3. F, p. 375	**12.** T, pp. 379–380	**21.** F, pp. 384–385
4. T, p. 376	**13.** F, p. 380	**22.** T, p. 385
5. F, p. 376	**14.** F, p. 380	**23.** T, pp. 385–386
6. T, p. 376	**15.** F, pp. 381–382	**24.** F, pp. 386–387
7. F, p. 377	**16.** F, pp. 381–382	**25.** T, pp. 387–388
8. T, p. 377	**17.** T, p. 382	
9. T, p. 377	**18.** F, p. 382	

MULTIPLE-CHOICE QUESTIONS

1. d, p. 374	**10.** d, p. 379	**19.** d, p. 383
2. a, pp. 375–376	**11.** c, pp. 379–380	**20.** c, p. 384
3. b, p. 376	**12.** b, p. 380	**21.** d, p. 384
4. d, p. 376	**13.** b, p. 380	**22.** c, p. 384
5. a, p. 376	**14.** b, pp. 380–381	**23.** c, p. 385
6. b, p. 377	**15.** a, p. 381	**24.** b, pp. 385–386
7. d, p. 377	**16.** b, p. 382	**25.** a, pp. 386–388
8. d, p. 378	**17.** b, pp. 382–383	
9. d, p. 379	**18.** c, p. 383	

PROBLEMS

1. *a.* C; *b.* A; *c.* E; *d.* D; *e.* B
2. *a.* L; *b.* S; *c.* L; *d.* L; *e.* S; *f.* S; *g.* L
3. *a.* 2312, 2550, 1750, 4450, 1842; *b.* D, C; *c.* would not, 2312, 1800, 80; *d.* would, 2550, 1000; *e.* would not, remain the same; *f.* would, would not
4. *a.* I, N; *b.* D, N; *c.* D, N; *d.* D, N; *e.* D, I

SHORT ANSWER AND ESSAY QUESTIONS

1. p. 374	**8.** pp. 378–379	**15.** pp. 382–383
2. pp. 375–376	**9.** p. 379	**16.** pp. 383–384
3. p. 376	**10.** pp. 379–380	**17.** p. 384
4. p. 376	**11.** p. 380	**18.** p. 385
5. pp. 376–377	**12.** pp. 381–382	**19.** pp. 385–386
6. pp. 377–378	**13.** p. 382	**20.** pp. 386–388
7. p. 378	**14.** p. 382	

CHAPTER 19

Agriculture: Economics and Policy

Agriculture is a large and vital part of the U.S. and world economies, and so it merits the special attention it receives in Chapter 19. As you will learn, the economics of farm policies of the federal government are of concern not only to those directly engaged in farming, but also to U.S. consumers and businesses that purchase farm products and to U.S. taxpayers who subsidize farm incomes. Agriculture is also important in the world economy because each nation must find a way to feed its population, and domestic farm policies designed to enhance farm incomes often lead to distortions in world trade and economic inefficiency in world agricultural production.

The chapter begins by examining a short-run problem of **price and income instability** and the long-run problem of the **declining output** of U.S. agriculture as a percentage of GDP. The short-run price and income instability results from farm prices and incomes having fluctuated sharply from year to year. Agriculture is a declining industry in the long run, and as a consequence, farm incomes have fallen over time. To understand the causes of each economic condition, you will have to use the concept of inelastic demand and your knowledge of how demand and supply determine price in a competitive market. The effort you have put into the study of these tools in previous chapters will now pay a dividend: an understanding of the causes of a real-world situation and the policies designed to address it.

The agricultural policies of the federal government have been directed at enhancing and stabilizing farm incomes by supporting farm prices. In connection with the support of farm prices, you are introduced to the **parity concept.** Once you understand parity and recognize that the parity price in the past has been above what the competitive price would have been, you will come to some important conclusions. Consumers paid higher prices for and consumed smaller quantities of the various farm products, and at the prices supported by the federal government, there were surpluses of these products. The federal government bought these surpluses to keep the price above the competitive market price. The purchases of the surpluses were financed by U.S. taxpayers. To eliminate these surpluses, government looked for ways to increase the demand for or to decrease the supply of these commodities. Programs to increase demand and decrease supply were put into effect, but they failed to eliminate the annual surpluses.

Over the years, farm policies have not worked well and the price-support system has been criticized for several reasons. First, the policies confuse the symptoms of the

agricultural economic condition (low farm prices and incomes) with its causes (resource allocation). Second, the costly farm subsidies are also misguided because they tend to benefit the high-income instead of the low-income farmer. Third, some policies of the federal government contradict or offset other policies to help farmers.

The politics of farm policy can also be studied from the public choice perspective first presented in Chapter 17. In this chapter you will learn how the special interest effect and rent-seeking behavior related to farm policies result in costly programs that have been supported by political leaders and subsidized by the federal government for so many years. Nevertheless, the political backing for farm price supports is declining because of a reduction in the farm population. There is also international pressure to reduce farm price supports in all nations to eliminate distortions in world trade and improve worldwide economic efficiency.

The chapter concludes with a discussion of the recent reform of agricultural policy in the United States. The **Freedom to Farm Act** of 1996 was an attempt to eliminate price supports and acreage allotments for many major agricultural products. In return, U.S. farmers were to receive income payments through 2002 to help them make the transition to working in a more competitive market. The deterioration in economic conditions before the end of the act led to emergency aid payments to farmers to stabilize crop prices and incomes for farmers. As you will learn, the features of that legislation have now been extended and expanded with the passage of the **Food, Conservation and Energy Act of 2008.** It provides direct payments, countercyclical payments, and marketing loans to help farmers. The subsidies and new legislation again demonstrate that U.S. agriculture retains strong special-interest and political support.

■ CHECKLIST

When you have studied this chapter you should be able to

☐ Give several reasons why it is important to study the economics of U.S. agriculture.

☐ Distinguish between farm commodities and food products.

☐ List three causes of the short-run price and income instability in agriculture.

☐ Explain why the demand for agricultural products is price inelastic.

☐ Cite a reason for the fluctuations in agricultural output.

☐ Discuss the fluctuations in domestic demand for agricultural products.

☐ Describe the instability of foreign demand for agricultural products.

☐ Identify the two major factors contributing to the long-run declining output in U.S. agriculture.

☐ Describe how technological change affects the long-run supply of agricultural products.

☐ Give two reasons why increases in demand lag increases in supply over time in U.S. agriculture.

☐ Use a supply and demand graph to illustrate the long-run declining output in U.S. agriculture.

☐ Explain the consequences of the long-run declining output in agriculture for industry structure, crop prices, and income.

☐ Compare farm-household income with nonfarm household income.

☐ List the six features of the "farm program."

☐ Give cost estimates of the size of U.S. farm subsidies in recent years.

☐ Present several arguments in support of farm subsidies.

☐ Define the parity ratio and explain its significance to agricultural policy.

☐ Use a supply and demand graph to identify the economic effects of price supports for agricultural products on output, farm income, consumer and taxpayer expenditures, economic efficiency, the environment, and international trade.

☐ Give examples of how the federal government restricts supply and bolsters demand for farm products.

☐ Explain criticisms of the parity concepts.

☐ Present three criticisms of the price-support system in agriculture.

☐ Use insights from public choice theory to discuss the politics of agricultural legislation and expenditures by the federal government for farm programs.

☐ Give two reasons, one domestic and one international, to explain the change in the politics of farm subsidies.

☐ Describe the major features of the Freedom to Farm Act of 1996.

☐ Explain the elements of the Food, Conservation and Energy Act of 2008 and how it affects crop prices, farm incomes, and subsidies in agriculture.

☐ Discuss the domestic and global effects of the U.S. sugar program (*Last Word*).

■ **CHAPTER OUTLINE**

1. The economic analysis of U.S. agriculture is important for several reasons: It is one of the nation's largest industries and is a real-world example of the purely competitive model; it illustrates the economic effects of government intervention in markets; it illustrates the special-interest effect and rent-seeking behavior; and it reflects changes in global markets.

2. The agricultural industry is very diverse because it covers many types of farm and ranch operations. Agriculture also includes farm products or **farm commodities** such as wheat, corn, soybeans, cattle, and rice, and also **food products** that are sold in stores. The major focus of the

chapter is on farm commodities (or farm products) because they tend to be sold in highly competitive markets. Some of these farm commodities are also subject to extensive government subsidies to maintain the prices for farm products or bolster farm incomes. Agriculture also has short-run and long-run problems. In the short run, there is price and income instability and in the long run there has been declining output as a percentage of GDP.

a. The reasons for the short-run price and income instability are several:

(1) The demand for farm products is inelastic, which means that the percentage change in quantity demanded is less than the percentage change in price;

(2) Weather or growing conditions cause fluctuations in the output of agricultural products; and

(3) Demand fluctuates in both domestic and foreign markets.

b. The causes of agriculture's long-run decline as an industry stem from two basic factors:

(1) The supply of agricultural products increased significantly over most of this century because of technological advances in agriculture.

(2) The demand for agricultural products failed to match the large increase in supply even though there were large increases in income (and population) because the demand for agricultural products is *income* inelastic (that is, increases in income lead to less than proportionate increases in expenditures on farm products).

(3) The consequences of the two factors are that there has been considerable consolidation in the number of farms and the emergence of **agribusiness,** or large corporate farms, in some types of farming.

c. Farm-household income used to be well below nonfarm household incomes, but that is no longer the case because of out-migration from farming, consolidation, rising farm productivity, and government subsidies. Many farmers also supplement their farm incomes with nonfarm income from jobs in towns. Some households also operate profitable commercial farms.

3. Since the 1930s, farmers have been able to obtain various forms of public aid, but the primary purposes of the federal **government subsidies** have been to enhance and stabilize farm prices and incomes.

a. Several arguments are used to justify these expenditures, such as the poor incomes of farmers, the importance of the family farm, the hazards of farming, and market power problems.

b. The cornerstone of the federal policy to raise farm prices is the **parity concept,** which would give the farmer year after year the same real income per unit of output. It is measured by the **parity ratio,** which is the ratio of the prices received by farmers divided by the prices paid by farmers.

c. Historically, farm policy provided **price supports** at some percentage of the parity price. But because the supported price was almost always above the market price, government had to support the price by purchasing and accumulating surpluses of agricultural products; while farmers gained from this policy, there were losses for consumers and society, and problems were created in the environment and international sectors.

d. To reduce the annual and accumulated surpluses, government attempted to

(1) reduce the output (or supply) of farm products by **acreage allotments** and soil bank programs and

(2) expand the demand for farm products by finding new uses for farm products, expanding domestic demand, and increasing the foreign demand for agricultural commodities.

4. Agricultural policies designed to stabilize farm incomes and prices have not worked well. The policies have been subject to **criticisms and political debate.**

a. Economists have criticized the **parity concept** for its lack of economic logic. There is no reason why the prices received by farmers should be about equal to the prices paid by farmers over time. Prices for commodities produced by farmers and prices for products purchased change because of changes in supply and demand in different markets.

b. There are three basic **criticisms of price-support programs.**

(1) Price-support programs have confused the *symptoms* of the agricultural economic condition (a low amount of farm products and low farm incomes) with its *causes* (resource allocation) and have encouraged people to stay in agriculture.

(2) The major benefits from price-support programs are *misguided* because low-income farmers often receive small government subsidies while high-income farmers often receive large government subsidies; price supports also affect land values and become a subsidy for owners of farmland who rent their land and do not farm.

(3) The various farm programs of the federal government have often *offset* or contradicted each other. Price-support programs have tried to stabilize prices, while other programs have increased supply, thus putting downward pressure on prices.

c. The **politics of farm policy** explain why costly and extensive subsidies have persisted in the United States.

(1) Four insights from public choice theory serve to explain this development: rent-seeking behavior by farm groups, the special-interest effect that impairs public decision making, political logrolling to turn negative outcomes into positive outcomes, and the clear benefits and hidden costs of farm programs.

(2) Changing politics also explains why there has been a reduction in the political support for agricultural subsidies.

(a) There has been a decline in the farm population and its political power.

(b) The United States also is committed to reducing agricultural subsidies worldwide because they distort world trade. This U.S. support for freer trade makes it harder to support domestic farm subsidies.

5. Since the mid-1990s there have been several attempts to reform farm policy to make the farm sector more market-oriented and less dependent on government subsidies, but they have met with mixed success.

a. The **Freedom to Farm Act** of 1996 tried to change 60 years of U.S. farm policy. The law ended price supports and acreage allotments for eight agricultural commodities. In return for accepting more risk, income payments were made to farmers through the year 2002 to help them make the transition to operating in a more competitive market. The change was expected to increase agricultural output, crop diversity, and risk management by farmers. The decline in several farm commodity prices in recent years created pressure to change the Freedom to Farm Act. The U.S. government responded to the problem by increasing subsidies to farmers with emergency aid, but it was only a temporary solution.

b. The **Food, Conservation and Energy Act of 2008** is the current law and it contains three types of subsidies for farm commodities. It continues the policy of giving farmers freedom to plant and provides constant **direct payments** to farmers that are based on past crop production levels. It provides **countercyclical payments (CCPs)** that cover any gap if the market price of a commodity falls below the target price. It offers **marketing loans** on a per-unit-of-output basis from a government lender with limits on the amount of loan repayment should crop prices fall below a certain level. The 2008 legislation makes it clear that the special-interest lobby for agriculture is still strong and that agriculture will continue to receive large government subsidies in spite of the market and output distortions that result from the large subsidies.

6. (*Last Word*). Price supports and import quotas have doubled U.S. sugar prices relative to world market prices. The estimated total cost to consumers is between $1.5 and $1.9 billion per year. Import quotas have been imposed to keep low-priced foreign sugar out of the U.S. market so that price supports can be maintained. In 1975, 30 percent of U.S. sugar was imported, but today only about 20 percent is imported. This import policy has had significant effects on less developed nations and the world market for sugar. The decline in potential sugar revenue has hurt developing countries. The sugar that could have been sold in the U.S. is dumped on world markets, where the world price is then further depressed. Overall, both domestically and worldwide, the sugar program has distorted resources allocation and world trade.

■ **HINTS AND TIPS**

1. This chapter applies several economic ideas—supply and demand, elasticity, price controls, and public choice theory—that you learned about in previous chapters. If your understanding of these ideas is weak, review supply and demand and price controls in Chapter 3, elasticity in Chapter 4, and public choice theory in Chapter 17.

2. Make sure you understand the distinction between the short-run and long-run economic conditions in U.S. agriculture. There is a short-run price and income instability that involves the year-to-year changes in the prices of farm products and farm incomes. The changes in supply and demand over time have made agriculture a declining industry in the U.S. economy over the long run.

3. Figure 19.6 and the related discussion are very important to your study. The figure illustrates the economic effects that agricultural price supports have on different groups and the overall economy.

■ IMPORTANT TERMS

farm commodities

food products

agribusiness

parity concept

parity ratio

price supports

acreage allotments

Freedom to Farm Act

Food, Conservation and Energy Act of 2008

direct payments

countercyclical payments (CCPs)

marketing loan program

SELF-TEST

■ FILL-IN QUESTIONS

1. It is important to study the economics of U.S. agriculture for many reasons; it is one of the (largest, smallest) _____ industries in the nation; it provides a real-world example of pure (monopoly, competition) _____; it demonstrates the intended and unintended effects of (consumer, government) _____ policies that interfere with forces of supply and demand; it reflects the (decreased, increased) _____ globalization of agricultural markets; and it illustrates aspects of (public, private) _____ choice theory.

2. The basic cause of the short-run price and income instability in agriculture is the (elastic, inelastic) _____ demand for farm products. This demand occurs because farm products have few good (complements, substitutes) _____ and because of rapidly diminishing marginal (product, utility) _____.

3. The elasticity of demand for farm products contributes to unstable farm prices and incomes because relatively (large, small) _____ changes in the output of farm products result in relatively _____ changes in prices and incomes and because relatively _____ changes in domestic or foreign demand result in relatively _____ changes in prices and incomes.

4. From a long-run perspective, the (demand for, supply of) _____ agricultural products increased rapidly over the past 60 years because of technological

progress, but the _____ agricultural products did not increase as fast, in large part because food demand is income (elastic, inelastic) _____ and because the rate of population increase has not matched the increase in production.

5. Four arguments used to justify expenditures for farm subsidies are: the (inelastic, low) _____ income of farmers, the (cost, value) _____ of the family farm as a U.S. institution; the (rent-seeking, hazards) _____ of farming from many natural disasters; and the fact that the farmers sell their output in (purely, imperfectly) _____ competitive markets and purchase their inputs in _____ competitive markets.

6. If farmers were to receive a parity price for a product, year after year a given output would enable them to acquire a (fixed, increased) _____ amount of goods and services.

7. If the government supports farm prices at an above-equilibrium level, the results will be (shortages, surpluses) _____ that the government must (buy, sell) _____ to maintain prices at their support level.

8. With price-support programs, farmers (benefit, are hurt) _____ and consumers _____. The incomes of farmers (increase, decrease) _____, while the price consumers pay for products _____ and the quantities of the agricultural product that they purchase _____.

9. Society also is hurt by farm price-support programs because they encourage economic (efficiency, inefficiency) _____, an (over, under) _____ allocation of resources to agriculture, and a (small, large) _____ government bureaucracy for agriculture.

10. Agricultural price supports have (increased, decreased) _____ domestic agricultural production and _____ the use of inputs such as pesticides and fertilizers, resulting in (positive, negative) _____ effects on the environment.

11. The above-equilibrium price supports make U.S. agricultural markets (more, less) _____ attractive to foreign producers who try to sell _____ of their agricultural products in the United States. This activity is likely to (increase, decrease) _____ trade barriers, and _____ the efficiency of U.S. agriculture. The trade barriers will have a (negative, positive) _____ effect on developing nations, which are often dependent on worldwide agricultural markets.

12. To bring the equilibrium level of prices in the market up to their support level, government has attempted to (increase, decrease) _____ the demand for and to _____ the supply of farm products.

13. To decrease supply, the federal government has used (acreage-allotment, rent-seeking) _____ programs. To increase demand, the federal government has encouraged (new, old) _____ uses for agricultural products and sought to increase domestic and foreign (supply, demand) _____ for agricultural products through the domestic food stamps program or the foreign Food for Peace program.

14. The policies of government to support agricultural prices and income (have, have not) _____ worked well over the past 60 years because they have confused the symptoms of the farm economic condition, which are (high, low) _____ prices and incomes, with its root cause, which is (efficient, inefficient) _____ allocation of resources.

15. There are two other criticisms. Many of the benefits from farm price supports go to (high, low) _____-income farmers instead of _____-income farmers. The effects of price-support programs of the federal government are (reinforced, offset) _____ by other government programs.

16. Despite these criticisms, farm policies have received strong support in Congress over the years; the result of this can be explained by insights from (monopoly, public choice) _____ theory. When farm groups lobby for federal programs that transfer income to them, they are exhibiting (parity, rent-seeking) _____ behavior. There is also a special-interest effect because the costs to individual taxpayers are (large, small) _____ but the benefits to farmers are _____ from farm programs.

17. In addition, when agricultural groups or farm-state politicians trade votes to turn negative into positive outcomes, they are using political (allotments, logrolling) _____. Another public choice problem with farm subsidies is that the benefits of farm programs are (clear, hidden) _____, while much of the costs are _____ in the form of higher consumer prices for agricultural products.

18. There are also world (aid, trade) _____ considerations from agricultural subsidies. The effects of supports for the prices of agricultural products in the United States and European Union (EU) have been to (increase, decrease) _____ domestic production in these nations, _____ export

subsidies for farm products in these nations, and _____ world prices for agricultural products, thus distorting worldwide trade in agricultural products.

19. Calls for reforms of farm policy in the United States led in 1996 to the Freedom to (Trade, Farm) _____ Act that sought to (expand, eliminate) _____ price supports for eight farm crops in return for giving farmers freedom to (plant, export) _____ crops. To make the transition from price-supported agriculture to market-oriented agriculture, farmers received transition (licenses, payments) _____, but the fall in several crop prices later in the decade led to emergency measures to (increase, decrease) _____ farm subsidies.

20. The Food, Conservation and Energy Act of 2008 continues the policy of freedom to (export, plant) _____, and provides income support for farmers in the form of direct (insurance, payments) _____. In addition, there are price-support subsidies in the form of countercyclical (insurance, payments) _____ and marketing (campaigns, loans) _____. As a result of the act, the government's subsidy for agriculture has (increased, decreased) _____, which in turn contributes to _____ crop production and low crop price. This resulting condition then leads to demands for (more, less) _____ farm subsidies.

■ **TRUE–FALSE QUESTIONS**

Circle T if the statement is true, F if it is false.

1. Agriculture experiences year-to-year fluctuations in farm prices and farm incomes.　**T　F**

2. The demand for farm products is price elastic. **T　F**

3. The quantities of agricultural commodities produced tend to be fairly *insensitive* to changes in agricultural prices because a large percentage of farmers' total costs are variable.　**T　F**

4. The foreign demand for farm products is relatively stable.　**T　F**

5. Appreciation of the dollar will tend to decrease the demand for farm products.　**T　F**

6. The supply of agricultural products has tended to increase more rapidly than the demand for these products in the United States.　**T　F**

7. Most of the recent technological advances in agriculture have been initiated by farmers.　**T　F**

8. The demand for farm products is income elastic. **T　F**

9. One reason for the lagging demand for U.S. farm products is a slow rate of population growth in the United States.   **T F**

10. The consequences over time of supply and demand conditions in agriculture are that minimum efficient scale has increased.   **T F**

11. The size of the farm population in the United States has declined in both relative and absolute terms since about 1960.   **T F**

12. The major aim of agricultural policy in the United States for the past 75 years or so was to support agricultural prices and incomes.   **T F**

13. If the prices paid by farmers were 500% higher than in the base year and the price received by farmers were 400% higher than in the base year, the parity ratio would be 125%.   **T F**

14. Application of the parity concept to farm prices causes farm prices to decline and results in agricultural surpluses.   **T F**

15. When government supports farm prices at above-equilibrium levels, it can reduce the annual surpluses of agricultural commodities either by increasing the supply or by decreasing the demand for them.   **T F**

16. The acreage allotment program was designed to decrease the supply of farm products.   **T F**

17. Restricting the number of acres that farmers use to grow agricultural products has been only a partially successful method of reducing surpluses because farmers tend to cultivate their land more intensively when the acreage is reduced.   **T F**

18. Public policy has been effective in alleviating the resource allocation problem in U.S. agriculture, not just the symptoms.   **T F**

19. The price-income support programs for agriculture have given the most benefit to those farmers with the least need for the government assistance.   **T F**

20. A political action committee organized by a group of sugar beet farmers to lobby Congress for subsidies for sugar beets is an example of political logrolling.   **T F**

21. The reason that farmers, who are a small proportion of the population, can impose a large cost to taxpayers in the form of agricultural subsidies is because the cost imposed on each individual taxpayer is small and not given much attention by each taxpayer.   **T F**

22. One hidden cost of agricultural price-support programs is the higher prices that consumers pay for the product.   **T F**

23. The decline in farm population and in the related political representation in rural areas is one reason why political support for farm subsidies has increased.   **T F**

24. Domestic farm subsidies distort world trade and contribute to the inefficiencies in the international allocation of agricultural resources.   **T F**

25. Although the Food, Conservation and Energy Act of 2008 helped reduce the risk for farmers and raised farm incomes, it continues the federal government policy of subsidizing agricultural production.   **T F**

■ **MULTIPLE-CHOICE QUESTIONS**

Circle the letter that corresponds to the best answer.

1. The inelasticity of demand for agricultural products can be explained by
(a) parity ratio
(b) economies of scale
(c) rent-seeking behavior
(d) diminishing marginal utility

2. The inelastic demand for agricultural products means that a relatively small increase in output will result in a relatively
(a) small increase in farm prices and incomes
(b) large decrease in farm prices and incomes
(c) small decrease in farm prices and a relatively large increase in farm incomes
(d) large increase in farm prices and a relatively small decrease in farm incomes

3. The reason that large declines in farm prices do not significantly reduce farm production in the short run is that farmers'
(a) fixed costs are high relative to their variable costs
(b) variable costs are high relative to their fixed costs
(c) prices received are greater than prices paid for agricultural products
(d) prices paid are greater than prices received for agricultural products

4. One reason for the year-to-year instability of agricultural product prices is
(a) stable production of domestic agricultural products
(b) stable production of foreign agricultural products
(c) fluctuations in incomes received for agricultural products
(d) fluctuations in the foreign demand for agricultural products

5. If, over time, the increases in the supply of an agricultural product are much greater than the increases in demand for it, the supply and demand model would suggest that the product price
(a) and quantity will both increase
(b) and quantity will both decrease
(c) will increase, but the quantity will decrease
(d) will decrease, but the quantity will increase

6. Which is a significant reason why increases in demand for agricultural products have been small relative to increases in supply?
(a) Increases in the population of the United States have been greater than increases in the productivity of agriculture.
(b) Increases in the population of the United States have been greater than decreases in the productivity of agriculture.

(c) Increases in the incomes of U.S. consumers result in less than proportionate increases in their spending on agricultural products.

(d) Increases in the incomes of U.S. consumers result in more than proportionate increases in their spending on agricultural products.

7. Given an inelastic demand for farm products, a more rapid increase in the

(a) demand for such products relative to the supply creates a persistent downward pressure on farm incomes

(b) supply for such products relative to the demand creates a persistent upward pressure on farm incomes

(c) supply for such products relative to the demand creates a persistent downward pressure on farm incomes

(d) demand for such products relative to the supply creates a persistent downward pressure on agricultural product prices

8. The consequences of the long-run supply and demand conditions in agriculture are that minimum efficient scale has

(a) increased and crop prices have decreased

(b) increased and crop prices have increased

(c) decreased and crop prices have increased

(d) decreased and crop prices have decreased

9. The migration out of farming over the years, consolidation in farming, greater farm productivity, and government subsidies have caused farm-household incomes to

(a) decrease relative to nonfarm household incomes

(b) increase relative to nonfarm household incomes

(c) stay about the same as nonfarm household incomes

(d) be more stable than nonfarm household incomes

10. Which is a major rationale for public aid for agriculture in the United States?

(a) Farmers are more affected by competition from foreign producers than other parts of the economy.

(b) Farmers sell their products in highly competitive markets and buy resources in highly imperfect markets.

(c) Technological progress in farming has greatly increased the demand for farm products.

(d) The demand for farm products is income elastic.

11. Farm parity means that over time,

(a) the real income of the farmer remains constant

(b) a given output will furnish the farmer with a constant amount of real income

(c) the purchasing power of the farmer's nominal income remains constant

(d) the nominal income of the farmer will buy a constant amount of goods and services

12. If the index of prices paid by farmers was 1000 and the price received by farmers was 600, then the parity ratio would be

(a) 2.1 (or 210%)

(b) 1.7 (or 170%)

(c) 0.6 (or 60%)

(d) 0.4 (or 40%)

13. The necessary consequence of the government's support of agricultural prices at an above-equilibrium level is

(a) a surplus of agricultural products

(b) increased consumption of agricultural products

(c) reduced production of agricultural products

(d) the destruction of agricultural products

14. Another consequence of having government support farm prices at an above-equilibrium level is that consumers pay higher prices for farm products, and

(a) consume more of these products and pay higher taxes

(b) consume less of these products and pay higher taxes

(c) consume more of these products and pay lower taxes

(d) consume less of these products and pay lower taxes

Use the graph below to answer Questions 15, 16, and 17. D *is the demand for and* S *is the supply of a certain product.*

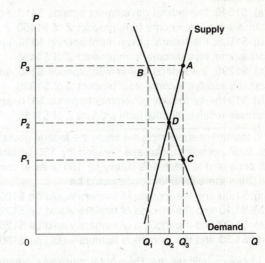

15. If the federal government supported the price of this product at P_3, the total amount it would have to spend to purchase the surplus of the product would be

(a) $0Q_3AP_3$

(b) Q_1Q_3AB

(c) P_1CAP_3

(d) $0Q_1BP_3$

16. With a support price of P_3, the total income of producers of the product will be

(a) $0Q_3AP_3$

(b) $0Q_1BP_3$

(c) $0Q_3CP_1$

(d) $0Q_2DP_2$

17. With a support price of P_3, the amount spent by consumers will be

(a) $0Q_3AP_3$

(b) $0Q_1BP_3$

(c) $0Q_2DP_2$

(d) Q_1Q_3AB

*Answer Questions 18, 19, and 20 on the basis of the demand and supply schedules for agricultural product **Z** as shown below.*

Pounds of Z demanded	Price	Pounds of Z supplied
850	$1.30	1150
900	1.20	1100
950	1.10	1050
1000	1.00	1000
1050	.90	950
1100	.80	900
1150	.70	850

18. If the federal government supports the price of **Z** at $1.30 a pound, then at this price, there is
(a) a surplus of 200 pounds of **Z**
(b) a surplus of 300 pounds of **Z**
(c) a surplus of 400 pounds of **Z**
(d) a shortage of 400 pounds of **Z**

19. With a federal price support of $1.30 a pound, consumers spend
(a) $1040, the federal government spends $410, and farmers receive income from product **Z** of $1450
(b) $1105, the federal government spends $390, and farmers receive income from product **Z** of $1495
(c) $1296, the federal government spends $240, and farmers receive income from product **Z** of $1320
(d) $1045, the federal government spends $110, and farmers receive income from product **Z** of $1155

20. If, instead of supporting the price, the federal government took actions to increase demand by 150 units at each price and to decrease supply by 150 units at each price, then the equilibrium price would be
(a) $1.00 and the income of farmers would be $1000
(b) $1.10 and the income of farmers would be $1320
(c) $1.20 and the income of farmers would be $1260
(d) $1.30 and the income of farmers would be $1300

21. To help eliminate the agricultural surpluses created by farm subsidies, the federal government has tried to
(a) increase supply and demand
(b) decrease supply and demand
(c) increase supply and decrease demand
(d) decrease supply and increase demand

22. Which is a major criticism of agricultural price supports?
(a) Restricting agricultural output increases farm prices but reduces farm incomes when demand is inelastic.
(b) The principal beneficiaries of these supports have been farmers with low incomes who would be better off in another type of work.
(c) They fail to treat the underlying problem of the misallocation of resources between agriculture and the rest of the economy.
(d) They duplicate other economic policies that are designed to increase the prices for agricultural products.

23. When farmers and farm organizations lobby Congress for a larger appropriation for agricultural price and income programs, according to public choice theory this action would be an example of
(a) confusing symptoms with causes
(b) misguided subsidies
(c) rent-seeking behavior
(d) political logrolling

24. Which has been a consequence of protective trade barriers for agricultural products established by the European Union (EU)?
(a) higher prices for U.S. agricultural products
(b) restriction of exports of EU agricultural products
(c) lower worldwide prices for agricultural products
(d) more sales of U.S. agricultural products to the EU

25. A consistent feature in both the Freedom to Farm Act of 1996 and the Food, Conservation and Energy Act of 2008 was
(a) decreasing crop price-support subsidies for farmers
(b) giving farmers the freedom to plant various agriculture crops
(c) bolstering of the domestic and foreign demand for U.S. agricultural products
(d) improving of the parity ratio so that the prices farmers paid for their inputs were similar to the prices they received for their output

■ **PROBLEMS**

1. The following table is a demand schedule for agricultural product **X.**

(1) Price	(2) Bushels of X demanded	(3) Bushels of X demanded
$2.00	600	580
1.80	620	600
1.60	640	620
1.40	660	640
1.20	680	660
1.00	700	680
.80	720	700
.60	740	720

a. Based on columns 1 and 2, is demand elastic or inelastic in the price range given? _____
b. Based on columns 1 and 2, if the amount of **X** produced should increase from 600 to 700 bushels, the income of producers of **X** would _____ from $ _____ to $ _____; an increase of _____% in the amount of **X** produced would cause income to _____ by _____%.
c. If the amount of **X** produced were 700 bushels and the demand for **X** decreased from that shown in columns 1 and 2 to that shown in columns 1 and 3, the price of X would _____ from $ _____ to $ _____; the income of farmers would _____ from $ _____ to $ _____.

d. Assume that the government supports a price of $1.80, that the demand for **X** is that shown in columns 1 and 2, and that farmers grow 720 bushels of **X**.
(1) At the supported price there will be a surplus of

_____ bushels of X.
(2) If the government buys this surplus at the support price the cost to the taxpayers of purchasing the surplus is $_____.
(3) The total income of the farmers producing product **X** when they receive the support price of $1.80 per bushel

for their entire crop of 720 bushels is $_____.
(4) Had farmers sold the crop of 720 bushels at the free-market price, the price of **X** would be only

$_____ per bushel, and the total income of these

farmers would be $_____.
(5) The gain to farmers producing **X** from the price-

support program is therefore $_____.
(6) In addition to the cost to taxpayers of purchasing

the surplus, consumers pay a price that is $_____ greater than the free-market price and receive a quan-

tity of **X** that is _____ bushels less than they would have received in a free market.

2. The following table gives the index of prices farmers paid in three different years. The price farmers received in year 1, the base year, for a certain agricultural product was $3.50 per bushel.

Year	Index of prices paid	Parity price	Price received	Parity ratio
1	100	$3.50	$3.50	100%
2	120	_____	3.78	_____%
3	200	_____	5.25	_____%

a. Compute the parity price of the product in years 2 and 3 and enter them in the table.
b. The prices received for the product in each year are also shown in the table. Complete the table by computing the parity *ratio* in years 2 and 3. (*Hint:* It is *not* necessary to construct an index of prices received in order to compute the parity ratio. This ratio can be computed by dividing the price received by the parity price.)

3. The demand schedule for agricultural product **Y** is given in columns 1 and 2 of the following table.

(1) Price	(2) Bales of Y demanded	(3) Bales of Y demanded
$5.00	40,000	41,000
4.75	40,200	41,200
4.50	40,400	41,400
4.25	40,600	41,600
4.00	40,800	41,800
3.75	41,000	42,000
3.50	41,200	42,200

a. If farmers were persuaded by the government to reduce the size of their crop from 41,000 to 40,000

bales, the income of farmers would _____ from

$_____ to $_____.
b. If the crop remained constant at 41,000 bales and the demand for **Y** increased to that shown in columns

1 and 3, the income of farmers would _____ from

$_____ to $_____.

4. Suppose the demand for sow jowls during a certain period of time was that shown in the table below and the federal government wished to support the price of sow jowls at $.70 a pound.

Price (per pound)	Quantity demanded (pounds)
$1.00	1000
.90	1020
.80	1040
.70	1060
.60	1080
.50	1100
.40	1120

a. If the output of sow jowls were 1100 pounds during that period of time, the market price of sow jowls would be

$_____ and the federal government would (buy, sell)

_____ (how many?) _____ pounds of sow jowls.
b. But if the output were 1000 pounds during that period of time, the market price of sow jowls would be

$_____ and the federal government would not have to intervene.

■ **SHORT ANSWER AND ESSAY QUESTIONS**

1. Why are the economics of agriculture and agricultural policy important topics for study?

2. What are the causes of the short-run price and income instability in U.S. agriculture?

3. Why does the demand for agricultural products tend to be inelastic? What are the implications for agriculture?

4. What have been the specific causes of the large increases in the supply of agricultural products over time?

5. Why has the demand for agricultural products failed to increase at the same rate as the supply of these products?

6. What have been the consequences of long-run supply and demand conditions in agriculture?

7. What is meant by "the farm program"? What particular aspect of the farm program has traditionally received the major attention of farmers and their representatives in Congress?

8. Why do agricultural interests claim that farmers have a special right to aid from the federal government?

9. Explain the concept of parity and the parity ratio.

10. Why is the result of government-supported prices invariably a surplus of farm commodities?

11. What are the effects of farm price-support programs on farmers, consumers, and resource allocation in the economy?

12. Identify and describe three ways that society at large loses from farm price-support programs.

13. Explain how U.S. farm policy may cause environmental problems.

14. Discuss the effects of farm price-support programs on international trade and developing nations.

15. What programs has the government used to try to restrict farm production? Why have these programs been relatively unsuccessful in limiting agricultural production?

16. How has the federal government tried to increase the demand for farm products?

17. Explain the three major criticisms of agricultural price supports.

18. How can public choice theory explain the persistence of federal government support for farm subsidies for so many decades? Discuss the application of rent-seeking behavior, the special-interest effect, political logrolling, and hidden costs to subsidies for agriculture.

19. What domestic and international factors are contributing to the reduction in political support for agricultural subsidies?

20. What are the key features of the Freedom to Farm Act of 1996 and the Food, Conservation and Energy Act of 2008? In what ways are the two acts similar and how are they different in terms of government intervention in agriculture, the provision of agricultural price supports, and income payments to farmers?

ANSWERS

Chapter 19 Agriculture: Economics and Policy

FILL-IN QUESTIONS

1. largest, competition, government, increased, public
2. inelastic, substitutes, utility
3. small, large, small, large
4. supply of, demand for, inelastic
5. low, value, hazards, purely, imperfectly
6. fixed
7. surpluses, buy
8. benefit, are hurt, increase, increase, decrease
9. inefficiency, over, large
10. increased, increased, negative
11. more, more, increase, decrease, negative
12. increase, decrease
13. acreage-allotment, new, demand
14. have not, low, inefficient
15. high, low, offset
16. public choice, rent-seeking, small, large
17. logrolling, clear, hidden
18. trade, increase, increase, decrease
19. Farm, eliminate, plant, payments, increase
20. plant, payments, payments, loans, increased, increased, more

TRUE–FALSE QUESTIONS

1. T, p. 392	10. T, pp. 396–397	19. T, p. 402
2. F, p. 392	11. T, p. 397	20. F, p. 403
3. F, pp. 393–394	12. T, p. 398	21. T, p. 403
4. F, p. 394	13. F, p. 399	22. T, p. 403
5. T, p. 394	14. F, p. 399	23. F, p. 403
6. T, pp. 395–396	15. F, p. 399	24. T, pp. 403–405
7. F, p. 395	16. T, p. 401	25. T, p. 406
8. F, pp. 395–396	17. T, p. 401	
9. T, pp. 395–396	18. F, pp. 402–403	

MULTIPLE-CHOICE QUESTIONS

1. d, p. 392	10. b, p. 398	19. b, p. 399
2. b, pp. 392–393	11. b, p. 399	20. d, p. 399
3. a, pp. 393–394	12. c, p. 399	21. d, p. 401
4. d, p. 394	13. a, p. 399	22. c, pp. 402–403
5. d, pp. 394–396	14. b, p. 399	23. c, p. 403
6. c, pp. 395–396	15. b, p. 399	24. c, pp. 403–405
7. c, pp. 396–397	16. a, p. 399	25. b, pp. 405–406
8. a, pp. 396–397	17. b, p. 399	
9. b, pp. 397–398	18. b, p. 399	

PROBLEMS

1. *a.* inelastic; *b.* decrease, 1200.00, 700.00, 16.67, decrease, 41.67; *c.* fall, 1.00, 0.80, fall, 700.00, 560.00; *d.* (1) 100, (2) 180, (3) 1296, (4) 0.80, 576, (5) 720, (6) 1.00, 100
2. *a.* 4.20, 7.00; *b.* 90, 75
3. *a.* increase, 153,750.00, 200,000.00; *b.* increase, 153,750.00, 205,000.00
4. *a.* .50, buy, 40; *b.* 1.00

SHORT ANSWER AND ESSAY QUESTIONS

1. p. 391	8. p. 398	15. p. 401
2. pp. 392–394	9. p. 399	16. p. 401
3. p. 392	10. p. 399	17. pp. 402–403
4. pp. 392–393	11. pp. 399–400	18. p. 403
5. pp. 393–394	12. p. 400	19. pp. 403–405
6. pp. 394–397	13. p. 400	20. pp. 405–406
7. p. 398	14. p. 400	

Income Inequality, Poverty, and Discrimination

Chapter 20 examines three current problems in the economy of the United States. The chapter begins with a look at the facts of **income inequality.** You will discover that there is substantial income inequality in the United States and learn how it is measured with the Lorenz curve and Gini ratio. You should also note that the degree of income inequality for individuals and households will be less over time because of income mobility and because government taxes and transfer payments reduce the amount of income inequality.

The chapter discusses the multiple factors that contribute to income inequality. The seven causes that are described should indicate to you that there is no simple explanation as to why some people have more income than others. It is not the result of some grand conspiracy; it can be attributed to ability differences, education and training, discrimination, preferences for jobs and risk, wealth, market power, and luck or misfortune.

Over time there have been changes in the relative distribution of income that indicate income inequality in the United States is increasing. In this section of the chapter, you will learn about the probable reasons for growing income inequality that include shifts in the demand for skilled labor, changes in the demographics of the workforce, and other factors.

A case can be made for both income equality and income inequality. Few people, however, would advocate that there should be an absolutely equal distribution of income. The question to be decided is not one of inequality or equality but of how much or how little inequality there should be. A major insight from the chapter is that there is a fundamental **trade-off between equality and efficiency** in the economy. If the society wants more equality, it will have to give up some economic efficiency in the form of less output and employment.

The reason for the focus on income distribution is ultimately the concern about **poverty.** In the later sections of the chapter you will learn about the extent of the poverty problem, who poverty affects, and the actions government has taken to alleviate it. Recall from Chapter 16 that one economic function of government is to redistribute income. Poverty and other income distribution problems are addressed through the federal government's income-maintenance system. This system consists of **social insurance programs,** such as Social Security, and **public assistance programs,** or welfare. You will discover how these programs are designed to meet the needs of different groups, either those who are poor or those who require more stability in their incomes.

Discrimination has always been present in labor markets in the form of wage, employment, occupational, or human capital discrimination. This discrimination causes significant costs for individuals who earn lower wages or have fewer work opportunities than would otherwise be the case. There are also costs to society because valuable labor resources are being inefficiently used.

The economic analysis of labor market discrimination gives you several insights into this significant problem. The taste-for-discrimination model explains the hiring practices of prejudiced employers and the effects on the wages and employment of nonpreferred groups. You will also learn how statistical discrimination, which bases decisions on average characteristics, may disadvantage individuals. The crowding model of occupational discrimination described in the chapter also explains how occupational segregation affects pay and output in an economy.

■ **CHECKLIST**

When you have studied this chapter you should be able to

☐ Describe income inequality in the United States based on the percentage of households in income categories.

☐ Describe income inequality in the United States based on the percentage of personal income received by households in income quintiles.

☐ Explain the Lorenz curve by defining each axis, the diagonal line, and the meaning of the curve.

☐ Use a Lorenz curve to describe the degree of income inequality in the United States.

☐ Use a Gini ratio to measure income inequality.

☐ Explain the effects of time on income mobility and the distribution of U.S. income.

☐ Discuss the effects of government redistribution on income equality in the United States and illustrate the effects using a Lorenz curve.

☐ Explain the seven causes of income inequality in the United States (ability; education and training; discrimination; preferences and risks; unequal distribution of wealth; market power; and luck, connections, misfortune).

☐ Identify three probable causes of growing income inequality in the United States over the past three decades.

☐ Present a case for income equality based on the maximization of total utility.

☐ Make the case for income inequality based on incentives and efficiency.

☐ Explain the trade-off between equality and efficiency in the debate over how much income inequality there should be.

☐ Give a definition of poverty based on U.S. government standards.

☐ Describe the incidence of poverty among different demographic groups in the United States.

☐ Describe the trends in the poverty rate in the United States since 1959.

☐ Explain issues or problems with the measurement of poverty.

☐ Identify the two basic kinds of programs in the U.S. system for income maintenance.

☐ Describe the characteristics of major social insurance programs (Social Security, Medicare, and unemployment compensation).

☐ Explain the purposes of the major public assistance programs (SSI, TANF, SNAP, Medicaid, and EITC).

☐ Define discrimination and give examples of it.

☐ Use a wage equation to explain the taste-for-discrimination model in labor markets.

☐ Use a supply and demand graph to illustrate the taste-for-discrimination model in labor markets.

☐ Explain and give an example of statistical discrimination.

☐ Use the crowding model of occupational discrimination to explain differences in wages among groups and efficiency effects.

☐ Describe the costs of discrimination for society as well as for individuals.

☐ Explain the changes in the amount and distribution of wealth among families from 1995 to 2007 (*Last Word*).

■ **CHAPTER OUTLINE**

1. There is considerable *income inequality* in the United States.

  a. One way to show this inequality is with a table showing the personal distribution of income by households. In 2008, 24.7 percent of all households had annual before-tax incomes of less than $25,000, but 20.5 percent had annual incomes of $100,000 or more.

  b. A table of the personal distribution of income by households in quintiles is a second way to show the inequality. In 2008, the 20 percent of households with the lowest incomes accounted for 3.4 percent of personal income while the 20 percent of households with the highest incomes accounted for 50 percent of personal income.

  c. The degree of income inequality can be shown with a *Lorenz curve.* The percentage of households is plotted on the horizontal axis and the percentage of income is plotted on the vertical axis. The diagonal line between the two axes represents a perfectly equal distribution of income. A Lorenz curve that is bowed to the right from the diagonal shows income inequality. If the actual income distribution were perfectly equal, the Lorenz curve and the diagonal would coincide. The visual measurement of income inequality described by the Lorenz curve can be converted to a *Gini ratio,* which is the area between the Lorenz curve and the diagonal divided by the total area below the diagonal. As the income inequality increases, the ratio will increase.

  d. Income data shows that there is considerably *less* income inequality over a longer time period than a single year. In fact, there is significant *income mobility* for individuals and households over time. The longer the time period considered for individuals and households, the more equal the distribution of income.

  e. Government redistribution has had a significant effect on income distribution. The distribution of income can be examined after taxes and transfer payments. When this adjustment is made, the distribution of income is more equal. *Noncash transfers,* which provide specific goods or services, account for most of the reduction in income inequality, and they include Medicare, Medicaid, housing subsidies, subsidized school lunches, and SNAP. The effect of the government transfers is to shift the Lorenz curve toward more equality.

2. The market system is impersonal and does not necessarily result in a fair distribution of income. At least seven factors explain *why income inequality exists:*

  a. Abilities and skills differ greatly among people, which influences the work they can do and their pay.

  b. There are differences in education and training that affect wages and salaries.

  c. Discrimination in education, hiring, training, and promotion will affect incomes.

  d. People have different preferences for certain types of jobs, for their willingness to accept risk on the job, and also for the amount of leisure that will be earned through their work.

  e. Wealth can provide a source of income in the form of rents, interest, and dividends, and since there are inequalities in the distribution of wealth, it will contribute to income inequalities.

  f. Some individuals have a degree of market power in either resource or product markets that creates higher incomes.

  g. Other factors, such as luck, personal connections, and misfortunes can play a role in contributing to income inequality.

3. Income inequality in the United States has changed over time.

  a. From 1970 through 2008, the distribution of income became more unequal. In 2008 the lowest 20 percent of households received 3.4 percent of total before-tax income compared with 4.1 percent in 1970. The highest 20 percent of households received 50 percent of total before-tax income in 2008 compared with 43.3 percent in 1970.

  b. Among the factors that explain the growing income inequality in the United States over the past three decades are:

  (1) increases in the demand for highly skilled workers compared with the demand for less-skilled workers;

  (2) changes in labor demographics from the influx of less-skilled baby boomers into the labor force, the increase in dual incomes among high-wage households, and more single-parent households earning less income; and

  (3) decreases in wages for less-skilled workers and less job security because of more international trade competition, the influx of less-skilled immigrants into the labor force, and a decline in unionism.

4. An important question to answer for an economy is not whether there will be income inequality, but what is an acceptable amount of inequality.

    a. Those who *argue for equality* contend that it leads to the maximum satisfaction of consumer wants (utility) in the economy.

    b. Those who *argue for inequality* contend that equality would reduce the incentives to work, save, invest, and take risks, and that these incentives are needed if the economy is to be efficient to produce as large an output (and income) as it is possible for it to produce from its available resources.

    c. In the United States there is an *equality–efficiency trade-off.* A more nearly equal distribution of income results in less economic efficiency (a smaller output and income) and greater economic efficiency (a larger output and income) leads to a more unequal distribution of income. The debate over the right amount of inequality depends on how much output society is willing to sacrifice to reduce income inequality.

5. Aside from inequality in the distribution of income, there is a great concern today with the problem of poverty in the United States.

    a. Using the generally accepted definition, the *poverty rate,* which is the percentage of the U.S. population living in poverty, was 13.2 percent in 2008.

    b. The poor are found among many groups and in all parts of the nation. Compared with the poverty rate for the population as a whole (13.2%), there are higher poverty rates among female-headed households (28.7%), African-Americans (24.7%), foreign-born who are not citizens (23.3%), Hispanics (23.2%), children under 18 years of age (19%), and women (14.4%).

    c. The poverty rate has varied over time, as shown in Figure 20.5 of the text. It fell significantly from 1959–1969 and was in the 11–13 percent range in the 1970s. The rate rose around periods of recession in the economy (early 1980s and early 1990s), and fluctuated in the 11–13 percent range in other periods.

    d. There are issues with the measurement of poverty. Some contend that it is understated because the official income thresholds are set low and do not cover the high cost of living in urban areas. Others contend that the poverty definition understates the standard of living for many who are classified as poor because the poverty rate is an income and not a consumption measure.

6. The *income-maintenance system* of the United States is intended to reduce poverty and includes both social insurance and public assistance (welfare) programs. These are *entitlement programs* because all eligible persons are granted or entitled to the benefits of the programs.

    a. The principal *social insurance programs* are *Social Security* and *Medicare.* They are financed by payroll taxes levied on employers and employees. The unemployment insurance programs that provide *unemployment compensation,* maintained by the states and financed by taxes on employers, are also social insurance programs in the United States.

    b. The *public assistance programs* include *Supplemental Security Income (SSI), Temporary Assistance for Needy Families (TANF),* the *Supplemental Nutrition Assistance Program (SNAP),* and *Medicaid.* The *earned-income tax credit (EITC)* is for low-income working households, with or without children. Other public assistance programs provide noncash transfers for education, job training, and housing assistance.

7. *Discrimination* involves giving people different and inferior treatment in employment or living situations (such as hiring, education, training, promotion, wages, working conditions, or housing) based on some unrelated factor or characteristic (such as race, ethnicity, gender, or religion). Discrimination reflects a personal bias or prejudice against a particular group.

8. The economic analysis of discrimination provides some insights even though the issue is complex and multifaceted.

    a. The *taste-for-discrimination model* explains prejudice using demand theory. The model assumes that a prejudiced employer is willing to pay a "price" to avoid interactions with a nonpreferred group.

    (1) The *discrimination coefficient* measures in monetary units the cost of the employer's prejudice. An employer will hire nonpreferred workers only if their wage rates are below those of the preferred workers by an amount at least equal to the discrimination coefficient.

    (2) In the supply and demand model for nonpreferred workers, an increase in the prejudice of employers will decrease the demand for this labor, the number of workers, and their wage rate. A decrease in the prejudice of employers will increase the demand for this labor, the number employed, and the wage rate.

    (3) The taste-for-discrimination model suggests that in the very long run, competition will reduce discrimination, but critics question this conclusion, given the insufficient progress in reducing discrimination over time in the United States.

    b. *Statistical discrimination* involves judging people based on the average characteristics of the group to which they belong instead of productivity or personal characteristics. In labor markets, employers may stereotype workers by applying the average characteristics of the group in work assessments of individual members of that group. The practice may be profitable and on average it may produce correct decisions, but it fails to take into account the individual skills and capabilities and limits opportunities for workers.

    c. The practice of *occupational segregation* suggests that women and minorities are crowded into a small number of occupations. In this crowding model, the supply of these workers is large relative to the demand for them, and thus their wage rates and incomes are lower in these crowded occupations. Eliminating occupational segregation would raise wage rates and incomes for these workers and also increase the economy's output.

    d. Discrimination imposes a cost to society as well as to individuals. The cost to individuals comes in the form of lower wages, fewer job opportunities, inferior treatment, and poorer working or living conditions. The costs to society come in the form of reduced total output and income for the economy. These costs arise because discrimination creates artificial barriers to competition.

9. (*Last Word*). The Federal Reserve's Survey of Consumer Finances shows that median and average family wealth, adjusted for the effects of inflation, rose considerably from 1995 to 2007. The distribution of this wealth is highly unequal and there has been a general trend to greater income inequality of wealth since 1995.

■ **HINTS AND TIPS**

1. The distribution of income, poverty, and discrimination raise issues of **normative economics.** For example, some people may say that "no person should be allowed to make that much money" when a high salary is reported in the media for a sports star or business executive. This chapter focuses on the **positive economics** related to the three topics. It explains and analyzes why incomes differ, why there is poverty, and why discrimination is costly for individuals and society.

2. The **Lorenz curve** looks more complicated than it really is. The curve shows how the cumulative percentage of income is distributed across the percentage of households. The easiest way to learn about the curve is to use income and household data to construct one. Problem 1 in this chapter will help you with that objective.

■ **IMPORTANT TERMS**

income inequality

Lorenz curve

Gini ratio

income mobility

noncash transfers

equality—efficiency
  trade-off

poverty rate

entitlement programs

social insurance programs

Social Security

Medicare

unemployment
  compensation

public assistance programs

Supplemental Security
  Income (SSI)

Temporary Assistance for
  Needy Families (TANF)

Supplemental Nutrition
  Assistance Program
  (SNAP)

Medicaid

earned income tax credit
  (EITC)

discrimination

taste-for-discrimination
  model

discrimination coefficient

statistical discrimination

occupational segregation

SELF-TEST

■ **FILL-IN QUESTIONS**

1. The data on the distribution of personal income by households suggest that there is considerable income (equality, inequality) _____ in the United States. The data show that households with annual incomes of less than $10,000 are about (7.1, 20.5) _____ percent of all households, and households with $100,000 or more in income are about _____ percent of all households.

2. Income inequality can be portrayed graphically by drawing a (supply, Lorenz) _____ curve.

a. When such a curve is plotted, the cumulative percentage of (income, households) _____ is measured along the horizontal axis, and the cumulative percentage of _____ is measured along the vertical axis.

b. The curve that would show a completely (perfectly) equal distribution of income is a diagonal line that would run from the (lower, upper) _____ left to the _____ right corner of the graph.

c. The extent or degree of income inequality is measured by the area that lies between the line of complete equality and the (horizontal axis, Lorenz curve) _____.

d. The Gini ratio measures the area between the line of equality and the Lorenz curve (multiplied, divided) _____ by the total area below the line of equality.

3. One major limitation with census data on the distribution of income in the United States is that the income-accounting period is too (short, long) _____. There appears to be significant income (mobility, loss) _____ over time. Also, the longer the time period considered, the (more, less) _____ equal is the distribution of income.

4. The tax system and the transfer programs in the U.S. economy significantly (reduce, expand) _____ the degree of inequality in the distribution of income. The distribution of household income is substantially less equal (before, after) _____ taxes and transfers are taken into account and substantially more equal _____ taxes and transfers are taken into account.

5. As described in the text, the important factors that explain income inequality are: differences in _____; education and _____; labor market _____; differences in job preferences and _____; the unequal distribution of _____; market _____; and _____, connections, and misfortune.

6. Since 1970, the distribution of income by quintiles has become (more, less) _____ unequal. The data show that since 1970 the lowest 20 percent of households are receiving a (greater, lesser) _____ percentage of total income and the highest 20 percent of households are receiving a _____ percentage of total income.

7. The causes of the growing inequality of incomes are (more, less) _____ demand for highly skilled workers, entrance into the labor force of _____ -experienced baby boomers, and _____ households headed by single-wage earners. Other factors include (more, less) _____ international competition that has reduced the average wage of low-skilled workers, _____ immigration that has increased the number of low-income households, and _____ unionism.

8. Those who argue for the equal distribution of income contend that it results in the maximization of total (income, utility) _____ in the economy, while those who argue for the unequal distribution of income believe it results in a greater total _____.

9. The fundamental trade-off is between equality and (welfare, efficiency) _____. This means that less income equality leads to a (greater, smaller) _____ total output, and a larger total output requires (more, less) _____ income inequality.

10. The economic problem for a society that wants more equality is how to (minimize, maximize) _____ the adverse effects on economic efficiency.

11. Using the official definition of poverty for 2008, the poor included any household of four with an income of less than ($21,834; $36,834) _____ and any individual with an income of less than ($10,201; $20,201) _____ a year. In 2008, (13.2, 26.4) _____ percent of the population, or about (39.8, 77.6) _____ million people were poor.

12. Poverty tends to be concentrated among the (children, elderly) _____, among (whites, African-Americans) _____, and in households headed by (men, women) _____.

13. The measurement of poverty rates is not without criticisms. Some contend that the high cost of living in major metropolitan areas means that poverty rates are (over, under) _____-reported by official statistics. Others contend that poverty rates would be lower in the United States if statistics were based on (income, consumption) _____ and the standard of living.

14. One part of the income-maintenance system in the United States consists of social insurance programs such as (Social Security, AFDC) _____, (Medicare, Medicaid) _____, and (employment, unemployment) _____ compensation.

15. The other part of the income-maintenance system consists of public assistance or welfare programs such as (Social Security, SSI) _____, (Medicare,

Medicaid) _____, and SNAP. Also included in public assistance programs are state-administered ones that provide cash assistance for households with children or (EITC, TANF) _____, and a tax credit program for low-income working households, or _____. Other public assistance programs offer help in the form of (cash, noncash) _____ transfers, such as rent subsidies for housing and education assistance such as Head Start.

16. In the taste-for-discrimination model, the discrimination coefficient *d* measures the (utility, disutility) _____ that prejudiced employers experience when they must interact with those they are biased against. This coefficient is measured in monetary units and becomes part of the (benefit, cost) _____ of hiring nonpreferred workers. The prejudiced employer will hire nonpreferred workers only if their wage rate is (above, below) _____ that of the preferred workers by at least the amount of the discrimination coefficient.

17. An increase in the prejudice of employers against nonpreferred workers will (increase, decrease) _____ their wage rate and the number employed; a decrease in the prejudice of employers against nonpreferred workers will (increase, decrease) _____ their wage rate and the number employed.

18. When employers base employment decisions about individuals on the average characteristics of groups of workers, this is (reverse, statistical) _____ discrimination. The decisions that firms make based on this type of discrimination may be (irrational, rational) _____ and profitable, on average, but hurt individuals to whom the averages (do, do not) _____ apply.

19. The occupational discrimination that pushes women and African-Americans into a small number of occupations in which the supply of labor is large relative to the demand for it is explained by the (managerial-opposition, crowding) _____ model. Because supply is large relative to demand, wages and incomes in these occupations are (high, low) _____. The reduction or elimination of this occupational discrimination would result in a (more, less) _____ efficient allocation of the labor resources of the economy and (an expansion, a contraction) _____ in the domestic output.

20. Discrimination (increases, decreases) _____ the wages of workers in the discriminated group and _____ the wages of workers in the preferred group; it _____ economic efficiency and _____ total output in the economy.

■ TRUE–FALSE QUESTIONS

Circle T if the statement is true, F if it is false.

1. If you knew the average income in the United States, you would know a great deal about income inequality in the United States.   **T F**

2. The data on the distribution of personal income by households in the United States indicates that there is considerable income inequality.   **T F**

3. In a Lorenz curve, the percentage of households in each income class is measured along the horizontal axis and the percentage of total income received by those households is measured on the vertical axis.   **T F**

4. Income mobility is the movement of individuals or households from one income quintile to another over time. **T F**

5. Income is less equally distributed over a longer time period than a shorter time period.   **T F**

6. The distribution of income in the United States *after* taxes and transfers are taken into account is more equal than it is *before* taxes and transfers are taken into account. **T F**

7. Differences in preferences for market work relative to nonmarket activities are one reason for income differences in the United States.   **T F**

8. The ownership of wealth is fairly equally distributed across households in the United States.   **T F**

9. Neither luck nor misfortune is a factor contributing to income inequality in the United States.   **T F**

10. From 1970 to 2008, there was an increase in income inequality in the United States.   **T F**

11. A significant contributor to the growing income inequality of the past three decades was the greater demand for highly skilled and highly educated workers.   **T F**

12. Growing income inequality means that the "rich are getting richer" in terms of absolute income.   **T F**

13. The basic argument for an equal distribution of income is that income equality is necessary if consumer satisfaction (utility) is to be maximized.   **T F**

14. Those who favor equality in the distribution of income contend that it will lead to stronger incentives to work, save, and invest and thus to a greater national income and output.   **T F**

15. In the trade-off between equality and economic efficiency, an increase in equality will lead to an increase in efficiency.   **T F**

16. Using the government definition of poverty, 13.2 percent of the population was poor in 2008.   **T F**

17. The incidence of poverty is very high among female-headed households.   **T F**

18. Social Security, Medicare, and unemployment compensation are public assistance or welfare programs.   **T F**

19. Social insurance programs provide benefits for those who are unable to earn income because of permanent handicaps or who have no or very low income and also have dependent children.   **T F**

20. The Temporary Assistance for Needy Families (TANF) has among its provisions work requirements for those receiving welfare and a specified limit on the number of years for receiving welfare benefits.   **T F**

21. In the taste-for-discrimination model, employer preference for discrimination is measured in dollars by discrimination coefficient *d*. These employers will hire nonpreferred workers only if their wages are at least *d* dollars below the wages of preferred workers.   **T F**

22. In the taste-for-discrimination model, a decline in the prejudice of employers will decrease the demand for black workers and lower the black wage rate and the ratio of black to white wages.   **T F**

23. Statistical discrimination occurs when employers base employment decisions about individuals on the average characteristics of groups of workers.   **T F**

24. The crowding model of occupational segregation shows how white males earn higher earnings at the expense of women and minorities, who are restricted to a limited number of occupations.   **T F**

25. Discrimination redistributes income and reduces the economy's output.   **T F**

■ MULTIPLE-CHOICE QUESTIONS

Circle the letter that corresponds to the best answer.

1. Recent data on the personal distribution of income in the United States indicate that
- **(a)** average incomes are falling
- **(b)** average incomes are constant
- **(c)** there is considerable income equality
- **(d)** there is considerable income inequality

Use the graph below to answer Questions 2, 3, and 4. The graph shows four different Lorenz curves (1, 2, 3, and 4).

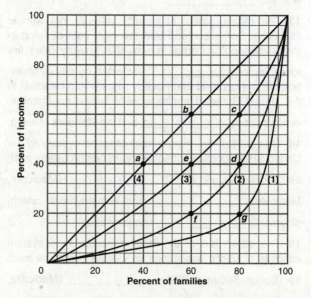

2. The greatest increase in income equality would occur with a shift in a Lorenz curve from
- (a) 1 to 2
- (b) 1 to 4
- (c) 4 to 1
- (d) 3 to 1

3. The movement from point *b* to point *f* in the graph would indicate that
- (a) 60% of households now receive 40% of income instead of 60% of income
- (b) 60% of income goes to 20% of households instead of 60% of households
- (c) 20% of income goes to 20% of households instead of 60% of households
- (d) 60% of households now receive 20% of income instead of 60% of income

4. Which change would indicate that there has been an increase in income inequality and an increase in the Gini ratio? A movement from point
- (a) *b* to *a*
- (b) *g* to *d*
- (c) *g* to *f*
- (d) *e* to *d*

5. Suppose that Laura earns $5000 in year 1 and $50,000 in year 2, while Kristin earns $50,000 in year 1 and only $5000 in year 2. Is there income inequality for the two individuals?
- (a) Both the annual and the 2-year data indicate equality.
- (b) Both the annual and the 2-year data indicate inequality.
- (c) The annual data indicate inequality, but the 2-year data indicate equality.
- (d) The annual data indicate equality, but the 2-year data indicate inequality.

6. The empirical data indicate that the tax system and the transfer programs of the government
- (a) significantly reduce the degree of inequality in the distribution of income
- (b) produce only a slight reduction in the degree of inequality in the distribution of income
- (c) significantly increase the degree of inequality in the distribution of income
- (d) produce only a slight increase in the degree of inequality in the distribution of income

7. Most of the contribution to government redistribution of income comes from
- (a) taxes
- (b) transfers
- (c) income mobility
- (d) unemployment insurance

8. Which is one cause of unequal income distribution in the United States?
- (a) an equitable distribution of wealth and property
- (b) differences in education and training
- (c) the high levels of noncash transfers
- (d) the low benefit-reduction rate

9. The fact that some individuals are willing to take riskier jobs or assume more risk in their businesses is one major reason why there are differences in
- (a) social insurance programs
- (b) entitlement programs
- (c) welfare
- (d) income

10. Inequality in the distribution of wealth contributes to
- (a) the same percentage of income received by the highest and lowest percentages of households
- (b) a smaller percentage of income received by the highest 20 percent of households
- (c) a greater percentage of income received by the highest 20 percent of households
- (d) a greater percentage of income received by the lowest 20 percent of households

11. Which would be evidence of a decrease in income inequality over time in the United States?
- (a) A decrease in the percentage of total personal income received by the lowest quintile
- (b) An increase in the percentage of total personal income received by the highest quintile
- (c) An increase in the percentage of total personal income received by the four lowest quintiles
- (d) A decrease in the percentage of total personal income received by the four lowest quintiles

12. A factor contributing to the increase in income inequality since 1970 has been
- (a) less international competition from imports
- (b) less demand for highly skilled workers in the labor force
- (c) more marriages among men and women with high income potential
- (d) more power by unions to obtain wage increases for union workers

13. Suppose Ms. Anne obtains 5 units of utility from the last dollar of income received by her, and Mr. Charles obtains 8 units of utility from the last dollar of his income. Assume both Ms. Anne and Mr. Charles have the same capacity to derive utility from income. Those who favor an equal distribution of income would
- (a) advocate redistributing income from Charles to Anne
- (b) advocate redistributing income from Anne to Charles
- (c) be content with this distribution of income between Anne and Charles
- (d) argue that any redistribution of income between them would increase total utility

14. The case for income inequality is primarily made on the basis that income inequality
- (a) is reduced by the transfer payment programs for the poor
- (b) is necessary to maintain incentives to work and produce output
- (c) depends on luck and chance, which cannot be corrected by government action
- (d) is created by education and training programs that distort the distribution of income

15. The debate over income redistribution focuses on the trade-off between equality and
(a) efficiency
(b) unemployment
(c) inflation
(d) economic freedom

16. What was the poverty rate for the U.S. population in 2008?
(a) 6.2%
(b) 9.1%
(c) 13.2%
(d) 21.5%

17. In 2008, which group had the *smallest* percentage in poverty?
(a) Hispanics
(b) households headed by women
(c) children under 18 years of age
(d) persons 65 years and older

18. An example of a social insurance program would be
(a) Medicare
(b) Medicaid
(c) SNAP
(d) Head Start

19. Which is designed to provide a nationwide minimum income for the aged, the blind, and the disabled?
(a) SSI
(b) FFS
(c) AFDC
(d) Social Security

20. The Temporary Assistance for Needy Families (TANF) program is administered by
(a) states and puts a lifetime limit of five years on receiving welfare payments
(b) religious institutions and places people in temporary jobs
(c) businesses and develops skills through education assistance
(d) the federal government and provides nutrition assistance for the needy

21. The purpose of the earned income tax credit (EITC) is to
(a) give a tax credit for spending on education and job training for welfare recipients
(b) give a tax break to businesses if they have low-income workers

(c) substitute the payment of cash for nutrition assistance if people are willing to go to work
(d) offset Social Security taxes paid by low-wage earners so they are not "taxed into poverty"

22. In a supply and demand model of the labor market for nonpreferred workers, an increase in employer prejudice will
(a) increase supply, raise the wage rate, and decrease the employment of these workers
(b) decrease supply, lower the wage rate, and decrease employment of these workers
(c) decrease demand, lower the wage rate, and decrease the employment of these workers
(d) increase demand, raise the wage rate, and increase the employment of these workers

23. Suppose the market wage rate for a preferred worker is $12 and the monetary value of disutility the employer attaches to hiring a nonpreferred worker is $3. The employer will be indifferent between either type of worker when the wage rate for nonpreferred workers is
(a) $15
(b) $12
(c) $9
(d) $3

24. When people are judged on the basis of the average characteristics of the group to which they belong rather than on their own personal characteristics or productivity, this is
(a) human-capital discrimination
(b) occupational discrimination
(c) employment discrimination
(d) statistical discrimination

25. The crowding of women and minorities into certain occupations results in
(a) higher wages and more efficient allocation of labor resources
(b) lower wages and less efficient allocation of labor resources
(c) lower wages, but more efficient allocation of labor resources
(d) lower wages, but no effect on the efficient allocation of labor resources

■ PROBLEMS

1. The distribution of personal income among households in a hypothetical economy is shown in the table below.

(1) Personal income class	(2) Percentage of all households in this class	(3) Percentage of total income received by this class	(4) Percentage of all households in this and all lower classes	(5) Percentage of total income received by this and all lower classes
Under $10,000	18	4	_____	_____
$10,000–$14,999	12	6	_____	_____
$15,000–$24,999	14	12	_____	_____
$25,000–$34,999	17	14	_____	_____
$35,000–$49,999	19	15	_____	_____
$50,000–$74,999	11	20	_____	_____
$75,000 and over	9	29	_____	_____

a. Complete the table by computing the
(1) percentage of all households in each income class and all lower classes; enter these figures in column 4.
(2) percentage of total income received by each income class and all lower classes; enter these figures in column 5.
b. From the distribution of income data in columns 4 and 5, it can be seen that
(1) households with less than $15,000 a year income

constitute the lowest _____% of all households and

receive _____% of the total income.
(2) households with incomes of $50,000 a year or more constitute the highest _____% of all households

and receive _____% of the total income.
c. Use the figures you entered in columns 4 and 5 to draw a Lorenz curve on the graph below. (Plot the seven points and the zero-zero point and connect them with a smooth curve.) Be sure to label the axes.
(1) Draw a diagonal line that would indicate complete equality in the distribution of income.

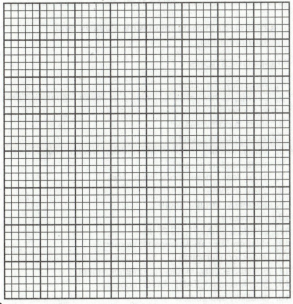

0

(2) Shade the area of the graph that shows the degree of income inequality.

2. Match the terms with the correct phrases below using the appropriate number.

1. entitlement programs **3.** public assistance programs
2. noncash transfers   **4.** social insurance programs

a. Government programs such as social insurance, SNAP, Medicare, and Medicaid that guarantee particular levels of transfer payments to all who fit the programs'

criteria.   _____

b. Government programs that pay benefits to those who are unable to earn income (because of permanent handicaps or because they have very low incomes and dependent children).   _____

c. Government transfer payments in the form of goods and services rather than money.   _____

d. Government programs that replace earnings lost when people retire or are temporarily unemployed.

_____

3. Suppose there are only three labor markets in the economy and each market is perfectly competitive. The following table contains the demand (or marginal-revenue-product) schedule for labor in each of these three markets.

Wage rate (marginal revenue product of labor per hour)	Quantity of labor (millions per hour)
$11	4
10	5
9	6
8	7
7	8
6	9
5	10
4	11
3	12

a. Assume there are 24 million homogeneous workers in the economy and that 12 million of these workers are male and 12 million are female.
(1) If the 12 million female workers can be employed only in the labor market Z, for them all to find employ-

ment the hourly wage rate must be $_____.
(2) If of the 12 million male workers 6 million are employed in labor market X and 6 million are employed in labor market Y, the hourly wage rate in labor markets

X and Y will be $_____.
b. Imagine now that the impediment to the employment of females in labor markets X and Y is removed and that as a result (and because the demand and marginal revenue product of labor are the same in all three markets) 8 million workers find employment in each labor market.
(1) In labor market Z (in which only females had previously been employed)

(a) the hourly wage rate will rise to $_____.
(b) the *decrease* in national output that results from the decrease in employment from 12 million to 8 million workers is equal to the loss of the marginal revenue products of the workers no longer employed, and it

totals $_____.
(2) In labor market X and in labor market Y (in each of which only males had previously been employed)

(a) the hourly wage rate will fall to $_____.

(b) the *increase* in national output that results from the increase in employment from 6 million to 8 million workers is equal to the marginal revenue products of the additional workers employed; the gain in each of these markets is $ million, and the total gain in the two markets is $_____.

(c) the *net* gain to society from the reallocation of female workers is $_____ million.

■ SHORT ANSWER AND ESSAY QUESTIONS

1. How much income inequality is there in the U.S. economy? Cite figures to support your conclusion.

2. What is measured along each of the two axes when a Lorenz curve is drawn?

(a) If the distribution of income were completely equal, what would the Lorenz curve look like?

(b) If one household received all of the income of the economy, what would the Lorenz curve look like?

(c) After the Lorenz curve for an economy has been drawn, how is the degree of income inequality in that economy measured?

(d) What is the difference between the Lorenz curve and the Gini ratio?

3. Explain how time affects the distribution of income and interpretations of income trends.

4. What effect do taxes and transfers have on the distribution of income in the United States? How much of this change in the distribution of income is the result of the transfer payments made by government?

5. What seven factors contribute to income inequality in the United States?

6. What has been the trend in income distribution in the United States since 1970?

7. What are three probable explanations for the increase in income inequality in the United States since 1970?

8. State the case for equal distribution of income.

9. Explain the advantage to the nation from an unequal distribution of income.

10. What is the fundamental trade-off involving income inequality? Explain the slicing the pizza pie analogy.

11. What is poverty? What is the minimum income level below which the federal government defines a person or household as "in poverty"? How many people and what percentage of the U.S. population are "in poverty" using this definition?

12. What characteristics—other than the small amounts of money they have to spend—do the greatest concentrations of the poor households of the nation *tend* to have?

13. What have been the trends in the poverty rate from 1960 to 2000? What were the trends since 2000?

14. What are some of the problems with measuring poverty that would cause it to be understated or overstated?

15. List and briefly describe three social insurance programs of the income-maintenance system of the United States.

16. Explain the major public assistance programs of the income-maintenance system of the United States. How do they cover welfare needs?

17. How can discrimination be viewed as resulting from a preference or taste for which the prejudiced employer is willing to pay? What will determine whether the prejudiced employer hires nonpreferred workers in this model?

18. How do changes in employer prejudice affect wage rates for nonpreferred workers and the ratio of wages between preferred and nonpreferred workers?

19. Explain the concept of statistical discrimination and give an example of it. How can it lead to discrimination even in the absence of prejudice?

20. Describe the economic effects of occupational segregation on the wages of women and minorities. How does this type of segregation affect the domestic output of the economy?

ANSWERS

Chapter 20 Income Inequality, Poverty, and Discrimination

FILL-IN QUESTIONS

1. inequality, 7.1, 20.5
2. Lorenz; *a.* households, income; *b.* lower, upper; *c.* Lorenz curve; *d.* divided
3. short, mobility, more
4. reduce, before, after
5. ability, training, discrimination, risks, wealth, power, luck
6. more, lesser, greater
7. more, less, more, more, more, less
8. utility, income
9. efficiency, greater, more
10. minimize
11. $21,834, $10,201, 13.2, 39.8
12. children, African-Americans, women
13. under, consumption
14. Social Security, Medicare, unemployment
15. SSI, Medicaid, TANF, EITC, noncash
16. disutility, cost, below
17. decrease, increase
18. statistical, rational, do not
19. crowding, low, more, an expansion
20. decreases, increases, decreases, decreases

TRUE–FALSE QUESTIONS

1. F, p. 411	**10.** T, p. 416	**19.** F, pp. 421–423
2. T, pp. 411–412	**11.** T, p. 416	**20.** T, p. 423
3. T, pp. 411–412	**12.** F, p. 417	**21.** T, pp. 424–425
4. T, p. 412	**13.** T, pp. 417–418	**22.** F, p. 425
5. F, pp. 412–413	**14.** F, pp. 418–419	**23.** T, p. 426
6. T, pp. 413–414	**15.** F, p. 419	**24.** T, pp. 426–427
7. T, p. 414	**16.** T, pp. 419–420	**25.** T, p. 429
8. F, pp. 414–415	**17.** T, p. 420	
9. F, p. 415	**18.** F, pp. 421–423	

MULTIPLE-CHOICE QUESTIONS

1. d, pp. 411–412
2. b, pp. 411–412
3. d, pp. 411–412
4. d, pp. 411–412
5. c, pp. 412–413
6. a, pp. 413–414
7. b, pp. 413–414
8. b, pp. 414–415
9. d, p. 414

10. c, pp. 414–415
11. c, p. 416
12. c, p. 416
13. b, pp. 417–418
14. b, pp. 418–419
15. a, p. 419
16. c, pp. 419–420
17. d, p. 420
18. a, pp. 421–423

19. a, p. 423
20. a, p. 423
21. d, p. 423
22. c, pp. 424–425
23. c, pp. 424–425
24. d, p. 426
25. b, pp. 427, 429

SHORT ANSWER AND ESSAY QUESTIONS

1. pp. 411–412
2. pp. 411–412
3. pp. 412–413
4. pp. 413–414
5. pp. 414–415
6. p. 416
7. pp. 416–417

8. pp. 417–418
9. pp. 418–419
10. p. 419
11. pp. 419–420
12. p. 420
13. pp. 420–421
14. p. 421

15. pp. 421–423
16. pp. 423–424
17. pp. 424–425
18. p. 425
19. p. 426
20. pp. 426–427, 429

PROBLEMS

1. *a.* (1) column 4: 18, 30, 44, 61, 80, 91, 100, (2) column 5: 4, 10, 22, 36, 51, 71, 100; *b.* (1) 30, 10, (2) 20, 49; *c.* graph
2. *a.* 1; *b.* 3; *c.* 2; *d.* 4
3. *a.* (1) 3, (2) 9; *b.* (1) (a) 7, (b) 18, (2) (a) 7, (b) 15, 30, (c) 12

CHAPTER 21

Health Care

Health care has been a topic of major national debate as shown in the 2010 passage of the **Patient Protection and Affordable Care Act.** The first few sections of the chapter discuss the twin problems that gave rise to the new legislation: rising health care costs and limited access to health care by many Americans. The economics you learned in previous chapters will now be put to good use in analyzing these twin problems of health care.

The explanations for the first problem—the rapid **rise in cost**—rely on your prior knowledge of supply and demand. Before you can appreciate the demand and supply factors that influence health care costs, however, you need to recognize the peculiar features of the market for health care that make it different from the other markets with which you are familiar. Society is reluctant to ration health care based solely on price or income, as is the case with most products. The market also is subject to asymmetric information between the buyer (patient) and seller (health care provider), with the seller making most of the decisions about the amount of services to be consumed and the prices to be paid. The system of third-party payments reduces the out-of-pocket price paid by buyers and thus distorts the traditional price signals in the health care marketplace. Medical care can generate spillover benefits to others who do not pay for these benefits (positive externalities), and thus government intervention may be necessary in this market to obtain these benefits.

With this background in mind, you are ready to read about the **demand for health care.** The demand factors have significantly increased the cost of health care. Health care is relatively price insensitive, so increases in price result in little reduction in the quantity consumed. The demand for health care increased as per capita incomes increased because health care is a normal good. Adding to the demand pressures are an aging population, unhealthy lifestyles, and the practices of physicians that are influenced by medical ethics and a fee-for-service payment system. The medical insurance system also contributes to increased demand by reducing the costs to the consumer, as does the federal government with its tax subsidy of employer-financed health insurance.

Supply has not increased at the same rate as demand in health care. Although the supply of physicians has increased, it has had little effect on reducing health care costs. Health care also is an area of slow productivity growth because of the personal attention required for services. The development and use of new medical technology also have increased cost pressures in health care rather than reduced them.

The various **reforms** for the health care system that you will read about near the end of the chapter focus on containing cost and achieving universal coverage. Suggestions for cost containment call for increased uses of incentives, such as increased deductibles and copayments for medical services, the adoption of more managed care such as is found in health maintenance organizations, and tighter controls over Medicare payments based on specific classifications of treatments. After describing these cost containment programs, the chapter describes the major provisions and controversies associated with **Patient Protection and Affordable Care Act,** which significantly expanded health care coverage in the United States.

■ CHECKLIST

When you have studied this chapter you should be able to

☐ Describe the major characteristics of the health care industry.

☐ Explain the reasons for U.S. emphasis on private health insurance.

☐ State the twin problems with the health care system.

☐ Cite data on total spending on health care and as percentage of GDP.

☐ Discuss the quality of medical care in the United States.

☐ Explain four economic implications of rising health care spending.

☐ Describe three effects on the labor market from rising health care spending.

☐ Discuss whether the United States is spending too much on health care.

☐ State reasons why people have limited access to health care.

☐ List four peculiarities of the market for health care.

☐ Discuss the four demand factors that have increased health care costs over time.

☐ Explain how health insurance affects health care spending by creating a moral hazard problem and tax subsidies.

☐ Use supply and demand analysis to explain the rapid rise in health care expenditures.

☐ Describe how rationing is used in other nations to control health care costs.

☐ Identify three supply factors affecting the costs of health care.

☐ Evaluate the relative importance of the demand and supply factors affecting health care.

☐ Discuss proposals to reform the health care system so that there can be universal access.

☐ Explain how incentives can be used to help contain health care costs.

☐ Describe the major provisions of the Patient Protection and Affordable Care Act.

☐ State the objections and alternatives to the Patient Protection and Affordable Care Act.

☐ Describe the features of Singapore's efficient and effective health care system (*Last Word*).

■ **CHAPTER OUTLINE**

1. The *health care industry* in the United States covers a broad range of services provided by doctors, hospitals, dentists, nursing homes, and medical laboratories. It employs about 16 million people, about 817,000 of whom are practicing physicians. There are about 5800 hospitals. Americans make more than 1 billion visits to physicians each year.

2. A large percentage of health care spending in the United States is provided through **private health insurance.** Many other countries such as Canada have systems of *national health insurance* where health care is provided at no cost or low cost for all residents and paid for with tax revenues. The system of private health insurance in the United States started mostly during the Second World War as a way for employers to recruit workers by offering health insurance as a "free" benefit. After the war the system continued to expand to other employers and businesses. One consequence of this system of private health insurance is that it creates incentives for the overuse of health care. Another consequence is that health care reform efforts have focused on regulating the existing system rather than considering other alternatives.

3. Two major problems face the health care system. The *costs* of health care are high and rapidly rising. Some U.S. citizens do not have *access* to health care or adequate coverage by the system.

4. *Health care costs* are rising for many reasons.

a. Costs have risen in absolute and relative terms.

(1) Total health care spending pays for many items such as hospitals, doctors, dentists, prescription drugs, nursing homes, and program administration and is obtained from many sources, such as private health insurance, Medicare, Medicaid, **copayments** and **deductibles,** and other sources, as shown in text Figure 21.1.

(2) Expenditures were about 17 percent of domestic output in 2009.

(3) The health care expenditures as a percentage of GDP are highest in the United States compared with other industrial nations.

b. There is general agreement that medical care in the United States is probably the best in the world, which is a consequence of its high expenditures for health care. That does not mean, however, that the United States is the healthiest nation. In fact, it ranks low internationally on many health indicators.

c. Rising health care expenditures and costs have at least four negative economic effects.

(1) Workers have reduced access to care because some employers reduce or eliminate health insurance.

(2) There are three adverse effects on labor markets: slower growth in wages as health care becomes a larger proportion of worker's total compensation; more use of part-time or temporary workers who do not receive health insurance; and outsourcing (and offshoring) of workers who are not covered by health care or work abroad.

(3) Medical bills for the uninsured or underinsured are a reason for an increase in personal bankruptcies.

(4) Health care costs put rising demands on budget expenditures at all levels of government.

d. The question of whether there is too much spending on health care is difficult to evaluate. Some economists argue that the greater spending contributes to society's GDP and well-being. Other economists argue that the basic problem is that there is an *overallocation* of resources to health care and *less* economic efficiency in the use of the nation's resources.

5. A major problem with health care is **limited access.** A large percentage of the population (about 15% in 2008) has no medical coverage. Those medically uninsured are generally the poor, although some young adults with good health choose not to buy insurance. Low-income workers and those employed in smaller businesses are less likely to be covered, or have limited coverage, because of the higher costs of health care for smaller firms.

6. There are many reasons for the *rapid rise in health care costs.*

a. The market for health care is different from other markets. Medical care has ethical and equity considerations not found in most other markets. Health care suppliers have more information than do buyers, so there is asymmetric information in the market. Medical care spending and treatment often create positive externalities. The third-party payment system for insurance reduces incentives to control health care spending and leads to overconsumption.

b. Several demand factors have increased health care costs over time.

(1) Health care is a normal good with an income elasticity of about +1.0, so that spending on it will rise in proportion to per capita income. Health care is also price *inelastic,* which means that total health care spending will increase even as the price of health care rises.

(2) The aging population of the United States increases the demand for health care.

(3) Unhealthy lifestyles because of alcohol, tobacco, or drug abuse increase the demand for and spending on health care.

(4) Doctors can add to costs because there is asymmetric information—the provider knows more than the buyer—and thus there is supplier-induced demand.

(a) Doctors have no strong incentive to reduce costs for the buyer and perhaps an economic interest in increasing them because they are paid as a *fee for service.*

(b) **Defensive medicine,** which involves the use of extra testing, may be used to prevent possible lawsuits, but it increases costs.

(c) Medical ethics require the best (and often the most expensive) procedures.

c. Although health insurance plays a positive role in giving people protection against health risks, it contributes to increased costs and demand for health care.

(1) It creates a *moral hazard problem* by encouraging some people to be less careful about their health and gives some people incentives to overconsume health care than would be the case without insurance.

(2) Health insurance financed by employers is exempt from both federal income and payroll taxation. This *tax subsidy* increases the demand for health care.

(3) From a supply and demand perspective, health insurance reduces the price to the buyer below the no-insurance equilibrium price. This lower price induces more health care consumption and creates an efficiency loss for society.

(4) Other nations use different nonprice methods to control or ration health care spending such as putting spending limits on paying for health care treatments in the national health care system and increasing waiting time to obtain health care services. In the United States, the system of private health insurance was regulated at the state level and state insurance commissioners or state politicians had more incentive to expand benefits that drove up health care costs. These higher costs were paid for by private insurers and there was no budget constraint as was the case with a national health insurance system.

d. Supply factors affect health care costs.

(1) The increase in the supply of physicians has not kept up with the increase in demand for health care, thus increasing physician costs. One reason is that the rising cost of education and training for physicians limits the number completing medical programs.

(2) The productivity growth in health care has been slow relative to other sectors of the economy.

(3) Most new medical technology has increased costs, despite the fact that some technological advances in medicine have decreased costs.

e. Only a relatively minor portion of the increase in health care costs can be attributed to increasing incomes, the aging of the population, or defensive medicine. The most likely explanations for the rise in health care costs are the use of advanced medical technology, medical ethics that require best treatment, and a third-party system of insurance payments with little incentive to control costs.

7. Different types of *cost containment* schemes that alter incentives have been used in the health care reforms over the years.

a. Insurance companies have increased *deductibles* and *copayments* to give consumers more incentives to reduce health costs.

b. *Heath savings accounts (HSAs)* were established as part of the 2003 Medicare reform. Individuals make tax-deductible contributions into their HSAs and they can use them to pay for qualified medical expenses. This program is thought to promote the use of personal savings for health care expenditures and add more incentives to reduce costs because bills would be paid directly by the account holder and not a third party.

c. Managed care organizations are being more widely used to control health care costs and are of two types. *Preferred provider organizations (PPOs)* offer discounts to insurance companies and consumers who use them. *Health maintenance organizations (HMOs)* are prepaid health plans that closely monitor health care costs because they operate with fixed budgets.

d. The *diagnosis-related-group (DRG) system* is used to classify treatments and fix fees to reduce the costs of Medicare payments, although the DRG systems may also reduce the quality of care.

e. There have been congressional efforts to limit the size of *medical malpractice* awards to contain health care costs. Thirty-three states have caps on "pain and suffering" provisions of malpractice awards.

8. The *Patient Protection and Affordable Care Act* (PPACA) of 2010 was not a cost containment program or a national insurance program, but rather focused on expanding the existing system of private health care insurance and public health care insurance (Medicaid and Medicare).

a. The major provisions of the act sought to expand coverage to more of the uninsured and pay for it with new taxes and a requirement to buy health insurance.

(1) Insurance companies cannot deny people coverage based on preexisting medical conditions, cannot impose annual or lifetime limits on spending for individuals, and cannot drop people from insurance rolls.

(2) The act imposes an *employer mandate* that requires every firm with 50 or more employees to purchase health care for them or pay a fine.

(3) The act has a *personal mandate* that requires individuals to purchase health insurance for themselves and their dependents if they do not already have private or government insurance.

(4) The PPACA tries to provide health insurance to those without coverage or with low incomes through the employer mandate, through the extension of Medicaid to people with incomes less than 133 percent of the poverty level, and by subsidizing the purchase of health insurance for those low-income individuals who have to buy their own insurance.

(5) *Insurance exchanges* that are government regulated will be established in each state so individuals can shop for their own insurance and thus more competition can be introduced into the private insurance market.

(6) Other provisions include coverage of adult children on parents' policies through age 26; no deductibles or co-pays for annual checkups or preventive care; and mandating that health insurance companies spend 80 percent of their revenue on health care.

(7) Taxes to pay for the PPACA come from a new 0.9 percentage point tax on Medicare for high-income earners, a new 3.8 percentage point tax on capital gains for high-income earners, a new 40 percent tax on employers who offer high-premium health care policies for individuals or families, a 2.9 percent excise tax on medical devices, and a 10 percent tax on indoor tanning.

b. The PPACA is not without its critics, who argue that it will create more bureaucracy and inefficiency and lead to the establishment of national health insurance. There also is concern that this new entitlement will be costly and expensive in the long run and may increase the demand for and consumption of health care rather than reducing demand and limiting costs. Other alternatives to the PPACA would be some system of health care that raises the percentage of health care spending that comes directly from the consumer rather than from private insurers.

9. (*Last Word*). Singapore has an efficient and effective health care system that relies on competition, consumer incentives, and saving. Competition is encouraged by requiring hospitals to post prices for services. The consumer is given an incentive not to over consume health care because there are high out-of-pocket consumer costs for using health care services. Consumers also are required to have medical saving accounts and deposit 6 percent of their incomes in these accounts. Several types of programs in the United States (for example, Whole Foods Markets and the State of Indiana) have incentive features similar to the Singapore system, particularly the use of high out-of-pocket deductibles, and they appear to be effective.

■ HINTS AND TIPS

1. This chapter contains many health care terms with which you may not be familiar. Make sure you review the meaning of each important term before reading the text chapter and taking the self-test in this chapter.

2. The two economic ideas that are the most difficult to comprehend are asymmetric information and moral hazard. The buyer and seller information problems were discussed extensively in Chapter 17. To remember the meaning of these ideas, associate them with examples from the text or ones that you construct.

3. This chapter uses the concepts of income elasticity and price elasticity of demand to explain the demand for health care. Reread the text discussion of these concepts in Chapter 4 if you cannot recall how these elasticities are defined.

4. The graphical presentation of a market with and without health insurance (Figure 21.3) is a relatively straightforward application of supply and demand. The one difficult concept is efficiency loss. This concept was discussed in Chapters 5 and 16; you will now see it applied to health care.

■ IMPORTANT TERMS

deductibles

copayments

fee for service

defensive medicine

tax subsidy

health savings accounts
  (HSAs)

preferred provider
  organizations (PPOs)

health maintenance
  organizations (HMOs)

diagnosis-related-group
  (DRG) system

Patient Protection and
  Affordable Care Act
  (PPACA)

employer mandate

personal mandate

insurance exchanges

SELF-TEST

■ FILL-IN QUESTIONS

1. In the United States, health care is one of the (smallest, largest) _____ industries. It employs about (2, 16) _____ million people, of whom about (235, 817) thousand _____ are physicians. There are about (2200, 5800) _____ hospitals in the industry.

2. In the United States a high proportion of health care spending is provided through (national, private) _____ health insurance, and such insurance is typically provided by (employers, government) _____ as a work benefit.

3. The twin problems facing the health care system are high and rapidly growing (benefits, costs) _____ and the fact that many U.S. citizens (do, do not) _____ have access to health care or adequate coverage by the system.

4. In 1960, health care spending was about (5, 17) _____ percent of domestic output (GDP), but in 2009 it was about _____ percent of domestic output. Compared to other industrialized nations, the United States has the (lowest, highest) _____ level of health care expenditures as a percentage of domestic output.

5. The economic effects of rising health care costs are (more, less) _____ access to health care and _____ coverage for workers. There are labor market problems, such as (more, less) _____ wage growth, _____ labor mobility, and (more, less) _____ use of temporary or part-time workers. Health care costs also create _____ demands on the budgets of governments at the federal, state, and local levels.

6. The basic problem with growing health care expenditures is that there is an (underallocation, overallocation) _____ of resources to health care. The large expenditures for health care mean that at the margin, health care is worth (more, less) _____ than alternative products that could have been produced with the resources.

7. The uninsured in health care are concentrated among the poor, many of whom work at (low-wage, high-wage) _____ jobs, (do, do not) _____ qualify for Medicaid, and may work for (small, large) _____ businesses. Others who are uninsured include (older, younger) _____ adults in excellent health and people with (minor, major) _____ health problems.

8. The market for health care is different from other markets because of (technology, ethical–equity) _____ considerations, (symmetric, asymmetric) _____ information, (positive, negative) _____ externalities, and (first-party, third-party) _____ payments.

9. Health care is (an inferior, a normal) _____ good with an income elasticity of about (0, 1) _____ for most industrially advanced nations. In this case, a 10 percent increase in incomes will result in a (1, 10) _____ percent increase in health care expenditures.

10. Health care is price (inelastic, elastic) _____, with a coefficient estimated to be (0.2, 1.5) _____. The price elasticity of demand for health care means that a 10 percent increase in price would decrease health care spending by (2, 15) _____ percent.

11. Other factors increasing the demand for health care include a(n) (older, younger) _____ population and lifestyles that are often (entertaining, unhealthy) _____.

12. The demand for health care is affected by the problem of asymmetric information in the practice of medicine, which means that the (demander, supplier) _____ will decide the types and amount of health care to be consumed. Physicians (have, do not have) _____ an incentive to reduce costs for the buyer and perhaps an economic interest in increasing them because they are paid on a (personal mandate, fee for service) _____ basis.

13. Increased demand and costs can arise from the practice of (offensive, defensive) _____ medicine to limit the possibility of a lawsuit or from medical (insurance, ethics) _____ that require the use of the best medical techniques by doctors.

14. Health insurance increases demand because it creates a moral (dilemma, hazard) _____ problem. It makes people (more, less) _____ careful about their health and gives people incentives to (underconsume, overconsume) _____ health care more than they otherwise would without health insurance.

15. Health insurance financed by employers is (taxed, tax-exempt) _____ at the federal level. This (tax, tax subsidy) _____ (increases, decreases) _____ the demand for health care.

16. In a supply and demand analysis, health insurance (raises, lowers) _____ the price to the buyer below the no-insurance equilibrium price. This (higher, lower) _____ price induces (less, more) _____ health care consumption and creates an efficiency (benefit, loss) _____ for society.

17. The supply factors that affect health care costs include the (high, low) _____ cost of physician services, (fast, slow) _____ growth in productivity in health care, and the use of (new, old) _____ medical technology.

18. Over the years, actions have been taken to contain health care costs. Insurance companies have (increased, decreased) _____ deductibles and copayments to provide incentives for consumers to reduce expenditures, and there has been _____ use of preferred provider organizations (PPOs) to get consumers to use lower-cost health care providers. Businesses and other organizations have formed health maintenance organizations (HMOs) that have prepaid health plans and use a (fee-for-service, managed care) _____ approach to control health costs. Medical treatments have been classified according to a diagnosis-related-group (DRG) system and the government has (fixed, variable) _____ fee payments for each treatment.

19. The primary goal of the Patient Protection and Affordable Care Act (PPACA) of 2010 was (cost containment, universal coverage) _____. Every firm with 50 or more workers is required to purchase health insurance for their workers as part of (a personal, an employer) _____ mandate and all individuals must purchase health insurance for themselves and their dependents as part of _____ mandate unless they are covered by other insurance. Individual shopping for insurance will be done in government-regulated markets designed to promote competition that are called insurance (exchanges, mandates) _____.

20. Critics of the PPACA argue that it is likely to (increase, decrease) _____ government bureaucracy, _____ the consumption of health care and its cost, _____ the federal budget deficit, and lead to nonprice rationing in a (private, national) _____ health insurance system.

■ **TRUE–FALSE QUESTIONS**

Circle T if the statement is true, F if it is false.

1. The twin problems of health care are the rapidly rising cost of health care and the general decline in the quality of health care. **T F**

2. Medicaid is the nationwide federal health care program available to Social Security beneficiaries and the disabled.   **T F**

3. Expenditures on health care are high in the United States but even higher in Japan and United Kingdom.   **T F**

4. Rising health care costs reduce workers' access to health care.   **T F**

5. Increasing health care expenditures cause problems for the budgets of federal, state, and local governments.   **T F**

6. Aggregate consumption of health care is so great that at the margin it is worth more than the alternative goods and services these resources could otherwise have produced.   **T F**

7. About 60 percent of the population of the United States had no health insurance in 2008.   **T F**

8. Minimum-wage workers have health insurance because their insurance premiums are covered by the federal government.   **T F**

9. There is asymmetric information in the market for health care because the supplier (doctor) acts as the agent for the buyer (patient) and tells the buyer what health care services should be consumed.   **T F**

10. The market for health care is characterized by negative externalities.   **T F**

11. Third-party payments are a factor in the health care market because about three-fourths of all health care expenses are paid through public or private insurance.   **T F**

12. The demand for health care is price elastic.   **T F**

13. There is a strong incentive to underconsume health care because consumers have little information about the costs of medical treatments and doctors are paid on a fee-for-service basis.   **T F**

14. "Defensive medicine" refers to the medical practice of physicians using preventive medicine to reduce illness and disease in patients.   **T F**

15. Health care insurance is a means by which one pays a relatively small known cost for protection against an uncertain and much larger cost in the future.   **T F**

16. A moral hazard problem arises from health insurance because those covered tend to take fewer health risks and consume less health care than would be the case without insurance.   **T F**

17. The demand for health care is increased by a federal tax policy that exempts employer-financed health insurance from taxation.   **T F**

18. There is overwhelming evidence that the American Medical Association has purposely kept admissions to medical school artificially low to restrict the supply of doctors.   **T F**

19. Productivity growth has been slow in the health care industry.   **T F**

20. The development and use of new technology in health care has been a major factor in increasing the costs of health care.   **T F**

21. The growth of managed care organizations has transformed the medical industry into one dominated by large insurance and health care firms.   **T F**

22. The diagnostic-related-group (DRG) system is a health maintenance organization that specializes in the diagnoses of illnesses to reduce costs.   **T F**

23. The primary goal of the Patient Protection and Affordable Care Act was the containment of health care costs.   **T F**

24. The Patient Protection and Affordable Care Act makes it illegal for insurance companies to deny coverage to anyone on the basis of preexisting medical conditions. **T F**

25. The cost of the Patient Protection and Affordable Care Act will be paid for by imposing several new taxes on individuals and employers.   **T F**

■ **MULTIPLE-CHOICE QUESTIONS**

Circle the letter that corresponds to the best answer.

1. The two major problems facing the health care system of the United States are
 (a) the formation of health alliances and preferred provider organizations
 (b) a decline in innovation and the rate of technological changes
 (c) increasing supply and decreasing demand for health care
 (d) access to health care and rapidly increasing costs

2. The health care industry employs about how many physicians?
 (a) 51,300
 (b) 150,700
 (c) 817,000
 (d) 1,984,000

3. What was total spending for health care as a percentage of GDP in 1960 and in 2009?

	1960	2009
(a)	1	4
(b)	2	6
(c)	5	17
(d)	9	18

4. The contradiction about health care in the United States is that the country's
 (a) medical care is the best in the world, but the nation ranks low on many health indicators
 (b) expenditures for health care are modest, but its medical care is the best in the world
 (c) expenditures for health care are the highest in the world, but its quality of medical care is the worst of all industrial nations
 (d) advances in medicine have fallen at a time when its need for better medicine has risen

5. Which is a labor market effect from rapidly rising health care costs?
(a) a decrease in the number of health care workers
(b) an increase in the rate of growth of real wages
(c) an increase in the use of part-time workers
(d) a decrease in the skill of the labor force

6. Which person is most likely to be uninsured or ineligible for health insurance?
(a) A college professor working at a state university
(b) A full-time worker at a big manufacturing plant
(c) An accountant employed by a large corporation
(d) A dishwasher working for minimum wage at a restaurant

7. Which would be considered a peculiarity of the market for health care?
(a) third-party payments
(b) employer mandates
(c) tax credits and vouchers
(d) fee-for-service payments

8. The demand for health care is
(a) price elastic
(b) price inelastic
(c) income elastic
(d) income inelastic

9. From an income perspective, health care is considered
(a) an inferior good
(b) a normal good
(c) a superior good
(d) a supply-induced good

10. Which is a demand factor in the market for health care?
(a) an aging population
(b) advances in new medical technology
(c) slow productivity growth in the health care industry
(d) the number of physicians graduating from medical school

11. Asymmetric information causes problems in the health care market because
(a) the buyer, not the supplier, of health care services makes most of the decisions about the amount and type of health care to be provided
(b) the supplier, not the buyer, of the health care services makes most of the decisions about the amount and type of health care to be provided
(c) government has less information than the health care providers and can inflate fees
(d) insurance companies, not the health care consumer, control deductibles and copayment policies

12. Unhealthy lifestyles may be encouraged by medical insurance because people figure that health insurance will cover illnesses or accidents. This attitude is characteristic of
(a) a personal mandate
(b) an employer mandate
(c) a moral hazard problem
(d) a reduced access problem

Answer Questions 13, 14, 15, and 16 based on the following demand and supply graph of the market for health care.

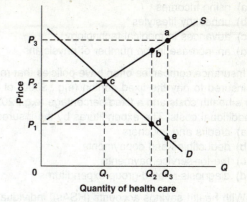

Quantity of health care

13. If there were no health insurance, the equilibrium price and quantity of health care would be
(a) P_1 and Q_2
(b) P_2 and Q_1
(c) P_2 and Q_2
(d) P_3 and Q_3

14. Assume that health insurance pays half the cost of health care. For the consumer, the price and quantity of health care consumed would be
(a) P_1 and Q_2
(b) P_2 and Q_2
(c) P_2 and Q_1
(d) P_3 and Q_3

15. With health insurance paying half the cost of health care, there is allocative
(a) efficiency because at Q_1 the marginal cost to society equals the marginal benefit
(b) efficiency because at Q_2 the marginal cost to society is less than the marginal benefit by the difference between points **b** and **d**
(c) inefficiency because at Q_2 the marginal cost to society exceeds the marginal benefit by the difference between points **b** and **d**
(d) inefficiency because at Q_3 the marginal cost to society exceeds the marginal benefit by the difference between points **a** and **e**

16. The efficiency loss caused by the availability of health insurance is shown by area
(a) Q_1caQ_3
(b) Q_1cbQ_2
(c) **cae**
(d) **cbd**

17. Which of the following would be a nonprice mechanism for rationing health care in a national health care system?
(a) insurance exchanges
(b) waiting for service
(c) defensive medicine
(d) an employer requirement

18. Which is a supply factor in the health care market?
(a) medical technology
(b) an aging population
(c) defensive medicine
(d) growing incomes

19. Most experts attribute a major portion of the relative rise in health care spending to
   (a) rising incomes
   (b) unhealthy lifestyles
   (c) advances in medical technology
   (d) an increase in the number of physicians

20. Insurance companies often have policies that require the insured to pay the fixed portion (e.g., $500) of each year's health costs and a fixed percentage (e.g., 20%) of all additional costs. The expenditures by the insured are
   (a) credits and vouchers
   (b) deductibles and copayments
   (c) fee-for-service payments
   (d) diagnosis-related-group expenditures

21. With health savings accounts (HSAs), individuals
   (a) make tax-deductible contributions to the accounts and then use the funds to pay for health care expenditures
   (b) contract with health maintenance organizations and use the accounts to get medical services at the lowest possible rate
   (c) obtain discounted prices for health care services that are provided by the diagnosis-related-group system
   (d) deposit money in a bank and receive a certificate of deposit that is indexed to the inflation rate for health care

22. An organization that requires hospitals and physicians to provide discounted prices for their services as a condition for inclusion in the insurance plan is a
   (a) health maintenance organization
   (b) preferred provider organization
   (c) fee-for-service organization
   (d) health alliance

23. The payment that the hospital receives for Medicare patients is based on
   (a) preexisting conditions
   (b) health savings account funds
   (c) the number of malpractice awards
   (d) a diagnosis-related-group system

24. One of the major ways that the Patient Protection and Affordable Care Act increases the number of people insured is through
   (a) managed care
   (b) Insurance exchanges
   (c) personal and employer mandates
   (d) increasing deductibles and copayments

25. Which is one of the new taxes used to help fund the Patient Protection and Affordable Care Act?
   (a) a 2 percent tax on fast food
   (b) a 10 percent tax on indoor tanning
   (c) a 12 percent tax on corporations
   (d) a 15 percent tax on the incomes of high-income earners

■ **PROBLEMS**

1. Following is a table showing a supply and demand schedule for health care. In the left column is the price of health care. The middle column shows the quantity demanded (Q_d) for health care. The right column shows the quantity supplied (Q_s) of health care.

Price ($)	Q_d	Q_s
3000	100	500
2500	200	400
2000	300	300
1500	400	200
1000	500	100

a. Assume that there is no health insurance in this market. At a price of $2000, the quantity demanded will be _____ units of health care and the quantity supplied will be _____ units. There will be (a surplus, a shortage, equilibrium) _____ in this market for health care at _____ units.

b. Now assume that health insurance cuts the price of health care in half for the consumer. The new price to the consumer will be $_____ and the quantity consumed will be _____ units. At this level of quantity, the marginal cost to society of a unit of health care is $_____ while the marginal benefit is _____.

c. Draw a supply and demand graph in the following graph based on the data in the preceding table. Make sure to label the axes and identify prices and quantities.

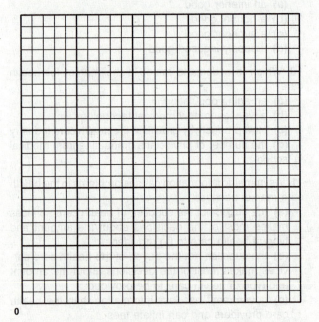

0

(1) Show the equilibrium point in a market without health insurance and label it as point *a*.
(2) Show the price to the consumer and quantity consumed when health insurance covers half of the cost of health care. At this quantity, indicate the marginal cost to society of this unit of health care and label it at point *b*. Also, indicate the marginal benefit to society of this unit of health care and label it as point *c*.
(3) Indicate the area of efficiency loss when health insurance covers half of the cost of health care.

HEALTH CARE 275

2. In the situations listed below indicate whether the events primarily affect the demand (**D**) for health care or the supply (**S**) of health care. Also, indicate whether it would increase (+) or decrease (−) the demand for or supply of health care.

	D or S	**+ or −**
a. An aging population	___	___
b. More use of defensive medicine	___	___
c. Healthier lifestyles	___	___
d. Less health insurance coverage	___	___
e. Increased productivity in health care	___	___
f. Newer and more costly medical technology	___	___
g. A sharp reduction in the number of physicians	___	___
h. A tax subsidy to consumers to cover health care	___	___
i. Rising per capita incomes	___	___
j. More use of a fee-for-service payment system	___	___

3. Match the terms with the correct phrases using the appropriate number.

1. copayments
2. employer mandate
3. diagnosis-related-group system
4. preferred provider organization
5. health maintenance organization
6. deductibles
7. personal mandate
8. insurance exchanges

a. A unit set up by insurance companies that requires hospitals and physicians to provide discounted prices for their services as a condition for being included in the insurance plan _____

b. The percentage of cost that an insured individual pays while the insurer pays the remainder _____

c. A health care organization that contracts with employers, insurance companies, and other groups to provide health care for their workers or others who are insured _____

d. The dollar sum of costs that an insured individual must pay before the insurer begins to pay _____

e. An arrangement that gives the hospital a fixed payment for treating each patient with the payments based on hundreds of detailed health categories for patient conditions and needs _____

f. A requirement of the PPACA that employers with 50 or more workers either provide insurance for their workers or pay a fine _____

g. Government-regulated markets established in states to promote competition and enable individuals to shop for health insurance at competitive rates as part of the PPACA _____

h. A requirement of the PPACA that individuals must purchase health insurance for themselves and their dependents unless they have other insurance coverage _____

■ SHORT ANSWER AND ESSAY QUESTIONS

1. Define and describe the major features of the health care industry.

2. Why has the United States relied primarily on private health insurance?

3. Explain the relationship between the cost of and access to health care.

4. What are the dimensions of the cost increases in health care in absolute and relative terms?

5. How do health care expenditures in the United States compare with those in other industrialized nations?

6. What are the economic implications of rising health care costs?

7. Why is the aggregate consumption of health care in the United States a basic problem?

8. Who are the uninsured in the United States? What are the characteristics of the uninsured?

9. What are four peculiarities of the market for health care?

10. How do income and price elasticity affect the demand for health care?

11. In what ways do an aging population and unhealthy lifestyles influence and shape the demand for health care?

12. What role do doctors play in increasing the demand for health care?

13. What role does health insurance play in affecting health care costs?

14. How do nations with national health insurance ration health care and control costs?

15. Why might physicians' high incomes have nothing to do with supply restrictions?

16. How have changes in medical technology affected health care costs?

17. What is the relative importance of demand and supply factors in affecting the rise in health care costs?

18. What actions have insurance companies and the federal government taken to reduce or contain health care costs?

19. Explain the major provisions of the Patient Protection and Affordable Care Act.

20. What some objections and alternatives to the Patient Protection and Affordable Care Act?

ANSWERS

Chapter 21 Health Care

FILL-IN QUESTIONS

1. largest, 16, 817, 5800
2. private, employers
3. costs, do not
4. 5, 17, highest

5. less, less, less, less, more, more
6. overallocation, less
7. low-wage, do not, small, younger, major
8. ethical–equity, asymmetric, positive, third-party
9. a normal, 1, 10
10. inelastic, 0.2, 2
11. older, unhealthy
12. supplier, do not have, fee for service
13. defensive, ethics
14. hazard, less, overconsume
15. tax-exempt, tax subsidy, increases
16. lowers, lower, more, loss
17. high, slow, new
18. increased, increased, managed care, fixed
19. universal coverage, an employer, a personal, exchanges
20. increase, increase, increase, national

TRUE–FALSE QUESTIONS

1. F, pp. 434–435	**10.** F, p. 439	**19.** T, p. 444
2. F, p. 435	**11.** T, p. 439	**20.** T, p. 444
3. F, p. 436	**12.** F, p. 439	**21.** T, p. 446
4. T, p. 437	**13.** F, p. 440	**22.** F, p. 447
5. T, p. 437	**14.** F, p. 440	**23.** F, p. 447
6. F, p. 438	**15.** T, p. 441	**24.** T, p. 447
7. F, p. 438	**16.** F, p. 441	**25.** T, p. 450
8. F, p. 438	**17.** T, p. 441	
9. T, p. 439	**18.** F, p. 444	

MULTIPLE-CHOICE QUESTIONS

1. d, pp. 434–435	**10.** a, p. 440	**19.** c, p. 445
2. c, p. 434	**11.** b, p. 440	**20.** b, p. 446
3. c, p. 436	**12.** c, p. 440–441	**21.** a, p. 446
4. a, pp. 436–437	**13.** b, p. 442	**22.** b, p. 446
5. c, p. 437	**14.** a, p. 442	**23.** d, p. 447
6. d, p. 438	**15.** c, p. 442	**24.** c, p. 447
7. a, p. 439	**16.** d, p. 442	**25.** b, p. 450
8. b, p. 439	**17.** b, p. 443	
9. b, p. 439	**18.** a, p. 444	

PROBLEMS

1. *a.* 300, 300, equilibrium, 300; *b.* 1000, 500, 3000, 1000; *c.* (1) the intersection of price of $2000 and quantity of 300, (2) point *b* is the intersection of $3000 and quantity of 500 units, and point *c* is the intersection of $1000 and quantity of 500 units, (3) the area of efficiency loss is the area in the triangle outlined by points *a*, *b*, and *c*

2. *a.* D, +; *b.* D, +; *c.* D, −; *d.* D, −; *e.* S, +; *f.* S, −; *g.* S, −; *h.* D, +; *i.* D, +; *j.* D, +

3. *a.* 4; *b.* 1; *c.* 5; *d.* 6; *e.* 3; *f.* 2; *g.* 8; *h.* 7

SHORT ANSWER AND ESSAY QUESTIONS

1. p. 434	**8.** p. 438	**15.** p. 444
2. p. 434	**9.** p. 439	**16.** pp. 444–445
3. pp. 434–435	**10.** pp. 439–440	**17.** p. 445
4. pp. 435–436	**11.** p. 440	**18.** pp. 445–447
5. p. 436	**12.** pp. 440–441	**19.** pp. 447–450
6. p. 437	**13.** pp. 441–442	**20.** p. 450
7. p. 438	**14.** p. 443	

CHAPTER 22

Immigration

Immigration is a topic often misunderstood and subject to heated controversy. The unique feature of this chapter is that it uses the power of economic information and analysis to offer significant insights and findings that should improve your understanding of this complex and controversial issue.

Simply stated, immigration involves the movement of labor resources from one nation to another. The chapter begins with a brief description of **economic immigrants** who typically move to the United States for some desired economic gain. These immigrants are of two types. They consist of **legal immigrants** who have permission to permanently reside in the United States or who have permission to work and live in the nation for a temporary period of time. They also include **illegal immigrants** who enter the country without the legal permission of the U.S. government.

The second section of the chapter explains the **economic reasons for immigration** into the United States from a cost and benefit perspective. A prime reason people make the move is to expand their opportunities to gain the benefits of a greater income. Moving costs, however, also influence the immigration decision because immigration can be considered an investment decision. Other factors also come into the cost–benefit decision such as the distance of the move, the age of the worker, and language skills.

The third section focuses on the **economics of immigration** in general. It uses a labor demand model to analyze what happens to wage rates, efficiency, output, and income. The conclusions drawn about immigration using the supply and demand analysis are definite, but as you discover at the end of the section, the real world is more complicated, so any conclusions will be modified by various factors such as the cost of migration, remittances, backflows, resource complementarities, capital investment, and unemployment.

The fourth section extends the economic analysis and applies it to **illegal immigration.** A supply and demand model for low-wage labor is used to illustrate the economic effects of illegal immigration on employment, wage rates, the prices of goods and services, and government. The analysis reveals that illegal immigration can have both negative and positive effects depending on the economic conditions and circumstances.

Immigration is one of those controversial issues that are the subject of ongoing debate in the United States. Although the issue can be viewed from a political, social, legal, or cultural dimension, this chapter shows how the basic economics you have learned throughout your textbook can be used to gain new understanding of this issue.

■ **CHECKLIST**

When you have studied this chapter you should be able to

☐ Explain how immigrants are classified as legal immigrants and illegal immigrants.

☐ Describe trends in the level of legal immigration since 1980.

☐ Identify the major categories of admission for legal immigration.

☐ List the major countries of origin for legal immigrants.

☐ Supply estimates of the number of illegal immigrants (average number per year in recent years and the total number overall).

☐ List three reasons why legal or illegal immigrants decide to migrate.

☐ Discuss the role of earning opportunities in migration decisions.

☐ Explain how immigration can be viewed as an investment decision.

☐ Discuss how distance and age, or other factors, affect the cost–benefit evaluation of the migration decision.

☐ Describe the personal gains from economic immigration.

☐ Use a supply and demand model to explain the economic effects of worker migration from Mexico to the United States in terms of wage rates, efficiency, output, and income shares.

☐ Explain how five factors complicate or modify the economic effects of migration on the two economies.

☐ Discuss the fiscal effects of the economics of migration between the two economies.

☐ Describe the research findings on the economic effects of immigration.

☐ Use a supply and demand model to explain the economic effects of illegal immigration on employment and wages.

☐ Explain how illegal immigration affects the prices of goods and services produced by illegal immigration.

☐ Discuss the fiscal impact of illegal immigration on state and local governments and other concerns.

☐ Offer a description of optimal immigration from an economic perspective.

☐ Describe some key elements in the history of immigration reform and recent attempts to offer a comprehensive reform (*Last Word*).

■ CHAPTER OUTLINE

1. The United States is a nation shaped and influenced by *economic immigrants,* who are motivated to move to the United States for economic gain. The number of immigrants consists of two types. First, there are legal immigrants who have been granted the right to live and work in the United States, some of whom are *permanent legal residents* (holding "green cards") and others who are *temporary legal immigrants* with permission to reside in the United States for a specific period. Second, there are illegal immigrants who have entered the country without legal permission or overstayed a temporary visa.

   a. The number of *legal immigrants* to the United States was about 500,000 from 1980 to 1988. From 1989 to 1992, it spiked to over 1.75 million because of an amnesty program, and then ranged from 750,000 to 1.25 million. From 2000 to 2009 it averaged 1 million a year; in 2009 it was 1.13 million. Legal immigrants are admitted for many reasons such as family sponsorship (66.1%), refugee status (15.7%), employment-based preferences (12.7%), diversity (4.2%), and other reasons (1.2%). Some are admitted through the *H1-B provision* of the immigration law that allows a limited number of high-skilled workers to be admitted to work in specialty occupations for six years. Among the top nations for legal immigrants are Mexico, China, the Philippines, India, Dominican Republic, Cuba, Vietnam, Colombia, South Korea, and Haiti.

   b. The number of *illegal immigrants* has averaged about 250,000 per year from 2000 to 2009 with over 60 percent coming from Mexico and Central America. In 2009 about 11 million illegal immigrants were residing continuously in the United States.

2. The three main *reasons that people immigrate* into the United States are to take advantage of better economic opportunities, to escape political or religious persecution, and to reunite with family members or friends.

   a. The main economic attraction of the United States for immigrants is the *opportunity for a higher-paying job.* Such jobs enable workers to get a better financial return on their stock of *human capital,* or the knowledge, know-how, and skills a person possesses. Typically, a large difference in wages increases the incentive to migrate from low-wage nations to high-wage nations or "magnet" countries such as Australia, Switzerland, the United States, and some Western European nations.

   b. The decision to immigrate is a *cost–benefit* calculation and entails giving up current income or consumption for future benefit. There are explicit costs such as paying for application fees and moving expenses for legal immigrants (or paying for an expeditor, or "coyote," for illegal immigrants). There are implicit or opportunity costs related to lost income while moving, and personal costs of leaving a family or culture. In making the decision, the immigrant evaluates whether the expected benefits of higher earnings and career possibilities are greater than the explicit and implicit costs of moving.

   c. *Nonwage factors* can affect the cost–benefit analysis of the immigration decision.

   (1) In most cases, the greater the *distance* required for migration, the less the likelihood that it will occur because more uncertainty and risk are associated with the move. These distance costs can be reduced if migrants follow *beaten paths,* or migration routes taken by family or friends who previously made the move. Previous immigrants can reduce the costs for prospective immigrants by providing vital information and connections.

   (2) *Age* too is a factor affecting the migration decision, with immigrants more likely to be younger than older. Younger workers can expect to accumulate more earnings benefits from the move because of their longer life spans. In addition, younger workers have lower opportunity costs, more flexibility, and fewer family responsibilities than older workers.

   (3) Other factors can affect the migration decision too such as English-language skills, lower tax rates, more entrepreneurial opportunities, or interest in the future welfare of children.

3. The *economic effects of immigration* involve personal gain, but also influence wage rates, efficiency, output, and income shares.

   a. The large inflows of legal and illegal immigrants to the United States are evidence that there is personal gain in the form of higher real wages from securing a job and working in the United States.

   (1) Nevertheless, the move may not produce the expected gains for some immigrants, so there can be major *backflows,* or return migration to the home country.

   (2) Although immigrants, on average, improve their standard of living, they may not achieve pay parity with native-born workers if there is a lack of work *skill transferability,* especially for those workers with poor English-language skills.

   (3) *Self-selection* may be a factor that helps to overcome some of the lack of skill transferability because only those immigrants who are strongly motivated to succeed make the move. The potential may be greatest for those immigrants who bring a high skill level (e.g., engineers or scientists).

   b. The impact of immigration on wage rates, efficiency, and output can be shown in a two-nation model, with one low-wage nation (Mexico) and one high-wage nation (the United States). The movement of workers from Mexico raises the average wages of workers in Mexico and lowers the average wage rates in the United States. Domestic output in Mexico will decline and domestic output in the United States will expand, but the net effect from an overall perspective is an increase in output and economic efficiency. The elimination of barriers to the international flow of labor can provide overall *efficiency gains from migration* because the same number of workers will produce more output.

   c. Immigration has three effects on output or income shares.

   (1) Output in the United States will increase, but output will decrease in Mexico. This outcome helps explain why

the United States has high annual quotas for immigration. Some poorer nations, however, may discourage emigration of their highly educated workers because such outflows of skilled labor create a **brain drain** in a nation.

(2) The wage income falls for native-born U.S. workers and rises for native-born Mexican workers who stay in Mexico. Total wage income (for native-born plus immigrant workers) in a nation may increase or decrease depending on the elasticity of labor demand. For example, if labor demand is elastic, a wage decrease will increase total wage income.

(3) The incomes of businesses in the United States will increase, but the incomes of businesses will decrease in Mexico because the United States gains "cheap" labor and Mexico loses "cheap" labor.

d. The conclusions from the model must be adjusted to take into account *complexity and modifications*.

(1) There is a cost to migration for workers that will reduce the world gain in output which wage differences between the two nations will not equalize.

(2) **Remittances** reduce the gains from immigration for the United States. If immigrant workers send some of their increased wage income to relatives in Mexico, then some income gain for the U.S. economy is lost to Mexico. Such remittances help explain why Mexico favors liberal U.S. immigration laws. In addition, the return of immigrant workers from the United States to Mexico creates an output and income loss for the United States. Such backflows alter output and income gains and losses.

(3) Whether workers in a domestic U.S. industry see their incomes fall because of the immigration of labor from Mexico depends on whether the workers in an industry are **complementary resources** or **substitute resources.** If such workers are complementary resources, then the lower wage rates caused by immigration may increase the demand for all labor because of an output effect and thus create more employment and income.

(4) The model assumes that the stock of capital is constant, but immigration can change investment in capital goods. In the long run an increase in business income in the United States from immigration may increase the rate of return on capital and stimulate more capital investment. The additional capital may increase labor productivity, lower production costs, and lower prices, and thus increase the demand for labor and increase wages. Conversely, the inflow of immigrants from Mexico into low-wage and labor-intensive occupations such agricultural harvesting in the United States may stifle capital investment in such industries.

(5) The model assumes full employment in both nations. If there is unemployment or underemployment in Mexico, it can increase domestic output in Mexico when the surplus workers move to the United States. And such immigrant workers may be less motivated and capable than the native-born Mexican workers who stay in Mexico. Such a **negative self-selection** may be a reason Mexico opposes strict border enforcement. Native-born workers in the United States may prefer strong border enforcement if such negative

self-selection means that the immigrant workers wind up being unemployed in the United States and require more government support that eventually decreases the after-tax income of U.S. domestic workers.

e. Immigration can affect government tax revenues and spending. If immigrants take advantage of welfare benefits in the United States, it imposes an additional cost on the nation. Prior to the 1970s immigrants were less likely to receive public assistance than domestic residents, but between the 1970s and 1998 immigrants used the welfare system more than domestic residents because more of the immigrants were low-skill workers. Welfare reform in 1996 reduced this public assistance at the federal level because the eligibility requirements for immigrants were changed to add a five-year waiting period. State and local governments, however, have to bear the burden of increased spending for public schools, health care, and other government services used by low-income immigrants.

f. The research findings indicate that immigration increases output and incomes in the United States and that the nation benefits from the human capital obtained from highly skilled immigrant workers. The effect of immigration on the wages of native-born U.S. workers is less certain, and estimates range from minus 3 percent to plus 2 percent. Immigration appears to reduce the wages of native-born U.S. workers with low education, and also perhaps reduces the wages of highly trained native-born U.S. workers.

4. The **debate over illegal immigration** has heated up because more low-skilled jobs are being filled by illegal immigrants. Their entry into the domestic labor markets for low-skilled workers is viewed as lowering wage rates and placing greater demands on public goods and services. A labor supply and demand model is used to evaluate these concerns.

a. The effects of illegal workers in a market for low-wage labor can be shown in a demand and supply graph that has a demand curve for labor and *two* supply curves. One supply curve is for domestic workers only and it is left of the total supply curve for all workers (domestic plus illegal). In equilibrium, the wage rate for all workers (domestic and illegal) will be lower than the wage rate for domestic workers alone. The model shows that the lower wage rate for all workers does reduce the employment of some of the domestic workers. Such domestic workers require a **compensating wage differential** to attract them to this otherwise undesirable work. The substitution of illegal workers for domestic workers, however, is not one-for-one, and it is less than the total amount of employment created by having both illegal and domestic workers in the labor force.

b. The model shows that the entry of illegal workers into low-wage markets for labor reduces wage rates in that market. The overall effect of immigration on average wages is either slightly negative or slightly positive. If illegal workers are complementary resources for domestic workers, the lower wage rate caused by the entry of illegal workers into a labor market can increase the demand for domestic workers in a complementary labor market. If, however, illegal workers are a substitute for domestic workers, the wage rates for domestic workers will decline. From a national or overall perspective, illegal workers do not affect the average wage rate for all workers because it is dependent on worker productivity, not illegal immigration.

c. The entry of illegal workers into particular industries puts downward pressure on the prices of goods and services produced by those industries. The lower prices for goods and services produced by these illegal workers can help increase the standard of living for all Americans.

d. Illegal immigration places a sizable burden on state and local governments with high concentrations of illegal immigrants because they use school, health care, and other public goods. Such immigrants pay for some of these public costs through sales taxes, gasoline taxes, and the property taxes built into rent. The state and local fiscal burdens for each low-skill immigrant household are estimated to be as high as $19,500 per year and for all such households in total about $50 billion annually. There is a lesser burden on the federal government than on state and local governments because illegal immigrants do not receive much federal assistance, but they do pay payroll taxes and income taxes.

e. There are other concerns about illegal immigration. It can undermine respect and support for laws and increase crime rates. It is unfair to legal immigrants who follow proper rules and procedures to enter the nation. There also are risks to national security from weak enforcement of borders.

5. Economic analysis can improve the discussion over immigration because the analysis suggests that immigration can make a positive or negative contribution to a nation, depending on such factors as the number of immigrants, the nation's capacity to absorb them into the economy, their level of education and skills, and their work ethic. Immigration is not an all-or-nothing decision. Economic analysis shows that a nation should expand its immigration until the marginal benefit equals the marginal cost. Also, some immigrants create more benefits than other immigrants, so not all immigrants should be thought of as the same.

6. (*Last Word*). Immigration quotas have been a mainstay of immigration law and reform since the 1920s although the preferences in the quotas and the legal limits have changed over time. In more recent years, the major concern with immigration has been with illegal immigration. In 2006, there were an estimated 12 million illegal immigrants residing in the United States. An attempt was made in 2007 in the U.S. Senate to address the illegal immigration issue with many proposed reforms, such as improved monitoring of the U.S. border, increased fines for employers hiring illegal immigrants, amnesty for illegal immigrants, and a guest-worker program. The reform legislation failed to pass and the debate over what to do continues.

■ **HINTS AND TIPS**

1. This chapter deals with the issue of immigration, which can provoke emotional reactions. Make sure you remember the distinction between *positive* and *normative* economics made in Chapter 1. The purpose of the chapter is to analyze and explain the economics of immigration (*what is*), and not the ideal world (*what ought to be*).

2. The graph in Figure 22.3 presents a simple model of immigration between two nations that shows only the demand curve for each nation and how the change in the equilibrium wage in each nation changes the quantity of labor. The wage rate is plotted on the vertical axis and the quantity of labor is on the horizontal axis. The graph shows how immigration affects the wage rate, employment, and domestic output. Problem 1 in this chapter will help you master this material.

■ **IMPORTANT TERMS**

economic immigrants	efficiency gains from migration
legal immigrants	
H1-B provision	brain drain
unauthorized (illegal) immigrants	remittances
human capital	complementary resources
beaten paths	substitute resources
backflows	negative self-selection
skill transferability	compensating wage differential
self-selection	

SELF-TEST

■ **FILL-IN QUESTIONS**

1. U.S. immigration consists of two basic types: those immigrants who have government permission to reside and work in the United States and are referred to as (legal, illegal) _____ immigrants, and those immigrants who are not authorized to reside or work in the United States, and are referred to as _____ immigrants.

2. In 2009, the number of legal immigrants to the United States was about (1, 6) _____ million. Almost two-thirds of legal U.S. immigrants get their legal status through ties to (employment, family) _____. The leading nation for legal immigration is (Russia, Mexico) _____.

3. From 2000 to 2009, the net annual flow of illegal immigrants was about (250, 950) _____ thousand. The number of illegal immigrants who reside continuously in the United States is about (2, 11) _____ million, and of this group, over half are from (China, Mexico) _____.

4. List three main reasons why people immigrate into the United States:

a. _____

b. _____

c. _____

5. Other things equal, if there are larger wage differences between nations, then incentives (increase, decrease) _____ for migrating to the nations providing higher-wage opportunities. An example of a "magnet country" that attracts a lot of immigrants would be (Vietnam, Australia) _____.

6. Immigration can be viewed as a(n) (consumption, investment) _____ decision. A person will migrate if he or she estimates that the stream of future earnings in a new nation is (less than, greater than) _____ the explicit and implicit costs of moving.

7. Other things equal, the greater the distance a person has to travel to migrate to another country the (more, less) _____ likely the person is to migrate; also, workers who migrate are _____ likely to be younger in age.

8. In general, the constant flow of immigrants to the United States indicates that the economic benefits to immigrants are (greater, less) _____ than the costs, but some immigrants may return to their home nation if they conclude that the benefits are _____ than the costs. Such return migration is referred to as (self-selection, backflows) _____.

9. The simple model of immigration shows that the movement of workers from a poor nation (Mexico) to a rich nation (United States) (increases, decreases) _____ wage rates in Mexico and _____ wage rates in the United States.

10. Movement of labor from Mexico to the United States (increases, decreases) _____ the real output of goods and services in the United States and _____ the real output of goods and services in Mexico, but from a combined or overall perspective, the total output _____, indicating that there are efficiency (gains, losses) _____ from migration.

11. The outflow of highly educated workers from one nation to another nation is commonly called a (self-selection, brain drain) _____, and this may be one reason why some nations that provide subsidized education for citizens (support, oppose) _____ such outflows.

12. Although an inflow of workers from Mexico to the United States will decrease wage rates in the United States, if the demand for labor in the United States is elastic it will (increase, decrease) _____ total wage income, but if the demand for labor is inelastic, it will _____ total wage income.

13. Unrestricted immigration of workers into the United States from Mexico will (increase, decrease) _____ business incomes in the United States and _____ business incomes in Mexico because the United States is (losing, gaining) _____ "cheap" labor and Mexico is _____ "cheap" labor.

14. The simplified model of immigration of workers into the United States from Mexico assumes that migration is costless. If there are costs to migration, then wage rates will remain somewhat (higher, lower) _____ in the United States, but the wage-rate difference between the two nations (will, will not) _____ encourage more migration of workers from Mexico to close the gap because the cost of migration is (greater, less) _____ than the expected benefit.

15. When Mexican workers who have immigrated to the United States send some of their wage income back to Mexico, they are making (remittances, backflows) _____, which can reduce the net gain from migration; and if some of these Mexican workers gain labor market skills in the United States and then return home, these _____ can reduce the net gains from migration.

16. If immigrant workers and domestic-born workers are complementary resources, then the lower wage rate resulting from large-scale immigration (increases, decreases) _____ production costs and creates an output effect that _____ the demand for labor.

17. The simple model of immigration assumes (full, partial) _____ employment, but in many cases Mexican workers are either unemployed or underemployed, and if these unemployed or underemployed Mexican workers immigrate into the United States, they (raise, lower) _____ the net gain from migration for Mexico. The movement of such workers may reflect (negative, positive) _____ self-selection if these workers who move are less capable or less motivated.

18. The introduction of illegal workers in the domestic U.S. labor market (increases, decreases) _____ the total supply of workers and _____ the wage rate from what it would be without illegal workers, and _____ the number of domestic workers employed. The deportation of illegal workers (will, will not)

_____ increase the wage rate for domestic workers, but the employment of domestic workers _____ increase on a one-for-one basis because the quantity supplied of domestic workers is less than the total demand for workers.

19. The entry of illegal workers into certain low-wage occupations will (increase, decrease) _____ the wage rate, but the overall effect of illegal immigration on average wage rates can be slightly positive if illegal workers are a (substitute, complementary) _____ resource for some domestic workers, or slightly negative if the illegal workers are a _____ for some domestic workers.

20. If illegal workers provide important help for producing goods and services in the U.S. economy, then prices of those goods and services will be (higher, lower) _____ than they otherwise would be without those illegal workers, and the standard of living for Americans will be _____.

■ **TRUE–FALSE QUESTIONS**

Circle T if the statement is true, F if it is false.

1. More than 10 million immigrants enter the United States each year, about half of whom are legal and the other half illegal. **T F**

2. The largest bulk of legal U.S. immigrants obtain their legal status via family ties to American residents. **T F**

3. The top country of origin for illegal immigrants is Cuba. **T F**

4. The main driver of economic immigration is the opportunity to improve the immigrant's earnings and standard of living. **T F**

5. Other things equal, larger wage differences between nations weaken the incentive to migrate and therefore increase the flow of immigrants toward the country providing the greater wage opportunities. **T F**

6. Immigration can be viewed as an investment decision because the prospective immigrant weighs all the costs of moving against the expected benefits. **T F**

7. Immigrants often reduce their costs of long moves by following beaten paths, which are routes taken previously by family, relatives, and friends. **T F**

8. From an economic perspective, a person who estimates that the stream of future earnings exceeds the explicit and implicit cost of moving is likely to migrate. **T F**

9. Younger workers are much less likely to migrate than older workers. **T F**

10. Immigrants who lack English language skills do not, in general, fare as well in the U.S. workforce as immigrants who have those skills when they arrive in the United States. **T F**

11. The sizable and continuous flow of immigrants to the United States shows that, overall, the economic benefits of immigration into the United States are greater than the costs for those who make the move. **T F**

12. Return migration or backflows seldom occur when people immigrate into the United States from other nations. **T F**

13. The lack of skill transferability means that although migrants may increase their wages through immigration into the United States, they may not earn as much as similarly employed domestic workers. **T F**

14. Economic immigration is characterized by self-selection, which means that migrants who choose to move may be more motivated and able to overcome the lack of skill transferability. **T F**

15. The simple demand and supply model of immigration suggests that the movement of workers from a low-wage nation to a high-wage nation decreases domestic output in the high-wage nation and increases domestic output in the low-wage nation. **T F**

16. An increase in the mobility of labor because of the elimination of barriers to the international flows of labor tends to increase the world's output of goods and services. **T F**

17. Brain drain in immigration refers to the fact that the rate of immigration is higher among illegal than legal workers. **T F**

18. If the demand for labor is elastic in the United States, then a decrease in wages from immigration will increase total wage income. **T F**

19. Mexican workers who have migrated to the United States and send remittances to their families in Mexico increase the gain to domestic output in the United States and reduce it in Mexico. **T F**

20. If immigrant workers and domestic-born workers are complementary resources, then the lower wage rate that results from large-scale immigration will create an output effect that increases the demand for labor among these domestic-born workers. **T F**

21. When unemployed or underemployed laborers from a poor nation migrate to a rich nation, the poor nation suffers a loss in domestic output because it loses workers. **T F**

22. The immigration of workers into the United States reduces domestic output and income in the U.S. economy. **T F**

23. In a market for low-wage labor in the United States, an increase in illegal workers increases the supply of labor in such markets and reduces the wage rate. **T F**

24. If illegal workers provide a substantial amount of low-wage labor in a particular industry, then the prices of goods and services in that industry will be higher. **T F**

25. Illegal immigration tends to impose a higher net fiscal burden on state and local governments. **T F**

■ MULTIPLE-CHOICE QUESTIONS

Circle the letter that corresponds to the best answer.

1. Immigrants who have permission to reside and work in the United States are
   (a) aliens
   (b) legal immigrants
   (c) illegal immigrants
   (d) undocumented workers

2. The H1-B provision of the immigration law allows
   (a) high-skilled workers in specialty occupations to enter and work continuously in the United States for six years
   (b) low-skilled workers in the agricultural industry to enter and work on a temporary basis during harvest season
   (c) "green card" holders to stay in the United States on an indefinite basis
   (d) the immediate deportation of those individuals who enter the United States illegally

3. Which one of the following is the major category for legal immigration?
   (a) diversity
   (b) refugee status
   (c) family sponsorship
   (d) employment-based preferences

4. What is the approximate number of legal and illegal immigrants who entered the United States *per year* in a recent year (2009)?
   (a) 350 thousand legal and 105 thousand illegal
   (b) 556 thousand legal and 221 thousand illegal
   (c) 1.13 million legal and 250 thousand illegal
   (d) 8.45 million legal and 3.47 million illegal

5. Which nation accounts for most of the legal immigrants admitted to the United States each year and also is the source of the largest number of illegal immigrants?
   (a) China
   (b) India
   (c) Cuba
   (d) Mexico

6. By moving from a low-wage nation to a high-wage nation, immigrants can increase the value of their
   (a) backflows
   (b) remittances
   (c) brain drains
   (d) human capital

7. Which nation would be considered a "magnet country" that attracts a lot of immigrants?
   (a) Japan
   (b) Sweden
   (c) Australia
   (d) South Korea

8. Other things equal, which person is more likely to migrate to the United States to work?
   (a) a younger worker, who lives in a nation near the United States
   (b) an older worker, who lives in a nation near the United States
   (c) a younger worker, who lives in a nation far from the United States
   (d) an older worker, who lives in a nation far from the United States

9. If there is full employment in both nations and unimpeded immigration, the effect of the migration of workers from a low-wage nation to a high-wage nation is to increase the
   (a) average wage rate in the high-wage nation
   (b) domestic output in the high-wage nation
   (c) business incomes in the low-wage nation
   (d) domestic output in the low-wage nation

10. In general, the elimination of barriers to the international flow of labor tends to
   (a) lower the wage rates for high-skilled labor
   (b) raise the wage rates for high-skilled labor
   (c) create worldwide efficiency gains from migration
   (d) eliminate worldwide efficiency gains from migration

Answer questions 11, 12, 13, and 14 on the basis of the following graph that shows a simple model of unimpeded immigration from Mexico to the United States as described in your textbook.

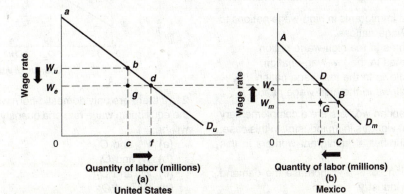

11. Before immigration is allowed from Mexico to the United States, what will be the wage rate and quantity of labor employed in each nation?
(a) U.S.: W_u and c Mexico: W_m and C
(b) U.S.: W_e and f Mexico: W_m and C
(c) U.S.: W_u and c Mexico: W_e and F
(d) U.S.: W_e and f Mexico: W_e and F

12. After immigration is allowed from Mexico to the United States, what will be the wage rate and quantity of labor employed in each nation?
(a) U.S.: W_u and c Mexico: W_m and C
(b) U.S.: W_e and f Mexico: W_m and C
(c) U.S.: W_u and c Mexico: W_e and F
(d) U.S.: W_e and f Mexico: W_e and F

13. With unimpeded immigration, what will happen to domestic output in the United States and in Mexico?
(a) increase in the U.S. from 0abc to 0adf and increase in Mexico from 0ADF to 0ABC
(b) increase in the U.S. from 0abc to 0adf and decrease in Mexico from 0ABC to 0ADF
(c) decrease in the U.S. from 0adf to 0abc and decrease in Mexico from 0ABC to 0ADF
(d) decrease in the U.S. from 0adf to 0abc and increase in Mexico from 0ADF to 0ABC

14. With unimpeded immigration, what will happen to business income in the United States and in Mexico?
(a) decrease in the U.S. from $W_e ad$ to $W_u ab$ to and decrease in Mexico from $W_m AB$ to $W_e AD$
(b) increase in the U.S. from $W_u ab$ to $W_e ad$ and increase in Mexico from $W_e AD$ to $W_m AB$
(c) increase in the U.S. from $W_u ab$ to $W_e ad$ and decrease in Mexico from $W_m AB$ to $W_e AD$
(d) decrease in the U.S. from $W_e ad$ to $W_u ab$ and increase in Mexico from $W_e AD$ to $W_m AB$

15. If the cost of migration from a low-wage nation to a high-wage nation is high, it
(a) increases immigration into the high-wage nation and keeps some of the wage-rate difference between the two nations
(b) increases immigration into the high-wage nation and closes the wage-rate difference between the two nations
(c) reduces immigration into the high-wage nation and keeps some of the wage-rate difference between the two nations
(d) reduces immigration into the high-wage nation and closes the wage-rate difference between the two nations

16. Remittances from immigrants in high-wage nations to their families in low-wage nations
(a) increase incomes in the high-wage nation
(b) increase incomes in the low-wage nation
(c) increase backflows in the low-wage nation
(d) increase backflows in the high-wage nation

17. Assume that American workers are a complementary resource to immigrant workers in an industry. In this case, an increase in the number of immigrant workers in this industry will
(a) lower production costs and increase the demand for all labor in the industry

(b) raise production costs and increase the demand for all labor in the industry
(c) lower production costs and decrease the demand for all labor in the industry
(d) raise production costs and decrease the demand for all labor in the industry

18. In the long run, some of the adverse wage effects of immigration on native-born workers may be mitigated by
(a) negative self-selection by unemployed workers
(b) compensating wage differentials for immigrants
(c) greater incentives for investment in capital goods to boost productivity
(d) more expenditures by state and local governments to cover the cost of immigration

19. Which would increase the gains realized in a low-wage nation from the migration of its workers to a high-wage nation?
(a) an increase in the explicit and implicit costs of migration
(b) a decline in the remittances of migrants to their low-wage nation
(c) an increase in the migration of unemployed workers from the low-wage nation to the high-wage nation
(d) a reduction in the welfare benefits in the high-wage nation for immigrants who come from a low-wage nation

20. The research evidence indicates that the overall effect of immigration on the average American wage ranges from
(a) zero to plus 10 percent
(b) minus 3 percent to plus 2 percent
(c) plus 8 percent to plus 12 percent
(d) minus 8 percent to minus 12 percent

Answer questions 21, 22, and 23 on the basis of the following graph which, shows the market for unskilled labor in agriculture. The demand for labor is shown by the demand curve D. The supply of domestic-born workers is shown by supply curve S_d. The total supply of domestic-born and illegal workers is shown by supply curve S_t.

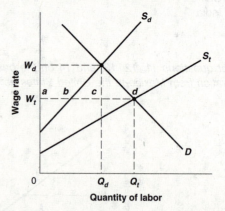

21. If there are only domestic-born workers in this market, the equilibrium wage rate and quantity of workers employed will be:
(a) W_d and Q_d
(b) W_t and Q_t
(c) W_d and Q_t
(d) W_t and Q_d

22. At a low wage of W_t what will be the quantity of domestic-born workers who will be employed and what will be the quantity of illegal workers who will be employed?

    (a) *bd* domestic-born workers and *ac* illegal workers

    (b) *cd* domestic-born worker and *ab* illegal workers

    (c) *ab* domestic-born workers and *bd* illegal workers

    (d) *ac* domestic-born workers and *cd* illegal workers

23. If illegal immigrants were originally able to work in this market, but then were excluded, the employment of domestic-born workers would increase by

    (a) *ac* and the total employment of all workers would increase by *cd*

    (b) *bc* and the total employment of all workers would decrease by *cd*

    (c) *ab* and the total employment of all workers would increase by *bc*

    (d) *ac* and the total employment of all workers would decrease by *cd*

24. Which of the following statements is generally valid about illegal immigration?

    (a) It imposes a high net fiscal burden on state and local governments.

    (b) It raises the prices for products in those industries where illegal workers are concentrated.

    (c) It reduces the standard of living of all Americans and their families.

    (d) It increases the employment of domestic-born workers on a one-to-one basis for the number of illegal workers who are deported.

25. From a strictly economic perspective, nations seeking to maximize net benefits from immigration should

    (a) expand immigration because it benefits society with a greater supply of products and increased demand for them

    (b) contract immigration because the benefits are minor and it reduces the wage rates of domestic workers

    (c) expand immigration until its marginal benefits equal its marginal costs

    (d) contract immigration until the extra welfare cost for taxpayers is zero

■ **PROBLEMS**

1. The two tables that follow show the demands for labor and the levels of domestic output that can be produced at each level of employment in two countries, **A** and **B**.

Country A		
Wage rate	Quantity of labor demanded	Real output
$20	95	$1900
18	100	1990
16	105	2070
14	110	2140
12	115	2200
10	120	2250
8	125	2290

Country B		
Wage rate	Quantity of labor demanded	Real output
$20	10	$200
18	15	290
16	20	370
14	25	440
12	30	500
10	35	550
8	40	590

a. If there were full employment in both countries and if

(1) the labor force in Country **A** were 110, the wage rate in Country **A** would be $_____.

(2) the labor force in Country **B** were 40, the wage rate in Country **B** would be $_____.

b. With these labor forces and wage rates

(1) total wages paid in **A** would be $_____ and the incomes of businesses (capitalists) in **A** would be $_____. (*Hint:* Subtract total wages paid from the real output.)

(2) total wages paid in **B** would be $_____ and business incomes in **B** would be $_____.

c. Assume the difference between the wage rates in the two countries induces 5 workers to migrate from **B** to **A**. So long as both countries maintain full employment,

(1) the wage rate in **A** would (rise, fall) _____ to $_____,

(2) and the wage rate in **B** would _____ to $_____.

d. The movement of workers from **B** to **A** would

(1) (increase, decrease) _____ the output of **A** by $_____,

(2) (increase, decrease) _____ the output of **B** by $_____, and

(3) (increase, decrease) _____ their combined (and the world's) output by $_____.

e. This movement of workers from **B** to **A** also (increased, decreased) _____ business incomes in **A** by $_____ and (increased, decreased) business incomes in **B** by $_____.

2. Consider the following wage and quantity of labor data for a low-wage market. The demand column shows the quantity of labor demanded at each wage rate. The domestic supply column shows the number of domestic-born workers willing to work at each wage rate. The total supply column shows the total number of workers (domestic-born plus illegal immigrants) who are willing to work at each wage rate.

Wage rate	Demand	Domestic supply	Total supply
$14	200	400	1100
13	300	300	900
12	400	200	700
11	500	100	500
10	600	0	300

a. What will be the equilibrium wage rate if there is no illegal immigration? _____ What is the quantity of domestic-born workers employed at this wage rate? _____

b. What will be the equilibrium wage rate if there is illegal immigration in this low-wage industry? _____ What is the quantity of total workers (domestic-born and illegal) employed at this wage rate? _____

c. At the equilibrium wage rate for total workers, how many workers will be domestic-born? _____ How many will be illegal workers? _____

d. How many more domestic-born workers will be employed if the wage rate for total workers rises to the wage rate for domestic-born workers only? _____ What is this compensating wage differential? _____

e. Do illegal workers reduce the employment of domestic-born workers by an amount equal to the employment of illegal workers? (Yes or No) _____ With illegal immigration, there are _____ illegal workers employed. If they are prevented from working, the employment of domestic-born workers at the total supply wage rate would only be _____ workers, and thus there would be another _____ illegal workers not replaced by domestic workers at this total supply wage rate.

■ **SHORT ANSWER AND ESSAY QUESTIONS**

1. Describe the numbers and trends in legal immigration in recent years. From where do most illegal immigrants come to the United States and for what reason do they get admitted?

2. Describe the estimated number of illegal immigrants who come annually, and also those who reside continuously, in the United States.

3. Use the concept of human capital to explain how earnings opportunities affect the decision to migrate.

4. How do moving costs affect the decision to migrate? What are these costs?

5. Discuss how distance, age, and other factors influence the decision to migrate.

6. How does the lack of skill transferability affect the wages earned by immigrants? What role does self-selection play in overcoming the wage differential?

7. Explain the effects of the migration of labor from a low-wage nation to a high-wage nation. Give your answer in terms of the effects on the wage rate, domestic output, and business incomes in the two nations.

8. Why might some high-wage nations encourage a relatively high level of immigration through its quotas? Why might some low-wage nations want to restrict the emigration of highly educated workers?

9. How does the cost of migration create rather than eliminate a wage gap between the equilibrium wages for workers in a high-wage nation and workers in a low-wage nation in similar industries?

10. What are remittances? What effect do they have on the gains and losses from the migration of labor from a low-wage nation to a high-wage nation?

11. Explain the economic effect on the demand for domestic labor when immigrant labor is a complementary resource rather than a substitute resource.

12. How might capital investment be affected by the use of immigrant labor? Describe a positive and negative scenario.

13. What effects will unemployment or underemployment in a low-wage nation have on the gains from the migration of workers to a high-wage nation?

14. Discuss the effects of immigrants on tax revenues and government spending in the United States. Which unit of government bears the largest net fiscal burden?

15. Offer a brief summary of the research findings about immigration on wages.

16. Describe the employment effects of illegal immigration for domestic-born workers in a low-wage industry in the United States. Do illegal workers fill most jobs that domestic-born workers do not want? Is the substitution one-for-one?

17. Why does illegal immigration have very little effect on the average level of wages in the United States?

18. What are the price effects from illegal immigration? In what way does illegal immigration affect the standard of living?

19. Describe the fiscal impact of illegal immigration and other concerns with it.

20. Explain from an economic perspective how a nation finds an optimal level of immigration.

ANSWERS

Chapter 22 Immigration

FILL-IN QUESTIONS

1. legal, illegal
2. 1, family, Mexico
3. 250, 11, Mexico

4. *a.* take advantage of employment opportunities; *b.* escape political or religious persecution; *c.* reunite with family or loved ones

5. increase, Australia

6. investment, greater than

7. less, more

8. greater, less, backflows

9. increases, decreases

10. increases, decreases, increases, gains

11. brain drain, oppose

12. increase, decrease,

13. increase, decrease, gaining, losing

14. higher, will not, greater

15. remittances, backflows

16. decreases, increases

17. full, raise, negative

18. increases, decreases, decreases, will, will not

19. decrease, complementary, substitute

20. lower, higher

TRUE–FALSE QUESTIONS

1. F, pp. 455–456	10. T, p. 458	19. F, p. 461
2. T, p. 456	11. T, p. 458	20. T, p. 462
3. F, p. 456	12. F, p. 459	21. F, pp. 462–463
4. T, p. 456	13. T, p. 459	22. F, p. 463
5. F, p. 457	14. T, p. 459	23. T, p. 464
6. T, p. 457	15. F, p. 460	24. F, p. 464
7. T, p. 458	16. T, p. 460	25. T, p. 467
8. T, p. 457	17. F, p. 461	
9. F, p. 458	18. T, p. 461	

MULTIPLE-CHOICE QUESTIONS

1. b, p. 455	10. c, p. 460	19. c, p. 462
2. a, p. 455	11. a, p. 460	20. b, p. 463
3. c, pp. 455–456	12. d, p. 460	21. a, p. 464
4. c, p. 456	13. b, p. 460	22. c, p. 464
5. d, p. 456	14. c, p. 461	23. b, p. 464
6. d, pp. 456–457	15. c, p. 461	24. a, p. 465
7. c, p. 457	16. b, p. 462	25. c, p. 467
8. a, pp. 457–458	17. a, p. 462	
9. b, p. 460	18. c, p. 462	

PROBLEMS

1. *a.* (1) 14, (2) 8; *b.* (1) 1540, 600, (2) 320, 270; *c.* (1) fall, 12, (2) rise, 10; *d.* (1) increase, 60, (2) decrease, 40, (3) increase, 20; *e.* increased, 220, decreased, 70

2. *a.* $13, 300; *b.* $11, 500; *c.* 100, 400; *d.* 100, $2; *e.* no, 400, 200, 200

SHORT ANSWER AND ESSAY QUESTIONS

1. pp. 455–456	8. p. 460	15. p. 453
2. p. 456	9. p. 461	16. pp. 464–465
3. pp. 456–457	10. pp. 461–462	17. p. 465
4. p. 456	11. p. 462	18. p. 465
5. pp. 457–458	12. p. 462	19. p. 465
6. p. 459	13. pp. 462–463	20. p. 467
7. pp. 459–461	14. p. 463	

CHAPTER 23

International Trade

After a brief review of the facts of international trade, the text uses the concept of production possibilities that you learned in Chapter 1 to explain why nations trade. Nations specialize in and export those goods and services in the production of which they have a **comparative advantage,** which means the domestic opportunity cost of producing a particular good or service is lower in one nation than in another nation. When nations specialize in those products in which they have a comparative advantage, the world can obtain more goods and services from its resources and each nation enjoys a higher standard of living than it would without trade.

Another question the chapter answers is what determines the equilibrium prices and quantities of the imports and exports resulting from trade. The text uses the **supply and demand analysis,** originally presented in Chapter 3, to explain equilibrium in the world market for a product. A simplified two-nation and one-product model of trade is constructed with export supply curves and import demand curves for each nation. Equilibrium occurs where one nation's export supply curve intersects another nation's import demand curve.

Regardless of the advantages of specialization and trade among nations, people in the United States and throughout the world for well over 200 years have debated the question of whether **free trade or protection** was the better policy for their nation. Economists took part in this debate and, with few exceptions, made a strong case for free trade. They also argued that protectionism in the form of tariffs, import quotas, and other trade barriers prevents or reduces specialization and decreases both a nation's and the world's production and standards of living. Despite these arguments, nations have erected and continue to erect trade barriers using an assortment of protection arguments that have questionable validity.

The latter sections of the chapter address questions related to how to make trade among nations work better and resolve trade disputes. **Multilateral agreements** have been made among nations and **free-trade zones** have been established to reduce trade barriers and increase worldwide trade. The World Trade Organization (WTO) is responsible for multilateral trade negotiations among member nations. The European Union (EU) is a free-trade zone among 27 European nations. The North American Free Trade Agreement (NAFTA) established a free-trade zone for the United States, Canada, and Mexico. The U.S. Congress developed policies to assist U.S. workers hurt by the expansion of trade.

Whether the direction of the trade policy in the United States will be toward freer trade or more protectionism is a question that gets debated as each new trade issue is presented to the U.S. public. The decision on each issue may well depend on your economic understanding of trade and the problems with trade protection.

■ **CHECKLIST**

When you have studied this chapter you should be able to

☐ Cite some key facts about international trade.

☐ State the three economic circumstances that make it desirable for nations to specialize and trade.

☐ Give examples of labor-intensive, capital-intensive, and land-intensive goods.

☐ Explain the difference between absolute advantage and comparative advantage.

☐ State the three assumptions made about the production possibilities graphs for two products in a two-nation example of trade.

☐ Compute the opportunity-cost ratio of producing the two products in the two-nation example.

☐ Determine which nation has a comparative advantage in the two-nation example.

☐ Calculate the range in which the terms of trade will occur in the two-nation example.

☐ Explain how nations gain from trade and specialization based on the two-nation example.

☐ Discuss how increasing costs affect specialization in the two-nation example.

☐ Restate the general case for free trade.

☐ Construct domestic supply and demand curves for two nations that trade a product.

☐ Construct export supply and import demand curves for two nations that trade a product.

☐ Explain how the equilibrium world prices and quantities of exports and imports are determined for two nations that trade a product.

☐ Define and explain the purpose of tariffs, import quotas, nontariff barriers, voluntary export restraints, and export subsidies.

☐ Explain the economic effects of a protective tariff for a product on consumption, production, imports, revenue, and efficiency.

☐ Analyze the economic effects of an import quota and compare them with a tariff.

☐ Discuss the problems with six major arguments for trade protectionism (self-sufficiency, diversification, infant industry, dumping, employment, and cheap labor).

☐ Describe the purpose and outcomes from the General Agreement on Tariffs and Trade (GATT).

☐ Discuss the purpose and controversies surrounding the World Trade Organization (WTO).

☐ Explain how the European Union (EU) operates as a free-trade zone.

☐ Describe the North American Free Trade Agreement (NAFTA).

☐ Discuss the reasons for the Trade Adjustment Assistance Act of 2002.

☐ Evaluate reasons for and outcomes from offshoring.

☐ Explain how Frédéric Bastiat satirized the proponents of protectionism (*Last Word*).

■ CHAPTER OUTLINE

1. Some key facts on international trade are worth noting.
   a. About 13 percent of the total output (GDP) of the United States is accounted for by exports of goods and services. The United States provides about 8.5 percent of the world's exports. The United States also leads the world in the combined volume of exports and imports.
   b. The United States has a trade deficit in goods and a trade surplus in services, and overall has a trade deficit in goods and services. The United States has a sizable trade deficit in goods and services with China. Canada is the most important trading partner for the United States in terms of the volume of trade.
   c. The major exports of the United States are chemicals, agricultural products, consumer durables, semiconductors, and aircraft. The major imports are petroleum, automobiles, metals, household appliances, and computers. Most of the U.S. trade occurs with other industrially advanced nations and members of OPEC. Canada is the largest trading partner for the United States.
   d. The major participants in international trade are the United States, Japan, China, and the nations of Western Europe. Other key participants include the Asian economies of South Korea, Taiwan, and Singapore.
   e. International trade links nations and is the focus of economic policy and debate in the United States and other nations.

2. The *economic basis for trade* comprises several circumstances. Specialization and trade among nations is advantageous because the world's resources are not evenly distributed and efficient production of different products requires different technologies and combinations of resources. Also, products differ in quality and other attributes, so people might prefer imported to domestic goods in some cases. Some nations have a cost advantage in making *labor-intensive goods* such as textiles or toys. Other nations have a cost advantage in producing *land-intensive goods* such as beef or vegetables. Industrially advanced economies have a cost advantage in making *capital-intensive goods* such as airplanes or chemicals.

3. Specialization and international trade increase the productivity of a nation's resources and allow a nation to obtain greater output than would be the case without trade. A nation has an absolute advantage in the production of a product over another nation if it can produce more of the product with the same amount of resources as the other nation. To specialize and benefit from trade, however, a nation only needs to have a comparative advantage, which means that it produces a product at a lower opportunity cost than another nation.
   a. The concept of comparative advantage is presented with an example using two nations (the United States and Mexico) and two products (beef and vegetables). The production possibilities curves are different straight lines because of the assumption of constant opportunity costs, but the curve for each nation is different because of different costs. The United States has an absolute advantage in the production of both beef and vegetables, which means that if all resources were devoted to one product or the other, the United States would produce more of both products (beef: United States 30 tons and Mexico 10 tons; vegetables: United States 30 tons and Mexico 20 tons).
   (1) The *opportunity-cost ratio* is what one nation has to forgo in the output of one domestic product to produce another domestic product. Using tons as units for beef (B) and vegetables (V), the opportunity-cost ratio for the United States is $1V = 1B$.
   (2) The opportunity-cost ratio for Mexico is $2V = 1B$.
   (3) If each nation is self-sufficient, they will pick some combination of the two products to produce. Assume this output mix for the United State is $18B$ and $12V$ and for Mexico it is $8B$ and $4V$.
   b. *Comparative advantage* explains the gains from trade and is directly related to opportunity cost. In essence, a nation has a comparative advantage in the production of a product when it can produce the product at a lower domestic opportunity cost than can a trading partner. A nation will specialize in the production of a product for which it is the low opportunity cost producer and trade for the other products it wants. Although the United States has an absolute advantage in producing both products, it does not have a comparative advantage because of the differences in the domestic opportunity cost of producing the products in both nations. The *principle of comparative advantage* says that total output will be greatest when each nation specializes in the production of a product for which it has the lowest domestic opportunity cost.
   (1) Returning to the two-nation example, for the United States, $1V = 1B$, but for Mexico, $2V = 1B$. The United States has a lower domestic opportunity cost for beef because for the United States to get $1B$ it gives up only $1V$ whereas for Mexico to get $1B$ it gives up $2V$.
   (2) Note that for Mexico, after dividing each side of $2V = 1B$ by 2 it becomes $1V = 0.5B$, Mexico has a lower domestic opportunity cost for vegetables because for Mexico to get $1V$, it gives up only $0.5B$ whereas for the United States to get $1V$ it gives up $1B$.
   c. The **terms of trade** or ratio at which one product is traded for another is between the opportunity-cost ratios of the two nations, or between $1V = 1B$ (U.S. costs) and $1V = 2B$ (Mexico's costs).
   d. Supposing that the terms of trade are $1V = 1.5B$, it is then possible to show a *trading possibilities line* that shifts outward from the original production possibilities line for each nation.
   (1) Each nation will be able to achieve a set of beef and vegetable alternatives by specializing in the production of the product for which it has a low opportunity cost

and trading its output of that product for the product for which has a high opportunity cost.

(2) Each nation gains from this trade because specialization permits a greater total output from the same resources and a better allocation of the world's resources. Given the terms of trade ($1V = 1.5B$), if the United States uses all its resources to produce beef ($30B$) and exports $10B$ to Mexico and in return gets $15V$, it is better off with trade ($20B$ and $15V$) than without trade ($18B$ and $12V$). If Mexico uses all its resources to produce vegetables ($20V$) and exports $15V$ to the United States and in return gets $10B$, it is better off with trade ($10B$ and $5V$) than without trade ($8B$ and $4V$).

e. If opportunity cost ratios in the two nations are not constant and there are increasing opportunity costs associated with more production of a product, then specialization may not be complete.

f. The basic argument for free trade among nations is that it leads to a better allocation of resources and a higher standard of living in the world because total output will increase from specialization and trade. Several side benefits from trade are that it increases competition and deters monopoly, and offers consumers a wider array of choices. It also links the interests of nations and can reduce the threat of hostilities or war.

4. Supply and demand analysis of exports and imports can be used to explain how the equilibrium price and quantity for a product (e.g., aluminum) are determined when there is trade between two nations (e.g., the United States and Canada).

a. For the United States, there will be *domestic* supply and demand as well as *export* supply and import demand for aluminum.

(1) The price and quantity of aluminum are determined by the intersection of the domestic demand and supply curves in a world without trade.

(2) In a world with trade, the export supply curve for the United States shows the amount of aluminum that U.S. producers will export at each world price above the domestic equilibrium price. U.S. exports will increase when the world price rises relative to the domestic price.

(3) The import demand curve for the United States shows the amount of aluminum that U.S. citizens will import at each world price below the domestic equilibrium price. U.S. imports will increase when world prices fall relative to the domestic price.

b. For Canada, there will be domestic supply and demand as well as export supply and import demand for aluminum. The description of these supply and demand curves is similar to the account of those of the United States previously described in point **a**.

c. The equilibrium world price and equilibrium world levels of exports and imports can be determined with further supply and demand analysis. The export supply curves of the two nations can be plotted on one graph. The import demand curves of both nations can be plotted on the same graph. In this two-nation model, equilibrium will be achieved when one nation's import demand curve intersects another nation's export supply curve.

5. Nations limit international trade by erecting **trade barriers,** which are of several types. **Tariffs** are excise taxes or "duties" on value or quantity of imported goods. They can be revenue tariffs, which typically are placed on products that are not domestically produced and whose basic purpose is to raise money for government. There also can be **protective tariffs,** which are designed to shield domestic producers from foreign competition by raising the price of imports. **Import quotas** are restrictions on the quantity or total value of a product that can be imported from another nation. **Nontariff barriers** are burdensome rules, regulations, licensing procedures, standards, or other practices that make it difficult and costly to import a product. A **voluntary export restraint (VER)** is an agreement among exporters to voluntarily limit the amount of a product exported to another nation; it has the same effect as an import quota. Governments also interfere with trade by giving a domestic producer an **export subsidy,** which is a government payment to a producer that helps the producer sell the product in an export market for a lower price than otherwise would be the case.

a. The imposition of a **tariff** on a product has both direct and indirect economic effects.

(1) The direct effects are an increase in the domestic price of the good, less domestic consumption, more domestic production, less foreign production, and a transfer of income from domestic consumers to the government.

(2) The indirect effects are a reduction in the incomes of foreign producers and thus the incomes of foreign nations to purchase products from the nation imposing the tariff, a shift of resources from efficient industries to inefficient industries, and thus less trade and worldwide output.

b. The imposition of a **quota** on an imported product has the same direct and indirect effects as that of a tariff on that product, with the exception that a tariff generates revenue for government use whereas an import quota transfers that revenue to foreign producers.

c. Special-interest groups benefit from protection and persuade their nations to erect trade barriers, but the costs of tariffs and quotas to consumers and nations exceed any benefits.

6. The arguments for **protectionism** are many, but each one can be challenged for its validity.

a. The military self-sufficiency argument can be challenged because it is difficult to determine which industry is "vital" to national defense and therefore must be protected; it would be more efficient economically to provide a direct subsidy to military producers rather than impose a tariff.

b. Using tariff barriers to permit diversification for stability in the economy is not necessary for advanced economies such as the United States, and there may be great economic costs to diversification in developing nations.

c. It is alleged that infant industries need protection until they are sufficiently large to compete, but the argument may not apply in developed economies: It is difficult to select which industries will prosper; protectionism tends to persist long after it is needed; and direct subsidies may be more economically efficient.

d. Sometimes protection is sought against **dumping,** which is the sale of foreign goods on U.S. markets at prices either below the cost of production or below the prices commonly charged in the home nation. Dumping is a legitimate concern and is restricted under U.S. trade law, but to use dumping as an excuse for widespread tariff protection is unjustified, and the number of documented cases is few. If foreign companies are more efficient (low cost) producers, what may appear to be dumping may actually be comparative advantage at work and domestic consumers can benefit from lower prices.

e. Trade barriers do not necessarily increase domestic employment because imports may eliminate some jobs, but create others, so imports may change only the composition of employment, not the overall level of employment. Also, the exports of one nation become the imports of another, so tariff barriers can be viewed as "beggar thy neighbor" policies. In addition, other nations are likely to retaliate against the imposition of trade barriers that will reduce domestic output and employment. The *Smoot-Hawley Tariff Act* is an example of legislation passed during the Great Depression that caused a trade war with other nations, thus hurting rather than helping the United States. In the long run, barriers create a less efficient allocation of resources by shielding protected domestic industries from the rigors of competition.

f. Protection is sometimes sought because of the cheap foreign labor argument that low-cost labor in other nations will undercut the wages of workers in the United States, but there are several counterpoints. First, there are mutual gains from trade between rich and poor nations and they lower the cost of production for products. Second, it should be realized that nations gain from trade based on comparative advantage, and by specializing at what each nation does best, the productivity of workers and thus their wages and living standards rise. Third, there is an incorrect focus on labor costs per hour rather than labor cost per unit of production. Labor costs or wages per hour can be higher in one nation than in another because of the higher productivity of workers (and it results in lower labor cost per unit of production).

7. International trade policies have changed over the years with the development of *multilateral agreements* and *free-trade zones.* They are used to counter the destructive aspects of trade wars that arise when nations impose high tariffs.

a. The *General Agreement on Tariffs and Trade (GATT)* that began in 1947 provided equal treatment of all member nations and sought to reduce tariffs and eliminate import quotas by multilateral negotiations. The Uruguay Round of GATT agreements that took effect in 1995 eliminated or reduced tariffs on many products, cut restrictive government rules applying to services, phased out quotas on textiles and apparel, and decreased subsidies for agriculture.

b. The *World Trade Organization (WTO)* is an international agency that is the successor to GATT. In 2010, 153 nations were members of the WTO. It is responsible for overseeing trade agreements among nations and rules on trade disputes. The WTO also provides a forum for more trade liberalization negotiations under the *Doha Development Agenda* that was begun in Doha, Qatar, in 2001. These negotiations focus on additional reductions in tariffs and quotas and cutbacks in domestic subsidies for agricultural products.

c. The *European Union (EU)* is an example of a regional free-trade zone or trade bloc among 27 European nations. The EU abolished tariffs among member nations and developed common policies on various economic issues, such as the tariffs on goods to and from non-member nations. In 2010, 16 EU nations shared a common currency—the *euro.* The chief advantages of such a currency is that it reduces transactions costs for exchanging goods and services in Euro Zone nations and allows consumers and businesses to comparison shop.

d. In 1993, the *North American Free Trade Agreement (NAFTA)* created a free-trade zone or trade bloc covering the United States, Mexico, and Canada. Critics of this agreement feared job losses and the potential for abuse by other nations using Mexico as a base for production, but the dire outcomes have not occurred. There has been increased trade among Canada, Mexico, and the United States because of the agreement.

8. Although increased trade and trade liberalization raise total output and income, they also create controversies and calls for assistance. The *Trade Adjustment Assistance Act* of 2002 provides support to qualified workers displaced by imports or plant relocations from international trade. It gives cash assistance, education and training benefits, subsides for health care, and wage subsidies (for those aged 50 or older). Critics contend that such dislocations are part of a market economy and workers in the international sector should not get special subsidies for their job losses.

9. The *offshoring* of jobs occurs when jobs done by U.S. workers are shifted to foreign workers and locations. While offshoring has long been used in manufacturing, improvements in communication and technology make it possible to do it in services. Although offshoring causes some domestic workers to lose their jobs, it can be beneficial for an economy. It allows an economy to specialize and use its labor resources in high-valued work for which it has a comparative advantage and obtain services for low-valued work that can be done more efficiently by foreign workers. It can increase the demand for complementary jobs in high-valued industries. It allows domestic businesses to reduce production costs, and thus be more competitive in both domestic and international markets.

10. (*Last Word*). Frédéric Bastiat (1801–1850) was a French economist who wrote a satirical letter to counter the proponents of protectionism. His "petition" to the French government called for blocking out the sun because it provided too much competition for domestic candlestick makers, thus illustrating the logical absurdity of protectionist arguments.

■ **HINTS AND TIPS**

1. In the discussion of **comparative advantage,** the assumption of a constant opportunity-cost ratio means the production possibilities "curves" for each nation can be drawn as straight lines. The slope of the line in each nation is the opportunity cost of one product (beef) in terms of the other product (vegetables). The reciprocal of the slope of each line is the opportunity cost of the other product (vegetables) in terms of the first product (beef).

2. The **export supply and import demand curves** in Figures 23.3 and 23.4 in the text look different from the typical supply and demand curves that you have seen so far, so you should understand how they are constructed. The export supply and import demand curves for a nation do not intersect. Each curve meets at the price point on the *Y* axis showing the equilibrium price for domestic supply and demand. At this point there are no exports or imports.

> **a.** The export supply curve is up-sloping from that point because as world prices rise above the domestic equilibrium price, there will be increasing domestic surpluses produced by a nation that can be exported. The export supply curve reflects the positive relationship between rising world prices (above the domestic equilibrium price) and the increasing quantity of exports.
>
> **b.** The import demand curve is down-sloping from the domestic equilibrium price because as world prices fall below the domestic equilibrium price, there will be increasing domestic shortages that need to be covered by increasing imports. The import demand curve reflects the inverse relationship between falling world prices (below the domestic price) and the increasing quantity of imports.

3. One of the most interesting sections of the chapter discusses the arguments for and against trade protection. You have probably heard people give one or more of the arguments for trade protection, but now you have a chance to use your economic reasoning to expose the weaknesses in these arguments. Most are half-truths and special pleadings.

■ IMPORTANT TERMS

labor-intensive goods

land-intensive goods

capital-intensive goods

opportunity-cost ratio

comparative advantage

principle of comparative advantage

terms of trade

trading possibilities line

gains from trade

world price

domestic price

export supply curve

import demand curve

equilibrium world price

tariffs

revenue tariff

protective tariff

import quota

nontariff barrier (NTB)

voluntary export restriction (VER)

export subsidy

dumping

Smoot-Hawley Tariff Act

General Agreement on Tariffs and Trade (GATT)

World Trade Organization (WTO)

Doha Development Agenda

European Union (EU)

Euro Zone

North American Free Trade Agreement (NAFTA)

Trade Adjustment Assistance Act

offshoring

■ SELF-TEST

■ FILL-IN QUESTIONS

1. In the United States, exports of goods and services make up about (13, 26) _____ percent of total U.S. output. The volume of exports and imports in dollar terms makes the United States the world's (largest, smallest) _____ trading nation.

2. A trade deficit occurs when exports are (greater than, less than) _____ imports and a trade surplus occurs when exports are _____ imports. The United States has a trade deficit in (goods, services) _____ and a trade surplus in _____.

3. Nations tend to trade among themselves because the distribution of economic resources among them is (even, uneven) _____, the efficient production of various goods and services necessitates (the same, different) _____ technologies or combinations of resources, and people prefer (more, less) _____ choices in products.

4. The principle of comparative advantage means total world output will be greatest when each good is produced by that nation having the (highest, lowest) _____ opportunity cost. The nations of the world tend to specialize in the production of those goods in which they (have, do not have) _____ a comparative advantage and then export them, and they import those goods in which they _____ a comparative advantage in production.

5. If the cost ratio in country X is 4 Panama hats equal 1 pound of bananas, while in country Y 3 Panama hats equal 1 pound of bananas, then

> **a.** in country X hats are relatively (expensive, inexpensive) _____ and bananas relatively _____,
>
> **b.** in country Y hats are relatively (expensive, inexpensive) _____ and bananas relatively _____,
>
> **c.** X has a comparative advantage and should specialize in the production of (bananas, hats) _____, and Y has a comparative advantage and should specialize in the production of _____.
>
> **d.** When X and Y specialize and trade, the terms of trade will be somewhere between (1, 2, 3, 4) _____ and _____ hats for each pound of bananas and will depend on world demand and supply for hats and bananas.

e. When the actual terms of trade turn out to be 3 1/2 hats for 1 pound of bananas, the cost of obtaining

(1) 1 Panama hat has been decreased from (2/7, 1/3) _____ to _____ pounds of bananas in Y.

(2) 1 pound of bananas has been decreased from (3 1/2, 4) _____ to _____ Panama hats in X.

f. International specialization will not be complete if the opportunity cost of producing either good (rises, falls) _____ as a nation produces more of it.

6. The basic argument for free trade based on the principle of (bilateral negotiations, comparative advantage) _____ is that it results in a (more, less) _____ efficient allocation of resources and a (lower, higher) _____ standard of living.

7. The world equilibrium price is determined by the interaction of (domestic, world) _____ supply and demand, while the domestic equilibrium price is determined by _____ supply and demand. When the world price of a good falls relative to the domestic price in a nation, the nation will (increase, decrease) _____ its imports, and when the world price rises relative to the domestic price, the nation will _____ its exports.

8. In a two-nation model for a product, the equilibrium price and quantity of imports and exports occur where one nation's import demand curve intersects another nation's export (supply, demand) _____ curve. In a highly competitive world market, there can be (multiple, only one) _____ price(s) for a standardized product.

9. Excise taxes on imported products are (quotas, tariffs) _____, whereas limits on the maximum amount of a product that can be imported are import _____. Tariffs applied to a product not produced domestically are (protective, revenue) _____ tariffs, but tariffs designed to shield domestic producers from foreign competition are _____ tariffs.

10. There are other types of trade barriers. Imports that are restricted through the use of a licensing requirement or bureaucratic red tape are (tariff, nontariff) _____ barriers. When foreign firms voluntarily limit their exports to another country, it would represent a voluntary (import, export) _____ restraint.

11. Nations erect barriers to international trade to benefit the economic positions of (consumers, domestic producers) _____ even though these barriers (increase, decrease) _____ economic efficiency and trade among nations and the benefits to that nation are (greater, less) _____ than the costs to it.

12. When the United States imposes a tariff on a good that is imported from abroad, the price of that good in the United States will (increase, decrease) _____ and the total purchases of the good in the United States will _____. The output of U.S. producers of the good will (increase, decrease) _____ and the output of foreign producers will _____.

13. When comparing the effects of a tariff with the effects of a quota to restrict the U.S. imports of a product, the basic difference is that with a (tariff, quota) _____ the U.S. government will receive revenue, but with a _____ foreign producers will receive the revenue.

14. There are counterarguments to the six arguments for trade protectionism.

a. The military self-sufficiency argument can be challenged because it is difficult to determine which industry is (essential, unessential) _____ for national defense and must be protected. A direct subsidy to producers would be (more, less) _____ efficient than a tariff.

b. Using trade barriers to permit diversification for stability in an economy is not necessary for (advanced, developing) _____ economies such as in the United States, and there may be great economic costs to forcing diversification in _____ nations.

c. The problem with the infant industry argument is that it is difficult to determine when (a mature, an infant) _____ industry becomes _____ industry.

d. The protection-against-dumping argument does not hold because the lower prices from alleged dumping may be a case of (absolute, comparative) _____ advantage at work and documented cases of dumping are relatively (common, rare) _____.

e. Trade barriers do not necessarily increase domestic employment because imports may change only the (level, composition) _____ of employment, such barriers (increase, decrease) _____ the incomes of trading partners thus hurting an exporting nation and other nations can (dump, retaliate) _____ by imposing their own trade barriers.

f. Proponents of the cheap foreign labor argument tend to focus exclusively on large international differences that exist in labor costs (per unit, per hour) _____ and fail to mention that these differences are mostly the result of large national differences in productivity that serve to equalize labor costs _____.

15. The three principles established in the General Agreement on Tariffs and Trade (GATT) of 1947 were

a. _____

b. _____

c. _____

16. The World Trade Organization (WTO) is the successor to GATT and it is responsible for overseeing multilateral trade (barriers, agreements) _____ and rules on trade (licenses, disputes) _____. The current round of multilateral trade negotiations is the (Abba, Doha) _____ Development Agenda that focuses on (increasing, decreasing) _____ tariffs, import quotas, and agricultural subsidies.

17. An example of a regional free-trade zone is the (Western, European) _____ Union. It abolished (imports and exports, tariffs and quotas) _____ among the participating members and established (common, different) _____ tariffs on goods imported from outside this free-trade zone. The common currency of many of the member nations of the regional free-trade zone is the (peso, euro) _____.

18. The North American Free Trade Agreement (NAFTA) formed a free-trade (barrier, zone) _____ among the United States, Canada, and Mexico. This agreement will eliminate (terms of trade, tariffs) _____ among the nations. Critics in the United States said that it would (increase, decrease) _____ jobs, but the evidence shows a(n) _____ in jobs and total output since its passage.

19. The Trade Adjustment Assistance Act of 2002 is designed to help some of the (workers, businesses) _____ hurt by shifts in international trade patterns. Critics contend that such job losses are a (small, large) _____ fraction of the total each year and that such a program is another type of special (tariff, subsidy) _____ that benefits one type of worker over another.

20. The shifting of work previously done by U.S. workers to workers located in other nations is (dumping, offshoring) _____. It reflects a (growth, decline) _____ in the specialization and international trade of services. It may (decrease, increase) _____ some jobs moved to other nations, but also _____ jobs and productivity in the United States.

■ **TRUE–FALSE QUESTIONS**

Circle T if the statement is true, F if it is false.

1. The combined volume of exports and imports in the United States as measured in dollars is greater than in any other nation.   **T   F**

2. A factor that serves as the economic basis for world trade is the even distribution of resources among nations.   **T   F**

3. People trade because they seek products of different quality and other nonprice attributes.   **T   F**

4. Examples of capital-intensive goods would be automobiles, machinery, and chemicals.   **T   F**

5. The relative efficiency with which a nation can produce specific goods is fixed over time.   **T   F**

6. Mutually advantageous specialization and trade are possible between any two nations if they have the same domestic opportunity-cost ratios for any two products.   **T   F**

7. The principle of comparative advantage is that total output will be greatest when each good is produced by that nation which has the higher domestic opportunity cost.   **T   F**

8. By specializing based on comparative advantage, nations can obtain larger outputs with fixed amounts of resources.   **T   F**

9. The terms of trade determine how the increase in world output resulting from comparative advantage is shared by trading nations.   **T   F**

10. Increasing opportunity costs tend to prevent specialization among trading nations from being complete.   **T   F**

11. Trade among nations tends to bring about a more efficient use of the world's resources and a higher level of material well-being.   **T   F**

12. Free trade among nations tends to increase monopoly and lessen competition in these nations.   **T   F**

13. A nation will export a particular product if the world price is less than the domestic price.   **T   F**

14. In a two-country model, equilibrium in world prices and quantities of exports and imports will occur where one nation's export supply curve intersects the other nation's import demand curve.   **T   F**

15. A tariff on coffee in the United States is an example of a protective tariff.   **T   F**

16. The imposition of a tariff on a good imported from abroad will reduce the amount of the imported good that is bought.   **T   F**

17. A cost of tariffs and quotas imposed by the United States is higher prices that U.S. consumers must pay for the protected product.   **T   F**

18. The major difference between a tariff and a quota on an imported product is that a quota produces revenue for the government.   **T   F**

19. To advocate tariffs that would protect domestic producers of goods and materials essential to national defense is to substitute a political-military objective for the economic objectives of efficiently allocating resources.   **T F**

20. One-crop economies may be able to make themselves more stable and diversified by imposing tariffs on goods imported from abroad, but these tariffs are also apt to lower the standard of living in these economies. **T F**

21. Protection against the "dumping" of foreign goods at low prices on the U.S. market is one good justification for widespread, permanent tariffs.   **T F**

22. Tariffs and import quotas meant to increase domestic full employment achieve short-run domestic goals by making trading partners poorer.   **T F**

23. The cheap foreign labor argument for protection fails because it focuses on labor costs per hour rather than what really matters, which is labor cost per unit of output. **T F**

24. Most arguments for protection are special interest appeals that, if followed, would provide gains for consumers at the expense of protected industries and their workers.   **T F**

25. The General Agreement on Tariffs and Trade sought to reduce tariffs through multilateral negotiations.   **T F**

26. The World Trade Organization (WTO) is the world's major advocate for trade protectionism.   **T F**

27. The members of the European Union (EU) have experienced freer trade since it was formed.   **T F**

28. The 1993 North American Free Trade Agreement (NAFTA) includes all Central American nations.   **T F**

29. The Trade Adjustment Assistance Act of 2002 provided compensation to U.S. workers who were displaced by shifts in international trade patterns.   **T F**

30. Although offshoring decreases some U.S. jobs, it also lowers production costs, expands sales, and may create other U.S. jobs.   **T F**

■ **MULTIPLE-CHOICE QUESTIONS**

Circle the letter that corresponds to the best answer.

1. Which nation leads the world in the combined volume of exports and imports?
 (a) Japan
 (b) Germany
 (c) United States
 (d) United Kingdom

2. Which nation is the most important trading partner for the United States in terms of the percentage of imports and exports?
 (a) India
 (b) Russia
 (c) Canada
 (d) Germany

3. Nations engage in trade because
 (a) world resources are evenly distributed among nations

(b) world resources are unevenly distributed among nations
 (c) all products are produced from the same technology
 (d) all products are produced from the same combinations of resources

Use the following tables to answer Questions 4, 5, 6, and 7.

NEPAL PRODUCTION POSSIBILITIES TABLE

	Production alternatives					
Product	A	B	C	D	E	F
Yak fat	0	4	8	12	16	20
Camel hides	40	32	24	16	8	0

KASHMIR PRODUCTION POSSIBILITIES TABLE

	Production alternatives					
Product	A	B	C	D	E	F
Yak fat	0	3	6	9	12	15
Camel hides	60	48	36	24	12	0

4. The data in the tables show that production in
 (a) both Nepal and Kashmir is subject to increasing opportunity costs
 (b) both Nepal and Kashmir is subject to constant opportunity costs
 (c) Nepal is subject to increasing opportunity costs and Kashmir to constant opportunity costs
 (d) Kashmir is subject to increasing opportunity costs and Nepal to constant opportunity costs

5. If Nepal and Kashmir engage in trade, the terms of trade will be
 (a) between 2 and 4 camel hides for 1 unit of yak fat
 (b) between 1/3 and 1/2 units of yak fat for 1 camel hide
 (c) between 3 and 4 units of yak fat for 1 camel hide
 (d) between 2 and 4 units of yak fat for 1 camel hide

6. Assume that prior to specialization and trade Nepal and Kashmir both choose production possibility C. Now if each specializes according to its comparative advantage, the resulting gains from specialization and trade will be
 (a) 6 units of yak fat
 (b) 8 units of yak fat
 (c) 6 units of yak fat and 8 camel hides
 (d) 8 units of yak fat and 6 camel hides

7. Each nation produced only one product in accordance with its comparative advantage, and the terms of trade were set at 3 camel hides for 1 unit of yak fat. In this case, Nepal could obtain a maximum combination of 8 units of yak fat and
 (a) 12 camel hides
 (b) 24 camel hides
 (c) 36 camel hides
 (d) 48 camel hides

8. What happens to a nation's imports or exports of a product when the world price of the product rises above the domestic price?
(a) Imports of the product increase.
(b) Imports of the product stay the same.
(c) Exports of the product increase.
(d) Exports of the product decrease.

9. What happens to a nation's imports or exports of a product when the world price of the product falls below the domestic price?
(a) Imports of the product increase.
(b) Imports of the product decrease.
(c) Exports of the product increase.
(d) Exports of the product stay the same.

10. Which one of the following is characteristic of tariffs?
(a) They prevent the importation of goods from abroad.
(b) They specify the maximum amounts of specific commodities that may be imported during a given period of time.
(c) They often protect domestic producers from foreign competition.
(d) They enable nations to reduce their exports and increase their imports during periods of recession.

11. The motive for barriers to the importation of goods and services from abroad is to
(a) improve economic efficiency in that nation
(b) protect and benefit domestic producers of those goods and services
(c) reduce the prices of the goods and services produced in that nation
(d) expand the export of goods and services to foreign nations

12. When a tariff is imposed on a good imported from abroad,
(a) the demand for the good increases
(b) the demand for the good decreases
(c) the supply of the good increases
(d) the supply of the good decreases

Answer Questions 13, 14, 15, 16, and 17 on the basis of the following diagram, where S_d and D_d are the domestic supply and demand for a product and P_w is the world price of that product.

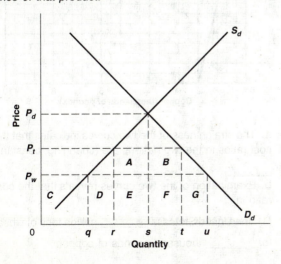

13. In a closed economy (without international trade), the equilibrium price would be
(a) P_d, but in an open economy, the equilibrium price would be P_t
(b) P_d, but in an open economy, the equilibrium price would be P_w
(c) P_w, but in an open economy, the equilibrium price would be P_d
(d) P_w, but in an open economy, the equilibrium price would be P_t

14. If there is free trade in this economy and no tariffs, the total revenue going to the foreign producers is represented by
(a) area C
(b) areas A and B combined
(c) areas A, B, E, and F combined
(d) areas D, E, F, and G combined

15. If a per-unit tariff was imposed in the amount of P_wP_t then domestic producers would supply
(a) q units and foreign producers would supply qu units
(b) s units and foreign producers would supply su units
(c) r units and foreign producers would supply rt units
(d) t units and foreign producers would supply tu units

16. Given a per-unit tariff in the amount of P_wP_t, the amount of the tariff revenue paid by consumers of this product is represented by
(a) area A
(b) area B
(c) areas A and B combined
(d) areas D, E, F, and G combined

17. Assume that an import quota of rt units is imposed on the foreign nation producing this product. The amount of *total* revenue going to foreign producers is represented by areas
(a) $A + B$
(b) $E + F$
(c) $A + B + E + F$
(d) $D + E + F + G$

18. Tariffs lead to
(a) the contraction of relatively efficient industries
(b) an overallocation of resources to relatively efficient industries
(c) an increase in the foreign demand for domestically produced goods
(d) an underallocation of resources to relatively inefficient industries

19. Tariffs and quotas are costly to consumers because
(a) the price of the imported good rises
(b) the supply of the imported good increases
(c) import competition increases for domestically produced goods
(d) consumers shift purchases away from domestically produced goods

20. The infant industry argument for tariffs
(a) is especially pertinent for the European Union
(b) generally results in tariffs that are removed after the infant industry has matured

(c) makes it rather easy to determine which infant industries will become mature industries with comparative advantages in producing their goods

(d) might better be replaced by an argument for outright subsidies for infant industries

21. Smoot-Hawley Tariff Act resulted in
   (a) a significant decline in tariffs
   (b) a trade war with other nations
   (c) the elimination of import quotas
   (d) the imposition of antidumping duties

22. "The nation needs to protect itself from foreign countries that sell their products in our domestic markets at less than the cost of production." This quotation would be most closely associated with which protectionist argument?
   (a) diversification for stability
   (b) increased domestic employment
   (c) protection against dumping
   (d) cheap foreign labor

23. Which is a likely result of imposing tariffs to increase domestic employment?
   (a) a short-run increase in domestic employment in import industries
   (b) a decrease in the tariff rates of foreign nations
   (c) a long-run reallocation of workers from export industries to protected domestic industries
   (d) a decrease in consumer prices

24. Which is the likely result of the United States using tariffs to protect its high wages and standard of living from cheap foreign labor?
   (a) an increase in U.S. exports
   (b) a rise in the U.S. real GDP
   (c) a decrease in the average productivity of U.S. workers
   (d) a decrease in the quantity of labor employed by industries producing the goods on which tariffs have been levied

25. Which of the following is characteristic of the General Agreement on Tariffs and Trade? Nations signing the agreement were committed to
   (a) the expansion of import quotas
   (b) the establishment of a world customs union
   (c) the reciprocal increase in tariffs by negotiation
   (d) the nondiscriminatory treatment of all member nations

26. One important outcome from the Uruguay Round of GATT was
   (a) an increase in tariff barriers on services
   (b) the elimination or reduction of many tariffs
   (c) removal of voluntary export restraints in manufacturing
   (d) abolishment of patent, copyright, and trademark protection

27. What international agency is currently charged with overseeing multilateral trade negotiations and with resolving trade disputes among nations?
   (a) World Bank
   (b) United Nations
   (c) World Trade Organization
   (d) International Monetary Fund

28. One of the major accomplishments of the European Union was
   (a) passing the Trade Assistance Act
   (b) enacting minimum wage laws
   (c) increasing tariffs on U.S. products
   (d) establishing the Euro Zone

29. An example of the formation of a regional free-trade zone would be the
   (a) Smoot-Hawley Tariff Act
   (b) Doha Development Agenda
   (c) North American Free Trade Agreement
   (d) General Agreement on Tariffs and Trade

30. The Trade Adjustment Assistance Act
   (a) increased funding for the World Trade Organization
   (b) provided more foreign aid to nations that trade with the United States
   (c) extended normal-trade-relations status to more less-developed countries
   (d) gave cash assistance to U.S. workers displaced by imports or plant relocations abroad

■ **PROBLEMS**

1. Shown below and on the next page are the production possibilities curves for two nations: the United States and Chile. Suppose these two nations do not currently engage in international trade or specialization, and suppose that points **A** and **a** show the combinations of wheat and copper they now produce and consume.

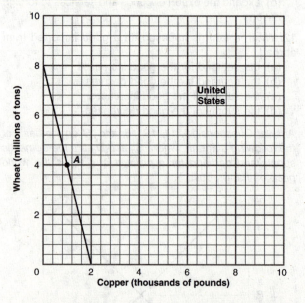

a. The straightness of the two curves indicates that the cost ratios in the two nations are (changing, constant)

_____.

b. Examination of the two curves reveals that the cost ratio in

(1) the United States is _____ million tons of wheat

for _____ thousand pounds of copper.

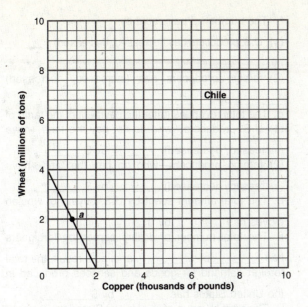

(2) Chile is _____ million tons of wheat for _____ thousand pounds of copper.

c. If these two nations were to specialize and trade wheat for copper,

(1) The United States would specialize in the production of wheat because _____.

(2) Chile would specialize in the production of copper because _____.

d. The terms of trade, if specialization and trade occur, will be greater than 2 and less than 4 million tons of wheat for 1000 pounds of copper because _____

_____.

e. Assume the terms of trade turn out to be 3 million tons of wheat for 1000 pounds of copper. Draw in the trading possibilities curves for the United States and Chile.

f. With these trading possibilities curves, suppose the United States decides to consume 5 million tons of wheat and 1000 pounds of copper while Chile decides to consume 3 million tons of wheat and 1000 pounds of copper. The gains from trade to

(1) the United States are _____ million tons of wheat and _____ thousand pounds of copper.

(2) Chile are _____ million tons of wheat and _____ thousand pounds of copper.

2. Following are tables showing the domestic supply and demand schedules and the export supply and import demand schedules for two nations (**A** and **B**).

NATION A

Price	Q_{dd}	Q_{sd}	Q_{di}	Q_{se}
$3.00	100	300	0	200
2.50	150	250	0	100
2.00	200	200	0	0
1.50	250	150	100	0
1.00	300	100	200	0

a. For nation **A**, the first column of the table is the price of a product. The second column is the quantity demanded domestically (Q_{dd}). The third column is the quantity supplied domestically (Q_{sd}). The fourth column is the quantity demanded for imports (Q_{di}). The fifth column is the quantity of exports supplied (Q_{se}).

(1) At a price of $2.00, there (will, will not) _____ be a surplus or shortage and there _____ be exports or imports.

(2) At a price of $3.00, there will be a domestic (shortage, surplus) _____ of _____ units. This domestic _____ will be eliminated by (exports, imports) _____ of _____ units.

(3) At a price of $1.00, there will be a domestic (shortage, surplus) _____ of _____ units. This domestic _____ will be eliminated by (exports, imports) _____ of _____ units.

NATION B

Price	Q_{dd}	Q_{sd}	Q_{di}	Q_{se}
$2.50	100	300	0	200
2.00	150	250	0	100
1.50	200	200	0	0
1.00	250	150	100	0

b. For nation **B**, the first column is the price of a product. The second column is the quantity demanded domestically (Q_{dd}). The third column is the quantity supplied domestically (Q_{sd}). The fourth column is the quantity demanded for imports (Q_{di}). The fifth column is the quantity of exports supplied (Q_{se}).

(1) At a price of $1.50, there (will, will not) _____ be a surplus or shortage and there _____ be exports or imports.

(2) At a price of $2.50, there will be a domestic (shortage, surplus) _____ of _____ units. This domestic _____ will be eliminated by (exports, imports) _____ of _____ units.

(3) At a price of $1.00, there will be a domestic (shortage, surplus) _____ of _____ units. This domestic _____ will be eliminated by (exports, imports) _____ of _____ units.

c. The following table shows a schedule of the import demand in nation **A** and the export supply in nation **B** at various prices. The first column is the price of the product. The second column is the quantity demanded for imports (Q_{diA}) in nation **A**. The third column is the quantity of exports supplied (Q_{seB}) in nation **B**.

Price	Q_{diA}	Q_{seB}
$2.00	0	100
1.75	50	50
1.50	100	0

(1) If the world price is $2.00, then nation (**A**, **B**) _____ will want to import _____ units and nation _____ will want to export _____ units of the product.

(2) If the world price is $1.75, then nation (**A**, **B**) _____ will want to import _____ units and nation _____ will want to export _____ units of the product.

(3) If the world price is $1.50, then nation (**A**, **B**) _____ will want to import _____ units and nation _____ will want to export _____ units of the product.

3. The following table shows the quantities of woolen gloves demanded (**D**) in the United States at several different prices (**P**). Also shown in the table are the quantities of woolen gloves that would be supplied by U.S. producers (S_a) and the quantities that would be supplied by foreign producers (S_f) at the nine different prices.

P	D	S_a	S_f	S_t	S'_f	S'_t
$2.60	450	275	475	_____	_____	_____
2.40	500	250	450	_____	_____	_____
2.20	550	225	425	_____	_____	_____
2.00	600	200	400	_____	_____	_____
1.80	650	175	375	_____	_____	_____
1.60	700	150	350	_____	_____	_____
1.40	750	125	325	_____	_____	_____
1.20	800	0	300	_____	_____	_____
1.00	850	0	0	_____	_____	_____

a. Compute and enter in the table the total quantities that would be supplied (S_t) by U.S. and foreign producers at each of the prices.

b. If the market for woolen gloves in the United States is a competitive one, the equilibrium price for woolen gloves is $_____ and the equilibrium quantity is _____.

c. Suppose now that the United States government imposes an 80 cent ($.80) tariff per pair of gloves on all gloves imported into the United States from abroad. Compute and enter into the table the quantities that would be supplied (S'_f) by foreign producers at the nine different prices. [*Hint:* If foreign producers were willing to supply 300 pairs at a price of $1.20 when there was no tariff, they are now willing to supply 300 pairs at $2.00 (the $.80 per pair tariff plus the $1.20 they will receive for themselves). The quantities supplied at each of the other prices may be found in a similar fashion.]

d. Compute and enter into the table the total quantities that would be supplied (S'_t) by U.S. and foreign producers at each of the nine prices.

e. As a result of the imposition of the tariff the equilibrium price has risen to $_____ and the equilibrium quantity has fallen to _____.

f. The number of pairs sold by

(1) U.S. producers has (increased, decreased) _____ by _____.

(2) foreign producers has (increased, decreased) _____ by _____.

g. The total revenues (after the payment of the tariff) of

(1) U.S. producers—who do not pay the tariff—have (increased, decreased) _____ by $_____.

(2) foreign producers—who do pay the tariff—have (increased, decreased) _____ by $_____.

h. The total amount spent by U.S. buyers of woolen gloves has _____ by $_____.

i. The total number of dollars earned by foreigners has _____ by $_____, and, as a result, the total foreign demand for goods and services produced in the United States has _____ by $_____.

j. The tariff revenue of the United States government has _____ by $_____.

k. If an import quota were imposed that had the same effect as the tariff on price and output, the amount of the tariff revenue, $_____, would now be received as revenue by _____ producers.

■ SHORT ANSWER AND ESSAY QUESTIONS

1. What is the economic basis for trade? Explain the underlying facts that support free trade and supply examples of three types of goods produced based on resource differences.

2. Explain the difference between absolute advantage and comparative advantage.

3. Provide a two-nation and two-product example that shows the gains from specialization and trade.

4. What is the case for free trade?

5. Explain how the equilibrium prices and quantities of exports and imports are determined. Why will exports in a nation increase when world prices rise relative to domestic prices?

6. What motivates nations to erect barriers to the importation of goods from abroad, and what types of barriers do they erect?

7. Suppose the United States increases the tariff on automobiles imported from Germany (and other foreign countries). What is the effect of this tariff-rate increase on
  (a) the price of automobiles in the United States;
  (b) the total number of cars sold in the United States during a year;
  (c) the number of cars produced by and employment in the German automobile industry;
  (d) production by and employment in the U.S. automobile industry;
  (e) German income obtained by selling cars in the United States;

(f) the German demand for goods produced in the United States;

(g) the production of and employment in those U.S. industries that now export goods to Germany;

(h) the standards of living in the United States and in Germany;

(i) the allocation of resources in the U.S. economy; and

(j) the allocation of the world's resources?

8. Compare and contrast the economic effects of a tariff with an import quota on a product.

9. Critically evaluate the military self-sufficiency argument for protectionism. What industries should be protected?

10. What is the basis for the diversification-for-stability argument for protectionism? How can it be countered?

11. Explain the arguments and counterarguments for protecting infant industries.

12. Can a strong case for protectionism be made on the basis of defending against the "dumping" of products? How do you determine if a nation is dumping a product? What are the economic effects of dumping on consumers?

13. What are the problems with using trade barriers as a means of increasing domestic employment?

14. Does the economy need to shield domestic workers from competition from "cheap" foreign labor? Explain using comparative advantage, standards of living, productivity, and labor cost per unit of output.

15. What was the purpose of the General Agreement on Tariffs and Trade (GATT), and what did it achieve?

16. Describe the purpose of the World Trade Organization (WTO). Why is it controversial?

17. What is the European Union? What has it achieved?

18. What is the North American Free Trade Agreement (NAFTA)? What do critics and defenders say about the agreement?

19. Discuss the purpose of the Trade Adjustment Assistance Act of 2002 and its advantages and disadvantages.

20. Explain the reasons U.S. businesses have turned to offshoring and evaluate the costs and benefits of such actions.

ANSWERS

Chapter 23 International Trade

FILL-IN QUESTIONS

1. 13, largest
2. less than, greater than, goods, services
3. uneven, different, more
4. lowest, have, do not have
5. *a.* inexpensive, expensive; *b.* expensive, inexpensive; *c.* hats, bananas; *d.* 3, 4; *e.* (1) 1/3, 2/7, (2) 4, 3 1/2; *f.* rises

6. comparative advantage, more, higher
7. world, domestic, increase, increase
8. supply, only one
9. tariffs, quotas, revenue, protective
10. nontariff, export
11. domestic producers, decrease, less
12. increase, decrease, increase, decrease
13. tariff, quota
14. *a.* essential, more; *b.* advanced, developing; *c.* infant, mature; *d.* comparative, rare; *e.* composition, decrease, retaliate; *f.* per hour, per unit
15. *a.* equal, nondiscriminatory treatment of all member nations; *b.* reduction of tariffs by multilateral negotiations; *c.* elimination of import quotas
16. agreements, disputes, Doha, decreasing
17. European, tariffs and quotas, common, euro
18. zone, tariffs, decrease, increase
19. workers, small, subsidy
20. offshoring, growth, decrease, increase

TRUE–FALSE QUESTIONS

1. T, p. 473	**11.** T, p. 481	**21.** F, pp. 488–489
2. F, p. 474	**12.** F, p. 481	**22.** T, p. 489
3. T, p. 474	**13.** F, pp. 482–485	**23.** T, p. 489–490
4. T, p. 474	**14.** T, pp. 482–485	**24.** F, p. 490
5. F, p. 474	**15.** F, p. 485	**25.** T, p. 491
6. F, p. 476	**16.** T, p. 486	**26.** F, p. 491
7. F, p. 477	**17.** T, p. 487	**27.** T, p. 491
8. T, p. 477	**18.** F, p. 487	**28.** F, p. 492
9. T, p. 478	**19.** T, p. 488	**29.** T, p. 492
10. T, p. 480	**20.** T, p. 488	**30.** T, p. 492–493

MULTIPLE-CHOICE QUESTIONS

1. c, p. 473	**11.** b, p. 485	**21.** b, p. 489
2. c, p. 473	**12.** d, p. 486	**22.** c, pp. 488–489
3. b, p. 474	**13.** b, pp. 486–487	**23.** c, p. 489
4. b, p. 476	**14.** d, pp. 486–487	**24.** c, pp. 489–490
5. a, p. 478	**15.** c, pp. 486–487	**25.** d, p. 491
6. a, pp. 478–480	**16.** c, pp. 486–487	**26.** b, p. 491
7. c, pp. 478–480	**17.** c, p. 487	**27.** c, p. 491
8. c, pp. 482–485	**18.** a, p. 487	**28.** d, p. 492
9. a, pp. 482–485	**19.** a, p. 487	**29.** c, p. 492
10. c, p. 485	**20.** d, p. 488	**30.** d, p. 492

PROBLEMS

1. *a.* constant; *b.* (1) 8, 2, (2) 4, 2; *c.* (1) it has a comparative advantage in producing wheat (its cost of producing wheat is less than Chile's), (2) it has a comparative advantage in producing copper (its cost of producing copper is less than the United States'); *d.* one of the two nations would be unwilling to trade if the terms of trade are outside this range; *f.* (1) 1, 0, (2) 1, 0

2. *a.* (1) will not, will not, (2) surplus, 200, surplus, exports, 200, (3) shortage, 200, shortage, imports, 200; *b.* (1) will not, will not, (2) surplus, 200, surplus, exports, 200, (3) shortage, 100, shortage, imports, 100; *c.* (1) A, 0, B, 100, (2) A, 50, B, 50, (3) A, 100, B, 0

3. *a.* 750, 700, 650, 600, 550, 500, 450, 300, 0; *b.* $2.00, 600; *c.* 375, 350, 325, 300, 0, 0, 0, 0, 0; *d.* 650, 600, 550, 500, 175, 150, 125, 0, 0; *e.* $2.20, 550; *f.* (1) increased, 25, (2) decreased, 75; *g.* (1) increased, $95, (2) decreased, $345; *h.* increased, $10; *i.* decreased, $345, decreased, $345; *j.* increased, $260; *k.* $260, foreign

SHORT ANSWER AND ESSAY QUESTIONS

CHAPTER 24

The Balance of Payments, Exchange Rates, and Trade Deficits

As you know from Chapter 23, nations buy and sell large quantities of goods and services across national boundaries.The residents of these nations also buy and sell such financial assets as stocks and bonds and such real assets as land and capital goods in other nations, and the governments and individuals in one nation make gifts (or give remittances) to other nations. In Chapter 24 you will learn *how* nations using different currencies are able to make these international financial transactions, the accounting system used to measure them, and what the accounts mean for a nation.

The market in which one currency is sold and is paid for with another currency is the **foreign exchange market.** When the residents of a nation (its consumers, business firms, or governments) buy products or real or financial assets from, make loans or give gifts to, or pay interest and dividends to the residents of other nations, they must *buy* some of the currency used in that nation and pay for it with some of their own currency. And when the residents of a nation sell products or real or financial assets to, receive loans or gifts from, or are paid dividends or interest by the residents of other nations, they *sell* this foreign currency in return for some of their own currency. The price paid (in one currency) for a unit of another currency is called the foreign exchange rate, and like most prices, it is determined by the demand for and the supply of that foreign currency.

At the end of a year, nations summarize their international financial transactions. This summary is called the nation's **balance of payments:** a record of how it obtained foreign currency during the year and what it did with this foreign currency. Of course, all foreign currency obtained was used for some purpose—it did not evaporate—consequently, the balance of payments *always* balances. The balance of payments is an extremely important and useful device for understanding the amounts and kinds of international transactions in which the residents of a nation engage. A balance-of-payments deficit occurs when the foreign currency receipts are less than foreign currency payments and the nation must reduce the **official reserves** of its central bank to balance its payments. Conversely, a balance-of-payments surplus occurs when foreign currency receipts are greater than foreign currency payments, and the nation must expand its official reserves to balance its payments.

How nations correct balance-of-payments deficits or surpluses or adjust trade imbalances often depends on the **exchange-rate systems** used. There are two basic types of such systems—flexible and fixed. In a flexible or floating system, exchange rates are set by the forces of the demand for and supply of a nation's currency relative to the currency of other nations. If the demand for a nation's currency increases, there will be an *appreciation* in its value relative to another currency, and if the demand of a nation's currency declines, there will be a *depreciation* in its value relative to another currency. Fixed-exchange-rate systems have been used by nations to peg or fix a specific amount of one nation's currency that must be exchanged for another nation's currency. Both types of systems have their advantages and disadvantages. Currently, the major trading nations of the world use a **managed float exchange-rate system** that corrects balance-of-payments deficits and surpluses.

The final section of the chapter examines the U.S. **trade deficits** that arise when the value of exports is less than the value of imports. As you will learn, these deficits are the result of several factors such as differences in national growth rates and a declining saving rate that have contributed to imports rising faster than exports. They also have several implications such as increased current consumption at the expense of future consumption and increased U.S. indebtedness to foreigners.

■ CHECKLIST

When you have studied this chapter you should be able to

☐ Describe examples of transactions in international trade and the role that money plays in them.
☐ Explain how money is used for the international buying and selling of real and financial assets.
☐ Give a definition of a nation's balance of payments.
☐ Use the items in the current account to calculate the balance on goods, balance on goods and services, and balance on the current account when given the data.
☐ Describe how balance is achieved in the capital and financial account.
☐ Explain the relationship between the current account and the capital and financial account.
☐ Use a supply and demand graph to illustrate how a flexible-exchange-rate system works to establish the price and quantity of a currency.
☐ Discuss the role of official reserves when there is a balance-of-payments deficit or balance-of-payments surplus.
☐ Describe the depreciation and appreciation of a nation's currency under a flexible-exchange-rate system.
☐ Identify the six principal determinants of the demand for and supply of a particular foreign currency and explain how they alter exchange rates.

☐ Explain how flexible exchange rates eventually eliminate balance-of-payments deficits or surpluses.

☐ Describe three disadvantages of flexible exchange rates.

☐ Use a supply and demand graph to illustrate how a fixed exchange-rate system functions.

☐ Explain how nations use official reserves to maintain a fixed exchange rate.

☐ Describe how trade policies can be used to maintain a fixed exchange rate.

☐ Discuss advantages and disadvantages of using exchange controls to maintain a fixed exchange rate.

☐ Explain what domestic macroeconomic adjustments are needed to maintain a fixed exchange rate.

☐ Identify three different exchange-rate systems used by the world's nations in recent years.

☐ Discuss the pros and cons of the system of managed floating exchange rates.

☐ Describe the causes of recent trade deficits in the United States.

☐ Explain the economic implications of recent trade deficits in the United States.

☐ Assess the role that speculators play in currency markets (*Last Word*).

■ **CHAPTER OUTLINE**

1. International financial transactions are used for two purposes. First, there is the international trade of goods and services, such as food or insurance, that people buy or sell for money. Second, there is the international exchange of financial assets, such as real estate, stocks, or bonds, that people also buy or sell with money. International trade between nations or the international exchange of assets differs from domestic trade or asset exchanges because the nations use different currencies. This problem is resolved by the existence of foreign exchange markets, in which the currency of one nation can be purchased and paid for with the currency of the other nation.

2. The **balance of payments** for a nation is a summary of all the financial transactions with foreign nations; it records all the money payments received from and made to foreign nations. Most of the payments in the balance of payments accounts are for exports or imports of goods and services or for the purchase or sale of real and financial assets. The accounts show the inflows of money to the United States and the outflows of money from the United States. For convenience, both the inflows and outflows are stated in terms of U.S. dollars so they can be easily and consistently measured.

    a. The **current account** section of a nation's balance of payments records the imports and exports of goods and services. Within this section

    (1) the *balance on goods* of the nation is equal to its exports of goods minus its imports of goods;

    (2) the *balance on services* of the nation is equal to its exports of services minus its imports of services;

    (3) the **balance on goods and services** is equal to its exports of goods and services minus its imports of goods and services; and

    (4) the **balance on the current account** is equal to its balance on goods and services and two other "net" items (which can be positive or negative). First there is net investment income (such as dividends and interest), which is the difference in investment income received from other nations minus any investment income paid to foreigners. Second, there are net private and public transfers, which is the difference between such transfers to other nations minus any transfers from other nations. This balance on the current account may be positive, zero, or negative. In 2009, it was a negative $420 billion.

b. International asset transactions are shown in the **capital and financial account** of a nation's balance of payments.

(1) The *capital account* primarily measures debt forgiveness and is a "net" account. If Americans forgave more debt owed to them by foreigners than foreigners forgave debt owed to them by Americans, then the capital account would be entered as a negative (−).

(2) The financial account shows foreign purchases of real and financial assets in the United States. This item brings a flow of money into the United States, so it is entered as a plus (+) in the capital account. U.S. purchases of real and financial assets abroad result in a flow of money from the United States to other nations, so this item is entered as a minus (−) in the capital account. The nation has a surplus in its financial account if foreign purchases of U.S. assets (and its inflow of money) are greater than U.S. purchases of assets abroad (and its outflow of money). The nation has a deficit in its financial account if foreign purchases of U.S. assets are less than U.S. purchases of assets abroad. The **balance on the capital and financial account** is the difference between the value of the capital account and the value of the financial account.

c. The balance of payments must always sum to zero. For example, any deficit in the current account would be offset by a surplus in the capital and financial account. The reason that the account balances is that people trade current produced goods and services or preexisting assets. If a nation imports more goods and services than it exports, then the deficit in the current account (and outflow of money) must be offset by sales of real and financial assets to foreigners (and inflow of money).

d. Sometimes economists and government officials refer to **balance-of-payments deficits or surpluses**. Whether a nation has a balance-of-payments deficit or surplus depends on what happens to its **official reserves**. These reserves are central bank holdings of foreign currencies, reserves at the International Monetary Fund, and stocks of gold.

(1) A nation has a *balance-of-payments deficit* when an imbalance in the combined current account and capital and financial account leads to a decrease in official reserves. These official reserves are an inpayment to the capital and financial account.

(2) A *balance-of-payments surplus* arises when an imbalance in the combined current account and capital and financial account results in an increase in official

reserves. These official reserves become an outpayment from the capital and financial account.

(3) Deficits in the balance-of-payments will happen over time and they are not necessarily bad. What is of concern, however, for any nation is whether the deficits are persistent over time because in that case they require that a nation continually draw down its official reserves. Such official reserves are limited and if they are depleted, a nation will have to adopt tough macroeconomic policies (discussed later in the chapter). In the case of the United States, there are ample official reserves and their depletion is not a major concern.

3. There are two basic types of exchange-rate systems that nations use to correct imbalances in the balance of payments. The first is a *flexible- or floating-exchange-rate system* that will be described in this section of the chapter outline. The second is a *fixed-exchange-rate system* that will be described in the next section of the chapter outline. If nations use a flexible- or floating-exchange-rate system, the demand for and the supply of foreign currencies determine foreign exchange rates. The exchange rate for any foreign currency is the rate at which the quantity of that currency demanded is equal to the quantity of it supplied.

a. A change in the demand for or the supply of a foreign currency will cause a change in the exchange rate for that currency. When there is an increase in the price paid in dollars for a foreign currency, the dollar has *depreciated* and the foreign currency has *appreciated* in value. Conversely, when there is a decrease in the price paid in dollars for a foreign currency, the dollar has *appreciated* and the foreign currency has *depreciated* in value.

b. Changes in the demand for or supply of a foreign currency are largely the result of changes in the *determinants of exchange rates* such as tastes, relative incomes, relative inflation rates, relative interest rates, expected returns, and speculation.

(1) A change in tastes for foreign goods that leads to an increase in demand for those goods will increase the value of the foreign currency and decrease the value of the U.S. currency.

(2) If the growth of U.S. national income is more rapid than other nations', then the value of U.S. currency will depreciate because it will expand its imports over its exports.

(3) *Purchasing-power-parity theory* is the idea that exchange rates equate the purchasing power of various currencies. Exchange rates, however, often deviate from this parity. If the inflation rate rises sharply in the United States and it remains constant in another nation, then foreign currency of the other nation will appreciate in value and the U.S. currency will depreciate in value.

(4) Changes in the relative interest rate in two nations may change their exchange rate. If real interest rates rise in the United States relative to another major trading partner, the U.S. dollar will appreciate in value because people will want to invest more money in the United States and the value of the other nation's currency will depreciate.

(5) Changes in the expected returns on stocks, real estate, and production facilities may change the exchange rate. If corporate tax rates are cut in the United States, then such a change would make investing in U.S. stock or production facilities more attractive relative to other nations, so foreigners may demand more U.S. dollars. The U.S. dollar will appreciate in value and the value of the foreigner's currency may depreciate.

(6) If speculators think the U.S. currency will depreciate, they can sell that currency and that act will help depreciate its value.

c. Flexible exchange rates can be used to eliminate a balance-of-payments deficit or surplus.

(1) When a nation has a payment deficit, foreign exchange rates will increase, thus making foreign goods and services more expensive and decreasing imports. These events will make a nation's goods and services less expensive for foreigners to buy, thus increasing exports.

(2) With a payment surplus, the exchange rates will increase, thus making foreign goods and services less expensive and increasing imports. This situation makes a nation's goods and services more expensive for foreigners to buy, thus decreasing exports.

d. Flexible exchange rates have three disadvantages.

(1) Flexible rates can change often so they increase the uncertainties exporters, importers, and investors face when exchanging one nation's currency for another, thus reducing international trade and international purchase and sale of real and financial assets.

(2) This system also changes the terms of trade. A depreciation of the U.S. dollar means that the United States must supply more dollars to the foreign exchange market to obtain the same amount of goods and services it previously obtained. Other nations will be able to purchase more U.S. goods or services because their currencies have appreciated relative to the dollar.

(3) The changes in the value of imports and exports can change the demand for goods and services in export and import industries, thus creating more instability in industrial production and in implementing macroeconomic policy.

4. If nations use a *fixed-exchange-rate system,* the nations fix (or peg) a specific exchange rate (for example, $2 will buy one British pound). To maintain this fixed exchange rate, the governments of these nations must intervene in the foreign exchange markets to prevent shortages and surpluses of currencies caused by shifts in demand and supply.

a. One way a nation can stabilize foreign exchange rates is through *currency interventions.* In this case, its government sells its reserves of a foreign currency in exchange for its own currency (or gold) when there is a shortage of the foreign currency. Conversely, a government would buy a foreign currency in exchange for its own currency (or gold) when there is a surplus of the foreign currency. The problem with this policy is that it only works when the currency needs are relatively minor and the intervention is of short duration. If there are persistent deficits, currency reserves may be inadequate for sustaining an intervention; so nations may need to use other means to maintain fixed exchange rates.

b. A nation might adopt trade policies that discourage imports and encourage exports. The problem with such policies is that they decrease the volume of international trade and make it less efficient, so that the economic benefits of free trade are diminished.

c. A nation might impose *exchange controls* so that all foreign currency is controlled by the government, and then rationed to individuals or businesses in the domestic economy who say they need it for international trade purposes. This policy too has several problems because it distorts trade, leads to government favoritism of specific individuals or businesses, restricts consumer choice of goods and services they can buy, and creates a black market in foreign currencies.

d. Another way a nation can stabilize foreign exchange rates is to use monetary and fiscal policy to reduce its national output and price level and raise its interest rates relative to those in other nations. These events would lead to a decrease in demand for and increase in the supply of different foreign currencies. But such macroeconomic policies would be harsh because they could lead to recession and deflation, and cause civil unrest.

5. In the past, some type of fixed-exchange-rate system was used such as the gold standard or the Bretton Woods system. The exchange-rate system used today is a more flexible one. Under the system of *managed floating exchange rates,* exchange rates are allowed to float in the long term to correct balance-of-payments deficits and surpluses, but if necessary there can be short-term interventions by governments to stabilize and manage currencies so they do not cause severe disruptions in international trade and finance. For example, the G8 nations (United States, United Kingdom, Canada, Germany, France, Japan, Russia, and Italy) regularly discuss economic issues and evaluate exchange rates, and at times have coordinated currency interventions to strengthen a nation's currency. This "almost" flexible system is favored by some and criticized by others.

a. Its proponents contend that this system has *not* led to any decrease in world trade, and has enabled the world to adjust to severe economic shocks throughout its history.

b. Its critics argue that it has resulted in volatile exchange rates that can hurt those developing nations that are dependent on exports, has *not* reduced balance-of-payments deficits and surpluses, and is a "nonsystem" that a nation may use to achieve its own domestic economic goals.

6. The United States had large and persistent *trade deficits* in the past decade and they are likely to continue.

a. These trade deficits are the result of several factors:
(1) more rapid growth in the domestic economy than in the economies of several major trading partners, which caused imports to rise more than exports;
(2) the emergence of large trade deficits with China and the use of a relatively fixed exchange rate by the Chinese;

(3) a rapid rise in the price of oil that must be imported from oil-producing nations; and
(4) a decline in the rate of saving and a capital account surplus, which allowed U.S. citizens to consume more imported goods.

b. The trade deficits of the United States have had two principal effects.
(1) They increased current domestic consumption beyond what is being produced domestically, which allows the nation to operate outside its production possibilities frontier. This increased current consumption, however, may come at the expense of future consumption.
(2) They increased the indebtedness of U.S. citizens to foreigners. A negative implication of these persistent trade deficits is that they will lead to permanent debt and more foreign ownership of domestic assets, or lead to large sacrifices of future domestic consumption. But if the foreign lending increases the U.S. capital stock, then it can contribute to long-term U.S. economic growth. Thus, trade deficits may be a mixed blessing.

7. (*Last Word*). Speculators buy foreign currency in hopes of reselling it later at a profit. They also sell foreign currency in hopes of rebuying it later when it is cheaper. Although speculators are often accused of creating severe fluctuations in currency markets, that criticism is overstated because economic conditions rather than speculation are typically the chief source of the problem. One positive function of speculators is that they smooth out temporary fluctuations in the value of foreign currencies. Another positive role speculators play in currency markets is that they bear risks that others do not want by delivering the specified amount of foreign exchange at the contract price on the date of delivery.

■ **HINTS AND TIPS**

1. The chapter is filled with many new terms, some of which are just special words used in international economics to mean things with which you are already familiar. Other terms are entirely new to you, so you must spend time learning them if you are to understand the chapter.

2. The terms **depreciation** and **appreciation** can be confusing when applied to foreign exchange markets. First, know the related terms. "Depreciate" means decrease or fall, whereas "appreciate" means increase or rise. Second, think of depreciation or appreciation in terms of *quantities*: what decreases when the currency of Country A *depreciates* is the quantity of Country B's currency that can be purchased for 1 unit of Country A's currency; what increases when the currency of Country A *appreciates* is the quantity of Country B's currency that can be purchased for 1 unit of Country A's currency. Third, consider the effect of changes in *exchange rates:* when the exchange rate for Country B's currency increases, this means that Country A's currency has *depreciated* in value because 1 unit of Country A's currency will now purchase a smaller quantity of Country B's currency; when the exchange rate for Country B's currency decreases, this means that Country A's currency has *appreciated* in value because 1 unit of

Country A's currency will now purchase a larger quantity of Country B's currency.

3. The meaning of the balance of payments can also be confusing because of the number of accounts in the balance sheet. Remember that the balance of payments must always balance and sum to zero because the current account in the balance of payments can be in deficit, but it will be exactly offset by a surplus in the capital and financial account. When economists speak of a balance-of-payments deficit or surplus, however, they are referring to adding *official reserves* or subtracting *official reserves* from the capital and financial account so that it just equals the current account.

■ IMPORTANT TERMS

balance of payments

current account

balance on goods and services

balance on current account

capital and financial account

balance on the capital and financial account

balance-of-payments deficit

balance-of-payments surplus

official reserves

flexible- or floating-exchange-rate system

fixed-exchange-rate system

purchasing-power-parity theory

currency interventions

exchange controls

managed floating exchange rate

trade deficit

trade surplus

SELF-TEST

■ FILL-IN QUESTIONS

1. The rate of exchange for the European euro is the amount in (euros, dollars) _____ that a U.S. citizen must pay to obtain 1 (euro, dollar) _____. The rate of exchange for the U.S. dollar is the amount in (euros, dollars) _____ that a citizen in the euro zone must pay to obtain 1 (euro, dollar) _____. If the rate of exchange for the euro is (1.05 euros, $0.95) _____, the rate of exchange for the U.S. dollar is _____.

2. The balance of payments of a nation records all payments (domestic, foreign) _____ residents make to and receive from _____ residents. Any transaction that *earns* foreign exchange for that nation is a (debit, credit) _____, and any transaction that *uses up* foreign exchange is a _____. A debit is shown with a $(+, -)$ _____ sign, and a credit is shown with a _____ sign.

3. If a nation has a deficit in its balance of goods, its exports of goods are (greater, less) _____ than its imports of goods. If a nation has a surplus in its balance of services, its exports of services are (greater, less) _____ than its imports of services. If a nation has a deficit in its balance on goods and services, its exports of these items are (greater, less) _____ than its imports of them.

4. The current account is equal to the balance on goods and services (plus, minus) _____ net investment income and net transfers. When investment income received by U.S. individuals and businesses from foreigners is greater than investment income Americans pay to foreigners, then net investment income is a (negative, positive) _____ number; when transfer payments from the United States to other nations are greater than transfer payments from other nations to the United States, then net transfers are a _____ number.

5. The capital account is a net measure of (investment, debt forgiveness) _____. When Americans forgive more debt owed to them by foreigners than foreigners forgive debt owed to them by Americans, the capital account has a (debit, credit) _____ that reflects an outpayment of funds.

6. The financial account measures the flow of monetary payments from the sale or purchase of real or financial assets. Foreign purchases of real and financial assets in the United States earn foreign currencies, so they are entered as a (plus, minus) _____ in the financial account, but U.S. purchases of real and financial assets abroad draw down U.S. holding of foreign currencies, so this item is entered as a _____.

7. If foreign purchases of U.S. assets are greater than U.S. purchases of assets abroad, the nation has a (surplus, deficit) _____ in its financial account, but if foreign purchases of U.S. assets are less than U.S. purchases of assets abroad, it has a _____.

8. A nation may finance a current account deficit by (buying, selling) _____ real or financial assets and may use a current account surplus to (buy, sell) _____ real or financial assets.

9. The sum of the current account and the capital and financial accounts must equal (0, 1) _____ so the balance of payments always balances. When economists or government officials speak of a balance-of-payments deficit or surplus, however, they are referring to the use of official reserves, which are the quantities of (foreign currencies, its own money) _____ owned by a nation's central bank.

10. If a nation has a balance-of-payments deficit, then its official reserves (increase, decrease) _____ in the capital and financial account, but with a balance-of-payments surplus its official reserves _____ in the capital and financial account.

11. If foreign exchange rates float freely and a nation has a balance-of-payments *deficit,* that nation's currency in the foreign exchange markets will (appreciate, depreciate) _____ and foreign currencies will _____ compared to it. As a result of these changes in foreign exchange rates, the nation's imports will (increase, decrease) _____, its exports will _____, and the size of its deficit will (increase, decrease) _____.

12. What effect would each of the following have—the appreciation (**A**) or depreciation (**D**) of the euro compared to the U.S. dollar in the foreign exchange market, *ceteris paribus*?

   a. The increased preference in the United States for domestic wines over wines produced in Europe: ____

   b. A rise in the U.S. national income: ____

   c. An increase in the inflation rate in Europe: ____

   d. A rise in real interest rates in the United States: ____

   e. A large cut in corporate tax rates in Europe: ____

   f. The belief of speculators in Europe that the dollar will appreciate in the foreign exchange market: ____

13. There are three disadvantages of freely floating foreign exchange rates: the risks and uncertainties associated with flexible rates tend to (expand, diminish) _____ trade between nations; when a nation's currency depreciates, its terms of trade with other nations are (worsened, improved) _____; and fluctuating exports and imports can (stabilize, destabilize) _____ an economy.

14. To fix or peg the rate of exchange for the Mexican peso when the exchange rate for the peso is rising, the United States would (buy, sell) _____ pesos in exchange for dollars, and when the exchange rate for the peso is falling, the United States would _____ pesos in exchange for dollars.

15. Under a fixed-exchange-rate system, a nation with a balance-of-payments deficit might attempt to eliminate the deficit by (taxing, subsidizing) _____ imports or by _____ exports. The nation might use exchange controls and ration foreign exchange among those who wish to (export, import) _____ goods and services and require all those who _____ goods and services to sell the foreign exchange they earn to the (businesses, government) _____.

16. If the United States has a payments deficit with Japan and the exchange rate for the Japanese yen is rising, under a fixed-exchange-rate system the United States might adopt (expansionary, contractionary) _____ fiscal and monetary policies to reduce the demand for the yen, but this would bring about (inflation, recession) _____ in the United States.

17. The international monetary system has moved to a system of managed (fixed, floating) _____ exchange rates. This means that exchange rates of nations are (restricted from, free to) _____ find their equilibrium market levels, but nations may occasionally (leave, intervene in) _____ the foreign exchange markets to stabilize or alter market exchange rates.

18. The advantages of the current system are that the growth of trade (was, was not) _____ accommodated and that it has survived much economic (stability, turbulence) _____. Its disadvantages are its (equilibrium, volatility) _____ and the lack of guidelines for nations that make it a (bureaucracy, nonsystem) _____.

19. In recent years, the United States had large trade and current account (surpluses, deficits) _____. One cause of these deficits was (stronger, weaker) _____ economic growth in the United States relative to Europe and Japan. Other contributing factors were a (rise, fall) _____ in trade deficits with China, a _____ in the price of oil, and a _____ in the saving rate.

20. One effect of the recent trade deficits of the United States has been a(n) (decrease, increase) _____ in current domestic consumption that allows the nation to operate outside its production possibility frontier, but may lead to a(n) _____ in future consumption. Another effect was a (rise, fall) _____ in the indebtedness of U.S. citizens to foreigners.

■ **TRUE–FALSE QUESTIONS**

Circle T if the statement is true, F if it is false.

1. The two basic categories of international financial transactions are international trade and international assets.   **T F**

2. The balance of payments of the United States records all the payments its residents receive from and make to the residents of foreign nations.   **T F**

3. Exports are a debit item and are shown with a minus sign (−), and imports are a credit item and are shown with a plus sign (+) in the balance of payments of a nation. **T F**

4. The current account balance is a nation's export of goods and services minus its imports of goods and services. **T F**

5. The capital account will be a negative number when Americans forgive more debt owed to them by foreigners than the debt foreigners forgive that was owed to them by Americans. **T F**

6. The nation's current account balance and the capital and financial account in any year are always equal to zero. **T F**

7. When a nation must make an inpayment of official reserves to its capital and financial account to balance it with the current account, a balance-of-payments deficit has occurred. **T F**

8. The two "pure" types of exchange-rate systems are flexible (or floating) and fixed. **T F**

9. When the U.S. dollar price of a British pound rises, the dollar has depreciated relative to the pound. **T F**

10. If the supply of a nation's currency increases, that currency will appreciate in value. **T F**

11. The purchasing-power-parity theory basically explains why there is an inverse relationship between the price of dollars and the quantity demanded. **T F**

12. If income growth is robust in Europe, but sluggish in the United States, then the U.S. dollar will appreciate. **T F**

13. If the expected returns on stocks, real estate, or production facilities increased in the United States relative to Japan, the U.S. dollar would depreciate in value relative to the Japanese yen. **T F**

14. The expectations of speculators in the United States that the exchange rate for Japanese yen will fall in the future will increase the supply of yen in the foreign exchange market and decrease the exchange rate for the yen. **T F**

15. If a nation has a balance-of-payments deficit and exchange rates are flexible, the price of that nation's currency in the foreign exchange markets will fall; this will reduce its imports and increase its exports. **T F**

16. Were the United States' terms of trade with Nigeria to worsen, Nigeria would obtain a greater quantity of U.S. goods and services for every barrel of oil it exported to the United States. **T F**

17. If a nation wishes to fix (or peg) the foreign exchange rate for the Swiss franc, it must buy Swiss francs with its own currency when the rate of exchange for the Swiss franc rises. **T F**

18. If exchange rates are stable or fixed and a nation has a balance-of-payments surplus, prices and currency incomes in that nation will tend to rise. **T F**

19. A nation using exchange controls to eliminate a balance-of-payments surplus might depreciate its currency. **T F**

20. Using the managed floating system of exchange rates, a nation with a persistent balance-of-payments surplus should allow the value of its currency in foreign exchange markets to decrease. **T F**

21. Two criticisms of the current managed floating-exchange-rate system are its potential for volatility and its lack of clear policy rules or guidelines for nations to manage exchange rates. **T F**

22. The trade deficits of the United States in recent years were caused by sharp increases in U.S. exports and slight increases in U.S. imports. **T F**

23. Improved economic growth in the economies of the major trading partners of the United States would tend to worsen the trade deficit. **T F**

24. The decline in the saving rate in the United States contributed to the persistent trade deficit of the past decade. **T F**

25. The negative net exports of the United States have increased the indebtedness of U.S. citizens to foreigners. **T F**

■ **MULTIPLE-CHOICE QUESTIONS**

Circle the letter that corresponds to the best answer.

1. If a U.S. citizen could buy £25,000 for $100,000, the rate of exchange for the pound would be
 (a) $40
 (b) $25
 (c) $4
 (d) $.25

2. U.S. residents demand foreign currencies to
 (a) produce goods and services exported to foreign countries
 (b) pay for goods and services imported from foreign countries
 (c) receive interest payments on investments in the United States
 (d) have foreigners make real and financial investments in the United States

3. Which of the following would be a credit in the current account?
 (a) U.S. imports of goods
 (b) U.S. exports of services
 (c) U.S. purchases of assets abroad
 (d) U.S. interest payments for foreign capital invested in the United States

4. A nation's balance on the current account is equal to its exports less its imports of
 (a) goods and services
 (b) goods and services, plus U.S. purchases of assets abroad
 (c) goods and services, plus net investment income and net transfers
 (d) goods and services, minus foreign purchases of assets in the United States

5. The net investment income of the United States in its international balance of payments is the
(a) interest income it receives from foreign residents
(b) value of dividends it receives from foreign residents
(c) excess of interest and dividends it receives from foreign residents over what it paid to them
(d) excess of public and private transfer payments it receives from foreign residents over what it paid to them

Answer Questions 6, 7, and 8 using the following table that contains data for the United States' balance of payments in a prior year. All figures are in billions of dollars.

(1)	U.S. goods exports	$+1149
(2)	U.S. goods imports	−1965
(3)	U.S. service exports	+479
(4)	U.S. service imports	−372
(5)	Net investment income	+74
(6)	Net transfers	−104
(7)	Balance on capital account	−2
(8)	Foreign purchases of U.S. assets	+1905
(9)	U.S. purchases of foreign assets	−1164

6. The balance on goods and services was a deficit of
(a) $107 billion
(b) $709 billion
(c) $816 billion
(d) $935 billion

7. The balance on the current account was a
(a) surplus of $739 billion
(b) deficit of $739 billion
(c) surplus of $816 billion
(d) deficit of $816 billion

8. The balance on the financial account was a
(a) deficit of $372 billion
(b) surplus of $479 billion
(c) deficit of $739 billion
(d) surplus of $741 billion

9. In a flexible- or floating-exchange-rate system, when the U.S. dollar price of a British pound rises, this means that the dollar has
(a) appreciated relative to the pound and the pound has appreciated relative to the dollar
(b) appreciated relative to the pound and the pound has depreciated relative to the dollar
(c) depreciated relative to the pound and the pound has appreciated relative to the dollar
(d) depreciated relative to the pound and the pound has depreciated relative to the dollar

10. Which statement is correct about a factor that causes a nation's currency to appreciate or depreciate in value?
(a) If the supply of a nation's currency decreases, all else equal, that currency will depreciate.
(b) If the supply of a nation's currency increases, all else equal, that currency will depreciate.
(c) If the demand for a nation's currency increases, all else equal, that currency will depreciate.
(d) If the demand for a nation's currency decreases, all else equal, that currency will appreciate.

11. Assuming exchange rates are flexible, which of the following should increase the dollar price of the Swedish krona?
(a) a rate of inflation greater in Sweden than in the United States
(b) real interest rate increases greater in Sweden than in the United States
(c) national income increases greater in Sweden than in the United States
(d) the increased preference of Swedish citizens for U.S. automobiles over Swedish automobiles

12. Under a flexible-exchange-rate system, a nation may be able to correct or eliminate a persistent (long-term) balance-of-payments deficit by
(a) lowering the barriers on imported goods
(b) reducing the international value of its currency
(c) expanding its national income
(d) reducing its official reserves

13. If a nation had a balance-of-payments surplus and exchange rates floated freely, the foreign exchange rate for its currency would
(a) rise, its exports would increase, and its imports would decrease
(b) rise, its exports would decrease, and its imports would increase
(c) fall, its exports would increase, and its imports would decrease
(d) fall, its exports would decrease, and its imports would increase

Answer Questions 14, 15, and 16 using the graph below.

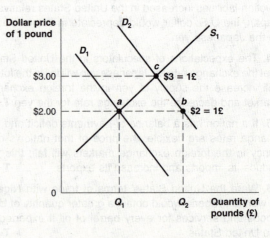

14. If D_1 moves to D_2, the U.S. dollar has
(a) appreciated, and the British pound has depreciated
(b) appreciated, and the British pound has appreciated
(c) depreciated, and the British pound has depreciated
(d) depreciated, and the British pound has appreciated

15. If D_1 moves to D_2, there will be a balance-of-payments
(a) deficit of Q_1
(b) surplus of Q_2
(c) deficit of Q_2 minus Q_1
(d) surplus of Q_2 minus Q_1

16. If **D₁** moves to **D₂**, but the British government seeks to keep the exchange rate at $2 = 1£, then it can do so through policies that

(a) increase the supply of pounds and decrease the demand for pounds

(b) decrease the supply of pounds and increase the demand for pounds

(c) increase the supply of pounds and increase the demand for pounds

(d) decrease the supply of pounds and decrease the demand for pounds

17. Which would be a result associated with the use of freely floating foreign exchange rates to correct a nation's balance-of-payments surplus?

(a) The nation's terms of trade with other nations would be worsened.

(b) Importers in the nation who had made contracts for the future delivery of goods would find that they had to pay a higher price than expected for the goods.

(c) If the nation were at full employment, the decrease in exports and the increase in imports would be inflationary.

(d) Exporters in the nation would find their sales abroad had decreased.

18. The use of exchange controls to eliminate a nation's balance-of-payments deficit results in decreasing the nation's

(a) imports

(b) exports

(c) price level

(d) income

19. Assume a nation has a balance-of-payments deficit and it seeks to maintain a fixed exchange rate. To eliminate the shortage of foreign currency, it may have to adopt monetary policies that

(a) lower the interest rate

(b) raise the interest rate

(c) reduce the tax rate

(d) increase the tax rate

20. A system of managed floating exchange rates

(a) allows nations to stabilize exchange rates in the short term

(b) requires nations to stabilize exchange rates in the long term

(c) entails stable exchange rates in both the short and long term

(d) fixes exchange rates at market levels

21. Floating exchange rates

(a) tend to correct balance-of-payments imbalances

(b) reduce the uncertainties and risks associated with international trade

(c) increase the world's need for international monetary reserves

(d) tend to have no effect on the volume of trade

22. The trade problem that faced the United States in recent years was a

(a) deficit in its capital account

(b) surplus in its balance on goods

(c) deficit in its current account

(d) surplus in its current account

23. Which was a cause of the growth of U.S. trade deficits in recent years?

(a) protective tariffs imposed by the United States

(b) slower economic growth in the United States

(c) direct foreign investment in the United States

(d) a declining saving rate in the United States

24. What would be the effect on U.S. imports and exports when the United States experiences strong economic growth but its major trading partners experience sluggish economic growth?

(a) U.S. imports will increase more than U.S. exports

(b) U.S. exports will increase more than U.S. imports

(c) U.S. imports will decrease but U.S. exports will increase

(d) there will be no effect on U.S. imports and exports

25. Two major outcomes from the trade deficits of recent years were

(a) decreased domestic consumption and U.S. indebtedness

(b) increased domestic consumption and U.S. indebtedness

(c) increased domestic consumption but decreased U.S. indebtedness

(d) decreased domestic consumption but increased U.S. indebtedness

■ PROBLEMS

1. Assume a U.S. exporter sells $3 million worth of wheat to an importer in Colombia. If the rate of exchange for the Colombian peso is $.02 (2 cents), the wheat has a total value of 150 million pesos. There are two ways the importer in Colombia may pay for the wheat.

    a. It might write a check for 150 million pesos drawn on its bank in Bogotá and send it to the U.S. exporter. The U.S. exporter would then send the check to its bank in New Orleans and its checking account there would

increase by $_____ million. The New Orleans bank would then arrange to have the check converted to U.S. dollars through a correspondent bank (a U.S. commercial bank that keeps an account in the Bogotá bank).

    b. The second way for the importer to pay for the wheat is to buy from its bank in Bogotá a draft on a U.S. bank for $3 million, pay for this draft by writing a check for 150 million pesos drawn on the Bogotá bank, and send the draft to the U.S. exporter. The U.S. exporter would then deposit the draft in its account in the New Orleans bank and its checking account there would increase

by $_____ million. The New Orleans bank would then collect the amount of the draft from the U.S. bank on which it is drawn through the Federal Reserve Banks.

2. The following table contains hypothetical balance-of-payments data for the United States. All figures are in billions. Compute with the appropriate sign (+ or −) and enter in the table the six missing items.

Current account

(1)	U.S. goods exports	$+150
(2)	U.S. goods imports	−200
(3)	*Balance on goods*	____
(4)	U.S. exports of services	+75
(5)	U.S. imports of services	−60
(6)	*Balance on services*	____
(7)	*Balance on goods and services*	____
(8)	Net investment income	+12
(9)	Net transfers	−7
(10)	**Balance on current account**	____

Capital Account and Financial Account

(11)	Capital Account	−5

Financial Account:

(12)	Foreign purchases of assets in the U.S.	+90
(13)	U.S. purchases of assets abroad	−55
(14)	*Balance on financial account*	____
(15)	**Balance on capital and financial account**	____
		$ 0

3. The following table shows supply and demand schedules for the British pound.

Quantity of pounds supplied	Price	Quantity of pounds demanded
400	$5.00	100
360	4.50	200
300	4.00	300
286	3.50	400
267	3.00	500
240	2.50	620
200	2.00	788

a. If the exchange rates are flexible
(1) what will be the rate of exchange for the pound?

$_____
(2) what will be the rate of exchange for the dollar?

£_____
(3) how many pounds will be purchased in the market?

_____
(4) how many dollars will be purchased in the market?

_____

b. If the U.S. government wished to fix or peg the price of the pound at $5.00, it would have to (buy, sell)

_____ (how many) _____ pounds for $_____.
c. And if the British government wished to fix the price of the dollar at £ 2/5, it would have to (buy, sell)

_____ (how many) _____ pounds for $_____.

■ **SHORT ANSWER AND ESSAY QUESTIONS**

1. Explain the two basic types of international transactions and give an example of each one.

2. What is meant when it is said that "A nation's exports pay for its imports"? Do nations pay for all their imports with exports? Explain.

3. What is a balance of payments? What are the principal sections in a nation's balance-of-payments, and what are the principal "balances" to be found in it?

4. How can a nation finance a current account deficit? Explain the relationship between the current account and the capital and financial account.

5. Why do the balance-of-payments balance? Explain.

6. What is a balance-of-payments deficit, and what is a balance-of-payments surplus? What role do official reserves play in the matter?

7. Is a balance-of-payments deficit bad or a balance-of-payments surplus good? Explain.

8. Use a supply and demand graph to help describe how exchange rates for a currency appreciate and depreciate.

9. What types of events cause the exchange rate for a foreign currency to appreciate or to depreciate? How will each event affect the exchange rate for a foreign currency and for a nation's own currency?

10. How can flexible foreign exchange rates eliminate balance-of-payments deficits and surpluses?

11. What are the problems associated with flexible-exchange-rate systems for correcting payments imbalances?

12. How may a nation use its international monetary reserves to fix or peg foreign exchange rates? Be precise. How does a nation obtain or acquire these monetary reserves?

13. What kinds of trade policies may nations with payments deficits use to eliminate their deficits?

14. How can foreign exchange controls be used to restore international equilibrium? Why do such exchange controls necessarily involve the rationing of foreign exchange? What effect do these controls have on prices, output, and employment in nations that use them?

15. If foreign exchange rates are fixed, what kind of domestic macroeconomic adjustments are required to eliminate a payments deficit? To eliminate a payments surplus?

16. Explain what is meant by a managed floating system of foreign exchange rates.

17. When are exchange rates managed and when are they allowed to float? What organization is often responsible for currency interventions?

18. Explain the arguments of the proponents and the critics of the managed floating system.

19. What were the causes of the trade deficits of the United States in recent years?

20. What were the effects of the trade deficits of recent years on the U.S. economy?

ANSWERS

Chapter 24 The Balance of Payments, Exchange Rates, and Trade Deficits

FILL-IN QUESTIONS

1. dollars, euro, euros, dollar, $0.95, 1.05 euros
2. domestic, foreign, credit, debit, −, +
3. less, greater, less
4. plus, positive, negative
5. debt forgiveness, debit
6. plus, minus
7. surplus, deficit
8. selling, buy
9. 0, foreign currencies
10. decrease, increase
11. depreciate, appreciate, decrease, increase, decrease
12. *a.* D; *b.* A; *c.* D; *d.* D; *e.* A; *f.* D
13. diminish, worsened, destabilize
14. sell, buy
15. taxing, subsidizing, import, export, government
16. contractionary, recession
17. floating, free to, intervene in
18. was, turbulence, volatility, nonsystem
19. deficits, stronger, rise, rise, fall
20. increase, decrease, rise

TRUE–FALSE QUESTIONS

1. T, p. 499
2. T, p. 500
3. F, p. 500
4. F, pp. 500–501
5. T, p. 501
6. T, p. 502
7. T, pp. 502–503
8. T, p. 503
9. T, pp. 503–504
10. F, pp. 503–504
11. F, p. 505
12. T, p. 505
13. F, p. 505–506
14. T, p. 506
15. T, pp. 506–507
16. T, p. 508
17. F, p. 508–509
18. T, p. 509
19. F, pp. 509–510
20. F, pp. 510–511
21. T, p. 511
22. F, pp. 512–513
23. F, pp. 512–513
24. T, p. 513
25. T, p. 513

MULTIPLE-CHOICE QUESTIONS

1. c, p. 499
2. b, p. 499
3. b, p. 500
4. c, pp. 500–501
5. c, p. 501
6. b, pp. 500–501
7. b, pp. 500–501
8. d, pp. 501–502
9. c, pp. 503–504
10. b, pp. 503–504
11. b, p. 505
12. b, pp. 506–507
13. b, pp. 506–507
14. d, pp. 506–507
15. c, pp. 506–507
16. a, pp. 508–509
17. d, pp. 507–508
18. a, pp. 509–510
19. b, pp. 510
20. a, pp. 510–511
21. a, pp. 510–511
22. c, p. 512
23. d, pp. 512–513
24. a, pp. 512–513
25. b, p. 513

PROBLEMS

1. *a.* 3; *b.* 3
2. −50, +15, −35, −30, +35, +30
3. *a.* (1) 4.00, (2) 1/4, (3) 300, (4) 1200; *b.* buy, 300, 1500; *c.* sell, 380, 950

SHORT ANSWER AND ESSAY QUESTIONS

1. p. 499
2. p. 499
3. pp. 499–502
4. pp. 500–502
5. p. 502
6. pp. 502–503
7. pp. 502–503
8. pp. 503–504
9. pp. 505–506
10. pp. 506–507
11. pp. 507–508
12. pp. 508–509
13. p. 509
14. pp. 509–510
15. p. 510
16. p. 510
17. pp. 510–511
18. p. 511
19. p. 512–513
20. p. 513

Glossary

Note: Terms set in *italic* type are defined separately in this glossary.

ability-to-pay principle The idea that those who have greater *income* (or *wealth*) should pay a greater proportion of it as taxes than those who have less income (or wealth).

absolute advantage A situation in which a person or country can produce more of a particular product from a specific quantity of resources than some other person or country.

accounting profit The *total revenue* of a *firm* less its *explicit costs;* the profit (or net income) that appears on accounting statements and that is reported to the government for tax purposes.

acreage allotments program A pre-1996 government program that determined the total number of acres to be used in producing (reduced amounts of) various food and fiber products and allocated these acres among individual farmers. These farmers had to limit their plantings to the allotted number of acres to obtain *price supports* for their crops.

adverse selection problem A problem arising when information known to one party to a contract or agreement is not known to the other party, causing the latter to incur major costs. Example: Individuals who have the poorest health are most likely to buy health insurance.

advertising A seller's activities in communicating its message about its product to potential buyers.

AFL-CIO An acronym for the American Federation of Labor–Congress of Industrial Organizations; the largest federation of *labor unions* in the United States.

agency shop A place of employment where the employer may hire either *labor union* members or nonmembers but where those who do not join the union must either pay union dues or donate an equivalent amount of money to a charity.

aggregate A collection of specific economic units treated as if they were one. For example, all prices of individual goods and services are combined into a *price level,* or all units of output are aggregated into *gross domestic product*.

agribusiness The portion of the agricultural and food product industries that is dominated by large corporations.

Alcoa case A 1945 case in which the courts ruled that the possession of monopoly power, no matter how reasonably that power had been used, was a violation of the antitrust laws; temporarily overturned the *rule of reason* applied in the *U.S. Steel case*.

allocative efficiency The apportionment of resources among firms and industries to obtain the production of the products most wanted by society (consumers); the output of each product at which its *marginal cost* and *price* or *marginal benefit* are equal, and at which the sum of *consumer surplus* and *producer surplus* is maximized.

anchoring The tendency people have to unconsciously base, or "anchor," the valuation of an item they are currently thinking about on previously considered but logically irrelevant information.

antitrust laws Legislation (including the *Sherman Act* and *Clayton Act*) that prohibits anticompetitive business activities such as *price fixing,* bid rigging, monopolization, and *tying contracts*.

antitrust policy The use of the *antitrust laws* to promote *competition* and economic efficiency.

appreciation (of the dollar) An increase in the value of the dollar relative to the currency of another nation, so a dollar buys a larger amount of the foreign currency and thus of foreign goods.

asset Anything of monetary value owned by a firm or individual.

asymmetric information A situation where one party to a market transaction has much more information about a product or service than the other. The result may be an under- or overallocation of resources.

average fixed cost (AFC) A firm's total *fixed cost* divided by output (the quantity of product produced).

average product (AP) The total output produced per unit of a *resource* employed (*total product* divided by the quantity of that employed resource).

average revenue Total revenue from the sale of a product divided by the quantity of the product sold (demanded); equal to the price at which the product is sold when all units of the product are sold at the same price.

average tax rate Total tax paid divided by total *taxable income* or some other base (such as total income) against which to compare the amount of tax paid. Expressed as a percentage.

average total cost (ATC) A firm's *total cost* divided by output (the quantity of product produced); equal to *average fixed cost* plus *average variable cost*.

average variable cost (AVC) A firm's total *variable cost* divided by output (the quantity of product produced).

315

backflows The return of workers to the countries from which they originally emigrated.

balance of payments (See *international balance of payments*.)

balance-of-payments deficit The net amount of *official reserves* (mainly foreign currencies) that a nation's treasury or central bank must sell to achieve balance between that nation's *capital and financial account* and its *current account* (in its *balance of payments*).

balance-of-payments surplus The net amount of *official reserves* (mainly foreign currencies) that a nation's treasury or central bank must buy to achieve balance between that nation's *capital and financial account* and its *current account* (in its *balance of payments*).

balance on capital and financial account The sum of the *capital account balance* and the *financial account balance*.

balance on current account The exports of goods and services of a nation less its imports of goods and services plus its *net investment income* and *net transfers* in a year.

balance on goods and services The exports of goods and services of a nation less its imports of goods and services in a year.

bankrupt A legal situation in which an individual or *firm* finds that it cannot make timely interest payments on money it has borrowed. In such cases, a bankruptcy judge can order the individual or firm to liquidate (turn into cash) its assets in order to pay lenders at least some portion of the amount they are owed.

barrier to entry Anything that artificially prevents the entry of firms into an industry.

barter The exchange of one good or service for another good or service.

beaten paths Migration routes taken previously by family, relatives, friends, and other migrants.

behavioral economics The branch of economics that combines insights from economics, psychology, and neuroscience to give a better explanation of choice behavior than previous theories that incorrectly concluded that consumers were always rational, deliberate, and unemotional. Behavioral economics explains: *framing effects, anchoring, mental accounting,* the *endowment effect,* and how people are *loss averse.*

benefits-received principle The idea that those who receive the benefits of goods and services provided by government should pay the taxes required to finance them.

bilateral monopoly A market in which there is a single seller *(monopoly)* and a single buyer *(monopsony)*.

bond A financial device through which a borrower (a firm or government) is obligated to pay the principal and interest on a loan at a specific date in the future.

brain drains The exit or *emigration* of highly educated, highly skilled workers from a country.

break-even output Any output at which a (competitive) firm's *total cost* and *total revenue* are equal; an output at which a firm has neither an *economic profit* nor an economic loss, at which it earns only a *normal profit.*

break-even point An output at which a firm makes a *normal profit* (*total revenue = total cost*) but not an *economic profit.*

British thermal unit (BTU) The amount of energy required to raise the temperature of 1 pound of water by 1 degree Fahrenheit.

budget constraint The limit that the size of a consumer's income (and the prices that must be paid for goods and services) imposes on the ability of that consumer to obtain goods and services.

budget line A line that shows the different combinations of two products a consumer can purchase with a specific money income, given the products' prices.

businesses Economic entities (*firms*) that purchase resources and provide goods and services to the economy.

business firm (See *firm*.)

cap-and-trade program A government strategy for reducing harmful emissions or discharges by placing a limit on their total amounts and then allowing firms to buy and sell the rights to emit or discharge specific amounts within the total limits.

capital Human-made resources (buildings, machinery, and equipment) used to produce goods and services; goods that do not directly satisfy human wants; also called capital goods.

capital and financial account The section of a nation's *international balance of payments* that records (1) debt forgiveness by and to foreigners and (2) foreign purchases of assets in the United States and U.S. purchases of assets abroad.

capital and financial account deficit A negative balance on its *capital and financial account* in a country's *international balance of payments.*

capital and financial account surplus A positive balance on its *capital and financial account* in a country's *international balance of payments.*

capital gain The gain realized when securities or properties are sold for a price greater than the price paid for them.

capital goods (See *capital*.)

capital-intensive goods Products that require relatively large amounts of *capital* to produce.

capitalism An economic system in which property resources are privately owned and markets and prices are used to direct and coordinate economic activities.

capital stock The total available *capital* in a nation.

cardinal utility Satisfaction (*utility*) that can be measured via cardinal numbers (1, 2, 3...), with all the mathematical properties of those numbers such as addition, subtraction, multiplication, and division being applicable.

cartel A formal agreement among firms (or countries) in an industry to set the price of a product and establish the outputs of the individual firms (or countries) or to divide the market for the product geographically.

causation A relationship in which the occurrence of one or more events brings about another event.

cease-and-desist order An order from a court or government agency to a corporation or individual to stop engaging in a specified practice.

ceiling price (See *price ceiling.*)

Celler-Kefauver Act The Federal law of 1950 that amended the *Clayton Act* by prohibiting the acquisition of the assets of one firm by another firm when the effect would be less competition.

central bank A bank whose chief function is the control of the nation's *money supply;* in the United States, the Federal Reserve System.

central economic planning Government determination of the objectives of the economy and how resources will be directed to attain those goals.

ceteris paribus **assumption** (See *other-things-equal assumption.*)

change in demand A movement of an entire *demand curve* or schedule such that the *quantity demanded* changes at every particular price; caused by a change in one or more of the *determinants of demand.*

change in quantity demanded A change in the *quantity demanded* along a fixed *demand curve* (or within a fixed demand schedule) as a result of a change in the product's price.

change in quantity supplied A change in the *quantity supplied* along a fixed *supply curve* (or within a fixed supply schedule) as a result of a change in the product's price.

change in supply A movement of an entire *supply curve* or schedule such that the *quantity supplied* changes at every particular price; caused by a change in one or more of the *determinants of supply.*

Change to Win A loose federation of American unions that includes the Service Workers and Teamsters and has a total membership of 6 million workers.

circular flow diagram An illustration showing the flow of resources from *households* to *firms* and of products from firms to households. These flows are accompanied by reverse flows of money from firms to households and from households to firms.

Clayton Act The Federal antitrust law of 1914 that strengthened the *Sherman Act* by making it illegal for firms to engage in certain specified practices.

climate-change problem The problem of rising world temperatures that most climate experts believe are caused at least in part by increased carbon dioxide and other greenhouse gases generated as by-products of human economic activities.

closed shop A place of employment where only workers who are already members of a labor union may be hired.

Coase theorem The idea, first stated by economist Ronald Coase, that some *externalities* can be resolved through private negotiations of the affected parties.

coincidence of wants A situation in which the good or service that one trader desires to obtain is the same as that which another trader desires to give up and an item that the second trader wishes to acquire is the same as that which the first trader desires to surrender.

COLA (See *cost-of-living adjustment.*)

collective action problem The idea that getting a group to pursue a common, collective goal gets harder the larger the group's size. Larger groups are more costly to organize and their members more difficult to motivate because the larger the group, the smaller each member's share of the benefits if the group succeeds.

collective bargaining The negotiation of labor contracts between *labor unions* and *firms* or government entities.

collective voice The function a *labor union* performs for its members as a group when it communicates their problems and grievances to management and presses management for a satisfactory resolution.

collusion A situation in which firms act together and in agreement (collude) to fix prices, divide a market, or otherwise restrict competition.

command system A method of organizing an economy in which property resources are publicly owned and government uses *central economic planning* to direct and coordinate economic activities; command economy; communism.

communism (See *command system.*)

comparative advantage A situation in which a person or country can produce a specific product at a lower *opportunity cost* than some other person or country; the basis for specialization and trade.

compensating differences Differences in the *wages* received by workers in different jobs to compensate for the nonmonetary differences between the jobs.

compensating wage differential (See *compensating differences.*)

compensation to employees *Wages* and salaries plus wage and salary supplements paid by employers to workers.

competition The presence in a market of independent buyers and sellers competing with one another along with the freedom of buyers and sellers to enter and leave the market.

competitive industry's short-run supply curve The horizontal summation of the short-run supply curves of the *firms* in a purely competitive industry (see *pure competition*); a curve that shows the total quantities offered for sale at various prices by the firms in an industry in the short run.

competitive labor market A resource market in which a large number of (noncolluding) employers demand a particular type of labor supplied by a large number of nonunion workers.

complementary goods Products and services that are used together. When the price of one falls, the demand for the other increases (and conversely).

complementary resources Productive inputs that are used jointly with other inputs in the production process; resources for which a decrease in the price of one leads to an increase in the demand for the other.

compound interest The accumulation of money that builds over time in an investment or interest-bearing account as new interest is earned on previous interest that is not withdrawn.

concentration ratio The percentage of the total sales of an industry made by the four (or some other number) largest sellers in the industry.

conflict diamonds Diamonds that are mined and sold by combatants in war zones in Africa as a way to provide the currency needed to finance their military activities.

conglomerate merger The merger of a *firm* in one *industry* with a firm in another industry (with a firm that is not a supplier, customer, or competitor).

conglomerates Firms that produce goods and services in two or more separate industries.

constant-cost industry An industry in which expansion by the entry of new firms has no effect on the prices firms in the industry must pay for resources and thus no effect on production costs.

constant opportunity cost An *opportunity cost* that remains the same for each additional unit as a consumer (or society) shifts purchases (production) from one product to another along a straight-line *budget line* (*production possibilities curve*).

constant returns to scale Unchanging *average total cost* of producing a product as the firm expands the size of its plant (its output) in the *long run*.

consumer equilibrium In marginal utility theory, the combination of goods purchased based on *marginal utility* (MU) and *price* (P) that maximizes *total utility;* the combination for goods X and Y at which $MU_x/P_x = MU_y/P_y$. In indifference curve analysis, the combination of goods purchased that maximize *total utility* by enabling the consumer to reach the highest *indifference curve,* given the consumer's *budget line* (or *budget constraint*).

consumer goods Products and services that satisfy human wants directly.

consumer sovereignty Determination by consumers of the types and quantities of goods and services that will be produced with the scarce resources of the economy; consumers' direction of production through their *dollar votes*.

consumer surplus The difference between the maximum price a consumer is (or consumers are) willing to pay for an additional unit of a product and its market price; the triangular area below the demand curve and above the market price.

consumption of fixed capital An estimate of the amount of *capital* worn out or used up (consumed) in producing the *gross domestic product;* also called depreciation.

copayment The percentage of (say, health care) costs that an insured individual pays while the insurer pays the remainder.

copyright A legal protection provided to developers and publishers of books, computer software, videos, and musical compositions against the copying of their works by others.

corporate income tax A tax levied on the net income (accounting profit) of corporations.

corporation A legal entity ("person") chartered by a state or the Federal government that is distinct and separate from the individuals who own it.

correlation A systematic and dependable association between two sets of data (two kinds of events); does not necessarily indicate causation.

cost-benefit analysis A comparison of the *marginal costs* of a government project or program with the *marginal benefits* to decide whether or not to employ resources in that project or program and to what extent.

cost-of-living adjustment (COLA) An automatic increase in the incomes (wages) of workers when inflation occurs; guaranteed by a collective bargaining contract between firms and workers.

countercyclical payments (CCPs) Cash *subsidies* paid to farmers when market prices for certain crops drop below targeted prices. Payments are based on previous production and are received regardless of the current crop grown.

craft union A labor union that limits its membership to workers with a particular skill (craft).

creative destruction The hypothesis that the creation of new products and production methods simultaneously destroys the market power of existing monopolies.

credible threat In *game theory,* a statement of harmful intent by one party that the other party views as believable; often issued in conditional terms of "if you do this; we will do that."

cross elasticity of demand The ratio of the percentage change in *quantity demanded* of one good to the percentage change in the price of some other good. A positive coefficient indicates the two products are *substitute goods;* a negative coefficient indicates they are *complementary goods*.

crowding model of occupational discrimination A model of labor markets suggesting that *occupational discrimination* has kept many women and minorities out of high-paying occupations and forced them into a limited number of low-paying occupations.

currency appreciation (See *exchange-rate appreciation*.)

currency depreciation (See *exchange-rate depreciation*.)

currency intervention A government's buying and selling of its own currency or foreign currencies to alter international exchange rates.

current account The section in a nation's *international balance of payments* that records its exports and imports of goods and services, its net *investment income,* and its *net transfers*.

deadweight loss (See *efficiency loss*.)

declining industry An industry in which *economic profits* are negative (losses are incurred) and that will, therefore, decrease its output as firms leave it.

decreasing-cost industry An industry in which expansion through the entry of firms lowers the prices that firms in the industry must pay for resources and therefore decreases their production costs.

deductible The dollar sum of (for example, health care) costs that an insured individual must pay before the insurer begins to pay.

defaults Situations in which borrowers stop making loan payments or do not pay back loans that they took out and are now due.

defensive medicine The recommendation by physicians of more tests and procedures than are warranted medically or economically as a way of protecting themselves against later malpractice suits.

demand A schedule showing the amounts of a good or service that buyers (or a buyer) wish to purchase at various prices during some time period.

demand curve A curve illustrating *demand.*

demand schedule (See *demand.*)

demand-side market failures Underallocations of resources that occur when private demand curves understate consumers' full willingness to pay for a good or service.

demographers Scientists who study the characteristics of human populations.

dependent variable A variable that changes as a consequence of a change in some other (independent) variable; the "effect" or outcome.

depreciation (of the dollar) A decrease in the value of the dollar relative to another currency, so a dollar buys a smaller amount of the foreign currency and therefore of foreign goods.

derived demand The demand for a resource that depends on the demand for the products it helps to produce.

determinants of demand Factors other than price that determine the quantities demanded of a good or service.

determinants of supply Factors other than price that determine the quantities supplied of a good or service.

developing countries Many countries of Africa, Asia, and Latin America that are characterized by lack of capital goods, use of nonadvanced technologies, low literacy rates, high unemployment, rapid population growth, and labor forces heavily committed to agriculture.

diagnosis-related group (DRG) system Payments to doctors and hospitals under *Medicare* based on which of hundreds of carefully detailed diagnostic categories best characterize the patient's condition and needs.

differentiated oligopoly An *oligopoly* in which firms produce a *differentiated product.*

differentiated product A product that differs physically or in some other way from the similar products produced by other firms; a product such that buyers are not indifferent to the seller when the price charged by all sellers is the same.

diffusion (Web chapter) The spread of an *innovation* through its widespread imitation.

dilemma of regulation The tradeoff faced by a *regulatory agency* in setting the maximum legal price a monopolist may charge: The *socially optimal price* is below *average total cost* (and either bankrupts the *firm* or requires that it be subsidized), while the higher, *fair-return price* does not produce *allocative efficiency.*

diminishing marginal returns (See *law of diminishing returns.*)

diminishing marginal utility (See *law of diminishing marginal utility.*)

direct foreign investment (See *foreign direct investment.*)

direct payments Cash subsidies paid to farmers based on past production levels; unaffected by current crop prices and current production.

direct relationship The relationship between two variables that change in the same direction, for example, product price and quantity supplied; positive relationship.

discrimination The practice of according individuals or groups inferior treatment in hiring, occupational access, education and training, promotion, wage rates, or working conditions even though they have the same abilities, education, skills, and work experience as other workers.

discrimination coefficient A measure of the cost or disutility of prejudice; the monetary amount an employer is willing to pay to hire a preferred worker rather than a nonpreferred worker.

diseconomies of scale Increases in the *average total cost* of producing a product as the *firm* expands the size of its *plant* (its output) in the *long run.*

dividends Payments by a corporation of all or part of its profit to its stockholders (the corporate owners).

division of labor The separation of the work required to produce a product into a number of different tasks that are performed by different workers; *specialization* of workers.

Doha Development Agenda The latest, uncompleted (as of mid-2010) sequence of trade negotiations by members of the *World Trade Organization;* named after Doha, Qatar, where the set of negotiations began. Also called the Doha Round.

dollar votes The "votes" that consumers and entrepreneurs cast for the production of consumer and capital goods, respectively, when they purchase those goods in product and resource markets.

domestic price The price of a good or service within a country, determined by domestic demand and supply.

dominant strategy In *game theory,* an option that is better than any other alternative option regardless of what the other firm does.

dumping The sale of a product in a foreign country at prices either below cost or below the prices commonly charged at home.

DuPont cellophane case The antitrust case brought against DuPont in which the U.S. Supreme Court ruled (in 1956) that while DuPont had a monopoly in the narrowly defined market for cellophane, it did not monopolize the more broadly defined market for flexible packaging materials. It was thus not guilty of violating the *Sherman Act.*

earmarks Narrow, specially designated spending authorizations placed in broad legislation by Senators and representatives for the purpose of providing benefits to firms and organizations within their constituencies without undergoing the usual evaluation process or competitive bidding.

earned-income tax credit (EITC) A refundable Federal tax credit for low-income working people designed to reduce poverty and encourage labor-force participation.

earnings The money income received by a worker; equal to the *wage* (rate) multiplied by the amount of time worked.

economic concentration A description or measure of the degree to which an industry is dominated by one or a handful of firms or is characterized by many firms. (See *concentration ratio.*)

economic cost A payment that must be made to obtain and retain the services of a *resource;* the income a firm must provide to a resource supplier to attract the resource away from an alternative use; equal to the quantity of other products that cannot be produced when resources are instead used to make a particular product.

economic efficiency The use of the minimum necessary resources to obtain the socially optimal amounts of goods and services; entails both *productive efficiency* and *allocative efficiency.*

economic growth (1) An outward shift in the *production possibilities curve* that results from an increase in resource supplies or quality or an improvement in *technology;* (2) an increase of real output *(gross domestic product)* or real output per capita.

economic immigrants International migrants who have moved to a country from another to obtain economic gains such as better employment opportunities.

economic investment (See *investment.*)

economic law An *economic principle* that has been tested and retested and has stood the test of time.

economic model A simplified picture of economic reality; an abstract generalization.

economic perspective A viewpoint that envisions individuals and institutions making rational decisions by comparing the marginal benefits and marginal costs associated with their actions.

economic policy A course of action intended to correct or avoid a problem.

economic principle A widely accepted generalization about the economic behavior of individuals or institutions.

economic profit The *total revenue* of a firm less its *economic costs* (which include both *explicit costs* and *implicit costs*); also called "pure profit" and "above-normal profit."

economic regulation (See *industrial regulation* and *social regulation.*)

economic rent The price paid for the use of land and other natural resources, the supply of which is fixed *(perfectly inelastic).*

economic resources The *land, labor, capital,* and *entrepreneurial ability* that are used in the production of goods and services; productive agents; factors of production.

economics The social science concerned with how individuals, institutions, and society make optimal (best) choices under conditions of scarcity.

economic system A particular set of institutional arrangements and a coordinating mechanism for solving the economizing problem; a method of organizing an economy, of which the *market system* and the *command system* are the two general types.

economic theory A statement of a cause-effect relationship; when accepted by all or nearly all economists, an *economic principle.*

economies of scale Reductions in the *average total cost* of producing a product as the firm expands the size of plant (its output) in the *long run;* the economies of mass production.

economizing problem The choices necessitated because society's economic wants for goods and services are unlimited but the resources available to satisfy these wants are limited (scarce).

efficiency gains from migration Additions to output from *immigration* in the destination nation that exceed the loss of output from *emigration* from the origin nation.

efficiency loss Reductions in combined consumer and producer surplus caused by an underallocation or overallocation of resources to the production of a good or service. Also called *deadweight loss.*

efficiency loss of a tax The loss of net benefits to society because a tax reduces the production and consumption of a taxed good below the level of *allocative efficiency.* Also called the deadweight loss of the tax.

efficiency wage A wage that minimizes wage costs per unit of output by encouraging greater effort or reducing turnover.

efficient allocation of resources That allocation of an economy's resources among the production of different products that leads to the maximum satisfaction of consumers' wants, thus producing the socially optimal mix of output with society's scarce resources.

elastic demand Product or resource demand whose *price elasticity* is greater than 1. This means the resulting change in *quantity demanded* is greater than the percentage change in *price.*

elasticity coefficient The number obtained when the percentage change in *quantity demanded* (or supplied) is divided by the percentage change in the *price* of the commodity.

elasticity formula (See *price elasticity of demand.*)

elasticity of resource demand A measure of the responsiveness of firms to a change in the price of a particular *resource* they employ or use; the percentage change in the quantity of the resource demanded divided by the percentage change in its price.

elastic supply Product or resource supply whose price elasticity is greater than 1. This means the resulting change in quantity supplied is greater than the percentage change in price.

emigration The exit (outflow) of residents from a country to reside in foreign countries.

employer mandate The requirement under the *Patient Protection and Affordable Care Act (PPACA)* of 2010 that firms with 50 or more employees pay for insurance policies for their employees or face a fine of $2000 per employee per year. Firms with fewer than 50 employees are exempt.

employment rate The percentage of the *labor force* employed at any time.

empty threat In *game theory,* a statement of harmful intent that is easily dismissed by the recipient because the threat is not viewed as being believable; compare to *credible threat.*

endowment effect The tendency people have to place higher valuations on items they own than on identical items that they do not own. Perhaps caused by people being *loss averse.*

entitlement programs Government programs such as *social insurance, Medicare,* and *Medicaid* that guarantee particular levels of transfer payments or noncash benefits to all who fit the programs' criteria.

entrepreneurial ability The human resource that combines the other resources to produce a product, makes nonroutine decisions, innovates, and bears risks.

equality-efficiency trade-off The decrease in *economic efficiency* that may accompany a decrease in *income inequality;* the presumption that some income inequality is required to achieve economic efficiency.

equilibrium position In the indifference curve model, the combination of two goods at which a consumer maximizes his or her *utility* (reaches the highest attainable *indifference curve*), given a limited amount to spend (a *budget constraint*).

equilibrium price The *price* in a competitive market at which the *quantity demanded* and the *quantity supplied* are equal, there is neither a shortage nor a surplus, and there is no tendency for price to rise or fall.

equilibrium quantity (1) The quantity at which the intentions of buyers and sellers in a particular market match at a particular price such that the *quantity demanded* and the *quantity supplied* are equal; (2) the profit-maximizing output of a firm.

equilibrium world price The price of an internationally traded product that equates the quantity of the product demanded by importers with the quantity of the product supplied by exporters; the price determined at the intersection of the export supply curve and the import demand curve.

euro The common currency unit used by 16 European nations (as of 2010) in the *Euro Zone,* which consists of Austria, Belgium, Cyprus, Finland, France, Germany, Greece, Ireland, Italy, Luxembourg, Malta, the Netherlands, Portugal, Slovakia, Slovenia, and Spain.

European Union (EU) An association of 27 European nations (as of 2010) that has eliminated tariffs and quotas among them, established common tariffs for imported goods from outside the member nations, eliminated barriers to the free movement of capital, and created other common economic policies.

Euro Zone The 16 nations (as of 2010) of the 25-member (as of 2010) *European Union* that use the *euro* as their common currency. The Euro Zone countries are Austria, Belgium, Cyprus, Finland, France, Germany, Greece, Ireland, Italy, Luxembourg, Malta, the Netherlands, Portugal, Slovakia, Slovenia, and Spain.

excess capacity Plant resources that are underused when imperfectly competitive firms produce less output than that associated with achieving minimum average total cost.

exchange controls (See *foreign exchange controls.*)

exchange rate The *rate of exchange* of one nation's currency for another nation's currency.

exchange-rate appreciation An increase in the value of a nation's currency in foreign exchange markets; an increase in the *rate of exchange* with foreign currencies.

exchange-rate depreciation A decrease in the value of a nation's currency in foreign exchange markets; a decrease in the *rate of exchange* with foreign currencies.

exchange-rate determinant Any factor other than the *rate of exchange* that determines a currency's demand and supply in the *foreign exchange market.*

excise tax A tax levied on the production of a specific product or on the quantity of the product purchased.

excludability The characteristic of a *private good,* for which the seller can keep nonbuyers from obtaining the good.

exclusive unionism The practice of a *labor union* of restricting the supply of skilled union labor to increase the wages received by union members; the policies typically employed by a *craft union.*

exhaustive expenditure An expenditure by government resulting directly in the employment of *economic resources* and in the absorption by government of the goods and services those resources produce; a *government purchase.*

exit mechanism The process of leaving a job and searching for another one as a means of improving one's working conditions.

expanding industry An industry whose firms earn *economic profits* and for which an increase in output occurs as new firms enter the industry.

expectations The anticipations of consumers, firms, and others about future economic conditions.

expected rate of return (Web chapter) The increase in profit a firm anticipates it will obtain by purchasing capital (or engaging in research and development); expressed as a percentage of the total cost of the investment (or R&D) activity.

expected-rate-of return curve (Web chapter) As it relates to research and development (*R&D*), a curve showing the anticipated gain in *profit,* as a percentage of R&D expenditure, from an additional dollar spent on R&D.

explicit cost The monetary payment a *firm* must make to an outsider to obtain a *resource.*

exports Goods and services produced in a nation and sold to buyers in other nations.

export subsidy A government payment to a domestic producer to enable the firm to reduce the price of a good or service to foreign buyers.

export supply curve An upward-sloping curve that shows the amount of a product that domestic firms will export at each *world price* that is above the *domestic price*.

external benefit (See *positive externality*.)

external cost (See *negative externality*.)

externality A cost or benefit from production or consumption, accruing without compensation to someone other than the buyers and sellers of the product (see *negative externality* and *positive externality*).

extraction cost All costs associated with extracting a natural resource and readying it for sale.

factors of production *Economic resources: land, capital, labor,* and *entrepreneurial ability*.

fair-return price The price of a product that enables its producer to obtain a *normal profit* and that is equal to the *average total cost* of producing it.

fallacy of composition The false notion that what is true for the individual (or part) is necessarily true for the group (or whole).

farm commodities Agricultural products such as grains, milk, cattle, fruits, and vegetables that are usually sold to processors, who use the products as inputs in creating *food products*.

fast-second strategy (Web chapter) An approach by a dominant firm in which it allows other firms in its industry to bear the risk of innovation and then quickly becomes the second firm to offer any successful new product or adopt any improved production process.

Federal government The government of the United States, as distinct from the state and local governments.

Federal Trade Commission (FTC) The commission of five members established by the *Federal Trade Commission Act* of 1914 to investigate unfair competitive practices of firms, to hold hearings on the complaints of such practices, and to issue *cease-and-desist orders* when firms are found to engage in such practices.

Federal Trade Commission Act The Federal law of 1914 that established the *Federal Trade Commission*.

fee for service In the health care industry, payment to physicians for each visit made or procedure performed rather than payment as an annual salary.

financial capital (See *money capital*.)

financial investment The purchase of a financial asset (such as a *stock, bond,* or *mutual fund*) or real asset (such as a house, land, or factories) or the building of such assets in the expectation of financial gain.

firm An organization that employs resources to produce a good or service for profit and owns and operates one or more *plants*.

first-mover advantage In *game theory*, the benefit obtained by the party that moves first in a *sequential game*.

fiscal policy Changes in government spending and tax collections designed to achieve a full-employment and noninflationary domestic output; also called *discretionary fiscal policy*.

fishery A stock of fish or other marine animal that is composed of a distinct group, for example New England cod, Pacific tuna, or Alaskan crab.

fishery collapse A rapid decline in a fishery's population because its fish are being harvested faster than they can reproduce.

fixed cost Any cost that in total does not change when the *firm* changes its output; the cost of *fixed resources*.

fixed exchange rate A *rate of exchange* that is set in some way and therefore prevented from rising or falling with changes in currency supply and demand.

fixed resource Any resource whose quantity cannot be changed by a firm in the *short run*.

flexible exchange rate A *rate of exchange* determined by the demand for and supply of a nation's money; a rate free to rise or fall (to float).

floating exchange rate (See *flexible exchange rate*.)

Food, Conservation, and Energy Act of 2008 Farm legislation that continued and extended previous agricultural subsides of three basic kinds: *direct payments, countercyclical payments,* and *marketing loans*.

food products Processed agricultural commodities sold through grocery stores and restaurants. Examples: bread, meat, fish, chicken, pork, lettuce, peanut butter, and breakfast cereal.

foreign competition (See *import competition*.)

foreign direct investment (Web chapter) Financial investments made to obtain a lasting ownership interest in firms operating outside the economy of the investor; may involve purchasing existing assets or building new production facilities.

foreign exchange controls Controls that a government may exercise over the quantity of foreign currency demanded by its citizens and firms and over the *rates of exchange* as a way to limit the nation's quantity of *outpayments* relative to its quantity of *inpayments* (to eliminate a *payments deficit*).

foreign exchange market A market in which the money (currency) of one nation can be used to purchase (can be exchanged for) the money of another nation; currency market.

foreign exchange rate (See *rate of exchange*.)

four-firm concentration ratio The percentage of total industry sales accounted for by the top four firms in the industry.

framing effects In *prospect theory,* changes in people's decision-making caused by new information that alters the context, or "frame of reference," that they use to judge whether options are viewed as gains or losses.

freedom of choice The freedom of owners of property resources to employ or dispose of them as they see fit, of workers to enter any line of work for which they are qualified, and of consumers to spend their incomes in a manner that they think is appropriate.

freedom of enterprise The freedom of *firms* to obtain economic resources, to use those resources to produce products of the firm's own choosing, and to sell their products in markets of their choice.

Freedom to Farm Act A law passed in 1996 that revamped 60 years of U.S. farm policy by ending *price supports* and *acreage allotments* for wheat, corn, barley, oats, sorghum, rye, cotton, and rice.

free-rider problem The inability of potential providers of an economically desirable good or service to obtain payment from those who benefit, because of *nonexcludability*.

free trade The absence of artificial (government-imposed) barriers to trade among individuals and firms in different nations.

fringe benefits The rewards other than *wages* that employees receive from their employers and that include pensions, medical and dental insurance, paid vacations, and sick leaves.

functional distribution of income The manner in which *national income* is divided among the functions performed to earn it (or the kinds of resources provided to earn it); the division of national income into wages and salaries, proprietors' income, corporate profits, interest, and rent.

future value The amount to which some current amount of money will grow if the interest earned on the amount is left to compound over time. (*See compound interest.*)

gains from trade The extra output that trading partners obtain through specialization of production and exchange of goods and services.

game theory A means of analyzing the pricing behavior of oligopolists that uses the theory of strategy associated with games such as chess and bridge.

GDP (See *gross domestic product.*)

General Agreement on Tariffs and Trade (GATT) The international agreement reached in 1947 in which 23 nations agreed to give equal and nondiscriminatory treatment to one another, to reduce tariff rates by multinational negotiations, and to eliminate *import quotas*. It now includes most nations and has become the *World Trade Organization*.

generalization Statement of the nature of the relationship between two or more sets of facts.

Gini ratio A numerical measure of the overall dispersion of income among households, families, or individuals; found graphically by dividing the area between the diagonal line and the *Lorenz curve* by the entire area below the diagonal line.

government failure Inefficiencies in resource allocation caused by problems in the operation of the public sector (government), specifically, rent-seeking pressure by special-interest groups, shortsighted political behavior, limited and bundled choices, and bureaucratic inefficiencies.

government purchases Expenditures by government for goods and services that government consumes in providing public goods and for public capital that has a long lifetime; the expenditures of all governments in the economy for those *final goods and services*.

government transfer payment The disbursement of money (or goods and services) by government for which government receives no currently produced good or service in return.

grievance procedure The method used by a *labor union* and a *firm* to settle disputes that arise during the life of the collective bargaining agreement between them.

gross domestic product (GDP) The total market value of all *final goods and services* produced annually within the boundaries of the United States, whether by U.S.- or foreign-supplied resources.

guiding function of prices The ability of price changes to bring about changes in the quantities of products and resources demanded and supplied.

H1-B provision A provision of the U.S. immigration law that allows the annual entry of 65,000 high-skilled workers in "specialty occupations" such as science, *R&D*, and computer programming to work legally and continuously in the United States for six years.

health maintenance organizations (HMOs) Health care providers that contract with employers, insurance companies, labor unions, or government units to provide health care for their workers or others who are insured.

health savings accounts (HSAs) Accounts into which people with high-deductible health insurance plans can place tax-free funds each year and then draw on these funds to pay out-of-pocket medical expenses such as *deductibles* and *copayments*. Unused funds accumulate from year to year and later can be used to supplement *Medicare*.

Herfindahl index A measure of the concentration and competitiveness of an industry; calculated as the sum of the squared percentage market shares of the individual firms in the industry.

homogeneous oligopoly An *oligopoly* in which the firms produce a *standardized product*.

horizontal axis The "left-right" or "west-east" measurement line on graph or grid.

horizontal merger The merger into a single *firm* of two firms producing the same product and selling it in the same geographic market.

households Economic entities (of one or more persons occupying a housing unit) that provide *resources* to the economy and use the *income* received to purchase goods and services that satisfy economic wants.

human capital The knowledge and skills that make a person productive.

human capital investment Any expenditure undertaken to improve the education, skills, health, or mobility of workers, with an expectation of greater productivity and thus a positive return on the investment.

hypothesis A tentative explanation of cause and effect that requires testing.

illegal immigrants People who have entered a country unlawfully to reside there; also called unauthorized immigrants.

imitation problem (Web chapter) The potential for a firm's rivals to produce a close variation of (imitate) a firm's new product or process, greatly reducing the originator's profit from *R&D* and *innovation*.

immigration The inflow of people into a country from another country. The immigrants may be either *legal immigrants* or *illegal immigrants.*

immobility The inability or unwillingness of a worker to move from one geographic area or occupation to another or from a lower-paying job to a higher-paying job.

imperfect competition All market structures except *pure competition;* includes *monopoly, monopolistic competition,* and *oligopoly.*

implicit cost The monetary income a *firm* sacrifices when it uses a resource it owns rather than supplying the resource in the market; equal to what the resource could have earned in the best-paying alternative employment; includes a *normal profit.*

import competition The competition that domestic firms encounter from the products and services of foreign producers.

import demand curve A downsloping curve showing the amount of a product that an economy will import at each *world price* below the *domestic price.*

import quota A limit imposed by a nation on the quantity (or total value) of a good that may be imported during some period of time.

imports Spending by individuals, *firms,* and governments for goods and services produced in foreign nations.

incentive function of price The inducement that an increase in the price of a commodity gives to sellers to make more of it available (and conversely for a decrease in price), and the inducement that an increase in price offers to buyers to purchase smaller quantities (and conversely for a decrease in price).

incentive pay plan A compensation structure that ties worker pay directly to performance. Such plans include piece rates, bonuses, *stock options,* commissions, and *profit sharing.*

inclusive unionism The practice of a labor union of including as members all workers employed in an industry.

income A flow of dollars (or purchasing power) per unit of time derived from the use of human or property resources.

income effect A change in the quantity demanded of a product that results from the change in *real income (purchasing power)* caused by a change in the product's price.

income elasticity of demand The ratio of the percentage change in the *quantity demanded* of a good to a percentage change in consumer income; measures the responsiveness of consumer purchases to income changes.

income inequality The unequal distribution of an economy's total income among households or families.

income-maintenance system A group of government programs designed to eliminate poverty and reduce inequality in the distribution of income.

income mobility The extent to which income receivers move from one part of the income distribution to another over some period of time.

increase in demand An increase in the *quantity demanded* of a good or service at every price; a shift of the *demand curve* to the right.

increase in supply An increase in the *quantity supplied* of a good or service at every price; a shift of the *supply curve* to the right.

increasing-cost industry An *industry* in which expansion through the entry of new firms raises the prices *firms* in the industry must pay for resources and therefore increases their production costs.

increasing marginal returns An increase in the *marginal product* of a resource as successive units of the resource are employed.

increasing returns An increase in a firm's output by a larger percentage than the percentage increase in its inputs.

independent goods Products or services for which there is little or no relationship between the price of one and the demand for the other. When the price of one rises or falls, the demand for the other tends to remain constant.

independent unions U.S. unions that are not affiliated with the *AFL-CIO.*

independent variable The variable causing a change in some other (dependent) variable.

indifference curve A curve showing the different combinations of two products that yield the same satisfaction or *utility* to a consumer.

indifference map A set of *indifference curves,* each representing a different level of *utility,* that together show the preferences of a consumer.

individual demand The demand schedule or *demand curve* of a single buyer.

individual supply The supply schedule or *supply curve* of a single seller.

individual transferable quotas (ITQs) Limits set by government or a fisheries commission on the total number or total weight of a species that an individual fisher can harvest during some particular time period; fishers holding the quotas can sell all or part of the rights to other fishers.

industrially advanced countries High-income countries such as the United States, Canada, Japan, and the nations of western Europe that have highly developed *market economies* based on large stocks of technologically advanced capital goods and skilled labor forces.

industrial regulation The older and more traditional type of regulation in which government is concerned with the prices charged and the services provided to the public in specific industries, in contrast to *social regulation.*

industrial union A *labor union* that accepts as members all workers employed in a particular industry (or by a particular firm).

industry A group of (one or more) *firms* that produce identical or similar products.

inelastic demand Product or resource demand for which the *elasticity coefficient* for price is less than 1. This means the resulting percentage change in *quantity demanded* is less than the percentage change in *price.*

inelastic supply Product or resource supply for which the price elasticity coefficient is less than 1. The percentage change in *quantity supplied* is less than the percentage change in *price.*

inferior good A good or service whose consumption declines as income rises, prices held constant.

inflation A rise in the general level of prices in an economy.

information technology New and more efficient methods of delivering and receiving information through the use of computers, fax machines, wireless phones, and the Internet.

infrastructure The capital goods usually provided by the *public sector* for use by its citizens and firms (for example, highways, bridges, transit systems, wastewater treatment facilities, municipal water systems, and airports).

injunction A court order directing a person or organization not to perform a certain act because the act would do irreparable damage to some other person or persons; a restraining order.

in-kind transfer The distribution by government of goods and services to individuals for which the government receives no currently produced good or service in return; a *government transfer payment* made in goods or services rather than in money; also called a noncash transfer.

innovation The first commercially successful introduction of a new product, the use of a new method of production, or the creation of a new form of business organization.

insurable risk An event that would result in a loss but whose frequency of occurrence can be estimated with considerable accuracy. Insurance companies are willing to sell insurance against such losses.

insurance exchanges Government-regulated markets for health insurance in which individuals seeking to purchase health insurance to comply with the *personal mandate* of the *Patient Protection and Affordable Care Act (PPACA)* of 2010 will be able to comparison shop among insurance policies approved by regulators. Each state will have its own exchange.

interest The payment made for the use of money (of borrowed funds).

interest income Payments of income to those who supply the economy with *capital*.

interest rate The annual rate at which *interest* is paid; a percentage of the borrowed amount.

interest-rate-cost-of-funds curve (Web chapter) As it relates to research and development (*R&D*), a curve showing the *interest rate* the firm must pay to obtain any particular amount of funds to finance R&D.

interindustry competition The competition for sales between the products of one industry and the products of another industry.

interlocking directorate A situation where one or more members of the board of directors of a *corporation* are also on the board of directors of a competing corporation; illegal under the *Clayton Act*.

international value of the dollar The price that must be paid in foreign currency (money) to obtain one U.S. dollar.

invention (Web chapter) The first discovery of a product or process through the use of imagination, ingenious thinking, and experimentation and the first proof that it will work.

inverse relationship The relationship between two variables that change in opposite directions, for example, product price and quantity demanded; a negative relationship.

inverted-U theory of R&D (Web chapter) The idea that, other things equal, *R&D* expenditures as a percentage of sales rise with industry concentration, reach a peak at a four-firm *concentration ratio* of about 50 percent, and then fall as the ratio further increases.

investment Spending for the production and accumulation of *capital* and additions to inventories.

investment goods Same as *capital* or capital goods.

investment in human capital (See *human capital investment*.)

"invisible hand" The tendency of firms and resource suppliers that seek to further their own self-interests in competitive markets to also promote the interests of society.

kinked-demand curve The demand curve for a noncollusive oligopolist, which is based on the assumption that rivals will match a price decrease and will ignore a price increase.

labor People's physical and mental talents and efforts that are used to help produce goods and services.

labor force Persons 16 years of age and older who are not in institutions and who are employed or are unemployed and seeking work.

labor-force participation rate The percentage of the working-age population that is actually in the *labor force*.

labor-intensive goods Products requiring relatively large amounts of labor to produce.

labor productivity Total output divided by the quantity of labor employed to produce it; the *average product* of labor or output per hour of work.

labor union A group of workers organized to advance the interests of the group (to increase wages, shorten the hours worked, improve working conditions, and so on).

laissez-faire capitalism (See *capitalism*.)

land Natural resources ("free gifts of nature") used to produce goods and services.

land-intensive goods Products requiring relatively large amounts of *land* to produce.

law of demand The principle that, other things equal, an increase in a product's price will reduce the quantity of it demanded, and conversely for a decrease in price.

law of diminishing marginal utility The principle that as a consumer increases the consumption of a good or service, the *marginal utility* obtained from each additional unit of the good or service decreases.

law of diminishing returns The principle that as successive increments of a variable resource are added to a fixed resource, the *marginal product* of the variable resource will eventually decrease.

law of increasing opportunity costs The principle that as the production of a good increases, the *opportunity cost* of producing an additional unit rises.

law of supply The principle that, other things equal, an increase in the price of a product will increase the quantity of it supplied, and conversely for a price decrease.

learning by doing Achieving greater *productivity* and lower *average total cost* through gains in knowledge and skill that accompany repetition of a task; a source of *economies of scale*.

least-cost combination of resources The quantity of each resource a firm must employ in order to produce a particular output at the lowest total cost; the combination at which the ratio of the *marginal product* of a resource to its *marginal resource cost* (to its *price* if the resource is employed in a competitive market) is the same for the last dollar spent on each of the resources employed.

legal cartel theory of regulation The hypothesis that some industries seek regulation or want to maintain regulation so that they may form or maintain a legal *cartel*.

legal immigrant A person who lawfully enters a country for the purpose of residing there.

liability A debt with a monetary value; an amount owed by a firm or an individual.

loanable funds *Money* available for lending and borrowing.

loanable funds theory of interest The concept that the supply of and demand for *loanable funds* determine the equilibrium rate of interest.

lockout An action by a firm that forbids workers to return to work until a new collective bargaining contract is signed; a means of imposing costs (lost wages) on union workers in a collective bargaining dispute.

logrolling The trading of votes by legislators to secure favorable outcomes on decisions concerning the provision of *public goods* and *quasi-public goods*.

long run (1) In *microeconomics,* a period of time long enough to enable producers of a product to change the quantities of all the resources they employ; period in which all resources and costs are variable and no resources or costs are fixed. (2) In *macroeconomics,* a period sufficiently long for *nominal wages* and other input prices to change in response to a change in a nation's *price level*.

long-run competitive equilibrium The price at which firms in *pure competition* neither obtain *economic profit* nor suffer economic losses in the *long run* and in which the total quantity demanded and supplied are equal; a price equal to the *marginal cost* and the minimum long-run *average total cost* of producing the product.

long-run supply In *microeconomics,* a schedule or curve showing the prices at which a purely competitive industry will make various quantities of the product available in the *long run*.

long-run supply curve A schedule or curve showing the prices at which a purely competitive industry will make various quantities of the product available in the *long run*.

Lorenz curve A curve showing the distribution of income in an economy. The cumulated percentage of families (income receivers) is measured along the horizontal axis and the cumulated percentage of income is measured along the vertical axis.

loss averse In *prospect theory,* the property of people's preferences that the pain generated by losses feels substantially more intense than the pleasure generated by gains.

macroeconomics The part of economics concerned with the economy as a whole; with such major aggregates as the household, business, and government sectors; and with measures of the total economy.

managed floating exchange rate An *exchange rate* that is allowed to change (float) as a result of changes in currency supply and demand but at times is altered (managed) by governments via their buying and selling of particular currencies.

managerial prerogatives The decisions that a firm's management has the sole right to make; often enumerated in the labor contract (work agreement) between a *labor union* and a *firm*.

marginal analysis The comparison of marginal ("extra" or "additional") benefits and marginal costs, usually for decision making.

marginal benefit The extra (additional) benefit of consuming 1 more unit of some good or service; the change in total benefit when 1 more unit is consumed.

marginal cost (MC) The extra (additional) cost of producing 1 more unit of output; equal to the change in *total cost* divided by the change in output (and, in the short run, to the change in total *variable cost* divided by the change in output).

marginal cost–marginal benefit rule As it applies to *cost-benefit analysis,* the tenet that a government project or program should be expanded to the point where the *marginal cost* and *marginal benefit* of additional expenditures are equal.

marginal product (MP) The additional output produced when 1 additional unit of a resource is employed (the quantity of all other resources employed remaining constant); equal to the change in *total product* divided by the change in the quantity of a resource employed.

marginal productivity theory of income distribution The contention that the distribution of income is equitable when each unit of each resource receives a money payment equal to its marginal contribution to the firm's revenue (its *marginal revenue product*).

marginal rate of substitution (MRS) The rate at which a consumer is willing to substitute one good for another (from a given combination of goods) and remain equally satisfied (have the same *total utility*); equal to the slope of a consumer's *indifference curve* at each point on the curve.

marginal resource cost (MRC) The amount the total cost of employing a *resource* increases when a firm employs 1 additional unit of the resource (the quantity of all other resources employed remaining constant); equal to the change in the *total cost* of the resource divided by change in the quantity of the resource employed.

marginal revenue The change in *total revenue* that results from the sale of 1 additional unit of a firm's product; equal to the change in total revenue divided by the change in the quantity of the product sold.

marginal-revenue–marginal-cost approach A method of determining the total output where *economic profit* is a maximum (or losses are a minimum) by comparing the *marginal revenue* and the *marginal cost* of each additional unit of output.

marginal revenue product (MRP) The change in a firm's *total revenue* when it employs 1 additional unit of a resource (the quantity of all other resources employed remaining constant); equal to the change in total revenue divided by the change in the quantity of the resource employed.

marginal revenue productivity (See *marginal revenue product.*)

marginal tax rate The tax rate paid on an additional dollar of income.

marginal utility The extra *utility* a consumer obtains from the consumption of 1 additional unit of a good or service; equal to the change in total utility divided by the change in the quantity consumed.

market Any institution or mechanism that brings together buyers (demanders) and sellers (suppliers) of a particular good or service.

market demand (See *total demand.*)

market economy An economy in which the private decisions of consumers, resource suppliers, and firms determine how resources are allocated; the *market system.*

market failure The inability of a market to bring about the allocation of resources that best satisfies the wants of society; in particular, the overallocation or underallocation of resources to the production of a particular good or service because of *externalities* or informational problems or because markets do not provide desired *public goods.*

market for externality rights A market in which firms can buy rights to discharge pollutants. The price of such rights is determined by the demand for the right to discharge pollutants and a *perfectly inelastic supply* of such rights (the latter determined by the quantity of discharge that the environment can assimilate).

market period A period in which producers of a product are unable to change the quantity produced in response to a change in its price and in which there is a *perfectly inelastic supply.*

market system All the product and resource markets of a *market economy* and the relationships among them; a method that allows the prices determined in those markets to allocate the economy's scarce resources and to communicate and coordinate the decisions made by consumers, firms, and resource suppliers.

marketing loan program A Federal farm subsidy under which certain farmers can receive a loan (on a per-unit-of-output basis) from a government lender and then, depending on the price of the crop, either pay back the loan with interest or keep the loan proceeds while forfeiting their harvested crop to the lender.

median-voter model The theory that under majority rule the median (middle) voter will be in the dominant position to determine the outcome of an election.

Medicaid A Federal program that helps finance the medical expenses of individuals covered by the *Supplemental Security Income (SSI)* and *Temporary Assistance for Needy Families (TANF)* programs.

Medicare A Federal program that is financed by *payroll taxes* and provides for (1) compulsory hospital insurance for senior citizens, (2) low-cost voluntary insurance to help older Americans pay physicians' fees, and (3) subsidized insurance to buy prescription drugs.

Medicare Part D The portion of Medicare that enables enrollees to shop among private health insurance companies to buy highly subsidized insurance to help reduce the out-of-pocket expense of prescription drugs.

medium of exchange Any item sellers generally accept and buyers generally use to pay for a good or service; *money;* a convenient means of exchanging goods and services without engaging in *barter.*

mental accounting The tendency people have to create separate "mental boxes" (or "accounts") in which they deal with particular financial transactions in isolation rather than dealing with them as part of their overall decision-making process that considers how to best allocate their limited budgets using the *utility-maximizing rule.*

merger The combination of two (or more) firms into a single firm.

microeconomics The part of economics concerned with decision making by individual units such as a *household,* a *firm,* or an *industry* and with individual markets, specific goods and services, and product and resource prices.

Microsoft case A 2002 antitrust case in which Microsoft was found guilty of violating the *Sherman Act* by engaging in a series of unlawful activities designed to maintain its monopoly in operating systems for personal computers; as a remedy the company was prohibited from engaging in a set of specific anticompetitive business practices.

midpoint formula A method for calculating *price elasticity of demand* or *price elasticity of supply* that averages the two prices and two quantities as the reference points for computing percentages.

minimum efficient scale (MES) The lowest level of output at which a firm can minimize long-run *average total cost.*

minimum wage The lowest *wage* that employers may legally pay for an hour of work.

monetary policy A central bank's changing of the *money supply* to influence interest rates and assist the economy in achieving price stability, full employment, and economic growth.

money Any item that is generally acceptable to sellers in exchange for goods and services.

money capital Money available to purchase *capital;* simply *money,* as defined by economists.

money income (See *nominal income.*)

monopolistic competition A market structure in which many firms sell a *differentiated product,* into which entry is relatively easy, in which the firm has some control over its product price, and in which there is considerable *nonprice competition.*

monopoly A market structure in which there is only a single seller of a good, service, or resource. In antitrust law, a dominant firm that accounts for a very high percentage of total sales within a particular market.

monopsony A market structure in which there is only a single buyer of a good, service, or resource.

moral hazard problem The possibility that individuals or institutions will change their behavior as the result of a contract or agreement. Example: A bank whose deposits are insured against losses may make riskier loans and investments.

MR = MC rule The principle that a firm will maximize its profit (or minimize its losses) by producing the output at which *marginal revenue* and *marginal cost* are equal, provided product price is equal to or greater than *average variable cost.*

MRP = MRC rule The principle that to maximize profit (or minimize losses), a firm should employ the quantity of a resource at which its *marginal revenue product* (MRP) is equal to its *marginal resource cost* (MRC), the latter being the wage rate in a purely competitive labor market.

multinational corporations Firms that own production facilities in two or more countries and produce and sell their products globally.

mutual interdependence A situation in which a change in price strategy (or in some other strategy) by one firm will affect the sales and profits of another firm (or other firms). Any firm that makes such a change can expect the other rivals to react to the change.

Nash equilibrium In *game theory,* an outcome from which neither firm wants to deviate; the outcome that once achieved is stable and therefore lasting.

national health insurance (NHI) A program in which a nation's government provides a basic package of health care to all citizens at no direct charge or at a low cost-sharing level. Financing is out of general tax revenues.

National Labor Relations Act (NLRA) Act first passed as the Wagner Act of 1935; as amended, the basic labor-relations law in the United States; defines the legal rights of unions and management and identifies unfair union and management labor practices; established the *National Labor Relations Board.*

National Labor Relations Board (NLRB) The board established by the *National Labor Relations Act* of 1935 to investigate unfair labor practices, issue *cease-and-desist orders,* and conduct elections among employees to determine if they wish to be represented by a *labor union.*

natural monopoly An industry in which *economies of scale* are so great that a single firm can produce the product at a lower average total cost than would be possible if more than one firm produced the product.

negative externality A cost imposed without compensation on third parties by the production or consumption of sellers or buyers. Example: A manufacturer dumps toxic chemicals into a river, killing fish prized by sports fishers; an external cost or a spillover cost.

negative relationship (See *inverse relationship.*)

negative self-selection As it relates to international *migration,* the idea that those who choose to move to another country have poorer wage opportunities in the origin country than those with similar skills who choose not to *emigrate.*

negative-sum game In *game theory,* a game in which the gains (+) and losses (−) add up to some amount less than zero; one party's losses exceed the other party's gains.

net benefits The total benefits of some activity or policy less the total costs of that activity or policy.

net taxes The taxes collected by government less *government transfer payments.*

network effects Increases in the value of a product to each user, including existing users, as the total number of users rises.

net worth The total *assets* less the total *liabilities* of a firm or an individual; for a firm, the claims of the owners against the firm's total assets; for an individual, his or her wealth.

NLRB (See *National Labor Relations Board.*)

nominal interest rate The interest rate expressed in terms of annual amounts currently charged for interest and not adjusted for inflation.

nominal wage The amount of money received by a worker per unit of time (hour, day, etc.); money wage.

noncash transfer A *government transfer payment* in the form of goods and services rather than money, for example, food stamps, housing assistance, and job training; also called in-kind transfers.

noncollusive oligopoly An *oligopoly* in which the firms do not act together and in agreement to determine the price of the product and the output that each firm will produce.

noncompeting groups Collections of workers who do not compete with each other for employment because the skill and training of the workers in one group are substantially different from those of the workers in other groups.

nonexcludability The inability to keep nonpayers (free riders) from obtaining benefits from a certain good; a characteristic of a *public good.*

nonexhaustive expenditure An expenditure by government that does not result directly in the use of economic resources or the production of goods and services; see *government transfer payment.*

nonprice competition Competition based on distinguishing one's product by means of *product differentiation* and then *advertising* the distinguished product to consumers.

nonrenewable natural resource Things such as oil, natural gas, and metals, which are either in actual fixed supply or which renew so slowly as to be in virtual fixed supply when viewed from a human time perspective.

nonrivalry The idea that one person's benefit from a certain good does not reduce the benefit available to others; a characteristic of a *public good.*

nontariff barriers (NTBs) All barriers other than *protective tariffs* that nations erect to impede international trade, including *import quotas,* licensing requirements, unreasonable product-quality standards, unnecessary bureaucratic detail in customs procedures, and so on.

normal good A good or service whose consumption increases when income increases and falls when income decreases, price remaining constant.

normal profit The payment made by a firm to obtain and retain *entrepreneurial ability;* the minimum income entrepreneurial ability must receive to induce it to perform entrepreneurial functions for a firm.

normative economics The part of economics involving value judgments about what the economy should be like; focused on which economic goals and policies should be implemented; policy economics.

North American Free Trade Agreement (NAFTA) A 1993 agreement establishing, over a 15-year period, a free-trade zone composed of Canada, Mexico, and the United States.

occupation A category of activities or tasks performed by a set of workers for pay, independent of employer or industry. Examples are managers, nurses, farmers, and cooks.

occupational licensing The laws of state or local governments that require that a worker satisfy certain specified requirements and obtain a license from a licensing board before engaging in a particular occupation.

occupational segregation The crowding of women or minorities into less desirable, lower-paying occupations.

official reserves Foreign currencies owned by the central bank of a nation.

offshoring The practice of shifting work previously done by American workers to workers located abroad.

oligopoly A market structure in which a few firms sell either a *standardized* or *differentiated product,* into which entry is difficult, in which the firm has limited control over product price because of *mutual interdependence* (except when there is collusion among firms), and in which there is typically *nonprice competition.*

one-time game In *game theory,* a game in which the parties select their optimal strategies in a single time period without regard to possible interaction in subsequent time periods.

OPEC (See *Organization of Petroleum Exporting Countries.*)

open shop A place of employment in which the employer may hire nonunion workers and the workers need not become members of a *labor union.*

opportunity cost The amount of other products that must be forgone or sacrificed to produce a unit of a product.

opportunity-cost ratio An equivalency showing the number of units of two products that can be produced with the same resources; the cost 1 corn $\equiv$ 3 olives shows that the resources required to produce 3 units of olives must be shifted to corn production to produce 1 unit of corn.

optimal amount of R&D (Web chapter) The level of *R&D* at which the *marginal benefit* and *marginal cost* of R&D expenditures are equal.

optimal reduction of an externality The reduction of a *negative externality* such as pollution to the level at which the *marginal benefit* and *marginal cost* of reduction are equal.

ordinal utility Satisfaction that is measured by having consumers compare and rank products (or combinations of products) as to preference, without asking them to specify the absolute amounts of satisfaction provided by the products.

Organization of Petroleum Exporting Countries (OPEC) A cartel of 12 oil-producing countries (Algeria, Angola, Ecuador, Iran, Iraq, Kuwait, Libya, Nigeria, Qatar, Saudi Arabia, Venezuela, and the United Arab Emirates) that attempts to control the quantity and price of crude oil exported by its members and that accounts for a large percentage of the world's export of oil.

other-things-equal assumption The assumption that factors other than those being considered are held constant; *ceteris paribus* assumption.

output effect The situation in which an increase in the price of one input will increase a firm's production costs and reduce its level of output, thus reducing the demand for other inputs; conversely for a decrease in the price of the input.

paradox of voting A situation where paired-choice voting by majority rule fails to provide a consistent ranking of society's preferences for *public goods* or services.

parity concept The idea that year after year the sale of a specific output of a farm product should enable a farmer to purchase a constant amount of nonagricultural goods and services.

parity ratio The ratio of the price received by farmers from the sale of an agricultural commodity to the prices of other goods paid by them; usually expressed as a percentage; used as a rationale for *price supports.*

partnership An unincorporated firm owned and operated by two or more persons.

patent An exclusive right given to inventors to produce and sell a new product or machine for 20 years from the time of patent application.

Patient Protection and Affordable Care Act (PPACA) A major health care law passed by the Federal government in 2010. Major provisions include an individual health insurance mandate, a ban on insurers refusing to accept patients with preexisting conditions, and Federal (rather than state) regulation of health insurance policies.

payroll tax A tax levied on employers of labor equal to a percentage of all or part of the wages and salaries paid by them and on employees equal to a percentage of all or part of the wages and salaries received by them.

P = **MC rule** The principle that a purely competitive firm will maximize its profit or minimize its loss by producing that output at which the *price* of the product is equal to *marginal cost,* provided that price is equal to or greater than *average variable cost* in the short run and equal to or greater than *average total cost* in the long run.

per capita GDP *Gross domestic product* (GDP) per person; the average GDP of a population.

per capita income A nation's total income per person; the average income of a population.

perfectly elastic demand Product or resource demand in which *quantity demanded* can be of any amount at a particular product *price;* graphs as a horizontal *demand curve.*

perfectly elastic supply Product or resource supply in which *quantity supplied* can be of any amount at a particular product or resource *price;* graphs as a horizontal *supply curve.*

perfectly inelastic demand Product or resource demand in which *price* can be of any amount at a particular quantity of the product or resource demanded; *quantity demanded* does not respond to a change in price; graphs as a vertical *demand curve.*

perfectly inelastic supply Product or resource supply in which *price* can be of any amount at a particular quantity of the product or resource demanded; *quantity supplied* does not respond to a change in price; graphs as a vertical *supply curve.*

per se violations Collusive actions, such as attempts by firms to fix prices or divide a market, that are violations of the *antitrust laws,* even if the actions themselves are unsuccessful.

personal distribution of income The manner in which the economy's *personal* or *disposable income* is divided among different income classes or different households or families.

personal income tax A tax levied on the taxable income of individuals, households, and unincorporated firms.

personal mandate The requirement under the *Patient Protection and Affordable Care Act (PPACA)* of 2010 that all U.S. citizens and legal residents purchase health insurance unless they are already covered by employer-sponsored health insurance or government-sponsored health insurance (*Medicaid* or *Medicare*).

per-unit production cost The average production cost of a particular level of output; total input cost divided by units of output.

plant A physical establishment that performs one or more functions in the production, fabrication, and distribution of goods and services.

policy economics The formulation of courses of action to bring about desired economic outcomes or to prevent undesired occurrences.

political corruption The unlawful misdirection of governmental resources or actions that occurs when government officials abuse their entrusted powers for personal gain.

positive economics The analysis of facts or data to establish scientific generalizations about economic behavior.

positive externality A benefit obtained without compensation by third parties from the production or consumption of sellers or buyers. Example: A beekeeper benefits when a neighboring farmer plants clover. An *external benefit* or a spillover benefit.

positive sum game In *game theory,* a game in which the gains (+) and losses (−) add up to more than zero; one party's gains exceeds the other party's losses.

***post hoc, ergo propter hoc* fallacy** The false belief that when one event precedes another, the first event must have caused the second event.

potential competition The new competitors that may be induced to enter an industry if firms now in that industry are receiving large *economic profits.*

poverty A situation in which the basic needs of an individual or family exceed the means to satisfy them.

poverty rate The percentage of the population with incomes below the official poverty income levels that are established by the Federal government.

preferred provider organization (PPO) An arrangement in which doctors and hospitals agree to provide health care to insured individuals at rates negotiated with an insurer.

present value Today's value of some amount of money that is to be received sometime in the future.

price The amount of money needed to buy a particular good, service, or resource.

price ceiling A legally established maximum price for a good or service.

price discrimination The selling of a product to different buyers at different prices when the price differences are not justified by differences in cost.

price elasticity of demand The ratio of the percentage change in *quantity demanded* of a product or resource to the percentage change in its *price;* a measure of the responsiveness of buyers to a change in the price of a product or resource.

price elasticity of supply The ratio of the percentage change in *quantity supplied* of a product or resource to the percentage change in its *price;* a measure of the responsiveness of producers to a change in the price of a product or resource.

price fixing The conspiring by two or more firms to set the price of their products; an illegal practice under the *Sherman Act.*

price floor A legally determined minimum price above the *equilibrium price.*

price leadership An informal method that firms in an *oligopoly* may employ to set the price of their product: One firm (the leader) is the first to announce a change in price, and the other firms (the followers) soon announce identical or similar changes.

price-level stability A steadiness of the price level from one period to the next; zero or low annual inflation; also called "price stability."

price maker A seller (or buyer) of a product or resource that is able to affect the product or resource price by changing the amount it sells (or buys).

price support A minimum price that government allows sellers to receive for a good or service; a legally established or maintained minimum price.

price taker A seller (or buyer) that is unable to affect the price at which a product or resource sells by changing the amount it sells (or buys).

price war Successive and continued decreases in the prices charged by firms in an oligopolistic industry. Each firm lowers its price below rivals' prices, hoping to increase its sales and revenues at its rivals' expense.

principal-agent problem A conflict of interest that occurs when agents (workers or managers) pursue their own objectives to the detriment of the principals' (stockholders') goals.

principle of comparative advantage The proposition that an individual, region, or nation will benefit if it specializes in producing goods for which its own *opportunity costs* are lower than the opportunity costs of a trading partner, and then exchanging some of the products in which it specializes for other desired products produced by others.

private good A good or service that is individually consumed and that can be profitably provided by privately owned firms because they can exclude nonpayers from receiving the benefits.

private property The right of private persons and firms to obtain, own, control, employ, dispose of, and bequeath *land, capital,* and other property.

private sector The *households* and business *firms* of the economy.

process innovation (Web chapter) The development and use of new or improved production or distribution methods.

producer surplus The difference between the actual price a producer receives (or producers receive) and the minimum acceptable price; the triangular area above the supply curve and below the market price.

product differentiation A strategy in which one firm's product is distinguished from competing products by means of its design, related services, quality, location, or other attributes (except price).

product innovation (Web chapter) The development and sale of a new or improved product (or service).

production possibilities curve A curve showing the different combinations of two goods or services that can be produced in a *full-employment, full-production* economy where the available supplies of resources and technology are fixed.

productive efficiency The production of a good in the least costly way; occurs when production takes place at the output at which *average total cost* is a minimum and *marginal product* per dollar's worth of input is the same for all inputs.

productivity A measure of average output or real output per unit of input. For example, the productivity of labor is determined by dividing real output by hours of work.

productivity growth The increase in *productivity* from one period to another.

product market A market in which products are sold by *firms* and bought by *households*.

profit The return to the resource *entrepreneurial ability* (see *normal profit*); *total revenue* minus *total cost* (see *economic profit*).

profit-maximizing combination of resources The quantity of each resource a firm must employ to maximize its profit or minimize its loss; the combination in which the *marginal revenue product* of each resource is equal to its *marginal resource cost* (to its *price* if the resource is employed in a competitive market).

profit-sharing plan A compensation device through which workers receive part of their pay in the form of a share of their employer's profit (if any).

progressive tax A tax whose *average tax rate* increases as the taxpayer's income increases and decreases as the taxpayer's income decreases.

property tax A tax on the value of property (*capital, land, stocks* and *bonds,* and other *assets*) owned by *firms* and *households*.

proportional tax A tax whose *average tax rate* remains constant as the taxpayer's income increases or decreases.

proprietor's income The net income of the owners of unincorporated firms (proprietorships and partnerships).

prospect theory A *behavioral economics* theory of preferences having three main features: (1) people evaluate options on the basis of whether they generate gains or losses relative to the *status quo;* (2) gains are subject to diminishing marginal utility while losses are subject to diminishing marginal disutility; (3) people are *loss averse*.

protective tariff A *tariff* designed to shield domestic producers of a good or service from the competition of foreign producers.

public assistance programs Government programs that pay benefits to those who are unable to earn income (because of permanent disabilities or because they have very low income and dependent children); financed by general tax revenues and viewed as public charity (rather than earned rights).

public choice theory The economic analysis of government decision making, politics, and elections.

public good A good or service that is characterized by *nonrivalry* and *nonexcludability;* a good or service with these characteristics provided by government.

public interest theory of regulation The presumption that the purpose of the regulation of an *industry* is to protect the public (consumers) from abuse of the power possessed by *natural monopolies*.

public sector The part of the economy that contains all government entities; government.

public utility A firm that produces an essential good or service, has obtained from a government the right to be the sole supplier of the good or service in the area, and is regulated by that government to prevent the abuse of its monopoly power.

purchasing power The amount of goods and services that a monetary unit of income can buy.

purchasing power parity The idea that exchange rates between nations equate the purchasing power of various currencies. Exchange rates between any two nations adjust to reflect the price level differences between the countries.

pure competition A market structure in which a very large number of firms sells a *standardized product,* into which entry is very easy, in which the individual seller has no control over the product price, and in which there is no nonprice competition; a market characterized by a very large number of buyers and sellers.

purely competitive labor market A *resource market* in which many firms compete with one another in hiring a specific kind of labor, numerous equally qualified workers supply that labor, and no one controls the market wage rate.

pure monopoly A market structure in which one firm sells a unique product, into which entry is blocked, in which the single firm has considerable control over product price, and in which *nonprice competition* may or may not be found.

pure profit (See *economic profit.*)

pure rate of interest An essentially risk-free, long-term interest rate that is free of the influence of market imperfections.

quantity demanded The amount of a good or service that buyers (or a buyer) are willing and able to purchase at a specific price during a specified period of time.

quantity supplied The amount of a good or service that producers (or a producer) are willing and able to make available for sale at a specific price during a specified period of time.

quasi-public good A good or service to which excludability could apply but that has such a large *positive externality* that government sponsors its production to prevent an underallocation of resources.

R&D Research and development activities undertaken to bring about *technological advance.*

rate of exchange The price paid in one's own money to acquire 1 unit of a foreign currency; the rate at which the money of one nation is exchanged for the money of another nation.

rate of return (Web chapter) The gain in net revenue divided by the cost of an investment or an *R&D* expenditure; expressed as a percentage.

rational behavior Human behavior based on comparison of marginal costs and marginal benefits; behavior designed to maximize total utility.

real capital (See *capital.*)

real gross domestic product (GDP) *Gross domestic product* adjusted for inflation; gross domestic product in a year divided by the GDP *price index* for that year, the index expressed as a decimal.

real income The amount of goods and services that can be purchased with *nominal income* during some period of time; nominal income adjusted for inflation.

real interest rate The interest rate expressed in dollars of constant value (adjusted for *inflation*) and equal to the *nominal interest rate* less the expected rate of inflation.

real wage The amount of goods and services a worker can purchase with his or her *nominal wage;* the purchasing power of the nominal wage.

recession A period of declining real GDP, accompanied by lower real income and higher unemployment.

regressive tax A tax whose *average tax rate* decreases as the taxpayer's income increases and increases as the taxpayer's income decreases.

regulatory agency An agency, commission, or board established by the Federal government or a state government to control the prices charged and the services offered by a *natural monopoly.*

remittances Payments by *immigrants* to family members and others located in the origin countries of the immigrants.

rental income The payments (income) received by those who supply *land* to the economy.

renewable natural resources Things such as forests, water in reservoirs, and wildlife that are capable of growing back or building back up (renewing themselves) if they are harvested at moderate rates.

rent-seeking behavior The actions by persons, firms, or unions to gain special benefits from government at the taxpayers' or someone else's expense.

repeated game In *game theory,* a game which is played again sometime after the previous game ends.

replacement rate The birthrate necessary to offset deaths in a country and therefore to keep the size of its population constant (without relying on immigration). For most countries, the replacement rate is about 2.1 births per woman per lifetime.

resource A natural, human, or manufactured item that helps produce goods and services; a productive agent or factor of production.

resource market A market in which *households* sell and *firms* buy resources or the services of resources.

revenue tariff A *tariff* designed to produce income for the Federal government.

right-to-work law A state law (in 22 states) that makes it illegal to require that a worker join a *labor union* in order to retain his or her job; laws that make *union shops* and *agency shops* illegal.

risk The uncertainty as to the actual future returns of a particular *financial investment* or *economic investment.*

rivalry (1) The characteristic of a *private good,* the consumption of which by one party excludes other parties from obtaining the benefit; (2) the attempt by one firm to gain strategic advantage over another firm to enhance market share or profit.

rule of reason The rule stated and applied in the *U.S. Steel case* that only combinations and contracts unreasonably restraining trade are subject to actions under the antitrust laws and that size and possession of monopoly power are not illegal.

sales and excise taxes   (See *sales tax; see excise tax.*)

sales tax   A tax levied on the cost (at retail) of a broad group of products.

saving   After-tax income not spent for consumer goods.

scarce resources   The limited quantities of *land, capital, labor,* and *entrepreneurial ability* that are never sufficient to satisfy people's virtually unlimited economic wants.

scientific method   The procedure for the systematic pursuit of knowledge involving the observation of facts and the formulation and testing of hypotheses to obtain theories, principles, and laws.

self-interest   That which each firm, property owner, worker, and consumer believes is best for itself and seeks to obtain.

self-selection   As it relates to international migration, the idea that those who choose to move tend to have greater motivation for economic gain or greater willingness to sacrifice current consumption for future consumption than those with similar skills who choose to remain at home.

seniority   The length of time a worker has been employed absolutely or relative to other workers; may be used to determine which workers will be laid off when there is insufficient work for them all and who will be rehired when more work becomes available.

separation of ownership and control   The fact that different groups of people own a *corporation* (the stockholders) and manage it (the directors and officers).

sequential game   In *game theory,* a game in which the parties make their moves in turn, with one party making the first move, followed by the other party making the next move, and so on.

service   An (intangible) act or use for which a consumer, firm, or government is willing to pay.

Sherman Act   The Federal antitrust law of 1890 that makes monopoly and conspiracies to restrain trade criminal offenses.

shirking   Workers' neglecting or evading work to increase their *utility* or well-being.

shortage   The amount by which the *quantity demanded* of a product exceeds the *quantity supplied* at a particular (below-equilibrium) price.

short run   (1) In microeconomics, a period of time in which producers are able to change the quantities of some but not all of the resources they employ; a period in which some resources (usually plant) are fixed and some are variable. (2) In macroeconomics, a period in which nominal wages and other input prices do not change in response to a change in the price level.

short-run competitive equilibrium   The price at which the total quantity of a product supplied in the *short run* in a purely competitive industry equals the total quantity of the product demanded and that is equal to or greater than *average variable cost.*

short-run supply curve   A supply curve that shows the quantity of a product a firm in a purely competitive industry will offer to sell at various prices in the *short run;* the portion of the firm's short-run marginal cost curve that lies above its *average-variable-cost* curve.

shutdown case   The circumstance in which a firm would experience a loss greater than its total *fixed cost* if it were to produce any output greater than zero; alternatively, a situation in which a firm would cease to operate when the *price* at which it can sell its product is less than its *average variable cost.*

simultaneous consumption   The same-time derivation of *utility* from some product by a large number of consumers.

simultaneous game   In *game theory,* a game in which both parties choose their strategies and execute them at the same time.

single-tax movement   The political efforts by followers of Henry George (1839-1897) to impose a single tax on the value of land and eliminate all other taxes.

skill transferability   The ease with which people can shift their work talents from one job, region, or country to another job, region, or country.

slope of a straight line   The ratio of the vertical change (the rise or fall) to the horizontal change (the run) between any two points on a line. The slope of an upward-sloping line is positive, reflecting a direct relationship between two variables; the slope of a downward-sloping line is negative, reflecting an inverse relationship between two variables.

Smoot-Hawley Tariff Act   Legislation passed in 1930 that established very high tariffs. Its objective was to reduce imports and stimulate the domestic economy, but it resulted only in retaliatory tariffs by other nations.

social insurance programs   Programs that replace the earnings lost when people retire or are temporarily unemployed, that are financed by payroll taxes, and that are viewed as earned rights (rather than charity).

socially optimal price   The price of a product that results in the most efficient allocation of an economy's resources and that is equal to the *marginal cost* of the product.

social regulation   Regulation in which government is concerned with the conditions under which goods and services are produced, their physical characteristics, and the impact of their production on society; in contrast to *industrial regulation.*

Social Security   The social insurance program in the United States financed by Federal payroll taxes on employers and employees and designed to replace a portion of the earnings lost when workers become disabled, retire, or die.

Social Security trust fund   A Federal fund that saves excessive Social Security tax revenues received in one year to meet Social Security benefit obligations that exceed Social Security tax revenues in some subsequent year.

sole proprietorship   An unincorporated *firm* owned and operated by one person.

special-interest effect   Any result of government promotion of the interests (goals) of a small group at the expense of a much larger group.

specialization   The use of the resources of an individual, a firm, a region, or a nation to concentrate production on one or a small number of goods and services.

SSI (See *Supplemental Security Income.*)

standardized product A product whose buyers are indifferent to the seller from whom they purchase it as long as the price charged by all sellers is the same; a product all units of which are identical and thus are perfect substitutes for each other.

Standard Oil case A 1911 antitrust case in which Standard Oil was found guilty of violating the *Sherman Act* by illegally monopolizing the petroleum industry. As a remedy the company was divided into several competing firms.

start-up firm A new firm focused on creating and introducing a particular new product or employing a specific new production or distribution method.

statistical discrimination The practice of judging an individual on the basis of the average characteristics of the group to which he or she belongs rather than on his or her own personal characteristics.

status quo The existing state of affairs; in *prospect theory*, the current situation from which gains and losses are calculated.

stock (corporate) An ownership share in a corporation.

stock options Contracts that enable executives or other key employees to buy shares of their employers' stock at fixed, lower prices even when the market price subsequently rises.

strategic behavior Self-interested economic actions that take into account the expected reactions of others.

strike The withholding of labor services by an organized group of workers (a *labor union*).

subsidy A payment of funds (or goods and services) by a government, firm, or household for which it receives no good or service in return. When made by a government, it is a *government transfer payment.*

substitute goods Products or services that can be used in place of each other. When the price of one falls, the demand for the other product falls; conversely, when the price of one product rises, the demand for the other product rises.

substitute resources Productive inputs that can be used instead of other inputs in the production process; resources for which an increase in the price of one leads to an increase in the demand for the other.

substitution effect (1) A change in the quantity demanded of a *consumer good* that results from a change in its relative expensiveness caused by a change in the product's price; (2) the effect of a change in the price of a *resource* on the quantity of the resource employed by a firm, assuming no change in its output.

sunk cost A cost that has been incurred and cannot be recovered.

Supplemental Nutrition Assistance Program (SNAP) A government program that provides food money to low-income recipients by depositing electronic money onto special debit cards. Formerly known as the food-stamp program.

Supplemental Security Income (SSI) A federally financed and administered program that provides a uniform nationwide minimum income for the aged, blind, and disabled who do not qualify for benefits under *Social Security* in the United States.

supply A schedule showing the amounts of a good or service that sellers (or a seller) will offer at various prices during some period.

supply curve A curve illustrating *supply*.

supply schedule (See *supply*.)

supply-side market failures Overallocations of resources that occur when private supply curves understate the full cost of producing a good or service.

surplus The amount by which the *quantity supplied* of a product exceeds the *quantity demanded* at a specific (above-equilibrium) price.

surplus payment A payment exceeding the minimum payment necessary to ensure the availability of a resource in a production process; for example, land rent.

TANF (See *Temporary Assistance for Needy Families.*)

tariff A tax imposed by a nation on an imported good.

taste-for-discrimination model A theory that views discrimination as a preference for which an employer is willing to pay.

tax An involuntary payment of money (or goods and services) to a government by a *household* or *firm* for which the household or firm receives no good or service directly in return.

tax incidence The degree to which a *tax* falls on a particular person or group.

tax subsidy A grant in the form of reduced taxes through favorable tax treatment. For example, employer-paid health insurance is exempt from Federal income and payroll taxes.

technological advance New and better goods and services and new and better ways of producing or distributing them.

technology The body of knowledge and techniques that can be used to combine *economic resources* to produce goods and services.

Temporary Assistance for Needy Families (TANF) A state-administered and partly federally funded program in the United States that provides financial aid to poor families; the basic welfare program for low-income families in the United States; contains time limits and work requirements.

terms of trade The rate at which units of one product can be exchanged for units of another product; the price of a good or service; the amount of one good or service that must be given up to obtain 1 unit of another good or service.

theoretical economics The process of deriving and applying economic theories and principles.

theory of human capital The generalization that *wage differentials* are the result of differences in the amount of *human capital investment* and that the incomes of lower-paid workers are raised by increasing the amount of such investment.

time-value of money The idea that a specific amount of money is more valuable to a person the sooner it is received because the money can be placed in a financial account or investment and earn *compound interest* over time; the *opportunity cost* of receiving a sum of money later rather than earlier.

total allowable catch (TAC) A limit set by government or a fisheries commission on the total number of fish or tonnage of fish that fishers collectively can harvest during some particular time period.

total cost The sum of *fixed cost* and *variable cost*.

total demand The demand schedule or the *demand curve* of all buyers of a good or service; also called market demand.

total fertility rate The average total number of children that a woman is expected to have during her lifetime.

total product (TP) The total output of a particular good or service produced by a firm (or a group of firms or the entire economy).

total revenue (TR) The total number of dollars received by a firm (or firms) from the sale of a product; equal to the total expenditures for the product produced by the firm (or firms); equal to the quantity sold (demanded) multiplied by the price at which it is sold.

total-revenue test A test to determine elasticity of *demand* between any two prices: Demand is elastic if *total revenue* moves in the opposite direction from price; it is inelastic when it moves in the same direction as price; and it is of unitary elasticity when it does not change when price changes.

total supply The supply schedule or the *supply curve* of all sellers of a good or service; also called market supply.

total utility The total amount of satisfaction derived from the consumption of a single product or a combination of products.

Trade Adjustment Assistance Act A U.S. law passed in 2002 that provides cash assistance, education and training benefits, health care subsidies, and wage subsidies (for persons age 50 or older) to workers displaced by imports or relocations of U.S. plants to other countries.

trade deficit The amount by which a nation's *imports* of goods (or goods and services) exceed its *exports* of goods (or goods and services).

trademark A legal protection that gives the originators of a product an exclusive right to use the brand name.

trade-off The sacrifice of some or all of one economic goal, good, or service to achieve some other goal, good, or service.

trade surplus The amount by which a nation's *exports* of goods (or goods and services) exceed its *imports* of goods (or goods and services).

trading possibilities line A line that shows the different combinations of two products that an economy is able to obtain (consume) when it specializes in the production of one product and trades (exports) it to obtain the other product.

tragedy of the commons The tendency for commonly owned *natural resources* to be overused, neglected, or degraded because their common ownership gives nobody an incentive to maintain or improve them.

transfer payment A payment of *money* (or goods and services) by a government to a *household* or *firm* for which the payer receives no good or service directly in return.

tying contract A requirement imposed by a seller that a buyer purchase another (or other) of its products as a condition for buying a desired product; a practice forbidden by the *Clayton Act*.

unemployment The failure to use all available *economic resources* to produce desired goods and services; the failure of the economy to fully employ its *labor force*.

unemployment compensation (See *unemployment insurance*).

unemployment insurance The social insurance program that in the United States is financed by state *payroll taxes* on employers and makes income available to workers who become unemployed and are unable to find jobs.

unemployment rate The percentage of the *labor force* unemployed at any time.

uninsurable risk An event that would result in a loss and whose occurrence is uncontrollable and unpredictable. Insurance companies are not willing to sell insurance against such a loss.

union (See *labor union*.)

unionization rate The percentage of a particular population of workers that belongs to *labor unions;* alternatively, the percentage of the population of workers whom unions represent in *collective bargaining*.

union shop A place of employment where the employer may hire either *labor union* members or nonmembers but where nonmembers must become members within a specified period of time or lose their jobs.

unit elasticity Demand or supply for which the *elasticity coefficient* is equal to 1; means that the percentage change in the quantity demanded or supplied is equal to the percentage change in price.

unlimited wants The insatiable desire of consumers for goods and services that will give them satisfaction or *utility*.

Uruguay Round A 1995 trade agreement (fully implemented in 2005) that established the *World Trade Organization (WTO)*, liberalized trade in goods and services, provided added protection to intellectual property (for example, *patents* and *copyrights*), and reduced farm subsidies.

user cost The *opportunity* cost of extracting and selling a nonrenewable resource today rather than waiting to extract and sell the resource in the future; the *present value* of the decline in future revenue that will occur because a nonrenewable resource is extracted and sold today rather than being extracted and sold in the future.

U.S. Steel case The antitrust action brought by the Federal government against the U.S. Steel Corporation in which the courts ruled (in 1920) that only unreasonable restraints of trade were illegal and that size and the possession of monopoly power were not by themselves violations of the antitrust laws.

usury laws State laws that specify the maximum legal interest rate at which loans can be made.

utility The want-satisfying power of a good or service; the satisfaction or pleasure a consumer obtains from the consumption of a good or service (or from the consumption of a collection of goods and services).

utility-maximizing rule The principle that to obtain the greatest *utility,* a consumer should allocate *money income* so that the last dollar spent on each good or service yields the same marginal utility.

value-added tax A tax imposed on the difference between the value of a product sold by a firm and the value of the goods purchased from other firms to produce that product; used in several European countries.

value judgment Opinion of what is desirable or undesirable; belief regarding what ought or ought not to be in terms of what is right (or just) or wrong (or unjust).

variable cost A cost that in total increases when the firm increases its output and decreases when the firm reduces its output.

VAT (See *value-added tax.*)

venture capital (Web chapter) That part of household saving used to finance high-risk business enterprises in exchange for shares of the profit if the enterprise succeeds.

vertical axis The "up-down" or "north-south" measurement line on a graph or grid.

vertical integration A group of *plants* engaged in different stages of the production of a final product and owned by a single *firm.*

vertical intercept The point at which a line meets the vertical axis of a graph.

vertical merger The merger of one or more *firms* engaged in different stages of the production of a final product.

very long run (Web chapter) A period long enough that *technology* can change and *firms* can introduce new products.

voice mechanism Communication by workers through their union to resolve grievances with an employer.

voluntary export restrictions (VER) Voluntary limitations by countries or firms of their exports to a particular foreign nation to avoid enactment of formal trade barriers by that nation.

wage The price paid for the use or services of *labor* per unit of time (per hour, per day, and so on).

wage differential The difference between the *wage* received by one worker or group of workers and that received by another worker or group of workers.

wage rate (See *wage.*)

wages The income of those who supply the economy with *labor.*

wealth Anything that has value because it produces income or could produce income. Wealth is a stock; *income* is a flow. Assets less liabilities; net worth.

welfare programs (See *public assistance programs.*)

Wheeler-Lea Act The Federal law of 1938 that amended the *Federal Trade Commission Act* by prohibiting and giving the commission power to investigate unfair and deceptive acts or practices of commerce (such as false and misleading advertising and the misrepresentation of products).

world price The international market price of a good or service, determined by world demand and supply.

World Trade Organization (WTO) An organization of 153 nations (as of mid-2010) that oversees the provisions of the current world trade agreement, resolves trade disputes stemming from it, and holds forums for further rounds of trade negotiations.

WTO (See *World Trade Organization.*)

X-inefficiency The production of output, whatever its level, at a higher average (and total) cost than is necessary for producing that level of output.

zero-sum game In *game theory,* a game in which the gains (+) and losses (−) add up to zero; one party's gain equals the other party's loss.

NOTES